BROOKLYN'S SCARLETT

SUSAN HAYWARD: FIRE IN THE WIND

GENE ARCERI

Published in the USA by:
BearManor Media
PO Box 1129
Duncan, Oklahoma 73534-1129
www.bearmanormedia.com

ISBN 978-1-59393-028-8

Printed in the United States of America.
Cover design by Christopher Jones.
Book design by Brian Pearce | Red Jacket Press.

TABLE OF CONTENTS

DEDICATION

A postman's delivery brought with it an introduction to Diana Adams. Fate interacted. A creative exchange evolved. Diana became a writer's hope, a colleague who was honest, intelligent, intrepid, dependable, encouraging and humorous. If I faltered, she persisted until the job was completed. I proudly dedicate this book to Diana with love and admiration.

ACKNOWLEDGEMENTS

I can almost hear their voices; see their faces. Throughout this book, you will meet them all. Though so many are gone now their words remain. They opened their homes — and hearts — to share their memories of Susan Hayward: Brooklyn school mate June O'Brien. Susan's brother, Wally, offered me a place to stay while in Hollywood. I slept on a rose covered sofa bed that Susan had bought so she could stay with her brother when he needed her. In Hollywood I sat by pools, met people I would interview in coffee shops, hotel lobbies. I went to Bel Air for a visit with Henry Hathaway, Danny Mann's office on Sunset Boulevard, and Nolan Miller's salon. I would go anywhere at anytime when and if they would see me. My travels led me to Baltimore to meet Father Thomas Brew–to Atlanta to see Father Morrow. In Carrollton, Georgia, I was the houseguest of Mary Williams and slept in Susan's bedroom where she would stay with Mary on occasion. A wonderful nostalgic journey walking through the town, stopping in the stores Susan frequented. I visited the church she built across from her home and Father McGuire.

All of this has been revisited on the following pages. Back in San Francisco, I was driven up to spend time with Ed Montgomery and his family. Over lunch at the SF Press Club Graham Kisinglinbury could not be more supportive. And I will never forget Curlee, Susan's housekeeper and confidant, who fixed a dinner for me and her family in the kitchen. My only wish is that I could not do it all over again. Still, as I read this book, a tribute to all those involved, in so many ways — I have!

PRELUDE

Her name was up in lights for the last time. The large unevenly placed faded red plastic letters SUSAN HAYWARD hung innocuously on the front wall of an undistinguished building along West Hollywood's La Cienega Boulevard.

The building at 526 No. La Cienega Boulevard in Los Angeles was not a movie house, nor a theatre, but the Arthur B. Goode Auction Gallery with its folksy slogan 'Buy or Sell the Goode Way.'

There was to be a Sunday afternoon session on June 13 and two evening sessions, June 14 and 15, 1976, with refreshments served and 'programs' printed on deep orange paper bearing an unmemorable photograph of the actress, wearing a very uncharacteristic wig, from her only stage appearance as Mane.

The Oscar Susan Hayward had won for *I Want To Live* sat on the top shelf of a locked display case along with her other awards. The David di Donatello from Italy, The Golden Gaucho from Argentina, the Silver Bear from Germany, The Mar del Plata from the South American Film Festival, Foreign Press Golden Globe for the World's Favorite Actress, and dozens more stacked up below on shelves in the main showroom of the auction gallery.

A Not For Sale sign had been scotch-taped under the Oscar making it, and the other awards, the only Hayward possessions in the place that didn't have price tags. The alloy objects, seemingly impervious to time, would escape the fate of the boxes of Christmas ornaments, kitchen utensils, books, prescription glasses, and such sentimental items as framed poetry readings and all the worldly goods left behind to be disposed of. The auction had been commissioned by the heirs and the probate division of the superior court of the State of California.

Her films had been packing them in for a long time and the Gallery was filled to the walls for each session. Some had known her or worked with her in one way or another, others were fans — but most were the curious, anxious for a look at what had filled her closets and dresser drawers. There were also the losers in the acting profession, people who had never made it — certainly never in the way she had. They came because they knew no matter how she had beaten them out during her lifetime they had finally won — because in June of 1976, they were still alive and Susan Hayward's life was over.

One lady faintly resembling the late star may have wondered silently alone among the numbered pieces — looking, touching, remembering — it would have been her older sister Florence Marrener, who was a stranger to her at the end of her life. Certainly one person who was there to inspect the assemblage was her brother Walter Marrener.

Walter, totally unknown to anyone, would be left to contemplate sadly where it would all go — as it did eventually; scattered around by the auctioneer's gavel as the vestiges of his sister's life went on the block. Green and yellow living room furniture, and earth toned clothes, a box filled with Bibles, towels with signs of the Zodiac on them, a fishing reel, jump rope, sewing box, espresso maker, a jade ring, and a plaque with a quote by Goethe — 'Nothing should be more highly prized than the value of each day', showed something of the fabric of her passage through life.

Arthur B. Goode, a tall heavyset man with a receding hairline and an auctioneer in Hollywood since 1936, boasted that his first memory in life was of his mother washing his mouth out with soap. Despite his 68 years, he conveyed the energy of a used car salesman and the patter of a stand-up comedian.

Eventually all the movie star estates seemed to end up at an Arthur B. Goode Auction. He had sold the remaining lifetime accumulations of Valentino, Bogart, Hedda Hopper, and John and Lionel Barrymore, to name but a few. For the movie stars who wanted to completely dispose of their pasts (like Hedy Lamarr who walked out of her house one day in 1950 and never went back) he listened to their weary instructions over the telephone to 'sell everything' and just took over from there.

Arthur B. Goode, who lives off the memorabilia of faded and fallen stars, is by default, a bit player acting out their last scenes. As for his nebulous audience, he bragged while chomping on a cigar: "People come to have fun. They don't know what they're doing, so I help them enjoy themselves. I also make money that way. I joke and laugh with 'em. And I never use a script. My secretary told me I'm the only guy who can get high without grass or liquor. I just turn myself on. We have X rated auctions." Goode added that most of his customers were upper middle class curiosity seekers.

Among the customers was a fussily dressed woman in the front row that eagerly chattered: "Auctions are one of the games people play, and I love to play it! It's an expensive hobby but my husband makes lots of money and it's something to show guests before cocktails."

A young couple had been there for the entire auction buying towels and pictures — the husband said sheepishly, "My wife has this thing for Susan Hayward and when we saw the estate sale advertised in the paper she just had to come down and get some keepsakes."

A couple of young men sat in the back row, nudging each other as pieces of Susan's life filtered through the auction, throwing out a bid for a dress, a pair of gloves, shoes, a handbag."

A serious man in a three-piece suit bought a ginger jar and some art supplies. An obese open shirted auction pro said, "This is the rag sale tonight. Oh I did pick up a few things for my kids to horse around with."

A woman wandering around the showroom was looking for bidder number 49. "Number 49 got a box of Hayward's panty hose for $4 and I bid $5. It was a good deal — I mean, they're all unused. I'm not here because I want a part of Susan Hayward. I'm no exhibitionist. In fact, I can't see why anybody would want to wear one of her wigs. That stuff gives me the willies. You know, she was completely bald from that tumor."

A meek young man bought a lovely chiffon green gown and red wig for his mother.

Standing off to one side behind a calculator was a tall blonde man watching everything with computer-like eyes, making notes, adding figures and giving nods of affirmation or denial to the auctioneer; squeezing every cent from the bidders with silent encouragement and smiling at Goode's tasteless jokes. A reporter went up to him, he was Timothy Barker, one of Susan's sons. But Barker was too preoccupied with the calling out of bids and the action going on to break his rapt concentration. He brushed the reporter aside as his wife came rushing up to him and in a thick German accent told him she had just gotten another parking ticket, which seemed to annoy him and he took her away to admonish her.

Near the close of the auction, members of the audience were still in a buying mood. They were like trick or treaters, and Goode had run out of candy to give them. No doubt about it, they were still hungry.

As the evening wore on, a carnival like atmosphere began to develop, particularly when the wigs went on sale.

The wigs were luxurious and red. Susan Hayward, one of the most famous titian-haired performers in the history of films, had been completely bald for the last painful years of her life.

"Come on kids," the auctioneer cajoled, "Somebody start the bidding. You too can be a Susan Hayward look alike. Remember that. And remember Halloween's coming."

"It'll be Halloween before you know it..."

The curtain came down. The lights dimmed. The audience left — and another lifetime of collecting was unraveled. It was finished; the show was over.

In a dimly lit corner, unnoticed and unsold, remained a stainless steel framed poster of soaring seagulls bearing four lines of poetry:

Hold fast to dreams,
For if dreams die,
Life is a broken-winged bird,
That cannot fly.

Sixteen months before on March 15th, 1975, Susan Hayward had departed Hollywood forever.

Susan had made a name for herself and finally came home. The name was Mrs. Floyd Eaton Chalkley, and home was Carrollton, Georgia — population 10,973. The girl who almost became Scarlett O'Hara was to be buried not fifty miles from that heroine's creator, novelist Margaret Mitchell.

At one time, Susan had reflected on becoming a southern 'lady' — making a home in the South. "This belle from Brooklyn had to be forty-five years old before she became a 'detoured Scarlett O'Hara,'" she quipped. "Mrs. Chalkley...and that's what I want to be called..."

Now she had come back to her adopted hometown, to her final resting place, to be buried beside her husband in a simple tomb honed from Georgia granite, designed and created by Susan herself with the aid of Georgia sculptor, Julian Harris.

The pink marble headstone was a sculptured head of the Agonizing Christ, bought by the Chalkleys in Italy. The plot, surrounded by pine and holly, overlooked the expansive rolling lands where she had spent 'the happiest years of my life' and now, with every dream she could have ever have dreamed come true, her last wish was to be laid to rest in the obscurity of rural West Georgia.

For Susan, the ten years with Eaton were the contented years. She had loved the 6'1" Chalkley far more than anyone Hollywood could have dreamed up for her. Chalkley was a Virginian who had made good as an FBI agent, a Washington lawyer, a gentleman farmer, and finally as the owner of the Chalkley Motor Company, adjoining the Carroll Theatre on Newman Street.

It was during their marriage that she had won the elusive Oscar... something she had been within Excalibur's reach of through five nominations before finally grasping it.

Susan was flown home to Carrollton — and Eaton. There was no fanfare. This time no crowds lined the path to the incoming plane. No motorcade of home folk led the parade toward the rolling green hills of Carroll County. There were to be no great speeches, no eulogy, no applause, and no laughter.

Susan Hayward Chalkley came home to Carrollton on her last earthly journey in peaceful dignity. The day ended in a rich sunlit glow that bathed the hills and etched the stark late wintry trees into a canvas of rare beauty.

On Sunday, March 16th, 1975, the day of the funeral, the people of Carrollton, following their tradition, baked cakes and hams. Ann Moran, a close friend of the Chalkleys, baked a special banana cake — their favorite.

They lined seven miles of highway between the funeral home and the cemetery. The message on the Village Theatre's marquee expressed the feelings of all Carrolltonians; SUSAN WE'LL ALWAYS LOVE YOU.

It was a gloomy, rainy, Sabbath morning as the townspeople assembled in the chapel of Our Lady of Perpetual Help Catholic Church. After the service, officiated by Father Thomas Brew from Baltimore, the mourners filed slowly past the coffin, which was heaped high with yellow roses — Susan's favorite flowers — and white orchids. The local grocery clerk paused and remembered seeing her in pedal pushers with her red hair tied back and driving a pick-up truck with CHAL-MAR (Chalkley-Marrener; Susan's given name) FARMS painted on the side. A country woman, with a small baby in her arms, recalled the day Susan sat on the back steps of her home, drinking cold buttermilk, and talking about 'so many things.' A bank teller remembered her standing patiently in line. People waved and she would return their greetings — almost saluting — as she passed them by dressed in her bandanas, western shirts and khaki cotton slacks.

Curlee Crowder, a Carrollton woman who had worked for the Chalkley's for many years, spoke about her: "Mrs. Chalkley liked the simple people. 'They were more sincere,' she used to say. She was bored by bridge, gatherings, teas and socio-charitable company."

Now, outside, a crowd gathered around the small Catholic Church in the misty drizzle. Only the clicking of television news cameras indicated that the rites being said there were for someone of international status.

Some 18 years had passed since Susan Hayward had made her home in Carrollton, following her marriage to Eaton Chalkley. Until his death in 1966, some ten years later, she was much a part of the local community 'as down to earth a person as anyone else.' She had only wanted to be with Eaton, in their home together, and the reason she had left that home was because of memories of him.

She was to be buried today, beside her husband, across from the home where they had lived; her last request. Although the wind was cold and the drizzle was turning to rain, the grass was green and the flowers, surrounding the grave, cast a brilliance of color against the granite marker placed there after Eaton's death.

The group seated underneath the canopy protecting the gravesite was small. Movie stars, jet setters, and dignitaries were noticeably absent at the gathering. Only Susan's immediate family attended, including her twin sons, and a brother. Onlookers kept a respectful distance, some no doubt disappointed by the lack of celebrities.

The Chalkleys had arranged for the building of the Chapel of Our Lady of Perpetual Help, in granite matching the rock of their own home, on a hill in the heart of their property and given the land to the parish.

Now, at graveside, before a tombstone engraved simply Mrs. F.E. Chalkley, the local residents knew they would not see the handsome couple dancing at the Carrollton Country Club again or share the small dinner parties for close friends, which Susan preferred.

The beautiful, willful, Mrs. Chalkley, born June 30, 1917 in Flatbush, Brooklyn as Edythe Marrener to Walter and Ellen Marrener was now buried beneath the red clay of Georgia. Mrs. Chalkley, dead at 57, survived by her sons, a grandson, a grand-daughter and millions of fans around the world, the star of more than 50 motion pictures and winner of numerous international awards…could it have been only 36 years ago that a young girl of 19 looking over her shoulder, red hair blowing in the wind, smiled to the future from the cover of the Saturday Evening Post…a color photograph that would take her to Hollywood, and, after much heartbreak, to fame and fortune.

To Eugene
best regards
Susan Hayward

CHAPTER 1

June 30, 1917 — worldwide newspapers carried headline coverage of World War 1 from the North Sea to the Mediterranean; President Wilson ordered 10,000 of our aircraft to fly to France to bomb the German lines. The War Department issued lists of casualties in the American army in France. Pope Benedict XV led the free world in prayers for peace, and King George and Queen Mary were approaching their silver wedding anniversary. Mary Pickford's latest picture *How Could You Jean* opened at the Strand and the Follies headlined W.C. Fields, Marilyn Miller, Will Rogers and Eddie Cantor. At battle outposts, with our boys in the trenches darkened by night against air raids, the sound of a newborn baby howling for attention in a railroad flat in Brooklyn could hardly have presaged the future headlines she would occupy.

The baby's mother just dreamed of 'getting out.' She had heard the clang of the Church Avenue trolley too many times, walked past the Jewish candy stores 'til she was sick of them, smelled the stale beer odors of the Irish bars and the sweet sticky ones of the German bakeries so often that they made her gag. But Ellen Marrener came from Swedish stock and the Swedes were clean, practical people and looking in a mirror in her drab, fourth-floor flat at 3507 Church Avenue, Brooklyn, she could plainly see that she was not quite young and no longer pretty.

As for Walter, her husband, she knew that there was no way to count on him. He was a slight, ineffectual man, who preferred words to action and drinking to either of them. He was a wireman for the Interboro Rapid Transit Company, the I.R.T., and the most exciting thing that happened in their lives these days were their fights when they both had too much to drink. (President Wilson had repealed the prohibition of beer and wine, and a pail of beer from the corner bar was a luxury they needed, to forget.) Walter would threaten her if she didn't stop nagging him and Ellen would go on nagging, safe in the sad knowledge that Walter could never do anything, not to her, and not for her either.

So much for herself. And Walter. That left the children. Florence, her girl, was beautiful and from her first steps displayed a talent for dancing. Along with her cornflakes, Ellen fed the child the notion that she was going to be a star.

Then there was Wally, two years younger, slight like his father, with an impish and adorable grin. He too danced like a dream. Her real hopes

This page, facing page: The Brooklyn Apartment Building where Susan grew up —
2568 Bedford Ave.

were with Florence but there was no telling — Wally might very well make it, too. After all, her kids had talent in their veins.

Walter was half-English and half-Irish but the Irish side was pure starshine. His mother had been an actress in the Old Country and was still known by her stage name of Katie Harrigan. His sister had been one of the original Ziegfeld Girls and one brother was a musician. The closest Walter himself had ever come to 'show business' was when he worked as a barker for a Coney Island rollercoaster. But Walter — what the hell!

At least he'd given them something — the gift of Katie Harrigan's blood. Lots of the Irish who lived around them in that corner of Flatbush still remembered her. And someday, Ellen Marrener was determined, every one of them and everyone else in the world, too, would know the names of Florence and Wally Marrener.

All she had to do, Ellen told herself, was get through the winters that were cold and drab and the summers, when the heat that gathered on the narrow streets steamed up towards her fourth floor 'penthouse', and the

only cool spots anywhere were on the fire escapes or on the roof of the building; where you could look across the East River, past the Brooklyn Bridge to the skyscrapers of Manhattan.

CHILDHOOD

*This I was born with: an imagination
and a natural talent for lying.
The perfect ingredients for an actor.*

CHAPTER 2

Flatbush, covering approximately three and a half square miles, is located in the center of Brooklyn, about thirty minutes from midtown Manhattan by car, train, or bus. Indians had once lived there and now it was the home of many ethnic groups to which the Marreners could claim affinity with English and Irish stock on the father's side and Swedish on the mother's, although both Ellen and Walter were born in America.

Ellen's third and last child, little Edythe Marrener was born on the 30th of June 1917 Saturday — 'Saturday's child has to work for a living.' She was a tiny baby with bright hazel eyes, long brown lashes, with a tilt to her nose and her father's flame colored hair.

After her birth, Walter and Wally moved into one bedroom and Ellen and the girls stayed in the other, and that was the end of any further additions to the Marrener family.

On the day she was born Wally and Florrie ran in and out of the flat giddy with excitement, as they showed friends their new sister. Right from the beginning, there were people who called her 'Red' or 'Carrot top'. With that hair, there was no way to avoid it, just as there was no way for the beautiful baby to avoid Ellen Marrener's dreams.

Edythe's first summer was so like so many summers in Flatbush. The horses and wagons clattered up the hot street, the kids, on vacation from school, ran bare-foot and the canaries, perched in their cages in front parlors, chirped along with the clang of the trolley car bells, sounding as they passed along the street.

For grownups, their neighborhood was drab and unfulfilling but for children it had its attractions, however temporary.

Years later, Wally Marrener would recall; "a block from where we lived, Church Avenue turned into a dirt road and even further out there was farmland. You could walk just a little ways and come to a farmer's market."

Walter Sr. who worked in the subways from four p.m. until midnight rarely came home before early morning, and he treasured the little time he had with his children. On his occasional days off, feeling like a visitor to the unfamiliar daylight, he would take them to an empty lot for one of his favorite activities.

According to Wally, "My father loved kites. Loved to make them and loved to fly them. And E — I always called Susan (Edythe) that, just plain E — and I would go along and watch them soar up into the sky."

Walter also understood his children in a way that Ellen who was pre-occupied with turning Florrie into a star never could.

When little Edythe began to attend P.S. 181, she took a lot of teasing because of her bright hair and sometimes words would turn to blows. Edythe quickly developed a defensive chip on her shoulder as a result of certain incidents, and it remained with her for the rest of her life.

One day walking home from school alone a boy teased her, she answered back and he socked her.

Gripping her schoolbooks, she sat down on the front steps of her building with tears in her eyes. Her father, coming downstairs on his way to work, sat down beside her. Fighting back tears, she told him what had happened. He looked at his youngest, detecting the fighting spirit and hot temper of his Irish forebears.

"Always hit back," he said to his daughter, "and remember this, the harder they hit you, the higher you'll bounce — if you're a good ball to start with. If you're not, you might as well give up anyway."

The thin, tired man brushed back her hair from her eyes, got up and walked away.

She sat, staring after him.

As back up to his advice, he urged her to practice sparring with Wally. Soon the schoolmates who called her 'red' and 'pepper pot' were surprised at the fierceness with which she fought.

When Edythe was seven, she lived through the first significant event of her life. Just barely.

Late one afternoon — her father had already gone off to the subways — she was standing at the window in their flat, watching her brother and some friends fly kites on the sidewalk in front of the house.

Eager to join them, she ran to her mother and asked for 3¢ to buy a paper plane at the neighborhood candy store. Mrs. Marrener thought carefully, along with everything else milk had just gone up to 12½¢ a quart and every cent mattered. She looked at her seven year old, who looked back at her hopefully.

Ellen carefully counted out the pennies and gave them to the little girl, who whooped happily, as she dashed down the four flights of stairs to the street.

"I'll be right back Wal," she announced as she crossed to the candy store.

Out of habit, Wally said, "Be careful, E —"

But she was too excited at the prospect of playing with Wally and the big boys to be careful and as she dashed back across the street, a speeding car turned the corner and tossed her to the ground.

"Lying there, she looked just like a broken doll," Wally would remember many years later. "On the ground next to her was that paper plane of hers just soaked with her blood. The driver of the car picked her up in his arms and ran up the four flights of stairs to our flat. Then," he added wryly, "he ran down the stairs, straight to his bank to withdraw all his savings."

Doctors at the Free Clinic where Ellen took the girl told the distraught parents that they must expect the worst. Edythe would probably not live. But the little red-haired youngster was tougher than anyone realized. She hung on, and hung on; finally, painfully, pulling herself out of death's reach. The doctors marveled.

"Yes," they finally told her parents, "She will live. But prepare yourselves. She has two fractured legs and a broken hip and she will be a cripple for the rest of her life. She will never walk again."

For six months, Edythe was a prisoner in a complicated structure of plaster casts and traction lines, unable to move, unable to do anything more than look out the window of the bedroom towards Manhattan.

The temperament that would so ably portray the courage of Jane Froman (herself crippled by a plane crash) in the screenplay *With A Song In My Heart* may have begun to take shape on that sultry day in Brooklyn, when a little girl, against all medical advice and odds, struggled to walk again.

But it was not a totally unhappy time. What had happened to the little Marrener girl was shocking enough to have touched a nerve in the entire neighborhood. The car that ran her down could just as easily have broken the bodies of any of their children. That's the way those things happened.

"After she was back from the hospital," Wally remembered, "the ladies from the church brought over a big bag of toys and she was allowed to open one each day that she was laid up in bed. She got a big kick out of that. It added a little surprise."

The reward for the pain and the suffering was her first taste of fame — and she liked it.

"Then when she got out of traction, we were able to take her out. But she still couldn't bend one leg and she couldn't walk at all, so my folks bought her the longest wagon they could find, and we used to pull her around in that."

The little girl in her wagon, with her crown of shining hair became a neighborhood favorite, a slum princess pulled through her streets by willing and loving hands.

Eventually, the wagon gave way to crutches.

"And those she hated. So she began spending most of her time alone in the flat, mostly in the kitchen — that was her favorite room."

Looking around her, at the tawdry furnishings, she began to be acutely aware of the drabness of her surroundings and looking out the windows of the kitchen, at the pole where all the washlines were attached, she realized that she hated the view. More and more the sheets on those washlines became curtains, which rose on the private dramas she began to act out in her imagination.

At the end of six months, she went back to school but she had changed. Always aloof, she became even more so, offering her friendship to very few of her schoolmates.

Edythe, even then, was not just a regular kid on the block.

"E was choosy in picking friends, if she didn't like you she would have nuthin' to do with you. The neighbors thought she was snobbish," said Wally. "I used to watch after E and after she got a little older she had her own friends. She brought kids home to do homework on the kitchen table, Martha and Sarah Finkelstein and Ira Gossell (who later became actor Jeff Chandler); he was a little fat kid from around the corner, about half a block away."

And she began to lie.

"I can still remember walking home from school," she was quoted as saying years later, "telling the other children about all the beautiful dresses I had at home in the closet — lying through my teeth! I guess that's when I first began acting, or at least getting interested in it. Pretending, making believe, using my imagination. This I was born with; an imagination and natural talent for lying. The perfect ingredients for an actor."

The accident brought with it another foreshadowing of the 'Susan Hayward' to come. As a result of it, her hips were unbalanced and one leg was a quarter of an inch shorter than the other. For the rest of her life, she wore a lift in one shoe. But even with the lift, she was left with an odd, rolling gait. At the time that it happened, it was one more part of her ordeal. Later on, it became the 'sexy' walk that characterized her to the world.

As a child, she was drawn to the bizarre and the dramatic. Sometimes when Ellen Marrener was busy, Edythe's sister, Florence, was forced to mind the two young ones and she would often take them to a nearby cemetery where they could wander through the grounds, pausing here and there to read a tombstone or two. Sometimes they would watch, spellbound, as a funeral procession moved slowly past them.

On days when they tired of reading who was resting in peace, Florence would take them to the Kings County Hospital; known throughout the Borough of Brooklyn as the place they put the "crazies." Standing safely outside the huge iron gates, they would make faces at the patients on the lawn inside until they finally caught someone's eye. When he or she came towards them, they would shriek in horror and run away.

The trips they enjoyed most were to nearby farms, not more than a five to ten minute walk away. They would pick tomatoes and eat them sprinkled with salt taken from their kitchen or try for a handful of corn stalks, until they were caught and chased out of the field.

Most of the time, Florence was too busy to bother with the other two. As she grew up, she remained pretty and proud of her good figure and her golden-reddish hair. Ellen Marrener had sold her own faith in Florence to a relative more solvent than the rest of the family who believing that Florence could indeed make it in the professional world, paid for her dancing lessons and encouraged her to devote all her time to preparing for a career.

More and more, Wally became responsible for entertaining Edythe.

There were places she disliked violently. One was the public swimming pool, which, to most slum children, was a glorious escape during the sweltering days of summer. To Edythe, it was disgusting, with towels that remained gray and dingy no matter how often they were laundered and a smell of sweat clinging to the locker rooms no matter how carefully they were cleaned.

She much preferred going to Coney Island with Wally, ambling down the boardwalk, smelling the cool salty air, listening to the waves, then finally going into Steeplechase 'the friendly place' as it was billed. The vast entertainment park with its rides and food stands and fun houses was the pride of Coney.

Once inside, the two youngsters would seek out 'the friendly people' with the Combination Tickets. Very often, when the happy possessors of these prizes left the park, they would turn over their tickets to Wally and E. The combination offered 10 rides for 50¢ and most of the time there were a few unpunched, and the two Marrener children would remedy that immediately.

She also loved going to the neighborhood library and almost as soon as she learned to read, Edythe developed an insatiable appetite, going through everything on the shelves, even the encyclopedias.

A few years later, she would discover Thomas Wolfe and devour every word he wrote. To her it seemed incredible that the North Carolina writer had actually lived in Brooklyn at the same time that she did. So deep was her devotion to him that the neighborhood librarians gave her a nickname. Privately, they called her "the Wolfe girl."

But true heaven was in the theatres — The Brooklyn Paramount, Fox, Flatbush and Kenmore. At the crack of dawn, she and Wally would stand in line and willingly trade in their hard-to-come-by 15¢ for admission to the First Show. When it was finished and the auditorium cleared, they would hide in the bathrooms, and then sneak back into the auditorium. By the time the theatre closed at night, they were heady not only from hunger, but from seeing three complete shows.

Vaudeville performers began to recognize them (whenever they could they sat in the front row) and they began to ask 'the little redheaded girl' to climb on stage to help with the magic tricks.

'The little redheaded girl' got another turn in the spotlight when she and Wally won an amateur dancing contest. They were there courtesy of Florence, who, at seventeen, was entering all the dance contests and talent competitions she could find in Brooklyn, Queens, Long Island and New Jersey. At one of them, there was a special competition for 'amateurs' and the two little ones, who'd picked up some of her routines, entered and won.

Florence, who had never actually won anything herself, shrugged it off. Let the children play if they wanted to. Florence was headed for more important things than "prizes."

Being a woman of limited emotional range, Ellen Marrener focused almost all of her attention on Florence. Though little Edythe talked all the time about being an actress, her mother paid no attention. To her it was just "child talk." As far as she was concerned, the accident had retired the girl permanently from the great game of success.

Besides making kites, Walter also made radio sets and on his few evenings away from his job, he would plant himself at the kitchen table and put sets together. Edythe and Wally would sit next to him, looking on in absolute fascination. When he had finished, he would give each of them a turn at the headset, letting them listen to music and voices that came in "out of nowhere."

Edythe's sense of responsibility was implanted at twelve years old, when she helped her brother deliver his newspapers for the Brooklyn Eagle.

"Years after the accident, she used to help me with the Sunday editions — they were so big. We'd pile the papers in the wagon and she'd help me deliver 'em. I used to give her money to go to the movies, and get ice cream — things like that," Wally explained, "she never tried to get out of it, even if it was cold and raining or snowing hard."

On such days, Wally would sometimes stop to cup his hands around his mouth and blow some warm breath through his fingers that were numb from the cold. E would wait a minute or two and say, "Come on Wal, let's get goin', sooner we'll get home," and give the wagon a push from behind.

Actually, she was learning many things. One was the fact that her family was poor, another that the neighborhood was poor. When the country ran crashing into the Depression, the Marrener's became even poorer. They had to move from their red brick 'penthouse' on Church Avenue to a shabbier, smaller and more crowded place at 2568 Bedford Avenue. Just hanging on became harder and harder.

Edythe and Wally, like a lot of Brooklyn kids, collected junk — mostly paper — in a wagon made from a wooden soapbox with solid wooden wheels. They would get about a penny for ten pounds of paper but pennies could be changed into nickels and dimes to buy a 10¢ gallery seat at a matinee.

Sometimes Ellen Marrener would give Edythe a few household chores, which she would try to get out of by offering to go to the stores for her mother. It was more fun to go to the bakery for a ¼ loaf of Jewish rye bread — 'and see that it's fresh' — , smell the fresh baked poppy seed rolls that she loved, and gaze longingly over all the trays of raisin and cinnamon buns with icing on top. And 'day olds' were always cheaper. At the butcher shop she would ask for a nickel's worth of tongue 'the end of the tongue' she would say. Then on to the local grocer.

"Hi, red," they would greet her. Her face burned at the name and seeing her reaction, they quickly became serious about her order. It would then be penciled in as a charge and a subtotal given, to be paid on a Saturday when Poppa got his bi-monthly paycheck.

On her way home she would go through Woolworth's Department Store, passing the perfume counters, 'just to smell it,' and look at the rhinestone jewelry and clothes racks. Walking slowly home, she would stop in front of store windows, to press her upturned nose against the glass and wonder what it would be like to have money.

Her arms filled with grocery shopping bags, she would pass the other little girls in ragged dresses, and scruffy boys in straggling knickerbockers and peaked caps.

Sometimes she would stop in front of a house to admire a shining brown gelding with black mane pulling a small wagon, with an old Italian man holding the reins. There were horses too, on the outskirts of her Aunt and Uncle's place in New Jersey, where she would occasionally be sent for a summer visit, which was as close to being in the country as she ever came.

"Birthdays at the Marrener home were no big deal. Mom baked a cake or pie, and that was it," Wally said, "at Easter time we'd get a chocolate egg, or a rabbit or something. On Thanksgiving, we used to dress up in a masquerade, fill up socks with chalk and whack people with it. Flo didn't go; didn't do much of anything except stay in her own little word, dancin' mostly."

"E loved Christmas," Wally continued. "She'd be makin' all kinds of things, paintin' pictures, cards; we hadn't any money for real gifts. We'd do our Christmas shoppin' in the 5 & 10, typical of families in Brooklyn in those days. We'd wait 'til Christmas Eve to get a free tree from the stands — 'cause you knew if they didn't sell the trees they were goin' to reduce them to practically nothin'. When it got to a certain point in the evening they figured they might as well give 'em away. We used to wait 'till the last minute, when they were throwin' trees away, and go down the street and pick one up and haul it home."

"Our parents gave us what presents they could. We'd always hang up stockings. We didn't have a regular fireplace, a mantle piece or something would do. As we got older, we got less and less. We used to get apples, oranges, candy and nuts. One time I got a bottle of medicine I had to take this fish oil, to build myself up, Scott's Emulsion."

One Christmas they got a sleigh. Bundled up they went to Prospect Park not too far away, where there were some hills. Then finally, there were only gift-wrapped lumps of coal. In the language of poverty, they said, "that's the end — no more toys for you."

No more toys for Edythe instead there were her own private pleasures that she began to seek out. Riding on an open-air double-decker bus, for instance, that could take her for a nickel, from the Battery in downtown Manhattan, past the lions of the Main Public Library, up Fifth Avenue and past Central Park.

Sometimes she'd get off at the library, go in and wander around, browsing through the books and soaking up the atmosphere of learning, which was later to become so much a part of her own life.

And sometimes — best of all — she'd walk along 42nd Street or Broadway, past the wonderful new Roxy Theatre that glittered and shone like no other place in the world.

She said from the beginning, that she intended to be an actress and she was diligent in pursuing the theatre, Flatbush style. No club, church or society in the neighborhood could start casting a play without the little Marrener girl turning up for it. When she wasn't cast in a part, she would volunteer to do costumes, begging and borrowing material to make her creations.

As she approached her teens, Edythe began to think again about her grandmother, Katie Harrigan, her aunt, the Ziegfeld girl, and her uncle who played in a combo in Coney Island. They had all made careers in show business. She would, too.

She was aware that she needed to study and learn, so she sought out a local drama 'coach' and told him that she was interested in taking lessons.

Looking at the youngster, it was clear to him that the only way she could take lessons would be as a "scholarship student." Nevertheless, he told her to recite something for him.

Although she'd acted in a number of shows, Edythe suddenly found herself on the verge of panic. This was serious business! This could make a tremendous difference in her whole life! The more she thought about it, the more nervous she became and her normally high voice pitched even higher.

After a few minutes, the coach indicated that she could stop.

"You have a bad voice," he told her. "It's high. It's squeaky. And you have an accent."

"What kind of an accent?" she asked.

"A Brooklyn accent."

"But *this is Brooklyn.*"

"The students I work with do not have Brooklyn accents."

Then grudgingly accepting reality, he added, "Or if they do, they lose them quickly."

Edythe refused to be put off. Sitting down, she pleaded her case. Her voice was steady but the handkerchief she kept twisting and untwisting, and her legs, which she kept crossing and uncrossing, indicated what was going on inside her.

"Well, that's why it's so important for me to study with you. So I can learn to speak right. I'm going to be an actress — a professional actress," she ended in an unusual burst of confidence.

The coach smiled thinly.

"I wouldn't waste my time if I were you, Miss…"

"Marrener. Edythe Marrener. Why not?"

"Because you're never going to make it. It's bad enough not to speak well. But even worse, you don't understand the basic responsibility of every actress."

"What do you mean —"

"You must be meticulous about your personal appearance."

She looked at him in amazement. She had dressed carefully putting on each newly laundered piece of clothing as if it were part of a nun's habit.

"You have a hole in your shoe."

Edythe nodded, too proud to explain that she had only one pair of shoes and the cardboard in them had just worn through.

Now that he had systematically destroyed the girl, the coach smiled — "Actually, you're a very pretty little girl and I'm sure there are all sorts of things in the cards for you — "

Without another word, Edythe got up to leave. His inability to evoke a subservient reaction irritated the coach.

"The most amusing part of this," he said, "is that you obviously came here expecting to win some sort of *scholarship.*"

In those days, daughters of the poor could put their time to more profitable use than going to High School. But when she graduated from grammar school, Edythe was determined to go on with her education, and she enrolled at Girls Commercial.

Here again, she was standoffish to the other students. Although she was scholastically eligible for the Arista, the Honor Society, she never made it because it required endorsements from all the other members. Edythe's often prickly tongue kept her from having many friends.

"What's she got to be so stuck up about?" the other girls asked each other, seeing in her nothing more than another product of the Brooklyn slums, no better than they were. If anything, she wasn't even as good as they were, with her one blouse that she wore every day and washed every night. Everyone was poor, but it seemed that the Marreners were even poorer.

What few people saw was that underneath the almost ludicrous snobbery was a very frightened youngster, mistrustful of everyone and constantly on her guard against ridicule.

"The only way I knew how to protect myself," she later explained, "was to try to scare people before they scared me."

At Girls Commercial, she spent a great deal of time in the library, letting herself get caught up in the shining web of words that Thomas Wolfe spun for her. It was also in that library, she read for the first time, George Bernard Shaw's play about Eliza the flower girl who becomes a great lady.

When she read Pygmalion, she might have wished for some Professor Henry Higgins to come into her life and turn it around but she knew that the chance of that was not too likely. What of it! She would be her *own* Professor Higgins and make herself into someone the whole world would know and admire.

No question about it. She would be an actress.

One of the women in the Dramatics Department was named Eleanor O'Grady. After she heard Edythe read for the first time, she called her into her office.

"I believe you have real talent," she told the girl. "Have you ever thought about making performing your career?"

Had she ever thought —!

If she hadn't been afraid to reveal herself to anyone, she might have told the nice looking middle aged woman that she had thought of nothing else since she was a little girl playing Cinderella at P.S. 181. She might have told her about Katie Harrigan, and about the times she'd been called onstage by the magicians at the Vaudeville Theatre.

She might have said that hearing someone else tell her she had talent had finally made it real. Instead, she said in a tone that was almost too self-assured, "I'm going to be an actress, Miss O'Grady. I decided that a long time ago."

Miss O'Grady was perceptive enough to see through the emotional armor Edythe wore as regularly as she did her one blouse.

She saw to it, from then on, that Edythe was given leads in school productions. Her undemanding faith finally paid off. The girl permitted her to become a friend.

She'd always been selective about her friends.

In grade school, one of the few kids who fit her standards for friendship was Ira Grossell, whose family owned a candy store. They'd been cast together in Cinderella. Ira had been the Prince until the onset of puberty suddenly made his voice crack and turned the Prince into a silent Stage Manager.

He was a chubby boy with warm, sensitive eyes and a sweet smile. The thing they had in common was their love of movies and plays and the fact that both planned to act for a living.

When Edythe went off to Girls Commercial High School, her friendship with Ira ended. Now and then, she would see him in front of his family's candy store, and though she was aware that he was getting taller and quite handsome, they never fell into the 'dating' pattern of most teenagers.

Both of them were too busy 'getting out' and in a hurry to do it.

For in those days, in her mid-teens, Edythe was very much a young girl in a hurry.

The boys who had called her 'red' as a child, the ones who had tied tin cans to her bicycle when she was a twelve year old tomboy, suddenly became more aware of her long flaming hair and her pretty face. They began calling her 'red' again but this time there was something different in the way they said it, something taunting and a little nasty. After all, she was a redhead, and everyone knew that redheads were fiery, selfish, mean — and sexy.

"You find, as you approach the dating age," said Susan, "that men are divided into two divisions; the curious and wary. The latter seem to give redheaded women a wide berth, probably figuring they're too hot to handle. The former take the attitude that inasmuch as there are fewer redheads than blondes or brunettes, they must be different somehow. And if you want to find out check with one of the curious type; pinned down, he'll admit it!"

But if you noticed her and sought her out, she couldn't care less. There was no place in her life for the likes of them. She had no intention of ending up in a Brooklyn tenement, tied down with children and a husband who worked in a dull routine job.

It was much safer, and more satisfying to concentrate on celluloid lovers. There were a series of them, but the object of her special adoration was Ronald Colman. Elegant, gentle and world weary though he was, perhaps the most appealing thing about him to the Brooklyn girl was the beautiful way in which he spoke English, turning words into music. Someday, she told herself, she too would speak like that.

Focused as she was on herself and her future, it was a shock sometimes to look up from studying at the kitchen table and look at her family for a moment.

Ellen Marrener's brown hair was almost entirely grey. Her father seemed even slighter than his five feet five and one hundred and forty pounds should make him. His flame-bright hair had turned white and the glasses that kept slipping off his nose made him seem almost a sad figure.

Florence had quit High School long ago. Though she had slipped and fallen, and hurt her tailbone, she was determined as ever to keep on dancing. Wally had quit High School too and was working full time during the day.

But she, Edythe, would never quit. Not High School. Not anything. The mirrors in the Marrener's flat told her she was young and healthy and beautiful. And whether the world went through a Depression again — or another War, from the way people were beginning to talk, didn't really matter to her. She would get through it just fine.

It was Saturday, June 30, 1934, and after three days of temperatures hovering near 100 degrees, the mercury mercifully dropped. That morning Edythe Marrener joined her mother and sister at the kitchen table.

Mrs. Marrener was talking to Florrie about Mrs. Anna Antonio, the twenty eight year old mother convicted with two men for the murder of her husband. For the second time in twenty-four hours, the condemned woman had won a reprieve from Governor Lehman. Florrie read the morning's headlines — Woman Again Gets Stay of Execution In The Final Hours.

"Mom, can't we talk about somethin' else, it's my birthday remember?" Edythe reminded her, "I'm seventeen today."

Edythe Marrener couldn't possibly know that twenty years later she herself would portray the role of another convicted murderess, suffering similar circumstances, in a performance that would shock the movie going public around the world.

A few years before, far away from Brooklyn in Atlanta, Georgia, an unknown woman of thirty-six, had been grinding out a manuscript for over ten years, despairing with it and stuffing chairs and cupboards with chapters wrapped in brown paper. When finally assembled it became one of the great classics that the 30's produced — *Gone With The Wind.*

If it had not been for that one (and only) book written by the Atlanta housewife, perhaps the destiny of Edythe Marrener might have taken a different path. For certainly, *Gone With The Wind* changed the lives of both women.

Something about its characters; Scarlett O'Hara, the beautiful willful Daughter of the Confederacy; Ashley Wilkes, the man she pursued; Rhett Butler, the romantic rogue who pursued her; Melanie Wilkes, the kindest and gentlest of women; captured the minds and hearts of the American public as no book had since perhaps, *Uncle Tom's Cabin* almost a century ago.

When it was announced that *Gone With The Wind* was going to be made into a film, the country went crazy and the search for a girl to play the stunning, half-Irish Katie Scarlett knocked almost everything else off the front page.

Her final starring role at High School…

Wally, her mother and her father sat in the audience. Florence, who was practically the financial mainstay of the family at that point, was out dancing professionally.

But it was she, Edythe, the one her mother never took seriously and the one with the lift in her shoe, who was center stage.

Even though she wasn't making a cent as an actress — yet — she was sure that someday soon she would be making real money. Then she'd show Florence who the star of the family really was.

Unfortunately for the poor, 'someday' doesn't pay the rent or put food on the table. The Marreners reminded her that they'd sacrificed enough just to keep her in High School long after other girls were working in shops or factories, or for the telephone company.

Susan under studio contract.

CAREER

If I were starting out in this day and age, I don't think I would choose an acting career. The motion picture has all changed so tremendously. I think I'd be much more attracted to a career in something like archaeology or geology. Acting, no.

CHAPTER 3

"Susan lived at home until she went to Hollywood," Wally told me. As for the boys she left behind — "There was only one boy who used to come down to the dances that she was interested in. He went to the same church as we did, Lenox Road Baptist Church. The boy was a piano player. Susan had a little crush on him but it didn't last. There were other boyfriends but her mind was on her career."

Graduating from Brooklyn's Girls Commercial High School, the highlight of her school days was a $75 prize she won in an art contest when she was eighteen.

She took the money to invest in a career on Broadway. Producers and directors weren't exactly waiting for her. Acting upon the advice of a friend, she enrolled in the Feagan School of Dramatic Arts in Rockefeller Center, New York City. She went after the much talked about 'experience.'

Lack of money resulted in her looking for work as a model. At this time, there was a big boom in color photography and a natural redhead would be in.

Edythe (she changed the spelling of her name to have a 'classier' sound to it) had grown up 'hand-me-down-dress-poor' in the shadow of her mother's favoritism toward her sister Florence. Ellen Marrener still dressed her in what she considered demure high school clothes. Her eyebrows weren't plucked, she wore no trace of make-up, lipstick or rouge, yet determined as she was, she started the rounds of modeling agencies.

As usual, always in a hurry and with her red hair flying she walked fast and furiously to save money. Her hip rolling gait was not affected by a reminder of her pelvic fractures, which had knit incorrectly when her mother had taken her to a free clinic instead of an orthopedist.

Edythe checked the yellow pages of the Manhattan phone book tearing off the listings for model agencies. On a hunch, she picked out what she thought were the best by their addresses. Acting impulsively on that same hunch she walked into the Walter Thornton Agency and asked for a job.

One of Edythe's girl friends from Astoria, Long Island, Margaret Lane reminisced about those days back in 1938.

"We had to break into modeling the hard way then. Armed with a folio of our pictures and a scrapbook, we'd call on photographers, artists and fashion directors — and there were about 500 of them on the list."

"When we waited in reception rooms together, clutching our scrapbooks and hoping, Susan was scared, but she was wise enough to concentrate on the positive — the strong belief she had in herself. She became artist Jon Whitcomb's most beguiling cover girl when he began to draw her wistful, saucy loveliness, and that was the start of her climb as a model."

Edythe not only found favor with the well known illustrator Jon Whitcomb but the Walter Thornton Agency needing a true red head, and not having one, they became interested.

With her red hair, hazel eyes, good teeth and small but well proportioned figure, she was registered.

"As a model," she said later, "I didn't get more than a few days work a month. At $35 a day, from ads — bread, cereal, toothpaste, soaps and appearing in mail order catalogues. I was always the other girl at the picnic."

Thornton himself said of her, "She was a real lone wolf, a girl with no time for friends or social life."

As a photographer's model, it was the color photographs taken by Ivan Dimitri, illustrating a national magazine article in the *Saturday Evening Post* that first got her attention.

Titled 'How Models Come To New York', Edythe was quoted as saying, 'in my case, by subway.'

"After the article came out," Wally remembered, "agents came to the house in Brooklyn. My father was in the hospital at the time, he had had a heart attack at work — so he had no say in the matter. My mother had to give her permission for her to go to Hollywood."

Edythe read everything about David O. Selznick searching for an unknown to play Scarlett O'Hara. Although the book emphasizes Scarlett's dark hair — this time the studio wanted some red heads. And she believed it all. She read the book. She was half-Irish like Scarlett and a redhead and wanted to get in on it somehow. Besides, she was no stranger to the camera, having done a Vitaphone short scene as a hat model.

Agents from the Warner Brothers New York office offered her a $50 a week contract. There were other offers but the one that most excited her was from the David O. Selznick New York office. The story goes that director George Cukor was thumbing through the magazine when his eyes lighted on Susan. Another was that Cukor saw her on the cover of the *Saturday Evening Post*, which would have been difficult as that issue with the Marrener model in color came out October 7, 1939 when *Gone With The Wind* had completed shooting.

Finally, George Cukor, bored with the 'discovery' story said over the phone, very succinctly — "She was brought to my office by her agent."

The only person available to go with 18 year old Edythe to California was Florence, 6 years her senior. Florence felt this was her chance too; she might get a test and break into the movies once they got to Hollywood. Edythe really wanted her brother Wally to go with her, but he was needed at home.

Edythe and Florence took the train to California. They found cheap rooms and began the rounds of agent's offices. The names vary, but Benny Medford's name appears more than any other, as the agent who brought her to George Cukor. She would be just one more girl in the hundreds who would get a test for Scarlett, in the biggest publicity gimmick of the year. There were girls from all over the country waiting for even a second look.

Streetwise Edythe sized up the situation — it was tough for girls trying to break into the movies.

Never, it seemed, had there been a place on earth where men enjoyed the privilege that they did in that community. The cause was obvious. Hundreds of the most beautiful girls in American — the majority sadly deficient in talent and worldly experience — flocked to Hollywood each year. Never more so than in the year of the casting for *Gone With The Wind*. The line stretched from the studio lots through every agent's office, to any party given by any man with some free money who wanted to provide someplace for food and drinks and, most importantly, contacts.

At these parties, most of the lovely girls met a few unattractive men with little influence. There were hundreds of pretty girls waiting to be discovered, but few with Edythe Marreners real talent, who through sheer perseverance and ability got up every time they were slapped down and finally literally demanded recognition.

On September 20, 1937 at $50 a week at the Warner Brothers Studios in Burbank, she began working as an extra on her six month contract.

In her very first film, *Hollywood Hotel* Louella Parsons, the powerful Hearst columnist would play herself in a movie based on her radio show. Edythe Marrener was put on the film as an extra.

Warners wanted to change Edythe's name and she was holding out for her grandmother's name, Katie Harrigan, but they laughed her down. From now on, it would be Susan Hayward.

The newly christened Susan Hayward made an important and influential contact on the set of *Hollywood Hotel*— the self-acclaimed Queen of Gossip, Louella Parsons.

Next at Warners, she did a small bit as a telephone operator in the Bette Davis — Erroll Flynn potboiler *The Sisters*. The unbilled Susan Hayward in the film would be billed over the formidable Miss Davis the next time they were in another picture together.

Following this, she was assigned to *Girls on Probation* putting her 10th in the credits under the up and coming Ronald Reagan. She was back to no billing again in *Comet Over Broadway* before her option was dropped by the studio. During this time, in between filming, she posed for cheesecake pin-up stills, which she disliked so intensely she would never agree to do the same again.

"Susan really got kicked around and I think it got to her," producer Marty Rackin said, "Jack Warner, the head of Warner Bros., used to say that an actor on his ass, was worth two on his feet and he kept them that way. Susan was shy and very insecure then and after the Warner treatment she never let down her guard."

While waiting for her chance to test for *Gone With The Wind*, Paramount OK'd a test for her at their studio, to be directed by Henry Hathaway.

Contrary to popular opinion, this, in fact, was her very first screen test, not the one for *Gone With the Wind*; "As a matter of fact I took her very first screen test. She was 18. I did the test that got her into Paramount. She chose a recitation *Alter Ego*, by Arch Obler. She recited that for the test. It was made in color because of her red hair. She was marvelous, just sensational. It was 15 minutes, a whole reel; it was made on nitrate (which disintegrates). She was not nervous or in awe. She wasn't in awe of anybody in her life, except maybe, Selznick. I wasn't around to know but maybe him. But he would be the only one that I would imagine she might be in awe of. Her *Gone With The Wind* test came *after* that," he repeated. "She did that *Alter Ego* test and eventually it got her a contract at Paramount."

Alter Ego was the story of a girl with a double-personality one good, one bad, with the evil one fighting to take over the weaker good side. It was a female version of Jekyll and Hyde and was made into a feature film in 1945 called *Bewitched* starring Phyllis Thaxter.

At 19 years of age, Susan did finally test for Scarlett, and then did over 100 other tests with young actors who were trying out for the part of Ashley Wilkes. While testing she held out hopes for Scarlett and resisted other studio possibilities.

Glenn Langan was one of the young actors who tested with Susan for the role of Ashley Wilkes. "The scene from *Gone With The Wind* used for my test was the one during which Scarlett, after the death of her second husband, washed her mouth out with cologne so Rhett Butler will not know she had been drinking." Langan believed Susan looked right for Scarlett, however inexperienced.

While she was awaiting word, Susan's father died in a Brooklyn hospital at the age of 59. "When he passed away," her brother said, "Susan called and asked us, "Why don't you come out to California? So I quit my job and my mother and I took the Greyhound bus to California, it was her first trip anywhere, her first time out of Brooklyn. That was early in 1938."

Meanwhile, Wally remembered, "Her agent told her, 'If you can hold out a little longer I'll get you a better deal on the contract.' She could have had a contract at $75 a week but this agent was holding out for $350 to start with, we all wanted it for her. She said, 'Once you start low you might stay low.' She had a good mind and she was pretty cagey with a buck."

Then, on November 18, 1937, in a memo to Mr. Daniel T. O'Shea Selznick wrote; "I think we can forget about Susan Hayward… we don't need her anymore as a stand-in for Scarlett, or to work with people we are testing for the other role, what with others around…"

According to Henry Hathaway, "The biggest disappointment in her life, that maybe set her off, was she thought she was going to be Scarlett. She was shook by it. They wanted some new person — what the hell! Vivien Leigh was unknown. She would have been equally as good as Vivien Leigh playing that part. Selznick didn't care at that time who it was, just so she was beautiful, brilliant, and full of belligerence — and she was. She was Scarlett! If ever there was one she was an instinctively good actress, she could have handled it."

Asked by a reporter about it years later, Hayward said, as if excusing herself for not getting the part; "It would have been the shortest career on record. I was 16½ (19) years old and I didn't know where the camera was. I was just one amongst many who were brought there — sort of a publicity thing. I think they knew all along who was gonna play Scarlett."

AT EASE

Some people have to be constantly amused. I don't. I don't have to be surrounded by people or "entertained."

CHAPTER 4

For quick money and because she had heard you got cases of the product, Susan anonymously took a posing job again for a Shredded Wheat advertisement. About this experience at that time, she said, "I glanced out of the window at the cheap bungalow court where we all lived, my mother, brother and sister. I studied the worn couch with broken springs, the splintering chairs causing runs in my nylons and all the free samples of Shredded Wheat from the company we had to eat..."

It was six months later that she landed her contract at Paramount, in 1939, cast in a small part replacing Frances Farmer who was tied up in a play in New York, or in a sanatorium as believed.

At Paramount, as one of the new starlets, she recalled; "What I remembered most was the mop closet (the dressing room) all the studios were crowded in those days and they stuck many of us brash upstarts into cubbyholes which barely gave us room to turn around in let alone change costumes and clean up."

At a starting salary of $250 a week, she made her first appearance in *Beau Geste*, with Gary Cooper and Ray Milland. She received fifth billing but no mention in the reviews. From there, she went up to second place for *Our Leading Citizen*, a minor effort, and dropped to fourth place in another poor film *$1,000 A Touchdown*. She began a new year and a new picture- *Among The Living*. This part, as a small town vamp, seemed to portend the role of a vixen, which she was to portray so well throughout her career.

The Scarlett test had an adverse effect on her when she was new at Paramount. She had preconceived, stubborn notions of her ability.

The studio gave a party to introduce all the young hopefuls and all the super-stars and successful actresses were there, Claudette Colbert, Paulette Goddard, and Marlene Dietrich, the studio's biggest box-office names of the time.

To Susan it was a learning experience: "All my life I've been terribly frightened of people. At the studio, it was the casting director, the cameramen, reporters and publicists who asked endless questions. I thought everyone was so brilliant and I felt so inadequate. At this party, those famous stars seemed so poised, so sure of themselves. Or so I thought. That's when I got the idea that I should try to be like them."

People at the studio advised her to change because her attitude was wrong. She stopped being herself and tried to copy everyone else. She got so mixed up and became more confused than ever. The ones who tried to help her make changes approached her the wrong way. They criticized her and as a result, she became belligerent.

"Her agent tried to get her to put on more of a front," Wally said, "he told her that she should have a house with a swimming pool and a big car."

She objected to this, "If you keep me working," she told her agent, "when will I be able to enjoy all of that. I don't need a swimming pool so all the drifters can come in while I'm working and use it." Later on when she could afford it, she would by herself Christmas presents, like a fur coat one year, a diamond ring the next. She enjoyed spending money but she was still careful.

Louella Parsons did not forget the little redhead who apple-polished her with attention while at Warners. She chose her along with a few other promising players, including Jane Wyman and Ronald Reagan to begin a Vaudeville Tour on November 13, 1939, in Santa Barbara; then on to the Golden Gate Theatre in San Francisco, Philadelphia, Pittsburg, Baltimore, New York, Washington D.C. and Chicago. Throughout the tour the cast did 4-5 shows a day of songs, dances and skits. Susan did sketches with Reagan in which she slapped his face after an innocent remark he made. She hit him hard enough for him to remember to this day. It was believed that Susan and Jane Wyman were enemies from the start, over Susan's interest in Reagan, who was Wyman's fiancé. Mostly Susan did an 'is anybody here from Brooklyn' routine. She endeared herself to Louella for the rest of the columnist's life, and when they returned to Hollywood, Louella would start the publicity ball rolling for the ambitious starlet."

Items began to appear with regularity in her column, usually telling the studio they should give her better parts. Meanwhile Susan's elocution lessons were laying on a finishing school accent over her pure Brooklynese. She joined the dozen promising players at Paramount — The Golden Circle.

One of that group Richard Webb has not forgotten their first meeting; "I met up with her around 1940. She was a beautiful gal with a husky voice that turned me on. I would say she was a 'ballsy' gal. I was under contract there and the guy who handled Veronica Lake's and my publicity was

Cecil Perril. They were trying to push their new actors all the time and Cecil arranged some things. Susan and I did some publicity poses around the pool of the Beverly Hills Hotel. One week they had me engaged to Martha O'Driscol in print, the next week to Ssan Hayward. Susan was highly intelligent, very alert, and had a tremendous character. I thought of all the girls, that she would make it."

Susan with Ronald Reagan.

Susan's advancing movie career affected her mother who became increasingly pretentious. Ellen Marrener still believed that when Florence got her break she would outdistance her younger sister. After all, Florrie was beautiful compared to Susan and she could dance whereas Susan could not. Florence was a hit in Holly wood with all the men who turned around for a second look at the lovely girl. While she looked back, Susan only looked straight ahead for better jobs and bigger parts in the business.

Susan took an increasing interest in astrology; looking for answers or guideposts to help direct her life. Commenting on this she said, "I've been interested in it for years. I have all the books and read them from cover to cover. I'm a Cancer with a Leo rising, which gives you a tip. I'm very much as my sign says, moody, the sensitivity and all that — but otherwise I'm much more a Leo."

Whether it was the planets or her intuition that moved her to step out of line in front of a studio sales convention for exhibitors she took the opportunity to speak her mind. Chosen to say welcoming words, Hayward said compulsively; "Several of you have asked why I'm not in more Paramount Pictures and that's a damned interesting question."

Then addressing herself directly to studio chief Y. Frank Freeman. "Well, Mr. Freeman do I get a break or don't I?"

"Things became easier after that," she said, "Anyway I always saw the thing as a job. I was never late. I always learned my lines and I did what the director told me to do because he was the boss. I didn't party. I went home and read or studied. I didn't romance anybody for work, no way. I wanted to make it right."

Susan fancied herself older than her years when she hit Hollywood. One evening, on one of her rare evenings on the town, at the nightspot Macambo, she was sitting with two overbearing young men who were giving her the full treatment in open admiration. Reporter Harry Evans spotted her and getting an introduction told her he'd like to do an article on here.

"Why?" Susan asked.

"Because I admired your work in your last picture very much," he replied.

"Oh yes," she said. "My latest non-starring film. If you decide to do this article, I have some special photographs to illustrate it — snapped from the neck down. You can reach me through any unimportant press agent at Paramount. And thanks for the compliment," she added, dismissing him. "I didn't know I looked so young and naïve."

To her he was just another aggressive Hollywood character trying to get her phone number. Her belligerence that night at the Macambo had become her natural reflex, developed as a kid from Brooklyn with a chip on her shoulder and a determination to beat every male Hollywood smarty. In all, she had become overly suspicious and very pugnacious. She would not be like some of the others who had their spirit beaten down to the point where they would play ball with anybody.

Henry Hathaway, among others, agreed with that comment; "She never slept around, not at all, she wasn't a flirt."

Susan handled men on their own terms, as she said, "I've been fortunate. I've always been liberated, but circumstances differ with each woman. I think that if a woman does the same job as a man, she should get the same respect but I personally don't want to be in competition with a man. I would rather have him lead the way, with slight encouragement from me, of course. And some nudging to make sure he leads me in the right direction. But I have no desire to go out and run some man's garbage truck."

Louella Parsons gave her another boost in her column when she told Paramount Studio that they had a young Bette Davis on the lot. Now she practically demanded they put her in a decent picture. So they loaned her out to Columbia.

Director Gregory Ratoff tested 35 girls for the Robert Sherwood production of *Legacy* before he found his Hester in 23 year old Hayward. The film was released under the title *Adam Had Four Sons* and in it, Susan as Hester, was hot for every one of them. As the nymphomaniac home wrecker, it was her best role to date and she took advantage of it. She got third billing to Ingrid Bergman and Warner Baxter. The New York Times critic wrote; "Susan Hayward so coyly overacts the romantically unlicensed mischief-maker that often she is ridiculous."

Susan was grateful to director Ratoff for her chance and she never forgot Bergman's professional manner and kindness toward her in helping her gain screen time and experience, as Bergman threw many scenes her way. Invariably, she said, Ingrid Bergman was her favorite actress and meant it. As for the critics: "I don't like critics very much; I don't read them. I have much more respect for my own opinion. If the work I've done pleases me, nothing a critic says is about to change my mind."

The Hollywood grapevine gossip was out. Hayward was good. One of the people who studied her work in the film was producer Walter Wanger. It was Wanger's opinion that Susan darned near stole the picture from a darned good actress, Ingrid Bergman. A fact that seemed never to have been publicized to any extent was that Susan was nominated for best supporting actress because of her work in the film.

Why didn't her employers do something then about this recognition? Why didn't they buy a special story for her and give her a star build up? *Adam* was produced at Columbia. Why did Paramount treat the whole matter as it were a freak of fortune and wasted her proven ability for another five years? This is one of the mysteries of the film business. Anyone can be ignored in Hollywood.

Possibly one answer was Hayward was a curious standout at Paramount. She displayed a flare for histrionics in front of the cameras, as she modified her artificially throaty voice into dramatically convincing inflections. More experienced actresses, noticing her fiery competence, felt threatened and pleaded with their directors not to be cast opposite her. Susan, without being arch or in any way showy, inspired a nervous watchfulness in her fellow starlets and either desire or impotent fear in the young men of the Golden Circle.

People seemed to be always angry with her, a condition of life that she not only tolerated but actually appeared to thrive on. Her world, inside and out, was one of ire.

Her career had hardly begun when she was sued by the Walter Thornton model agency in New York and her first agent in Hollywood, in both cases for breach of contract.

Thornton claimed; "I made her famous. When she left for Hollywood on a contract I got for her (Warner Bros.) her name was Edythe Marrener then and she was a very discouraged looking little girl. She came to me in 1937 after having been tested and turned down by several movie studios. Then I went to work to build her into a star. I taught her make-up, grace, gave her confidence in herself, spent lots of money getting her good publicity, and my wife and I helped her with her clothes to make her look smart when she went for jobs. We made contacts for her career. Then came a contract for Hollywood, which we got for her. When she left she kissed us good-bye and swore she would never forget all we had done for her and cried when the train pulled out."

Possibly Susan was too busy now to try to remember or too young at the time to give it much more thought or attention than the casual remark that almost anyone might make in similar circumstances. Who has not made similar promises on an emotional parting?

While other girls were going right to the top, she was given the parts nobody else wanted. Susan, now back at her home studio, was shipped off to the lower rated Republic Studio for a B picture, *Sis Hopkins*, with Judy Canova and Jerry Colona.

At Republic, she met studio contract player John Carroll, a Rhett Butler type, who made a play for her and this time she let herself get caught — just briefly.

The country was at war that December of 1941 and Susan was in a warring mood at the studio. Things went from bad to bedlam. Then suddenly she was called into the front office and told they would be loaning her out for the important lead in *Dark Waters*. Louella was pleased and gave her readers the scoop. Susan's faith was restored, but just as swiftly as it came, it went.

Unexpectedly, Merle Oberon was available. Hers was a box office name, so the deal was called off. Hurt and humiliated she stormed into the front office demanding to know the reason why. Why hadn't they protected her when the contract was already signed? A top executive then told her he had deliberately okayed the cancellation to teach her a lesson. She knew then in some way she would have to start all over again.

Paramount sent her to Kentucky to judge a horse race. She went cooperatively. They loaned her a creamy beige molded-to-her-figure gown to wear. It was originally made for Carole Lombard. When she returned to Hollywood there was a studio wardrobe woman waiting at the station to take the gown back. She took score of the incident and one day would give back as good as they gave.

Cecil B. De Mille, the king of showmanship at that time on the lot, was preparing *Reap The Wild Wind*.

Jesse L. Lasky, Jr. had never forgotten his experience with her on that film; "I met her and knew her through *Reap The Wild Wind*. I was fortunate to be one of the writers on it and there was a day I remember, I was working on some sort of scene. De Mille read the scene; it was a rough draft. They were going to test Susan and De Mille said, 'Jesse I'm interested in this girl, because you know, the moment in the film is coming when the divers go down and they open the chest, and the first thing they see is this great streaming blaze of red hair coming out of the chest at the bottom of the sea in this wrecked ship. She has the right color hair. Whether she has the right color acting, we must learn. Now you go out Jesse and work the test with her."

I went out and I worked the test with them and read with her, rehearsing. I thought she was quite promising even then and I went back afterward and told De Mille, which was dangerous. Saying someone was marvelous could have been the kiss of death — 'writer's don't cast pictures my dear boy,' De Mille would have said. It could have been that way but in this case he looked at the test and he was very moved, very impressed. That was her first break at Paramount."

Lasky continued, "I certainly couldn't have imagined how far she would go. When I saw her, I thought she was very promising and certainly a beauty. I had no idea she would become the actress that she did."

"I had to learn to channel my energy very early in my career," Susan had said, "In the old days of movie making, when a director said 'Action!' and he meant for tears or laughter or whatever mood was needed, you had to be ready — or they'd get someone else to do the job. You couldn't take time to get in the mood; you were paid to *be* in the mood."

"You had to have your emotions right on tap, to turn it on — snap!

Reap the Wild Wind.

Like that. I got my early training with some very good directors, William Wellman *(Beau Geste)* Gregory Ratoff *(Adam Had Four Sons)* De Mille *(Reap The Wild Wind)* — and they weren't about to sit around and wait for me or anyone to get in the mood. I didn't spend time between scenes joking with the crew or playing poker with the wardrobe women. I saved my energy so that when they said, 'Action!' I was ready. I learned it because it was part of my trade. And by the same token, I learned to turn the emotions off just as quickly."

Reap The Wild Wind opened at the Radio City Music Hall that March in 1942. Hayward got 6th billing below John Wayne and Paulette Goddard, with whom she had competed for the role of Scarlett just a few years before.

She was so effective that Paramount gave her *The Forest Rangers* again with Goddard — competing with her for Fred MacMurry, the male lead.

I Married A Witch and *Star Spangled Rhythm* with an all studio cast, in which she sang with her voice dubbed, completed her 1942 film schedule.

Republic released *Hit Parade of 1943* with Susan and attentive John

Ray Milland, Paulette Goddard, Susan Hayward and John Wayne in Reap the Wild Wind.

Carroll, a comedown for her that was most discouraging. Louella wrote, "redhead Susie Hayward and John Carroll will soon announce their engagement."

Susan, however, called the whole thing off when she found Carroll to be a cheapskate. It appeared to be a wise decision in light of Carroll's later troubles; when a lawsuit by a seventy year old widow demanded the return of $228,000 she claimed to have loaned him.

The studio publicity departments tended to inspire a sexual laissez faire attitude among the starlets in those days, with their constant inventions of romantic liaisons, and the gossip columnists ate it up.

Susan, fitting into this 'norm', began having romantic attachments. Ellen Marrener, dependent on her daughter for support, could say little about Susan's conduct, which was discreet enough and in a way, almost expected by her peers and superiors. If she was going to make a career by playing mean little sex kittens on the screen, there had to be a certain amount of real life initiation.

William Holden and Susan began a lengthy affair during the making of *Young And Willing*. After they finished the film, they went to Paris, passionately inseparable for the time.

Eddie Bracken who was in *Young And Willing* with Holden and Hayward recalled a scene between Susan and himself off camera; "Everybody was telling dirty jokes and she walked into the dressing room. I had told a joke and everybody was on the floor laughing at it. It had a four-letter word in it. They asked me to tell the story to Susan and a couple of others. When Susan heard the four letter word, she slapped my face. It was such a stinging blow; I can feel it to this day. I didn't realize it, but I hit her. After that Susan and I were fastest of friends, maybe she liked to get hit, I don't know. I had never hit a woman, never would. I felt terrible, but because of my alertness, of hitting in the prize ring, I just reacted too fast."

Susan was receiving mail from her brother who was now in the army. "That was a sad portion of my life," he recollected, "you had to be at least five feet. I just made it. I got into a transportation outfit, driving jeeps. Susan joined a nanny outfit down at Long Beach. She had a uniform and everything. She would go and spend a few hours there each week. She did volunteer service and sold war bonds."

Wally had a picture by his bunk from his sister inscribed: "To Wally from his little sister Susan, also known as Edythe, Momma, movie actress, Miss Hayward and hey Red! Love and kisses — Susan." All of his buddies in the army wanted autographed photos from him when they found out Susan Hayward was his sister. As Wally said, "Getting those pictures of Susan to give around kept me outta a lot of K.P."

In 1944, after Susan returned from San Francisco for the premier of *Jack London*, in which she played Charmian Kittredge, the sweetheart of the author. She began volunteering some evenings at the Hollywood Canteen as part of the war effort to help servicemen's morale. She was serving behind a snack bar at the canteen when she saw a young Leslie Howard type emceeing the show. The tall blonde actor's name was Jess Barker.

Jess Barker, born in Greenville, South Carolina in 1912, was a better than average athlete during his High School days and aspired to a baseball career. An opportunity came for Barker to go to New York; here he made the acquaintance of several theatrical people, and an inflated ego prompted him to take 'a fling at acting.' A course of study at the Theodora

To Wally - from his little sister Susan also known as "Edythe" - "mama" "movie actress" "Mrs Barker" "Miss Hayward" and "Hey Red!" Love and kisses

Irvine Studio for the Theatre in New York, led to stage engagements. For a dozen years, he trouped in New York and on the road, playing opposite such luminaries as Ina Claire, Tallulah Bankhead and Lenore Ulric. Plays in which he appeared included such hits, as *You Can't Take It With You*, *Allure*, *Magic* and so on. Then came a low period, between seasons in 1940-1942 during which time Barker was out of work because of a dearth of theatre productions.

So, he made the acquaintance of several Hollywood people and an increasingly inflated ego prompted him to take 'a fling at movies.' Under a studio contract, he got work in Hollywood because being 4F, he was available and the crop of Hollywood leading men was lean; the six foot, blue-eyed blonde actor of Irish-English descent made his screen debut in *Cover Girl* at Columbia Studios opposite red-headed Rita Hayworth.

Oddly enough, Susan had wondered at one time if she should have changed her name because of Rita Hayworth who occupied an adjoining dressing room at Paramount, thinking the public might get their almost similar sounding names confused.

Later, as movie magazine columnists would say, "He (Jess) found his heart at the Hollywood Canteen — in Susan Hayward."

nother version is that Gregory Ratoff who had just completed *Adam Had Four Sons* with Susan was on a trip to New York and caught Jess in a stage show. Seeing him, he thought that Barker would be the ideal leading man to play opposite Susan in real life.

But whatever fates brought her and Jess Barker together in 1943, soon there was no turning back. She became pregnant by Barker that same year.

While Susan was attracted by the up and coming actor, she didn't consider him stable husband material and for a time toyed with the idea of having his child out of wedlock. When she finally went to the studio heads and told them of her condition, they informed her that if she didn't marry Barker her contract would be terminated. The studio had told her who to date, how to dress, what to say to the press, and now they were telling her whom she should marry. Determined to become a movie star she never defied the studio's dictatorial hold over her life. She married him.

Jess hardly knew the emotional hurricane he was marrying, and little suspected the furies that would engulf him over the next ten years of his life. He should have been forewarned when Susan, acting on her mother's advice, insisted that they sign a prenuptial financial agreement in which they each waived their right to community property should there be a divorce.

"My mother won't come to the wedding unless you do (sign)" Susan pleaded to Jess.

Mother Marrener went to the wedding without protest, as Jess had signed the document. Susan judged correctly that she, the more ambitious one, would outdistance her husband professionally and wanted her future bank account protected.

The marital storms between the Barkers began almost immediately. After three months, they broke up, only to have the studio decree that they reconcile for the sake of appearance.

On February 19, 1945 at St. John's Hospital in Santa Monica Susan gave birth to non-identical twins, Timothy and Gregory. Gregory was named after Gregory Ratoff who gave Susan her break as a shrew in

Barker Family.

Adam Had Four Sons. (She remembered he chose her from among the 35 actresses trying out for the part.)

The span of the time between the marriage ceremony and the birth of the twins, seven months, was just long enough for the studio to issue a news release about the 'premature' birth. To Paramount's relief, none of the columnists had guessed the hoax. Susan's forced marriage to Barker was just an opening to the shattering circus of publicity that would later sweep over the couple.

Louella, who was at the wedding in St. Thomas Episcopal Church in Hollywood stuck up for her protégé when she and Jess started to battle. "Susie said they are temperamentally unsuited to each other." She added, "Susie led a sheltered life up until her marriage."

Susan got lost in *The Fighting Seabees*, again with John Wayne and again on loan to Republic. She did get second billing to the increasingly popular box office star.

"John Wayne is my favorite leading man of all time," she would repeatedly say, "He's so big and rugged and so strong and can do practically anything, yet he's so gentle. I've always adored him, always, but then so has the whole world."

In her next picture, Eugene O'Neil's *The Hairy Ape*, she got second billing next to William Bendix. A reviewer wrote, "Miss Hayward who is achieving a type of ultimate odiousness, resorts at times to artificiality, but generally contributes her full share to the picture."

Louella kept mentioning Susan for several leads at Paramount, in fact several in a week, but they generally went to someone else.

The Barkers rented a modest house in Beverly Hills, then Columbia Pictures dropped Jess and his agent signed him up with Universal. Susan's contract was to end with her next film, *And Now Tomorrow*. She had several offers at this point and one was from David O. Selznick, the mogul who memo'd her out of work in 1939.

Louella spoke for Susan in her column when she wrote, "Susie says Life is beautiful, my career is moving along and you should see my babies, you've never seen anything so cute. Jess has been a good boy. I believe we're making a success of our marriage."

Susan had decided on an offer, 'because, she said, the moon was right.' But first, she had to do one for Howard Hughes' studio RKO, *Deadline At Dawn*. She would play a dance hall girl who helps clear a naïve sailor of a murder charge.

Director Harold Clurman spoke enthusiastically: "The whole experience is very vivid. Susan Hayward was very nice, but she was not in the best state there, because for some reason they (Paramount) had lost interest in her. One thing the film did for her was to make her rise again, until she became a star, as we all know. Clifford Odets wrote some good lines, it got good notices, and it's played all over the world. Considering it took only about $500,000 to make I am sure the studio made a lot of money on it."

Bill Williams, her co-star, who played the sailor in the movie couldn't forget something that had happened; "She was a heck of an actress and a lovely human being. The last shot in the picture was when I was sitting in the bus with her; remember she was going to go with me. We had to kiss and it wasn't right. Either I was holding her too tight or was a little too innocent about it. It went on about 3-4 hours. I said, "Gee Susie, it's been a long time kissing you hasn't it?"

"Bill," she said, "I gotta tell you something, you didn't do anything for me, either."

One of the reasons was probably Barbara Hale. After the premier of *Deadline At Dawn* in Rockford, Illinois, Bill Williams married Barbara Hale on June 22, 1946.

Susan went to Universal Pictures under personal contract to producer

And Now Tomorrow.

Walter Wanger.

As Susan told publicity director Graham Kislingbury at Universal, "I had two opportunities. Selznick offered me a contract but he had no definite plans for me. Wanger said, you come in and do this picture for me, and sign a contract and I will build you into a star. That's why I went with Wanger."

Susan now had someone who believed in her and she had great confidence in him. That was all she needed.

Wanger said, "They've sprung a redheaded Bette Davis on me. She reads every book written, printed and pesters me to buy stories for her. If Susan had her way, I'd own more literature than the public library."

"I have an insatiable appetite for reading," she admitted, "I'll read anything that comes along, even the encyclopedia if I run out of other things.

I consider it all grist for the mill; it all goes into the burner and something worthwhile is bound to come out."

Wanger first put her in a technicolor Western *Canyon Passage* with Dana Andrews. The world premier of *Canyon Passage* was held in Portland, Oregon, home of its author Ernoe Laycox — which is possibly why the movie out grossed *Gone With The Wind* in the State of Oregon.

Smash Up: The Story of a Woman.

But it was her next Walter Wanger picture that was the turning point for Susan. Wanger bought a property, tailored made for her untapped talents. *Smash Up: The Story of a Woman*. In it, she would portray the neglected wife of a crooner. It was said it was based on the life of Dixie Lee, the wife of crooner Bing Crosby.

Susan really needed a big hit because by this time she was supporting her unemployed husband, her mother, and giving handouts to her sister.

Wanger had an original screenplay written for Susan from the story by Dorothy Parker and Frank Cavett. Miss Parker's reputation speaks for itself. Cavett was one of the most proficient and successful writers in Hollywood. The original title of the Parker-Cavett opus, written for Susan, was 'Angelica.' It was later changed to *Smash Up*.

She was being given the chance of a lifetime as the dipsomaniac and she reached out for it with both hands, determined to make every scene count in her favor. As the unhappy alcoholic wife, Hayward worked on her part every second she had on and off the camera.

Wanger's former publicity man, Graham Kislingbury said on the making of *Smash-Up*; "Mrs. Marty Mann, who was director for National Education on Alcoholics, and her assistant came out as technical advisors on the picture, both of them having been alcoholics. My wife and I took Mrs. Mann and her assistant to Lucy's, which was a famous place for dinner in those days in Hollywood. Mrs. Mann gave Susan a lot of background for the film."

Susan commented to the press; "Women should not drink. Women are not constituted like men; they're too emotional and can't take a lot of liquor. A woman spends hours making herself beautiful and then after two drinks her face falls."

Her director on *Smash-Up*, Stuart Heisler, became wise to her method of whipping up her emotions: "Susan had so many emotional crises on tap that she arranged a set of signals, like a lifted finger or a nod of her head, to let me know when she was in the proper mood to start the scene."

She was afraid to speak, for fear it would break her emotional pitch. Heisler became so sensitive to her vibrations that he shared every moment of anguish with her, he said, "What an ordeal that picture was. I was limp as a rag every night."

So was her co-star Lee Bowman, but for different reasons. He found her cold, difficult to relate to and remained bitter about the whole experience. In later years, he said he would not even speak of it to anyone as long as she was alive.

Marsha Hunt, an excellent actress, co-starring as well in the picture recalled: "Sadly she had absolutely nothing to do with me. I never understood why. I finally realized it wasn't personal, I couldn't have offended her. This was a person so private and so closely involved with her job at hand that all relationships with others were nonexistent. After the scene (in which she attacks Miss Hunt in the powder room — giving her a beating) she went back to her dressing room. She would turn on her heel and walk away. I don't think I ever worked with anyone more private, more excluding. Maybe she felt it might break the spell."

After the picture was in release, Miss Hunt met Susan in a department store in Beverly Hills.

"She was dressed as for a garden party. I don't mean she was badly dressed; she was extremely feminine, in a floating chiffon gown, wide picture hat, and little white gloves. She was gorgeous, a beautiful woman, and so gowned that your eye was fastened on her. She was standing in front of can openers, strainers, utensils, and kitchen supplies. When I glanced up from the counter where I was shopping, there she was facing me, without a sign of recognition."

Someone who knew Susan well said, "She was painfully shy, a trait which takes the form of brutal frankness. She is almost sullen with strangers, making no effort to please them. She goes out of her way to make an unfavorable impression. She used to say, 'you have to accept me at my worst or not at all.' She didn't want to wear glasses, and half the time she couldn't make her way without them. That's why she didn't recognize people — she couldn't see them."

Graham Kislingbury had further recollections on *Smash-Up*, "I remember when the picture was completed. I came up with an idea that if I could get Susan to Sacramento, we would screen the movie for the Legislators at a midnight preview. I was sure we could get it presented before the assembly in the Senate, before the Governor. We then could probably get some good wire breaks out of it. I talked Susan into going. I found out that somewhere along the line, somebody must have pushed her around, maybe they pushed too hard. I never did. So maybe she trusted me?"

We went to San Francisco first and had a press conference with the critics at the St. Francis Hotel. (Susan sipped sherry — publicly). Later we were driving from San Francisco up to Sacramento and Susan said to Jess on the way up, 'I think I'm gettin' too old for this sort of thing.' She was 30 years old."

At a dinner party before the preview that night, for the leaders of the assembly and the Senate with Governor Earl Warren there, and other dignitaries, Susan made a little speech before dinner.

"It's just wonderful, to meet you men who run the State. This is my adopted State, I come from Brooklyn. It's a beautiful State, but there is just one thing I wish you gentlemen would do. I wish you would remove those atrocious billboards from our highways."

Fru Morton, the lobbyist for Foster & Kleiser, the big outdoor sign company turned red as a beet.

During dinner, two highway patrolmen came in and put handcuffs on Jess Barker and arrested him for impersonating the husband of Susan Hayward.

"This beautiful girl couldn't be married to a guy like this," they admonished as they hauled him off.

"You bring back my husband, bring him back," Susan shouted. They all broke up laughing, as the assembly was in on the gag.

Susan wasn't laughing, and neither was Barker.

The New York Times film critic Bosley Crowther wrote: "Susan Hayward performs the boozy heroine with a solemn fastidiousness which turns most of her scenes and drunken fumbling and heebies into key burlesque."

Life magazine gave the film a four page spread. The public went for it and found Hayward's performance very sympathetic and other critics singled out her performance as one of the most revealing character portraits of a woman alcoholic as one of the most memorable of the year.

Susan Hayward got her first 'best actress' nomination from the Academy of Motion Pictures Arts & Sciences.

She was headed for triumph and disaster.

Loretta Young, who won the Oscar (1947) as Best Actress for *The Farmer's Daughter* said, "I personally voted for Susan Hayward, because I was absolutely stunned by this performance, and when I saw it, I knew I couldn't do it as well. I knew that woman had done that part magnificently. And I voted for her because I think she deserved it."

Loser, Susan Hayward, kept her chin up for the press. "I'll be nominated for an Oscar again," she swore. "Maybe not next year. Maybe I'll have to wait until the fifties. (1958 exactly) But I intend to win someday."

GOSSIP

---

*I have no interest in gossip. I think
people who repeat tales about other people
should have their mouths taped.*

CHAPTER 5

Susan's career was ignited by her mentor Walter Wanger, and really caught fire after her performance as an alcoholic wife in *Smash-Up*. As Susan's star rose, Jess's burned up. His yearly income from his acting would usually be counted in the hundreds of dollars, not the thousands. His first few films shortly after his marriage to Susan were hits with the bobby soxers. Yet soon afterwards, he seemed to take a back seat to his ambitious wife, looking after the children in the daytime and not particularly looking for work. Was Jess lazy or was he merely becoming what he felt Susan needed to become a success herself — who can really say? Could Susan have stayed married to a driving, self-realizing, ambitious male? Or was she too competitive?

She had little or no time to be a good mother, giving every waking moment over to her career. Jess became both mother and father, taking the boys out shopping and on outing sprees while his wife spent long hours at the studio.

About her ambition Susan was quoted as saying, "I feel sorry for anyone who doesn't have some drive or ambition. If you don't have it, you're nowhere and going nowhere. You have to have a purpose in life, a reason for being. Otherwise why be here?"

Susan who said she needed very strong men in her life, contradicted herself by falling for their weaknesses, and then resented them for it.

She was a moody creature and became very aggressive during periods of strenuous work. There were continuous arguments with Jess over his failure to find work, and sometimes they became violent. What she may have failed to realize, were the boys to lose the one steady parent they had, and Susan's 'masculine' ego would have been damaged if Jess had donned the normal worldly role of a husband. In this, she was like her mother in her neurotic refusal to face up to her true feelings about her husband and children. As a result of all this Jess drank more and more and the boys became confused. Susan lied to journalists, spinning her quaint homey stories of family togetherness with as much conviction as she read dialogue in front of the cameras.

To ease his sense of lost confidence, Jess would invite his other 'at liberty' actor friends over for cocktails around the pool. Susan, coming home after a hard day at the studio, would go to her room and stay there until he got rid of them.

When he didn't and arguments ensued, she fled from their home and sought sanctuary with understanding friends who would hide her from Jess. She slept on their couch. On one occasion, she spent two weeks in the small apartment of a girl press agent. There she cooked her meals (usually pot roast) washed the dishes, cleaned the house, and spent half the night sitting on her friend's bed pouring out her troubles.

When her friend suggested a divorce, Susan replied, "When there's a divorce, it's the woman who gets it in the neck…"

Her friends asked naturally enough, "but why go back to him?" "Why did she keep going back when there was so much friction in their lives?"

"The answer is a question," she told her friend, "Have you ever been lonely?"

Susan didn't need a crowd around her in her free time at hone, "When I'm not working I do as little as possible. I read, I swim, I go to new places and travel. But my idea of relaxing is just doing nothing. Stretching out and looking at the sky. I can do that for hours. Some people have to be constantly amused or entertained. I don't."

Graham Kislingbury commenting on a long and friendly association with Susan recalled one particular incident: "Susan and Jess and her two sons were living in a rented home in Beverly Hills. They were being evicted and they were going around separately in different parts of the area they wanted to live, looking for an apartment where they could live with their kids. Eventually they moved into a hotel in Santa Monica. The telephone rang in my office and I answered.

"Are you Graham Kislingbury, this is Hedda Hopper — look you, I understand that Barker and Hayward have split up, he's looking for an apartment."

"I said, 'I don't know anything like that at all.'

"'Where's Susan?' she demanded.

"'I don't know where she is right now.'

"'You don't know where Hayward is? What kind of a press agent are you anyway!'

"'I truthfully don't know. They moved out of their house because they were evicted.'

"'Where's she staying,' said Hopper impatiently.

"'I don't know.'

"'You're one hell of a press agent. Look you find out where she is and you call me right back, you understand' — and she slammed down the phone.

"I called Susan at the hotel and told her about the conversation," Kislingbury said.

"Just ignore her and if she calls you back hang up on her," she told him.

Jess, Susan and the twins.

Susan resented this scandal hunter rummaging around in her closet looking for skeletons. She liked Louella Parsons, Hopper's rival, but couldn't care less about Hopper because Hopper was only out to hurt her, ready to break a scandal, which wasn't happening.

The truth was that the lease on their rented house was expiring, and the place was being sold for a huge amount of money. Susan and Jess moved four times in two years. She refused to pay black market rentals and she would definitely not pay cash under the table.

"The Barkers had been house hunting for weeks," said Kislingbury, "Walter Wanger backed them for a loan and they bought a house out in the Valley."

The house was a simple two-story affair on an unfashionable street in the San Fernando Valley, with two garages for their medium priced cars. There was a small lawn in front of the house with a swimming pool in the back yard. Their neighbors had nothing to do with the movie business. The price was $25,000, which was considered quite high in 1946. According to the newspapers on the day following the sale, it was reported that when it was discovered that the perspective buyer was Susan Hayward the price was jacked up by another $10,000.

Susan must have reflected at that moment on the Brooklyn drama coach who years before took one look at her and rated her below the crowd because of a hole in her shoe. Today, the mere mention of her name to the real estate salesman had rated her above the crowd — by $10,000. The ivy covered, English cottage in the Valley meant so much to her as it was the very first home she had ever owned.

Graham Kislingbury had to make frequent calls at the house to discuss things they were going to be doing. "They had no furniture in the living room at all," he remembered. "Susan made it clear that 'we're not going to put a piece of furniture in here until we can afford it.'"

Gradually they furnished the house, 'at least we are better off now than when we moved in Christmas Eve. About all we were able to set up except for the beds, was the Christmas tree,' she said.

"When they were married they were just about on a par — in their careers. Then Susan began to go and Jess didn't move. I asked Wanger to give Jess a role," Kislingbury said, "and Susan tried to help."

To the press, she stated that she would not permit her husband an experienced theatre trained actor to take inferior film roles. She added she felt handicapped by having never been on the stage. Barker pursued his hobbies, photography, horse racing and drinking, and Susan began another picture.

Alfred Hitchcock's associate Joan Harrison borrowed her for *They Won't Believe Me* and Wanger then put her into *The Lost Moment*. Susan got a chance at an *Alter Ego* character in *The Lost Moment* playing the schizophrenic lead, Tina Borderau. She also fought frequently with its director Martin Gable.

"He," said Susan, "was a great genius — he thought. You couldn't even walk into the room properly for him. I had a long difficult speech in a long scene. It was going well, but he stopped me at the same point, each time I got to a certain word. It was some simple word. I've even forgotten what it was, but he insisted I was mispronouncing it. By the twelfth take, I thought surely I had said it the way he wanted, but it still didn't suit him. I told him, "If you stop me once more, I am surely going to haul off and hit you. He answered, 'Ho, ho, ho!' Sure enough in the middle of the next take, he stopped me again. Well, being a lady, I didn't punch him. Instead, I picked up a lamp. It connected. Oh, yes I paid for the lamp! Of course, it was just one of those things; emotion building up until it is released like a typhoon — and over just as quickly."

Director Martin Gabel, who came from the New York theatre, went back to it after this one film, as a character actor.

One day Kislingbury called Louella to get a Sunday feature story on Susan's role in the film and she asked to see the children. Kislingbury and Susan gave each of the boys a little bouquet of posies to give to Louella and they prompted them as to what to say. When they arrived at her front door and rang the bell, it was opened by the black maid and the kids said, "These are for you Miss Parsons." While Susan doubled up laughing, Kislingbury, restraining himself, instructed them, "Not yet, not yet."

Louella wrote about it for her readers, "My adopted daughter Susie brought the twins over. They sang and did their little routines. You know, Tim is the serious one and Greg the comedian and Susie said, 'I think Greg will be an actor and Tim will write the scripts.' "

Hayward, the dark horse in the Oscar race that year, 1947, lost to the venerable Loretta Young. The nomination did however advance her career. Susan was determined to try harder.

"Susan came into my office in the rickety old writers' building at Universal one day," Kislingbury recalled. "It was down at one end of the studio. Every time you walked up the stairs, the building shook. As she came in I said, 'isn't this awful?'"

" 'It's all right', she smiled, "some day you'll have a good office, you gotta have faith, it sure carried me a long way.' She always had just a little bit of that Brooklyn manner."

Susan, going from one picture into another, barely had time to keep in touch with her mother. Her sister, Florence was married and Wally, just out of the army, went to work for the Race Tracks in Santa Anita and Hollywood, where he would be for the next 30 years.

"Susan was a hard worker", Kislingbury recalled. "We went up to North Carolina to make *Tap Roots* and she would have to be up at 5 o'clock in

Susan and her brother Wally.

the morning to be at the hairdresser and into make-up before we drove 50-60 miles to location that day. She did not party at night, though the rest of the cast did. Sometimes she would get back from location at 7 o'clock at night. She would call me 2 or 3 times a week. She knew I was going back and forth from the location to the studio and she would ask me to take her out to dinner when the rest of the cast went off partying. We would try to find a new place to eat each time. I remember one time we got a cab to go somewhere to some restaurant we had heard about, up in the mountains there. The cab driver kept looking in the rear view mirror, and finally turned around."

"You're Susan Hayward," he blurted out.

Then he whirled the cab around, turned down a side street, and start speeding off.

"Where are you going?" Kislingbury said, but he wouldn't answer.

Susan shouted at him, "What are you trying to do?"

He drove up to a house in a nearby small town and grabbed the ignition key and ran inside.

Kislingbury turned to Susan, "You know what he's going to do? He's going to bring the whole family out to meet you."

"You're kidding!" she said.

Sure enough, out came the whole family—"you're our favorite star," exclaimed the cab driver, and Susan had to meet the entire family.

"We have a very tight schedule, and I asked him, 'can we go now?'" the publicity man said. "He drove us out to the restaurant and he wanted to come back to pick us up."

"Oh, no, thank you," we replied quickly. "We have a limousine coming." We weren't going to get caught again.

Susan confided in a trusted friend during the North Carolina shooting of *Tap Roots*, "I'm having a rough time with Jesse. I wouldn't care if he got a job in a department store as a clerk; he just lies around the house all day. He criticizes me constantly. If he was working this wouldn't happen. He's very down, he hasn't been able to get acting work and he won't do anything else. What the heck, if I couldn't make it in this business, I would do something else."

Jess did do something else — he applied for unemployment insurance.

Susan's brother very often went over to the house to check up on the boys who had to be looked after when their mother was not at home. One mid-day when Jess came down from his bedroom, having been awakened by the twins on the front lawn circling around on their bikes, he was very upset about getting up so late, and having missed his appointment at the unemployment office. Wally was fixing lunch for the boys, and Jess wanted him to stop and squeeze some fresh orange juice for him. Wally refused. Jess went back to bed.

In November of 1947, Susan sued Jess Barker for divorce but just before Thanksgiving they reconciled, Susan couldn't go through with it so close to the Christmas holidays because of what it would do to the family.

Interviewed by the press, she said, "When I start a picture, Jess and I study the script together. If I give a good performance, he is greatly responsible. I could never have played the role in *Smash-Up* if it weren't for Jess. Not because he drinks, but because he's a fine actor. Even the best talent has to wait for a chance to make good. That's the routine in this town. Jess will get his". Who was Susan trying to convince — herself?

While on location for *Tap Roots* Susan wasn't needed for one particular days shooting and she didn't have anything to do, so as Graham Kislingbury was going to the airport, to pick up cast member Ward Bond, Susan decided to go along just for the ride. While waiting at the airport a middle-aged society woman approached Susan.

"Oh, you're Susan Hayward," she gushed. "Well, I'm having a party at my home, tomorrow night, and I want you to come."

"Thank you," Susan replied. "But I am working very hard and while I'm working, I just cannot accept social engagements."

"Well!" snapped the woman, "Of course movie stars mean nothing to us out here. I just thought it would be nice for you," and walked away in a huff.

Susan blew a puff of smoke from her cigarette. "You'll find one in every town", she said to Kislingbury.

After *Tap Roots*, the British froze the pound sterling and the film companies couldn't get their money out of England. This threw Hollywood into a real tailspin towards the end of summer of '47.

"We were just winding up Tap Roots when Wanger announced out of the blue, that he was going to leave Universal and go to Eagle Lion. Of course that meant that she would go with him," Kislingbury related, "and Wanger wanted me to go to Eagle Lion too, but my wife and I had enough of Hollywood, so we decided to go back to San Francisco. When Susan heard the news she called me. 'Can we have lunch?' she asked. 'Sure!' I replied and we went across the street from the studio.

"'Gee,' she said over lunch, 'I feel terrible — you're the one person I really have gotten along with.'"

Susan, who had responded easily to the soft, spoken Kislingbury, felt protected with the publicity front man who gave her fatherly advice and the warmth of his presence. His like were not replaceable.

"One day I got a call from Dave Lipton at Eagle Lion," Kislingbury continued. "Susan had moved to Eagle with Walter and was making a picture called Tulsa. He said she didn't want to go to San Francisco to plug the premier of Tap Roots and could I go down there and try to persuade her. I flew down to the studio and Dave and I drove out. She was working in the picture and didn't know I was coming. We went to the sound stage and she was in her dressing room so I knocked on her door. The door opened. 'Graham!' she screamed and threw her arms around me and took me inside. She wanted to know what I was doing and I asked her if she liked it there. 'one studio's like another,' she sighed.

"I asked her about the opening of Tap Roots in San Francisco and told her that Boris Karloff was going, Julie London and Dick Long and some more of the cast but without her, it would be a flop.

"Why don't you come up, and we'll have some fun.

"She though a moment, 'O.K. Graham, I'll do it.' And that was that."

During the filming of *Tulsa*, she had a scene in which she was supposed to crack up with remorse. The way the scene was planned, the camera followed her across a room until she went out, slamming the door behind her. During rehearsals, she raved and ranted at that door. She kicked it, and slammed it and yelled at it, while most people watched in astonishment. Director Stuart Heisler, her director from *Smash-Up*, merely sat back in his chair, waiting for the tears to come. To whip up her emotions she had to have something to get mad at, he was wise to her technique.

Tulsa was to be her last picture with Walter Wanger under his personal sponsorship. She went, on loan, almost immediately into another picture, *The Saxon Charm* at Universal.

Susan collapsed on the set of *The Saxon Charm* — reported Louella in her column. She, however, would not hold up production and forced herself into a quick recovery.

"Days off get me out of the rhythm and take the edge off my characterization," she stated.

Walter Wanger, who had controlled her professional destiny up to this point, sold her contract to 20th Century Fox for $200,000. Wanger felt a mixture of relief and regret. Although his contract with her had more than 2 ½ years to go he felt it was time for Susan to move away and go ahead; but it was believed he simply needed the money.

Susan signed a 7 year no option contract at a sliding annual increase salary beginning at $150,000. It raised the eyebrows of the economy-minded industry. From now on, Susan really got the star treatment.

"I couldn't care less — and I never did care — about the A number one treatment, the star's dressing room, the limousine. That's all junk," she declared. "Oh, it's nice if you can have it, but it was never important to me. I never cared if I had to dress in a broom closet or a tent as long as I had privacy to change my costumes. Some performers wouldn't work if their dressing room wasn't as posh as someone else's and that's junk. Just externals; it means nothing. The only thing that's important is what you put on film and what it does to your audience. Of course now that I've said that, the next time I work they'll probably make me dress in a broom closet."

What Hayward did put on film in her first picture for 20th Century Fox was *House of Strangers*. Director Joseph L. Mankiewicz and Susan battled from the start. The fireworks were over her red hair. Mankiewicz said there was too much of it and wanted her to cut it.

"Every other producer and director wanted me to cut my hair and my answer was 'No!'" Susan said defensively her first day at work. "I refuse to be led around by fashion dictators who say women have to have short hair. I know I look better with a long bob and I'm going to keep it!"

Susan's proudest possession was her long, luxurious red hair. She regarded it as an identifying trademark. No studio hairdresser was allowed to touch it and her present contract prevented Fox from ever calling for any change in her hairdo without her consent.

The veteran actors in the cast of House of Strangers, working with her for the first time, were taken aback by her coldness. During the production, she thoroughly upset Joe Mankiewicz — a director noted for his informal approach to life — by calling him Mr. Mankiewicz. He called her Susie. As the picture was winding up, Susan completed a scene and asked, "How was it, Joe?"

Mankiewicz, startled by her sudden familiarity, replied, "It was fine, Miss Hayward."

Samuel Goldwyn wanted Hayward for the lead in My Foolish Heart and made a deal with Darryl Zanuck at Fox studio. Having seen the script, Susan wanted the part, feeling that it was a perfect part for her. During the shooting of the picture director Mark Robson was amazed at her stamina, which enabled her to remain in front of the cameras for nine weeks of non-stop shooting. As she appeared in all but two scenes, it was a tremendous physical task.

"Susan may look frail," a friend commented. "But she's got the constitution of a truck driver."

Susan was up at 5 a.m. each day to keep up with the increasing schedule of films lined up for her at Fox, leaving her non-acting husband in bed to sleep until noon. She left money around the house, in a handbag or bureau drawer, to get what was needed in the way of groceries, etc. She was becoming increasingly successful, and more moody and unhappy with her personal and home life — what was left of it.

Her brother didn't bother her, knowing how hard she was working. Her mother was off to Reno and Vegas on gambling trips, sponsored by Susan. Florence, by this time was completely out of the picture, with a husband and children, struggling to make ends meet.

In fact, Susan's life now seemed to rotate entirely around the studio. She was now 33 years old and had been working steadily for the past 15 years.

My Foolish Heart opened on New York City's Radio City Music Hall and for her performance in this film; she would be up for her second best actress academy award nomination. The movie going public took her to their hearts as the unhappy girl caught up in an ill-starred wartime romance, and she became bigger box office than ever before.

Her new home studio then gave her an inconspicuous little comedy entitled *Stella*, which she rightfully refused. They signed another redhead Ann Sheridan to replace her.

It was, to her, a decided comedown with the possible Oscar staring her in the face. Now that she knew what her box office draw was the ambitious and riled redhead went to the front office and asked why she wasn't being given better parts.

It was the same old story but one she was familiar with. She had learned one hard method of competition; to get your way frighten your peers with arrogance, and pretend submission to your bosses.

To her co-stars, during the making of films, she was frigid — coldly detached — never mingling and only friendly to non-threatening lessers like hairdressers and make-up artists. For top directors, she was always admirably efficient, doing difficult scenes in fewer takes than it took other actresses. To lesser-known directors, who were intimidated by her on-set frostiness, she behaved like a shrew, losing her temper and issuing ultimatums. When told a hairdresser she wanted was in London on an assignment, she told the director, "Well, bring him back!"

Her coldness, mingled with her usually superior work in front of the cameras, inspired a fearful awe.

True, most actors wanted to keep their distance from her, seldom putting her on dinner party lists, but they also rarely dared to compete and often moved aside to make way for her to go on to increasing success.

Her climb to become America's biggest grossing actress, during the early 50's, was as much a matter of steely and unscrupulous will power as of talent.

Veteran director Henry Hathaway, who was a pioneer in the industry and learned his craft from the days of silent epics like *Ben Hur*, was a tough taskmaster.

A Hathaway picture was done on time. He was a company man who didn't tolerate any temperament and he was tough, but he was good. The studio knew Susan needed an iron hand at times and that Hathaway couldn't be browbeaten. He was also an expert Western director and a man's director. Wayne, Cooper and others of their like worked with him and became lifelong friends. It was Hathaway's direction of John Wayne in *True Grit* that landed him an Oscar.

"She was a bitch!" said director Hathaway. "Anybody who is a bitch to work with has got to be a bitch to live with. That's an inherent thing, a part of your make-up, to be an obstruction to everything. She was a little twisted, she was twisted in her walk, she always walked a little sideways, stood a little sideways, it's a thing that was in her nature. It was in her head, her look, her walk, in the way she stood, that girl was twisted."

Susan's first film back at Fox after they had suspended her for refusing *Stella* was *Rawhide* to be directed by Henry Hathaway, and co-starring Tyrone Power.

But Hathaway said emphatically; "There was not a speck of trouble with her on that picture. In the beginning, in her earlier pictures she was never any trouble. Oh, she was aloof and went off by herself, didn't mingle, didn't go out to the cafés or join in on anything. Up in Arrowhead on location, the cast and crew — all of us — went to the San Louie Café and we'd all sit together, but she would go with her maid or hairdresser to some other place. It sort of bothered her to be friendly, she didn't want to get into any traps or make any commitments. I think her children were a disappointment and I think her marriage to Barker was a disappointment. She had a lot of inherent hurts, the same thing happened to Gene Tierney."

"She spent all her free time up in the mountains with those two kids of hers looking for arrowheads", Hathaway mused in mystification, "always going up to Lone Pine and Bishop, taking the kids on trips when she could have taken them up to Arrowhead and Big Bear where we were working."

20th bought the play rights to *What Makes Sammy Run*, a hard hitting play about the New York garment industry and the ruthless Sammy

Glick. They changed the sex of the anti-hero to that of Harriet Boyd, a hard-shelled dame, especially for the Hayward talents. It was tailor made for her.

The studio sent her to New York for location shooting. With the boys in school and looked after by their grandmother and uncle, Jess went along for the ride. They stayed at New York's Hampshire House on West 58th street and made the most of their visit; with Susan leading the way now very much back on home ground, but with a much different perspective than the one that she had departed Brooklyn with some years earlier.

Following the New York location, the studio planned to send her to Dawsonville, Georgia. She would replace Jeanne Crain in the film *I'll Climb The Highest Mountain* as Miss Crain had become pregnant.

Here Susan met restaurateur Harvey Hester, who owned Aunt Fanny's Cabin where the crew often went for dinner, and finding him as comfortable as an 'old shoe' she struck up a meaningful friendship with him which was to last the remainder of her life.

Harvey Hester, a large, very rotund man, took a small part in the film as one of the local characters.

Susan enjoyed the location and rural scenery, and made headlines May 31, 1950, in Georgia when she lost her footing while trying to take snapshots of the 729 ft. Amicola Falls. She was saved by 20th Century Fox chauffeur Will Gray who caught her, but almost went over the Falls with her while doing so.

Fellow actress on the picture Lynn Bari when asked of their working relationship could only comment; "She had nothing to say to me."

Susan endeared herself to her fans again, as the backwoods minister's wife. However, when a reporter told her it was one of his favorite films, she scoffed, "You gotta be kiddin'. I never saw myself as much of a preacher's wife. I didn't like wearing all those pretty dresses or having to be so genteel."

Cast next as Bathsheba to Gregory Peck's *David*, Hayward commented that she would have preferred it if the film were called Bathsheba and David, instead of the other way around. Either way, on investment alone 20th proved that she was their most valuable player. They tied up $12,500,000 in her films that year alone (1951) a quarter of the studio's annual production budget.

The one memorable thing to her about the biblical technicolor opus was that she caught a cold during the famous bathing scene, when she had to stand up all day on the sound stage in a waist high tub while a female slave poured water over her.

Susan had to cancel plans for a European trip with Jess when Fox gave her what she really wanted. The Jane Froman Story, 'I'll See You In My Dreams,' changed finally to *With a Song In My Heart*. Jeanne Crain was originally cast, but lost to her Brooklyn opponent; and this time Miss Crain was not pregnant.

Two of the dancers in the musical biography with her were Herman Boden and Frank Boden told this version, "Susan preferred tall fellows, we were all over six feet. She was just 5'6" in heel. She worked very hard, and she was a perfectionist, a real pro. No matter how many times they wanted her to re-do anything, she did it; she wanted people to help her. I remember the first tine she came into the rehearsal hall; she looked at everybody and wanted them to like her. She was warm and natural. We then rehearsed with the piano..."

On the other hand Frank commenting on the same movie told his version, "When we met her she was pleasant, but quiet and not particularly warm. She didn't know anyone and was standoffish. She sang along with the soundtrack and we thought she must have had coaching prior to her coming onto the sound stage, because she fell into the dance steps pretty fast. It took between 3-5 days to film the 'Song In My Heart' sequence. Herman and I did a lift with her and she was tense and Froman was there, watching from a wheelchair. She liked what she saw (in Susan playing her). Susan would ask 'is this right? — Am I holding myself correctly? — Doing this the right way?'"

"Even to me," he said. "Susan became Jane in the movie. Jane also mentioned Susan visiting her in New York and how they preferred the same perfume, hair color, clothes, etc. to a point it was like a psychic experience. They got along beautifully.*

"It was an elaborate set on a big stage, and Susan often sat with Billy Daniels, the choreographer (who was later to commit suicide) and Richard Allen, Her dancing partner in the sequence (who now works in a massage parlor). It was a very subdued atmosphere and we kept our distance. When they were finally ready to shoot the number she was very serious, and they must have really practiced to get to that point. After we shot the number, she thanked everyone and left at 6 o'clock, she didn't like to shoot after 6 p.m. It wasn't like working with Betty Grable, which was fun, Betty broke us up constantly."

The story was about Singer Jane Froman who surmounted crippling injuries in an airplane crash in 1943 while going overseas to entertain the troops.

Susan spent hours in her dressing room with Jane Froman going over the script, scene by scene. She asked her about her childhood, she wanted to know what kind of clothes she wore, what her drives were, her tastes, and interests. How she felt after the Clipper crashed finding herself in the water.

Every time Froman looked around the darkly lit recording studio during the recording sessions of the 26 song soundtrack, she would see Susan sitting somewhere in the back watching her every move, every gesture.

With a Song In My Heart.

Jane Froman's husband Rowland Smith of Columbia, Missouri, mentioned a conversation he held with his now deceased wife about the movie, "I remember Jane telling me how impressed she was with Susan Hayward. Susan watched her as she recorded, dubbed the soundtrack, and she copied so many mannerisms of hers that it was uncanny."

Costumer Charles La Maire created "the most expensive wardrobe I have ever designed and we used colors that went with Susan's red hair."

While Susan had made four pictures in that year (1950), Jess had a bit part in a B movie *The Milkman*.

Susan, who herself had stepped into the footprints of other stars in the forecourt of Grauman's Chinese Theatre when she first arrived in Hollywood, now immortalized herself by putting her own footprints and signature in cement that same year.

She received her third Oscar nomination for Best Actress for *With A Song In My Heart* and garnered many awards from magazines but most importantly, from the public. The Foreign Press gave John Wayne and Susan Hayward their award in 1952 as the World's Favorite Actor and Actress — the most popular stars in the world.

The American Beauticians Congress voted her "the most beautiful

With a Song In My Heart.

redhead in the world" and the National Florists Association crowned her their Queen.

Susan spoke contemptuously of her screen allure, calling it gimmicky, and in tossing her long red mane, exclaimed, "I feel like whinnying when I do it."

But for all that, at night Susan went home to her English Ivy covered cottage exhausted to an inebriated husband, sleeping children and loneliness.

Movie making is a business normally involving enormous costs, much elaborate equipment and complex inter-relationships among gifted and talented people, with profit usually as the motive. Susan was used as a yardstick for measuring profit and while she was on top she was kept working constantly. In the film industry, the profitable was generally the beautiful, but the beautiful was not necessarily the popular.

Susan at the top was an easier target for those a step below and her detractors were waiting, hoping for her to topple, and again there were those who with praise and smiles who were working to dislodge her.

She had entered the film industry as a teenager, and through hard driving, competition, and versatility she had fought to get where she was and now had to fight to stay there.

"My life is fair game for anybody. I spent an unhappy, penniless childhood in Brooklyn. I had to slug my way up in a place called Hollywood where people love to trample you to death. I don't relax because I don't know how. Life is too short to relax," she said.

The climb took its toll on both her and her family. She stayed home at nights, reading books, searching for screen parts. There was enough fighting on the set and to unwind she took those few extra drinks at night.

She couldn't beat her husband at his hobby so she joined him. If the Barker's drank heavily and fought, they did it at home; they seldom went out in public.

Now whenever she was approached by anyone seeking favors she fired first before they could ask, "Whatever it is, the answer is *no!*"

Darryl Zanuck put her next into Ernest Hemingway's *The Snows of Kilimanjaro* along with Gregory Peck and with Ava Gardner borrowed from MGM to co-star.

Famed astrologer Carroll Righter did her daily charts while she was filming the picture: "I'm like a doctor; they come to me when they have problems. I would do 40 pages a month for her. I was on the set of *The Snows of Kilimanjaro*, doing her chart and Hildergard Neff's, she was a typical Moonchild, moody, up and down that is why she was such a fine actress. Jess Barker was a Gemini, and the twins, Pisces. She needed a Taurus."

When Susan was undecided about whether to take a long-term contract at Fox as opposed to freelancing, I advised her as her astrologer to sign the contract, as her chart imposed this direction. I could foresee a slide in her career if she were on her own. She wanted to know what time of the day she should sign it. I gave her 3:23 a.m. She set her alarm, awoke during the early morning hours turned on her bedside lamp and signed the contract and then went back to sleep."

Susan was warned by her astrologer to be cautious. The studio giving some of the best scenes in the picture to Ava Gardner were careful to shoot them all after Susan was off the lot and Susan piqued at Fox over this turned down a series of their next scripts.

Howard Hughes wanted her back at RKO and got her for *The Lusty Men* with Robert Mitchum. However, she was happier on *The President's*

Lady with more her kind of man, Charlton Heston, on her Fox schedule. But she still felt they weren't treating her properly and she did not like the next script *White Witch Doctor*, set to co-star again with Robert Mitchum.

Henry Hathaway, on directing *White Witch Doctor*: "She would sulk if they tried to make her do something she didn't want to. And when women get angry about something and get a chip on their shoulder they're never good in films then and it's true with men too. Suddenly there would be one person she would get mad at, or the studio, and then she would slack off a little bit. You know what happens to some of these people then, they don't want to do this picture or that one. That was why Wayne was such a big guy, a big star (he didn't do that kind of thing).

"I got a call from Zanuck's office and he said, "I have this picture, it has to start and both she and Mitchum came in here and said they will not make the picture, and it has to start in two weeks. They said it was a terrible script they just wouldn't do it. Besides, they didn't have any faith in the director. Will you read it and see what the hell's the matter with it."

A worried Zanuck went on, "I have a commitment with these people and if they don't make it, I have to pay them."

"I read the script and called Zanuck — 'Jesus, Darryl. I don't blame them. It's a lousy, awful, unbelievable script.'"

Zanuck called off the picture temporarily, cancelled the director and debated the situation, having spent over 600 thousand dollars in one of the units for exteriors with a million tied up in the production so far, including pre-production costs. Shortly afterwards Zanuck called Hathaway.

"Henry, do you think you can do anything with it at all. I'll give you a couple of writers. I can't lose a whole million if I make this picture. There's no way to lose with those two people in it."

Hathaway was given the script assignment, and total directorial control. He rewrote the script in two weeks but he said, "I didn't do it as good as it should have been done."

"There was no romance between the two of them (Hayward and Mitchum). As soon as you said 'cut,' she went off to her little cabin and went either right inside or sat in the doorway — or the chair outside the doorway. I think she got along with Mitchum because anybody can get along with Bob. He's such a sweet man; he's on a level with Cooper.

"She had no sense of humor — none. She would stay where she was and wouldn't crack a smile, then turn around and walk away and never say anything. She was a fully competent actress, capable of any kind of emotion, and doing it well. She never had to be prodded into doing anything."

Director Hathaway elaborated, "You could talk to her about what should be done and that was it. She was camera-wise and always tilted her face in her favor. She had a way of standing and always ended up in the same position no matter what the hell happened, she would end up with her hand on her hip. Very characteristic and a little awkward, I thought."

With a Song In My Heart.

June O'Brien of San Jose, California was almost 18 years old in 1952 and a senior at Girl's Commercial High School in Brooklyn, "One of my warmest memories," she said, "was in the spring of that year. *With A Song In My Heart* was about to open in New York City at the Roxy Theatre and there was quite a fuss being made. Susan Hayward was coming back to visit her old alma mater. The assembly hall was jammed with maybe, 1,000 students, and we were all singing 'With A Song In My Heart' as she walked in.

"She was truly the most beautiful woman I had ever seen. It wasn't make-up either. It was a look on her face. As she reached the stage, tears were running down her face. She looked at us all with such feeling. Jess Barker was at her side. When all the excitement died down, our principal started to speak and pay much tribute to Susan. She began to list her accomplishments while a student there. In the middle of it the principal mentioned Susan had been a member of the Arista Society, which was the Honor Roll Society for students who managed an A average all through school.

"Susan stood up and interrupted the principal at this point and brought

With a Song In My Heart.

the house to its feet when she said, 'I never made Arista once during my years here.' The girls just ate it up.

"She then spoke to us of her memories of her school days and how she was so torn between her schooling and costume designing, and her tremendous desire to be an actress. She told how she had this wonderful English teacher who had encouraged her in her acting and talked to her many times, continually encouraging her, and Susan gave all the credit to this wonderful teacher, her true friend in High School. This teacher had told her to leave school and try her hand at acting in Hollywood. Then Susan pointed up to the balcony in the assembly hall and said, 'There she is sitting right up there, now.'

"It was Miss O'Grady, the little white haired teacher sitting in the back off to the side. It was really a tear filled moment when the teacher got up and slowly made her way down the stairs to the center aisle and up on to the stage.

"Susan moved towards her, helped her up the steps and embraced her with such love. It was really a tear filled moment.

"Outside in front of the building Susan standing in her mink coat, pressed her heel hard on the cigarette she had dropped to the sidewalk, stepped into her limousine and sped off, leaving it all behind, without looking back."

Susan picked up awards everywhere; The *Photoplay* Magazine Award; at the Del Mar Club for International Good Will; the Gold Medal for *With A Song In My Heart* (along with Gary Cooper who accepted his for *High Noon*). Not only was her performance nominated for best actress but the picture brought in over 10 million dollars at the box office.

She felt she deserved a vacation so she and Jess left for Europe in May leaving the twins in the care of her mother and brother.

Upon her return and in spite of her contemporary look in *David and Bathsheba*, for which she and the film were accorded poor reviews, Fox assigned her to *Demetrious and The Gladiators*, a super cinemascope technicolor biblical potboiler. She was cast as the wicked Messalina and she sneered her way all through the film.

Louella Parsons quoted Susan as saying, "I'm (practically) a split personality. Through my screen roles I live many lives in one; here at home I'm happy to be just Mrs. Barker who goes shopping at the supermarket like any other housewife."

Then the night of July 16, 1953, Susan ran shrieking into the night, 'Don't kill me! Somebody help me!' she screamed as she fled naked from her home in the valley, with her husband hot on her heels.

In court, Jess explained what had happened preceding the escape that Susan believed had threatened her life.

After dinner that evening (July 16, 1953), he and Susan were sitting in front of the television set and browsing through the newspapers. There had been a discussion between them about families in Hollywood and during the conversation, Susan brought his mother into it.

Questioned in court Barker said, "Well, it wasn't very pleasant. It was about an incident when I was a child that I had told her about."

"Possibly," she had retorted, "that's what's wrong with you."

Jess said that he had then sat in stunned silence while Susan told him all the worst things she could about him. Then she had leaned across him to reach for a cigarette and said, "Besides, I think you're queer."

Jess then slapped her and the struggle began. As he tried to quiet her down, she bit him in the left arm, and then ran outside. He brought her back inside and gave her a spanking, picked her up and put her to bed. He told her, "to be quiet, the children were upstairs."

Susan got up and ran outside with Jess threatening her that if she didn't keep quiet, he would cool her off. He caught up with her, picked her up and threw her into the pool. The robe that Susan was wearing slipped off. Jess went back to the den and Susan back to her room. He then decided to take a walk and was in front of the house when Susan appeared fully dressed, carrying the dog in her arms.

She was heading down the street. He tried to get her back and asked Susan's friend, Martha Little, who was staying with them convalescing from an illness, to get her inside and put her to bed.

Susan then told her story: It was late at night because Jess had gone to get the late edition of the papers. She said she had been studying a script and Jess was watching television. They were in the living room when the argument started. She asked him for a divorce, as she felt it was the only solution to their problems. He said "never."

"If you don't love me, and don't want to do what I consider right, why do you want to hang on?' she asked him.

"You're a good meal ticket," he replied.

Susan looked at him and said, "I don't understand you. I think you're very queer." And he walked over to her and slapped her in the face.

Susan told the court that he then threw her on the floor, pulled off her robe and beat her. She managed to get free and ran into the back garden. He caught up with her but she broke away again and reached for the phone to call the police. He came after her, knocked the phone from her hand and dragged her outside into the garden and up the steps to the swimming pool and threw her in. She was panicked as she was pulled down into the water by the heavy pink terry cloth robe. She struggled to the surface and started screaming for her life and he pushed her head under the water. When she came up for the second time, she remained silent and he allowed her to climb out of the pool.

She, considering that he might have become deranged, quietly went indoors, leaving the heavy wet robe by the pool.

Once inside her room Susan just wanted to run and dressed swiftly to make her escape. She opened the side door of the bedroom and walked quietly past the den and out to the garden, then around by the kitchen door, which lead to the driveway — and freedom.

Barker intercepted her by the kitchen door and grabbed her, pulling her inside with such force that she arrived practically effortlessly at the front door, which she opened and ran down the driveway. He caught up with her and started to beat her, as she screamed for help.

"Don't kill me. Somebody help me!" she cried into the night. The critically ill Martha Little ran out and begged him to stop as Susan ran into the house and called the police. He chased her and grabbed the phone out of her hand. Then suddenly there was a commotion outside. Someone had called the police.

Susan asked them to get a cab and they offered to drive her but she refused. The cab came and Martha Little and Susan sped away, to Ellen Marrener's house.

The next day, Susan returned with her brother and Martha to ask Barker to leave. She had also called her business manager Mr. Wood to have him meet here there.

Susan described her injuries in court, "I had a black eye, bruises on the left side of my face, on the temple, the jaw, the nose and I thought my jaw was broken. The eyeball was injured — it was all bloody. My body was covered with bruises, mostly on my fanny, and my feet and legs were scratched and bleeding from being dragged up and down the steps and knocking against things."

A witness was called to describe the incident. She was a maid at the house next door to the Barker's and her room overlooked their garden and pool. Dodee Hazel Swain said she had been awakened by screams, a woman's screams, in the early morning of July 17th. "From the lights in the backyard I could see a woman running, her hair was kind of red — reddish like — and I hear a big splash and a man mumbling, 'you goin' sign that deal' and the woman says, 'no-no.' She ran over to the back door, close to where I am — she was naked. I hear some slaps and her screamin', 'don't kill me — somebody help me!' Then I hear the man voice, 'you're goin' to sign that deal' an' he throwed her into the pool. I didn't call the police 'cause I didn't want to interfere. It went on quite a while because I went and laid down."

Whichever version is closer to the actual happening, this you can be certain of; Susan and Jess had been drinking and started another fight that this time got completely out of control. The dunking and the swimming pool splash were heard around the world. The Hollywood press had a field day, and Susan Hayward's image as a tempestuous fiery woman was enhanced.

Following these proceedings that Labor Day weekend Susan returned from Hawaii where she had taken her sons for a respite and Jess called to take the boys out for Labor Day. Susan agreed.

She had guests at the house, a Mr. and Mrs. Dorsen, when Jess and the twins returned at 6 o'clock. They were all out by the pool having drinks and Susan politely asked Jess if he would like a drink. He said he would like to talk to her, and the Dorsen's left the pool and went indoors.

"Please, Jess," Susan said, "will you please be sort of quick about it, dinner is almost ready."

He started to speak of reconciliation but she flatly said that it was impossible, and he made it clear that he wouldn't leave. This caused delays in the kitchen for her guest and the children, who ate at this time every day and wondered what was happening. Susan tried to persuade him to go suggesting another time to talk about it.

He would leave when he was ready he told her. There was an argument and a scene and Susan said in court, "Well I was furious. I tried to get him to leave peacefully. He was sort of standing near me and I had a cigarette in my hand; it was lit, and I have a temper and I said, 'I would like to push this cigarette right in your eye.'"

"You haven't got the guts," he challenged her.

She then shoved it in his face. He smacked her across the mouth and Susan yelled. Then Thelma Dorsen came running out holding a drink in her hand — which Susan grabbed, throwing the contents in Jess's face.

The next day Susan called her lawyer Martin Lang, "I want that divorce, and fast!"

Susan who gave glowing reports of her marriage to movie fan magazines appeared in court in a chic black dress and dark glasses, to cover the bruises and commenting about all the false quotes, said, "After all, I am an actress and wanted things to look right."

Following the filing of her suit for divorce, on September 10, 1953, Susan left on November 22nd for Mexico to go on location for *Garden of Evil*.

Regarding the marital agreement, which Barker had signed, forever separating their income, he later said he was too busy buying the wedding cake to really read the agreement.

Henry Hathaway met up with 'her' again in Mexico when he directed *Garden of Evil*, "I never found her to be friendly, cooperative or anything. I never did have a good relationship with her, even down in Mexico with *Garden of Evil*.

"She was very objectionable and nasty. For instance, I like to start early, with energy. I like to shoot what I call my master shots in the morning and catch up with some close-ups and take a little time, and quit early.

I have always done that because mostly I have worked outdoors and the very early morning light is the best light to photograph — anyway, before the sun gets in right up ahead. We were all ready, not too early, at 8:30 in the morning. I saw that she was sitting in her dressing room and I said to the assistant director, Stan Huff, 'Stan, go over and tell her its time to work, that we're ready.' She was all ready, so Stan went over and came back.

"I don't want to tell you all this but she looked at her watch and asked if it was 9 o'clock. It wasn't."

Hathaway walked towards her, "I went over to her dressing room and said, we're ready to work and I see you're ready."

"Is it 9 o'clock?" she asked.

"No!"

"My contract says I work at nine!" was her snappy answer.

Hathaway now, with barely unrestrained anger, spoke with strong deliberation; "Your contract also says you work from 9 to 6, and I want to tell you something, Miss Lady. I am going to work you every fucking night until 6 o'clock. You've been getting off at 4:30 and 5 and you don't say 'I have to work until 6,' when you leave early. What else can we do?

"I am not only going to do that," he continued. "I'm gonna shoot every fuckin' close up of you after 5 o'clock at night. How do you like that?"

"You can't take a joke can you?" she looked up at him exhaling her cigarette.

"Fuck you!" he said and walked away.

"Then," he went on. "She came over and said she was ready to work. She's just nasty. Like there is something about her that she can't help; for no reason.

"Gary Cooper, Richard Widmark and Cameron Mitchell were all part of the cast. She never got along with anybody. Cooper was the sweetest man in the world and so is Widmark and I'm not hard to get along with either.

"We were all invited by a friend of mine Bruno Pagliai down to Cuernavaca (Bruno later married Merle Oberon) to his place New Year's Eve. He's a genteel man, an aristocrat. When he arrived, there was this great big long table and on both ends were silver buckets of ice with caviar, champagne and other things. She came in (Susan) with the assistant director, Stan Huff, a sweet guy. She picked up with him right away and I think she did it out of protection. She went over and looked at the table and said, 'When the hell do we eat?'

"Pagliai said we would be eating later.

"'Look I eat at 7:30 to 8 o'clock and if this is all you got to eat — good-bye!' and she left.

"She raised a stink about when and what she wanted to eat and they don't eat there in Mexico until 10:30. She wasn't drunk — she's just god-damn mean, and she may be sitting up there listening too!" the director said looking up.

"Later on, New Year's Eve, just before midnight, we went down to a café, and she came back after she had had her dinner, and sat down. We were sitting around the tables and midnight comes and a couple of the guys, Cameron Mitchell was one, went around kissed several of the dames. Mitchell wished her Happy New Year and reached down to kiss her. She reached up and clawed her nails down his face and drew blood."

Hathaway shook his head, "We had to lay off shooting for two days because his face was full of scabs — and that for no particular reason. She's just a mean son-of-a-bitch."

"I have a scar on my face from Susan, runs right down here," Cameron Mitchell pointed out, "We were doing a film in Mexico. It was lovely." According to Mitchell, "you couldn't leave Mexico if you had a work permit at the time, unless you saw the president."

Susan had left the children in the care of her mother and brother to go to Mexico, during the months following her separation from Jess Barker. At Christmas time, she flew back to spend a day and a half with the family. To make this trip, Susan fought with the studio brass and got a special dispensation from the President of Mexico to break the period of her work permit to leave Mexico and re-enter.

Mitchell continued his story, "Susan was having a big love affair then with Jeff Chandler and she wanted to go back and see him. She got permission and left. The rest of the company all wanted to go home for Christmas too. They thought it was not too nice of Susan to do that. So they excommunicated her for a week when she got back. The thing with Jeff was not a happy one and poor Susan incommunicado — she was blacked out for a week. On New Year's Eve, I couldn't take it anymore 'cause I really liked her. I had a crush on Susan and I went up to her to wish her well, the Happy New Year stuff. She had had a few brandies and she went just like a cat — (Mitchell clawed and made sounds) just like that and blood came out, in front of 900 Mexicans."

Mitchell told of another encounter, "Another time we were in a very primitive place called Paracutine — that was the volcano — you've heard the story about the peon who was pounding the fields with his bare feet, felt the earth get warm and this huge volcano sprang up. It was that way with Henry Hathaway. I'm sure you've heard stories about him too, a nice man, but on the set, he's a maniac. He couldn't drink coffee in the morning and he resented other people drinking it. We were in this primitive location and Hank, the generator man, who was Italian, would make this marvelous coffee. Susan was the drinking coffee and with that long beautiful hair and that feminine way of hers. Hathaway would never yell at her, he would yell at Stan Huff, our assistant, who is now married to the ex Mrs. Howard Hughes, Jean Peters. Anyway, Hathaway yelled at Stan, 'Stan I told you we won't have any goddamn coffee drinking on this set, anyone drinks coffee they can get their ass off my set, and when they finish they can come back and go to work.' So Susan very quietly took her cup of coffee and went to Mexico City for a week. Every time they called her, she said she wasn't finished with her coffee. She was lovely — like little children.

"Hathaway took her out dancing one night with his friends, Richard Widmark and Gary Cooper, 'Let's take her out,' they told me, but when Widmark danced with her, after the dance he came back and said, 'I can't dance with that dame, she leads.'" Hathaway broke up laughing, "She'd grab a guy and away she'd go. She was gorgeous."

Susan once said — on being difficult: "I've never been difficult to work with, just ask any director I've ever had. I'm difficult only to myself and I'm very hard on me. I think I've learned a great deal — patience for one thing — but I still have a tremendous amount to learn."

At about the same time of the filming of *Garden of Evil* in Mexico Susan was very upset over the imprisonment of her champion Walter Wanger, who was now serving a jail sentence for the shooting of Jennings Lang over Lang's attentions to Wanger's wife, Joan Bennett. She realized now that Walter had sold her contract to Fox to pay off creditors against the multi-million dollar fiasco of his independently produced *Joan of Arc*.

He had given her a strong boost to the top. She had made it and he'd fallen off the heap, and now she was looking for a way to help him out. Wanger had reshaped her whole professional life, pointing her in the direction of what most would have considered Utopia.

"Utopia, the word should be struck from the dictionary," said Susan, "Do you know of anybody who's every found it? Anyone who's even visited it or been there? I don't. The politicians all guarantee it but I don't think there is any such thing; if there were we'd probably all get tired of it very fast. Life seems to be a constant battle with a few moments out now and then for relaxation. If there is a Utopia, you probably find it only when you're dead."

For all her success she was desperately lonely, "I know it well," she said.

On being asked to comment about a book on Susan Hayward, Henry Hathaway could only say, "The only way I could see a book about her would be about a woman who destroyed herself. Like the movie about the drunk she played — everything she did was destroying herself, her marriage, her children, her mode of living, her attitude, and to spite all that she survived. Just to destroy herself many times over. The only kind of book about her that would make any sense would be like the part she played, of a person who absolutely destroyed herself. It should be called 'Self-Destruct!' That's a good title, 'Self-Destruct!' There is nothing good you can say about Susan — except that she was a good actress."

---

* The one time Rowland Smith saw his wife perform, it was in Germany during the war. She took the stage on crutches, a 50 pound cast from her hip to her toes, to perform for the wounded and dying. Smith was an officer of war information.

When Froman died, at 72, in her Columbia home, Rowland spoke about her life. She was born in University City in St. Louis County on November 10, 1907. Although she wasn't a Roman Catholic, until high school she attended a Catholic convent school in Clinton. Her mother was a piano teacher. After graduating from Christian College, she enrolled in the University of Missouri, Columbia School of Journalism. "Actually she flunked out of the school of journalism so her mother whisked her off to Cincinnati Conservatory of Music. Her first paid performance was an ad for Tom's Toasted Peanuts.

However, her big break came as a singer for the Paul Whiteman band. From Cincinnati, she went to Chicago and landed a full-hour Sunday afternoon radio show. After four years in Chicago, in 1935 she was voted top girl singer on the air. Venturing into New York, she landed a job with the Chesterfield Hour until 1943.

Credited with being the first USA volunteer, she boarded a plane for Europe to sing for allied troops in a USO show, the plane crashed into the Tagus River near Lisbon, Portugal. She was saved from the wreckage by co-pilot John Burns, whom she later married and divorced. The scene became a highlight of a 1952 movie about her life called, *With a Song in My Heart*. With Froman's voice dubbed in, Susan Hayward won an Oscar nomination for the part.

After the plane crash, doctors wanted to amputate her crushed leg but she refused. More than 35 operations later, she was back on the USO tour. It was on that tour that Smith heard her sing. The US Congress promised to pay off her mountainous doctor bills- but reneged on it. In 1962, she married Rowland Smith. Although Froman stuttered throughout her life and feared the telephone, she never had any problems before an audience. Contributions in her name were to be made to the Jane Froman Foundation for Emotionally Disturbed children at the Menninger Foundation. She was a humanitarian to the end.

JOHN WAYNE

John Wayne is my favorite leading man of all time. Why? He's so big and so rugged and so strong and can do practically anything, yet he's very gentle. I've always adored him, always, but then so has the whole world.

CHAPTER 6

Susan's emotional life had all the security of a floating crap game. Now, of all the people to gamble on, she took a chance on Howard Hughes. Not even her astrologer, Carroll Righter, could have predicted what would happen in that relationship.

Choreographer Bob Sidney was called in by the director and ex-song and dance man Dick Powell to choreograph a sequence in *The Conqueror*, produced by Howard Hughes at his RKO Studios. He would spend over six million dollars on this epic story of Mongol King Genghis Khan, who would be portrayed by the totally unexotic John Wayne, who turned it into an oriental western. To assist him in making it even more unbelievable Hughes finally got Susan Hayward for RKO as Bortai, the Tartar princess captured by Khan en route to her wedding. As the plot churned, Genghis wants to honeymoon Bortai — first. The casting could not have been worse if Charlie Chan had been cast as Rhett Butler and Anna May Wong as Scarlett in *Gone With The Wind*. In the film, Susan defends her honor for almost two hours, but not before her misplaced Salome dance in which she wants to slice Khan's head off with a sword, between bumps and grinds.

Bob Sidney, who had worked with Dick Powell before has never forgotten the experience; "She did not want to do the picture. She wanted no part of it."

"It was thought that it was Hughes 'way of getting her', but Susan was a very direct person. She would have said; 'Look Buster, to take me out you don't have to make a movie.' She was a very defiant person, a strong lady. Hughes borrowed her and she was told by Fox if she didn't do it, they would put her on suspension. Hughes was powerful and the Zanuck clan and Hughes were very close anyway. That business of her not going to do *The Conqueror*, well it was not so much that the picture was lousy; it was more like 'OK Mr. Howard Hughes, you want a match!'"

She fought him to a point where he said she was going to do it or else. The only reason she did it, she said, was because they gave her a lot of money. Susan was a businesswoman, she was not going to go on suspension and lose all that money. She was the top-notch star at Fox, too.

"Dick told me that Michael Woulf, the designer, was going out to see Susan at her home in Sherman Oaks, and I went with him. She knew he was coming and she opened the door herself.

"'I'm Michael Woulf,' he said.

"'Yes, and who are you?' she asked, looking at me.

"'Why, I'm Bob Sidney the choreographer,' I replied. I'll never forget her next comment; this is exactly what she said:

"Why are you here, who needs you!

"I was shocked. 'Well, I was told once, that people are hospitable here, and if I come to your house, you have got to be polite, don't you?'

"Susan broke up, 'Oh, come in.'

"Poor Michael Woulf, who was under personal contract to Hughes, was a very important guy at the studio and he designed these wonderful clothes for her," Sidney carried on. "He knew exactly the kind of things Susan like. She hated 'la-de-da' things, she had a very specific taste, not frilly, she liked things that might cling. Woulf showed her each sketch and with each one she said, 'Hate it! Hate it! Hate it! I don't like anything!'

"When we got back to the studio, Dick Powell asked how it went. 'She's a monster!' I said and told him what happened and he went hysterical.

"Powell finally had a talk with Susan, "Look Susan if you really hate the clothes fine, but if they are any good at all, you can't say they're horrible. There's a guy involved and he has a job to do."

"When she heard that she might jeopardize this guy's job, which wasn't the case," Sidney went on. "She said that some of the designs were O.K. Michael made them like sheets, they would cling, that's the only thing she would wear. She never had good legs; they were thin and weak. Her hips were good and she had this beautiful bust — that was real, she needed nothing to support them."

On one occasion, when a female columnist purred that Susan augmented nature with a bit of padding, La Hayward picked up the phone and quickly set the lady straight, the columnist backtracked, "Darling, can't you take a little joke?"

Said Susan, "Darling, I have no sense of humor about my bust!"

"Susan was very conscious of her legs, because they were thin and that's why I think she always diverted your attention. She always insisted on her left profile. In the early films, she looked wonderful no matter how you shot her. Perfect face for the camera. Later, she always posed from that left side and by doing that no one would look at her lower body. From the knees up she was damn good."

Sidney had to work up the dance routine for *The Conqueror*, in which Susan would be doing some motions in 'close-up' to drums, as they didn't know what the music would be. He met her again on the sound stage.

"She couldn't dance at all, but I thought from looking at her body that she had hips, so I tried to devise something which she as a non-dancer could do well as a dancer; something that was based on a certain line of her body. We showed it to her — she already said she would not dance — and she agreed to do two inserts, two close-ups. The dancer would do the long shots and Susan would come in for the close-up, smiling. I told her, 'when we say "close up" you do this with the knife.'"

She was supposed to get up from a reclining position in the scene when she sees the two knives hanging on a wall, about 18 feet high. She had to keep leaping in the scene until she got a knife and threw it at Khan.

"Did you read this thing," she said. "No pole vaulter can go that high — that's why I hate this dumb script."

"Well, anyway we lowered the knives," Sidney continued. "And she did the two close ups."

The professional dancer stand-in was waiting to do the full dance routine and Susan wanted to watch.

"Why, should I audition for you?" Sidney told her. "Then you'll do what you did to Michael Woulf's clothes. I was there and you tried to throw me out, too."

"You're a real son-of-a-bitch," she said. "Now if I'm nice and won't even tell you if I hate it can I watch?" (Of course she did.)

The girl, a very exciting dancer, did the number. When she finished, Susan asked where the close-ups went. Sidney brushed aside any further curiosity from her, "That's it, you can't help, I don't want any complaining about the dance. You didn't want to do it, now you don't have to."

"What do you mean I don't have to," she kicked off her shoes. "O.K. let's start!" she said. "But really, Bob, if I'm lousy, don't let me do it, let the girl do the long shots."

"Came the day of the shooting and the poor girl never even got lined up with the camera. I asked Susan to please, let her do it, just once; she wanted to earn her salary. She answered, 'Screw her! I'm doin' it. She'll get paid anyway.'

"She was fabulous for a girl who couldn't dance. She worked hard — we would rehearse every day (for six weeks). I gave her exercises and she'd say 'look at these legs, what can I do?' She looked forward to these exercises. She knew she was killing me during the sessions and she enjoyed it.

"I screamed, 'Enough!' she came back with, "you're supposed to have strong legs."

"'You know you never take me to the commissary," I said to her one day. "I want to look glamorous going in there with a star."

"'Yeah, sure," she'd say.

"For lunch she'd have a piece of cheese that she brought from home. 'It's lunchtime,' I always reminded her. 'No!' the same answer — but finally she went with me.

"All the dancing girls came on the set in costumes when they heard John Wayne was there, they could hardly wait to see him, and they were absolutely disenchanted. (Wayne wore pantaloons and was heavily mustached.)

"A fire broke out on the set and everyone ran screaming to put it out the crew, all the men, everyone but Susan. She thought if the set burned down it would take them days to rebuild it and they'd get extra money. She was afraid of nothing. She jumped the horse's side saddle, and she wasn't afraid of Wayne."

An amused Sidney related this episode: "Susan had this scene with John Wayne where he grabs her. She had all that red hair and another fall on top of her head to make her look taller. I asked her what she was doing with all that growth on top of her head 'You bitch,' she said. Wayne shook her so violently in the scene that this thing flew off her head. They reshot the take, and did it over and over, and then they were going to do it without her hairpiece. She said to me 'he's hurting me that son-of-a-bitch.' Her arms were black and blue. I said why don't you let him have it (in the groin) — she loved it!"

Sidney went over to John Wayne — "He's very macho and wanted every one to call him 'Duke.'"

"So I purposely said — 'Mr. Wayne.'

"He said, 'call me Duke.'

"I said, 'Mr. Wayne — this thing with Susan, well she's frail and she's not feeling well; its ladies day. I know she's the last person to admit it but couldn't you go easier, you're hurting her.'

"Wayne cried out, "Look she's so damn strong, she's stronger than I am. I don't want to come across as though she's putting me down.'

"He had a devil of a time controlling her, she raised her knee — you know where — and she let him have it. He really got it. They yelled, 'Cut!'"

"Susan respected talent," Sidney said. "She wasn't too fond of women. The women she liked were wardrobe women, hairdressers. Jokingly, she referred to herself as a nice Jewish girl from Brooklyn. She spoke very grand. She worked hard to get that deep, rich, low tone — then she would slip into Brooklynese kiddingly, she'd say, 'so wadda ya want me ta do?'"

"When she came into a room she would give this furtive look, because she couldn't see, and she wouldn't wear glasses because that would give her the excuse to end up with the left profile. I told her I didn't like that profile, the other one was better, and she said, 'How much did they pay you to say that?' 'A lot!' I said, because it meant redoing a whole damn scene. When she was being fitted she would say — 'lower,' 'higher' — sharply. She was not coy. She never used her wiles. If she didn't like something she'd say it."

Sidney found this difference, "She never gave a party for the crew after the picture was finished, no presents, none of that. I asked her to give a party after this picture, but she wouldn't do it. Dick Powell didn't like to spend money either (ask June Allyson, his wife at that time.) Susan would say, "If you don't like what you're doing, why take the job. And as for a party? We're all working in the same business. They get paid.""

Sidney reminded her one day, "I had met you years ago at Dick Wyman's house when you were married to Jess Barker."

"You must have not made any impression," she replied. "I didn't remember you."

"You're sweet," he said. "The only reason I remembered you was because you had all this dyed red hair."

"It wasn't dyed — then," she said. Now she was angry, "You're going too far. If I hit you, you'll know it."

She liked Bob Sidney and they were to remain friends.

As for *The Conqueror*, she said, "I had hysterics all through that one. Every time we did a scene, I dissolved in laughter. Me, a red-haired Tartar princess! It looked like some wild Irishman had stopped off on the road to Cathay a few years back."

Although Susan had legal custody of the children, Jess Barker tried to throw up as many legal roadblocks as possible.

In March, he tried to stop her from taking them on location with her to Utah, where she was filming Hughes's technicolor bonanza *The Conqueror*, but he failed.

Barker's lawyer S.S. Hahn, pleading Barker's case, told the judge — "to melt the ice in the heart of that woman with the legal whip...a river of gold has blinded that woman to her responsibilities to her children and husband...that woman is an absent mother with an icy heart..."

That same month Jess Barker met bit player Yvonne Doughty when he visited the restaurant operated by her mother. On their second date, she became intimate with him in an apartment in Sherman Oaks.

Susan would be absent again, but not from her children as she took them with her when the cast and screw were scheduled to go for exterior shooting on the picture to St. George, Utah.

The site was the main fallout zone for America's worst nuclear accident, the explosion known as "Dirty Harry'; one of the 87 open air atomic tests conducted at the nearby Nevada range between 1951-1962. On May 19, 1953 a sudden wind change, as Dirty Harry was detonated at 5:05 a.m., carried a more intense cloud of radioactive fallout than had been measured in a populated area, even in Japan after the explosion of two wartime atomic bombs.

In between May and August 1954, Susan Hayward and John Wayne and members of the cast and screw shot scenes in the thick of the fallout zone, unaware of the dangers of radiation.

Tons of the red earth, which had absorbed lethal radiation doses, was loaded into huge carriers and carted back to Hollywood, where it was used to construct huge indoor sets. Hayward, Wayne and the others left St. George and followed the caravan of big trucks and trailers which began rolling back to the studio with the red Utah earth which was to be used to make exterior scenes filmed in the studio for the six million dollar production.*

Susan had found something of a match in Howard Hughes. Both were extremely independent and very much loners, and both had peculiar sex problems. Hughes was very much attracted to the unpredictable, untamed redhead. She at least fulfilled one of his sexual fantasies with the required attribute of well-formed breast. Hughes certainly had power and money and that appealed to Susan, but his enigmatic attraction soon bored her.

During the divorce trial, Barker's lawyers called Hughes to the witness stand.

Hughes testified that his visits to Susan's home in Barker's absence were strictly business; he wanted her for his film *The Conqueror*. Barker countered that as a result of Hughes' visits his sons' attitude toward him had changed since the break-up. They told their father that Mr. Magic — as Hughes was introduced to the boys by their mother — had promised to take them for an airplane ride. They said his name was Howard Hughes, but that 'Mommie said we shouldn't tell Daddy his name.'

Susan, called back to the stand, admitted that Hughes had been to her home but denied having told the boys to keep the meeting a secret. Why should she, he was there to discuss a contract. Besides, Susan felt

Hughes could distract the boys from the recent split between the parents by taking them on trips, plane rides and sport outings (making Howard Hughes sound like a Boy Scout Master). To add to all this, the Marrener clan encouraged the liaison.

With Hughes in the picture, Barker fought to regain custody of his sons.

Susan with Timothy and Gregory.

Herb Caen, in his column in the *San Francisco Chronicle,* reported his arrival in San Francisco to retain lawyers Melvin Belli and Kathryn Gehrels. Later, Barker dropped by Peter Arnesto's restaurant on Geary Street, ordered coffee and a bromo seltzer and signed an autograph for waitress Nela Kennedy, still a celebrity coasting on his wife's fame.

Hughes was always amazed that he could call Susan quite spontaneously and say they were going out someplace and she would say she would be ready in ten minutes.

One time, they flew to Las Vegas in his private plane. His reasons, never truly explained, seemed unimportant to her. Seated in the lounge of the Sands Hotel, with two bodyguards at the next table, Susan and Hughes ordered dinner. Brooklyn born opera singer Robert Merrill was currently appearing there. After his nightclub act was over, Jack Entratter

who books the acts brought Merrill over to the corner table to be introduced to the famous pair. Hughes did not look up or stop eating; Susan
however, commented on how much she had loved his show. Hughes
mumbled that the mike was too loud and Susan gave him a sideward
glare.

"That Pagliacci aria, it almost made me cry," she said.

"Opera leaves me cold," said Hughes.

Susan gave him a menacing look and said sharply, "We Brooklyn
people stick together."

Hughes, who was embarrassed by her putting him down in public,
ignored the remark and asked her if she wanted anything for dessert.

Susan shook Merrill's hand as he excused himself to get ready for the
next show. Hughes did not offer his hand and Susan was annoyed by his
rudeness.

At 3 a.m. that morning, one of Hughes aides phoned Merrill in his
room in the hotel.

He offered Merrill a contract at Hughes studio, RKO, almost certainly
resulting from Susan's intercession. Merrill fended the offer with a 'speak
to my agent' answer.

Hughes could counter act what he supposed was Susan's interest in
Merrill by tying him up under contracts with options and dangling him
for years, which could kill his operatic career. Whereas Jane Russell, Ava
Garner and Lana Turner would placate Hughes, Hayward would tell him
off and say that he was acting like a spiteful little boy. Afraid to fight back
and incur her rejection, he would then go around her back to retaliate. In
the end, Merrill refused the offer.

On September 2, 1954, Susan was awarded custody of the nine-year-
old twins, with visitation rights for Barker.

Susan continued to live at 3737 Longridge Avenue Sherman Oaks in
her San Fernando Valley home — which remained half-furnished — and
her old friend, Martha Little, continued to live with after the divorce
from Jess.

Though critically ill with cancer, and certainly a handicap during
this period, Susan especially wanted her friend to enjoy Christmas. She
secretly paid thousands of dollars in medical bills for the incurably ill
sister of one of her schoolmates. She planned the Christmas holidays
for Martha and her family. It was to be Miss Little's last Christmas with
Susan, as shortly afterwards Miss Little returned to New York.

On New Year's Eve, Susan planned to have dinner with Howard
Hughes in the Polo Lounge of the Beverly Hills Hotel and he arranged

for one of his chauffeurs to pick her up at home. Susan was beautifully dressed and might have expected on this special evening that Hughes would make some commitment about their uncertain relationship.

He was waiting for her in a private dining room dressed in sneakers, jeans and open nick white shirt. They ordered drinks and Hughes in his soft nervous voice avoided her attempts at a serious conversation to clarify her position in his life. She was interrupted anyway by an aide calling Hughes away from the table when the midnight hour struck amid loud screams of 'Happy New Year' and the sound of horns and bells bringing in 1955.

He returned and was very apologetic but became more restless than ever. He was beckoned once again by another of his men from the dining room entrance. Susan had had it. She was suspicious and furious by this time and got up from the table and followed him into the main dining room, where she saw him sit down in a secluded corner next to actress Jean Peters.

Absolutely enraged by this double date maneuver she pushed through the crowd and stood before the startled Miss Peters and the now shaken Howard Hughes. She denounced him with Brooklyn adjectives in a very loud voice and stormed furiously out of the room.

Howard Hughes was now struck out as any possible contender for the man she needed in her life.

Meantime, Jess, who was penniless, counter-sued for a community property settlement and custody of the twins. The courts found that because of the pre-nuptial agreement with his wife, he was not entitled to community property but eventually awarded him $10,000 to help him begin a new life.

"Susan was more fortunate than I," Barker told the divorce court judge. "She became a star."

The Conqueror would be in production for the next two years and Susan would be working in two pictures at the same time as she was back and forth between RKO studios to complete her scenes while working on her next picture for 20th Century Fox.

When asked about a possible reconciliation with Jess, she replied, "Not a chance in the world, I know now I should have left Jess a long time ago. He'll be better off without me to depend on and I'll be better off not having to worry about him."

As a divorcee, Susan became the target for every prowling caballero in Hollywood. According to a friend, one gallant phoned for a date and got this reply, "See here, my friend, why do you want to go out with me, besides the fact that I'm rich, famous and beautiful."

When he hesitated a second too long, she hung up. Susan appreciated a quick response and if he'd come across with one she might have made a date with him.

"I pity the poor devil who takes me out in public the first time," she said, "We'd both be miserable. I haven't had a 'date' in so long I hardly know how to talk to a man except career wise, and I'm sure he will be uncomfortable with all the romance rumors the most casual dinner engagements will bring forth."

When Susan got the news of the death of Martha Little she dropped everything and flew to New York for the funeral. She was very disconsolate and back in Hollywood after the funeral. Jeff Chandler offered Susan a shoulder to cry on. Chandler, Susan and Martha Little were all old friends from their Brooklyn childhood days, he was now separated from his wife and with their mutual broken marriages; it was one more bond to share.

---

* John Wayne, Susan Hayward, Dick Powell, Agnes Moorehead and most of the top production people on the same movie developed cancer later on. Character actor Pedro Armendariz, Carroll Clark died, production manager of the film, his wife, the make-up chief and so many others working on this film all died of cancer related illnesses.

THE DARK

I'm terrified of the dark; always have been. I don't like the night and I keep the lights on — all the time. I can remember the very moment it happened when I was a child. I was in my grandmother's house and an uncle scared me by telling me there was a bogeyman waiting for me on the second floor. I can still remember that moment — vividly. I've been afraid of the dark ever since; not too crazy about that uncle, either. I'm also nearsighted and that doesn't help; it adds to my lack of security in the dark.

CHAPTER 7

She was the top woman star of the entire world in the fifties, with Gary Cooper and John Wayne running neck and neck for top male star. Her contract at 20th Century Fox brought her $250,000 a year and she was up to three academy award nominations. She had played fiery, tempestuous women in her last three pictures (*Demetrius and The Gladiators, Garden of Evil* and *Untamed)* — and she was now told she would have to begin her fourth picture. The studio was using her name at the box office for all it was worth. She paid off!

Clark Gable, through with his contract after twenty three years at MGM (the only studio contract he ever had), made a deal with Darryl Zanuck at 20th Century Fox for two films a year, for $400,000 guaranteed up front and 10% of the gross.

The first, *Soldier of Fortune* — obviously a title to throw the spotlight on him — would start in Hong Kong late in 1954. Gable wanted his young flame from MGM, Grace Kelly, to be cast as his co-star. At a press conference to publicize his new studio contract with Fox, he was quizzed about his first film and his new leading lady, Susan Hayward. Gable looked dumbstruck and muttered, 'Who's she?' The reporters thought it was a joke and kidded him along. But to Susan it was no laughing matter, she was furious.

Susan had tested for Scarlett O'Hara to appear opposite Gable's Rhett Butler decades ago when she was a fresh kid from Brooklyn and he was king of the movies. They almost met at a party given for him after he came out of the service. The whole town was throwing parties for him and he escorted singer Jan Clayton to one particular party, and was very attentive to her until Susan Hayward walked in — then his attention was gone. Gable was fascinated by the way Hayward looked 'sexily' at men. It wasn't sex, it was myopia. She was trying to find them without her glasses. Hayward didn't respond to Gable by going into a swoon. When Jan Clayton told her after the party that Gable stared at her all night she said, "He did? Why didn't somebody tell me?"

20th Century Fox told Susan she would have to go to Hong Kong for foreign location shooting. She couldn't legally take her sons out of the country without their father's and the court's permission and she didn't want to leave them in Barker's custody, as they never came back the same after their visits with him, and she feared further damage to her position as their mother and refused to go.

The chief of 20th Century Fox, Darryl F. Zanuck, who had guided Hayward's career to further prominence at Fox, was in his office in the executive building when a furious redhead stormed in, leaving behind her a secretary with mouth agape.

Zanuck started to rise.

"Stay right there Darryl!" she said.

Seated behind his mahogany desk in a tweed jacket and knitted tie, his moustache pressing an expensive cigar he sized up the situation as Hayward tore into him, pounding on his desk.

"I'm not leaving California, and I'm not going to do this picture."

"Now Susan," he said calmly, "This will be very good for you, after all this is Clark Gable and —"

"Screw Gable," she snapped back, "Get him Grace Kelly."

"Darryl I can't go — I won't!" she said, trying not to go into all the details.

"Susan," Zanuck said. "Now listen — you want to do *I'll Cry Tomorrow*, we all know — I've agreed to loan you to MGM — but first you'll have to wrap up this picture with Gable…"

And so they compromised.

When they eventually teamed up on the lot for shooting, she was very cool.

The scene came where Susan was to slap Gable across the face, after he had made an inopportune remark.

Gable grinned and told her not to feel shy; to let him have it — to make it look convincing. If not they would have to do another take.

She said she'd try her best. The director called for action — and got it; Susan hauled off and swung her right hand, landing a hit that sent Gable staggering off balance.

The making of this film was to run concurrently with the beginning of *I'll Cry Tomorrow* and towards the end of the shooting, a meeting was arranged between the producer of *I'll Cry Tomorrow* and her new director, Daniel Mann.

It was Daniel Mann's first meeting with Susan Hayward. He had only recently arrived in Hollywood from the New York theatre. Studio boss

Hall Wallis of Paramount Pictures had brought him out to direct Shirley Booth in *Come Back Little Sheba*, and the Italian actress Anna Magnani in *The Rose Tattoo*. Both pictures had brought considerable acclaim to the director and an Academy Award to each of the stars.

Larry Weingarten of Metro-Goldwyn-Mayer, the producer of *I'll Cry Tomorrow*, asked Mann to direct Susan Hayward in this film and

Susan and Clark Gable.

pre-production meetings were arranged. Weingarten, a mild mannered individual, was not cast in the usual mold of Hollywood producers. In fact, at a casual glance he could easily have been mistaken for an English professor from a nearby university.

Mann had never met a Hollywood movie star; Shirley Booth was from the stage and Anna Magnani was a star of the Italian screen. Hayward was a true product of the Hollywood system.

For their meeting, she wore a plain suit, blouse and gloves and a light make-up, not chic, but well groomed.

"There was an innate shyness, a self protectiveness about her, particularly in meeting new people and especially producers and directors. As soon as she felt you were honest with her," said Mann. "Her natural instincts as an outgoing lusty dame from Brooklyn came through.

"Susan was really keen on the role," he went on. "Very receptive about the meeting. There was nothing grand about her, but she certainly had all the professional concern about who she was going to be dealing with in a film of this nature.

"As I remember it our meeting was friendly; she was observing me, and I was observing her. She represented to me a lovely young talented lady who was going to have to go through a great big emotional role about somebody who became addicted to alcohol, the story of Lillian Roth."

Susan looked Mann over appraising, the individual who was going to be her director as she had director approval. She saw someone with an athletic build, dark hair and blue eyes, a serious, intelligent man whom, she must have decided, she could get along with.

She lit a cigarette and listened as Weingarten spoke to Mann and herself about general schedules and the target date for the completion of the movie. Following this Mann talked to Susan about the essence of the character of Lillian Roth, with all her strengths and weaknesses, the role that Susan would practically adopt as her own nature. Susan must have wondered how deep he was going to dig, how much he was going to probe. There would be areas where they would be on no man's land together and with her highly personalized acting, they would either have to meet or cancel each other out.

"Larry," Susan said to Weingarten during a break in Mann's talk, "It's imperative that whoever is going to direct this role — the role of a woman's life and her attempted suicide — had to be somebody I can accept; not simply accept legally but accept in a sense of working with extremely closely. I want to do this role right," she emphasized. "And I cannot accept someone I am not at ease with."Thus, she made her position clear to her new director.

Susan said very little else at the meeting in the executive's office. She never was a big talker but she didn't miss very much either. She had easily detected in Mann his sensitivity, and his air of self-assurance. He could be strong with her without pushing too hard, something she needed. Also,

Susan in I'll Cry Tomorrow.

had he not brought two middle aged actress's performances on screen to the critical acclaim of the industry and public's acceptance at the box office?

Shooting was to begin with the last scene of *I'll Cry Tomorrow*, the scene at the El Capitan theatre in Hollywood and Vine. In this scene, the regenerated torch-singer walks down the aisle to tell her story on the television show *This Is Your Life* to a television and studio audience of a combined total of some 40,000,000 people. The host of the television program, Ralph Edwards, introduces the honored guest to the audience. Susan, as Lillian Roth, meets the people who were responsible for saving her, after being helped on stage by members of Alcoholics Anonymous.

"We were going to open with that and all my instincts told me this is not the way to *start* the picture," Mann reflected. "This is a moment of climax of her coming back as a whole person again."

The house was full of people who had come to see the Ralph Edwards show. Edwards was on stage and Susan was waiting to make her entrance from the lobby through the doors of the theatre and down the center aisle.

A ramp was built from the back of the theatre over the top of the seats the full length of the theatre so that the camera could move with Susan. It would be on her as she walked down and would move with her and arc over to make the audience visible. They were ready for a rehearsal of the first scene.

Susan walked down the aisle with Mann looking through the lens. The elevation of the camera cut off the heads of the audience and all he could see was Susan's head and shoulders so he told the crew to put the camera down as low as it would go. The theatre had been contracted for and was loaded with lighting and other equipment for the shooting. There were hundreds of extras and Susan was being very patient as they launched into their first day. She was aware that the director had a shooting problem. In fact, it was obvious to her he was not at all happy with the shot. She heard him say it would not really do justice to the dramatic impact of her being aware of people staring at her and the moment — soon — that she was going to have to come down and face the truth; to be stripped emotionally naked and exposed to a world wide audience.

They rehearsed again and Mann asked that the camera be lowered even more to capture the expression on the audience's faces, only to make the discovery that it could not be lowered anymore. He turned to the assistant director and the MGM chiefs standing by.

"I am not going to do this shot," he said, "it doesn't make sense. My responsibility is to you, the studio, and the studio is synonymous with Susan, the audience, myself — and it just doesn't make sense."

He went into a huddle with the men surrounding him. Whilst directing each shot he would mentally fuse it into his image of the completed film and he was not prepared to compromise on this image. This had a tremendous impact on Susan who standing by watching and listening.

The executives were overwhelmed that Mann would take this position. It was unimaginable to them — even worse, it was his first picture at MGM.

"Danny you gotta do this!" said one of the studio executives.

"Look I'm not going to argue with you," he replied. "This is not a question of temperament or other nonsense. My first responsibility is to make this picture, and my making this picture means that this scene is the reaching of a climax — a lifetime of what she has gone through, and not to get the dramatic impact would be a terrible loss, and wouldn't really be right for me as a director and certainly not for Susan. No, no way! I'll go home. I have a nice backyard and I'll sit there and when you want me..." he broke off and walked away.

It was then that Susan realized that she had, as a director, a man who was going to be involved with only the best that could possibly be achieved, both cinematically and regarding the development of the character. Mann and Susan never discussed the decision, however, her attitude towards him was very much affected by it and she began to open up to him a little, feeling that she could trust him.

Ironically, when they got around to the scene again and decided to rebuild the ramp, there was a problem, which evidently disallowed them, as a movie company, to go into a theatre and film a TV show for a movie. They finally built the ramp on the MGM lot.

Another important moment came when Susan and Daniel Mann were to test each other. Cinematographer James Wong Howe was going over the script with Mann. The Oscar winning Howe was one of the greatest cameramen in the business, and was brilliant at underlying moods.

In preparing for her role, Susan had studied the mannerisms of seriously ill alcoholics and visited the cells of unfortunates in the Los Angeles County Jail. Through the bars of their cells, she has studied women with the "shakes."

In one scene, Susan had to play Lillian Roth at her absolute rock-bottom, lost in her alcoholic obsession as she sat in the bar with the winos, it would be very important now not only to photograph Susan's emotional involvement in that atmosphere but literally (if possible), to photograph the reflection of the place as registered in her face. She was to be completely lost, not aware of what she was doing, because she had been wandering around drunk for nobody knows how long.

"Danny, I'll tell you what; I want to make a test of Susan without make-up," Howe told Mann, "Susan has freckles, which are kind of a wholesome thing — but if I use a blue light the freckles will give us a texture to her skin and make her look really wasted."

Mann went to see Hayward, to talk about it.

"What! You want me to appear without any...Danny..." she said. "I-I don't know."

"Alright Susan, I am not asking you to appear unpleasant or ugly. I am asking you to appear as she did at this point in her life. Make-up can't create that. With no make-up and Jimmy's ability to get it, it will give us tremendous sympathy for Roth's appallingly wasted life at this moment."

She thought for a moment, "I've never done anything like that I've always tried to cover these things up, but I'll do it — O.K. I'll do it."

The scene in the barroom is where Lillian, now a chronic alcoholic, is living in almost complete forgetfulness. She makes drunks laugh by reciting a childhood job seeking speech — 'I'm Lillian Roth, I'm eight years old, I do imitations and dramatic parts' — and the winos finally discover that this *is* the lady they remembered. They laugh at her while Susan sits there laughing too; and as she's laughing big tears, like drops of blood, are pouring out of her eyes. It became one of the most unforgettable moments in the picture.

Susan changed a lot during this period, very much aided by the story of Lillian Roth's torment, and often went into long trances and became at times quite unreachable. She brooded and had frequent fits of severe nervousness and bouts of delirium tremens, similar to those that Lillian Roth must have experienced. The pain of her early years, which she was summoning for the role, sent her, in the early part of the filming especially, into desperate depressions. She could portray the lonely, desperate, frustrated singer so well because she had experienced similar emotions; despite the fact that many of her troubles were self made.

"It was one of the great moments in my whole career," Mann said about the barroom scene not simply because it was a classic moment of laughter and tears, but that she had the freedom and capacity to involve herself in a very personalized moment."

"Only an actress of great courage, talent and magic could have done it. It could have looked phony to be laughing and crying at the same time, big thing about Susan's talent is that none of this was representative.

What Susan did is what she experienced — that's why the audience experienced it."

As an actress and as an individual, Susan understood the story very thoroughly she was able to involve herself in these 'magic' moments, helping to make her the actress she was. In Susan's tragic life, there was a deep understanding of irony and pain. Mann picked up on this and was determined not to close her off or risk invading her with intimacies that might cause her to reject his direction.

A week later Susan Hayward tried to kill herself.

She was alone in the living room of her house in Sherman Oaks on that Monday night, April 25, 1955. She must have heard the grandfather clock strike midnight as she slammed the phone down on Jess Barker over another argument about the upbringing of their sons. Her thoughts circled hopelessly. The marriage had blown up the year before in a flare of headlines. She had seen him just four days ago — very reluctantly — and he had challenged her custody of the twins. She was driven to distraction by Barker's threats to take her boys away from her.

Sitting barefoot on the couch, dressed in pajamas, her head thrown back in exhaustion, a wave of depression must have swept over her. She could still hear his angry voice echoing in her ears. Divorce yes, but no end to the recriminations and quarrels. Timmie and Greg were sleeping upstairs, but they had never seemed so far away from her. Kept late at the studio for a conference, she had come home after their bedtime and crept up to look in on them, their two motionless forms outlined under the covers with only their heads visible. She couldn't just take them away someplace else, she was on the treadmill of her career and obligations she had built up did not allow her to break away from the only 'security' she had every known.

The house was so noisy during the day with the boys tearing about and Cleo the housekeeper trying to keep some kind of control. In the evenings Cleo's daughter, Willy Mae, joined her mother to help out with the boys when Susan worked late at the studio.*

At night, everything was deathly quiet. She had tried to go to sleep, but could not rest so she had gotten out of bed and gone downstairs to have a drink and a cigarette, and curl up on the couch. When she was found later that night, beside her lay the script of I'll Cry Tomorrow. She had probably been going over it before her suicide attempt.

Now, in her highly emotional and suggestible condition some of the thoughts in the script may have begun to work on her mind, so that her interpretation became even more personalized than usual, assuming a new significance.

Reading the scenes, she must have been aware of how the conflicts and fights with her own mother had much in common with the characters in the script. Susan's own mother was constantly badgering her about her drinking which had worsened considerably since her marriage to Barker and had continued to increase since the separation.

At some point, she took a large handful of sleeping pills, washed down with her usual bourbon, and decided at the last moment to call her mother.

Ellen Marrener, awakened by the ringing telephone in her home, picked up the receiver, angry and irritated at this interruption to her sleep but she quickly focused her attention as she heard her daughter's slurred speech, barely voicing the words, "Don't woo-ry Ma, you, you're taken care of."

Alarmed, she told her daughter she would call her right back and immediately phoned her son Wally, who remembered the call vividly.

"Wally, Susan just called me, she's talkin' kinda funny Wal, somethin' is goin' on out there. I'll call her and keep talkin' you get out there right away," his mother said.

Wally, following his mother's orders, jumped into his clothes, got into his car and in fifteen minutes was at Susan's home in the valley.

"When I arrived," he said, "the maid had heard the noise of her falling and had called the police. They hadn't arrived, neither had the ambulance and Susan's lying on the floor by the couch."

Shortly afterwards, speeding through the quiet suburban streets, a squad car screeched to a halt at the house on Longridge Avenue. Two police officers rushed across the patio and pounded on the door. They rushed past Wally as he opened it, and found Susan Hayward lying unconscious on the floor of her living room. The clock in the living room showed three o'clock. In Susan's bathroom cupboard upstairs, the detectives found two empty bottles of sleeping pills.

There are conflicting reports surrounding this incident — one of them had her mother calling the police department and saying, "My daughter is Susan Hayward. I'm afraid she's going to commit suicide." Another had Detective Wilkerson pounding on her front door yelling, "Susan, this is Wilkerson of the Detective bureau. Let us in!" — and getting only a 'yeah!' as reply, kicking in the patio door; there does appear to be validity in the patio-door incident as the L.A. Police Dept. used the Hayward suicide attempt case in a brief which was part of a move to reverse a Supreme Court ruling on illegal trespass. Chief William H. Parker contended that if his men had not broken down Miss Hayward's door, though it violated the law, she might have died.

"They just stood there," Wally said, "What are you gonna do," he cried out. "Just let her lie there until the ambulance gets here? Why don't you put her in your car! That might have been against the law," Wally went on, "but anyway the police put her in their car. They picked her up, one grabbin' her under the arms, the other by the legs with me holdin' her under the middle."

Reporters had just arrived at 3801 Longridge Avenue as Susan was being carried out of her house down the steps. The flashlights from the cameras lighted up the scene like a movie set. They yelled at the Detectives Wilkerson and Brondell for information. Wilkerson asked them to clear a way to the squad car and Brondell bit harder on his cigar and ignored them.

"Who are you?" they asked Wally.

"Who?" they said when they couldn't make out what his answer was.

"Her brother?"

"He don't look like her brother," they shouted as they scrambled over one another to get a closer shot of Susan — without make-up, her hair matted, pajamas disheveled and her face cold and expressionless.

"Once the police put her in the car," Wally continued. "I followed, and we got down to Ventura Blvd. about a half mile away and here comes the ambulance. Anyway, I followed the police car — I asked them if I go through a red light O.K.?" They said, 'Follow us.'"

The car raced to North Hollywood Receiving Hospital. In the emergency room, a team of doctors and nurses syringed out her stomach and she was prepared for transfer to Cedars of Lebanon Hospital.

Hovering between life and death, the woman who managed her career, home and family with computer-like efficiency had crashed.

Susan's mother sat at the kitchen table, on Longridge Ave. with her son Wally and her daughter Florence. Wally had returned from the hospital with the report that Susan's condition was critical. (Ellen Marrener and Florence were not very much in touch with Susan at this point and Wally had to keep them informed). They were having a drink to console themselves. The twins had been sent back to bed by their grandmother, "Mommie had a stomach ache and she was going to be fine," they were told. Nine-year-old Timmie crept downstairs and listened by the door.

He overheard his grandmother and his Aunt Florence arguing over what would happen to Susan's money and property if she didn't pull through. Grandmother was fearful of Jess Barker's claims to Susan's estate. Florence could have all her sister's clothes, furs, jewelry, and Wally would get what they worked out for him. Timmie never forgot what he overheard and the results of this conversation would considerably affect his feelings towards them in later years. During the divorce hearings, one of the children had reported hearing something his Grandmother said right after his father left home. In talking to his father just before he left he said he couldn't understand why Grandma should say, "She would kill you," and urge his mother to get rid of Daddy." No matter how these remarks were intended the effect of them on an eight year old must have been traumatic.

At Cedars of Lebanon, the chief medical resident was alerted to take charge as Susan was brought to her hospital room. She was given intravenous feeding so that drugs could be given to correct shock and during the pre-dawn hours, the nurse would check her pulse, respiration, blood pressure and the pupils of her eyes repeatedly.

At the root of her being, Susan must have wanted to live and some three hours after her arrival, she awakened from the coma.

A photo of the nearly dead Susan being carried from her home made the front page, with headlines bannering her suicide attempt. During her recovery in the hospital, an endless stream of 'Why-did-Susan-do-it?' articles appeared. Most of the articles assumed, at first that the strain of the divorce from Jess had caused her to overdose on barbiturates. Mystery lovers (including Howard Hughes, whom she had been dating) were later dragged into the conjectures. Jess himself, believing that he was the cause of the incident, told the newspapers that he had never stopped loving Susan; he wanted reconciliation and tried to visit her in the hospital, but he was the last person she wanted to see. Billy Graham shouted from his lectern, 'Movie stars are unhappy, miserable people' and went on to sermonize on Susan Hayward's attempt to kill herself. It all made hot newspaper copy.

The morning had come after all. Susan opened her eyes as daylight filled the hospital room. She was weak and her mind was in a daze as she laid there welcoming the sensation of being alive.

"She was kind of miserable you know," Wally said. "They stationed a guard at the door so you couldn't get in to see her. She said she didn't want anybody to see her. After two days my mother and myself were allowed in."

"She looked kinda sheepish, cause my mother was ready to ball her out, but I told my mother, "Now don't say anything to her — if she wants to tell us anything, let her do it."

Susan did tell them something, but it wasn't very much, she simply said that she was reading the script and forgot how many pills she had taken. She would neither admit nor deny that she had tried to take her own life.

On the third day in the hospital, Susan ordered a steak for lunch. She changed into a pink negligee and a filmy pick sleeveless jacket. Softly made up, her red hair brushed back shiny and loose, she was ready to meet the press, which had been waiting for her around the clock.

"Dr. Imerman says I can leave the hospital within the next day or two. I am very anxious to get back to my children and back to work. No, there's not the slightest possibility of a reconciliation — if Mr. Barker can discuss the future of our children in a rational manner I shall be willing to confer with him." — was all she would say about the whole affair. It sounded like a press release. So far as any other enquiries were able to determine, she never talked to anyone about that night. She did make one further statement, "There are some things that are between you and God only," she said, and putting her hand on a reporter's knee, continued, "Don't ever believe there isn't a God. There is. I know there is a God."

The following day, shortly after breakfast she put on a bright print dress and was ready to leave the hospital. An attendant brought a wheelchair into her room.

"What's that for?"

"Hospital rule, Miss Hayward."

"That's nonsense; I can walk alone — now!"

"The impact on me was terrifying," Daniel Mann said when he saw the morning paper, "Here was a human being whom I was concerned with on a very personal level and she had tried to take her own life. She would not see anybody at the studio, but she would see me. The studio sent a limousine over and I was driven out to her house in Sherman Oaks. This was a day or two later."

"When I arrived at the house there were reporters outside. I rang the bell and the door was opened about four inches wide by the housekeeper and when I announced who I was she said, "Yes, come in." It was all very magic and hocus pocus, like a bad mystery. She ushered me into the living room and I sat down."

"Miss Hayward will be down shortly," she said.

"The last I had seen of her was the picture in the newspapers as she was carried out inert. Now I heard footsteps on the staircase behind me and I turned around. There was Susan coming down the stairs, her hair all beautifully coiffured, and wearing an organdy dress and looking absolutely marvelous. As she entered the room, I made the faux pas of my life. She came bouncing in and said, "Hello Danny."

"Susan, you look so alive!" I exclaimed.

"Oh!" she laughed.

"Oh, no, no, no, excuse me," I said, "I didn't mean to be facetious, but you look wonderful, marvelous."

"She laughed again and I embraced her."

A few days later Susan returned to work at MGM. The first scene to be filmed, on her first day back, was a big musical production number, built around the song 'Sing You Sinners', (insert photo of sing your sinners) in which she performed on a multi level set with a platoon of dancers.

Veteran costume designer Helen Rose, who had been assigned to do Susan's clothes on the picture, was one of the first people on the set to see her that day.

"Susan was being given the star treatment; a dressing room in the star building and a portable dressing room on the set. She was not at all fashion conscious but she was easy to work with — that is, for me she was. Danny was the one who got friendly with her. I was happy to be working with Danny Mann again; we had had a great rapport when we did *Butterfield 8* with Elizabeth Taylor."

"Susan was very lonely and very unfriendly and I knew she was going through some big personal problems. I remember when she came back following her suicide attempt. She was in a black mood that day and when I was alone with her in her dressing room, I told her off; 'Susan, when are you going to wake up and stop feeling sorry for yourself.' Her response to this was a sharply withdrawn silence but from that time on she seemed to perk up," the designer said.

Up to this point Susan had never sung professionally, but during the course of some routine pre-recording tests, MGM's musical chief Johnny Green was astonished by her signing voice. Green urged her to do her own singing rather than use a recording of Lillian Roth's voice for the soundtrack. He coached her privately. The first song was 'Red, Red, Robin, etc.'

"When they played it for the studio chief's they all agreed Susan could do her own soundtrack. She did her own singing though with the reservation that when they discovered that she really couldn't do it they would replace her with a professional, about the only recorded incident in which she insisted she couldn't do something.

Susan sat in her dressing room until she was called or. The knock on her door told her they were ready on the set. She looked into the dressing room mirror, checking make-up, hair and the low-cut, sleeveless beaded evening gown Helen Rose had designed to display her beautiful shoulders and arms. She put on her shoes and stepped out.

She came out looking absolutely radiant, although serious, and the set was 'electrified.' Something changed — became super-charged — in the atmosphere on the stage. Every one pivoted in her direction, not a word was said, but there was a powerful undercurrent of suspense. It was virtually impossible to go on as though nothing had happened, though there was a real attempt on everyone's part to ignore the facts of the shocking headlines just a few days ago. The entire crew was focused on her as she made her way, stepping over wires and in between lights and cameras. She climbed the ladder to the top of the set. (It was two floors of a building, with the fourth wall cut out and a camera boom ready to shoot by rising up to look into the house on either floor). She would begin on the top floor. It was one of the big MGM stages and there was a large assembly of technical staff with recording and other equipment, and legions of dancers and extras — all in the best tradition of MGM musicals.

Jimmy Wong Howe had the light he wanted, the dancers and the extras were posed for their cue, the boom camera advanced towards her, then — ACTION!

The music blared out and her tight serious look vanished as the energy of the performance, the lights, movement and action of the whole scene seemed to release her, "Brothers and sisters, startin' today, you can lose your blues whenever you choose by singing your troubles away," she belted out.

After the scene she ran, not walked, to her dressing room. She ran daintily like a ballet dancer. Her body small and playful, but her eyes were sad and serious again. She had returned, and now it was business as usual.

Susan never sat around to shoot the breeze with anyone. She followed an almost invariable pattern of returning to her dressing room between takes. One time during a break, she asked a chorus boy, in costume as a sailor for the number, "Got a cigarette?" As she sat down next to him, he gave her one and lit it for her. They called for the next take. "Thanks sailor," was all she said, as she took up her position, warmed up to a smile, and waited for her cue to go into her number again.

Once the musical numbers were shot, they went back into the heavy dramatic scenes. "I surprised Susan with this one," Mann said, "The boy-friend had passed on in the picture and there was a scene where she gets a drink from the nurse. I made an inquiry and found out that Susan liked bourbon so I said to the prop man get me the best bourbon in the world. I didn't tell Susan. I knew she would respond perfectly to it."

She always threw herself almost violently into her parts. She was an honest actress. When the director called for her, she was ready. She knew her lines. She did not always rise easily to the emotional peaks her roles required, she sometimes had to work up to them, feeling her way. Now she had to try to work her way out of this one — and there was no one around to direct her.

In preparing for bed, before going downstairs, she had evidently taken some of the sleeping pills her doctor had prescribed. They must not have had much effect, as there was evidence that she had been downstairs and awake for some considerable time before she was found on the floor of the living room.

She had never liked the nights alone and she kept some lights on all the time. As a child, staying at her grandmother's house, an uncle had terrified her by telling her there was a bogeyman waiting for her upstairs. She had always remembered that and had been afraid of the dark ever since. She never outgrew that bogeyman and her nearsightedness didn't help either, it only added to her fear of what she couldn't see and her lack of security.

She probably tried to distract herself by going over the script and coming across a particularly violent scene between Lillian Roth and her mother, she had underlined the words — "<u>don't worry, Mom — you're taken care of</u>."

"The shot is where the nurse sees that she can't sleep because she is in such pain and anguish and she decides she is going to give her a drink. She took the real bourbon and poured some of it into a glass. The shot follows the nurse handing her the glass, and I didn't tell Susan it was bourbon. She took hold of the drink and brought it to her lips. It grabbed her in the throat, but instead of stopping the act she finished the drink, put the glass down and dropped her shoulders — and you knew she was hooked."

"You son-of-a-bitch," she smiled slowly at Mann.

She started every morning by involving herself totally in her role and worked towards achieving the highest emotional key. She was appreciative of everybody on the set but very detached.

"She maintained a certain distance. It was not a conscious attempt to be different, she was concentrating on her work, which was very personal to her," was how Mann described the detachment, "nothing needed to be superimposed for effect."

Mann had young children and sometimes they would exchange small talk about them but that was about as personal as she got. Anything that was not strictly relative to the shooting was organized so that it would not interfere and Susan made one exception. She knew Daniel Mann's birthday and that he was crazy about the number nine so she sent him ninety-nine long stem roses, in a huge bowl. He was very touched by this gesture. Another small deviation to this rule was when Irene Pappas was in Hollywood at MGM. She was on a working visit from Greece and she asked Mann's permission to visit the set to watch Susan at work. She had been an admirer of hers and Susan was very popular in Greece. Mann agreed but kept the socializing between them distinctly minimal, as Susan preferred.

They worked until six o'clock every day but if they ran over to six thirty, she would never complain but she would say, "I'm coming in a half hour late tomorrow to make up for it." She was very accurate about her work hours, very professional.

Director Mann reflected on the suicide scene, "It was a very special scene because it had nothing to do with her playing alongside another actor. The circumstances were that she had left her mother (Mrs. Roth) and she was to go to the hotel and enter the room after registering."

Before all of these important takes, Mann would talk to Susan. He demanded that the stage be absolutely quiet, that everyone sit down.

"I would talk to Susan," he said, "and tell her the circumstances leading up to the point where she would make her entrance."

"She would become very upset and being crying and making other sounds — like animal noises — whilst I was talking to her. She would generate this terrible, painful emotion from deep inside herself, this searing conflict that was Susan, and she would begin to whimper and cry, and finally shout, 'ALL RIGHT!' Now I'd watch her start to walk onto the set. Then she would grab hold of me and I'd push her back and we'd shoot the scene. At the end of the day, I would really be involved in the most amazing kind of nervous energy her pain being the source of it. Somehow, she would generate it and use it in the scene. On some days she would start crying at nine o'clock in the morning and keep it going all day."

"Susan, this is a rehearsal darling, don't, don't, I would plead with her."

"No, Danny it's all right."

"She would go into rehearsal again and again with this great release of all that terrible pain this poor woman, Lillian Roth, had experienced. Now the actual suicide scene came and I sat down with her again. Everybody else was sent away."

"We're going to do the suicide scene and you know all about it. I can't tell you about suicide. Whatever that pain is you can't live with anymore, that's an area of yours alone. I'll leave it that to you. We're not going to pretend to deal with the actual experience; your life's worth — to live or not to live — is going through your mind. They way we're going to dramatize it, is not to try to understand or discuss it, but what I want you to do is to look 'now' and hear 'now' and see 'now,' all the things you are never going to be able to see, hear and touch again. This is your last time."

"Jimmy Wong Howe lit the set, the hotel room high up, which Lillian Roth has taken with the intention of jumping out of the window — and there was a silence, and Susan did one of those great scenes of which she was so capable as an actress."

When she touched the table it had all the moment of feeling 'she may never touch this again.' She looked at the walls — it wasn't just looking, it wasn't just seeing, it was measuring, remembering, a lifetime in a moment. She had an involvement with all these objects and lifeless as they were, they were going to be her last link with a life she was about to throw away, hoping perhaps that at the last moment even one of these lifeless objects would give off some kind of reaction to stop her and make her life seem necessary.

When the bellboy came in again, it was relating to him not only in thoughtfulness (a tip) but, 'I must see a moment of some recognition of me,' and as these moments built up so did the desperation and pain of decision, 'should I, shouldn't I, will I have enough courage — please God make it quick for me — let it happen,' and so she vacillated alternating between what little strength she had left and the weakness which was overcoming her, and all this vacillation finally heaped up in over powering, mind numbing confusion. Then not necessarily wishing to die, but finally giving up and being overtaken, perhaps by the thought that the anguish would at least end on death, or the hope, maybe, that one would survive in the end but the pain would all be gone, or would at least be recognized by others in the statement of the attempt, Susan, as Lillian Roth, finally got to the window ledge and looked down; when she saw far below her the traffic and the people; and as she actually sat on the ledge, she fainted, and by a stroke of good fortune instead of falling out she fell — in.

"I really believed that Susan got back on her feet from that experience in playing that role of Lillian Roth," Mann said, "that was the road back, so to speak, from personal problems, her mother, her marriage. She could have gone one way or another — like the suicide scene. I was with her and walked this path with all its pitfalls."

Susan became a firebrand right after finishing *I'll Cry Tomorrow*. The film would be a gripping experience for moviegoers, generate her fourth academy award nomination, and bring to her a new respect in the movie industry.

Then scandal and headlines struck Susan again when the police were called in for the third time in recent months. Small time actress, Jill

Jarmyn, dropped in unexpectedly early one morning at her fiancé Don Barry's apartment, 'for a cup of coffee.' Miss Jarmyn told the cops that she found Miss Hayward there wearing blue-and-white-polka-dot pajamas and a surprised look. Jarmyn called Susan 'a bitch' so Susan socked her, giving her a black eye. Jarmyn attempted to hit her back and Susan worked her over with a clothes brush and a stream of truck driver four-letter words. They wrestled around, smashing some furniture in the process, until Barry came out of the kitchen and pulled them apart. Jarmyn filed an assault and battery complaint against her attacker but later dropped it, saying, 'a public hearing on this situation would be bad for the motion picture industry.' An odd statement after the fact of her 'pose' for the press; a picture complete with black eye. More than likely, she was paid off to drop the charges.

When Susan was queried by the press as to what she was doing at Barry's place that time of the morning, she quipped, "He makes good coffee." Later, when Hayward learned about the engagement, she dropped Barry completely and never spoke to him again.

Though her position was clearly indefensible to Miss Jarmyn there is an illuminating unreleased item on Hayward's file at the 20th Century-Fox — "I'm a sucker for anyone who comes offering honey instead of vinegar. But if someone comes along with a chip on their shoulder I'm agin' 'em pronto. Life's too short to waste on phonies. The psychologists have been saying for years, 'get it off your chest.' It's the people who never blow up who wind up paying the piper or rather the psychiatrist. I am extremely touchy. Unless I'm approached in the proper manner I won't play."

One of her paramours, during this overwrought period described her as a "prowling animal," obsessed with sex. Susan's urgent need for a man caused her to feel, unrealistically, that her old friend Jeff Chandler, might be the one to end her sleepless nights, but nothing ever came of that. Susan had a serious sexual problem, which had begun years before. She was inherently frigid and could not achieve an orgasm.

She finally went to what she called her Hollywood psychosexual shrink for aid. He told her how brilliant she was — she had an IQ of almost 170, in spite of her lack of formal education — at which she stood up and leaned across his desk, "If I'm so smart," she said, "why am I paying you $500 an hour?" and walked out.

She gave up on that idea completely and her final solution was to become a virtual wildcat during her love making encounters, acting out the thrill of the orgasm as a substitute for experiencing it. Some men would respond to this, others could not and when a man couldn't Susan would become furious with him, although she was fully aware all along that the trouble was with her.

Yet in spite of everything that was heard or written about her there were important people in the film industry who still described her as an innocent. They even held that her innocence helped catapult her into stardom, giving her international star status. As one of her directors put it, "She had status, recognition and money but she would have given it all up in two minutes for some real love."

At five thirty on the afternoon of August 19, 1955, on Stage 19 of the MGM studios in Culver City, the shooting of the last scene of *I'll Cry Tomorrow* wound up with pickup shots of a sequence in which Susan — her hair matted, her face tear-streaked, and her clothes filthy with grime from the streets and wino bars — wrecked her mother's living room. While she went off to her dressing room to clean up and put her face back on, the rest of the cast gathered around the remains of a small nightclub layout on another part of the big stage. Food was stacked on a row of tables, and a couple of bartenders began operating behind a bar, which had been previously used in the filming *Occasion* to celebrate the close of the picture.

A four-piece orchestra began playing songs from the picture and about a hundred or so people were gathered around slapping each other on the back, congratulating each other, sampling the buffet and dancing.

Soon, Susan reappeared wearing dark glasses, a blouse and black toreador pants, all vestiges of her afternoon as a sodden drunk having vanished. Someone clapped for attention and Director Mann made a short speech thanking everybody for their efforts and cooperation, which was followed by a long round of applause.

"And now," he said. "Let's hear from Miss Hayward."

Susan stood up, "I've loved every minute of it," she said. "And I've never had to work harder, or felt such a wonderful sense of achievement. Bless you all — I love you dearly."

Some of the wardrobe women dabbed at their eyes, and other members of the crew were swallowing hard.

Susan slipped away early. She went back to her dressing room to pick up her belongings and walked out of Stage 19 alone; a small frail looking figure making her solitary trek across the parking lot, she stepped into her car and drove off without looking back.

What of her future? As far as her career was concerned, she had nothing to fear, but what about 'the great void' in her personal life. What kind of man would be attracted to a domineering, career-conscious actress, after all, the glamorous, introspective, redheaded Susan Hayward was not necessarily the most popular girl in Hollywood. She had lived through this crisis, but who would pick up the pieces if there were another.

Part of her, the celluloid Susan Hayward, was now placed and stored in neatly labeled cans in a biographical story that would be forever identified with her. In retrospect, her recent experiences would be mild compared to what she had yet to face.

For the moment, there was to be a reprieve from some of her frustrations and uncertainties. In December of that year, she was to meet a man unlike anyone she had ever met before, a gentleman from Georgia by the name of Eaton Floyd Chalkley.

* After the scene when Susan goes shopping on Rodeo Drive Cleo continues…"Pam she was 5 or 6 and goin' round tellin' all the kids Susan Hayward is my Auntie, these black kids in the neighborhood, you gotta be a nut, as black as you are, how can Susan Hayward be your Auntie.

"I was at Fox MGM Paramount, I been on all these sets and Jess took me in one day, what's she doin'? Bathsheba, he said, and I was out there all day watchin them kill each other then she'd go in her make up place and get made up again, do the same scenes over again, same, same, over and over. She wanted me to play the Negro part in *The President's Lady*, the maid, the black woman. I wouldn't take it, even her mother got on me about that, she said," Cleo why don't you accept it Susan wants you so much." I said, I don't think I can make it, but they needed a woman who could speak southern and I'm southern and my vocabulary is kinda southern. So she wanted me to do this part. I wish I had now, after I grew older. I must a been 'bout 33, at that time. I was afraid I would embarrass everybody and myself. And I didn't want to be embarrassed. You see uneducated people can be very shy, I was afraid I couldn't remember the lines.

OSCARS

Awards are beautiful to win; everytime you get a prize, it's a magnificent feeling. I was very happy to get an Oscar — I'd lost out four times before I finally won — but it wasn't the highpoint. The big treat was winning the New York Film Critics Award. That's a tough one to win, not because they know so much but because most of them are such rats and they don't like to give anybody a prize, especially anybody from Hollywood.

CHAPTER 8

It was Washington in the early twenties — a frightening time to be young. The uncertainties of a post world war were being felt everywhere and America was going on a gaudy spree. Morality was undergoing a revolution and Calvin Coolidge prosperity embraced an era of zooming stocks, emancipated women, rum running and rebellious youth.

On the corner of 6th and B Street was the usual corner drug store. It was owned and operated by the most unusual Doc Geiger. He would oversee the crowd of boys, sometimes as many as twenty-five or more, who congregated there until around 8 o'clock each night before leaving to keep their dates. In Washington as in all cities at that time, there would be complaints about gangs loitering on street corners and disturbing the peace of neighborhoods. Many of the guys went around to Doc's protected territory, and when the police came to break up a mob near the store Doc's boys would leave by the back door. The cops, seeing the place empty, would then leave the area. After this had happened a few times Mrs. Geiger, a kind old lady who knew her husband enjoyed the company of the youths in the store, with their discussions about politics and one thing or another, called the 90th Precinct and strongly defending the boys — asked the cops to leave them alone; they wanted them there at the store.

Doc, a fallen away Catholic, repeatedly said, "None of my boys ever went bad."

One of his boys, Tom Farrell, was in the seminary and Doc promised that when Tom was ordained he would go to confession and make his peace with the Almighty.

Tom Farrell was one of the 'Renroc' team of four boys, who were as close as brothers. They were all good ballplayers, good athletes and they formed the team and called it 'Renroc' — which was corner spelt backwards — after Doc's place on the corner, as it was the most important influence in their lives at the time.

The eldest of the foursome was Vincent Flaherty. Vinnie, as he was known, stuttered badly all his life, but he went on to become an ace sportswriter in spite of his hardship with words. Tom Farrell was going to become a priest; Thomas Brew, who was also to enter the priesthood, was the lynchpin of the group, and Eaton Chalkley completed the foursome.

Virginia born (1909) Eaton Floyd Chalkley was the tallest of the four and at 17 was a robust, handsome youth who took good care of his appearance, prompting Thomas Brew's mother to remark to the boys, 'Why don't you all look more like Eaton?'

Thomas Brew, who was to become a lifelong friend and an important spiritual influence in Eaton Chalkley's development, accepted his scholarship for athletics to Georgetown University, the oldest Catholic college in Washington. Eaton, a year behind his friend Thomas was in his last year at Eastern High School in Washington.

Eaton and Thomas, the closest of the four friends, parted when Thomas switched to Mount St. Mary's College at Emmitsburg, Maryland in June 1934.

After graduation, Eaton went off to Xavier College in Cincinnati, Ohio and not long afterwards, he rejoined his friend, Thomas, at Mount St. Mary's. Now reunited, they became closer than ever.

Eaton's strict upbringing at home must have contributed considerably to what Thomas Brew was later to describe as an air of very assured self-passion. The Chalkley's attended St. Mark's Episcopal Church faithfully, where Eaton once had been an altar boy and had sung in the choir, and while he continued to practice his religious beliefs in the faith into which he was christened he was also taking another path at the Catholic College. It was whilst at Mt. St. Mary's, especially during the months of October and May (the months of the Blessed Mother) that Eaton, a non-catholic, was first in the morning to say the rosary in the grotto behind the college. He went to all the devotions in the chapel because there wasn't an Episcopal church nearby, and it was here that the interest and the seed for his conversion to Catholicism took place.

Thomas Brew graduated 18 months ahead of his friend, in 1932, at the lowest point in the depression. Over 13 million people were unemployed and the bottom dropped out of his father's work putting him among them. Thomas was the eldest of the Brew family and felt it was up to him to do something about their dire straights.

Although he had had ideas about entering the priesthood — which had become more specific during his last year in college — he found work as a teacher. During this period, he thought he might be making a mistake about his desired vocation in the priesthood and considered going to Law school at night whilst teaching days. The teaching was very badly underpaid and though he wasn't really interested in becoming a lawyer, he felt he needed some kind of professional training. Hopefully, he thought, the situation at home would stabilize itself when the others got older and he might then reconsider his vocation in the priesthood.

While Brew was teaching at Gonzaga High School, where he had once been a student, Eaton was preparing to leave Mt. St. Mary's.

At around this time, the Federal Bureau of Investigation had begun to expand from a rather small insignificant department to what it was later to become under the guidance of native Washingtonian J. Edgar Hoover. Hoover gave special consideration to boys living in Washington who wanted to work for him and Eaton Chalkley began as a clerk for the Department — June 1934 — making $1200 a year, a good salary for a young man of 21 during the depression. Eaton now wanted to advance to special agent and began attending law classes in the evenings, eventually working his way up during the late 30's.

It was then that Eaton and Thomas Brew decided to enter law school together, beginning in the same class.

During his early years with the FBI, Eaton struck up a friendship with a rather plain, quiet girl by the name of Dorothy Rowland. Always smiling and outgoing himself, for some reason he took to the inhibited and withdrawn girl. Dorothy was a catholic and once again, Eaton was drawn into the catholic religion by his association with her.

Vincent Flaherty was by this time a sports reporter for the Times Herald and he would soon write about Thomas Farrell's first mass in his sports column. Father Farrell was quite a football and baseball player, as were all of the 'graduates' of Doc Geiger's drugstore, and among other things, Flaherty mentioned "that Doc Geiger was at St. Joseph's for the first time in 40 years." True to his promise, when the day came in 1936 for Tom Farrell's lifetime vows into the priesthood, Doc Geiger sat in the front pew with Tom's closest friends, the old 'Renroc' team from the early twenties in Washington, Vincent Flaherty, Thomas Brew and Eaton Chalkley.

The next night the newly ordained Father Farrell went to Doc Geiger's place and, following Doc upstairs, heard his confession.

Several months later, with Tom Farrell now Father Tom of St. Mary's Govans and Vincent Flaherty having moved out West to a spot as a sports reporter for the Los Angeles Examiner, Thomas Brew and Eaton still probably the closest of the original team, confided in each other; Brew on his calling to the priesthood and Eaton on his plans to marry Dorothy Rowland, now that he was feeling more secure in his job with the F.B.I.

In November of 1936, Eaton and Dorothy were married in St. Patrick's Church in Washington by a priest from Mount St. Mary's. Because of their mixed faiths, they were married in the rectory. Thomas Brew was Eaton's best man.

Eight months after the wedding, Eaton and Thomas finished law school giving them both an L.L.B. degree from George Washington Law School in June 1937.

Four months out of law school in September of 1937 Thomas Brew entered the Jesuit Novitiate to begin his studies for the priesthood where he would remain for the next eight years and set his course for his calling in the priesthood.

Eaton was promoted to FBI agent and was sent to Indianapolis, Indiana on his first assignment. Dorothy Rowland Chalkley cried miserably as she left Washington, her home, and her family.

At around the same time that Eaton and Dorothy were leaving Washington, young Edythe Marrener, of Flatbush, was joyously packing to leave Brooklyn. She couldn't wait to "get out," hoping — swearing — that she would never return. She was leaving for Hollywood, California to test for the part of Scarlett O'Hara in *Gone With The Wind*.

While Eaton took to his new home and made fiends easily, Dorothy was homesick, lacking the self-confidence, to make in it — what was to her — the outside world. Later, when she learned she was pregnant she wanted to go home to be with her mother, to return to Washington and familiar surroundings.

But it was there in Indianapolis that their first child was born, to the unhappy mother, a son to be christened Joseph after the choir director of St. Mark's; the church that Eaton had attended in Washington.

When Eaton was transferred to Seattle by the FBI things got worse for Dorothy and the first cracks appeared within the marriage.

Eaton left the FBI in December 1940 and went to work in the legal department of General Motors at their headquarters in Detroit. He had finally converted to Catholicism having come into the Catholic Church of his own choosing after many years of exposure to it and many years of self-discovery. Once he moved into his new faith, he committed himself devoutly and forever.

Dorothy could find ample excuse to stay at home now with Joseph to take care of and another child expected. But after the birth of their daughter, she became more somber and withdrawn.

Eaton took his family back to the Washington area and they bought a home in Falls Church, Virginia. A large colonial house on a hilltop

Dorothy was back home and close to her family and she could no longer complain of being away. Now she was unhappy because Eaton was away on business trips. Even after the birth of a second daughter June, and with three children to care for she was not happy with her life. No matter what Eaton did, it was not right for her.

Eaton had developed an ulcer and in Chicago, it began to bleed profusely, to the danger point. He had to be given blood transfusions and in those transfusions, he was being given tainted blood.

In Hollywood, meantime, Susan Hayward's — the ex-Edythe Marrener — popularity zoomed to the top with a second Oscar nomination for My Foolish Heart. Her studio kept her busy and (as a replacement for Jeanne Crain) she was sent on location to Georgia for the filming of I'll Climb The Highest Mountain.

One of Georgia's most beloved characters in the 50's was restaurateur, Harvey Hester, who seemed to know just about everybody. Harvey owned the most famous restaurant in Georgia, a picturesque old place 20 miles out of Atlanta known as Aunt Fanny's, which was an unreconstructed slave quarters with brick floors and huge fireplaces, named after a famous old slave who had lived there. The film company went to Aunt Fanny's often and one day the director asked Harvey if — just for fun — he would take the role of a southern gentleman in the movie they were shooting. He agreed, and Hester and Susan hit it off beautifully right from the start and he became her "Uncle Harvey."

Following his divorce from Dorothy, "Eaton continued to work for General Motors, travelling to every state in the union on his investigative work. On his trips to Los Angeles, he customarily looked up his boyhood friend 'Vinnie' Flaherty. He preferred staying with him rather than going to a hotel, it was more like home. They often talked about the old neighborhood, the three schools they had attended together, and the other two members of the Renroc team, now Fathers Farrell and Brew.

During his travels, Eaton discovered Carrollton, Georgia. Fifty miles out of Atlanta, with a population of under 10,000, on the Little Tallapoosa River, it was fertile farm area. He liked it right from the start. Divorced and a confirmed bachelor, he decided to settle just outside the quiet, pleasant town. He was going on 42 years of age that May.

Eaton had met a man in Carrollton who owned a GM agency. He was getting ready to retire and was looking for a buyer. Eaton made his interest known to General Motors, clearly stating that this was the place for him. His reputation and the impact he made on the agency owner closed the deal. Eaton knew he had a good investment in the Cadillac agency but he also knew he was going into strange territory. He didn't know a solitary person in Georgia.

However, he also intended to go into private practice as a lawyer and he expected that that would involve some travel, which would allow him to keep in touch with his old friends around the country.

As it happened, Vincent Flaherty did know someone in Georgia; he knew Harvey Hester, and Eaton could not have wanted a better introduction into that part of the world. Hester was in Los Angeles visiting a friend and his visit there coincided with one of Eaton's visits. To introduce Eaton to Hester, Flaherty threw a cocktail party at his home in Westwood just before Christmas.

Eaton was with an attractive girl, his date for the evening, when Hester arrived with a familiar redhead on his arm, Susan Hayward, who he never failed to keep in touch with and always looked up when he was in the area.

The two were met by their host and Susan looking over Flaherty's shoulder, quickly noticed the tall stranger looking very assured and confident standing beside the tinseled Christmas tree, alone at the moment. She noticed him first because he was so tall. She was squinting a bit to focus in on him and Eaton Chalkley smiled at her across the room. Then people came between them and cut off their view and she lost him in the crowd.

Flaherty walked towards Susan a moment later to see if she wanted anything and out of the corner of her eye, she again saw the stranger who had smiled at her walk past them.

"Yeah, Vince," she murmured.

Flaherty caught on and talking Eaton's arm, said, "You haven't met have you?"

She looked up at him.

"Merry Christmas Miss Hayward," he said in his deep rich voice.

"Is that Dixie I hear?"

"Carrollton, Georgia," he laughed.

"Where's that!"

"About 50 miles out of Atlanta. It's a small place but it's growin'."

"Are you vacationing out here Mr. Chalkley," she said always one to get to the point.

"No, it's a business trip. I have a car agency in Carrollton, but my law practice takes most of my time. Anti-trust cases mostly."

"Does it bring you to the coast pretty often?"

"Why, yes!"

"Well, tell me more Mr. Chalkley."

She listened and gradually the other voices at the party faded out of focus leaving only his voice in her ears. Later when the group broke up, Flaherty suggested that the few remaining guests go over to Mocambo for Sunday night dinner.

At Mocambo, Susan was sitting out most of the evening, as Hester didn't dance. She and 'Uncle Harvey' were talking about the trip to New

Susan and Eaton

York for the World Series when they had gone to Yankee Stadium to watch the Dodgers in Susan's native Brooklyn, on one of the brief visits she allowed herself there. Her interest in baseball caught his interest in her, among others. Susan kept her eyes on Eaton as he danced with his date. Flaherty told Chalkley he should ask Susan for a dance.

"Why should she want to dance with me?" he asked.

"Just ask her, you'll see," said Flaherty.

Meanwhile he told Susan that Eaton wanted to dance with her, as he escorted Eaton's date to the dance floor. The moment the two were alone at the table, Susan said, "Well, shall we?"

Vincent Flaherty telephoned Father Brew to tell him about Eaton and Susan. He enjoyed playing Cupid in this romance.

Susan wasn't taking any chances and breaking all the rules in courtship, she went after him with all the energy of one of her movie characters.

Father Brew vividly recalls Susan saying right from the start, "This is the guy I want to get."

Producer Marty Rackin's wife, Helen, who had seen them together a number of times, said just about the same ting; "Eaton was quiet and reserved, he brought out the best in her and she brought out the best in him. He was a real southern gentleman, and Susie being in this kind of atmosphere, the movie industry — well, let's face it — these are not southern gentlemen. He was like a breath of fresh air to Susan. Maybe this is the kind of man she had in mind all her life. When she met him at this party, just before Christmas he was with another woman. But Susan looked at him and must have thought — 'this is for me' and went after him. She fell in love then and there."

Susan used Chalkley's friends as romantic go betweens to lure him time and again from his Georgian home in Carrollton to Hollywood, where she was completing *I'll Cry Tomorrow*, and she pursued him in the grand style.

When the picture was finished publicity man Stanley Musgrove was hired to campaign for an Oscar for her performance, as everyone knew she was going to be nominated for it. Musgrove had been recommended to her by Mike Connelly, who was on the Hollywood Reporter and was a writer on the script for *I'll Cry Tomorrow* with Gerald Frank.

Susan had recently moved into the house in Sherman Oaks following her divorce from Jess Barker, and the don 'Red' Barry headlines and the suicide attempt.

Musgrove told about his first meeting with her at 3801 Longridge Avenue and how startled he was to find the house practically empty.

"At first it was tough going dealing with her because I felt like I was up against a stone wall. Then all of a sudden, she was different and I told her so. She said, 'My doctor put me on something new and it makes me feel better!' — I asked her what it was. She said 'miltown,' which was new at that time. I told her I was going to get some dolls' and if ever you run out, I'll keep you on it.

"I leveled with her and she had a little humor about it. She had met Chalkley and she wanted him. He was a marvelous guy. A real dude. A real hunk, who had marvelous manners, a lovely sense of humor, and she set her cap for him. She was relentless about it."

Susan phoned Musgrove, "I want to see you, Stan. I want to give a party and I don't know how. I've never given one before. This place needs all kinds of fixin' up. And who is the right caterer?"

"I recommended the character actor Eric Blore's wife, Clara, a classy kind of woman," Musgrove said, "and Clara went over to the house, took a look around and nearly fainted. There was nothing to work with."

"Do you realize the only glasses in that house are Kraft cheese jars," she told Musgrove unbelievingly.

"It was true; everything had to be brought in. Furniture had to be rented. She only wanted to make an impression on Eaton, to show him she could entertain and do things in style so that when she got to his home in Carrollton she would be able to do it," Musgrove said.

Clara Blore did a miraculous job, transforming the place into an elegant setting for the party. She put gardenias in little urns in the powder rooms — that kind of thing — she ordered wonderful food and it was all first class. Susan made up her own guest list, which Musgrove thought peculiar. After reading it he asked her if she wanted any help with it, 'No!' she replied sharply.

Musgrove, at the party that night, recalled it this way: "Susan purposely invited only a handful of Hollywood people, like her agent Hugh French, and no name stars. She wanted to fill the house with what she thought were the intelligentsia, educated people, like doctors, dentists, psychiatrists and friend's of theirs, she figured this was the way to go. The way to impress Eaton."

The house was jammed with people and there was an evident strain among the guests. Nobody knew anyone else, but, as so often happens in Hollywood, everybody went anyway.

"Suddenly everybody seemed to get drunk and the whole party took off. They turned out to be the worst behaved bunch I've ever seen in my life. They got smashed and jumped into the pool with their clothes on. It had her crazy, she was about to pass out, until she saw that Eaton loved it."

Undaunted, Susan planned another party for Oscar night. It was planned as a winner's party. Clara Blore was called in again to make it work.

For her performance in *I'll Cry Tomorrow*, Susan got glowing reviews everywhere. Honors for her role continued to pile up. She and James Cagney were the recipient's of Best Actor — Best Actress Award from *Look* magazine in 1955. *Redbook, Motion Picture Exhibitor* and Englan's *Picturegoer* also named her best actress. She was a sure bet to win.

On the night of the Oscar presentations, looking radiantly happy and beautiful, Susan was seated between her 11-year-old sons. She was more hopeful than ever as her chance of getting the Award was now as great as it had ever been.

She came home from the theatre stunned; she couldn't believe she hadn't won. Louella Parsons was there waiting with a few close friends to console her. Stanley Musgrove brought actress Mary McCarthy, and Eaton waited, quietly watching her.

It was generally believed (though it was never mentioned publicly) that the academy was full of uptight members and that she had lost the Oscar because of the scandalous headlines, such was the climate of things in Hollywood in the mid 50's.

Anna Magnani won Best Actress Oscar as the neurotic Sicilian born seamstress in *The Rose Tattoo*, directed by Daniel Mann.

Susan was aware of Eaton standing alone in the background as she moved around the room to see everybody, hugging Louella, talking to everyone, behaving as though she had won and soon the whole thing took on a climate of real joy. Susan had lost the Oscar but she was winning what she wanted even more — Eaton.

Going up to Musgrove, she gave him a kiss and said, "You were supposed to get a $5,000 bonus if I got the Oscar, I am sorry you won't get it now."

Musgrove was taken aback, "Susan had been so unstable; been going to a shrink, had been in all this trouble, was bitter about losing the Oscar, yet she was so sweet about my not getting the $5,000 bonus."

Little was mentioned about the Italian actress Anna Magnani who won over Susan's performance until Mary McCarthy, after a few stiff drinks, went up to Susan (never one to kid around with about herself) and said, "Let's all go over to Joe's Little Italy and have some spaghetti." Everyone screamed laughing. Susan froze.

One evening, shortly after the Oscar party Mary McCarthy was having dinner with a friend at the Villa Nova, a popular Italian place on the strip. Susan, who loved Italian food, showed up with Eaton and they all met briefly.

Mary McCarthy, again feeling no pain, thanked Susan for the party 'the other night' but before she left them, she attempted another half-hearted job, "You know you should have won that Oscar Susan but you were drunk too much, you could tell in every scene that you'd been drinking." As McCarthy said, "The look that Susan gave — I just prayed that the floor would open up and dump me into hell."

Musgrove explained it this way, "I never heard Susan laugh. Susan was humorless, even Garbo had humor. Susan was the only one I've been around — and I've been around plenty. Some roared with laughter, I mean Ava Gardner, Myrna Loy, and Mae West, but Susan — nothing. That's why I think she was a little more cracked than the rest of them."

Whatever plans Eaton and Susan made for the future they kept to themselves. He went back to Carrollton and she stayed in Hollywood. Other men would have been overwhelmed by Susan, but Eaton held his own and was not overpowered. She was frustrated by his lack of commitment. She was in love with him and wanted to get married. She also wanted to get out of Hollywood, especially after getting a backhand swipe from the industry by their voting a foreign actress for the Oscar. She worked hard to get Eaton's approval, but felt rejected by him, and Hollywood.

With the twins in boarding school, she packed and left for Europe for the Cannes Film Festival.

On Saturday morning May 14, 1956, arriving at London airport she immediately landed in trouble. She was changing flights for a plane to France and under her mink coat; she hid a toy Yorkshire terrier. As she walked to the plane, quarantine officials spotted it and they politely explained the situation to her. She lost her temper, held the plane up and fought to keep the dog. She lost the argument and the dog.

Outfitted in a tight fitting pink sweater, Susan posed for French photographers in Cannes when she arrived for the festival. With her red hair flying wildly as she posed on the French Riviera she asked them where the men were, 'No actors," she emphasized. "I mean *men!*'

It can only be surmised what Eaton must have thought on reading this in the newspapers back in the United States.

In Cannes, she shared the spotlight briefly with Hollywood's and Europe's luminaries. Diana Dors, Kim Novak, Ginger Rogers and her old friend, Ingrid Bergman among others, all wearing their hair combed back neatly and primly as Hayward took the spotlight with her windswept mane winning the Festivals' 'Best Actress in the World' award — that May 23, 1956.

She triumphed with the equivalent of the Foreign Oscar sweepstakes picking up top honors at the Cork Festival in Ireland, and the Mar del Plata in South America. Out for a good time she also picked up a few admirers along the way. She cabled home the news of her victory and signed the cable — Susan Maganini. Susan had grown distrustful of Hollywood people after being shunted by them, and accepted by the world.

When she got back, she stayed for a while with her sons, and then took unexplained weekend trips alone. She dated a philosophy professor Dr. Frederick Mayer at the University of Redlands who fell in love with her. She switched partners and went from publisher Gordon White to disc jockey Bill Ballance, her agent Hugh French, followed by Brazilian millionaire Jorge Guinly. But with all of them, in the middle of the night she yearned for Eaton Chalkley.

Susan's agent at that time was Jack Gardean and he called her about doing a picture *Top Secret Affair* at Warner Bros. for producer Martin Rackin. It had been originally intended for Humphrey Bogart and Lauren Bacall, prior to Bogart's death.

Helen Rackin who often came on the set to be with her husband Marty, said about Susan: "She was basically not a Hollywood person. She was aloof and didn't go to many parties. I think she would have liked to have been a singer — she used to sing for friends. Anyhow, Eaton Chalkley was flying in regularly from Georgia to see her again. When Eaton came back, Susan was divinely happy and she looked marvelous, you could see that she was very much in love with him. Eaton was a big strapping guy, very tanned. He stayed at the Beverly Wilshire while she was filming *Top Secret Affair* — six to eight weeks. My husband called Susan 'hooligan' and they were very, buddy-buddy, got along great. Eaton sent her yellow roses during the picture. She loved them — kept them in her dressing room. When we went to lunch one day, with Kirk Douglas, I remember they were talking about how they hoped their children wouldn't go in the business. Susan wanted to give her sons a life away from Hollywood."

Because of her happiness at being reunited with Eaton, Susan was much better than expected in the sophisticated comedy. With the picture over, Susan planned Christmas for her sons and Eaton. It was her favorite holiday and she decorated the house in Sherman Oaks, giving every detail her personal attention.

Stanley Musgrove was invited out to Susan's for a Christmas party that year — 1956.

"By this time the house was first rate. It was incredible, the transformation, from the silver and the crystal to the linen, she did it for him. She even had a friend of hers, an editor of *House Beautiful*, come out and help her get the house ready. It was lovely, nothing lavish. For instance, the Christmas tree was all done up in ribbons and bows, it was just a lovely party. She really wanted this guy, she was madly in love with him, and she gave up practically everything to get him — he was the boss."

Susan, who always based her decisions on her hunches and emotions rather than reason, with her sons in Palos Verdes boarding school, left Hollywood in January 1957 and went to Carrollton for a dress rehearsal of what life would be like there; seeing Eaton's home, meeting his friends and driving with him around the quiet town.

Eaton had an instinctive nose of phoniness and since the movie, industry had more than its fair share he made it clear that he did not intend to live in Hollywood. If they were to be married, he wanted to live in Carrollton, where he had a home, a large piece of land and cattle and horses.

The rural beauty and peace of the countryside were the answer to a prayer to a woman who had been managing her own life, and fighting in the Hollywood jungle for a career since she was seventeen.

Back in Hollywood after her visit with Eaton, columnist Earl Wilson was warned about questions in an interview with Susan, with no mention to be made about Jess Barker. (Jess Barker had just been ruled the father of a daughter born out of wedlock to Yvonne Doughty he was ordered to pay $50.00 a month support. Miss Doughty screamed, 'I hate you. I hate you!' at Barker in court. Their daughter, born December 9, 1956 in an Encino Hospital, was named Margana Ruth Barker).

Wilson humorsly chided Susan about this before the interview, somberly she replied, "You ask me and we'll see."

Wilson: "Are you going to marry Don Barry, the cowboy star?"

Hayward hollered: "Who? It never entered my thoughts, it's a very distasteful subject and actually I think you're no gentleman to bring it up."

Wilson: (about Lillian Roth) "Didn't she have guts to write that book?"

Hayward: "She had guts to live it; I just hope the movie will make everybody more tolerant of people who are going through their own personal Gethsemane."

With that, Susan pushed a cigarette out in the ashtray, got up and left.

Susan was offered every script in Hollywood with her choice of leading men. She chose a role on location in Georgia — in real life — with the one man she hoped would star with her for the rest of her life.

Friday evening February 9, 1957, Marty and Helen Rackin were expecting Susan for dinner, to celebrate their move into their new house in Benedict Canyon. Edmund O'Brien, the actor, who had gone to school with Susan in Brooklyn, made a foursome. They held up dinner when Susan didn't show up at the expected time and waited and waited but still she didn't arrive. Getting no reply from her telephone number, they finally sat down to dinner. Then there was a knock on the door and a telegram arrived — "Sorry couldn't make dinner — married Eaton Chalkley." No one had to look around for small talk for the remainder of that evening.

Susan took out a marriage license under her maiden name, Edythe Marrener. Justice of the Peace Stanley Kimball performed the ceremony in Phoenix, Arizona and with Eaton firmly grasping her hand; she looked up at him and said, "I don't want to look back. From now on I'm going to look forward, always." Eaton would be 48 years old that May and Susan 40 in June. His boyhood chum Vincent Flaherty was his best man and Father Brew and Father Farrell were given the long awaited news by phone.

Ellen Marrener was surprised at the news when she heard it over the radio. When reporters phoned her home for a comment she declared, "I haven't talked to her in weeks. I don't know what she's up to."

"When I read in the papers they had flown to Phoenix and got married. I just wanted to yell and cheer. She got him!" cheered Stanley Musgrove.

There was a shadow over their happiness because in the eyes of the Catholic Church Eaton was still married to Dorothy Rowland. To the residents of the small town of Carrollton, Georgia, the worldwide publicity surrounding the marriage of the red headed movie star to the devout catholic Eaton Chalkley was all rather shocking — to be talked about in hushed tones. After all, Susan Hayward was a common law wife.

On April 4, 1957, Eaton went to the Superior Court of the State of California in Los Angeles, to sign an affidavit allowing him to take the Barker children back to his home in Georgia. They were now 14 years old and were to be enrolled at Georgia Military Academy. He also went ahead with plans to build a new and larger home on a 100-acre tract, which he owned in Carrollton. Susan, despairing of ever winning an Oscar or even finding another role to equal *I'll Cry Tomorrow*, just wanted to complete her contractual obligations and forget Hollywood. Behind the scenes, however, things were taking place, which were yet to lead to her much-coveted Oscar.

It began June 3, 1955 with a woman whose life was terminated for a crime for which she was sentenced to death. Barbara Graham was executed in the gas chamber in San Quentin prison, a short distance away from San Francisco. Public Relations man Graham Kislingbury, who was working for producer Louie De Rochemont of Cinerama, told De Rochemont about his college roommate Ed Montgomery who was an ace crime reporter with the *San Francisco Examiner*.

Ed Montgomery had won the Pulitzer Prize for 'best local reporting' work for the investigation for the bureau, then known as the Internal Revenue, in 1950, which lead to the Kefauver hearings. He was also the crime reporter on the Barbara Graham case. De Rochemont liked what he heard so Kislingbury put De Rochemont and Montgomery in touch with each other and Montgomery agreed to go to New York and do a working script about the Graham story. Soon afterwards, De Rochemont became interested in the Cinemiracle and dropped his option, leaving Montgomery with a script and no producer.

However, Kislingbury now heard that his former boss, producer Walter Wanger, was in San Francisco with his actress wife Joan Bennett who was to appear at the Alcazar theatre in *Janus*. He called them at their hotel and they made a luncheon date for the next day in the Redwood Room of the Clift Hotel.

Wanger, who had been a pillar of Hollywood and six times president of the Motion Picture Academy, had lost a fortune with his picture, *Joan of Arc*. Ingrid Bergman, the star of the film, had fallen from public grace and was deadwood at the box office then over her scandalous affair with the Italian film producer Roberto Rossellini. Wanger had to vacate a tiny office he had been reduced to taking in Hollywood. Washed up and broke, in a fit of rage probably fuelled by his despondency he shot agent Jennings Lang in the groin over Long's attentions to his wife, Joan Bennett. He was sentenced to 90 days in jail.

Over lunch, Kislingbury told Wanger about the Montgomery script and offered it to Wanger.

"I've got nothing better to do," said the former producer. "Why not?"

Ed Montgomery joined them later and from the letters of Barbara Graham, the court transcriptions and his articles about the case they completed the script, The Barbara Graham Story — retitled *I Want To Live* — from a line in one of Miss Graham's letters.

Walter Wanger, as an independent producer, had given Susan some good breaks and she felt she owed him a favor now that the chips were down. She had been looking for a chance to return something to him.

She was no longer under exclusive studio contract so he had a copy of the script mailed to her in Georgia.

It was eighteen months since she made her last film and Susan, never a lover of city life, felt released from 'the cage' now that she could fully indulge herself in outdoor activities.

When the script arrived, it was put in Eaton's office; she would get around to it in due course — she really had no great desire to return to Hollywood, away from Eaton, and she had agreed to read the script purely as a favor to Wanger. One day, Eaton found it tossed among his papers, read it and talked it over with Susan.

Even in Carrollton, Georgia, Hollywood was only a telephone call away. Susan always said, "I hate to pick up the telephone. It's always bad news!" Eaton picked up the phone call from Wanger and she encouraged by Eaton, set up a meeting in Hollywood with him.

Wanger and Ed Montgomery were waiting in a Hollywood restaurant when the Chalkley's walked in. Over a three-hour luncheon, they mapped out the story of the B-girl, accused of murder, railroaded to a conviction and executed in a gas chamber. During the discussion Susan watched for Eaton's reactions to the various facets of the story and what its require-ments would be in production, time, etc. and having satisfied herself, by a private code of silent communication with Eaton (which they often used in company), that he was in agreement she agreed to do the role. Now for the first tine, protected by her husband's business acumen, she would also get 37½% of the movie profits. A gentlemen's agreement was reached without the aid of agents, contracts and lawyers.

In March 24, 1958, Susan went back to work on the Samuel Gold-wyn lot for Walter Wanger. She had a mobile trailer for her dressing room and during the difficult months of shooting ahead Eaton would be unfailing support. The long stemmed yellow roses from Eaton would be ever-present on her dressing room table, a constant reminder of his love and encouragement.

At one end of the trailer was a reception room and she would often invite Ed Montgomery — who was the consultant on the film — in there to sit and talk. Striving for authenticity, she questioned him on every possible detail to help in conveying the character of the doomed woman. Susan was fascinated by the contradictory traits of personal-ity in the controversial woman, who had had an extraordinary effect on everyone she met.

"There was nothing flim-flam about Susan Hayward," Montgomery said. "It was all business. Eaton would sit off to one side on the set, quietly observing never interfering and Susan would ease up and smile when she looked his way."

"Eaton was a good listener, he asked questions and he listened. He didn't talk a lot, he didn't have too much to say but when he said something, it usually made sense," Montgomery remembered, "it wasn't just idle chatter. He wasn't running around the place letting everybody know he was Susan Hayward's husband. He took an interest in my family. On one occasion, my wife and our three children came down to visit me. Susan did a rare thing, mainly because Eaton shared it with us. She took time to show us around the studio, and around the set, explaining things."

No one ever talked to her when she was walking onto the set. They were warned not to talk when she came out of her dressing room and started toward the set because she had established a mood and was ready for the scene.

Eaton walked on the set on the morning of Monday, April 15, 1958 and asked the director Robert Wise to halt the shooting.

Mrs. Ellen Marrener, Susan's seventy-year-old mother, was in Mount Sinai Hospital with a heart attack and Eaton brought Susan the news that her mother had died. She lit a cigarette and stared indifferently toward an empty spot on the sound stage, silently angry with Eaton for stopping the scene. She felt nothing. The only one of the Marrener's who meant anything to her now was her brother Wally. Susan and her sister Florence were no longer on speaking terms.

Following the funeral, her mother's ashes remained in a box with a vault number attached, stored on a shelf in the crematorium funeral parlor. Ellen Marrener wasn't officially buried until several years later.

"Yes, my mother was cremated," Wally said. "I had a deed to a place back in Brooklyn, where my father is. There was a place for my mother's ashes, but I decided to keep her ashes out here in the Chapel of the Pines."

Stanley Musgrove, who was working on the picture as assistant to Robert Wise, spoke of one of his visits to the set around this time, "When Susan's mother died during the making of *I Want To Live* — to her it was like closing a door. She was *not* inconsolable. I can tell you that."

Director Wise went to San Quentin and witnessed an actual execution. Susan went too, though it is not certain that she witnessed the execution with Wise but she did sit in the chair in the gas chamber. Robert Wise said she was wonderful professionally but he found it impossible to relate to her personally. The only time he felt any warmth or real contact with her as a human being instead of as his star actress was when they were shooting in downtown Los Angeles one night. Some ragamuffins were leaning against the fence, watching.

Susan stared at them and said to Wise, "See those kids over there?"

He looked over; "Yes", he said.

"Those are like Park Avenue kids compared to the gang I grew up with," she said reflectively.

That was the only time she was ever less than totally professional in her conversations with him.

Wise said of her that, "She had a chemical combination that could excite and hold audiences as surely as Garbo and a few others. She was one of the few actresses who could hold up a movie all by herself."

On completion of the picture Musgrove, as publicity director, had to plan ads, publicity, tours and so forth and was told by Wise to check with Susan, just to be sure, that she was clear (Susan was also working at 20th Century Fox on *Woman Obsessed* directed by Henry Hathaway).

The producers of the Figaro Production of *I Want To Live* paid Barbara Graham's five-year-old son and her husband a total of $500 for any damages that they may suffer as a result of the movie based on her life. A deplorable compromise.

Stanley Musgrove recognized the additional motivation Eaton had given her and told her, "You're going to win (the Oscar) this time." She never said, 'I know it,' but felt good about it," he said.

"What will you say when you win?" he asked her.

"I know what I would like to say," she replied. "There is one person I would like to thank above all others — Me!"

With Eaton by her side, Susan went out on tour to sell the picture. Ed Montgomery, who was portrayed by Simon Oakland in the film, on tour with them commented, "We were on tour at Thanksgiving and we stopped off at their place in Georgia. This was the new house. They were in the process of moving from their last place. It was on a rise over-looking a lake. The twins were there — although you wouldn't know they were twins. One was tall and redheaded, the other short and of a different stature. Susan was very friendly; her husband was a very independent individual. Susan was going to cook the Thanksgiving dinner and the day before Thanksgiving, we went into Carrollton to do some shopping. Everywhere we went it was 'Mrs. Chalkley;' she was just Eaton Chalkley's wife."

Frankly, she wasn't the best cook in the world and she knew it.

"You know, I haven't done enough of this," she said, "but I'm learning."

Eaton laughed as he watched her and went on dicing the celery to go into the stuffing.

"I'm glad you're here, Eaton I wouldn't have remembered to put that in," she quipped.

"On Thanksgiving morning I can remember the twins being out in the field with a horse, Gregory was stroking the horse's neck and mane, and the back of his ears. Timothy was standing alongside, not touching the horse — just watching."

Montgomery continued, "Eaton brought over a dinner set and extra chairs from the other house. They apologized for the fact that their dining room furniture hadn't arrived, so this was sort of a makeshift affair. We all pitched in and did the dishes afterwards.

Eaton did the washing, I did the drying and the boys helped a bit. Susan sat on the kitchen stool, over to one side, smoking a cigarette. Eaton told her she had done a good job, put out a good Thanksgiving dinner — to relax and let the men work.

"'Thank heaven, it's over,' she said smiling.

"After dinner, we went to the cabin by the lake. She liked to pump the piano player there and change the piano rolls. She would sing and Eaton would sing along."

After Thanksgiving, they continued the promotion tour, in all travelling to over 12 cities as the picture was being released around the country.

"She had a certain shyness about her," Montgomery said, "I don't think it was because she 'thought I'm above all this,' but she didn't like to give autographs and the fans could think up the darndest things to ask her. That used to annoy her and then she didn't sign."

Susan, commenting on the fan syndrome: "I don't think there are as many fans around now as there used to be; maybe for rock musicians, but not for actor's and that's good. People are more sophisticated; they can accept a performer for what he does and idolize him. I could never understand youngsters putting actors on a pedestal. It should be men and women who really contribute something to humanity. The man who makes a really fine law or does something for humanity in medicine — they're the ones who should have fans. Even as a child, I don't remember idolizing an actor. It seemed so — misplaced."

Eaton tried to be with Susan in as many cities as his business would allow, she always wanted him with her, and they were on the phone all the time if they were not together. Eaton never missed Sunday mass or Holy Days of obligation wherever he happened to be.

"We went to Chicago, Philadelphia, and Boston, and Eaton and I had gone ahead to New York. When Walter Wanger and Susan arrived at La Guardia airport, we met their plane. Eaton had a surprise for Susan and handed her a huge box at the airport. She couldn't wait and opened it right there. It was a mink coat. She put it on and wouldn't take if off."

"Susan hardly drank at this time," Ed Montgomery went on. "Often at around 10:30 at night in the Chalkley's hotel suite, Eaton would call room service and order drinks for Wanger, me and himself. Susan usually 'didn't care for one.'"

The Chalkleys went abroad to France, Germany and Italy to promote the movie. She, in turn, was honored by a Golden Globe Award; the David di Donatello, Sicily; the Silver Bear from Berlin; Golden Gaucho, Argentina and more, when the time came to choose the most outstanding performance by an actress in these foreign countries, making her an international favorite.

Back in the States, after the promotional tour, they would occasionally go to Santa Anita racetrack to place some bets and to see Susan's brother, Wally.

"Hey Wal can you get us a table at the racetrack?" Susan would ask her brother.

"This would be on a Friday or Saturday, it would be a big day. I'd say 'I'll do my best' 'cause I'd have to go through channels but being there so long they'd say 'for you Wally?' and I'd say, 'it's not for me, it's for my sister.' 'For you and your sister, anything.'"

"When I would visit them at their table she'd say, 'Here Wal, here's twenty bucks go bet it for us and we'll split.' So I made her a little money. But I'd tell her she'd have to take care of the maître d' and the waiters, and she said, 'Don't tell me all about that. Eaton takes care of all that.' 'OK!' I said, 'but remind him will you, 'cause you're puttin' me on the spot.'"

One day, while they were driving home from Santa Anita after a not-so-lucky day at the races, they heard on the radio that Susan had been nominated for the Oscar.

On April 6, 1959, Eaton Chalkley's big hand was folded reassuringly over his wife's, as they sat in the Pantages Theatre the night of the Academy Awards.

Susan's heart was beating very fast as she watched Kim Novak and James Cagney up there on the dais as they opened the white envelope which contained the name of the winner for Best Actress of 1958.

The applause almost deafened the next words as the name of the winner, Susan Hayward, was given over the microphone. Susan kissed her husband and like a long-coiled spring suddenly released she springed from her seat. She gathered the folds of her black satin dress lifted them slightly and ran prettily like a ballet dancer to the stage — in those twelve seconds that it took to arrive there were twelve long years of grueling work.

The night of the awards Walter Wanger gave Susan a gold religious medal — on one side is the figure of St. Gemesius and the words *"please guide my destiny"* on the other side is engraved — *"To Susan — Best Actress and Best Friend — WW"*

Susan on Oscar night 1958 with David Niven.

She thanked Walter Wanger, the man who had helped her get her First Best Actress Nomination and had given her the part that got her her Fifth Nomination — and the Oscar.

All of Carrollton Georgia was watching on their television sets — and on a portable TV set in a school classroom, Susan's two sons, given special permission to stay up, watched the Oscar telecast.

Stanley Musgrove thought it odd that she didn't thank her director Robert Wise — as usually those best performances are heavily credited to the director.

Henry Hathaway had this to say, "Of course when she made *I Want To Live* and the other one about the drunk (*I'll Cry Tomorrow*), being mean was part of that picture. She came on as Fuck You! That's her nature, that's why she was so good in them. No, she never said that — I never heard her swear — to tell you the truth."

The police had to extricate Susan and Eaton from the Pantages Theatre and carve a pathway for them through the crowd as they arrived to enter the Beverly Hilton Ballroom where the Academy's annual dinner dance was being held. Seated inside at a table on the perimeter of the dance floor with Joan and Walter Wanger and Bob and Dolores Hope, the table was bombarded with a barrage of camera flashes from the surrounding photographers. Eaton tried to duck out of range and let Susan take the spotlight. He joked with them saying, "I didn't win anything."

Susan chimed in, "If it hadn't been for him, I wouldn't have either."

A photographer asked her to pose for a photo kissing the Oscar statue, "I don't kiss anyone but my husband," she quipped.

Strangers jammed the dance floor to congratulate her and to get autographs but Susan only wanted to get away as soon as she could and Eaton wanted to run, too.

This time she had a home to go to and someone she loved to go with her.

Of all the reporters' questions, the one she answered most easily was, "What was she going to do next?" She turned wearily to Eaton and said, "We're just anxious to get home."

"He" stood on the table in their Beverly Hills Hotel suite, slim, golden and small to have created such a fuss that was heard around the world surrounded by a forest of red roses tagged with congratulatory cards.

Susan stared at him, "I've wanted him for so long — "

"I know," Eaton said his arm around her.

"But we still have a plane to make. We're going back home tonight."

With her, Oscar cradled in her hands, Susan walked across the room and opened the lid of her suitcase, and packed Oscar inside.

"He'll look wonderful over our fireplace," she said.

Just before they left the suite, she took his bouquet of yellow roses in one arm and grabbing Eaton by the other, said, "I'm ready — let's go home."

CAPITAL PUNISHMENT

I'm in favor of it. I can only judge by my own feeling and I take it very personally. If somebody hurt anyone who was close to me or whom I loved and they weren't put to death for it, I would kill them myself. I am not a bleeding heart; I am not inclined to say "oh well they can be rehabilitated." If someone commits a crime — he should be punished for that crime, whether he's sane or insane. I don't believe in just letting people commit crimes and then go unpunished.*

* It's interesting to note Miss Hayward won an Academy Award for her performance in *I Want to Live!*, one of the movies' most potent anticapital punishment statements.

MORALITY

Morality today (1972) is so much looser at the seams. People of my generation were brought up in a much more strict fashion— there were certain things you simply did not do. All this sexual freedom the kids have today can hurt later on, especially the women. You've got to be able to respect yourself and if you just sleep around with anybody, how can you have respect? They might not think it's important now but there's going to come a time when it's going to hurt inside.

CHAPTER 9

Fifty miles from Carrollton, Georgia, in the Catholic Church in Cedartown, Father Charles Duke addressed his congregation from the pulpit at Sunday morning mass. Many of them were from Carrollton where, on the following morning, Mr. and Mrs. Eaton Chalkley were expected home.

When they returned, Father Duke told them, their relationship toward Eaton Chalkley would have to change. Chalkley was the first Catholic to go into business in Carrollton and in the beginning; he was regarded with wonder, a certain amount of suspicion and some definite prejudice. His charm and friendliness, however, worked very much in his favor and their doubts about him soon disappeared. There were many 'closet' Catholics there at that time, in this heavily Protestant and Southern Baptist area, but Eaton was proud of his chosen faith. He joined the Rotary International Organization and suggested that they have a catholic priest come in to say grace once in awhile, and he was the reason why people down there who either through fear or timidity, had given up going to church now came out of the 'woodwork' to attend.

Although Cedartown was regarded as the parish and Carrollton the Mission, Carrollton in fact, had the larger parish taking into account the Georgetown University students and their families.

Father Duke somberly told his congregation that Chalkley was setting a bad example that he had done wrong.

His marriage to this woman was not celebrated in the church and it was a matter of deep sincere regret. He may have gotten a civil divorce from his catholic wife but in the eyes of the church, he was still married to her. She was an adulteress.

"These people will always be welcome in the church," he said. "But they were not to get extraordinary attention."

The congregation filed out silently after the service.

The next day Eaton Chalkley arrived in town bringing with him his world famous redheaded movie star wife and Carrollton went crazy. They were met at Atlanta airport by a delegation headed by Mayor Stewart

Martin, and then a two and a half mile long motorcade drove the 50 miles to Carrollton, where another throng of local people were waiting to greet them.

The red carpet was rolled out and they were met with a parade, four bands, the keys to the city, a special edition of the local newspaper and with banners flying everywhere.

Susan couldn't make out what the banners said, because she didn't have her glasses on, but she knew what they meant.

Among the cheering crowd, Father Duke watched for a few moments then withdrew, and his friendship with Eaton Chalkley was over — forever. The loss of his friend left Eaton with a deep sense of unworthiness, and may also have eventually contributed to leaving a mark on his health.

Now, fallen from the church, deprived of the sacraments and unable to receive communion he was left only with the privilege of his devotions, which he practiced assiduously.

To Susan, it was such a perfect marriage. Nothing was missing — everything and everyone was so wonderful.

The Chalkleys came home to their new air conditioned modern ranch style house, faced with granite from the famous Stone Mountain nearby and roofed with crushed Georgia marble. It was situated in a pine grove that overlooked a man-made 15-acre lake on their 450 acres of land and was complete with a guesthouse.

The twins were attending the Chadwick School in Rolling Hills, California, completing their school semester, after which Susan intended to move them out to Georgia permanently. Again, she appealed to Superior Court in Los Angeles to get permission to take them out of the state, removing them from their Hollywood — Bel Air environment. Susan spoke of the advantages to the children of growing up in the atmosphere of a small town, living a normal life. Their father would, of course, be allowed proper visitation rights.

"The boys will share a paneled bedroom when they come home on weekends from the Military Academy. We have a playhouse on the grounds where we entertain neighbors and friends and have barbecues and parties. On Sundays, the family drives in to church. Whatever mistakes I have made as a mother, I want to put them behind me."

To anyone who had doubts, Susan explained, "I like being just plain Mrs. Chalkley. I love my husband and I want to be his full-time wife. I want to be with him all the time. This is the way I want to live."

A different point of view was being voiced out West; "They always come back," said one Hollywood cynic. "She's too much of a fighter to stop fighting, too much of an actress to stop acting, too accustomed to Hollywood excitement to retire."

When Susan first came to town, she decided to go to the First Baptist Church on Dixie Street but when she arrived at the church there were crowds of people outside, watching for her to make an entrance. The curious among the crowd thought she looked odd; slender, thin legs, with freckles on her arms, face, and that red hair — very Irish looking for a Baptist out of Brooklyn. She turned around and walked away and never went back.

The boys were finally allowed to leave California and shortly after their arrival, they were enrolled in the Georgia Military Academy, and while Eaton was attending to the farm and his various other business interests Susan began to organize the house.

It had black Georgia slate floors, walls of tongue-and-groove logs, painted white, and a huge fireplace in the living room connected with the one in the master bedroom on the other side of the wall. She would interrupt Eaton from time to time to ask his advice about certain things, such as whether they should have one or two sofas in the living room near the fireplace, and so on. She hired two black servants, Katie, a small, round, 'Mammy' type and a tall attractive, light-skinned young woman, Curlee.

Used to sleeping until noon when she was not working, Susan now insisted on getting up every morning to fix Eaton's breakfast. She tried her hand at cooking and baking and did the gardening. Meanwhile she had to juggle movie commitments to complete works in progress, which took her away from her home for weeks at a time.

Woman Obsessed was in release and Walter Wanger wanted her for *Cleopatra* but 20th Century Fox wanted Elizabeth Taylor. She was offered some of the prize roles of that decade but listened with total disinterest, as they would only be breaks in her newfound happiness. Because of his waning career, she did accept a plea for help from her old friend from Flatbush, Jeff Chandler, to make *Thunder In The Sun*. It meant going on location to Lone Pine, near San Diego, for some time and being separated from Eaton, which was distressing to her. She could never bring herself to say goodbye to him and would make a salute on leaving, 'I'll see you in the funnie papers,' * she would say, as she left; then she would keep looking back until he was no longer in sight.

* Referring to *Peanuts* by Charles Schultz; Sunday, May 21, 1972.

Her love for him made any parting almost impossible but, as Eaton agreed, Jeff Chandler needed her support to get another foothold in his career.

Late one night at the lodge in Lone Pine, a telephone call from Carrollton woke her up. She heard that Eaton, suddenly taken ill at home, had been rushed to the hospital. The news of her husband's collapse after

Curlee Mae — Susan and Eaton's maid.

midnight on July 24th, 1958, only 18 months after their marriage, sent her racing in a studio car to Los Angeles Airport to make an emergency flight to Atlanta at 1:20 A.M. When she arrived at the hospital in Atlanta, Eaton was being treated for a kidney ailment. He calmed her fears and insisted that she return to Lone Pine and not hold up production. Very unwillingly, she left with a promise she would be back as soon as possible to take care of him. "I'll see you in the funnie papers," she said, more cheerfully than she felt, as she left. His yellow roses arrived as usual the next day.

Bob Sidney, her 'pal' from *The Conqueror* movie answered Susan's call for some advice on a Flamenco dance she was called upon to do in *Thunder In The Sun*. It was about the only memorable moment in the entire picture.

Susan now had to meet her commitments for Fox's *Marriage-Go-Round*, and MGM's *Ada* with Dean Martin before she could settle down again at the ranch with Eaton. She wanted to quit the movies, but Eaton felt that she had this gift, this talent, and she should use it, and she was guided by him in this as in practically everything else.

None of the films she made at this time were of any importance to the public, to the critics, and least of all to Susan. She was much more concerned with playing the country wife, and she entered this role with the same determination that she came to be known for in her more memorable screen characters.

She just simply wanted to be with Eaton, almost trying to make up for the years without him. She hated location shooting which took her away from him.

At twilight one evening, she heard the faint sound of a car approaching along the winding road through the pinewoods. It grew louder, then stopped and she heard the familiar rumble of the garage door closing. Then came the click of a key in the front door and the voice that said, "I'm home!" She greeted him with a hug and kisses then went into the kitchen to prepare dinner. When she came into the living room, she noticed the kindling in the hearth had already caught alight, and Eaton was stretched out across the couch. He had turned on the television and she heard the announcer give the title of the feature film to be shown that evening *Adam Had Four Sons*, starring Ingrid Bergman.

"That's an old one," Susan called out. "I was in it too," she added, looking at Eaton.

Then the announcer said, "I wonder if Susan Chalkley is watching tonight?"

"Is she watching?" Eaton asked, as she sat down beside him.

"Only if you want to. I can run out and put on the steak — during the commercial."

She got up and walked back to the kitchen. She wasn't Susan Hayward — all that was past — as Susan often said to Eaton, "It's all yesterday's spaghetti." She was now Susan Chalkley!

Eaton promised her that when she was free, they would take a trip to Greece and Italy and when they were finally able to leave it was as the leaves were turning, heralding the arrival of fall.

"When Eaton and Susan first went to Rome on a trip, it so happened that Father McGuire was stationed in Rome at the headquarters of the Jesuits," said Father Brew. "I got in touch with him and told him they were coming and to do what he could for them. He would get them into places they would not be able to get into on their own. That was the beginning of their friendship. I first met Father McGuire at Gonzaga High School, I was the teacher there and he was student in my class."

In Rome, Eaton introduced Susan to the Reverend Daniel J. McGuire who was serving as American secretary to the Jesuit headquarters at the Vatican. It was Eaton's heartfelt desire that Susan would move toward his religion and her introduction to the Vatican would be another step in that direction for her.

While on a stop over in England, Susan signed to do *I Thank A Fool*, when her friend Ingrid Bergman had to bow out of the film, which was to have reunited Bergman with Cary Grant. When they returned from Europe in October, there were a pile of scripts awaiting her. (One of them, *Back Street*, sent by producer Ross Hunter would give her a sympathetic role.)

For now, with the holidays approaching, she was becoming very excited about her first real Christmas in her Georgian home amidst the pine trees. A firm believer in astrology, Susan believed that the stars were right and things were falling into their allotted placed. Best of all, she knew where she belonged.

Father Morrow, a young priest in Cedartown, recalled that particular Christmas Eve; "The first time I saw her was in our older church in Carrollton. This had been an Episcopal church, the oldest structure in town, but the Catholics had bought it when the Episcopalians moved out when they outgrew it. The building leaned in both directions and could only hold about 60 people. When they kneeled on the kneelers, they would sink to the floor. Eaton had arrived with Susan, she had furs on and I recognized her from the movies. When the midnight mass was over they left and I didn't get to greet them. Harvey Hester was with them too."

"Two or three days later when I was in town a pick up truck came along and the driver was a lady wearing a scarf over her hair, slacks, and a jacket. She was blowing the horn and yelling 'Hey, Father!' She pulled the truck over to where I was and started to chat right away. I wondered who she was, for the first minute or two, then I realized that it was Susan, and she was saying how badly she and Eaton felt that there had been no introductions, and she made up for it."

Eaton wanted to go to Mass every morning, not just on Sundays. Cedartown near Rome, Georgia, was almost 50 miles away, a 2-hour drive from Carrollton. The church in Carrollton, opened only on Sundays, was too small now and Eaton felt a new church would be desirable. Father Morrow, in agreement with him, urged the Bishop that Carrollton needed its own church; Eaton had started the parish interest in the Catholic faith and would now donate the land. Susan and he would provide funds for building the church on 14 acres of land across the lane from their home, and they would seek a resident pastor.

Bishop Hyland called Father Morrow that December of 1960 and asked him to become pastor of the churches in Cedartown and Carrollton, and to 'oversee' the construction of the new church.

One day Father Morrow drove by the Chalkley home and found Eaton, dressed as usual in shirt and tie, in the gatekeeper's little red house which he had converted into an office. From there you looked out over the fields, and down below was a road that led about a half mile to the house — a rather grand stone house where they lived. "I thanked them for their donation. I was working with the architect and Eaton was very interested in the plans. He would explain to Susan what was happening. The name of the church was to be Our Lady of Perpetual Help. Susan said, 'Father we are never going to leave here. We chose the highest piece of land to build the church on, so we could see it from the house.'"

"The building of the church brought me close to them and I started to go out in public with them," Father Morrow said, "I could easily see their beautiful personalities and I was able to ignore who Susan was as far as the rest of the world was concerned. I subscribed to Worldwide Marriage Encounter — 'don't be afraid to hold your honey's hand' — but because of my Irish background and being raised in staid Connecticut I was not used to it. In restaurants, they both looked at the same menu, sometimes holding hands while looking at it. The looks back and forth whether of disappointment or affection — you could see it always. All she needed was security.

"She would say to a waiter on walking into a restaurant, 'No, we don't want that table we want *that* table,' though she would be unrecognized. She had 'that voice' and in dealing with the plumbers or anyone on the farm, she had 'that voice' — you're not getting her money until the work is done right. There was no softness in dealing with people like that. He was the same way if you were not doing your job. Susan was always afraid of somebody taking advantage of her."

"They went often to Aunt Fanny's Cabin, owned by Harvey Hester. He wasn't pleasant to look at — extremely stout — but he had a smile and a personality, a sort of old shoe kind of guy."

Near the completion of the church, Father Brew came down to stay with them, and to place the outdoor Stations of the Cross, on the church grounds.

"I lived at the gatehouse when I went down to visit them, which was as often as I could, Eaton would say, 'I'm just a half-ass Catholic, but I'm going to keep my foot in the door, no matter what.' The worst language Eaton ever used was a 'hell' or 'damn.' Susan made a real effort to eliminate that kind of talk. She could talk like the best of ladies, and most of the time when she was with Eaton, she did."

Father Brew was right, for all the nine years that Susan was married to Eaton, living with him in Carrollton; she played the role of a sweet, well-bred small town wife and believed in it. For Susan did love Eaton and the daily use of her acquired play-acting skills was the only method she had of subordinating her feverish temperament to the requirements of Eaton's refined lifestyle. She learned how to be just folks. She gave to charities and went to church picnics, waiting in line for her turn at the buffet table. And made friends of his friends (like Mary Williams).

The telephone operator at the Wedgewood Motel outside Carrollton had the following story to tell: Susan used to race through a small town called Ranburne, Alabama, on her way to Carrollton, Georgia. The speed limit was such that you more or less had to creep through Ranburne.

One time, when the cops pulled her over to the side, she got out slammed the door and shook her fist at them in fury. "If you stop me one more time," she shouted, "I'm going to buy this goddamn town and build a bridge over it." Then she sped off, refusing a ticket and cursing like hell.

Mary Williams was one of the few Catholics in Carrollton when Eaton Chalkley first moved into town. Mary always said, about Susan, 'She was as Irish as Patti's pig and she didn't have that red hair for nuthin'."

"I moved to Carrollton in 1947 when my Paw saw the sign to buy this place, 'comin down from Savannah to see his mother. The property dated back to 1880 when they raised cotton on the land," Mary told strangers.

When Eaton first brought Susan to Carrollton (before the house was built on their land) they rented barn space for their two horses from Mrs. Williams, who had a home on fifty acres of land, and they would go horseback riding on the property. Mary Williams was in her 50's at that time, a mischievous little lady who loved to dance — especially the tango. Trim and nice looking, with grey hair, she lived in a brick house, built by her husband, which was completely pine paneled throughout the first floor. It had a disordered comfortable atmosphere and in the living room was a huge brick fireplace. The large kitchen with its built in preserve cabinets had windows over looking a garden patch, which you passed when you came through the side door.

Susan became very fond of Mary Williams and they spent hours drinking coffee and smoking cigarettes at her kitchen table. She would enjoy 'Miss Mary's' antics, especially when she did a tango while drying the dishes in her kitchen — much to her black kitten's wonderment. Susan treated that kitchen like her personal domain and there is a sign there written in a bold hand that reads: THIS IS THE KITCHEN OF MISS SUSAN I AM THE BOSS IF YOU DON'T BELIVE IT START SOMETHING.

Seated one day at the large round kitchen table, holding a cigarette Susan said to Mary, 'I guess you heard I make the boys work. I worked hard and God willing I stay alive long enough to raise them. But if I shouldn't those boys have got to know they have to work for a living. I am not going to give them everything they want so they can go around and waste it and be bums.' (During the summer, Greg worked as a mechanic in car dealerships and Timmie worked in one of the department stores as a salesman.)

Content and happy, Susan gained weight and let her hair get a shade darker. She saved store coupons and when she had enough for something she wanted she would pick up her friends, Mary Williams and Ann Moran, and take them to the stamp redemption center. Ann teased her about this one day. "Susie, you saving stamps and pasting them in books, you got to be kidding."

"Well, I need things too!" she answered with a pout.

Father Morrow, who was the first pastor at the Church of Our Lady of Perpetual Help and became a very close friend of the Chalkley's, remarked about the times he spent with them: "Eaton wanted to stay on the farm, he told me that. Susan liked to fish, so occasionally they went to Florida. They bought their own boats and stayed at Pier 66, where they also docked, before they bought a house on Nermi Drive in Ft. Lauderdale. They had a flat boat for fishing on the lake near the house, but the serious fishing was done in Florida where they had three boats. One was a party boat, one was for racing — this boat they took to Bermuda — and the third was for fishing. The boats berthed in Ft. Lauderdale where they usually stayed."

When Susan knew it was time to go back to work she followed a strict regimen. "If she knew she was going to make a movie a masseur would come out from Atlanta. She would get more circumspect about what she would eat. She knew I liked brownies and often she would bake them for me. Susan told me, 'Eaton won't eat many of these, but my will power is not strong.' I knew if a movie were coming around I wouldn't be offered any brownies."

Father Morrow would have to do without brownies for months to come as Susan (and often Eaton) left periodically for picture assignments. He would phone the house and Curlee, answering would say, 'They flew to California Father — you know how it is."

At that time, Susan started filming two pictures to be released the following year; Ross Hunter's *Back Street* and *The Marriage Go-Round*, which was Susan's last picture under her old Fox contract and would wind up a ten year association. Asked if she had any regrets about leaving the old home lot, she replied, "Not the slightest. Let's face it — what have I done here in the last five years? One, *Soldier of Fortune*, in which I played a mishmash; and two, *Woman Obsessed* about which I have no comment. The picture I'm doing is all right, but the studio has nothing planned for me. They used to plan things when Darryl Zanuck was in charge. But since he left — nothing. It's the old question of being a stepchild everyone takes for granted."

Susan's independent air was, of course, largely due to her happy marriage to Eaton and her life in Georgia.

"I love the life down there. If you want to fish or hunt you don't have to drive a hundred miles, it's right there. And it's faster to drive to Atlanta 50 miles away, than it is from the Beverly Hills Hotel to the Los Angeles Airport 15 miles away. But I also like the way of living; it's much easier and more relaxed. We have a lot of good friends down there; none of them in show business. I like it that way."

Actress Vera Miles, who was in *Back Street* with John Gavin and Susan, told Stanley Musgrove that while working with Susan she tried to get to know her.

She had met her through Musgrove some years before. After Susan had finished a particularly difficult scene — doing it sensationally — Vera, trying to lighten the mood, humorously told her, "It must be terrible to be such a lousy actress.' If looks could kill, Susan gave her one that would have done so on the spot. Vera later told Musgrove that there was just nothing she could say, and if she had said anything, it would have made it worse. As she explained, it was just her way of saying, 'how great you are.'

Susan defended the picture after it was released by saying, "These days, unless you have incest and a couple of rapes, the critics are not impressed. *Back Street* is a love story. It's a simple old-fashioned love. And I think audiences have liked it. You didn't feel dirty when you came out of the theatre."

In June of that year (1961), her long time friend and trusted Hollywood ally Jeff Chandler, died in the hospital of blood poisoning. Susan was deeply affected by this loss and fighting mad with the hospital. She claimed that they had killed him by their incompetence in mistreating his condition and considered suing the hospital for malpractice, but it never went any further than that. Her distrust in doctors and hospitals was compounded by this latest tragedy. The muscular handsome star with premature steel grey hair was dead at 44.

Susan had one more picture to do before she could return to Carrollton. She was reunited with her *I'll Cry Tomorrow* director, Daniel Mann, at MGM to do *Ada*, with Dean Martin.

On Susan's birthday June 30, 1961, Marty Rackin gave her a party. It was at agent Jay Bernstein's home on Doheny Drive. Her old beau Bill Holden showed up to wish her well, and the guests all were happy to see Eaton with her; he visited her often on the set and whether or not he was there his long stem yellow roses came faithfully each day.

That month an article appeared in an issue of *Confidential* magazine provoked by her sister Florence entitled, 'My Sister Susan Hayward Has Millions, But I'm On Relief.' Pictures of the sisters stared from the magazine cover.

She was very upset by the newspaper accounts and spoke to Ann Moran about it, "What would you do Ann?" she asked her plain speaking friend. "Let her go to work," Ann told her. "Yes," Susan agreed. "Let her go out and get it the way I got it — work for it."

Over for lunch one day, Father Morrow mentioned other articles recently prompted by Florence Marrener's pleas for help. "I had heard about these magazines and newspaper stories, they weren't complimentary. They said things about their marriage and her previous marriage. I asked them why they didn't do something about it in court. I said if somebody lied about me like that, I'd take them to court. They both said the publishers would love the publicity and they had concluded that there would be no point to it. You would sue someone this month and someone else six months later."

The knowledge of all this, however, did not help Eaton with his strong religious beliefs. He felt badly about all the adverse publicity since he had married a movie star, and thought of how it may have affected his children.

Eaton was in touch with his family and was always concerned about them.

"Eaton's son Joe was a high strung nervous kid," said Father Brew. "He was a nice kid, but he wasn't the best student. He couldn't stick to the books but he eventually made it. He graduated from St. Joseph's Academy, in Bardstown, Kentucky. His mother came to the graduation and, of course Eaton, and I was between them at dinner. Eaton had high hopes for the boy, but one thing — Joe could not reconcile himself to this new set up, he never accepted Susan."

There were many activities in preparation for the new church. Ann Moran, "the best baker south of the Mason Dixon Line," and chairperson for these functions recalled one of them.

"We had what we call a rubbish sale, and Eaton gave us some clothes to sell and Susan did the same. Anyway, I baked him a banana cake in return. On Sunday morning, he came in and gave me a check, saying, 'Ann that was the best banana cake I ever ate.' I gave the check to Father Morrow. He looked at it and when I explained he looked at the check again and said, 'that's the most expensive banana cake I ever saw.' I though the check was for five dollars — it was for fifty."

"Susie and I became friends through Eaton," Ann continued. "She would come over for a social gathering once in awhile and she suggested I turn the banana cake into the Pillsbury contest. So I put it in one year and nothing happened. She said I should try again, and to put her name on it, 'Just say, I love your banana cake, Maybe it will help.'"

Father Morrow, talking to Ann one day graphically described Susan's appetite during this period. "Honest Ann," he said. "I saw that woman eat a half of a cake at one sitting. But she did give me a little piece."

In Griffin's, Carrollton's only department store, the town electrician stopped a neighbor, "I just came from Susan Chalkley's house and you know what she was doing, she was freezing vegetables. Well, I never expected a movie star to freeze her own vegetables."

In answer to a reply that 'she is just like you and me,' the electrician could only say, "Well, she sure surprised me."

"She did do her own freezing," Ann verified. "And she used to do her own cooking too. One time I called her up and said, "Susie, do you think Eaton would like some city chicken?'

"What's city chicken?"

"Ask Eaton."

"Oh, my God yes," he said. "That's mock chicken."

"You get a wooden skewer, put pork and veal on it," Ann explained. "You dip it in egg and roll it in cracker meal and brown it — ."

"Well — I was cooking Eaton some curry."

"Alright then I'll give it to him tomorrow," Ann told her.

"Oh, no, the curry goes off — the city chicken comes in," Susan insisted.

"With her, anything he wanted he got."

Thinking back, Ann went on, "She would go into town with a babushka tied around her hair — she did her own hair. She'd wear a hat and sunglasses and off she'd go. Nobody had to deliver anything; she went after it. I spotted her in Bohanas's store one time and I walked in and said, "Susie, you stranded?"

"Yeah! Eaton's down the way."

"Do you want me to take you home?"

"No, when he gets through he'll pick me up."

"The heck with that, no sense waiting here. I'll give you a lift," Ann offered.

"I couldn't do that to Eaton, he'll come and get me sooner or later," she said patiently.

In town, nobody stared at her but they would look back after she went by. They would turn around and say, 'Hey, there goes Susan Hayward!'

"I know they see me," said Susan, "and they are surprised to see me but they leave me alone. We can go and come as we please. I can be myself in Georgia."

At first, the students from Carrollton College and West Georgia College rang their bell constantly, asking for her autograph, until they locked the gate that led to the main house down the road.

One of the storekeepers near Adamison Square in town described what happened when Eaton drove Susan into town: "The pick up truck would pull up and Eaton would lift Susan off the truck and raise her high over his head. She would laugh and he'd kiss her, then he would let her down and she would dash into J. Carl's Cleaners while he went off somewhere else. She would take up a position outside, along the street, and wait for him to come and get her."

"She followed him around like a puppy. So he wouldn't run off I guess. No matter where he moved she'd have to be with him," said the counter girl in McGee's Bakery off the Square.

Susan could often be seen standing among the cattle — no milk cows, only steak cows — with her hands on her hips just watching Eaton in the fields doing his daily chores, ready to assist in anything if he needed her — even to putting up a concrete fence post for the farm.

When the front gate was locked, Susan told Ann to drive around the back to the neighbors and drive up from there to her back door. Ann drove around to the back of the Chalkley house with her young daughter Judy one afternoon to pick up a puppy — one of her Dalmatians had had puppies and she gave Judy one and kept one for herself. Hers had one blue eye and one brown, "she just loved it." They walked in through the kitchen and called out to Susan who was upstairs.

"Her bedroom was huge and it overlooked the lake," said Ann as she remembered. The king-size white and gold bed. The master bedroom done in white and yellow. The white walls and rugs. The golden yellow chairs and chaise lounge. And the gold bedspread. "She was straightening up her dressing table, on which were huge bottles of colognes and perfumes."

"I noticed the two bathrooms off the bedroom and I asked her about them. She said, 'Well Ann, you know, when Eaton gets in there he's worse than a woman. I always have to hurry up and get out. So I just put another one in.' Her dressing room was about the size of the kitchen. Susan had many dresses from her movies hanging there."

She invited Ann and a few friends to a private screening of *Gone With The Wind* in the tiny Carroll theatre in town because Eaton wanted to see the film with her.

Susan was very contented with her life in Carrollton and told the cynics back in Hollywood who bet she wouldn't be.

"We have hills and streams, foxes, raccoons and possums right on our own land. The crickets serenade us at night. There are all kinds of things to do. We ride over our land throughout the seasons. The countryside is so green, the air is so clear. There is a deeper satisfaction in being told you're wonderful by the man you love than having a big raise in salary."

Susan never affected a honeysuckle and magnolia accent but her Brooklynese, Hollywood cultivated, Southern assimilated speech confused on old-time shopkeeper.

"Are you from England?" he questioned her.

"No, I'm from a place called Brooklyn," she told him.

"Where's that?"

"That's up North."

"Oh, I see. Well I knew you weren't anywhere's around here."

Christmas in Carrollton was always one of Susan's happiest times. The change of seasons brought with it cold weather and sometimes snow,

warm kitchens and a fire in the living room. The snow-covered countryside brought a lot of joy to Susan as she and Eaton scurried around
buying presents and searching out a pine tree for the decorations, which
she added to each year. Eaton was always very happy when Father Brew
could be with them. Susan must have been pleased for Eaton but one
wonders if she might not have been somewhat jealous of her husband's
uncommonly close relationship with Thomas Brew — a relationship that
in many ways closed her off. In particular, over Father Brew's deep interest for Eaton's health, which Susan must certainly have considered her
own special concern.

All in all though, with Greg and Timmie, Mary Williams, Ann Moran,
Harvey Hester and some of their other special friends it was always a true
family Christmas. They had more to celebrate than ever before with the
completion of Our Lady of Perpetual Help Church.

The entrance to the church was black slate and the inside was done in
earth tones, with beamed ceilings and paintings in the Eastern European
style. The Second Vatican Council called upon simplified churches, so as
not to be distracted by a lot of statues, giving attention to the altar and the
pulpit. The dark woods, white and gold background with gold candlesticks
on a simple white and gold altar conformed to the design requested.

About the only time Susan went to Mass with Eaton was on Christmas
Eve. The church was appropriately decorated for the holy season and Ann
Moran handed out the hymn books for the choral singing.

Susan, on being offered one, said, 'I can't sing!' Ann shoved a book at
her anyway, 'just make some noise then…' she said.

Father Brew said the Christmas Eve Mass, and afterwards Susan and
Eaton would invite their friends over.

Ann Moran — asked every time — remembered: "We always went in
on Christmas Eve for a holiday drink, right after the midnight Mass. They
had a gorgeous tree with golden angels, red ribbons, and silver bells. The
fireplace was ablaze, casting a golden glow on her Oscar on the mantle
and there were huge silver trays of food and silver coffee urns filled and
placed around. I said to her, 'Susie, they are gorgeous; just beautiful silver.'"

"Ann, if every you need them or anything for a church affair come over
and get them," she offered.

"I always baked her a special Christmas fruit cake which she was wild
about — we had such a lovely time those evenings," Ann said thoughtfully.

A shadow fell over their happiness, however, which no one spoke about
that night. Father Duke was invited to the dedication of the church and
later to Christmas Eve Mass and a visit with the Chalkley's and their

friends. He refused to come, saying, 'it would be like patting Eaton on the back for what he had done." Soon afterwards, Father Duke asked for a transfer from the area and left Carrollton and his one time close friend forever.

Father Morrow, who on this occasion could not make the Christmas Eve party, arrived the next day for a Christmas lunch. He recalled that visit.

"I arrived at the ranch and there was Harvey Hester. Eaton used to egg me on to get Susan to Mass more often, and 'Uncle' Harvey as well. He called them pagans, jokingly, but without smiling. I said, 'Harvey I missed you last night at the Mass.' They all started laughing. It seemed Harvey had spent the night in the pokey. He would go around with bottles of liquor as Christmas gifts and have a drink with everybody. He was heading out of Carrollton for another party by way of Buchanan. I guess he was weaving and he ended up in the pokey. He couldn't get anybody to get him out until finally he got hold of Eaton who arranged it for him."

"It was nice having you with us last night," Father Morrow said to Susan.

"Well, the day will come when I will be there every Sunday but not until I can receive communion," she emphasized.

The Chalkley's were leaving Carrollton again, this time for the United Kingdom, early in 1962, taking Curlee the maid with them. Susan was to begin shooting *I Thank A Fool*. Most of the location scenes were to be filmed in the tiny fishing village of Crookhaven in County Cork, Ireland — the same part of the country where Susan's grandmother Katie Harrigan had been born.

Her next film in England was the prophetic *Stolen Hours*, a remake of the earlier Bette Davis hit *Dark Victory*. In the movie, Susan has her hair shaved off for a brain tumor operation and then has to wear a wig. A portend of a true-life part she would, in time, be destined to live next time off-camera.

While not working on the Shepperton Studio set, where the non-location shooting was done, Susan spent quiet hours in her dressing room knitting Eaton a sweater. She always had his picture in a silver frame on her dressing room table — next to which were the ever present yellow roses. It was her favorite photograph of him, one of many they had taken on their travels. She fell in love with the Cornwall coast of England while filming some of the concluding scenes for the picture, and they considered buying property there.

The New York Times reviewer later wrote of her performance, "Susan Hayward is never allowed to go off the deep end. Her first fears of the unknown malady that afflict her are honest and real. As to her refusal to face up to the seriousness of her condition and her terror stricken resistance to medical help, especially impressive is her reaction and that of the people around her when she discovers that she has only a few months to live — there is no hand wringing martyred posturing of playing to the grandstand…"

Susan found some brocaded material of gold and white, which was later used on the chapel wall of the church. Whenever she traveled abroad, she and Eaton would visit as many churches as possible and Susan would always point out the statues of the saints. When they came back Susan spoke to Father Morrow about this, 'Father you have to put statues in the church, I want to buy them.'

Father Morrow explained how it would hurt the simplicity of the décor and Eaton agreed.

"Well Father," Susan promised. "You won't be Pastor here always and someday I'll get my statues in."

Helen Rackin talked about Susan's next movie, "My husband was head of production at Paramount Studios and they were going to make *Where Love Has Gone*, and he got in touch with Jack Gordean, Susan's agent, and told him about a great part in the picture for Susan. Mary Rackin phoned Susan and discussed the story based on Harold Robbin's novel, which seemed to be a left-handed account of the Lana Turner — Johnny Stompanato murder case of 1958.

"My husband was a great salesman, before she knew it he had talked her into saying she would do it. She read the script, but a week before starting she had second thoughts about it and called Marty."

"Marty, I don't know if I want to do this," she said.

"Suddenly she decided it wasn't right for her and she wanted to get out of it. That's where Eaton came in, he said, 'Listen Susan you did promise Marty you would do it, it would put him in a bad spot.' Then he said to my husband, 'Marty, Susan will do it.' I must say Eaton is the one who talked her into doing it.

"Eaton and Susan came out and stayed at the Beverly Wilshire Hotel. My husband had cast Bette Davis as the mother. Knowing what I knew about Bette Davis, I didn't think that she and Susan would get along. And they didn't."

"Bette Davis was a pain in the ass on that picture and Susan was patient with her but in the end she even drove Susan mad. I asked Marty why he didn't get Barbara Stanwyck for the part of Susan's mother? And he replied that 'Bette Davis was 'hot' right now.' I think he realized he had made a mistake because had he used Barbara Stanwyck, she would have been far superior."

At the press conference for the historic signing of the contracts for the film Davis and Hayward were photographed together. Susan had just completed the remake of Davis's *Dark Victory* (*Stolen Hours*) and Davis said, "some pictures should never have been re-made."

The script called for the stars to hate each other, which seemed to be less of an acting chore than a reality.

"She's a bitch!" Susan confided to a close friend. "— but a real pro!"

Bette Davis answered a question about Hayward to her interviewer saying, that she remembered with sadness Susan's unkind treatment of her during the shooting. She admitted she admired Susan's performances immensely up until the point that she had to work with her.

"Where indeed has love gone," Miss Davis pondered.

Hayward countered that Davis wanted to rewrite the script, naturally throwing more scenes her way, and wanted the death scene, which was originally intended for her, to last for pages.

A witness to it all said, "They were jealous of each other. Susan was frightened of Bette, who came on too strong, and reacted with obstinacy. Bette had just made a terrific re-emergence with *Baby Jane* and Susan was afraid of her walking away with the picture. The old fighting spirit returned to Hayward and eventually she stormed the front office demanding they shoot the film the way the script was written when she had signed for it, or she wouldn't continue.'

Eaton kept her under control and the picture was completed. He promised to take her home as soon as possible. Before they left town Marty and Helen Rackin invited 'Hooligan' over to their house for dinner.

"She loved steak, very rare, it had to be bloody. She told Marty she liked several of the outfits in the movie. Mary said, 'Look, Hooligan, they're a gift from me.'"

"No," she said. "I never want anything for nothing, what ever I want I pay for." She made a check out right there and then, Helen recollected.

A few days later back in her home in Carrollton, Susan, who had not seen her sister since 1958 when her mother had died, was shocked to read about her again in the headlines;

'SISTER OF FILM STAR FIGHTS FOR HER BABY' told the story of Florence having to appear in court to retain the custody of her two children. A son, 17, in a foster home and a baby girl in General Hospital. Susan's older sister confessed she was on welfare and destitute. The papers mentioned that she bore a striking resemblance to her actress sister.

The reports showed that Susan had helped her many times in the past but that she had not given any assistance recently. Susan's attorney said his client had 'no comment,' this having been a long drawn out situation and Miss Hayward and her husband preferred not to discuss it.

Eaton could not help thinking of his own family, under the circumstances.

Joe Chalkley, who never accepted his father's marriage to Susan Hayward, wanted — in some way — to prove himself. He tried several things — but mostly he wanted to fly, and his father made it possible for him to get his license.

Father Brew had never forgotten the outcome: "I was in Detroit on retreat. I got this call from Eaton. Joe had been killed in a plane crash — a storm someplace out of Louisville, Kentucky. I expressed my sympathy. I couldn't say anything definite to him at this point, about my joining him as I was out there attending a seminar. I did go to the funeral and Eaton met me at the airport. He had not expected me to be able to attend. I shall always remember what he said, 'This is more that I hoped for.' We went from Louisville to Atlanta and then to Washington. Again, it was this in-between thing which I was caught up in. Susan wanted to go, but Eaton insisted that she not go. The three of us, Harvey, Eaton and myself went to Washington alone, on a dreary September day in 1964."

Alone, at home in Carrollton, Susan came face to face with the reality of her husband's ties to his family and his religion and her unaccepted position as his lawful wife. Eaton's marriage to her was not a true one according to his church. Now, for a man of his conscience, fallen from the church unable to receive the sacraments Eaton's guilt gravely darkened with his son's sudden and tragic death — leaving her the outsider.

She did everything she could in acting the part of a catholic wife, as well as she knew how.

One wonders whether Eaton might subconsciously have held himself responsible for his son's death. The building of a church may have been partly for the community, but as much to amend for his religious indiscretion in marrying out of his faith. Susan, knowing all this, would have accepted any faith he was attached to — out of love for him.

How idyllic her life seemed, but underneath it all were serious problems. Eaton was deeply disturbed over his religion. Susan did everything she could to lessen his guilt and to make the marriage appear morally and socially correct. That was part of the reason she worked so hard to become part of the local scene.

In fact, Eaton sensing her dilemma once asked, "Where does the acting stop?"

Susan tried to take his mind off the tragedy by taking him close to the sea in Florida. For the next two years, she absolutely refused to leave him no matter how great the challenge of a movie role. They settled into the house at 220 Nermi Drive in Ft. Lauderdale where she wanted him to rest and regain his failing health and she was determined she would make it happen.

THE STAGE

The stage is the hardest work in the world. Doing the same performance night after night after night sent me right up the wall! I've had only one experience with the stage, in Las Vegas a few years ago doing Mame, *but that was enough. It was a challenge for me and I did the best I could at the time, but I was terribly glad when I lost my voice and had to quit the show. I learned my craft entirely in front of the movie camera and I must say I much prefer making movies, where every day is a different experience. And, too, I have no great feeling or awe about 'the theatah;' I don't consider myself an 'artiste.' I'm just a working woman, that's all, and I'd much rather work where there's a little variety.*

CHAPTER 10

Susan's agent Jack Gordeane phoned her. He wanted her to come to Hollywood to discuss a part in her old friend Joseph L. Mankiewicz's next film *The Honey Pot* to be filmed in Venice. Susan, knowing how much Eaton loved to go to Rome, and Venice, readily agreed to it, believing that this change would be just the ticket.

She told reporters: "My specific reason was Joe Mankiewicz. He's brilliant and what's more, he has heart. Nowadays I simply won't do a picture unless I know the director and his work." She added humorously, "I was getting restless anyway. It's good for me to work, its good discipline. I was getting lazy and a little fat. My husband realized this about me — "

While in Hollywood, she met up with the Marty Rackin's again; about this time, Helen said, "There was a big change in Eaton. He had gotten very, very, thin. He laughingly said that on the boat, he had tripped and had hurt his leg and it was giving him trouble. My husband said, "My God Eaton, you've lost a lot of weight.' Susan cut in defensively, 'He looks marvelous!' I think she felt that Eaton was seriously ill and you know she just didn't want to face it."

Father Brew said that Eaton's illness had originally started with an ulcer in Chicago. This went back to his first marriage. The bleeding was quite profuse, to a point of danger and they had to give him blood transfusions, and in those transfusions, he was getting tainted blood. It showed up as Hepatitis in the last three years of his life. His spells got progressively worse.

"You could see the color of his infection. This big, strong guy was wasting away; it was his good health that kept him alive as long as it did."

Eaton, not wishing for Susan to go to Italy alone and — perhaps — having a premonition of his approaching end, summoned up from some hidden reservoir the strength to join her on this trip. Before they left for Italy, he wanted to see as many of his old neighborhood friends as possible, it was as though he were tying together any loose ends of his life and saying his farewells.

"There was a reunion in Washington at the Carlton Hotel with as many of the old gang there as could be reached on short notice," said Father Brew, "everyone there was shocked by Eaton's appearance, this yellowish tinge to his skin. He did not look like himself. He was but a shadow of what everybody remembered. He knew his time was running out and he wanted this reunion with his old friends."

A bittersweet happiness warmed by memories of earlier visits journeyed with them as they arrived in Rome that September of 1965. The last time they had seen Rome, Eaton had found a renewal of spiritual solace in visiting the many churches. Now, Susan prayed fervently that he would find, in addition, a renewal of his former strength.

She hoped she could make it so, far away from all that could remind him of the death of his only son. As they disembarked from the plane in Rome that fall, Susan was very watchful of Eaton, though careful not to betray the fear for him within herself.

While shooting during the day, Susan constantly checked up on her husband at the hotel. She noticed his old enthusiasm returning, as he gave her that familiar smile when she left for the studio, and when she returned.

"I'll be right back, sailor," she would say, and salute him a goodbye. When she arrived at the studio, she found his yellow roses in her dressing room.

Actress Edie Adams working on the picture in Rome said sadly, "We all had a bad time. It was just a hard luck picture. Cinematographer Gianni di Venanzo died suddenly during the shooting. The movie was plagued with so many misfortunes. It read beautifully, a clever satire. We worked eight months on it, from August 1965 to March 1966. I got everyone to take hepatitis shots at my house; everyone took them — but Susan. She said, "I'm lettin' no doctor near me!"

"She was a small gutsy lady, she let nobody near her — we all kept away. She trusted only Joe Mankiewicz."

"I arranged for gamma globulin shots for the cast as well. Susan was under some kind of strain. I would have liked to have gotten close to her — to get to know her but she wouldn't join in with the cast on any social level. She seemed — bitter," was all that Edie Adams could finally say, to sum up her impression.

Eaton's condition worsened. He came down with the recurring liver ailment. He sought medical treatment in Rome but had to return to the

United States for more extensive care. Susan arranged to take her husband back to be hospitalized in Fort Lauderdale at Holy Cross Hospital, the first week in December.

By one of life's fortuitous coincidences the chaplain at Holy Cross was a priest from Mount St. Mary's who knew of Eaton Chalkley, but had never met him. He also knew of Eaton's invalid marriage to Susan Hayward, and through this, his removal from the practice of the sacraments, except when there is danger of death. The hospital chaplain absolved the dying man, heard his confession, anointed him and administered Holy Communion. Eaton Chalkley was at peace with himself at last. The albatross had dropped from around his neck.

Father Brew hastened to the bedside of his friend at Holy Cross Hospital, "I want to speak with Tom alone, please — " Eaton asked Susan to step out of the room. Hurt and confused by his request she left them to themselves. They talked privately. He also told his friend that he had made his confession, received communion and that he was happy to be back in the church.

"When he came home from the hospital, he had to have nurses around the clock." Father Brew said. "Then he insisted that she go back to work on the picture that she had contracted for. He said to her, 'you agreed to do it, do it. I'll be alright.'"

A helpless and desolate Susan flew halfway across the continent of Europe, leaving Eaton in the care of nurses, and doctors and Father Brew, to spend the unhappiest Christmas of her life.

"The next few weeks were rather difficult," Father Brew said, "She was calling every day, asking how he was. What can you tell a person on the telephone? He wasn't getting any better and it came to a point where the doctor said, 'you have to tell her.' So she came home."

From that moment on, Susan never left his side. That January, Father Morrow called from Carrollton.

"I would call periodically and ask how he was. Susan asked me to come down, 'You've been talking about coming and if you want to see him again…'"

Father Morrow left Carrollton for Lauderdale and the Chalkley home on Nermi Drive.

"I took a cab to the house and when I arrived she was waiting outside in front of the driveway. 'He's excited about your coming, but he's sleeping, suppose we wait awhile, let him get as much sleep as he can. He'll wake up after awhile," she said, as she led the way around the house to the canal. "I'll take you out to the boat."

She wanted everything very quiet for him. Then we went back inside because she said, "I don't want to leave him too long."

"She was very gentle with him. She was doing the nursing. Walking back and forth." "Father, you know he's receiving communion now and it had made him so happy."

"What about you?" I asked.

"I started the instructions, but I am more concerned about easing him through this. Then I'll look after myself."

"We went on in, this time, he was awake."

He had the rosary in his hand. I made a comment about it and Susan said, "Oh, he's constantly got those in his hands."

"Eaton and I had a nice visit, but Susan was either running for the water or running for the medicine. When we got a few moments to ourselves, she voiced something that was troubling her. She knew that Eaton wanted to be buried on the church grounds. From the first day that we ever talked about a church going up there, they also said there should be a cemetery.

The church wanted to avoid getting all tangled up as it could be a big business, running a cemetery. When I mentioned it to the Archbishop he wasn't keen on it."

"During the conversation, I interrupted Susan and asked her if I could use the phone. I didn't tell her but I called the Arch Bishop and told him Eaton Chalkley is back receiving the sacraments. He was entitled to a full Catholic funeral and would like to be buried at the Church of Our Lady. Susan would like him to be buried at the church. Why can't we?"

After a long pause, the Archbishop answered Father Morrow; "When you get back you announce that the parish is going to have a cemetery, so the announcement will precede the one that Eaton Chalkley is going to be buried there."

Father Brew, who had to leave, returned to his dying friend as soon as possible, "In the interval when he was home I would go say mass and bring Holy Communion back to him (from the church nearby)." In his waking moments, Eaton prayed with Father Brew, while holding on to a crucifix.

"That crucifix did not come from Pope John XXIII (as has been reported) it came from a priest of whom Susan and Eaton were very fond. It came from Father Samuel Robb — it was his crucifix, one that all Jesuits receive when they make their vows. Father Robb had died and the crucifix was given to me. I took it to Eaton and he kept it right beside him until he died."

Susan picked up the crucifix, she knew its background and where it came from.

"May I have it?" she whispered.

"Yes," said Father Brew.

She was to keep the crucifix with her always right up until her death, clutching it as she died.

She was there at the end. She held his hand. His last words were of his concern about her — not materially but spiritually. He was concerned about her soul.

Susan called Father Brew with the expected sad news of Eaton's death. She wanted to take her husband's body back to Washington so that his old friends would have the opportunity to pay their last respects. More importantly, she wanted to make it easier for Eaton first wife, Dorothy Roland, and his family by her to attend. Susan's one and only meeting with Eaton's first wife was to be at the funeral. The following night she took Eaton back to Carrollton for his burial.

The winter sun was filtering thinly through the windows in the chapel of Our Lady of Perpetual Help. Dressed somberly in black, Susan stood erect, looking straight ahead during the service conducted by Father Brew. Her diminutive figure now seemed an even more pitiful defense against the world of which Eaton had been her fortress and protector. This was one role for which no amount of preparation could have been made. Susan, though she covered it well was shocked and bereft.

The small gathering moved outside in silence to the open grave, where Eaton's boyhood friend Father Brew intoned a final blessing as the coffin was lowered into the ground.

"She was very composed," Ann Moran remembered, "They invited everyone there to go back to the house. Harvey Hester had the people from his restaurant bring food over to the Chalkley house."

Mary Williams walked Susan back from the church and was the last one to leave the house, leaving Susan by herself. After everyone had gone, Father Brew, who had returned to the gatehouse, left to return to the church for some private moments of prayer.

It was dusk when he stepped out of the church. Below him across the way, he heard the pitiful wailing sounds of a woman crying. He could see a form stretched out across the recently filled grave. Susan Chalkley was clutching at the earth and sobbing uncontrollably.

On that cold January night, she was wearing only the simple black dress that she had worn for the funeral service as she lay face down stretched across the grave.

Father Brew walked over to the prostrate and forlorn figure and helped her gently up from the ground.

"I want to be with Eaton," she cried, "I want to be with Eaton." Thomas Brew put his arms around her and held her, silently.

Susan Hayward, the widow Chalkley, boarded a plane for Venice a few days after the funeral of her husband. She was returning to complete the filming of *The Honey Pot*, and for the first time in almost ten years, there were no yellow roses from Eaton to greet her in her dressing room.

"My husband wouldn't be very proud of me if I hadn't finished what I'd already started, she said stoically, in response to suggestions that she could probably have arranged a release from her contract.

She returned to the set locked in the prison of her grief. Her co-star Rex Harrison must have sympathized with her remembering his own sorrow when his wife Kay Kendall died. Director Joe Mankiewicz offered what help he could but was unable to communicate with her beyond the perfunctory necessities of moving the shooting along.

"I came in on page 20 and got murdered on page 45," she later said about the assignment. She might have been talking about the way she felt about her own life now that she was without the one person who had given it meaning. When she was through with her scenes, she returned to Carrollton, Georgia.

The loneliest woman in the world now stood often and seemingly endlessly at the graveside of her departed husband, until finally in deep mourning, she would retreat, and close the door behind her inside the house she had once shared with Eaton.

Unable to sleep at night she sought refuge from her private agony in Mary William's home, staying with her for the first few days, sleeping in the upstairs bedroom. She then asked her friend if she would come back with her to the ranch and stay with her there for a while. Susan drank heavily now, trying to find an escape from her loss and relax herself enough to bring on some badly needed sleep. She had much to think about but uppermost in her mind was her determination to convert to Catholicism. Only as a catholic could she be buried in the consecrated ground next to her husband and that, she determined, was to be.

Susan spoke to Father Morrow about the possibility of conversion during her first visit with him since Eaton's death. "You try to see what the reasons are behind it," he said, and questioned her at length about her intentions. She became impatient with him, "I always wanted to,' she said, 'but the church wouldn't let me."

"You know what it will mean," he cautioned her. "You will have to be very circumspect about whom you might marry in the future."

Susan must have thought he was out of his mind to ever suggest she might marry again.

"Never, never, will there be another man. I could never meet a man like Eaton Chalkley," she cried.

Father Morrow urged her to follow the instructions. "It will take awhile," he said. Susan was upset by any suggestion of delay.

Susan knew Father Brew would be firm in his attitude toward her conversion, and that there was no way in which he would speed up the procedure for her.

"Susan went enough times to Mass with Eaton to get some idea of the Mass and its meaning," he said. "I think being with Eaton and seeing his principles and ideals had a lot to do with her interest in Catholicism. When she told me she was going to do it, I didn't get overly enthusiastic about it because I thought she was going too fast. I wanted to be sure it was a calm reason judgment, rather than an emotional reaction. Also, I wanted to be sure she got a good knowledge of the catholic faith (in) assuming a few obligations that she did not have before — something you don't jump into feet first and then ask afterwards, what have I gotten into?"

"I wanted to be sure she had an understanding of the church's laws on marriage lest the whole thing comes up again, but she was determined and she had this date fixed in her mind — June 30th."

Alone at night in the house, Susan would look over towards the church and its recently consecrated graveyard with its one grave and her own words came back to her, "Father we are never going to leave here. We chose the highest piece of land to build on, so we could see it from the house."

Six months after Eaton's death, Susan travelled incognito to Pennsylvania. She was preparing to be received into the catholic faith in the church of Saints Peter and Paul in the Pittsburg suburb of East Liberty and she was going to meet with Father McGuire, with whom she had been in contact.

Susan had told Father McGuire that she had come to a decision in her hours of grief that she could only find solace and comfort in Catholicism, and had asked for his help. She flew up to Pittsburgh on the Wednesday night of June 29th, 1966 and went directly to the church, arriving at 7:30 p.m. The next day, Thursday June 30th, the day of her 49th birthday, she returned to the noon Mass and stood before the altar in Saints Peters and Paul Church and was baptized into the Catholic faith by Father McGuire.

"What I feared might happen did!" said Father Brew. "Father McGuire happened to be Pastor of the church up there in Pittsburgh and he could arrange everything very quietly, the way she wanted it. The church was called St. Peter and Paul and her birthday coincided with the feast of St. Peter and Paul.

"I felt her knowledge was a bit on the superficial side," Father Brew commented, "I first met Father McGuire at Gonzaga High School where I was teaching and he was a student in my class. He is a very pleasant, kind, thoughtful person."

Father Morrow, observing Susan's six hour crash course in Catholicism said, "She went up to Pittsburgh and found a Jesuit up there who gave her a quick study — she found a guy who would do it for her — he was not a man of the Parish."

Of her conversion Susan said, "I became deeply interested in Catholicism when I went to Rome with my husband in 1958. My husband introduced me to the Reverend Daniel J. McGuire, who was serving as American secretary in the Jesuit headquarters at the Vatican.

"From that time on, I began to move toward this beautiful and moving religious faith with deliberate and determined steps. The more I attended Mass, the more I became convinced that someday I would convert."

Susan was baptized just before the noon Mass on that Thursday receiving her first Holy Communion. Several persons attending Mass recognized her and gathered around her after the service. The press was alerted, but Susan, distraught over having lost an earring that Eaton had given her, said little about her conversion.

She left Pittsburgh shortly afterwards and few to Fort Lauderdale where she was greeted and congratulated by her two sons, now both grown young men attending Auburn University.

Now a catholic, Susan probably hoped that her new religion would bring her the peace of mind that Eaton had once given to her and would have wanted her to have.

Back in Georgia, she asked Mary Williams to "walk behind me when I go up to receive communion for the first time at Our Lady of Perpetual Help on Sunday."

She still could not bear to be alone in the house and Mary Williams spent a great deal of time there with her.

"The maids didn't spend the nights, so I stayed with her. One time I was in the living room and I could hear her talking on the telephone from the bedroom. Some feller called her from Atlanta, I don't know what it was about, but she really let him have it. I said, 'Lord, I feel sorry for you poor fella' on the other end of the line — she was really sounding off."

"The next day I got up early and I told the colored woman if Susan wants to know where I am, tell her I'm in the yard (all 450 acres of it). I stayed with her cause she didn't want to be by herself."

Three months later Susan sold the farm.

"There are certain times in your life when you have to jump in the stream and swim," she said, "and there are other times when you jump out of the stream and watch it go by — until the time comes to jump in again."

She decided to move permanently to Ft. Lauderdale. Rather than run away from the past completely Susan felt sure she would be happier there where she had spent so many good times with Eaton. Much as she loved the ranch in Carrollton, it was not the place for her — alone.

"A woman can't manage a cattle ranch alone," she said, "at least not this woman. The cows scare me." Then she added, "You need a man like Eaton to run things on a ranch and know what should be done."

It was a difficult decision to sell that vast acreage of field and stream. "I loved our life out there, so had the boys, we enjoyed every minute of it."

Father Marrow thought back on this time, recalling that Susan had sold the house for only $250,000, including all the furnishings, and her comment on its sale, "I don't want anything to remind me."

Susan had changed a great deal by this time. She remarked that nothing has ever been smooth sailing for her, "Nothing but the wonderful ten years of total happiness with Eaton. When you say ten years, it sounds like a long time. When you live it and are truly happy, it is only a moment."

Susan was trying to pick up the pieces of her life in her own way and turned down all offers of work and any kind of interview saying that she "craved anonymity."

For the next eight months, Susan sat and stared at the water. She smoked five packs of cigarettes a day, rarely leaving the house on Nermi Drive. She drank Jack Daniels and Johnnie Walker Black Label and Beefeater martinis in huge brandy snifters and talked about her life with Eaton to Curlee, who listened patiently, and went along with her ramblings.

She continued to refuse all requests for interviews and seldom spoke to anyone on the phone with the exception of her brother and a few close friends.

Eventually, through an influential connection, a young man with the Heart Association managed to catch her interest. His southern drawl and polite, charming manners coupled with a racy sense of humor made an impression on her. She talked to him often and accepted invitations for benefits and charity affairs on behalf of the Heart Fund. Ron Nelson, the public relations man with the outfit, took up with the lonely star, becoming an escort and a personal friend. Susan learned to relax, joke and drink with him, and through it all she felt no pressures as he made no advances. It was a strictly platonic and easygoing friendship. She slowly came out of her shell and then joined him in a whirlwind of social activity, usually revolving around frequent cocktail hours. Dressed in her favorite uniform of white slacks and a navy blue shirt, with her hair tucked under a floppy white hat and wearing the inevitable sunglasses, she either went out on her boat or sat on the deck behind the house with her new buddy, Ron Nelson.

In May of 1967, 16 months after Eaton's death, there would be a break in the routine of sun and fishing, and drinking. She was offered a movie role, a cameo part, in *Valley of the Dolls*, at $50,000 for two weeks work at her old studio, 20th Century Fox, when Judy Garland was released from her commitment for the role.

Ken Dumaine, an actor on the Hollywood scene for years, worked on the picture and talked about why Garland was let go. "I remember when I went over to Fox to do Valley of the Dolls they knew right away Judy was having problems because she recorded the big number 'I'll Plant My Own Tree' and a few days later they had her back to redo a few bars that were not too good in the playback. They told her that Friday that they were shooting the number the following Monday and she said, 'Oh, we must have a playback before we can do it.' She didn't even remember having just done it. Each morning that she was due at the studio, they had a driver go over to her apartment to call for her. He would arrive there at 6:30 a.m. to pick Judy up at 7 a.m. and he'd wait throughout the morning, sometimes up to 12 noon, before he could even get to her and bring her back to the studio. Suddenly, Mark Robson, who was directing the picture said we can't put up with this. So they called Susan in. She had no time to prepare for it. She jumped in at the last minute and started working on the number."

"Nowadays I simply won't do a picture unless I know the director and his work," Susan said, "Mark Robson is directing it (*Valley of the Dolls*) and I first worked with him 24 years ago. We did *My Foolish Heart* together. Another reason is that the part's short, and good, and the salary's terrific."

Susan expressed regret at Judy Garland's leaving the film and she insisted that Garland be paid in full before she would sign for it. She got the part away from Jane Wyman and Bette Davis. She said of Garland, "She's such a talent, such a fine actress. I guess I don't understand these things though. I've enjoyed every minute of my career. It isn't art to me, its work, and darn good work, but it's never been my life. There are other things vastly more important to me."

Now that Susan was back in the news, she began to open up and talk to interviewers about her return to the cameras, seemingly enjoying all the attention she was getting again. She told one Ft. Lauderdale reporter:

"I was getting restless. It's good for me to work, it's good discipline. I was getting lazy and a little fat." As for her life in Lauderdale, the so — called Venice of the North, "I never really like the city. When I was a kid in Brooklyn, I used to hate taking subways. I think finally settling here was what I was looking for, the clear air and most of all the fishing."

For the moment Susan put aside her rods and reels, said goodbye to her stuffed marlin and other prize catches, and with Curlee following behind she left Florida for Hollywood.

Stanley Musgrove met up again with Susan at the Fox studios while she was there for her two week stint for *Valley of the Dolls*.

"I realized she was slightly mad. She was very sweet, too much so."

"I'm just in agony, still, over Eaton's death," he told her.

"Oh, I'm not. I just have joy, for the time we had together. I don't resent it. I am not bereaved. I don't think of it that way. I just think of him with joy for the wonderful times we had together. A lot of people didn't have the times we had."

"Susan," Musgrove asked her, "What do you do?"

"I go fishing all the time," she enthused, and repeated things she had told other people, how she loved fishing and, "Just before coming to Hollywood, I caught a 7 foot 1 inch sailfish." She had two boats — "and I'm the captain of both."

"She had skin that if she were out in the sun for three minutes it would burst, and she told these incredible stories. She would have looked so awful, freckled and everything if she had done all the fishing she said she did. There was a kind of madness about her. Also, she wasn't very good in her work, the picture stunk. But something was off kilter there. She never got into the role. I think the tumor had begun. Maybe a combination there — he died and the brain tumor started."

Susan wrote from her Beverly Wilshire Hotel suite one Sunday to her new friend Ron Nelson, thanking him for a gift he had sent.

Dear Ron,
The book is just charming. Thank you!
Worked this past Friday, and very happily too.
Of course it was like old home week when I went

on the set. Know most of the 'crew' from years
back and they all like me — and I like them.
Hope to be back in time for your birthday — but
also want the musical number to be as good as
possible so might ask for more rehearsal time.

Will keep you posted, my friend.
Best — Susan

Choreographer Bob Sidney was assigned to do the solo dance number for the film.

"Judy was doing the part of Helen Lawson. And poor Judy, it was very sad. I was introduced to her. I auditioned the 'I'll Plant My Own Tree' number that Susan finally did. I had it laid out for Judy and we already had it arranged, we had the chart done in Judy's key. We had had five days of her locking herself in her trailer and not coming out 'til 6 p.m. The first time I sang the song for her, I had to get under the table. She did the most outlandish things. Then I had to do it for her and Roger Eden. I had to audition it, I don't sing. Judy liked it; she liked the excitement of it.

"She would lock herself in her dressing room. They had people there just to see she had no booze. Lorna (her daughter) was a teenager then. She came running out of the room one day saying 'Mommie was strange, Mommie was taking something.' They had to dismiss her, nobody could handle her.

"Susan was called in and they paid her plenty because she had to come up from Florida, she had to give up her little fishing fleet. She came on the set a real pro. She arrived absolutely letter perfect. Everybody was impressed. Patty Duke was there and she was flip and all that, but the minute she met Susan she knew she was a strong lady, and it was no nonsense. None of the four letter words, Susan was a stickler for that. She never held up anyone. I can never remember them holding the camera for her — if they said let's go, she was there. She would let out an ungodly yell to clear her throat sometimes," Sidney screamed to illustrate.

"What the hell is that," I shrieked.

"You try it, it's good for you, you need it for your voice," she told him referring to Sidney's raspy, throat register.

"She was a big star when she left to go live in Ft. Lauderdale. She realized she had paid her dues and she wanted some personal happiness.

Wherever she met this Charlton Chalk, whatever the hell his name is —
he had to be a strong man. Susan would not respect a weak man; I asked
her if he was as strong as she was."

"You really are a problem," she smiled.

"She was delighted that I was on the picture. The first thing she said
to me was, 'When do we do the exercises?' Every damn day I used to get
black and blue because she never stopped.

"She's the only actress I know who never had any comment about
any other actress. When we did *Valley* [*of the Dolls*] and we were alone
she could have asked me about Judy Garland. She never once discussed
it, she never gossiped about her. Yes, she did make sure that Judy got
paid."

Sidney was waiting in her dressing room one day, "I had to know so
I asked her to tell the truth. 'Didn't you dunk Barker in the pool?'" He
was referring to the headlines before the divorce with Jess Barker where
the newspapers, in explicit detail, wrote of Susan's being thrown into the
pool at their home and Barker shoving her underwater.

"What do you mean?" Susan said defensively.

"I believe you did the dunking, you are stronger than he was," Sidney
suggested.

"I could do it!" she boasted.

"What do you do down there in Florida?" Sidney teased her.

"I look at the water. I have my fishing fleet."

"Oh, come on, what kind of fishing fleet, what kind of crap is that?" he
kidded her, "Really, don't you miss it here?"

"Miss what? This is a place to work. I'll always come back to work if
the price is right. I don't have many friends here anymore. I love living
down there."

Sidney was concerned about the scene in which Patty Duke pulls the
wig off Helen Lawson, played by Susan, and exposed a head of white
hair underneath. Susan insisted her hair be bleached white for that scene.

"Don't let them do your hair," he advised her.

"It won't work; you don't know what you're talking about. When you
change color, it isn't that bad. Don't worry I'm not paying for it!"

"Oh wear a wig Susan."

She explained to him how she had to be conscious in the whole scene
that when they pulled the wig off she would be exposed as the aging star
with the white hair. If she wore a wig underneath the top wig, it wouldn't
have felt the same to her and she would have affected her reaction. It
wouldn't have been honest.

Sidney watched her limber up for the dance routine, dressed in slacks and a tied up blouse and when she saw him looking, she tied a shirt around her waist.

"A little bit of a belly there?" he said.

"I didn't ask for your anatomical opinion," she answered him while exercising a good hour and a half.

Privately she asked him what he really thought about her condition.

"I remembered Susan in *Adam Had Four Sons*; she played such a bitch in it. I loved her so and when I got he chance to work with her I was delighted." Actor Ken Dumaine recalled first working with Hayward in *My Foolish Heart*, as a sailor in a scene at Grand Central Station, and then he did some standing scenes in *I'll Cry Tomorrow*. The last time, "I saw her was when she took over for Garland. I was one of the audience as she was doing this number for the camera.

"She had that great facility for lip syncing, and even though it was Margaret Whiting's soundtrack you could have sworn that she, Susan, was actually singing.

"I had seen Susan Hayward in public a time or two. She was not too friendly, she sort of played Miss Movie Star. She would arrive at a place and it was an — 'Out of my way — let me through', kind of attitude as she walked in and right through the crowd."

As for the role of Helen Lawson in Valley of the Dolls Susan remarked, "She's not exactly a person you'd take home to mother. She's a woman with a backbone of steel."

The critics singled out her brief appearance in the film as, 'like watching a Sarah Bernhardt' compared to the amateur histrionics of the rest of the cast.

After two weeks in Hollywood, Susan was back home in Ft. Lauderdale. "I wouldn't want to live in Hollywood all the time. It's like coming to a brilliant, creative, dream world. I like the simpler kind of life."

The simpler life that Susan returned to was another bout with the bottle, boredom, restlessness and more frequent forays into the local social scene on the arm of Ron Nelson. She was the prize catch of the community — the local legend living in their midst.

The twins were now 22 years old, with Gregory studying veterinary medicine at Auburn University and Timothy in the Armed Forces.

Susan phoned her brother in Hollywood at all hours of the night and sometimes she would phone Father Brew, or anyone who could talk to her about Eaton. In public, she would ramble on about fishing.

"I adore fishing in Florida — deep-sea fishing. You know — Hemingway, the big stuff. I love having a boat and being on the ocean. I'm out there every day. There are two fish I haven't caught yet and still must. I want a black marlin and a swordfish — they're very difficult to get, I've caught the other ones; I have them mounted and hanging like trophies all over my house."

Whatever she was doing, whether it was fishing or partying, flirting with the idea of meeting someone new, nothing worked. She didn't seem particularly happy with her freedom.

"I'm an independent," she said. "Very. Too much so. I always have been except when I was married to my second husband. You can't be totally independent when you have another human being to consider especially if you like the person and in my case, I adored him. I enjoyed that period of being — or rather, making believe — I was helpless. I could have stayed that way for the rest of my life but things didn't work out that way."

Back in Hollywood, Susan's brother Wally married for the first and only time. "I was working part of the time for Crown Management and they had this circus comin' to town. Carol (his future wife) was workin' in this gas station on Beverly Blvd. I knew the people there and one of the attendants said, 'Hey, look who's leading the parade.' Well, that was me in a jeep leading the route downtown. Behind me were the elephants."

Wally met Carol that day and as he said, "I kept this to myself — I'm like Susan that way — it was a kind of quiet thing. We took off and went to the Justice of the Peace. Later when Susan met Carol they hit it off right away."

Wally talked about Susan's behavior at this time. He was fearful that she might try to end her life because if ever she would have thought of such a thing it would have been after Eaton died, "because she loved him so much."

"What she did do," Wally said, "was get on the juice. She used to call from Florida and my wife would answer the phone and Susan would say, 'You takin' care of my brother? You feedin' him right? You doin' this for him or that for him?' So I would say to Carol, "Maybe you better get off the phone and I'll talk to her." And she would talk for a couple of hours — just to have somebody to talk to. She tried to get us to Carrollton at first and then when she moved to Florida, she wanted us to move down there. She said she could get me a job at the racetrack. But I knew at that time down there the racetracks were way underpaid. Out in California we were getting' the highest pay of any racetrack in the United States. So we never did go."

Father Brew had his own fishing tale to tell: "When Susan called me one time I told her my sister Ann was going down to Ft. Lauderdale to visit a friend. She said, 'tell her to call me.' Ann did and Susan said, 'You have to come out on the boat and we'll go fishing tomorrow.' So on my sister's line came this swordfish. I can't picture her reeling it in. Susan congratulated her and put a flag up. She had the swordfish mounted and sent it to my sister. It must have cost $300."

There were bigger fish in Florida who angled for a chance to catch her interest. Ed Lahey, for one, had his own special reasons.

Susan was asked to make a speech September 16, 1967, in Jacksonville, to all Republican leaders for Ed Lahey. There were rumors about her and the politician resulting from her help with his campaign for Governor of Florida. She told Father Morrow about being involved in his campaign, saying how much she enjoyed the contest. Father Morrow also read where she was dating other men (including Tom Shelton and Claude Kirk) and he mentioned it to her.

"Yes," she said. "But like I told you before there never will be another Eaton."

After all that build up, she withdrew, both from Ed Lahey and politics. Her experience with these politicians led her to say, "I've had enough of this! Dealing with these people!" When Susan felt she was being used, for whatever reasons, she walked out.

When Susan flew back to Carrollton, on rare visits, she saw her old friends Mary Williams and Ann Moran.

Ann and her daughter Judy took over a banana cake to Mary William's house for Susan. After they had caught up with the local happenings Susan rather apologetically asked Judy, "Did you hear Mrs. Chalkley is going out with another man?"

"Yes, Mrs. Chalkley," said the 12 year old.

"You know Mrs. Chalkley has to go out with a man once in awhile to these Oscar shows and these big things."

Judy shrugged her shoulders, "Oh that's all right, Mrs. Chalkley."

"You know if Mrs. Chalkley ever married a man he is going to have to be exactly like Mr. Chalkley, is that OK with you?"

"Sure that's OK!"

With tears in her eyes, Susan hugged her.

Susan heard jazz organist Jack Frost play one day in Lauderdale and thought he was great. She sent one of his records to her agent Jack Gordeane with instructions to get it over to Joey Bishop. "You tell Joey, Jack would be wonderful on his show." Bishop said fine only if Susan would make an appearance and introduce Jack. Susan went with Frost and his wife to Hollywood.

Backstage at the 'Joey Bishop Show' there was an aura of excitement Accustomed as the crew was to celebrities, there was something special about Susan Hayward, the lady from Florida. You didn't see her often in Hollywood — "she didn't do the town" — or make the personal appearances, even when she lived there. She moved through the backstage bedlam of the TV show creating a wake of curiosity.

Susan talked to TV host Bishop about her seafaring life in Ft. Lauderdale, and catching her first white marlin. She talked about the boats moored right behind her house — one for everyday use another for Sundays. She barely spoke of her past life other than saying it was a dream come true.

"I've learned to live again and I've learned to live alone." Her 23-year-old son Timothy was now at Fort Bennington, Georgia in intensive training for the Green Berets. Redheaded, freckled face Gregory was still studying veterinary medicine at Auburn University.

Susan was projecting a carefree image, attempting to conceal the deep-rooted emptiness that was invading her.

Her bogeyman had returned and was taking over. Then she was rescued by the offer of work from her old friend Marty Rackin. Rackin believed he had just the right vehicle to attract Susan to get her out of her lethargy.

He knew she couldn't even look at anything she and Eaton had been involved in, including the movie business (with the exception of a small part in *Valley of the Dolls*, which she did as a favor for Mark Robson). He realized too that after selling out all their holdings in Georgia, she had buried herself in her home in Florida. She had also tried big game fishing, safaris in Africa, motorcycle riding — but nothing erased the memory of her life with Eaton. She was living artificially, in a hazy cloud of alcohol.

Helen Rackin, speaking about her late husband said, "Marty got involved with Caesar's Palace and they were looking for somebody to play Mame. Mame is a gutsy dame and he thought it would be great for Susan because that's what Susan was."

Marty Rackin told his fellow investors that Susan was a 'buddy' of his and he called her at home in Florida from Las Vegas.

"Hey, Hooligan, how long you gonna sit there with the old folks in Sun City? How about coming to Vegas to do *Mame* for me on the stage at Caesar's Palace," Rackin goaded her.

Helen recalled Susan's reply to her husband, "Gee Marty, I don't know. This is what I'll do. I'll go to New York and see *Mame* and see if I can do it." Susan flew into New York to see Angela Lansbury in the stage hit and loved her and the play.

"My husband conned her into coming out here (to California) — urging her — 'Come on out here and we'll fly to Vegas and talk to the men there.'"

A month later Susan was in Vegas and that September 1968, she would begin rehearsals for *Mame*. First, she decided to make another visit to Carrollton. Susan was staying at Mary Williams' home when Ann Moran paid her a visit.

"Ann what do you think of me doing *Mame*?"

"Why not, all those other gals that can't carry a tune did it. I heard you sing, you got a rough voice, but you'd make a beautiful Auntie Mame."

Susan laughed and told them, "You know — I think I'm gonna do it!" They all cheered her, wishing her luck!

The director of *Mame*, John Bowab, had worked with practically every Mame who ever appeared in the role on stage. However, this was to prove a very new and extraordinary experience.

He began: "Susan was the only lady in a major company who did not audition for the role, everybody auditioned, from Ann Miller to Judy Garland. Caesar's has star approval, however. It was the only time we cast a lady without auditioning her. She was written into the contract by Caesar's Palace. They wanted her and they wanted her badly. Hers was the name they thought would be the big drawing card, and so did we. Except she was a lady who had never set foot on a stage. We knew she sang, how well we didn't know.

"It was big news and caused a lot of excitement. When she was finally introduced to us we were all really stunned. Susan had absolutely no figure at all. The body that all of us knew and loved, the great walk and the look and everything was gone. Her figure looked like an avocado or a round pear. The lady was dissipated, bloated."

Susan had flown up from Florida to New York to get into a rehearsal set up at The Broadway Arts rehearsal studio and to meet the cast. Her understudy Betty McGuire also playing another featured role in the production never forgot that meeting.

"We all were just waiting with bated breath for Susan Hayward to walk in. Now I had an image, we always have an image of somebody we've seen up on the screen. I thought she was taller and in walks this pint — sized lady. She's what — like 5'2" very plain, she had a kerchief on, a sweater over an aquamarine slacks outfit. No make-up with these wonderful freckles. It blew my mind. I went, "Oh my God anybody who was willing to walk in that ready, that prepared with the image of 'here comes the star' is some lady.

"We were all in awe. She had a wonderful black lady with her who had been her maid for years. Everybody just stood up and applauded and everything and she said, "Hey, wait a minute, hold the applause until you can see whether I can do it or not.'"

The highly acclaimed and awarded choreographer Oona White said, "When I first came to New York to meet with her and give her some exercises she looked like humpty-dumpty. She had no waist at all. It was a long pull. I sent a dancer with her back to Florida to make sure she did these exercises. She asked for it actually, she said, 'I can't do it alone. If I have to go back I know I'll just dissipate.' Her legs looked like matchsticks; I had to build up her legs. When I saw her standing at the dancers bar I thought, "Oh my God this is going to be a job getting her back in shape.""

Diana Baffer, the young, pretty, dance captain, was introduced to her on that first day at the studio and had her own impression: "This little tiny thing looked more frightened that I was. I was with her a week in New York then they decided they wanted to send me down to Fort Lauderdale for a couple of weeks. I stayed with her in her house working with her every day for a long time. I adored her. Unfortunately, she was in such bad physical shape she never did build up the stamina that she needed for the part of *Mame*. She had little spindly legs and she was heavy around the torso. She had what I would call the typical drinker's body. Poor little thing it took her a couple of days in rehearsal just to do a knee bend. She was over 50 and it was an impossible thing to ask her to try one of the hardest parts in musical comedy.

"She did so many things that were so sweet. She had a terrific house-keeper, Curlee, the black woman. Boy was she close to her. Curlee took care of her more than anybody did."

Susan and the young woman had dinner together each night and over a glass of wine, Susan opened up and began to confide in her. Susan confessed that she had lost her will to live. That after she had met Eaton Chalkley she realized that everything she had done in her life to that point just didn't seem nearly as important. She just couldn't believe that he was taken away from her at such a young age.

Diana would listen to her talk about her religion and other things she seemed to believe in, "She asked my astrological sign and she wasn't a bit surprised to learn that I am a Leo. Her son Gregory was in vet school when I was there and she thought the world of him. She spoke very highly of him, how bright he was, what a great child he was."

When Susan introduced Diana to her other son Timothy she insisted Diana go out with him, "I only went out with him one evening. He was into a lot of pot smoking; there was no doubt about it. Susan said she was going to bed early so I went out with him and his friends. I was introduced to them by him as 'his old lady's dancing teacher.'

"I had mentioned that I liked steamed clams once and on my last night in Ft. Lauderdale she had, my God, like a bushel full of clams delivered. I ate until I just couldn't eat anymore."

Director John Bowab remembered that, "Oona White had a wonderful regimen of exercises and it was Diana's job to implement them. Susan phoned and said she wanted to be back up North with us. She didn't feel she was under the right kind of discipline, which was a stunner for us and we were thrilled.

"It was with pride that she could see the waist coming back, the bust like getting firmer but the thing she took the greatest pride in were her legs, which were pencil thin. The face was wonderful, the hair was long — which became a problem. To see her in a rehearsal studio, which was all mirrored, when Oona or one of us would come around she'd say 'Look what's happening' and point to the muscles in her legs — they were still thin but now they had shape and texture and resiliency to them. That seemed to generate the most excitement to her. Any of those ladies who have had a big drinking problem for some reason lose their texture, their muscle tone. The exercises she did were incredibly difficult, I wouldn't do them," said the director. "She worked at it, I mean an 8 hour day — at the same time she was doing her vocals every day with the coach."

"While Susan was rehearsing for the Vegas company, Jane Morgan was rehearsing to take over the New York company and Janis Paige was doing an understudy rehearsal. We had all three ladies on stage one Saturday at the Winter Garden Theatre. I'll never forget Susan was sitting on the floor; she was changing her shoes. Jane Morgan was on one side and Janis Paige on the other. Jane did a back flip with a couple of boys and Susan's face went absolutely green."

"What's that?" she asked unbelievingly, thinking it was something she would have to do while thinking they were holding back to give her a little at a time. Luckily, it was not part of the act.

While in New York in training for her singing and dancing stage debut for the scheduled Christmas holiday opening, she replied to a letter from Ron Nelson:

November 21, 1968

Dear Ron —
It's colder than a well diggers ass here in Fun City — and in a few moments I'll be in the Epsom salt tub.

*Your letter was here at lunch time — when I returned to the apart-
ment for a diet Pepsi before starting the four hour dance and exercise
grind. Before Pepsi is always vocal exercises and singing time. On
Mondays — Wednesdays and Fridays — after dance — Masseuse
time — then there are always ten thousands incidentals!*

*I really collapsed with laughter at your version of the upcoming Har-
ness Ball bit — I would say without hesitation that the lady will fill the
bill amply — fore and aft!*

Oona White.

The work here — as you can well imagine — is at this point at which we separate the men from the boys — I screamed with pain and wailed that I was not a man or a boy but a poor weak female — and got a loud round of applause — but no sympathy.

I'd just as soon have brought in Chinese dinner for Thanksgiving but made the mistake of asking a few people over. I intend to kick them out after they eat.

I am enjoying it though — in spite of my foolish gripes, it seems to bring out the fighting Irish in me which has been too long buried under the veneer of being a lady.

One of the loveliest things is discovering so much in common with super active people — there is a deep simpatico that extends between us.

I'm pleased to hear that some of the Ft. Lauderdale crowd will come to Vegas but regret that my job will make me unavailable for any kind of social life — beyond ten minutes after the last show.

Give Kelly and Helen and the Seropians and the Erdmans my dearest love. Received a nice letter from Nixon. Miss everybody — but have too much to do to really be homesick.

Be good — be happy,

Your affectionate friend,
Susan

They had scheduled a Benefit Performance at the Winter Garden with Susan doing *Mame* for the first time in front of an audience. She was excited and frightened at the same time, but because of union complications, it was cancelled.

John Bowab recalled that promised event, "The interest in New York was maniacal. When people heard that a run through was going to be done 4,000 people would have killed me for tickets, they all begged to come."

Weeks later Susan and Oona White flew out to Las Vegas for the highly publicized opening. On the plane Oona said to her, "You've been such a good girl I'm going to let you have one brandy after dinner." It was Susan's reward for not drinking while in training in New York.

Vegas' Caesar's Palace, a $25 million caravansary, blossoming in the cool desert with white hot fury on 34 acres, 1500 employees in Greco Roman costumes, a $125,000 chandelier with 10,000 crystals. $200,000 worth of Italian statues for starters, attracted a multitude of people from all over the globe. Now with Susan Hayward playing in the Greco-Roman room, crowds would line up for hours to try to make one of her two evening shows.

Susan and Oona went right to Caesar's Palace but before they could get to their rooms, they were ushered into the dining room, and seated. Frank Sinatra who was appearing there introduced Susan and as Oona said, "the whole room fell apart." Now that the fiery redhead had come out of her cocoon, she was going full blast.

The first week in Vegas was a repeat of what she had done in New York. Dress rehearsals continued right up to Christmas day. During a break in rehearsals, Susan and the cast were invited by the hotel to have dinner in a private dining room. Then it was back to the show. Ann Moran sent up a five pound fruitcake from Carrollton to her, which she shared with the cast.

Scheduled to open the following night, on the afternoon of December 26, 1968, *Mame* was previewed for an invited audience of Air Force Personnel. When Susan made her entrance sliding down a banister blowing a bugle and singing, 'It's Today,' the men went wild. It could have been a scene from *With A Song In My Heart* when, Susan as Jane Froman, entertained servicemen on the U.S.O. tours.

Opening night, the room, which seated 1,300, was packed, with movie stars, who had flow up from L.A., the press, hotel management and any VIP that could use his influence to acquire a seat. The curtain rose on the smallest, most glamorous *Mame* in theatrical history, to great applause.

Director Bowab watched it all anxiously, "It didn't go as well as we wanted it to. The show was difficult to cut — it was a 90-minute version. She was too vulnerable, too soft, you wanted to reach out and protect her. With the other Mames you felt — well screw it — so what if there was a stock market crash she'd go on to something else — with Susan the audience wanted to go up there and take care of her.

"Susan, who did not wear a body mike, or use stage microphones felt that she had to fill the room and belted out every number. She felt more at ease with the ballads and when she sat down with the little boy, her nephew Patrick, and sang, 'If He Walked Into My Life,' she did it with a tenderness that was heartbreaking. The emotional rendering of the lyrics got in her way. The part of *Mame* calls for a player who can be cold, bitchy, and flippant. Ironically, for an actress who gained her reputation for tough portrayals on the screen, came across as femininely dependant. Every gesture, every line and lyric was listened to with extraordinary attention. I am sure many were wondering if she were going to make it. As one critic put it 'when Susan Hayward grabbed both thighs hard and with moist eyes and pouty lips told us that we need a little Christmas right this very minute, she was Barbara Graham pleading for her very life."

They also said she lacked stage authority, her timing was bad but still they found her a curiously affecting Mame and for certain, one the likes of which would not be seen again. The audience was in effect helping her through the performance cheering every gesture.

Stanley Eichelbaum of the San Francisco Examiner remarked, "I'm glad it's Las Vegas and not New York or Los Angeles. It's like a charity turnout for Princess Margaret — they even applaud her costumes."

Susan who had never faced a live audience in her 30 years of performing — determined to beat this latest challenge — won the first round.

In her dressing room after her opening night performance, the press bombarded her with questions, which she responded to with her usual direct honesty.

"You mean it didn't show?" she said when someone asked her if she were nervous, doing a little pirouette through forests of flowers and finding a free wall to lean against. "I'll tell you truthfully, I was really scared stiff the first 15 minutes on that stage."

"It's fun. It's not exactly easy — twice a night. But is anything worthwhile easy? After 30 years, I'm finally in the theatre! Still I'll be glad when it's over — I'll have new muscles." Then she swept everyone aside, "Okay fellas, that's it," she said. "I still have another show to do. But if you're ever down around Ft. Lauderdale and spot my boat, the 'Oh Susannah,' give a holler."

She and Curlee had taken a house in the desert, where Susan slept 'till noon to recover from the two shows the night before. Then she would spend the rest of the day indoors, taking her hot Epsom salt baths, reading and on occasion seeing a few people, such as Ron Nelson who made frequent trips to Vegas and, her new press agent, Jay Bernstein and some of the company members.

Betty McGuire was the only person in the musical history of *Mame* who understudied for Mame, Vera and, playing the role of Sally Kato, did all three. McGuire knew the rigors of performing and was amazed at Susan's labors. Susan was practically never off stage.

She stripped down for costume changes as her dressers pulled her in, between scenes, and pushed her right again on stage. There was no intermission break for *Mame*, it went right into the second act nonstop. Susan having to do all the dance numbers from the Mame cakewalk to the jitterbug, the songs, the comedy and the dramatic interludes. As her energy gave way, she would fall into the arms of the two dressers as they

literally lifted her up under the armpits, dressed her, wiped off the drench-
ing perspiration and toss her back in front of the footlights. They told her,
"you'll have to project more." To the screen actress, who misunderstood
the meaning, she shouted more to fill up the enormous room. In spite of
all this, Susan began being Mame rather than Mame taking over Susan.
When she was not on stage, she stayed in her dressing room to recharge
her energy. However, she found some relaxation playing the slot machines.
Before the first show and after the second show Susan disguised in dark
glasses, kerchief covering her red hair wearing slacks and sweater stood
by the one arm bandit and yanked it for all it was worth. Standing beside
her, Curlee holding a cup of money watched intently as Susan fought
with the machine to win. The hardened Las Vegas types surrounding her
never noticed her; she was just another small time gambler in the crowd.

Ruth Gilette, who played Mother Burnside, fretted over her wearing
her emeralds, coming to work. "She used to wear her jewels and everybody
was worried to death about it," Ruth said, "She and her maid would get
out of the car in the parking lot and walk into the hotel and she would be
wearing her emeralds. We'd say, 'Honey, you must not do that somebody
is going to hit you over the head.'"

"No darling," she would smile. "I don't think so. I don't want them in
a safe deposit box — I wanna use 'em."

There was only one stage level dressing room, which, of course, the star
had. The cast had to run up steps to reach theirs. Susan became concerned
for the older Ruth Gilette who had to dash up and down three times
a performance. She insisted that her friend share her dressing room for
her changes — no one else even thought of the ordeal it must have been
for the portly woman.

Susan spoke to Ruth about her late husband, how much in love she was
with him and that she did the show to get over all that she missed being
with him. Ruth and a few special people in the company that she became
friendly with often went back to her house after the show. Now that the
excitement of opening night had passed and the routine of fourteen shows
a week began to be a grinding reality, she started to become restless and
bored. There were surprises from time to time that picked up her spirits.

Her son Timmie had just married and as Susan had been unable to
attend the wedding, he brought his bride to Caesar's on New Year's Eve.
They watched his mother do her first show and at the end when Susan
was taking her curtain calls, a spotlight was thrown on the newlyweds.
Susan introduced them to the delighted audience and asked them to
come up on stage.

Rackin had shuttled between Hollywood and Vegas, trying to find ways to keep her going. They looked for every conceivable way to save her energy. As the weeks passed, the situation grew hopeless. Hayward was a box office bonanza and Caesar's was in a panic.

"She developed Vegas throat," John Bowab explained. "There is something about the air in Vegas that affects singers vocally, she got it but kept pushing to overcome it."

The examining doctors warned her that she should either have throat surgery or quit the show. She had developed nodes, little tumors, on her vocal chords. Within the past year, she had had a hysterectomy because of a benign tumor, now for a second time Susan had shown herself prone to growth formations.

Marty Rackin went into long conferences with the management of Caesar's. Something had to be done, and quickly.

Ron Nelson, who was practically in absentia from his job at the Heart Fund in Ft. Lauderdale, stood by Susan in this crises. One night while she was resting in her rented home in the desert, he went sightseeing near The Strip. He spotted a crowd of gawkers standing in front of a store window. Curious, he made his way up behind them. In the window was artist Ralph Cowan, painting a life sized portrait of Susan in her closing costume from *Mame*; a white gown with a white fox collar trim. The figure in the painting was like a Barbie doll with a cut out of a Susan Hayward face pasted on, except for the exaggerated pert nose and heart shaped mouth. She stood on huge rocks against a turbulent brooding sky, the artist's interpretation of Susan's private life; the moon (her astrological sign) casting its light on restless waters. Every day he painted in the window before an every increasing, curious audience. As the painting neared completion, the artificially technicolored little doll, staring off into space became an unbelievable caricature of Susan Hayward.

Nelson, at the sight of the oil painted monstrosity, hastened back to tell Susan, thinking it would be just the kind of joke she needed to "crack her up," it was so Las Vegas phony.

"You've got to see it. It's so funny you won't believe it!" he howled. In disbelief, she questioned Ron further about the painting. She also found out that the artist had been given permission by Caesar's Palace to attend numerous performances of *Mame* to study his subject. "How dare they permit that," she exploded.

She refused at first to even look at the outrage but her curiosity got the best of her and the following night after the show, in her usual disguise outfit, she went with Ron to inspect it.

She stood unnoticed among the crowd of people staring up at the cartoon Hayward on its easel resisting the impulse to throw a brick through the window. "Just look at that candy box crap," she said just a bit too loudly as Ron pulled her away before a scene developed.

Curlee would shake her head in sympathy saying, "Ain't it exhausin'?" In truth it was more than exhausting it was slowly taking its toll on her health — dangerously so.

Her feet started to give out long before her voice. The producers were on the alert for any last minute problems. She was in no condition to continue to perform one night and they told Betty McGuire to standby to take over for her. Betty saw her in her dressing room trying to force her tiny feet, which had swollen up to five times their size into boots for the big Mame number. Betty finished the show that night and continued for the next few performances until the swelling subsided.

Susan watched Betty perform from the control booth. She marveled at how the stage trained McGuire did the part with such ease. With years of experience behind her the musical comedy performer, as Irish as Susan herself, with her red hair, freckles and big blue eyes, breezed through the show. One of the reviewers catching her performance gave her a wonderful write up.

Susan came into Betty's dressing room with the review crumpled up in her fist, and threw it at the dressing table. "Here, put this in your scrapbook. They loved you and hated me!" and walked out.

Susan remained distant and aloof to her understudy and Betty, awestruck by the superstar, kept her distance. With Susan back in the role, Betty then had to go on for the actress who played Vera Charles. Previously, during the Bosom Buddy number the other actress tried to upstage Susan. That night Susan missed a cue and tripped, falling on top of Betty.

Betty pulled herself together and in return did the same thing to Susan making it seem like part of the act. The audience caught on, howled with laughter and applauded as Susan and Betty broke up laughing as they untangled themselves.

"She called me into her dressing room after the show," Betty said, she said how much fun she had on stage that night. That broke it. She knew that I was out to help her not hurt her."

From that time on Susan trusted her and warmed up considerably, even asking her advice.

"How the hell do you keep that energy going? And where does that voice come from? What is that?"

"You must remember Susan that I'm a stage lady — that's what I'd be asking you if I were in front of a camera. That's what I've been trained for, it's years and years of training."

After that Betty began to give Susan breathing exercises and explained what stage projection meant. It was too late into the show for this kind of help and Susan resorted to a body mike to preserve what strength she had left in her voice.

During these times together, Susan would often speak about Eaton saying she really thought that for the first time in her life she had someone who wanted her just for herself. She felt used up and Betty remembered specifically her saying, "You don't know how bloody the nails became, climbing my way up."

But there was one man who cared and looked out for her and that was Marty Rackin. "He was down there faster than you can say scissors when something was going wrong or when Susan wanted to know anything," Betty said.

The sold out houses, the applause and the compliments coming from all directions had rejuvenated her and she was feeling in top form for a time. After the discipline of her months in New York and the rigors of performing every night began to fade, she became moody without a man like Eaton around to help her get through this taxing job. She went back to drinking and started to smoke heavily again. Feeling trapped in her desert home she grew frustrated and nervous. She was fighting an uphill battle.

She became distrustful of her understudy Betty McGuire. As an actress from Hollywood used to people stabbing at you from right to left she looked at McGuire as a threat — the understudy who can't wait to get on. Another time she found a dislike in the precocious child actor who played Patrick. Then it was the actress who played Vera. An unknown member of the cast who played the homely Agnes Gooch was the then unknown Loretta Swit, who later gained fame as the character Hot Lips in the television series *M*A*S*H*. Swit ingratiated herself with Susan and joined the select group surrounding her along with warm and motherly Ruth Gilette and hairdresser Charles La France who comprised the trio of her close friends.

Director Bowab conspired with La France to cut Susan's long hair. Her perspiration problems left her hair damp and limp after a short time on stage. Without telling her — to even it out — he clipped away until it was shortened to the right length.

The ever-faithful Curlee stood by to comfort and calm her during any darkening moods. She would stand in the wings each night. To relieve the monotony she would sing along while watching Susan perform. But when it came to 'If He Walked Into My Life,' she just knew that Susan was singing about Eaton Chalkley.

After 17 weeks and 96 performances, Susan faced the press. In a hoarse whisper and with tears in her eyes she said; "My doctors insisted I leave *Mame* and do nothing but rest my voice for several months. I love the show and the cast, and I hate to walk out on Caesar's Palace. What really breaks my heart is I've never copped out on any role or anybody in my 30 years as a performer."

Betty McGuire wept for her. Others choked up. She planned a big farewell party for the cast, "I want to go out in style and say thank you in style."

The party was held in one of the most stylish rooms in the hotel, with its white leather covered circular dining booths; two orchestras playing all the tunes from *Mame*; waiters pouring champagne; and a splendid dinner waiting to be served. All the guests at the private party were waiting for the star to make her entrance.

The doors to the room opened and there stood the 'hostess' dressed in a sequin-sprayed beige and lavender gown and her lavish display of emeralds. When the conductor struck the overture from *Mame*, Susan Hayward walked into the room on cue, every inch the star. Graciously, she greeted her guests and wasted no time in being served from the bar.

Unannounced, and at the management's invitation, the next Mame, Celeste Holm, suddenly appeared, dressed in simply street clothes. Photographers covering the event engineered a situation between the outgoing star and her incoming replacement by pushing them together to pose for publicity shots. Members of the cast who had worked with Miss Holm during the National Tour told stories of how temperamental and difficult she had been. Susan, resenting her presence, marched off to the powder room. As if searching for a weapon, she took her lipstick from her handbag and scrawled in big red letters across the mirror:

CELESTE WHO????????

Then she had the audacity to sign it:

SUSAN HAYWARD

The entire cast made trips back and forth to the ladies room when word spread of Susan's angry graffiti to Miss Holm.

Celeste Holm came to the party, intending to stay only long enough 'for a visit' as requested by the hotel. She was brought over to Susan who was now seated next to Ron in one of the white leather circular booths, to be introduced. Betty McGuire, the on going Mame at that time, was seated to the far left, making an uncomfortable study of the three Mames.

According to an eyewitness Susan turned to speak to Celeste Holm confidentially, "I want you to know that these are great people you're working with."

Miss Holm listened perplexed, and smiled.

"I don't think you heard me right," Hayward said menacingly, "and if I hear of you abusing them, so help me, I'll come back here and kick your ass all the way back to Toledo, Ohio."

Every eye in the room turned toward them. When the publicity man said he had enough shots, Miss Holm excused herself and walked out.

Elated Susan got up and joined the merry group, ordering another drink. She signaled to those around her to begin dancing and was just about to take Ron onto the dance floor when he spotted artist Ralph Cowan coming through the door.

Ron quickly warned her that the gatecrasher was heading her way. She motioned for him to stand aside. She had taken care of Celeste "Who?" — now she would demolish Ralph "Who?"

Cowan introduced himself and proceeded to go into a long dissertation about his admiration for her ending with, "I'm such a devoted fan of yours, Miss Hayward. I've seen every movie you ever made..."

"Uh-huh," Susan said shaking her head.

"You're my favorite actress...and..."

"Uh-huh."

Cowan then made his pitch and told her of the thousands of dollars he had spent in paint, canvas and time to do the immortal portrait of her and for his labors of love, he was willing to sacrifice it — but only to her — at the give away price of $10,000.

"Really," she said in amazement then lowering her voice she yelled for the guards. "I want this man thrown out! How dare he crash my party — get him out of here!"

Everyone looking on loved it. Good old Susan she hadn't let them down. She stood with hands on her hips, giving them a scene they would never forget — just like in her movies.

As Cowan was being escorted out by the security guards to the exit, Susan tossed off a closing line in appraisal of his efforts.

"I saw your candy box crap, your little Susan Hayward doll that looks like if you wind it up it will cry tomorrow. Throw the bum out!" she ordered and lit up a cigarette.

The party was taking on a decided atmosphere of melodrama — starring the Hollywood redhead at her sharpest, meanest and most emasculating.

Curlee stood alone in the background quietly observing the scenes, and when Ron asked her to join in and have a drink, she simply and politely made it clear that she was just there to look after Susan.

Susan now took off her emeralds finding them an uncomfortable weight around her throat and gave them to Curlee. Curlee stood like a sentinel. She had important things on her mind and would break the news to Susan at the right moment the next day.

Marty Rackin bragged about his 'Hooligan,' "She lasted 17 weeks, 16 more than I expected, and she packed the room every night. Then she came down with desert throat and went back to Florida. I thought we had lost her."

Back in Ft. Lauderdale Curlee broke the news to her mistress; she was going back to Carrollton to marry the Reverend Frank Crowder. Crowder, a man much older than Curlee and in poor health, has proposed to her a long time ago, but out of loyalty and devotion to Eaton and Susan, she had stayed on long after Mr. Chalkley died. It was now time to return to Georgia and marry him.

Susan was now experiencing severe headaches, bad coordination, and even worse depression, when she came back to the house on Nermi Drive, which she had shared with Eaton. She could bear the memories it contained no longer and put it up for sale, still trying desperately to escape the past. Now, with Curlee leaving, another link with her past life was to be broken. She would truly be alone.

She had to make a change in her life whatever the risk.

She said later — after she had moved; "I don't keep scrapbooks. I have no interest in the past; why hang on to a dim memory of it? My husband once collected prints of my films to give me as a gift and I appreciated the thoughtfulness but I never showed them; they just took up space. When I gave up my house in Florida, I gave them all to a neighbor who I knew was interested in films and taking photographs. You see, things like that — holding on to the past — would just bog me down. Not everyone, perhaps, but me, yes."

Susan bought a condominium on the 9th floor of the Four Seasons building about a mile away from Nermi Drive, from which she could look down on the crisscrossing waterways. Not long afterwards, a surprise housewarming gift arrived at her new home. Caesar's Palace had shipped, by Air Express, a painting of herself as Mame by artist Ralph Cowan. She called Ron Nelson and told him to get over as fast as he could. She asked him to bring along a pair of garden shears, "I'm going to cut it up into little pieces and throw it into the canal," she said, inviting him to the ceremony.

When Ron arrived, they had their quota of drinks to get in the mood for their ceremony of vandalism. They began laughing hysterically, recalling that night of the farewell party and Cowan's comically aided departure.

They laughed even harder at Caesar's paying him $10,000 for it, as a gift to her. Eventually Ron convinced her it was so campy, he must have it for a place of honor in his apartment, to be illuminated and seen by his guests as they first entered his foyer. Somehow, this appealed to her and she made him a gift of the huge painting, with the promise that he burn it if he ever wanted to get rid of it. It still hangs in his apartment.

Susan looked marvelous as she approached her 52nd birthday in June of 1969. After the workout of *Mame,* she was trim and looking better than she had in years. Men tried to date her, hoping to use Ron Nelson's friendship as a means of reaching her. Apathetically, she dismissed any overtures. She would not let go of Eaton. She seemed imprisoned in a state of sad reflection almost preferring it to any change, ever after three years of grieving. She could not find love. She couldn't even find herself. She was still living for a man who was gone — kept alive only by his hold on her memory. She was so insecure; she felt that men only wanted her for her money or to use her for their own ambitions.

She sought no sexual liaisons, it was not in her true nature to be promiscuous and without a sincere, honest emotion; she withdrew from any momentary sexual encounters. Left by her sons for marriages of their own, with families to raise and lives of their own, she depended more on her friendship with Ron Nelson. The bond between them grew stronger, and he matched Susan drink for drink. It was a way to get through the long days and endless nights.

Ron was readily available to Susan for her sudden whims of coursing recklessly through the waterways of Ft. Lauderdale. If he complained of becoming seasick, she would laugh it off and tease him, "Poor Captain Tuna, the chicken of the sea."

She had with her on deck of the 'Oh Susannah' the mechanical bird in the gilded cage that William Holden had bought for her in Paris in 1942, and as they roared through the canals she sang along with its tweetering of 'Let's All Sing Like The Birdies Sing, Tweet, Tweet, Tweet, Tweet' as the 'Susanna's' tall antennas and fishing lines scraped the roofs of the bridges as she raced the boat under them.

She was warned many times by the Coast Guard to temper her maneuvers and be more cautious about ripping through the waters. They warned the other boats to beware, "the 'Oh Susannah' was loose on the waterways." Still, the resident celebrity got away with it every time.

Ron badgered her to attend parties with him. He needed her to support his activities with the Heart Fund. Her appearance insured a successful event. She in turn relied upon him to escort her to exclusive gatherings that she could not refuse. President Richard Nixon sent Susan an engraved invitation to the White House, which also included Nelson's name. Ron sitting next to Susan in a White House dining room overheard Richard Nixon confess to Hayward, 'You know, you have always been my favorite actress.'

Their play could sometimes take a serious turn. Susan and Ron were leaving a supermarket one afternoon when she caught sight of a Cadillac speeding away from a parked car it had just side-swiped. She jumped into her car and with Ron at the wheel yelled at him to catch up with the other driver. They managed to get near enough to the Cadillac for Susan to jot down the license number on a scrap of paper — next to it she wrote in capital letters CULPRIT. They returned to the parking lot and took down the number of the damaged car and next to this; she wrote VICTIM and left it on the sideswiped car's windshield. She called the police and reported it, also getting the victim's telephone number. When she called, the grateful woman wanted to thank her with a gift of some sort and asked to whom she was speaking. Susan said that didn't matter, but in her sailor's slang to 'help another person in trouble,' told the woman — "Throw someone a lifeline sometime."

If only someone could have thrown Susan one. She needed desperately at this time, as she sat and drank in her splendid penthouse apartment at the Four Seasons.

Ron took her to one particularly smart party and during the evening, they disagreed about something that left her very angry and she put him down in front of his friends. Insulted and extremely embarrassed by this time he remained silent for the remainder of the evening. The next day, as if nothing happened, she called him about going out on the boat. "No, I don't think I can make it this afternoon," he told her, making up some feeble excuse.

"What do you mean Ronsy-Ponsy," she said calling him by her pet name, trying to humor him.

"I just think it might be a good idea if we just didn't see each other for awhile."

"OK, have it your way," she said trying to hide her annoyance.

She called him again a few days later and he was very cool and excused himself, saying he had much work to do. This made her angry and hurt and she called him back and said he must come over; she had to see him, to tell him something. Still she did not apologize for the incident the other evening. She called again, in tears this time, and he could no longer resist

Four Season Apartments, where Susan lived from 1966 through 1971

and went right over to see her. After too many drinks, an argument flared up and she repeated the attack on his manhood that she had made at the party. He got up saying he had had enough and made as though to leave.

"You leave and I'll set this place on fire," she screamed at him, waving a lighted cigarette around.

He was used to her threats and left. As soon as he entered his apartment the phone rang, "I set fire to the apartment," she told him, "just wait a minute…"

"Susannah you're crazy."

"Oh yeah, well listen to this…" she held the phone out and crashing sounds came over the line. What he actually heard was the sound of firemen chopping down the door. She was almost certainly drunk. When she came back on the line, she said she had to go and tie her silk bed sheets into a rope and let herself down the balcony of the floor below.

He rushed out of his house over to the Four Seasons. He found her in the apartment below her penthouse, in the shower washing off the black soot.

The firemen, wearing gas masks, had broken into her apartment and found her on the balcony. They had given her oxygen to prevent any damage to her lungs, and put out the flames in the living room with hand extinguishers, and then escorted Susan to the apartment of Mrs. Carson, below. Mrs. Carson let Ron in when he arrived.

Susan's apartment was repaired and refurbished and several months later, on April 15th, she fell and broke her arm, while she said, she was waxing the floor. She had been drunk as she poured the wax and promptly slipped on it. Shortly after that, she broke her foot and moved around the apartment in a wheelchair. She was becoming self-destructive. She was also lonelier than she had ever been in Hollywood. She could have gone back to work, but she found this retirement community an excuse for not wanting to take any particular action. Bored and restless, she drank far too much and was plagued with persistent headaches, which she attributed to too much drinking.

She needed help, but refused any offers or suggestion of it, and though she seemed helpless to help herself, she just waited for someone who didn't come. She wanted something to happen — and it did.

Marty Rackin called her again "Hello, Hooligan," he began. He was making a picture in Mexico called *The Revengers*. There was a great cameo part for her, opposite her old buddy, Bill Holden.

Helen Rackin remembered her reaction, "He sent her a script and she called him, 'listen Marty, you've always been a good friend. I'll do it for nothing. I don't want any money.' He then said he would give her the minimum anyway and she flew out here. My husband was already in Mexico and Susan and I flew down to join him. It was in mid 1971 and Susan said she had to lose five pounds and went on hard-boiled eggs and liver twice a week. She did her own hair color and make-up and made no demands. It only took a week."

She was back in front of the cameras again, being watched over by Holden and Rackin. It was a lot better than sitting on the balcony of her apartment smoking a cigarette and holding a drink. She was glad to be back working again. After her scenes were completed, she returned to Hollywood, looking for offers.

She returned to the Hollywood limelight the night of the Motion Picture Relief Fund's big affair. It was an all-star benefit and it was also the night that Frank Sinatra announced his retirement, starting rumors that he was dying of cancer.

Afterwards, John Bowab and Oona White were sitting outside the Dorothy Chandler Pavilion waiting for their car and Susan spotted them and called out.

"She came running across over to us," Bowab recalled, "not at all like her. Hugging and kissing Oona — so very effervescent. It really threw us because we had heard all these stories about her. She looked breathtaking, prettier than when she did *Mame*. She was wearing green chiffon. They took a lot of pictures of her — photographers were snapping away like crazy. "Susan was in a bubbly mood, just radiant — that was the last time we saw her."

She was just happy to be back. She signed with Norman Brokaw of the William Morris Agency and was making the rounds with her new publicity agent, Jay Bernstein.

Norman Brokaw spoke of his meeting with Susan at this time, "She sat opposite me on the couch in my office and I couldn't believe it. She looked so young. I have always represented big stars like Barbara Stanwyck and Loretta Young, but this one looked as if the clock had stopped for her twenty years ago."

Brokaw, who knew of her temper and enormous talent, carefully brought up the fact that television was the big thing now. He had in fact put together a 90-minute movie-for-television written for Barbara Stanwyck. He said he would like to find another property of the same quality for her.

A few days later, Barbara Stanwyck was rushed to the hospital to have a kidney removed. Suddenly the property Brokaw had mentioned to Susan became available for her. It took him less than 30 seconds to convince CBS and Metromedia to continue *Heat of Anger*, the Stanwyck vehicle, with Susan in the lead.

Hollywood designer Nolan Miller was asked to take the script to Susan's home in Ft. Lauderdale. He took along his sketch pad, a case of fabric samples and a close friendship with the ailing Barbara Stanwyck, as well as an understanding of the role.

As he said, "Susan Hayward knew how close I was to Barbara Stanwyck. I was doing the TV movie with her. We'd been shooting two days when she got ill she was taken to the hospital and they didn't think she was going to live. They had to remove a kidney. For several days, it was will she live or die. The studio decided there was no way they could shelve the project, they'd gone too far and they couldn't hold it up. The doctor said if Missy (his name for Barbara Stanwyck) could ever work again, it would be at least a year, maybe two. So they decided to replace her and offered it to Susan. She said yes, she told me, because she had such a thing about Stanwyck. They were both from Brooklyn. As a young girl, Stanwyck used to support her family and the family would cash her checks at the local butcher at the corner. Susan used to hear a lot about Barbara Stanwyck and she identified with her. They were both very strong, very definite about likes and dislikes, fiercely loyal to people they love."

When Susan came to Hollywood, she patterned herself after her. She used to say she loved the way Stanwyck walked, like a cat, and she wanted to walk like that too. She wanted to wear the clothes Nolan had designed for Stanwyck but they were of such a different size it wasn't possible.

"I came back to work," said Susan, "because the grief finally was all wrung out of me and I had finished my job in raising the boys. They were both graduated from college, they both got married, and Gregory had already made me a grandmother. Besides, I looked around Fort Lauderdale and realized I was a freak in that society. I suddenly had an overwhelming desire to get back to Hollywood, where I could be a freak among freaks."

TELEVISION

I love television, especially the Movies-for-TV. That's 'where it's at' right now. I like the pace. You have to be there and ready, and deliver. Of course, once it's over, you collapse, but it's exciting.

CHAPTER 11

In the fall of 1971, Susan Hayward Chalkley sold her Four Seasons condominium, shipped her furniture to Los Angeles and rented a luxurious house above Sunset Blvd. She was 54 years old and returning to work in front of the cameras as a star actress.

She talked about the work itself on her return, to shoot *Heat of Anger,* "I feel like a pianist who hasn't touched a piano in years. You wonder if you can still play, and you're terrified, but then you hit the first note and it all comes back to you. It was easier I guess because I found myself in the midst of old friends. My co-stars are Leo J. Cobb and Fritz Weaver. The director is Don Taylor, who played the part of one of my husbands in *I'll Cry Tomorrow.* I knew the producer and writer from my Paramount and 20th Century Fox days; even many of the electricians and grips were familiar faces from movie productions I'd done. The only thing unfamiliar was the pace. I was frantic when I had to learn ten pages of dialogue every day, instead of the three we used to do in films, but I soon found out I was able to handle it. Fortunately my brain was in good shape."

Susan had to meet the press again for pre-publicity on her return to work in Hollywood. Her old time adversaries, including Hedda Hopper, were almost all gone, and Louella Parsons, her trusted friend, was in a sanitarium (and was to die in 1972).

Sitting in the Polo Lounge of the Beverly Hills Hotel in a navy and white pantsuit, wearing the familiar dark glasses and lighting up cigarette after cigarette, she fenced with a reporter. Her life long disdain for interviews and her grudging response to questions was evident over lunch. Her answers were either short or totally scrupulous.

The reporter complained that he hadn't been able to get a single good quote. "Then make them up." Hayward said in her familiar style, "You would have, anyway."

She spoke to others about her return to work and her future plans for settling into the right house, etc. and answered one contemporary question by saying: "I don't know anything about women's' lib. It's just that there are problems in the world today; such as a woman alone. Ten days ago I was willing to marry the plumber — not that he asked me."

She told an anecdote about her son Tim, then 26, who was working in the music department of Jay Bernstein's public relations firm. "Tim began in the mail room for 90 minutes. Then he went on to handle performers. He hated performers. He thought they were crazy. I said, "Maybe that's because you grew up with one.""

Her sons were trying to find a husband for their mother. Marty, and Helen Rackin knowing how lonely Susan was, were attempting to do the same in their own way, "Hey, Hooligan, we got a guy for you," Rackin enthused over the phone, "an Italian, a very good looking man in the wine business."

Helen continued, "It was a blind date. She gave in and said, 'Oh, alright!' He picked her up and brought her over to our house for dinner. She looked just beautiful. He was younger, a man in his 40's. Susan was in her 50's then. I called her up as soon as she got in the house and asked her how it went."

"Helen, I think I'm too old a broad for him: she said rather tiredly, "he probably would have wanted somebody younger anyway!"

Susan was back seeing some of her old Hollywood friends, in addition to her brother and his wife. However, something was wrong with her condition that she was trying to ignore or not admit to and perhaps she thought if she kept herself busy it might even go away.

Early in 1972, she reported to work on *Heat of Anger* for the first day of shooting and in her dressing room were two dozen long stem roses. Her heart skipped a beat and for a moment, she stood motionless, then she picked up the card and read, it then telephoned the sender. "Who told you that yellow roses were my favorite flower?"

"Nobody told me," replied Nolan Miller, "You just look like yellow roses to me."

She hesitated, "That's incredible," she said faintly. "When I get depressed or unhappy I send myself yellow roses." She explained about Eaton's yellow roses, always there, when she began something new or needed them.

"I honestly didn't know it," Nolan said, surprised at the coincidence, "so from then on I sent her yellow roses once or twice a week."

Nolan was on the set with her continuously for the next three weeks. "How's Miss Stanwyck?" Susan asked him the minute he walked in. "Have you called the hospital?"

"After awhile when 'Missy" Stanwyck was well enough to be aware of anything going on, Susan said she wanted to send her flowers and asked what were her favorite. I told her she liked anything pink, pink carnations, pink roses — pink or red."

Susan phoned the Beverly Hills Florist Harry Findley and told him to send some pink roses to Barbara Stanwyck. He asked if she wanted maybe two or three dozen.

"No Harry, I said I would like to send roses!"

"What does that mean?" he said not quite understanding.

"At least 12 dozen," she explained.

"They were not allowing Missy to keep flowers, there were so many coming in", Nolan said, "They couldn't let her have them in the room. They took the cards off and let her see them and sent them, as she requested, to the wards."

Susan Hayward's flowers arrived looking like a huge rose bush as they were carried in by the two deliverymen. On seeing the display, Barbara Stanwyck pleaded with her nurse, "Oh please couldn't I keep them." It was necessary to set up a special table in her hospital room to accommodate them."

The headaches Susan had been suffering for months were getting worse. Now she was never free of them. Her vision became blurred and she seemed to squint more than ever. She had a strange feeling in her right arm and the cigarette burns on her fingers, due to a lack of sensation in her hands, could no longer be ignored. She still consumed an unreasonable amount of alcohol and smoked incessantly through many sleepless nights. What she tried to keep secret was noticed by some people around her, Nolan Miller for one. He saw her lack of coordination and noticed her dizzy spells and occasional losses of equilibrium. Susan, who didn't like to talk about her health, would soon have to face up to it. For the time being, she was too busy to give it very much attention.

Through a decorator friend of Nolan Miller's, she found a house atop the highest hill in Beverly Hills. It stood at the end of a winding road on Laurel Way and was fronted by palm tress and Italian Cypress. Beyond its two huge oak doors were spacious rooms all on one level that looked onto a swimming pool which sat on the edge of a startling drop overlooking the whole of Los Angeles.

A long hallway led to a sunken living room with a round fireplace in its center. The property was priced suspiciously low for such a valuable site with its spacious dwelling. She had to find out why it had been on the market for such a long time and a shadow fell across her joy when she learned that the previous owner, a homosexual man, had shot himself and his nude body had been found floating in the swimming pool.

Somehow, Susan — will all her superstitions, which included some rather odd ones such as a fear of walking into a room which had peacock feathers as decoration — brushed aside the idea of any form of jinx on the house. With new furnishings and her own strong vibrations, she felt she could exorcise any bad omens.

When she was settled in, she made plans to have her usual annual check up and to catch up with Father Brew after two years.

"It was March in 1972 when she came to Washington to see Dr. Kellerer, an old friend of mine," said Father Brew. "We were in the same class in High School. I induced Eaton to go to him when he first started having his sickness (the ulcer trouble and hepatitis). Susan was very impressed by him. He is without doubt a top flight internist — a Doctor's Doctor. All his life he was crippled from infantile paralysis."

Susan had flown to Georgetown University Hospital to see Dr. Kellerer. As part of his extensive examination, he injected a dye into her bloodstream to enable him to check for growths, using a scanner. She was familiar with the procedure, although this time it was taking much longer and the physician's manner was more guarded. To confirm his findings another dye test was done and it showed that a tumor was definitely growing on one of her lungs. If it showed a malignancy, the lung would have to be removed. Susan sat frozen with fear and disbelief as the doctor talked about major surgery, the possible removal of her lung, the prognosis for total recovery, and cancer — a word that struck terror in her heart. Horribly frightened by her prospects she left the hospital to return to her new home making a stopover in Ft. Lauderdale to see Ron Nelson.

She fled to escape, however temporarily, the fact of the encroaching malignancy. Her nerves were very much on edge and though she didn't want to admit it she couldn't deny what she had learned. She told Ron of Dr. Kelleher's findings. Her life was threatened and could only be pro-longed by prompt action. Dr. Kellerer had urged with her to deal with the tumor immediately. When she left (at her request), he sent her hospital records to another doctor, Dr. Davis in Los Angeles.

On her return to Los Angeles, her brother called her with the news that his wife Carol was ill. She had tuberculosis, from which she suddenly died when complications arose. Susan put all concern for herself aside to help her brother through this sad period. Carol was to be cremated and her ashes were to be scattered over the Pacific Ocean.

Wally said, reflecting on this time, "It was arranged by the funeral direc-tor. First, they said they had a single engine plane, but Susan and I told them, 'we're not going up in a single plane.' When we got to the airport, the guy had a twin engine Cessna and we flew out over the ocean. The pilot had her ashes in a cloth bag." According to safety regulations, the pilot himself had to sprinkle the ashes over the ocean, but he asked Wally if he wanted to hold onto the bag until the last moment. "OK," said Wally indifferently, "it's just a bag of ashes as far as I'm concerned. He told us that when he got to this spot he would open the little side window and 'out it goes.' The wind from the propellers made everything open, I guess. That was it."

Later, Wally took a test for tuberculosis and was relieved to find that he had not caught it.

Dizzying headaches now plagued Susan and she drank to relieve the pain but it only increased. She just hoped it would miraculously go away as she approached the start of her next TV movie pilot, *Say Goodbye, Maggie Cole*. However, she was not sufficiently concerned to fly back to Georgetown University Hospital for another examination.

The news this time was critical. X-rays revealed growths in her brain as well. By the time, she returned to Los Angeles, she was already showing a loss of weight and was pale and unsteady. Determined not to back out of a commitment she made it through the filming of *Say Goodbye, Maggie Cole*, giving a remarkable performance considering the circumstances. "I can't hold up the whole crew. It cost them money," she told her brother. Hayward fans, however, could see a change in Susan, particularly as her hair, her proudest possession, was constantly covered over with various wigs. It could only be surmised that it had been cut for the hospital tests. Ironically, in *Say Goodbye, Maggie Cole* she was playing Dr. Maggie Cole, who saves a patient by operating on a brain tumor.

By the end of the year, she was back in Georgetown and during the Christmas season, she had a convulsive seizure. For the first time she faced up to the truth of her dangerous illness and she was sent home to L.A. under medical supervision.

For the next few months, she didn't know what was happening to her body. She continued to drink, and she continued to use the prescribed painkillers. The first sign of changes was in her hampered movements. At times, she had difficulty walking and she would drop things. Then she couldn't light her cigarettes.

With no particular sign of panic or depression Susan appeared to have faced up to the facts when one day, as Wally said, "'I don't know what brought it about,' she said to me, 'don't you know I'm dying.'"

"Oh, come on, quit your kidding," was all that Wally could reply. But he fell silent and though nothing more was said he began to brood over it. It was quite a shock to him.

Early in 1973, director Henry Hathaway celebrated his 75th birthday. The Rackin's attended the party; "It was at the Beverly Hills Hotel. They invited all the big movie stars who had appeared in pictures directed by him, Cary Grant, Bob Mitchum, John Wayne, Susan — everybody. That was the night when it started."

Henry Hathaway recalled seeing her that night, March 12, 1973, at his birthday party; "She was sitting at a table with Rita Hayworth and both of them were drunk."

In front of a crowd of her fellow stars, Susan had her first seizure. Medically it was much like an epileptic fit; the brain growths had caused a cerebral "electrical storm." Her body jerked spastically. Her hands became grasping claws and her face grimaced and went through agonizing contortions. When the seizure ended, she went into deep sleep.

She was taken to Century City Hospital where rigorous tests uncovered no less than twenty tumors growing at an incredible rate in her brain. They were inoperable and only immediate massive chemotherapy and radiation treatments could possibly save her from immediate death.

She was told that she would not leave the hospital alive without the treatments. If she could endure them, to Susan this was a way to fight back.

The nightmare began.

Monstrous machines circled her body, menacing needles jabbed her flesh, vile pills were forced down her throat, and gadgets were stuck on her head with trillions of wire tentacles running to scopes. She drank potions to kill the things in her brain. She was drugged and nauseous most of the time, and between two worlds.

Rumors quickly spread all over Hollywood — "Susan Hayward was dying." The switchboard at Century City buzzed with incoming calls to doctors, staff and Susan, all looking for news — some scoop, some last words. She was secretly moved to Cedars of Lebanon Hospital under the name of Margaret Redding.

Six weeks later, she was released, still alive but looking as though she had returned from the dead. Her five foot one inch frame held a mere eighty-five pounds and the chemotherapy and radiation treatments had caused all of her gorgeous red hair to fall out.

Dr. Lee Siegel, her doctor, told Ron Nelson, who had flown in from Ft. Lauderdale, that she soon would be dead. "It could be a week, a month, but she won't be alive by July 4th."

On the 4th of July, two months after Susan was released from Cedars of Lebanon, Wally's brooding over Susan caused him to have a heart attack.

He had continued his daytime job as a page at the racetrack and spent every evening with his sister on Laurel Way, keeping her company and having dinners with her.

"When we had dinner at her home, she was having trouble cutting her food. She then had to have a nurse. When we went out to dinner, I would have to get on one side of her with the nurse on the other side. We'd park our car and going into the restaurant, she would move real fast, each of us holding her up on either side. She would go like fire."

Wally's feelings of helplessness about his sister caused him to literally worry himself sick. He collapsed while on duty at the Hollywood Rack Track and was rushed by ambulance to the Intensive Care Unit of Centinela Hospital. His condition was labeled as stable. Susan, who wasn't permitted to see him immediately, telephoned him first thing the next morning. The nurse came into Wally's room to tell him they had a call from him from a woman, 'who said she was Susan Hayward, the actress — Susan Hayward the movie star.'

"Fine, she's my sister," Wally said, smiling at the surprised look on the nurse's face.

"Wal, don't let this get you down," Susan said. "When we're on our feet again you and I are going to take a trip around the world. Just us — and nobody else. We'll show 'em they can't keep a Marrener down."

"I didn't know I had heart trouble," Wally said. "When Susan came to see me she brought me stuffed animals, the first time, it was monkeys."

She went often and each time brought him a stuffed animal until he had a menagerie. Wearing her inevitable dark glasses, she made her unsteady way to the hospital room to cheer him up. They were alone and needed each other, as in the old days some forty years ago in Flatbush, when they had clung to each other to get through the disheartening family hardships of their childhood — when — little Edythe had helped her brother to deliver his newspapers and, stopping to rub his hands warm, she would say, "Come on Wal, let's get goin' sooner we'll be home,' giving his wagon a push from behind. Now, both in middle age, and both weak from illness, it was again Susan who gave Wally 'that push' to get him up and well enough to leave the hospital.

When he returned to his apartment, his condition required that he move to a more convenient place so he had to make a change, leaving the place where he lived with Carol.

Susan insisted on apartment hunting with her brother to make sure he found the right place for himself, in the same neighborhood. They liked a building on Hauser Blvd. and found an apartment there that was just about right. She checked out the lease with Wally in the rental office. Worried about his heart condition, she helped him carry things from his old place, piling them onto the elevator and scolded him if he tried to exert himself, while he was anxiously watching out for her. Patricia Morison, who lived in the buiding, met them on the elevator. Morison had achieved great success on the Broadway stage, creating roles in what now have become classic Broadway musicals, and hadn't see Susan since their early days at Paramount. When she saw her carrying a shopping bag full of clothes she couldn't help herself and said, 'Why Susan you're looking so well.'

"Did you think I wasn't?" Susan chided her as she introduced her brother to the singer.

Susan sent over some of her own furniture to the new apartment and bought herself a small sofa bed to sleep on when she stayed overnight. They would go shopping at the Farmers Market just across the way from the apartment building, with Susan pushing the heavy shopping cart around, in the early mornings when it wasn't so crowded, breathless, but determined that her brother would not have to exert himself. He allowed this so not to upset her, worried all the time that she might lose her balance and fall.

Susan, wearing big dark glasses, a scarf covering her red wig holding onto her brother's arm went unrecognized.

"She would buy a leg of lamb and have it cut in half," Wally said. "She gave half to me to take back and told the butcher to cut the other half up for lamb stew. She loved to cook. She didn't like to clean up 'cause she used every pot and pan in the kitchen. She'd pile everything in the dishwasher. She loved hot stuff — Italian and Mexican food, which I can't eat. I'd go out with her and order something else — but it didn't seem to bother her," he said as he shook his head.

They drove around in Wally's old car to all her old favorite places, Nate and Al's on Beverly Drive for corned beef sandwiches, or Senor Pecos in Century City for guacamole (near 20th Century Fox where she had worked for so many years), Howard Johnson's for breakfast, the Tick Tock off Hollywood Blvd. for lunch, and Frank and Musso's for dinner.

Eventually, a nurse had to be hired, for despite Susan's independent front, she needed constant supervision. Louisa was an attractive dark haired woman of Italian descent. She had an authoritative manner and when she moved into the house, she began to take complete charge of Susan. Her professional expertise was added to by growing devotion, as her interest in her patient became more and more a matter of deep personal concern. She wanted to provide the strength that Susan was quickly losing and accompanied her everywhere, jealously guarding her every moment.

"She smoked right up to the end," said Wally. "I would light her cigarette for her and I had to watch her so that she wouldn't drop it. She lost the feelings in her fingers. I cautioned the nurse up there about it. I told her to please watch that she didn't drop it in bed or on the couch."

Susan, now approaching the end of her life, was asked to appear practically everywhere. As is often the case many people wanted to be able to talk about seeing her during the last months of her life. Desperate to make her time count for something and fearing loneliness, she went out as often as she could. Wigs to compliment her gowns were set off by pieces of dazzling jewelry from her extensive collection. An experienced hand at make-up, she still managed to create a glamorous illusion. Fortified with drugs, including the necessary Dilantin, to help ward off any possible seizure, she made every effort to get out while she still could.

Her sons were constantly alert for news of her condition. Greg would fly up to visit his mother from Florida, and Timothy watched and waited for any reports from his home ground in L.A. having witnessed his mother's seizures at Hollywood parties. Behind the scenes, he had been working to gain control of his mother's estate, on grounds of incapability of reason and suffering delusions — irresponsibility. On March 30, 1973, he filed a petition with the courts, through his lawyers, Gerald Lipsky Inc., to gain control of her cash and property holdings claiming that his mother was unable to care for herself or her property. Susan had been served a summons prior to her long confinement at Cedars, but was so seriously ill that at the time that she had not understood the meaning of the papers ordering her to appear in court to defend her competence. Upon her release from the hospital, and when she realized what Timothy had been trying to do, she was outrage and angry and proved that she was as competent as she had ever been.

She challenged the original petition, through her lawyer, Charles Beardsley. On May 1st her son gave up the fight by filing a petition of Termination of Conservatorship with the Los Angeles Court — but not before asking in the same document that his mother pay his attorney feels and other costs, amounting to $3,725.00.

Susan was to face yet another heartbreaking conflict with her son when on July 1st, 1973, she saw herself in a shocking photograph on the cover of *The National Enquirer* with the caption — SUSAN HAYWARD NEAR DEATH.

The National Enquirer had contacted Jay Bernstein's office for a story on their client Susan Hayward's condition. Timothy who still worked as a publicist at the office made a deal with the publisher for an exclusive scoop on his mother and arranged to have a photographer take a picture of her at a party during one of her seizures. For this, he would be paid $5000. And for the estimated 20 million readers of *The National Enquirer*, 26-year-old Timothy Barker talked, "Nobody can hide this anymore. She has multiple brain tumors and they're inoperable. My mother could live for only a few more days or she could live for another six months. No one can answer that question — not even the doctors. It's in the hands of God. My mother knows, but she hasn't accepted it. She keeps telling me she's going to beat it. But in her heart, she knows…When I saw my mother, she was alert. But under the circumstances because you're dealing with a portion of the body that controls everything else, sometimes she's in, sometimes she's out. She fluctuates….She forces herself to stay awake for long periods. She's in good spirits. She's a fighter."

Susan Hayward was at death's door as *The Enquirer* went to press — they editorialized — and because there is a time lag between printing the paper and getting it onto the nation's newsstands you may have heard of her death before you read this story…they warned their readers.

Susan fought to survive every hour of every day. She also fought to have the article of her impending death denied. The whole world had seen the ghastly photograph of her; somehow, she had to erase that picture from their minds. In someway she would find a means to leave the world with the impression of the Susan Hayward they had come to know and admire. She would get that chance and grab at it before the next twelve months passed.

Louisa hated Timothy for what he had done to his mother. Her attentions toward Susan now became overtly possessive and she displayed her feelings to such an extent that others around them could easily see that her feelings went far beyond her duties as Susan's private nurse. Whether Susan herself sensed this was not known, but Louisa's devotion, her emotional commitment and loyalty gave her a sense of protection and encouragement. Lou, as she was called, gave her hope daily for some kind of recovery. The radiation treatments had controlled the metastasizing of the brain tumors. Louisa herself a Catholic, prayed with Susan, reassuring her of a Hereafter, and bathed her in holy water shipped from Lourdes.

Ron Nelson remained as close as ever, even more so, but this time the nurse stood between them. Timothy was received at the house with considerable trepidation by Louisa, she accepted him only because his mother wished no lingering estrangement from her son at this crucial time. As for the unassuming Wally, Lou struck up an immediate rapport with him. Wally and Ron had nothing in common and could barely communicate, each holding on to his private and separate concern for Susan.

In the center of all this was Susan slowly being torn apart by the self interest of those she loved, but through her faith in God and with what she had learned from her years with Eaton, she held on with uncharacteristic control for someone in such critical health.

She had already lived past the date predicted for her demise by her doctors. She wanted now to look for help from another source that had helped guide her through her life.

Ron and the nurse helped a thin, drawn, confused Susan up the steps toward the front door of the home of her old and trusted astrologer friend, Carroll Righter. He too was older, but as bright as ever, with a twinkle in his eye, and a very active, wry sense of humor. Tall and slim, Righter, welcomed the tiny, frail woman into his living room as her companions went out to sit by the pool, leaving them alone.

After some of the usual social trivialities, she came to the point. "Do I have cancer?"

He avoided the question by saying her chart showed a "professional decline," but added, "I see you will be alive in January 1975."

Instantly, her depression vanished and her face lit up with excitement, "I'm going to get well!" she cried.

In that moment, she knew the doctors to be wrong and Carroll Righter, who had never failed her, to be far more accurate than they.

The professional decline he mentioned probably had to do with her next scheduled TV pilot, which could possibly be cancelled. What did that matter she would be alive for at least another year and a half, and maybe for years after that. As she was preparing to leave Righter's home, her escorts stood on either side of her to help her down the stairs — "No!" she said firmly. "I can do it alone." With her spirit renewed, she held herself straight and for the first time in months took off her sunglasses and waving goodbye to her friend, walked unaided down the front steps.

Believing the doctors to have grossly miscalculated her condition, she made plans to have further tests done at Boston's Massachusetts General

Hospital, to get a completely different point of view and, hopefully, some different results. Ron Nelson had flown back to Ft. Lauderdale and she would join him there after her tests. Wally moved temporarily into her Laurel Way home to be close to his sister in case anything happened very suddenly.

On the other hand, Susan was worried about her brother being alone after his heart attack. She was alone too, and would see that he had care and rest.

"I still rented this place," said Wally, referring to his apartment on Hauser Blvd. "I would come back weekends to check the mail and things. There was a day nurse on duty as well. I gave up my bedroom at Susan's to the nurse, who stayed full time."

Susan wanted to go back to Carrollton for a visit before her stay at Massachusetts General Hospital. In October of 1973 with Wally and Lou in company, she arrived in the town that had once been her home.

It was really to be a long look at the past, her last one, she must have suspected, despite her desperate hopes. When the plane landed in Atlanta, they checked into the nearby Hilton Hotel. Susan called Monsignor Reagan, now pastor of Our Lady of Perpetual Help, and Mary Williams and Ann Moran.

"I was working in a beauty shop in White Springs when my daughter called and said, "Mother, Mrs. Chalkley is coming and she wants banana cake. I got chilled when I knew she was in town," remember Ann Moran. "I didn't have any banana cake — and it was strange because I just bought bananas that mornin'. I had put them in my car thinking well, I'll just make a couple in case I see her. I'll have them in the freezer."

Ann told the beauty shop owner that she, 'had to leave suddenly — cause Susie was comin' over to my house." The proprietor knew Mrs. Chalkley from the church and sent Ann off with get-well wishes for Susan.

Susan hired a limousine and, with Wally and Lou, made the journey toward tiny Carrollton, along the avenues of great elms wearing their autumn colors and arching gracefully over the roads, and beyond to the spacious woods.

T.S Elliot's October his 'cruelest month' could not have referred to the sleepy, timeless town that Susan came back to.

The limo drove another five miles to Ann Moran's house. Ann was waiting and watching by the window as the car pulled up in front. Ann knew of her illness, but, no matter what, she would not say anything about it. As soon as Susan walked in the front door, heavily bundled up in furs, Ann hugged her and saying she still looked very pretty, but too thin.

The two of them chatted, Susan asked about everybody they both knew and Ann told her of all the local gossip. Susan showed her snap shots of her new house in Los Angeles. Then Ann fussed about the kitchen making them coffee — she told Susan she would bake that night.

"I'll make a banana cake and a fruit cake," she told Susan.

Susan's eyes lit up. Ann turned to Wally and Louisa; "Susie loves my fruit cake and Eaton my banana cake," then looking over at Susan's sudden downcast expression, realizing what she said she quickly added, 'my fruit cake doesn't have all that gook in it, right Susie?'

Susan looked up, smiled and nodded. Before Ann went ahead with the cake preparation Susan suggested they all go along to Harvey Hester's for dinner.

On their journey back towards town, many memories were stirring within Susan. They drove along Main Street, then on Dixie Street, passing the places where she and Eaton had shopped together; and the post office, the library, the courthouse. Wally had never seen any of it and Susan kept saying, "Look Wally there's so and so and over there, that's so and so…" They passed placid old homes with their white picket fences set back from the wide sidewalks and marking out the big front lawns.

Wally was sorry he had waited until now to see his sister's land of treasured memories; Susan, in her grief over Eaton, had almost forgotten the beautiful, gentle peace of Carrollton.

They drove down the lane to the ranch house and the land that she and Eaton had owned and cared for together. They got out of the car and strolled for a while in the late autumn air, still warm, but with a perceptible nip in it. They stood in front of Monsignor Reagan's rectory across the road from the little red gatehouse, from where the road led down the lane to the big house overlooking the lake. The house was now owned by strangers and Susan looked at it for only a moment. She took Wally inside to meet Monsignor Reagan.

The affable Irishman welcomed them at the door with huge Irish Wolfhounds by his side. Susan rested inside for a few minutes, in front of the fireplace — 'Wally that fireplace is exactly the same as the one we had in our house.' When she talked it was yesterday again, and Eaton was by her side, he had, 'brought this from Europe and he wanted to build this, and would one day add something else.' There was so much they had planned to do — then she became silent.

Susan's eyes wandered over the grounds as Lou joined them and they made their way to the church. Animals and creatures of all sorts roamed the yards. There were dogs, cats, hamsters, chickens, peacocks, donkeys; it was as though Noah's Ark had landed there. Monsignor Reagan opened the church doors and the first thing she saw was a number of statues of different saints standing on pedestals near the altar. She smiled, remembering her words to Father Morrow; "You won't always be pastor here Father and someday I'll get my statues in."

The October wind was rising and the air filled with leaves as the twilight hour brought a melancholy glow. She left her brother and Lou with Monsignor Reagan and walked over to Eaton's grave. The beautiful autumn background of the countryside was almost a stage set to the once beautiful dying woman as she stood quietly looking at the tombstone — "F. Eaton Chalkley 1909-1966" — for what she must have known would be the last time. These moments brought back overwhelmingly the happy life they had shared. Tears filled the corners of her eyes. She slowly and painfully kneeled down and with the palms of her hands pressed against the cool grass she leaned forward and kissed the earth, and then she placed some fresh flowers on the grave and struggled slowly to her feet. In Eaton, she had found herself and had found her peace with God, which had led her finally to enter the Catholic faith. It was the only consolation she had left. She looked at the place next to Eaton, where she would join him.

She turned around, put on her dark glasses again and was ready to leave. They walked toward the waiting limousine, entered and drove off as the sky darkened and the wind started to turn chilly.

Ann Moran called Susan the following morning. It was another windy day and now the wind was cold.

"I don't think you ought to get out in that wind," Ann told her over the telephone, regarding her plans to meet at Aunt Fanny's Cabin restaurant.

"Ann, God bless you," Susan said. "I was thinking about it too, but I don't want to renege on the invitation."

"No!" Ann said firmly, "You just stay and eat dinner there at the hotel and I'll call Mary Williams and we'll come over and have cake and coffee." Susan now realized that Ann must have known about her illness.

Ann Moran put down the receiver and cried, but she would never mention a word about it to Susan.

After Carrollton, Susan flew to Massachusetts General for more probing, more robot machines, more needles, chemotherapy, radiation, nausea and the cold clinical eyes of another team of doctors.

The moment Ron Nelson saw her emerge from a plane in Ft. Lauderdale International Airport; he knew what the news from Boston had been. She had waited until all the other passengers had left before attempting to leave the jet with Wally and Lou. Dressed in a sable coat and wearing now once again the inevitable dark glasses she held on to the nurse, dragging her right foot as she moved.

He reached forward to embrace her. "Don't touch me," she said.

That night, after they were all settled into his house on Fiesta Way he offered her a drink of her favorite Chivas Regal.

"She can't have that," snapped Lou.

"Who the hell says I can't drink!" Susan shot back. "I can do anything I please!"

After a couple of drinks, she collapsed from exhaustion and was put to bed. As the days passed, Nelson could see that her condition was growing worse. The dragging of her left foot was the result of one of the tumors in her right brain lobe growing large and beginning to paralyze the left side of her body.

Back in her Laurel Way home, after three weeks with Ron in Florida, Susan saw what was happening to her and made some decisions not to undergo any further chemotherapy and radiation treatments, and she would only accept narcotic pain killing drugs now in moderation. The painful, nerve racking effort to save her life seemed increasingly futile, robbing her of the relative peace of what had to be her last months. She appeared to be giving up the fight.

"I don't want any more life-saving crap!" she cried out to Wally.

She wavered, between courage and terror, conviction and uncertainty. Despite her brave words, she told Wally and Nolan Miller, "If I thought it would help, I'd travel anywhere, take anything, even rat poison."

Laetrile was just beginning to be known in the United States so she begged her doctors to give her some laetrile treatments — which were illegal — and they refused. Still it could be gotten illegally from Mexico if you had the right connections.

Lou knew how to get it. She would do anything for Susan and she purchased the drug (manufactured from the insides of apricot pits) and began giving Susan injections, knowing that she was risking her R.N. license, her career, even a jail sentence. Her love for Susan came before all of this.

Whatever happened, there was a remission in the early months of 1974. Was it the miracle Susan had prayed for? Was it the results of the laetrile treatments? Whatever it was, it happened — to the absolute amazement of her doctors. Susan was once again filled with hope.

LONELINESS

I know it well.

CHAPTER 12

Susan had heard that astrologer Walden Welch was staying at a Redondo Beach Motel and made an appointment to see him.

She talked about business matters, discussed the effects of laetrile and repeatedly asked for some kind of conformation about life after death. She asked questions about reincarnation. When he told her he was a Catholic, she again wanted to be convinced in the belief of a Hereafter, through her faith.

Welch, like so many others, was surprised at how petite she was. He felt that she was gracious, but there was a wall she kept up in front of her. He never forgot her telling him that when they were shooting a scene for *David and Bathsheba* she was lying on the ground, looking up at Gregory Peck, with her arm at her side when suddenly she realized her hand had invaded an anthill. She jumped up in fright when she saw the huge red ants crawling about.

"You know," she said to Welch. "I've put my hand in anthills all my life."

Katherine Hepburn had never met Susan before her illness, yet was one of the first to call on her when she knew of her condition. Once Hepburn followed Wally's car into Susan's Laurel Way driveway and as she stepped out of her 1961 Thunderbird, in blue jeans and jacket, she spied Wally's license plate KHH and laughed when she told him he had her initials — Katherine Houghton Hepburn. Wally opened the front door with his key, to Hepburn's surprise, "Oh, I'm Susan's brother," he explained. From then on Hepburn always brought with her a bouquet of flowers from her own garden — because as she told Susan, "The florists around here are a rip-off." Susan adored it and her visits did wonders for her as they talked honestly, as few could, to each other.

Barbara Stanwyck had not forgotten the flowers Susan had sent when she herself was in the hospital and sent frequent notes to the younger actress, even though they still had not met.

Nolan Miller, another of Susan's visitors and Stanwyck's friend, carried messages back and forth between them. He told Susan about a visit to the Getty Museum that he was planning with Stanwyck.

"When Susan found out we were going to the Getty Museum she asked if she could join us. We said of course. Her limousine arrived ahead, with her nurse. Susan and Missy met and said 'Hello! Wonderful to meet you' — very casual about it all. We did the entire museum. Missy was constantly saying to Susan, 'Are you tired! Susan, do you want to sit down,' like best girlfriends. After we had spent the day there, we had lunch. When we got to the parking lot the two of them were in tears, hugging and kissing goodbye. You couldn't believe it was their first meeting. Every time we talked after that Susan kept saying she wanted Missy and I over to dinner. But it never happened."

Susan would not see many people, but she was always pleased to hear from Ruth Gilette, her Mrs. Burnside from *Mame*, and Helen Rackin.

Ron Nelson was a constant visitor and one time when he was there, with another loyal friend of Susan's, Loretta Swit arrived unexpectedly. She walked in, sat on the floor at Susan's feet, crying crocodile tears and pressing her hand and saying, "Oh, my beautiful, Oh, my darling," and went on and on. Someone present that day was moved to say afterwards, "Save your performance for the stage, Loretta I've had my fill."

Susan would usually be most conscious around 5 o'clock in the morning and Ron who was by her side that morning asked her, "Did you know Ruth Gilette came to see you today?" She mumbled, like a child — "Yes" — "Did you know that Loretta Swit came to see you today?" — "Yes — she's full of shit!"

When another friend heard this she said, "That shows you she was not out of it, for a woman half dead to get that."

It was rumored that Jess Barker had reentered Susan's life, that he had been seeing her on and off since Eaton died. There were those who said he was after something, possibly an inheritance. Barker himself said, "I never stopped loving her." Diana Baffer recalling all of the times Susan and she talked to each other said, "Susan never put him down." If Susan heard that Jess ever needed anything, she quietly found a way to help him. Someone close to her reported, "I don't know if she was seeing Jess Barker. At one time, his teeth were going bad and she foot the bill for new dentures for him. She didn't want her sons to see their father in that condition, with bad teeth."

Susan was receiving mail from all over the world. Fans sent her religious medals, cards, rosary beads, various relics that were intended as cures and letters, which Wally would read to her. One came from Richard Nixon at San Clemente. Susan was moved by the fact that, despite Watergate and his own health problems, which reportedly including drinking, he cared enough to call a mutual friend in Hollywood for her address. He and Pat were praying for her and hoped she would visit them as soon as she was able. She made only one comment about his troubles — "he got a raw deal."

Evangelist Kathryn Kulman told her TV viewers that she could save Susan Hayward. She also sent her a tape recording of some very special healing prayers.

Nolan Miller received a mysterious phone call from Susan, at his Custom Gown Salon on So. Robertson Blvd. She made an appointment to see him.

"She came with her nurse, we sat down and I waited for her to speak," said Nolan.

"I am going to make a public appearance," she told him.

"You're what?" he said.

"They have asked me to be on the Academy Awards, What do you think I should wear — how should I look?"

Hollywood had learned of Susan's remission and the Academy had sent her a formal invitation to appear live on television to present the 1974 Best Actress Award with David Niven, at the April 2nd Oscar ceremonies. The Academy was well aware of the risk of a seizure in front of the audience and the millions of viewers, but the spectacular effect of Susan stepping, Lazarus-like, up from her deathbed to make this appearance was the kind of drama from which Academy history was made.

Nolan, recovering from the shock, looked at her, "Let's get you the goddamnest Susan Hayward wig they ever made — lots of red hair." Then I did some sketches for her. As soon as she saw this dress (sketch) she said, 'this is what I want.' We were sitting here in the salon looking over fabric when she said she had no jewelry with her! It was all in Florida in the bank."

"So I called Huey Skinner at Van Cleef and Arpels and told him we were doing a gown for Susan and is there anyway you can loan her some jewelry (they never do this). He said to bring her over and let her pick out what she wanted so we drove over to Van Cleef and Huey put out three trays of diamond necklaces, bracelets and earrings in front of her, 'pick out what you want,' he said. She made every effort to look good that night."

Well aware of what was happening, she said, "This will be the last time the public will ever see me so I want to look beautiful."

She now had the chance that she had been waiting for to erase from the public's mind the grotesque photograph on the cover of *The Enquirer* nine months earlier.

The day of her highly publicized appearance before 53 million tele-viewers, she began to decline. Unhappy and worried over the way she might come across, she had second thoughts about being on the show. She told Lou to call the Academy and tell them she had changed her mind — but Louisa spoke to someone else about Susan's decision and then Katherine Hepburn was asked for advice. Hepburn rushed over to the house to bolster Susan's flagging spirits and to encourage her, insisting that she must go on. "Why?" Susan asked, "You never did."

Katherine Hepburn had never appeared at the Oscars not even to accept her own awards. Invited once again by the Academy this time she agreed to go to present the Irving Thalberg special award. She promised that she would be backstage to help Susan through her ordeal.

Make up artist Frank Westmore of the famous Westmore Brothers of Hollywood went to her home that afternoon and seeing the ravages of the cobalt treatments was shocked to find only the remains of the former unique look that was Susan. Only his knowledge and experience in recalling the Susan Hayward he remembered could bring back a transformation. Westmore literally reconstructed her as she had been 30 years ago.

Nolan Miller's dress would go up to her neck and arms with glistening sequins; Nolan added, "She was going to treat herself to something and she bought this sable coat and paid about $40,000 for it. She referred to it as the 'goddamnest sable coat anybody had ever seen.'"

She was very nervous. It must have been hard for any woman who had been that beautiful facing the facts that it had taken a real toll on her. When she was ready to leave, she said, "Well, I guess that's as much as anybody can do to help out, so we might as well get on with it."

Dressed in her black sable and holding on to the arm of her agent Jay Bernstein, Susan made her way through the side entrance of the Pantages Theatre.

Groucho Marx had the dressing room that was reserved for her and reluctantly gave it up. Her nurse, Lou, Ron and her doctor — who gave her an injection of Dilantin to prevent an on-camera seizure — were hovering around her. Frank Westmore was checking her hair and make-up and Nolan, the beautiful gown he had designed. A concerned Katherine Hepburn kept an anxious lookout.

The most awaited moment of the evening arrived, with the audience wondering whether she was really going to appear. David Niven introduced her and her co-presenter Charlton Heston.

"Mr. Heston has created many miracles — just illusions on the screen. But in presenting our next award, he brings with him the real thing — Miss Susan Hayward. She is no illusion."

Susan, leaning on Heston's arm was welcomed with a respectful, warm and restrained ovation. "Don't stop for a moment when you hear the applause," Hepburn had whispered to her just before she made her entrance, realizing that any over excitement might bring on a collapse.

The suspense backstage was gripping as everyone held their breath. Susan looked beautiful through the color cameras. There were no close-ups, the cameras kept a respectful distance.

Dr. Siegel's wife, Noreen, who was sitting in the audience never forgot, "The biggest recollection I have is the night of the Academy Awards. I was so furious — whether people were just stunned when she walked out, looking so pretty, so lovely, I don't know." Noreen Siegel felt the applause was not what it should have been. For so many people it was like watching a beautiful ghost, and they were dumbstruck they were so busy staring they kept applauding almost as though in a trance."

"I shall never forget the sight of Susan walking bravely out on that stage, in her high heels, straight and proud, holding her head up as if to say, 'I'll show the world,'" said Noreen Siegel.

In her dressing room, she was helped off with the 30-pound dress and the wig. She looked at herself in the mirror, seeing her bald head with some little tufts of hair beginning to grow back, her skinny arms and wasted body, and laughed as her friends stood around her watching, "If they could only see me now." She said cynically. "That's the last time I pull that off." She called it 'a miracle of faith.' Fifteen minutes later, she collapsed. She was carried out of the Pantages on a stretcher.

The Enquirer ran a story some weeks later — SUSAN HAYWARD'S MIRACULOUS RECOVERY FROM EDGE OF DEATH — 'I knew my faith in God would pull me through" — was the captioned quote, "Don't believe what those doctors are saying," she said. "I don't have cancer. Believe me, they're wrong. I know they think I have cancer in my head and that I'm going to die, but it's not so. The public will know how well I am when they see me working again."

Susan was gratified at last having vindicated *The Enquirer* story of July 1st, 1973.

Norman Brokaw remarked, "I think Susan demonstrated just how well she's feeling when she made the presentation of the Best Actress Award at the April 2nd Oscar Awards."

Stanly Musgrove was interested in her doing a television special about Sally Stanford — the infamous San Francisco Madam. Sally Stanford's first choice was Greer Garson, but Musgrove said he didn't think she would be quite right and 'what about Susan Hayward?' Stanford replied that she would be acceptable. Musgrove talked to Norman Brokaw who said it sounded great and to keep him posted.

Jay Bernstein told the press, "She's now reading TV scripts and even considering doing some TV commercials."

"As for Susan," *The Enquirer* noted that "*I Want To Live* has now become more than just a movie title — it is, for her, a very personal credo."

Susan the consummate actress had scored again.

Shortly after this news, Susan's remission ended. The tumor on the right side of her brain was enlarging again, causing further paralysis of her left side and occasional comas. She had to use a wheel chair, crutches, and leg braces to keep the partially paralyzed and wasted leg from breaking under the weight of her body.

"I had to build a ramp from her dining room into the living room," Wally said. "There were three steps and I got a friend of mine to get some plyboard and nail it in place. This way she didn't have to be carried back and forth. We used the wheelchair."

Wally, who was there practically 24 hours a day, did all he could for his sister, with the help of the two nurses — Lou overseeing the routines. As for her sons, Greg flew in from Florida every so often — when things were looking bad and Timothy, though she had a few hassles with him, was always forgiven — "blood is thicker than water" — she would say.

Timothy would stay away for weeks at a time and then would suddenly show up at the house with his wife Ilsa, and their young daughter. Susan called Timothy's German wife "The Kraut." Lou, who found Timothy abrasive, was not pleased with his sudden visits. She felt he was protecting his inheritance and was most interested in that than anything else. The nurse stood between Susan and her son shielding her from whatever might occur between them. The tension between the nurse and Timothy came to a climax when he arrived at the house one day and she would not let him in. He phoned later and she told him that Susan was still too tired to talk to him and hung up. He became infuriated and called back screaming and demanding that he be allowed to speak to his mother. The nurse coldly refused, reminding him that his mother was under supervision, and she would not risk her having another — possibly fatal — seizure.

A witness to this altercation watched the battle over the dying woman with horror.

Looking for revenge, Timothy went to the police to report the nurse who wouldn't allow him in the house. But worse, he also reported the illegal laetrile injections, which he had found out about. The police could only act on the charges if he would file a suit against the nurse and give evidence. His reaction was to call Lou and threaten to expose her, thereby having her license revoked. The nurse quickly flushed the evidence down the toilet and when the police came the next morning with a search warrant they found nothing.

Spurred on by this, Timothy found another way to get rid of the nurse. He contracted the testimony of one of the doctors, gained his father's support, his brother's and oddly enough even Wally's to declare his mother incompetent, to break Louisa's authority.

White uniformed men arrived at the Laurel Way house, waving official papers at the distraught nurse. They gave the helpless Susan a sedative and trussed in up in a straight jacket as if she were some hopelessly insane person. She tried to resist and told them that she would go, but must have her black onyx crucifix, which was always near her. She grasped it protectively as they carried her out on a stretcher to a waiting ambulance that sped off to a sanatorium.

Susan, who wavered in and out of comas, suddenly became alert sensing the danger. Propped up in the hospital bed strapped in the straight jacket she watched the doctors and nurses rushing around, nervous and uncertain as to what they were doing. The moment she was alone with one jittery nurse, she asked for a cigarette.

The frightened nurse obtained one from her belongings. Needing a light Susan pointed to a cigarette lighter in her bag. It was a rather large one, used by arthritics, that was built to operate at the touch of a fingertip. While the nurse was trying to operate the unfamiliar lighter, Susan, using her free arm, reached for her crucifix, lying on the night table next to the bed, she swung it will full force across the nurses' face. The nurse fell backward as blood smeared her cheek. Susan screamed for help, shouting for a telephone.

The attendants came rushing into the room followed by doctors. She threatened them with lawsuits, charges against the hospital; she would bring the full force of the press down on them all.

"I know my legal rights," she yelled at them. "I want my lawyer. NOW!"

They stood frozen before the wealthy and powerful actress. In control of herself, coherent and articulate her demands were met. Her lawyer secured her release and she was back home soon after.

Susan, wary of her son, at the same time tried to understand the actions of all involved. She would now have to be even more on her guard.

On her last birthday, June 30, 1974, she was 57 years old. She was very weak but she surprised everyone when she asked for a chocolate birthday cake. After a quiet dinner at home, Ron and the cook brought out a big chocolate cake aglow with candles.

She ate almost half of it. She looked at the other half and sympatheti-
cally suggested they drive over to her estranged son Timothy's house with
it, to share the remainder of her birthday evening with him. Later that
evening, mother and son, reached an unspoken truce.

On the 4th of July, Susan wanted an old-fashioned cook out, like
the ones she and Wally went to in Brooklyn when they were kids. They
planned an all-American party celebration with hot dogs and hamburgers
on the grill, corn on the cob, potato salad and all the fixings. She asked
Dr. Lee and Noreen Siegel, Marty and Helen Rackin, Timothy and Ilsa,
and her very special friend cinematographer Stanley Cortez and his wife
to join her, Wally and Ron.

In the later part of July, Susan, in need of more treatments, went back
to Emory University Hospital in Atlanta. She again phoned Mary Williams, Ann Moran and a few others.

"I went to the hospital with a banana cake, paper plates and plastic
knives and forks," Ann said, "and I went up to the information desk and
said I'd like to see Susan Chalkley."

"There is no one here by that name," the nurse on duty told her.

Ann told her the room number, Susan's private nurse's name and other
identifying information, assuring her that she knew she was there.

"Just a minute," she said, and phoned Susan's room.

"There is someone here with the right answers from Carrollton," she
said into the telephone. Then she turned to Ann and told her that Susan
had had a very bad night.

"I see. Well, that's all right. I understand. If someone will just come
down and get this cake," Ann said to the nurse. When she wakes up, she
can have it. I know she will want some."

Ann left the cake, with a note, and went home, knowing that Susan
would call her as soon as she could. As she walked into the house, the
phone rang. It was the nurse, "Mrs. Chalkley wants to talk to you."

"She balled me out for leaving," said Ann. "She was very upset when
she woke up and saw the cake and knew I had been there."

Ann, not wanting to say how much she really understood simply said,
"Susie you didn't feel good and you needed your rest more than you needed
company. I'll see you again, some other time." Susan went silent for what
seemed a long time.

Then she asked Ann if she would please come back to see her that
Wednesday. Ann asked that she have her nurse leave a message at the
desk giving her permission to go upstairs to visit with her.

"Moma's leaving Friday," Susan told her, "and — I'm gonna be fine."

"Good for you Susie — we'll keep you in our prayers."

That Wednesday, Ann went back to Emory Hospital. She inquired at the reception desk if there was any message for her, any word from Susan Chalkley's nurse. The nurse on duty said no, there wasn't. Ann Moran paused for a moment then turned around and walked away.

Father Brew, who had not seen Susan since their last meeting in Washington in 1972, met her again that September of 1974.

"She had been at Tufts Medical Center in Boston. Then she came down to Emory in Atlanta. She had to wait a couple of weeks to get the results of this test, so she spent some time in Ft. Lauderdale and asked me to come down. I arranged to make the trip and she said she would meet me at the airport. When I got there I didn't see Susan."

At the Miami airport, a man walked up to the priest and asked him if he was Father Brew, he was then asked over to the waiting limousine. Susan was seated in the back with Lou and Father Brew sat in front next to the driver. As they drove off to Ft. Lauderdale, the priest turned to Susan and started a conversation.

"From a distance she looked as she always did. Only later did I see that her red hair was a wig. She asked about mutual friends in Washington, all about Eaton's friends. I had no reason to suspect things were as bad as they were. In other words, she was really putting up a front. It wasn't until we got to the place where she was staying down there that I realized," Father Brew said. "The driver got out, opened up the back, took out a wheelchair and lifted her into it. She had not said anything about it. She had reserved a room for me at Pier 66. It was about two blocks from where she was staying in a private house. There was nobody there, just the two of them. She suggested that we have dinner that night and asked how soon I could be ready. I was still in shock about the wheelchair and her condition. I didn't want to let on to her. The way she presented it, well that's the way I was going to take it."

Susan told him she would pick him up around 7:30 this Friday night and they would have dinner at MacDonald's Sea Grill. The owner was from Washington and both Eaton and Father Brew had known him from there. It had been one of Eaton's favorite fish restaurants in Ft. Lauderdale. At 7:30, they called for Father Brew and drove over to MacDonald's. Again, she was lifted into the wheelchair, and taken inside the restaurant. From there she pulled herself to the table.

"After dinner I could see she was tired so I said I would see her the next day — when she called and told me we were going out to dinner that night. I said, 'Again?' But she insisted. This time she was with Ron Nelson."

Nelson made all the arrangements for dinner that Saturday night at the Tower Club atop Ft. Lauderdale's Landmark Building. The Tower management placed American Beauty roses at a corner table and printed special Miss Susan Hayward matches. The room was softly lit and there was an air of expectancy as the staff watched the Tower elevator doors.

When Susan arrived in her wheelchair, all beautifully done up in a long gown, with her buddy Ron and Father Brew walking on either side and the nurse pushing the wheelchair, the combo which featured an organist, began to play 'With A Song In My Heart,' 'No Foolish Heart,' and other songs from her motion pictures, as she was wheeled through the candlelit room. A hush fell over the room as she passed the other diners.

"She was clear in everything she said," Father Brew recalled, "I remember her signing a couple of autographs, but at the same time the people in there didn't embarrass her. I don't know what she was suffering, what she was feeling. There was no indication. I thought this girl has got a lot of courage. It was a pleasant dinner.

"When we left there and drove back to Pier 66 I said, as I got out of the limousine — 'good night, wonderful dinner, see you tomorrow.' 'No,' she said, 'we are going to have a nightcap.' She was put into her wheelchair and we went to the revolving roof cocktail lounge."

The four of them spent another hour or so there before they said goodnight to Father Brew in the lobby. As he went to his room, he wondered why she would put on a public performance like that for his sake? They could have dined privately at her home. He reflected on the time he was in England in 1962 with Eaton while Susan was making *Stolen Hours*, the story of a woman dying of a brain tumor. The dramatics of the evening left him pulsed — and then he recalled Eaton's words, "It's difficult to tell when the acting stops."

The next day Father Brew went across to Susan's home. From there they went to Holy Cross Hospital — where Eaton Chalkley had been hospitalized with his final illness. Father Brew was to say Mass at 2 p.m. that afternoon during which Susan received Holy Communion at the last Mass she would be able to attend.

Four days later, she was flown back to Emory. Neurosurgeon Dr. George Tindall performed a biopsy after telling Susan that if the results were positive there was no hope for a prolonged survival. With the biopsy procedure completed, she waited in her hospital room. The reports were back from pathology and Dr. Tindall and his associates came into her room.

According to Ron Nelson, who was with Susan, she looked at them and said to him, "If he's gonna tell me what I think he's gonna tell me, you'd better leave."

Standing outside in the corridor, he heard a heart-rending scream — then dead silence. The physicians left and he went back into the room.

A brain scan showed rapid brain tumor growth. Doctors concluded she would soon lose her speech and memory, then her swallowing reflex. Because she had explicitly forbidden any intravenous or other lifesaving devices she would die once she could no longer swallow.

"I don't want anybody to push me over," she said, "and I don't want anybody to hold me back."

Susan returned to Ron's home in Ft. Lauderdale, but by the end of September, she became so feeble that further care was needed and she was flown back to Emory in Atlanta, on October 5th. She went into a coma and doctors were now certain she would not regain consciousness and notified the family. Monsignor Reagan from Carrollton brought her Holy Communion.

On October 21st, she rallied and regained consciousness. The doctors were amazed. She simply refused to submit. With only a few months at best she did not want to go to Ft. Lauderdale with Ron because Eaton had died there. She wanted to go back to California, to her own home and Ron rented a plane to fly her back to Los Angeles.

Ron told Susan that his doctors had detected a mild heart condition and before Susan boarded her plane, she said to him, "Look, they think I've got cancer. We know you've had a heart attack. Make a deal? We won't talk about this anymore, but let's keep this special thing we've got til one of us kicks the bucket. If it's you, I'll try to be there — If it's me you goddam well better be or I'll haunt you."

Before she left him, she looked back and smiled, "I'll see you in the funnie papers."

Back home in L.A., Lou would sometimes carry Susan into the living room and place her on a chaise lounge, where she would greet visitors such as Kate Hepburn, Ruth Gilette, Nolan Miller and her sons.

Susan would wake up from sleeping and see yellow roses and say, "Oh, they must be from Nolan." Lou called Nolan at his salon and asked him if when he finished working for the evening to drop in for a while. It would cheer Susan up.

"I would go and have something to eat with the nurse, Susan would sit there. Sometimes she was propped up in bed, sometimes in a wheelchair. She wouldn't eat with anyone looking at her."

"One night I was at the house and one of her early films was on television — *Reap The Wild Wind* — and we watched part of it. 'Dear God, how did they ever give me a second chance?' The way she threw her head around and rolled her eyes,' she said about herself. 'I can't imagine they would ever give me a second chance...'"

Susan refused to see Marty Rackin and many others who wanted to call — probably because of the way she looked. Helen Rackin tried many times to see her but, "she was sleeping most of the time. Some times I talked to her on the phone, but she couldn't talk too well as the paralysis had really taken hold."

"I'd say, 'Susie, can I come up and see you?' She'd say, 'fine Helen, but call first.' By the time I got there, she was already asleep. I would always leave a little note for her."

Most of the time Susan was heavily sedated and she had a horror of old friends seeing her as she was, and a growing disinterest in the things outside her home.

She called Father Brew to arrange to see him just one last time. Eaton's friend was her closest link in this world to Eaton and possibly, she might have thought it the next world as well. Saying goodbye to him would be in a way, saying goodbye to Eaton as well.

"In December she called and said she would appreciate it, if I could come to see her, she was pretty bad. So about the middle of December I went out there. She was heavily sedated and sleeping most of the time, but we had a couple of conversations. She still put on that brave front and kept her sense of humor. There was no indication of fear or rebellion. She went through each one of the stages that Elizabeth Kubler Ross wrote of in Death and Dying. On my last visit she accepted, and in her own way was consoled by, the catholic belief of life Hereafter. The sermon I made at the Mass (at her funeral) was all on the idea — that this is not the end."

The house was decorated for Christmas. There were poinsettia plants, wreaths, a big Christmas tree and there were four choir boy figures in front of the house with Christmas carol recordings piped outside. To the dying woman in her bedroom all of this could hardly have mattered but it was the well-intended idea of the people around her to make an attempt at capturing the holiday spirit for her — almost certainly for the last time.

Weeks later, on February 7, 1975, Susan phoned Ron Nelson and told him that 'it was time.' He left his job, once again, to go to her side. Ron arrived at the Laurel Way home for the death watch and found the household in a state of subdued hysteria. A strange interplay of intrigues manifested itself. Timothy approached Ron asking him to testify, at the right time, to help him break the will to have his Uncle left out. As it stood Timothy and Greg were to be left a million dollars apiece, their Uncle the interest from $250,000 held in trust for him for the rest of his life, the principal to revert back to Timothy and Greg only upon his death. Ilsa, who obviously distrusted her husband (later she would divorce him), also went to Ron to ask him to testify in court to have her daughter receive a share of her grandmother's estate.

Susan's estranged sister, Florence, knowing about the terminal illness, had been trying to see Susan for months to plead with her not to leave her out of her will. Susan hadn't seen her sister for 15 years and wanted no reunion now — it was too late.

It was revealed later that the desperate woman came to the house one day wearing only a barrel with a sign on it saying, in effect, my sister Susan Hayward won't give me any money and I'm starving. The publicity stunt was not recorded by the press, however.

Helen Rackin recalled that, "My husband and I had friends in the Real Estate business and they heard that Susan was very bad. They wanted to know if her house was up for sale and if my husband would put in a good word for them" (After Susan died they were all after the house — for when a movie star or personality has owned a home — the price almost doubles.)

Susan's poolside bedroom, which she seldom left during her last months, became the focal point of all the intrigues and often took on an atmosphere of frenzy. Ron, guarding the bedroom, finally not able to bear it any longer at one point yelled at them all, "Will you stop this fighting and let her die in peace."

Timothy at last won his battle with Louisa when the bookkeeper, who took care of Susan's taxes, files and checks, told him that he had discovered records of the payments for the laetrile. Now he had the evidence he wanted and his lawyer informed Lou that she must leave the premises immediately or he would turn the cancelled checks over to the authorities and see to it that she would never work again as a private nurse.

Louisa went to say goodbye to the woman she had deeply loved and cared for. With tears streaming down her cheeks, she pleaded with her, "Susan can you hear me? Can you hear me? They're forcing me out."

Susan turned her head toward Louisa's voice and slowly opened her eyes, looking at her with understanding, but unable to speak. Tears came to her eyes and fell down her cheeks as she realized Louisa's desperate position and enforced exile, and her own powerlessness to do anything about it.

Angry and hurt, Lou packed her belongings. Before leaving, she warned Ron, "If you ever try to make money on Susan, I'll take care of you."

Standing by the front door she turned and looked at Timothy who was watching her leave, "You'll pay for this," she said as she left them all standing at the open door watching her walk down the driveway.

In late February, no non-family members, apart from Ron, Katherine Hepburn and Ruth Gilette were allowed to see her — with one exception. One day a woman arrived dressed in a long black cape with a hood and said she wished to see Miss Hayward. The nurse answered the front door bell did not recognize the mystery woman as Greta Garbo, and replied, "Miss Hayward can't see anyone."

"I think she will see me," Garbo said softly and when she made herself known was led in immediately to see Susan.

The enigmatic legend flew in from Florida to share some personal health secrets she hoped might pull her through. Susan was her favorite star and she left very saddened after seeing her.

Ron kept his watch at Susan's bedside, taking his own sleep either alongside her on the same huge bed or in the big armchair placed close to it. He didn't get much sleep and hardly ever bothered to undress. Dr. Siegel prescribed Valium and gave him an insomniac's clock. It flashed the hours and minutes on the ceiling in hypnotic red digits.

Timothy could no longer bring himself to enter his mother's bedroom because of the foul odors. "I can't go in there. It makes me sick. I can't take it, the smell or look at her."

"Go in there!" ordered Ron. "She's your mother. She's dying." Timothy fortified himself with liquor before going into the room and when he came out, he turned a sickly yellowish color. "Don't ever ask me to do that again. I'll never go in there. Not even after she's dead."

Ron asked Dr. Siegel to let him know of some sign that would tell him when it was all about to end. He wanted Susan to die in peace, not to just hang on in this horrible way. Dr. Siegel instructed him on how to check various vital signs, like the pulses of the carotid artery in the neck, and the wrists, to listen to her heartbeats, to gauge the blood pressure, and to listen to the breathing.

Practically overtaken by nervous exhaustion he pleaded with Dr. Siegel, "When in God's name, when?"

"You'll know."

One tormented night Ron called Siegel at his Beverly Hills home, saying he had to talk to someone. "I called him at about 1:30 a.m. and talked to him until 5 a.m." Ron said, obviously much in appreciation of the Doctor's counsel.

After four days of unconsciousness, she roused on March 10th and called her son, Gregory in Jacksonville, Florida. Greg though fully aware that his mother was soon to die had never actually discussed it with her. It was to be their last conversation.

"You know I'm dying," she said.

Greg, who had been shuttling between his veterinarian practice in Jacksonville and her bedside for the past 30 months in response to the alarms of doctors, spoke affectionately to her.

"Is there anything I can do?"

"You're a veterinarian," his mother said, "I thought you might be able to fix up this old horse."

They talked about his wife and the practice and little bits of small talk, until finally she said, "This is my nickel — so I'm signing off now. I want you to remember something, though....remember that I love you."

Soon afterwards, she lost her speech.

Dr. Siegel visited her a total of fifteen times in the last 12 days of her life. Her bills were $100 a visit, to which Timothy objected strongly saying his mother would die whether or not Siegel was there and why did he have to come every day?

Louisa, who was friends with the housekeeper, called her to let her know that she was coming over to see Susan, and would she give her an all clear signal and let her in. The housekeeper was afraid to take the chance and when Lou appeared at the door, she told her she couldn't let her in.

On the night of Tuesday, March 11th an old speckled hoot owl perched on the diving board of the swimming pool under Susan's bedroom. When Ron saw it, he turned ice cold. He had remembered Susan telling him of the superstition that the appearance of an owl meant imminent death.

The hoot of the owl sound through the stillness of the night almost gave his heart palpitations, he was terrified that Susan would somehow hear it, but she lay still in her bed her hands clasping the crucifix that Eaton had held on his deathbed.

Stanly Cortez who had known Susan for over 25 years, the cameraman on so many of her movies, who had been very close to her came to see her for the last time, "Throughout it all, she was so brave, so typically Irish in her fighting spirit. I was in Susan's room to visit her a few days before she died. She was holding that crucifix in her hand, saying, in a faint whisper — 'Gotta work a little harder for me.' She looked up at me with that face that expression that always spoke a thousand words and breathed, 'Don't worry about me, Stan — I'll make it.'"

On Wednesday, March 12th, Susan was in a stupor all day and that night Ron was awake all night by her bedside and the same owl came back and sat by the pool on the diving board. When it began to hoot Ron ran through the house practically verging on a nervous breakdown. He found what he was looking for — an old shotgun. Standing by the pool, he aimed at the owl silhouetted against a sky lit by a new moon. Ron was shaking so badly from his nervous state that he missed the owl completely and even the blast from the gun failed to frighten the bird from its post.

The echoing of the gunshot brought the Beverly Hills police to Susan's home and after a bizarre explanation and knowing some of the circumstances of the dying actress — they gave him a warning not to fire the gun again, and left.

The owl screeched relentlessly throughout the night and Ron stared at it transfixed practically the whole time. He fell into slumber for a short period just before dawn and when he opened his eyes, the owl had gone.

On Thursday, March 13th, the owl returned for the third night in a row. Now Ron was waiting for its return, accepting it as, perhaps, some form of mystic messenger, hooting its message that Susan would soon be taken from the living, released from her pain and suffering. On this the third night, the owl could again be seen by the light of the fading new moon, and the following day, March 14th while Ron watched Susan clutching the cross against her body he had a sense of time standing still.

The new R.N., Sidney Miller, walked in and out of the room, but Ron was alone with Susan when the end came.

Suddenly, Susan was aroused from her inertia by a great inner storm as a massive seizure seemed to grip every part of her body. The muscle spasms that attacked her face, and clamped her jaws violently together, caused her to bite off part of her tongue; though much of it had been bitten off during several other seizures. With eyes bulging, her head wrenched sharply one last time and the spasms came to an abrupt halt. Ron paused a moment then checked her pulse. It was gone and the breathing had stopped.

Edythe Marrener Barker Chalkley, known to the world as Susan Hayward, rested peacefully at last. Ron's eyes were drawn to the 'insomniac's clock' it read 2:24 pm. For some reason he remembered that in the TV movie she had made, *Say Goodbye, Maggie Cole*, Susan, playing the part of a doctor, wrote down the time of death of her patient in the last scene. The time had been 2:24 pm.

Her films had involved many excruciating reprieves from moments of death and she had played a woman dying of a brain tumor, — a tormented alcoholic, a woman on crutches…and on and on — now that was probably all she would be remembered for, since she was always bound to lose this last fight in the end.

Ron picked up the bedroom phone and dialed Dr. Siegel. The doctor ordered him not to tell anyone. Just guard the body and let no one in the bedroom until he arrived.

Ron dipped his fingers in the bowl of Holy Water, which had been kept near Susan and administered extreme unction, according to instructions given to him by a local priest. He made the sign of the cross, gently touching her and closed her eyelids.

Then he sat in the armchair near the bed staring at the tiny figure wrapped in a pink blanket with her right arm stretched out clutching the cross and her heard turned to the left. She was still beautiful.

Now that she was laying there lifeless, the cancer that had consumed the flesh of her body seemed not so much to have affected her face, which was now relaxed and peaceful. Her long lashes, enhancing her vivid eyes, had remained despite the loss of her hair. He covered the top of her head with a pink chiffon scarf to hide the baldness, reached for his camera and took a last photograph of her.

Dr. Siegel slipped quietly into the room within the hour and told Ron his plan. He wanted to have an autopsy done as soon as possible. He — along with others in the medical profession — was astounded that Susan had remained alive for two years with malignant brain tumors that medical science had said should have taken her life within two weeks. Possibly, they might find within that corpse an answer to some peculiar cancer-delaying process to advance their search in helping others. Ron, having been associated with the Heart Association for years, understood his meanings.

Even in death, Susan perhaps to throw out another lifeline.

Siegel, Ron and Nurse Miller devised a plan to get Susan's body out of the house before the press found out about her death. They propped her corpse in a sitting position in her wheelchair and the pink chiffon scarf was removed and replaced by a red wig. Dark glasses were put on her face, and a wrap pulled over her shoulders and the cadaver was wheeled out of the house and into a waiting ambulance. A neighbor peering from a window could only surmise that Susan was being taken to the hospital for some further treatments.

Shortly afterwards, Ron called Timothy to notify him of his mother's death, and he took over from there, being quite adept at handling the media a necessary part of this operation. Ron went ahead with the funeral arrangements for her burial in Carrollton, according to her wishes. Timothy told reporters the funeral would be on Monday in Carrollton and actually planned it for Sunday.

Wally was on the freeway driving back from his job at the racetrack when he heard on the radio the news that his sister had died hours earlier.

"I asked Ron, if anything should happen to call me at work and I would come right home. He never did. I found out on the radio coming home from work and rushed right up there," said Wally. "She died Friday (March 14th) and late Friday night we were on the plane heading for Atlanta. Gregory and his wife came up from Jacksonville and Timothy and his wife, Ron Nelson and myself were on the plane with the body."

The autopsy at the hospital room was prepared for the arrival of Susan's body. The pathologist's knife found, as they had suspected, that the cancer had developed in the right lung and had spread to the brain. Nothing unusual was discovered to explain her amazing remissions and survival. It was concluded that the answer lay in her incredibly strong constitution, and her strong heart, which refused to release her until the biggest of the multiple brain tumors had snapped the vagus — or cranial nerve, which originates in the part of the brain that keeps the heart beating. The final massive seizure broke the vagus nerve link. Not to be overlooked was Susan's strength of character and her determination to hold on for as long as she could; this surely had to be just as responsible for the miracle of her survival.

That night, with Susan's body in the cargo compartment of the Delta flight out of L.A., Ron sat alone in the first class section, numbed, silently ruminating — Susan would have told him, "Have a drink on me. Come on Ronsy-Ponsy — it's all yesterday's spaghetti."

When the plane landed in Atlanta, newspapers at the airport magazine stands carried the headlines — SUSAN HAYWARD DEAD. The limousine drove the party to the Wedgewood Inn, not far from town, and took Susan's body to the Almon Funeral Home.

Susan had asked that she be buried in the gown that she had worn for her last academy award appearance — the one in which she had been seen in public for the last time. She had also requested that Frank Westmore make her up once more. Ron had the gown prepared and took it to the undertakers.

The following evening at 9:00 pm, there was a rosary in the chapel of the Funeral Home. The casket was closed and Ron asked that it be opened so that he could see her again for the last time. She looked quite beautiful, recreated as the illusion she had been for the millions of filmgoers. Frank Westmore's artistry was just perfect, though the bosom — because of the autopsy — looked puffy, stuffed with a pillow. To hide this, flowers were placed over her bosom and she held the rosary blessed by Pope John. The casket was bronze and of the same style — at her request — that Eaton had been buried in. Nelson recalled Susan complaining about the inflationary price, whereas Eaton's casket had cost $5,000, to her, a few years later, it was now $8,000.

Talking about her own death one day, Susan had said, "I've never thought about it much, but I don't suppose people will remember me very long. There's a new actress coming along every day. As a person, though, a few people will remember me and that's all that's important."

It seems only fitting that this book close with a farewell from Susan in the way she would have preferred with an expression that she used when she was parting from friends. She would look up at you with those big sad eyes and smile, "I'll see you in the funnie papers," — she would say and put her right hand up to her forehead in a salute — a farewell.

She lived like a star, worked like a trouper, and died a heroine. She was buried next to her beloved husband on the grounds where they had built a Catholic church, in the red clay of Georgia.

EPILOGUE

THE CLEO MILLER INTERVIEW
(NOVEMBER 1984)

The Beginning of Friendship

"I started workin' for her (Susan Hayward) in 1953 to 1957 — she was a doll. We moved down from one house to another house, 3737 Longridge ñ that's where the big battle took place, then she divorced him and we moved, a house away 3801 Longridge Avenue, and that's the house she tried to kill herself. They (other domestics) said, 'You working for Susan Hayward?' I said yes. 'You can't stay there. She threw a bowl of salad at one of her maid's head. That woman is the meanest one on the block. You can't stay there.' I said, she ain't thrown one at mine yet. I'll wait 'till the salad start to fly then I'll go. We got along beautifully, she loved me and I loved her. I went on location to Utah. I could have gone to many places (except) I was scared to fly. She wanted to take me to Hawaii, Florida, Hong Kong, all over and I wouldn't fly."

Authors note: Cleo had the very first flight in her life when Susan sent a car to her house, airline tickets, and had her brought to the plane, put on board and flown to Utah with her daughter Willie Jean.

Susan "The Breadwinner" and the Suicide Attempt

"We both ate together in the kitchen, smoke, the whole works. She talk to me confidential. She couldn't stand her mother, her mother was jealous, her mother thought she should give her more than what she was giving. Susan was the support. Wally was a small man, out at the race track. Florence wasn't doin' anything. Susan was the bread maker. The whole thing supporting Jess, the kids, mother, Wally and Florence…and he (Jess) said he got tired carryin' her bags for her on trips. She was doin'

BROOKLYN'S SCARLETT

the payin' and he was doin' the carryin' — so he got tired of carryin'. He was a louse. He was never any good. His own kids don't respect him. He used her. Her son Timothy called me up, he said, 'Cleo I don't know what to do with this old man, he can't even go on unemployment.' No, honey he can't go on unemployment 'cause he never worked enough to draw on unemployment. He said, 'I don't know what my old man's going to do. She stuck by him for ten years."

"My (Cleo's) husband, Mathew Miller, and I were sleeping in the maid's room. 3 o'clock there was a horrible knock on the door, which I didn't hear because I'm way back; maid's rooms are always in the back. When I wake up I hear all this rumblin' goin' on, they (detectives) had broken in the den door. There was Susan Hayward laying on the floor, nuthin' on but a terry cloth robe…I jumped outta' bed, threw a robe on and ran through the kitchen…he said, (the detective) 'Why didn't you answer the door?' I said who are you? What are you here for? 'I came — Susan Hayward attempted suicide.' I said you gotta be kiddin'. He said 'yes, she's laying on the living room floor dying.' I ran into the living room and here she was, one leg stretched out on the floor, the other rockin' and I waved my hands over her eyes and said, "Miss Hayward, Miss Hayward, this is Cleo honey. This is Cleo baby." She just kept smilin' and lookin' up at the ceiling. She was goin' very fast. They said, 'where's the bathroom.' I showed them, there were three bottles of pills; she had emptied every one of them into her body. She called her mother and said, Mother if anything happens to me, you ain't got nuthin' to worry about. You got it made! This is unknown to me at the present time. They had to take her out in the police car rush her to Cedars Lebanon. She called me the next day and she said 'Cleo, I goofed! I've been to hell and back. I died and came back.' That's what she told me."

"She was depressed. She was terribly, terribly unhappy. She loved Jess Barker. He just weren't the man she wanted him to be. She didn't know much about men. She didn't play around like the others. She was interested in her career. She wanted to be a good actress and she were. She was the best. But she was lonely. She was shy and withdrawn from the public but with the ones she loved that she wanted around, she trusted, she was a doll.

They sent Bette Davis' limousine to pick up Susan when she left the hospital, after she committed suicide and Bette Davis was mad. She blast them all out."

Susan and the Twins

"Timothy would listen behind doors — overhearing anything. Florence would come over with her son. Timothy called me and he wanted me to help him with his book about his mother and he said, 'you know a lot that happened in that house Cleo. I was a little boy. I don't remember, you can enlighten me on a lot of things that happened that I was too young to understand'.

With Florence, the boys were quite young and when they seen her a couple of times with her son they never gotten along because her boy was born of a German father. He was really rough and nasty and they always fight. So then Florence didn't come with the kid anymore, then she came to see Susan maybe 3-4 times. Timothy could be quite nasty, we would take them up to school when Mama was away on location and we'd pick them up. One time Timothy wanted to sleep out on the hill, behind the pool. I went to Arizona, my daughter was there. I let them sleep out and they camped and everything. So he talked to me all the way into Tucson the next day. He said, 'Cleo can we sleep out again tonight?' I said no, you can't sleep out again tonight because I'm not there and Willie Jean can't be responsible for you sleepin' out on the hill. He screamed 'You bitch!' He threw the phone down he didn't hang up. I said, he called me a bitch Willie Jean, call him back to the phone. She said he will not come back Mama. I said, OK leave him alone I'll take care of him when I come home 'cause he was goin' to the Chapman school up in the Bowen Hills and we'd have to give them the limousine to take them every week. So when I came home from Arizona I called the school and I talked to the principal. I said, now Gregory can come home on the next weekend but Timothy can't come home. Why not Cleo? I'll tell you why, we had a little misunderstanding on the telephone. I was out of town. He called me a bitch. I said, I don't want him home this weekend. Ok she said. Whatever you say. I went up in the limousine, picked up Gregory, brought him home kept him the whole weekend and left Timothy there. That was his punishment."

"When he came home on the next weekend, the limousine went back up to pick them up, my daughter went up with him, brought them down for the weekend. Timothy ran into the house threw his books down, threw his arms around my neck and said, 'I love you Cleo. I'm sorry I called you a bitch'. He was 10-11 so I never heard a bitch from him again I heard him call his mother a bitch when his mother was messin' around with this guy and that guy after the divorce. Tim was Susan's favorite. She loved them both but she loved Timothy more. So he said, 'you bitch'! He had that down fine, he loved to say bitch. Susan didn't punish him, she just talked to him."

Susan and Jess Barker

"Jess was in the Valley, around Studio City, down Coldwater CanyonÖ.. the old house where they had the fight before the divorce. When I came back-from my day off — the house was a mess. Ok, I didn't know what's goin' on until Susan Hayward walks in with black and blue eyes, beat all over her body and the flowers was all over the floor so I knew somethin' terrible took place. The fight was over the money 'cause he had approached her, this what she told me. She told me he ask her to loan him $3,000 or so many thousands of money. He wanted to buy some shares in Dallas, Texas oil. She said, 'No, you go out and get yourself a job'. He said, 'I'm an actor!' So what do you want me to be a department store clerk or a filling station attendant. She said, whatever, if it's an honest living. But I am not going to let you have the money.' That's when the fight came. I was off that night. My sister worked in my place. Always had somebody to replace me when I wasn't there. When I was, then I'd get the kids off to school in the morning, make their lunch, get them breakfast, teeth brushed, the whole works, get them off to school. Then I get his note, on the cabinet, wake me up Cleo at one o'clock with my juice. I go to his bedroom with his juice, and he's in bed nude, of course he's covered, but he's nude. He comes in the kitchen and drinks two pots of coffee, sat there and yap, yap, yap, yap all day. He said to me one day, 'if anybody had said to me in Georgia, sitting under my grandfather's pecan trees that I would be sitting on my fanny today I never would have believed it'. I said, Really Now!"

"He'd get dressed bout 3 o'clock and go to the market and bring home the green stuff and the food for dinner. I'd prepare the dinner. He'd sit and read his paper and at 12 o'clock he'd go out and get the late paper and he'd read 'til 6 o'clock in the morning. He didn't go to bed until daylight. That was the whole time I was there — more or less. He had dinner with the boys, because Susan was often late coming home from the studio, very seldom she'd be home on time for dinner 'cause the boys had to be in bed by 8-8:30."

"He threw her in the pool, over the money, she had a terry cloth robe on, no clothes at all underneath. He threw her in and she swim to the other side. He go over and poke her down in the pool. The black girl next door who was living in also, it was her night on. She saw the whole stuff.

She was in court with us. She testified to it. I was in court but never had to testify. I was there every day but I was never called. She (Susan) aimed at him with a cigarette. The judge said, 'did you poke him in the eye with the cigarette?' 'No, I didn't but I aimed.' Like that — we smoked the same I'm a chain smoker too."

"He acted like a queer, in fact her mother called him a queer. She said, there's something wrong with that man with his swishin' butt. He was always swishin', so she thought there was something queer about him. The mother never liked him 'cause he was a bum. He was really a bum, I'm sorry to say it but he was a bum! He drank Vat 69. He'd start about 4-5 o'clock in the afternoon. No, not during the day, he drank coffee all day, then the booze in the afternoon. And all the rest of the night. No, the mother didn't come too often 'cause she and Susan didn't get along too well, and the mother didn't like him. She'd only visit when Susan went to New York, going to Europe vacations, or away doin' a picture. I was there with the children, the mother would come down to stay with me and be there on my days off. She was on the prejudice side. She thought I was a black gal takin' over Susan's home. But I had my chores, things to do, and Susan and me got along very well. When she was home I'd take her orange juice too and we'd sit on the bed reading dream books. 'What did you dream last night Cleo?' She'd ask so excited I'd dream so and so... What did you dream Susan? I'd dream so and so and we'd compare our dreams. Horoscope everything, look up the story...and she'd tell me all her secrets."

"She had quite a temper, she's a Cancer, Cancer people got a temper. She told me I didn't know men had big ones, short ones, medium size. She didn't know 'cause she never experienced it. She was only used to Jess Barker. Everything she knew about a man was Jess Barker until she divorced him. She just didn't play around with the other guys."

Susan and Superstitious

"Susan threw salt over her shoulder if she spilled it; said a man was coming if a fork dropped, etc."

"The cutest thing, when she was goin' for that Oscar for "I'll Cry Tomorrow" — she broke a mirror. I said, 'Miss Hayward let me go and bury this mirror', 'cause we were goin' to have our big party at the house, and catered it, she got a beautiful gown for the occasion and were goin' to have a big party afterward. The Academy thing that night 'cause she was so sure she gonna' win. So she breaks this mirror, I picked it all up and I said, let me take it down and bury it on its face, break the spell and you'll have good luck. You, Cleo, superstitious? I said, well you know you're up for the academy so you better let me go bury it on the face to bring good luck. So she said, 'No, on Cleo superstitions. Ok, I didn't bury it, threw it away. She didn't win it. She came home and cried on my shoulder and said, I should have listened to you Cleo. I should have let you bury the mirror the way you said'.

She was lookin' forward to it, she was sure she's gonna' win this time. This big party, in this $100,000 home, all the food and the people came and she came home and she had lost."

John Wayne, Howard Hughes, and Eaton Chalkley

"She wasn't too friendly with the movie stars; she didn't have parties in her home. She didn't like entertaining, she didn't like to go out to entertainments. No, John Wayne never visited the house. No movie screen in the house, just TV. She didn't glory in these fabulous things most people did. She threw away a $3,000 diamond in the desert of Utah. She went out riding in a car with John Wayne one night, and my daughter. She pulled it off 'cause she was in the process of divorce at that present time, A great big diamond wedding ring -square big diamond, she throw it out in the desert. No, Jess never gave her that, he never had that much money she bought it herself. And you can believe that me and my daughter walked down in 120∞ heat the next day. She said, maybe you'll find it somewhere on the freeway on the side of the road, if you can find it you can keep it. We didn't. We was in St. George, Utah, there's no black people, Indians, Mormons, and stuff like that. John Wayne and Susan had a house, he lived about a block from her, we had a lot of fun. She kicked him all the way to the house one night. You know he married Pillar, he and Pillar were shakin' together at that time, that was before they were married. Oh, yeah! Susan had a crush on him. We had a party at the Wayne house. Susan pulled off her shoes and said Pillar let's fight. She made him take her down to her house which is a block away and she kicked him in the butt all the way down. Then they got in the car, that night, the night she threw away the diamond."

"Howard Hughes, yes, I was in his company I'll say 6 to 9 months. I served him dinner in the dining room. He was kinda cold, you know, he's southern, not so hot on Negroes any way. (Cleo was born 125 miles from Dallas in a little town near Jacksonville). But he was nice — sometimes. Susan felt sorry for Hughes and always had Cleo bake him an apple pie and he would eat the whole thing. But Susan would pump him up. I had my little nephew out there and she said, 'Oh, Howard look at this nice little ole baby, isn't he sweet'. He went ohhhh, moanin' and held back like he was scared it was goin' to rub off on him. Honey, he didn't make it with any of those women. He couldn't make it with any. I don't know his story. He was shy. I don't know whether because of sex, but he was a shy, sexless man. He brought her yellow roses, beautiful yellow roses, dozens and dozens. Yellow roses, that were her favorite. Other than that I don't know what else she got (she laughs wickedly). She wasn't a flashy woman, she didn't deal in wealth like the others."

"My family came to visit and she said, 'invite them here Cleo, they can sleep in any bed they want to sleep in, cook them anything you want, there's a freezer full of food if not I'll order it.' She said 'your Mama and Daddy can stay here with you'. So my mom and dad and any of my relations come from out of state stay in Susan Hayward's home. Oh, she was a doll. (This drove Eaton mad and they had cutting arguments.) He was goin' around with Susan before they was married. He came to the house, stayed there. He'd come in from Georgia, spend maybe a week at a time. They would go up to Big Bear and spend some time there. He just couldn't stand her servants because we all was black. This one incident — Susan told my husband Matthew to have a beer, to go to the bar and get a beer, which she knew he liked, she always offered him one, and meanwhile open a bottle of champagne, 'cause they were leavin' that night for Big Bear. That night after they left they got into a big fight but not before us. He gave her hell, he said, 'I don't like your servants'. She said, 'Why? What's wrong with them? 'They are Negroes and I don't believe in negroes speakin' until they are spoken to. He was a bachelor and only paid his housekeeper $30 a month. They went to Big Bear, they had this fight and she left him in Big Bear. She came home and she told me, Well — it's all over between Chalkley and me. But it weren't all over because in a week they made up again. The next thing I knew she was announcing they were goin' to get married".

Susan's Gifts

"She had a heart of gold. She loved us so much. She loved my children, my daughter, Willie Jean, she was 17 years old. I said, Miss Hayward I'm livin' out here and my daughter is in the city and I'm worried about her runnin' around not bein' supervised. So Susan and I talked it over and she said, 'let her come here. She can take care of the boys. She can be the second maid. She can have room and board and I'll give her a salary'. She'd take the boys biking in the hills, go to the movies, she did all the small errands. So my daughter worked under me for 5 years. Susan gave me that break so I can bring my daughter from a rough city where I can keep an eye on her. Yes, she slept right upstairs with the boys. She look after 'em just like a second mother. No, Susan wasn't tough on the boys. Sometimes I'd tell her when they got me upset. She said, 'well Cleo, the kids gotta' throw off steam just like us grownups'."

"When my baby came, my baby Pamela was the first black baby that ever went to a doctor in Van Nuys. They didn't have no black patients. So she called up and got an appointment for my baby. She paid all the doctorr's bills, bought all the food, all the milk. She said, 'this is my adopted daughter'. So we goes down to Studio City and Susan says, 'Cleo let's go buy Pamela some clothes'. She's about 2 months old. She bought her a new baby bed. So, we goes to Studio City to Babytown. She bought little shoes, little clothes and this English carriage, great big beautiful thing, with the shield over it. So she goes over to the cashier, the sales girl says, 'Oh, Miss Hayward I didn't know you had a new baby. Susan says, 'Oh, didn't you know it honey. I had it by Sammy Davis, Jr.'

Gang, Kopp & Tyre — Attorneys arranged the adoption papers (April 4, 1957).

Pamela went around tellin' all these black kids Susan Hayward is my Auntie, these black kids in the neighborhood. You gotta be a nut, they told her, as black as you are, how can Susan Hayward be your Auntie."

"Willie Jean did sleep upstairs with the boys. We didn't have enough room. My husband and I had one bedroom, the maid's room. The first house was small, only 3 bedrooms, 2 downstairs. The second house had 17 rooms, pool houses, and dressing room, a whole hill, cost $100,000.

She didn't care about money, she never cared about money. One day she dropped $150 in the driveway in a paper bag. I found it layin' out there, this is your money, Oh, I guess I dropped it getting out of the car. She did some shoppin' and just dropped some money change in the paper bag…"

"I was at Fox, MGM, Paramount, I been on all these sets and Jess took me in one day. She was doin' Bathsheba, I was out there all day watching her and watchin' them kill each other. She wanted me to play the Negro part in "The President's Lady", the maid, the black woman. I wouldn't take it, even her mother got on me about that, she said, 'Cleo, why don't you accept it, Susan wants you so much'. I said, 'I don't think I can make it', but they needed a woman who could speak southern and I'm southern. I wish I had now, after I grew older. I must a been 'bout 33 at that time. I felt my education might not bring me up to the part. I was afraid I would embarrass everybody and myself. I was afraid I couldn't remember the lines."

Susan and Loyalty

Authors note: What was amusing was how Cleo would read scripts with Susan in the living room, often playing Gregory Peck, John Wayne or whatever co-star Susan co-starred with. Sometimes they would reverse roles and Susan would take the male leads and Cleo, in that southern way, would be Susan. Of course, they had a great time doing it, laughing, nevertheless Susan learned her part. Also Susan would help her with the big words and her reading.

"A little ole girl came from outta' state and sat on my back step for a whole day wantin' to get Susan's autograph. Susan was home that day. I say, Miss Hayward, please write somethin' on this piece of paper for this kid so she can go away. She said, 'when I'm home, I'm home. If they want to get in touch with me, they can go through The Screen Actor's Guild, the studio; all my fan mail goes there. I'm not taking it here. This is my house. When I'm home, I'm private; I don't want to be bothered with people'. Now, Susan Hayward was shy, very shy, she shied away from people and never wanted anyone to see her before she was made up. She was proud of her hair and her boobs. Nice figure, skinny legs like me."

"I took the children to the Baptist Church, she didn't go. I took them to be baptized in Van Nuys. John Wayne and his wife, Roy Rogers and his wife belonged to the same church in Van Nuys. Every Sunday morning I'd get 'em up and take them to Sunday school to the Baptist Church. I never know Susan to attend the church, she believed but she didn't attend. But she wanted the kids to have that background of religion."

"I got her juice one morning, and there was this old man at 6 o'clock in the morning on the couch, I never been so shocked in all my life. So she must have been really out of it that night in alcohol. She was drinking heavy, even went out to the car with no make up on, so this day she walked him to the car, he was all crippled, on crutches, she stayed down in the livin' room with all night. He worked at the studio, somethin' to do with the studio 20th Century Fox, but I forgot. That was the only one time. She eat very good. She liked steak, salad, fresh vegetables, desserts. She started on wine before she got goin' on another picture. She got off the heavy booze and got on the wine. She said wine kept her weight down."

"The last Christmas tree we had in 1956 touched the ceiling, she had a high beamed ceiling. It cost $55, the Christmas tree. We had a little lady named Martha Little. Martha Little was a doll. She came down every year to decorate; she was so artistic with her hands. She could make anything out of a weed, a flower, a branch, with her hands, so Miss Hayward would always pay her a salary to come down from New York to do our Christmas decorations. Oh, we had fabulous Christmas, the most gorgeous Christmas presents on the Christmas branch with a couple of hundred dollars in it, my name on it. Sarah came too and after her sister died, the last Christmas Martha was there, I made her breakfast, 2 soft boiled eggs, I'll never forget, a piece of toast and a cup of coffee. She said, 'Cleo, this the last Christmas I'll be with you'. I said, 'no Miss Martha honey'. I put my arms around her, we hugged and kissed. Sarah came after her sister died and she decorated the tree."

Susan and the final days with Cleo

Susan pleaded with Cleo to come with them to Georgia to be her housekeeper.

"I just refuse to go to Georgia. The farther south you go down south, the worse it got. Susan said, 'I'll change things, I'll change the law", in front of Chalkley. He said, 'They'll burn crosses on your lawn'. Her lawyer got me to sign a paper. I didn't read it. The next day she said, "Girl, I put you in my will."

"When she moved to Georgia she dumped everything. She didn't want to take with her, the old days, you know. She was married to Chalkley and got rid of the diary and she said, 'Cleo, anything you want here you can have, anything you don't want here dump it. I came across the diary so I collected it. It were a high school diary. She were 63 when she died. Jess looked through all my stuff. How'd you get all this stuff Cleo? This is all I want. I would love to have the diary. I don't have no use for the diary so I gave it to him. I didn't realize it — didn't mean anything to me at the present time, it was her private life. Yes she was 63, which the diary proved. 63 when she died not 56…63. I know how old she is, they quoted 55, you know how people do. They don't quote the real age. I saw the passport, the diary and she told me".

"I saw her on TV at the academy awards, you saw how ill she was. One day Jess called me from the Beverly Hills home and that was the last time I talked with her. He said, 'Cleo, I have someone I'd like to have talk to you'. I said, Oh, who? He said, 'I'll let you hear the voice. She spoke to me and told me how much she loved Chalkley and Jess were there. She said, 'Oh Cleo I loved my husband so much'. I begged her to let me come see her and she said, 'I'll let you know. I didn't want her to think I wanted anything from her; I wanted to visit her, be with her, comfort her, whatever I could do for her. She wouldn't let me — see her that way".

"We got boxes and boxes of fan mail and she said, 'Go ahead Cleo and dump it'. I said, is it all right if I open it. She said, sure-do anything you want with it. I found money — 50 cents, sometimes dollars, quarters, I collected much money out of the fan mail. Paintings, pictures, all kind of stuff. She didn't want no parts of it. They would send money for an autograph she never returned photographs. She didn't have the time but she had a studio girl to take care of all this but a portion of the mail come to the house. So we all collected boxes for them, there was money in just about every letter and if I hadn't just took the boxes I would have dumped all the money. I said, Miss Hayward these letters have money. She said, you keep it. I was opening mail like mad, every letter had change in it, and from all over the world".

"Susan gave me a bonus when she went to Georgia and with that I purchased a home in the San Fernando Valley. I saw her a few times after she left, she called me. He (Chalkley) was snobbish, he kept us apart. Timothy asked me to help him write a book on his Mama. He was so mad over the separation. He wanted to exploit his mother. I said to him, 'You don't want to do that honey. He said, yes I do'. I said I know a lot of dirty things that went on. He knew I knew. He wanted me to put in the loose ends, he didn't remember 'cause he was a little boy."

Author Notes: They — Jess and Timothy love to come to dinner. I make charcoal broiled steaks, or southern fried chicken, tossed green salad, apple pie, sweet potato pie, all kinds of pies, we do a lot of things. I'll get 'em here and you (this author) come over. I'll get them to talk to you, if I can find him. (This never happened).

Susan Hayward could never forget the depression years, the Flatbush neighborhood where she lived as a girl. Neither could Cleo: "She (Susan) goes down every day to get day old bread, she helps Wally, shine shoes, throw papers, that's how tough it were. Her father worked on the railroad. They were very, very poor livin' in Brooklyn. That's how tough her life was, that's how she came up. She was tryin' to make somethin' of herself."

Pulitzer Prize Winner Ed Montgomery. Twice President of the San Francisco Press Club, who†was also responsible for the story of Barbara

Graham which won the Academy Award for Susan Hayward in "I Want To Live", remembered vividly, when he went to stay with the Chalkley's in Georgia (in 1958). He recalled…"It's just possible that Miss Hayward had in mind the role she never got to play. Scarlett O'Hara, had in mind the home Tara, with the columns and all when she and Eaton Chalkley built their new home there in Georgia. Come to think about it it's very much like the plantation in "Gone With the Wind."

Possibly Susan was exorcising figments of her childhood. And as the Flatbush beauty who lost out on Scarlett but, finally, became a Southern Belle she wanted to recreate, in some way, a lost dream, a memory that lived within her, when she came to the home she really wanted with the one man she truly loved.

Grauman's Chinese Theatre, August 1951.

FILMOGRAPHY

Hollywood Hotel
December 1937, Warner Bros.
D: Busby Berkeley
Hello from Hollywood: Louella Parsons takes her radio program, and herself, to the screen. Highlights 30's Hollywood places of interest, including exterior of famed Hollywood Hotel on Hollywood Blvd. — Dick Powell, Lola and Rosemary Lane and Hollywood hopefuls, along with 19 year old Susan Hayward, as cinemaella to Louella's fairy godmother.

The Sisters
October 1938, Warner Bros.
D: Anatole Litvak
Good period piece. Three sisters and their soap-opera loves. Nice Bette Davis, naughty Errol Flynn, great Frisco quake. Susan unbilled as telephone operator, and unseen every time it's shown — must have been out to lunch. Anita Louise; Jane Bryan; Henry Travers; and Beulah Bondi. *(95 minutes)*

Girls on Probation
October 1938, Warner Bros.
D: William McGann
Prison and probation 'B' melodrama with Jane Bryan and Ronald Reagan — "a lightweight as District Attorney, is perhaps a little too soft for that kind of job." Susan got 10th billing and a pardon for inexperience. *(63 minutes)*

Comet Over Broadway
December 1938, Warner Bros.
D: Busby Berkeley
Faith Baldwin story fashioned for Kay Frances. Starlet Susan, a walk on. No billing, no mention. Ian Hunter. CAMERA: James Wong Howe.

Beau Geste
July 1939, Paramount Studio
D: William A. Wellman
Susan fifth billed as Bel-Ami to brothers Geste, and Bel-Amour to one — Ray Milland. A pretty and patient ingénue, had little to do and does it forgetably. Gary Cooper; Robert Preston; and Brian Donlevy. *(120 minutes)*

Our Leading Citizen
July 1939, Paramount Studio
D: Alfred Santell
A Bob Burns (Will Rogers type) vehicle. Paramount apprentice Susan decorative as his daughter. Romantic interest was newcomer Joseph Allen Jr., who went on to *It Happened in Flatbush,* and oblivion. Elizabeth Patterson; Gene and Kathleen Lockhart; and Charles Bickford. *(87 minutes)*

$1,000 A Touchdown
October 1939, Paramount Studio
D: James Hogan
What used to be tagged a lightweight programmer. Two of the biggest mouths in the movies, Joe E. Brown and Martha Raye, took up most of the screen, squeezing out Eric Blore and fourth billed Susan. *(71 minutes)*

Adam Had Four Sons
March 1941, Columbia
D: Gregory Ratoff
Warner Baxter had four sons and Susan, as nymphomaniac Hester, wanted them all. Susan a standout, under Ratoff's direction, as the scheming, conniving wife of Johnny Downs. Saintly Ingrid Bergman comes to the rescue, but not until 23 year old Susan and the audience gets their kicks. (80 minutes)

Sis Hopkins
April 1941, Republic
D: Joseph Santley
A Judy Canova hayseed special, with Jerry Colonna. Cooked up Canova corn for her fans. Susan 5th billed as snotty, society debutante until she finds her true hillbilly heart. Picture cost half million, "It Ain't Hay," one of the songs played by Bob Crosby and band. *(97 minutes)*

Among The Living
August 1941, Paramount Studio
D: Stuart Heisler

Picture a sleeper. Susan second billed over Frances Farmer. Susan, at 23, plenty sharp as Millie Perkins — a sociological study, as the clothes hungry sexy daughter, of a rooming housekeeper, who nearly gets herself strangled by the unsuspected killer Albert Dekker, as twins, who also got good notices. Richard Webb; Harry Carey; and Maude Eburne. *(68 minutes)*

Reap The Wild Wind
March 1942, Paramount Studio
D: Cecil B. DeMille

De Mille's 30th anniversary production. Susan, 7th billed, is Drusilla, secondary romantic interest to Robert Preston, left firsthand impression. Best acting honors go to giant rubber squid who wraps up the picture with all ten arms. Susan's first with John Wayne, and Technicolor — looking lush. Paulette Goddard; Ray Milland; and Charles Bickford. *(124 minutes)*

The Forest Rangers
September 1942, Paramount Studio
D: George Marshall

Susan third billed over Albert Dekker, this time, is pert and sassy snitching scenes from Fred MacMurray's fiancée Paulette Goddard. The threesome bedding down for the night just passed the Hayes office by a pine needle, in those days. Susan's red-headed spark and a forest fire keep the picture hot in color. *(87 minutes)*

I Married A Witch
October 1942, United Artists
D: Rene Clair

Veronica Lake, of the peek-a-boo-bang, is the witch; Susan, with hair pins in place, the bitch — a cool, society snob. Camera Witchcraft effects, best thing going for it. Fredric March; Robert Benchley. *(82 minutes)*

Star Spangled Rhythm
December 1942, Paramount Studio
D: George Marshall

A Christmas tree of 16 Paramount stars, to boost wartime morale, 20 featured players, including Susan, doing a swing shift number for defense. A swell movie, even more fun to watch today. Bing Crosby; Betty Hutton; Preston Sturges; Cecile B. DeMille; Bob Hope; Mount Rushmore and Old Glory. *(99 minutes)*

Young and Willing
February 1943, United Artists
D: Edward H. Griffith

Six stage-struck kids out to break Broadway. Susan fourth billed vamps producer/chef Robert Benchley — apartment below — for big chance. Interesting today, to watch the young and willing players on their way up. William Holden; Eddie Bracken; Barbara Britton; and Martha O'Driscoll. *(82 minutes)*

Hit Parade of 1943
March 1943, Republic
D: Albert S. Rogell

Susan is Jill Wright, a talented tunesmith. John Carroll a two timing plagiaristic lothario. Eve Arden is Eve Arden — a highlight. Variety show 'mostly colored'. Count Basie, Dorothy Dandridge and Harlem talent Freddie Martin, Ray McKinley orchestras. This movie is often shown, by Susan's friends, on the anniversary of her death because in it she appears so young, vivacious and happy. Retitled *Change of Heart* for TV, from the Oscar nominated song. *(90 minutes)*

Jack London
November 1943, United Artists
D: Alfred Santell

Susan's entry into a series of biographical ladies. Susan, as Charmian Kittedge, London's second wife, in period costume, upswept hairdo, is lovely and ladylike but on screen only last half of film, unfortunately. Mrs. Jack London visited Susan on set during shooting. Michael O'Shea; Virginia Mayo; and Louise Beavers. *(92 minutes)*

The Fighting Seabees
January 1944, Republic
D: Howard Lydecker

Susan with World War II hairdo is wire service correspondent Constance Chesley who gets her wires crossed between Dennis O'Keefe and John Wayne. Triangle gets untangled when Navy Hero Wayne gets killed fighting Japs. Plenty of action for Wayne fans. *(100 minutes)*

The Hairy Ape
May 1944, United Artists
D: Alfred Santell

Susan returns in role as snobbish, spoiled, selfish daughter of a steel tycoon, while travelling on a freighter, she sees stoker Bill Bendix, calls him 'a hairy ape', and engages in brain over brawn gutter dialogue. Good adaptation of Eugene O'Neill play, impressive Hayward 40's acting style. John Loder and Dorothy (Mrs. Citizen Kane) Comingore. *(92 minutes)*

And Now Tomorrow
November 1944, Paramount Studio
D: Irving Pichel

Loretta Young suffering from mastoiditis finds love with shanty town doctor Alan Ladd, who restores her hearing. Susan, as Young's younger sister, tries to be bad but script won't let her. Familiar tale well told, Beula Bondi; Cecil Kellaway; and Helen Mack. *(84 minutes)*

Deadline At Dawn
February 1946, RKO
D: Harold Clurman

Top billed Susan is June, a dime-a-dance joint hostess, who picks up a dumb but sweet sailor, Bill Williams, involved in a New York murder. The couple team up as Nick and Nora to find out who done it. Picture tries to be arty. Wise cookie Susan interesting to observe. *(83 minutes)*

Canyon Passage
July 1946, Universal
D: Jacques Thourneu

Walter Wanger's Technicolor western filmed in Oregon. Indian fight-ing with pauses for songs by Hoagy Carmichael. Susan, third billed, as Lucy Overmire simmers with unrequited love for Dana Andrews. In color she is competition for beautiful scenery. Brian Donlevy, Patricia Roc. *(90 minutes)*

Smash-Up, The Story Of A Woman
February 1947, Universal
D: Stuart Heisler

Susan's lost weekend. As chanteuse Angelica Evans, 29 year old Susan gets biggest break to date as girl who becomes a dipsomaniac to overcome her inferiority complex. Cast overshadowed by her histrionics — she steals everything but the props. Reward — best actress nomination. Lee Bowman; Eddie Albert; Marsha Hunt; and Producer Walter Wanger. *(113 minutes)*

They Won't Believe Me
July 1947, RKO
D: Irving Pichel

Weak married playboy Robert Young and the three women in his life. Susan is Verna, a file clerk, who fools around with Young, goes straight and gets killed in a car crash. A budget picture that scores, for all con-cerned. Rita Johnson and Jane Greer exceptional. *(95 minutes)*

The Lost Moment
October 1947, Universal
D: Martin Gabel

Demented in Venice. Susan, as Tina, goes schizophrenic over dead poet's love letters. When she's normal her hair is up, when it's down she becomes unbalanced. Fire, attempted murder, and 105 year old Agnes Moorehead add up to a moody yet fascinating movie. Beautifully lensed and scored. Robert Cummings; Joan Lorring; John Archer. Susan delighted in panning this film, but it's a lot better than she made it out to be. *(89 minutes)*

Tap Roots
August 1948, Universal
D: George Marshall

Mississippi belle Susan fights both the North and South during the civil war. As the neutral Morna Dabny, she uses sex as a sacrifice for the cause, and with tossing shoulder length red hair, in color, she plays it to the hilt. Van Heflin; Boris Karloff; Ward Bond. A Walter Wanger color epic. *(109 minutes)*

I Can Get It For You Wholesale
March 1951, 20th Century Fox
D: Michael Gordon

Scheming Susan in the New York garment trade, ambitious to the last stitch, she wises up before it's too late to a smooth finish. Dan Dailey; George Sanders. Filmed in New York City. *(91 minutes)*

I'd Climb the Highest Mountain
May 1951, 20th Century Fox
D: Henry King

Sweet Susan, as minister's wife Mary, in the Georgia countryside. Heartwarming episodes, in color, set against the red clay hills makes for charming family movie — the kind they hardly make anymore. William Lundigan; Rory Calhoun; Barbara Bates; and Lynn Bari. *(88 minutes)*

David and Bathsheba
August 1951, 20th Century Fox
D: Henry King

Susan and God. As Bathsheba Susan makes her biblical debut becoming King David's obsession. Susan looks more solemn than sinful. A peeping Gregory Peck eyes the temptress bathing, and from then on all holy laws are broken. Israel was never the same. Raymond Massey, Jayne Meadows. *(153 minutes)*

With A Song In My Heart
April 1952, 20th Century Fox
D: Walter Lang

Susan's 3rd biographical role as songstress Jane Froman, crippled in a plane crash, courageously returns to show business. Moving drama gave Robert Wagner, as shell shock soldier, his stardom. Thelma Ritter as nurse Clancy, from Flatbush, a joy. Susan punches over the vocal simulation of Froman's voice masterfully, received many awards, scoring her third Oscar nomination, at age 34. A Technicolor box office smash. Rory Calhoun; David Wayne; and Helen Westcott. *(117 minutes)*

The Snows of Kilimanjaro
September 1952, 20th Century Fox
D: Henry King

A travelogue in cinemascope and color of Ernest Hemingway short story. Gregory Peck and Ava Gardner, out front all the way, until the closing sequence where Susan comes wonderfully into her own. Hildegarde Neff. *(114 minutes)*

Untamed
March 1955, 20th Century Fox
D: Henry King

Susan, is Katie O'Neill, a kin to Scarlett O'Hara, who goes to South African, fights Zulu warriors and generally goes through hell, looking sublime throughout in period costume, with a follow-that-horse determination. This one would have been tough on any actress but gutsy Susan achieved the improbable. Tyrone Power, Richard Egan. *(111 minutes)*

Soldier of Fortune
May 1955, 20th Century Fox
D: Edward Dmytryk

Red China next stop: Susan's, Vinnie Holt, husband disappears on a photographic trip, she goes to Hong Kong to find him (on the back lot) while seeking help from Clark Gable. What should have been a hot team as seen in the studio tests, only steams in the final takes. Gene Barry, Michael Rennie. Cinemascope and color. *(96 minutes)*

I'll Cry Tomorrow
December 1955, MGM
D: Daniel Mann

This is it! Susan, as a soul in torment, plays alcoholic singer Lillian Roth, who came back. Susan's own song belting, powerful acting from the heights to the depths of skid row, at 38, gives the performance of her life. A can't miss Oscar — that did! Danny Mann's direction -superb. Jo Van Fleet; Richard Conte; and Eddie Albert. Susan wins foreign award. *(117 minutes)*

The Conqueror
March 1956, RKO
D: Dick Powell

Howard Hughes's version of "The Khan and I". A sex and sand camp classic. John Wayne, as the Mongol leader Gengis Kahn and Susan as his desired hot-blooded Tartar Princess, were never more marvelously miscast. Susan even does a hooch dance to stay in the mood. However tragic consequences, from filming near an atomic blast fall out, dissuade one's enjoyment. Agnes Moorehead, Pedro Armendariz, cinemascope and color. *(111 minutes)*

Top Secret Affair
January 1957, Warner Bros.
D: H.C. Potter

Susan tries comedy role in a light, harmless, slapstick quickie. As magazine publisher, Dottie Peal, she is out to bring General Kirk Douglas, "Old Ironpants", to his knees. Best scene, a tipsy Susan doing a balancing act on a diving board. Paul Stewart, Jim Backus. *(100 minutes)*

I Want To Live
October 1958, United Artists
D: Robert Wise

No other actress could have done it! Susan, as Barbara Graham, party girl, convicted of prostitution, perjury, and murder reached new stature as an actress. The gas chamber scenes make a powerful indictment against capital punishment, Susan's work, at 41, received unanimous acclaim including Oscar, after 5 nominations, and about time. Bravo! Simon Oakland, Virginia Vincent, Theodore Bikel. Incisive wise direction. *(120 minutes)*

Thunder in the Sun
April 1959, Paramount Studio
D: Russell Rouse

Susan is ridiculous as Gabrielle Dauphine, with a French/Flatbush accent burning up the road in a covered wagon with a cargo of grapevines. No greater love than she that lay her career, for Brooklyn school chum Jeff Chandler, who gives her the hot and cold Basque treatment. Susan with eyes flashing, bosom heaving, stomps out a wine festival dance, between Indian fighting and a grape crushing break. Jacques Bergerac. *(81 minutes)*

Woman Obsessed
May 1959, 20th Century Fox
D: Henry Hathaway

We now find Susan, Mary Sharron, in Northeastern Canada. As the angry widow who remarries for the sake of her fatherless son, all she has to do in this one is fight a forest fire, a blizzard, her new husband and the script. Nature wins out in cinemascope and color. Hayward and Hathaway square off again. Stephen Boyd, Theodore Bikel, Barbara Nichols. *(103 minutes)*

The Marriage-Go-Round
January 1961, 20th Century Fox
D: Walter Lang

As a college professor's wife, in Florida, Susan manages to keep their Swedish houseguest, a sexy smorgasbord amazon, away from her hungry husband. As the understanding, wisecracking spouse, content, Susan appears anything but. James, Mason, Julie Newmar. *(98 minutes)*

Ada
July 1961, MGM
D: Daniel Mann

Susan, as Ada Dallas, a trollop from down on the farm becomes lieutenant governor of Georgia by default — Governor Dean 'Bo' Martin's, to be precise. As the reformed prostitute and first lady Susan cleans up political graft and corruption, putting a high voltage charge into her lines, and figure as dressed by Helen Rose. Director Mann gambol's for fun. *(109 minutes)*

Back Street
October 1961, Universal
D: David Miller

Susan moves to a luxurious back street address for the love of gorgeous but wed, John Gavin, glamorous Jean Louis clothes, and career independence, which most women would kill for. But she's miserable because she had everything but a wedding ring. As the long suffering other woman she follows' her lover all over Europe, first class, in the artificial world of producer Ross Hunter. Women love its soap operatics and *Back Street* is popular TV fare today. Vera Miles, Virginia Grey. *(107 minutes)*

I Thank A Fool
September 1962, Metro-Goldwyn-Mayer
D: Robert Stevens

Susan's back in jail, this time in London, on a murder charge for unprofessional medical practice. Seems her mercy killing when as a Canadian doctor, who follows her lover to England is under question. So is the picture, an implausible mish-mash that foolish Susan had no one to thank for. Peter Finch, Diane Cilento. Cinemascope and color. *(100 minutes)*

Stolen Hours
October 1963, United Artists
D: Daniel Petrie

Susan now takes on a remake of the 1939 Bette Davis classic *Dark Victory*. Made in Britain, it is visually effective, as is Susan as the doomed Laura, a woman facing death as a result of a brain disease. In retrospect it cannot help but arouse compassion when viewed today. A fated irony of the real life tragedy to come of Susan's own illness. Unconditionally guaranteed — a good cry at the end. Michael Craig. Color. *(97 minutes)*

Where Love Has Gone
November 1964, Paramount Studio
D: Edward Dmytryk

Susan in San Francisco is, Valerie Hayden Miller, a successful sculptress with a lot of overtime for sex. Bette Davis is her aristocratic mother, and their scenes together sizzle. Plot thickens when Susan's daughter stabs her lover — a script out of the headlines of that famous movie queen. Susan pays for all the fun, she's had in the script, by stabbing herself with a chisel, which should have pleased Bette Davis. Michael Connors; Jane Greer; and Joey Heatherton. Cinemascope and color. *(114 minutes)*

The Honey Pot
May 1967, United Artists
D: Joseph L. Mankiewicz

Elegant sophisticated comedy set in Venice, about a fading fox and his three hens flocking to his bedside, before the scheming millionaire's will is documented. Susan, Mrs. Sheridan, does her best as the wisecracking, hypochondriac from Texas. Mankiewicz brilliance cannot be disguised by choppy editing. Rex Harrison; Maggie Smith; Edit Adams; Capucine; and Cliff Robertson. Cinemascope and color. *(131 minutes)*

Valley of the Dolls
December 1967, 20th Century Fox
D: Mark Robson

Slick gimmicky, guess-who about show-biz pill popping personalities. Susan, as Helen Lawson, comes over like a Sarah Bernhardt as compared to the others in the cast. She also belts out "Plant Your Own Trees" with the help of Dionne Warwick's voice. Trashy film, big box-office. Barbara Parkins; Patty Duke and Sharon Tate. Cinemascope and color. *(123 minutes)*

INDEX

UNDERSTANDING LAWYERS' ETHICS

Third Edition

By

Monroe H. Freedman

Professor of Law
Hofstra University
School of Law

Abbe Smith

Professor of Law
Georgetown University

```
Library of Congress Cataloging-in-Publication Data
Freedman, Monroe H.
  Understanding lawyers' ethics / by Monroe H. Freedman, Abbe Smith.-- 3rd ed.
     p. cm.
  Includes index.
  ISBN 0-8205-6117-7 (softbound : alk. paper)
  1. Legal ethics--United States. 2. Attorney and client--United States. I. Smith, Abbe. II. Title.
KF306.F76 2004
174'.3'0973--dc22
                                                                    2004009535
```

ISBN#: 0-8205-6117-7

Editorial Offices
744 Broad Street, Newark, NJ 07102 (973) 820-2000
201 Mission St., San Francisco, CA 94105-1831 (415) 908-3200
701 East Water Street, Charlottesville, VA 22902-7587 (804) 972-7600
www.lexis.com

(Pub.876)

DEDICATION

In Memory of Audrey and Caleb
and
For Benjamin, Andrew and Adrian

and

For David and Anita Smith
Models of Devotion and Zeal
In Their Own Right

ACKNOWLEDGMENTS

Several people made helpful suggestions about drafts of chapters. We are particularly grateful for editorial comments to Laura Cecere, Audrey Freedman, Caleb Freedman, Sally Greenberg, Judge Roger J. Miner, Ellen Schauber, Ilene Seidman, and Ralph Temple.

Parts of this book have appeared in earlier versions in the ABA Journal, the ABA Litigation Manual, the American University Law Review, the Catholic University Law Review, Criminal Defense Techniques, Criminal Justice Ethics, the Fordham Law Review, the Georgetown Journal of Legal Ethics, the Georgetown Law Journal, the Hofstra Law Review, the Journal of Legal Education, the Journal of the Legal Profession, the Michigan Law Review, the Pennsylvania Law Review, the Stanford Law Review, and the Yale Law Journal.

PREFACE

This book presents a systematic position on lawyers' ethics. We argue that lawyers' ethics is rooted in the Bill of Rights and in the autonomy and the dignity of the individual. This is a traditionalist, client-centered view of the lawyer's role in an adversary system, and corresponds to the ethical standards that are held by a large proportion of the practicing bar.

From this perspective, we analyze the fundamental issues of lawyers' ethics, and particularly the ABA's Model Rules and Model Code. Also, we discuss the principal views of lawyers' ethics that differ from ours, and explain why we think they are wrong.

Students, in particular, should be aware that this book takes a distinct position in a continuing and often heated controversy regarding the lawyer's role. We hope we can persuade you to our point of view. Even if you are not persuaded, however, you can benefit from the presentation, because it challenges you to come to grips with the underlying reasons for the position presented. The best way to achieve a real understanding of legal rules is to test them against your own moral standards and reasoned judgment.

If you do that, the book will have been a success, regardless of whether you end up saying, "I agree with the authors because . . . " or "I disagree with the authors because . . . " The whole thing is in the "because . . . "

TABLE OF CONTENTS

———

Page

Chapter 11 PROSECUTORS' ETHICS

Page

Chapter 1

UNDERSTANDING THE RULES OF LAWYERS' ETHICS

§ 1.01 INTRODUCTION

Understanding the rules of lawyers' ethics is essential because so much turns on them. Wherever you practice in the United States, ethical rules will determine whether you can be a member of the bar and how you conduct your practice. Disciplinary sanctions against lawyers include private reprimands, public censure, suspension of the right to practice, and disbarment.

In addition, although rules of ethics are drafted principally with a view to professional discipline, courts are increasingly turning to ethical rules as sources of law in litigation. One area of major importance is malpractice actions, in which lawyers can lose substantial fees or suffer compensatory and even punitive damages for conduct that falls short of professional standards. Also, motions to disqualify counsel from representing adverse parties are increasingly common. As a result, lawyers are being ordered to stop representing valued clients, sometimes in circumstances in which disqualification could have been avoided by taking appropriate precautions in accordance with the rules.

The rules governing lawyers' conduct also have a profound effect upon the rights of our clients. In some cases these rights run against us, the lawyers. If a client has the power to discharge a lawyer without cause, for example, the lawyer has lesser contract rights than, say, a construction worker who has been hired for the duration of a building project. Other obligations that we owe to our clients may have considerable effect on the interests of others. For example, a rule of lawyer-client confidentiality might prevent the lawyer from informing the victim of a client's fraud when the lawyer has learned of the fraud from the client. Of course, if that rule were changed to permit the lawyer to help the victim to remedy the fraud, the client's rights would be diminished and some clients might be less willing to confide in their lawyers.

A further reason for studying the ethical codes is to learn how to draft and analyze statutes. Some of the ethical rules deal with specific, narrow issues, like forbidding a lawyer to commingle her funds with a client's or to talk with a judge about a case when the other party's lawyer isn't present. Others are the loosest of canons, forbidding conduct that "adversely reflects on [the lawyer's] fitness to practice law" or that is "prejudicial to the administration of justice." All the rules present questions of policy, drafting, and interpretation.

§ 1.02   SELF-GOVERNANCE

Because of the far-reaching effects of lawyers' ethical rules — extending as broadly as the administration of justice itself — we might wonder why the Congress and state legislatures have, for the most part, delegated this important public function to lawyers. With the exception of occasional statutes that deal with specific issues, the rules that govern lawyers' professional conduct have been drafted into comprehensive codes by a private organization, the American Bar Association, and these codifications ordinarily have been adopted by state courts rather than by legislatures.[1] Whatever merit it may have, this procedure is contrary to democratic ideals.

One justification might be that law practice is too esoteric and complex for nonlawyers to regulate. When we consider, however, that legislatures regularly draft laws governing criminal law and procedure, taxation, nuclear policy, and defense procurement, it becomes obvious that legislators are not ordinarily discouraged by the fact that they do not fully understand everything they are legislating about.

The suggestion is sometimes made that self-regulation is essential to maintaining the independence of the bar.[2] On one reading, the proposition is tautological: to be independent means simply to be free of regulation from others. It is true that *legislative* regulation of lawyers' ethics would impose restraints on lawyers, but any ethical regulation imposes restraints on lawyers. Another reading might be that the independence of lawyers to represent their clients zealously and without conflicting obligations to others would be in jeopardy if legislatures were to write rules of professional ethics. There is no evidence that supports that notion, however, and the established bar has not been constant in its dedication to zealous representation free of conflicting obligations to others. In fact, as we will see, the principal concerns of the established bar often have been elsewhere.

Another reason for delegating such vast public responsibility to a private organization might be that the ABA has done the job so disinterestedly and so well. That proposition does not hold up either. Three times in the past century the ABA has attempted to draft a comprehensive, coherent, and enforceable code of professional conduct for lawyers, and each time it has failed to do an adequate job.

§ 1.03   THE ABA'S ETHICAL CODES

The ABA's first codification of ethical rules was the Canons of Professional Ethics in 1908. The Canons consisted of about forty numbered paragraphs,

---

[1] Before a code or rule of ethical conduct can be enforced against a lawyer, it must be adopted by the jurisdiction in which the lawyer is practicing. A private bar association can criticize a lawyer who acts contrary to its rules, and can expel the lawyer from membership in the organization, but it cannot affect the lawyer's status as a member of the bar.

One lawyer, upon being expelled from the American Bar Association for "advertising" himself in an autobiographical book, commented that it was a little like being told that you can no longer belong to the Book of the Month Club.

[2] *See, e.g.,* Model Rules of Professional Conduct, Preamble (1983).

each expressing a norm and, in some instances, a brief explanatory comment or explanation.

The Canons were not inspired purely by disinterested concerns with improving the ethical conduct of lawyers. Rather, they were largely motivated by the influx of Catholic immigrants from Italy and Ireland and Jews from Eastern Europe in the latter part of the nineteenth century. Just as labor unions of the time joined in demanding restrictive immigration laws to restrain competition for jobs, the established bar adopted educational requirements, standards of admission, and "canons of ethics" designed to maintain a predominantly native-born, white, Anglo-Saxon, Protestant monopoly of the legal profession. It is not coincidental that immigration into the United States reached an all-time peak in 1908, the year the Canons were promulgated by the ABA.

As Jerold Auerbach has shown in his excellent book, *Unequal Justice*, leaders of the bar left no doubt about why the new Canons of Professional Ethics were necessary. "What concerns us," said a member of a bar admissions committee, "is not keeping straight those who are already members of the Bar, but keeping out of the profession those whom we do not want."[3] In other public statements, establishment lawyers identified the ethical threat as second-generation Americans who, they said, "are almost as divorced from American life and American traditions as though they and their parents had never departed from their native lands."[4] Because of the "historical derivation" of these new citizens, "it will be impossible that they should appreciate what we understand as professional spirit."[5] As if these failings were not enough, the pained observation was made of these aspiring lawyers that even their "gestures are unwholesome and over-commercialized."[6]

One of those who spoke out about the threat posed by new citizens to the bar's ethical standards was Henry S. Drinker, a chairman of the ABA's Committee on Professional Ethics and Grievances, and long regarded as the bar's leading authority on lawyers' ethics. Drinker complained publicly of lawyers who had come "up out of the gutter," and who were "merely following the methods their fathers had been using in selling shoe-strings and other merchandise."[7] His particular concern was those he referred to as "Russian Jew boys."[8] Drinker's own ethical sensitivity is illustrated further by his analysis of the meaning of "conduct involving moral turpitude" as a ground for professional discipline.[9] A case that Drinker considered "difficult" to judge in terms of moral turpitude was that of a lawyer who had participated in the lynching of an African-American.[10]

---

[3] Jerold Auerbach, Unequal Justice 125 (1976).

[4] *Id.* at 123.

[5] *Id.*

[6] *Id.*

[7] *Id.* at 127.

[8] *Id.*

[9] *See, e.g.*, Model Code of Professional Responsibility, DR 1-101(A)(3) (1969).

[10] Henry Drinker, Legal Ethics 43 (1953). Another close case of "moral turpitude" in Drinker's view was that of a bona fide conscientious objector who had refused to further the war effort. *Id.*

Women, African-Americans, and lawyers of Asian and Latin descent were not a principal focus of the bar's new "ethical" rules because they were being excluded from the profession by rules and practices that denied them admission to law schools and membership in the bar. In addition, those few who finally did get into law schools faced widespread discrimination. Until 1954 the ABA denied membership to African-Americans.[11] When A. Leon Higginbotham, Jr. graduated from Yale Law School in 1952 with an outstanding record and a high recommendation from the Dean, he was told by a Yale alumnus in Philadelphia that his only chance of a job was with "two colored lawyers" who practiced in the city. Years later, Higginbotham became the Chief Judge of the U.S. Court of Appeals for the Third Circuit.

Few law schools admitted women until the middle of the twentieth century, and then only in small numbers. When women were belatedly admitted to Harvard Law School, they were welcomed by the Dean with the announcement that he had opposed their admission because each of them was "taking the place of a good man." In 1952, Sandra Day O'Connor graduated near the top of her class at Stanford Law School. The future Supreme Court Justice was then offered a position at a good law firm as a secretary. Five years later, Justice Ruth Bader Ginsburg graduated first in her class at Columbia Law School, but was rejected by law firms in New York City. As recently as 1964, Roberta Cooper Ramo (who became the first woman president of the American Bar Association in 1995), could not find a law firm position in the Raleigh-Durham-Chapel Hill area because of her gender.

Because the 1908 Canons of Professional Ethics were vague and self-contradictory, they were effective weapons for discriminatory enforcement. Predominant attention in enforcement was given to the canons proscribing advertising and solicitation — rules that were designed to make competition from nonestablished lawyers more difficult. As is shown in Chapter Twelve, *infra*, some of the early solicitation rules that overtly discriminated on socioeconomic grounds have been carried over in ABA codes and in state and federal ethical rules that are still being enforced.

The 1908 Canons governed lawyers' conduct for about sixty years. They were finally repudiated by the ABA, with the explanation that the Canons failed to give adequate guidance, lacked coherence, omitted reference to important areas of practice, and did not lend themselves to meaningful disciplinary enforcement.[12] That is, of course, a devastating indictment of the rules under which the established bar had been governing the profession for over half a century.

The next comprehensive body of ethical rules was the ABA's Model Code of Professional Responsibility in 1969.[13] The Model Code was quickly adopted,

---

[11] The National Lawyers' Guild, an organization committed to pursuing social justice, was founded in 1936 as an alternative to the ABA. Black lawyers were welcomed into the Guild. *See* Ann Fagan Ginger & Eugene Tobin, The National Lawyers' Guild: From Roosevelt Through Reagan (1988).

[12] Model Code, Preface.

[13] The word "Model" was actually a later addition to the title, in order to persuade the Department of Justice that the codification was merely an academic model and not a scheme among bar members to lessen competition in fees and advertising in violation of the antitrust laws.

with some variations of substance, by virtually all jurisdictions, and remains in force in a small number of states, notably New York.

In 1977, only eight years after promulgating the Model Code, the ABA appointed a commission to reconsider it. The commission was chaired by Robert J. Kutak, and became known as the Kutak Commission. Kutak characterized the Model Code as incoherent, inconsistent, and unconstitutional, and noted that its ambiguous and contradictory language could be used unfairly against lawyers in malpractice actions. The Model Code was also attacked by Robert W. Meserve and Geoffrey C. Hazard, Jr. Meserve was a former president of the ABA and succeeded Kutak as Commission Chairman; Hazard was Reporter for the Commission. Meserve and Hazard condemned the Model Code as internally inconsistent, ambiguous, unrealistic, and harmful to effective service to clients.[14] Anyone who thinks the ABA's Model Code is working well, they concluded, is "living in a dream world."[15]

Once again, therefore, the failure of the ABA to produce a serviceable codification of ethical rules for lawyers was acknowledged in the strongest terms by the ABA's own leadership.

The work of the Kutak Commission culminated in the ABA's adoption of the Model Rules of Professional Conduct in 1983.[16] Almost all jurisdictions have adopted the Model Rules, California[17] and New York being the major exceptions.[18] The Model Rules improve upon the Model Code in some respects. However, we believe that the Model Rules are, in many respects, less satisfactory overall than the Model Code. Our reasons are given throughout this book.

The way the ethics codes are interpreted and redrafted will be influenced by the American Law Institute's Restatement of the Law Governing Lawyers (Third) (1998).[19] The Restatement is a mix of improvements, failed opportunities, and bad rules, but it is a major work and cannot be ignored in attempting to understand the rules of lawyers' ethics.[20]

---

[14] Robert Meserve & Goeffrey Hazard, *We Should Adopt the Model Rules of Professional Conduct*, 26 BOSTON BAR J. 6, 7 (April 1982). Ironically, both the authors had previously defended the Model Code against similar criticisms that Professor Freedman had made.

[15] *Id.*

[16] The names are, unfortunately, confusingly similar. The best thing to do is to memorize which is which and be done with it.

[17] California has a distinctive set of rules and statutes.

[18] The District of Columbia has adopted a variant of the Model Rules, but the District's version is substantially different in many important respects.

[19] The ALI is a private organization of lawyers, law professors, and judges that publishes what it calls "Restatements" of various areas of law. Although the Restatement of the Law Governing Lawyers is called the "Third" (because of the date of its adoption), it is the first Restatement of the Law Governing Lawyers.

[20] *See* Monroe Freedman, *Caveat Lector: Conflicts of Interest of ALI Members in Drafting the Restatements*, 26 HOFSTRA L. REV. 641 (1998); Monroe Freedman, *The Life-Saving Exception to Confidentiality: Restating the Law Without the Was, the Will Be, or the Ought to Be*, 29 LOYOLA (L.A.) L. REV. 19 (1996).

§ 1.04 THE PURPOSES OF CODES OF LAWYERS' ETHICS

Presumably, we write, interpret, and apply rules of lawyers' ethics for one or more purposes. What purposes, then, are we trying to achieve with these rules? Obviously, the answer to that question will make important differences in the rules themselves.

For example, in drafting rules on advertising and solicitation by lawyers, a desire to prevent competition among lawyers will produce a restrictive rule. However, a policy to maximize access to legal services for people who are ignorant of their rights and their need for a lawyer will produce a more liberal rule. Also, a concern that some lawyers might take unfair advantage of unsophisticated clients might require a modification of the latter rule or the inclusion of a separate rule specifically addressing that problem.

Yet another purpose of ethical rules (including those on advertising) might be to improve the "image" of the profession, either by adopting rules that will appear to say the "right" thing or by forbidding conduct considered unseemly. For example, during consideration of the ABA's Model Rules, the managing editor of a news journal for lawyers wrote an opinion piece titled, *Ethics Review Needed to Polish Public Image of Bar*.[21] The same concern with image was expressed by the then-Chairman of the committee that produced the Model Rules. Upon adoption of the Model Rules by the ABA, Meserve announced with satisfaction that "[t]he legal profession has taken a step which should improve its image."[22] As we will see, some of the ABA's difficulties in drafting coherent rules appear to have come from a reluctance to make hard decisions on issues raising problems of image.[23]

§ 1.05 LAWYERS' ETHICS AND CLIENTS' RIGHTS

Some issues of lawyers' ethics require us to go deeper into our purposes and our values than others. In the past thirty years or so there has been an intense debate over whether one can be a good lawyer and a good person at the same time. Put otherwise, can effectively representing a client's lawful interests properly subject a lawyer to criticism on moral grounds?[24]

---

[21] Diana Huffman, *Ethics Review Needed to Polish Public Image of Bar*, LEGAL TIMES, Jan. 31, 1983, at 9.

[22] Robert Meserve, as quoted in Kathleen Sylvester, *At the ABA: From Bias to Ethics; Humor in the Court*, NAT. L. J., Aug. 15, 1983, at 5.

[23] Similarly, Professor Ted Schneyer has commented: "To maintain its authority inside as well as outside the bar, the ABA must in a time of professional ferment display its authority. One way to do so is to refurbish its image as lawgiver for the entire profession." Ted Schneyer, *Professionalism as Bar Politics: The Making of the Model Rules of Professional Conduct*, 14 LAW & SOC. INQUIRY 677 (1989). Schneyer's article shows that a concern with institutional image affected the substance of important ethical rules. *See also* William Glaberson, *Lawyers Consider Easing Restriction on Client Secrecy*, N.Y. TIMES, July 31, 2001, at A1, A17 (noting the concern about the public image of lawyers at the 2001 ABA annual meeting at which rules changes were considered).

[24] As Charles Curtis noted a half century ago, "[w]e are not dealing with the morals which govern a man acting for himself, but with the ethics of advocacy. We are talking about the special moral code which governs a man who is acting for another." Charles Curtis, *The Ethics of Advocacy*, 4 STAN. L. REV. 3, 16 (1951).

For example, what should the lawyer do when a client insists upon taking action that is lawful but that, in the lawyer's view, is also immoral? Does the lawyer hire out her conscience when accepting a retainer? Is it justifiable for the lawyer to impose her values on the client? The subject is developed in Chapter 3, but it is useful to introduce it here.

In analyzing the issue of the "good lawyer," commentators have analogized the lawyer's relationship to the client to that of a friend.[25] or even of a spouse.[26] Thus, Professor Charles Fried argues that a lawyer, like a friend, will not (or should not) impose her moral values on the other, while Luban argues the opposite — that a lawyer, like a spouse, will (or should) prevent the other from acting immorally. You might find both of these analogies to be somewhat strained and artificial, and the conclusions that are drawn from them to be less than compelling.

Professor Thomas Shaffer has suggested that we can best understand the issue of the good lawyer by looking to "[t]he distinctive feature of ethics in a profession":[27]

> The distinctive feature of ethics in a profession is that it speaks to the unequal encounter of two moral persons. Legal ethics, which is a subject of study for lawyers, then often becomes the study of what is good — not for me, but for *this other person, over whom I have power.* Legal ethics differs from ethics generally: Ethics is thinking about morals. *Legal ethics is thinking about the morals of someone else.* It is concerned with the goodness of someone else.

Shaffer thus identifies two aspects of the lawyer-client relationship that will affect our view of lawyers' ethical obligations. One is the inequality inherent in the relationship, in which the lawyer frequently has considerable power over the client. The second is a concern with the client's goodness (or, more accurately, the client's lack of it) and with the extent of the lawyer's responsibility (and perhaps risk) through association with the client as a lesser moral being. As Shaffer accurately observes: "Modern legal ethics assumes that clients corrupt lawyers — that they are, to use an old Catholic notion, occasions of sin, like R-rated movies and bad company."[28]

Although we agree that the concerns expressed by Shaffer are important to lawyers' ethics, our approach to clients and, therefore, to the ethical issues, has a different emphasis. In expressing the distinctive feature of ethics in the legal profession, we would identify the client not as "this other person, over whom I have power," but as "this other person whom I have the power to help." In this view, the central concern of lawyers' ethics is not (as Shaffer says, quoting Plato) how my client "can be made as good as possible." Rather, it

---

[25] Charles Fried, *The Lawyer as Friend: The Moral Foundations of the Lawyer-Client Relation*, 85 YALE L. J. 1060, 1071 (1976).

[26] DAVID LUBAN, LAWYERS AND JUSTICE 166–69 (1988); *compare* Curtis, *supra* note 24, at 8 (stating that "[t]he relation between a lawyer and . . . client is one of the intimate relations").

[27] Thomas Shaffer, *Legal Ethics and the Good Client*, 36 CATH. U.L. REV. 319 (1987) (first emphasis added). *Cf.* Monroe Freedman, *Legal Ethics and the Suffering Client*, 36 CATH. U.L. REV. 331 (1987). *See also*, THOMAS SHAFFER, AMERICAN LEGAL ETHICS (1985).

[28] Shaffer, *supra* note 27, 36 CATH. U.L. REV. at 320.

is how far we can ethically go — or how far we should be required to go — to achieve for our clients full and equal rights under law.

Put otherwise, Shaffer thinks of lawyers' ethics as being rooted in moral philosophy, while we think of lawyers' ethics as being rooted in the moral values that are expressed in the Bill of Rights. In the words of Justice William Brennan, Jr., "Our Constitution is a charter of human rights, dignity, and self-determination,"[29] and, as explained in Chapter Two, these values have been incorporated into the American adversary system and should inform our rules of lawyers' ethics.

Again, these are differences in emphasis only. Shaffer is not unconcerned about individual human rights nor are we unconcerned about the personal morality of ourselves, our clients, and others. Nevertheless, these differences in emphasis are important when it comes to drafting or interpreting rules of lawyers' ethics.

In varying degrees, the codes of lawyers' ethics reflect the drafters' conceptions of the lawyers' role and of the lawyer-client relationship.[30] To the extent that such a conception is expressed and consistently carried out, a code will at least have coherence. One thing you should watch for, therefore, is the extent to which the rules in each code succeed in carrying out the drafters' expressed conception of the lawyers' role.

The Model Code of Professional Responsibility recognizes that the lawyer's role is grounded in "respect for the dignity of the individual and his capacity through reason for enlightened self-government."[31] Thus,

> The professional responsibility of a lawyer derives from his membership in a profession which has the duty of assisting members of the public to secure and protect available legal rights and benefits. In our government of laws and not of men, each member of our society is entitled to have his conduct judged and regulated in accordance with the law; to seek any lawful objective through legally permissible means; and to present for adjudication any lawful claim, issue, or defense.[32]

At the same time, the Model Code is affected by a concern with public image. According to the Model Code, ethical conduct is not impelled principally by what the 1908 Canons called the lawyer's "conscience" or the lawyer's "own sense of honor and propriety."[33] Nor does the Model Code view the lawyer's ethical conduct as deriving from what Shaffer calls "character" or "integrity."[34] Rather, for the drafters of the Model Code, "in the last analysis it is the desire for the respect and confidence of the members of his profession and of the society which he serves that should provide to a lawyer the incentive for the highest possible degree of ethical conduct."[35] The Model Code also says

---

[29] William J. Brennan, Jr., *What the Constitution Requires*, N.Y. TIMES, Apr. 28, 1996, at D13.

[30] *See, e.g.*, THE AMERICAN LAWYER'S CODE OF CONDUCT, Preamble.

[31] Model Code, Preamble.

[32] *Id.*, EC 7-1.

[33] Canons of Professional Ethics 15 and 24.

[34] Shaffer, *supra* note 27, 36 CATH. U.L. REV. at 329–30.

[35] Model Code, Preamble.

that the professional judgment of the lawyer must be exercised "solely for the benefit of his client and free of compromising influences and loyalties."[36] Note, however, how an undue concern for "the respect . . . of the members of . . . society" could be the kind of compromising influence that the Model Code warns against, particularly if the lawyer is representing an unpopular client or cause.

The Model Rules of Professional Conduct reflect a significantly different view of the lawyer's role and of the lawyer's relationship to the client. As expressed by Professor Norman Redlich, who was one of its strongest proponents, the Model Rules "project a different set of values" from those of the Code, and "[t]he fate of the entire project may well hinge on the bar's willingness to accept the altered role model that the Model Rules envision."[37]

Those differences are apparent in the Model Rules' description of the lawyer in the opening sentence of its Preamble. As we have seen, the Model Code begins by stressing the client — "respect for the dignity of the individual and his capacity . . . for enlightened self-government." By contrast, the Model Rules begin: "A lawyer is a representative of clients, an officer of the legal system and a public citizen having special responsibility for the quality of justice." In a sense, of course, the description is simply a truism, but the difference in emphasis is intended to convey the altered role model to which Redlich referred.

§ 1.06   THE LAWYER AS "OFFICER OF THE COURT"

Particularly significant in the Preamble to the Model Rules is the phrase "officer of the legal system," which is similar to "officer of the court." Those who seek to minimize the lawyer's role of service to individual clients commonly characterize the lawyer as an "officer of the court."[38] The implication is that the lawyer's job is primarily to be an agent of the state. The Supreme Court has recognized, however, that the lawyer's traditional function is to serve the lawful interests of individual clients, even against the interests of the state.

For example, Justice Lewis Powell made only perfunctory reference to the lawyer as an "officer of the court" in writing for the Supreme Court:

> [T]he duty of the lawyer, subject to his role as an "officer of the court,"
> is to further the interests of his clients by all lawful means, even when
> those interests are in conflict with the interests of the United States

---

[36] EC 5-1.

[37] Norman Redlich, *Disclosure Provisions of the Model Rules of Professional Conduct*, 1980 A.B.F. Res. 981–982. Redlich was referring specifically to the disclosure provisions of the 1980 Discussion Draft of the Model Rules. However, he reprinted this portion of his article subsequent to adoption of the present version of the Model Rules. *See* Norman Redlich, Professional Responsibility: A Problem Approach (2d ed. 1983). Moreover, as we will see below, the Model Rules also project a different set of values with regard to the client's autonomy. The "altered role model" to which Redlich referred, therefore, is no less significant than his comment suggests.

[38] The question-begging nature of that characterization has been recognized for some time. *See, e.g.*, ABA Opin. 287 (1953); Monroe Freedman, *Professional Responsibility of the Criminal Defense Lawyer: The Three Hardest Questions*, 64 Mich. L. Rev. 1469, 1470 (1966).

or of a State. But this representation involves no conflict of interest in the invidious sense. Rather, it casts the lawyer in his honored and traditional role as an authorized but independent agent acting to vindicate the legal rights of a client, whoever it may be.[39]

Eight years later, writing for a majority of eight, Justice Powell sharpened the point: "[A] defense lawyer best serves the public, not by acting on behalf of the State or in concert with it, but rather by advancing 'the undivided interests of his client.' "[40] In short, in a free society the lawyer's function, as an officer of the court, is to serve the undivided interests of individual clients.

In recasting "the officer of the court" as "an officer of the legal system," the drafters of the Model Rules appear to be seeking a substitute for discredited rhetoric. In any event, the intention of some supporters of the Model Rules to reject the client-centered values of the Model Code is clear, and troubling.

§ 1.07 MORAL VALUES AND ETHICAL CHOICES

As this discussion suggests, you will find it extremely useful in understanding the rules of lawyers' ethics to have an opinion (however tentative) about your role as a lawyer and what your relationship should be to your client. You can then analyze and appraise each rule by asking whether the ethical purpose being advanced by the rule is consistent with your own model of the lawyer's role and of the lawyer-client relationship. That observation takes us to the ultimate reason for understanding the rules of lawyers' ethics — the self-understanding that can come from applying our own moral values to important issues of lawyers' professional responsibilities. An anecdote illustrates the point.

Several years ago, a friend of Freedman's expressed his disappointment that he could never serve on a jury. At that time, the Jury Commission used a questionnaire that asked, among other things, whether the potential juror had moral objections to the death penalty. Anyone answering yes to that question was automatically disqualified from serving. Since Freedman's friend believed, as a matter of religious conviction, that human life is sacred and paramount to all other moral values, he was disqualified each time he submitted the questionnaire.

Freedman suggested to his friend that his conduct was inconsistent with his asserted moral priorities. Human life was not paramount for him — telling the truth to the Jury Commission was. His scruples about answering the questionnaire truthfully made it impossible for him to serve on a jury and, as a juror, to vote against death. On reflection, Freedman's friend decided to lie on the next jury questionnaire.

This decision by Freedman's friend can be, and has been, debated. Our concern here, however, is not whether the decision was right or wrong, but only that you cannot have it both ways. Either telling the truth is more

---

[39] *In re Griffiths,* 413 U.S. 717, 724, 93 S.Ct. 2851, 2856, n. 14 (1973). *See also* Justice Powell's quotation from *Cammer v. United States,* 350 U.S. 399, 76 S.Ct. 456 (1956), Application of *Griffiths,* 413 U.S. 717, 728–29. *Cf.* Justice Burger's dissent in *Griffiths,* 413 U.S. at 731–32.

[40] *Polk County v. Dodson,* 454 U.S. 312, 318, 102 S.Ct. 445, 450 (1981).

important than saving life, or saving life is more important than telling the truth. Accordingly, when moral values are in conflict, the ways in which we resolve those conflicts show what our true moral priorities are. In that sense, ethics is applied morality, or morality in action. In making a series of ethical decisions, we create a kind of moral profile of ourselves.

You should be conscious, therefore, of how your own decisions on issues of lawyers' ethics establish your moral priorities and thereby define your own moral profile. In understanding lawyers' ethics, you may come to better understand your moral values, and yourself.

Chapter 2

THE ADVERSARY SYSTEM

§ 2.01   INTRODUCTION

In its simplest terms, an adversary system resolves disputes by presenting conflicting views of fact and law to an impartial and relatively passive arbiter, who decides which side wins what. In the United States, however, the phrase "adversary system" is synonymous with the American system for the administration of justice — a system that was constitutionalized by the framers and has been elaborated by the Supreme Court for two centuries. Thus, the adversary system represents far more than a simple model for resolving disputes. Rather, it consists of a core of basic rights that recognize, and protect, the dignity of the individual in a free society.

The rights that comprise the adversary system include personal autonomy, the effective assistance of counsel, equal protection of the laws, trial by jury, the rights to call and to confront witnesses, and the right to require the government to prove guilt beyond a reasonable doubt and without the use of compelled self-incrimination. These rights, and others, are also included in the broad and fundamental concept that no person may be deprived of life, liberty, or property without due process of law — a concept which itself has been substantially equated with the adversary system.[1] An essential function of the adversary system, therefore, is to maintain a free society in which individual human rights are central.[2]

Former Federal Judge Marvin E. Frankel has written that the adversary system is "cherished as an ideal of constitutional proportions," in part because it embodies "the fundamental right to be heard,"[3] and Professor Geoffrey Hazard adds that the adversary system "stands . . . as a pillar of our constitutional system."[4] Accordingly, the Supreme Court has reiterated that the right to counsel is "the most precious" of our rights, because it affects one's ability to assert any other right.[5] It follows, therefore, that the professional responsibilities of the lawyer, serving as counsel within our constitutionalized adversary system, must be informed by the same civil libertarian values that are expressed in the Constitution.

---

[1] GEOFFREY C. HAZARD, JR., ETHICS IN THE PRACTICE OF LAW 122 (1978).

[2] Code of Professional Responsibility, Preamble:

The continued existence of a free and democratic society depends upon recognition of the concept that justice is based upon the rule of law grounded in respect for the dignity of the individual and his capacity through reason for enlightened self-government. Law so grounded makes justice possible, for only through such law does the dignity of the individual attain respect and protection. Without it, individual rights become subject to unrestrained power, respect for law is destroyed, and rational self-government is impossible.

[3] MARVIN E. FRANKEL, PARTISAN JUSTICE 12 (1980).

[4] HAZARD, ETHICS IN THE PRACTICE OF LAW 123.

[5] *United States v. Cronic*, 466 U.S. 648, 654 (1984), *quoting* Schaefer, *Federalism and State Criminal Procedure*, 70 HARV. L. REV. 1, 8 (1957).

§ 2.02 CRITICISMS OF THE ADVERSARY SYSTEM

During the past few decades, attacks on the adversary system have been unprecedented in their breadth and intensity, and at times have been "scathing [and] venomous."[6] For example, at a conference of twenty-five of the country's "professional elite,"[7] most of them lawyers and judges, the adversary system was "thoroughly savaged."[8] Efforts by the conferees to produce an acceptable alternative to the adversary system ended unsuccessfully on a "note of resignation."[9]

It is not coincidental that these attacks on the adversary system have taken place in the context of critical analyses of lawyers' ethics. Critics concerned with the negative aspects of zealous, client-centered advocacy have recognized that the reforms they believe necessary in lawyers' ethics can come about only through restructuring the adversary system itself.

For example, in the cause of correcting the "excesses, distortions, and perversions" of the adversary system with regard to truth-seeking,[10] former Federal District Judge Marvin Frankel has proposed significant restrictions on traditional lawyer-client confidentiality and loyalty.[11] Frankel acknowledges that his proposals would effect "an appreciable revolution" in procedure, in lawyer-client relations, and in the lawyer's self-image.[12] Although professing "a profound devotion to a soundly adversary mode of reaching informed decisions,"[13] he concedes that his reforms will be impossible "until or unless the adversary ethic comes to be changed or subordinated."[14] Indeed, an entire chapter of his book is titled "Modifying the Lawyer's Adversary Ideal,"[15] and another chapter closes with a hope for "wiser, more effective ideas for breaking the adversary mold."[16]

From a very different perspective — that of postmodernism and multiculturalism — Professor Carrie Menkel-Meadow has also challenged the

---

[6] Jethro K. Lieberman, Book Review, 27 N.Y.L. REV. 695 (1981).

[7] Joseph N. Green, Jr., *Forward* to HAZARD, *supra* note 1, at ix.

[8] HAZARD, *supra*, n. 1, at 123.

[9] *Id.* at 126.

[10] FRANKEL, PARTISAN JUSTICE 9.

[11] *Id.* at 83; *see also* Marvin E. Frankel, *The Search for Truth: an Umpireal View*, 123 PA. L. REV. 1031 (1975); Monroe H. Freedman, *Judge Frankel's Search for Truth*, 123 PA. L. REV. 1060 (1975). The merits of Frankel's proposals are discussed in Chapter Five, *infra*.

[12] *Id.*

[13] *Id.* at 9.

[14] *Id.* at 18:

> The key point at every stage . . . is that the single uniformity is always adversariness. There are other goods, but the greatest is winning. There are other evils, but scarcely any worse than losing. Every step of the process, and any attempt to reform it, must be viewed in this light until or unless the adversary ethic comes to be changed or subordinated.

[15] *Id.*, Ch. 6.

[16] *Id.* at 100. Frankel has protested that the phrases quoted from his book do not fairly characterize his position. Frankel, *Some Comments on Our Constitutionalized Adversary System by Monroe H. Freedman*, 2 CHAPMAN L. REV. 253 (1999). He does not deny, however, that they are phrases that he himself has used in characterizing his position. Indeed, the very title of his book, Partisan Justice, implies a critique of an adversarial mode of seeking justice.

adversary system.[17] She argues that "we need to reexamine the attributes of the adversary system as the 'ideal type' of a legal system, and also reexamine the practice based on the premises of that system."[18] It is not clear, however, what alternative system, or systems, Menkel-Meadow favors. As she says:

> After I critique the adversary system, you will wonder what I would substitute for it. It should be obvious that as a postmodern, multicultural thinker, I have no one panacea, solution, or process to offer. Instead, I think we should contemplate a variety of different ways to structure process in our legal system to reflect our multiple goals and objectives.[19]

At one point, Menkel-Meadow does suggest a system with a "greater multiplicity of stories [or narratives] being told, of more open, participatory and democratic processes, yielding truths that are concrete but contextualized, explicitly focused on who finds 'truth' for whose benefit."[20] The vague and unwieldy nature of this proposal explains, perhaps, why some postmodern analysis "would reject any legal system," including, of course, the adversary system.[21] In any event, in a postmodern, multicultural system, the professional responsibilities of lawyers would be profoundly affected.

In short, Menkel-Meadow represents those who want different kinds of "truth" in dispute resolution, while Mr. Frankel represents those whose main concern is "the truth" in legal proceedings.[22] From both perspectives, however, the adversary system has become the battleground on which fundamental issues of lawyers' ethics are being fought out.

§ 2.03   THE ADVERSARY SYSTEM AND INDIVIDUAL DIGNITY

It is not surprising that in totalitarian societies, there is a sharp contrast in the role of a criminal defense lawyer from that in the American adversary system. As expressed by law professors at the University of Havana, "the first job of a revolutionary lawyer is not to argue that his client is innocent, but rather to determine if his client is guilty and, if so, to seek the sanction which will best rehabilitate him."[23]

Thus, a Bulgarian attorney began his defense in a treason trial by noting that "[i]n a Socialist state there is no division of duty between the judge, prosecutor, and defense counsel. . . . The defense must assist the prosecution

---

[17] See, e.g., Carrie Menkel-Meadow, The Trouble With the Adversary System in a Postmodern, Multicultural World, 38 Wm. & Mary L. Rev. 5 (1996). See also Monroe H. Freedman, The Trouble With Postmodern Zeal, 38 Wm. & Mary L. Rev. 63 (1996).

[18] Id. at 5.

[19] Id. at 11–12.

[20] Id. at 23–24.

[21] Id. at 16, n.23.

[22] M. Frankel, Partisan Justice at 77 (1980).

[23] J. Kaplan, Criminal Justice 264–265 (1973); Berman, The Cuban Popular Trials, 60 Colum. L. Rev. 1317, 1341 (1969).

to find the objective truth in a case."[24] In that case, the defense attorney ridiculed his client's defense, and the client was convicted and executed.[25] Similarly, in the trial of anti-Hitler bomb plotters in July, 1944, the court-appointed lawyer for one of the defendants "expressed horror at his client's actions and closed by demanding the death penalty for him."[26]

A Chinese lawyer, Ma Rongjie, has described the role of counsel in comparable terms.[27] Lawyers are "servants of the state."[28] The function of the defense lawyer in criminal cases is, at most, to plead mitigating circumstances on behalf of clients whose guilt is largely predetermined.[29] Mr. Ma represented Jiang Qing, widow of Mao Tse Tung, in the trial of what was called the "Gang of Four." Jiang Qing had requested a lawyer who would assert her innocence, but such a request was impossible to honor, Mr. Ma said. On the contrary, in representing "the criminals" (as Mr. Ma referred to his clients) he and the other defense lawyers conducted no investigations of their own, objected to no prosecution questions, cross-examined no prosecution witnesses, and called no witnesses themselves. Nor did the defense attorneys even meet with their clients. "There was no need to talk to them," Mr. Ma explained. "The police and the prosecutors worked on the case a very long time, and the evidence they found which wasn't true they threw away."[30]

Commenting on a similar legal system in the Soviet Union, Alexander Solzhenitsyn wrote sardonically:

> On the threshold of the classless society, we were at last capable of realizing the conflictless trial — a reflection of the absence of inner conflict in our social structure — in which not only the judge and the prosecutor but also the defense lawyers and the defendants themselves would strive collectively to achieve their common purpose.[31]

Under the American adversary system, a trial is not "conflictless," because the lawyer is not the agent or servant of the state. Rather, the lawyer is the client's "champion against a hostile world"[32] — the client's zealous advocate against the government itself. Unlike Mr. Ma, therefore, the American defense

---

[24] *Id.* at 264–265.

[25] Sometime later the verdict was found to have been erroneous, and the defendant was "rehabilitated." *Id.*

[26] V.R. Berghahn, *The Judges Made Good Nazis*, N.Y. *Times Book Rev.*, p.3, April 28, 1991, reviewing I. MULLER, HITLER'S JUSTICE (Harvard 1991).

[27] *N.Y. Times*, Jan. 6, 1982, p. B5.

[28] *Id.* As we have seen in Chapter One, the phrases used in the United States to convey a similar notion is "officers of the court" or "officers of the legal system."

[29] *Id.*

[30] *Id. See also*, Wu Dunn, *In Murky Trials, China Buries Tiananmen Affair*, N.Y. TIMES, Jan. 20, 1991, p. 10 (describing the trials of the leaders of the 1989 democracy movement).

The Chinese system remains the same. "The Chinese judiciary is an agency of the government and subject to influence by politicians . . . ." American Judicature Society, *Report for Members*, p. 1, Winter, 1999. Chinese judges told representatives of the American Judicature Society that they are "envious" of the independence of American judges. *Id.*

[31] ALEXANDER SOLZHENITSYN, GULAG ARCHIPELAGO 374 (Harper & Row, 1974), quoted in Ralph Temple, *In Defense of the Adversary System*, ABA LITIGATION, vol. 2, no. 2, 43, 44 (Winter, 1976).

[32] *See* ABA, Standards Relating to the Defense Function 145–146 (Approved Draft, 1971).

lawyer has an obligation to conduct a prompt investigation of the case.[33] All sources of relevant information must be explored, particularly the client.[34] Rather than accepting the government's decision to preserve or destroy evidence, the defense lawyer has a duty to seek out information in the possession of the police and prosecutor.[35] Defense counsel has those duties, moreover, even though the defendant has admitted guilt to the lawyer and has expressed a desire to plead guilty.[36] As explained by the ABA Standards for Criminal Justice, the client may be mistaken about legal culpability or may be able to avoid conviction by persuading the court that inculpatory evidence should be suppressed; also, such an investigation could prove useful in showing mitigating circumstances.[37]

Such rules, reflecting a respect for the rights even of the guilty individual, are a significant expression of the political philosophy that underlies the American system of justice. As Professor Zupancic has observed, "In societies which believe that the individual is the ultimate repository of existential values, his status vis-a-vis the majority will remain uncontested even when he is accused of crime. He will not be an object of purposes and policies, but *an equal partner in a legal dispute*."[38]

§ 2.04 THE ADVERSARY SYSTEM AND INDIVIDUAL RIGHTS

There is also an important systemic purpose served by assuring that even guilty people have rights. Jethro K. Lieberman has made the point by putting forth, and then explaining, a paradox:

> The singular strength of the adversary system is measured by a central fact that is usually deplored: The overwhelming majority of those accused in American courts are guilty. Why is this a strength? Because its opposite, visible in many totalitarian nations within the Chinese and Russian orbits, is this: Without an adversary system, a considerable number of defendants are prosecuted, though palpably innocent. . . . In short, the strength of the adversary system is not so much that it permits the innocent to defend themselves meaningfully, but that in the main it prevents them from having to do so.[39]

Lieberman concludes that "[o]nly because defense lawyers are independent of the state and the ruling political parties and are permitted, even encouraged, to defend fiercely and partisanly do we ensure that the state will be loathe to indict those whom it knows to be innocent." This benefit, however, is largely invisible. "We rarely see who is not indicted, we never see those

---

[33] ABA Standards for Criminal Justice 4-4.1 (1979).

[34] *Id.*, 4-3.2, 4-4.1.

[35] *Id.*, 4-4.1.

[36] *Id.*, 4-4.1.

[37] *Id.*, Commentary to Standard 4-4.1.

[38] Zupancic, *Truth and Impartiality in Criminal Process*, 7 Jour. Contemp. L. 39, 133 (1982) (emphasis added).

[39] Lieberman, Book Review, 27 N.Y.L. Rev. 695 (1981).

whom a prosecutor, or even a governor or president might like to prosecute but cannot."[40]

There is another systemic reason for the zealous representation that characterizes the adversary system. Our purpose as a society is not only to respect the humanity of the guilty defendant and to protect the innocent from the possibility of an unjust conviction. Precious as those objectives are, we also seek through the adversary system "to preserve the integrity of society itself . . . [by] keeping sound and wholesome the procedure by which society visits its condemnation on an erring member."[41]

In an insightful article, Professor John B. Mitchell has explained how defense counsel serves to make our criminal procedures consistent with our ideals.[42] By providing a vigorous defense, even for someone the lawyer knows is guilty, Mitchell says, defense counsel "makes the screens work."[43] Mitchell's "screens" are the procedures and standards that we use to protect individual rights in the criminal process (and to protect those who should not become entangled in the criminal process). These standards include reasonable suspicion for a stop on the street, probable cause for an arrest, sufficient evidence to indict and go to trial, and guilt beyond a reasonable doubt at trial.

Mitchell shows how zealous defense tactics have served to make the screens work as they should, for example, by improving the professionalism of police work.[44] In one community, defense counsel argued in narcotics cases that the prosecution had presented only the uncorroborated testimony of a single police officer. After four acquittals in such cases, the police began to corroborate drug buys with concealed transmitters and marked money. In other cases, acquittals resulted from the failure of investigators to dust for fingerprints; thereafter, a suspect tentatively identified as a robber was not tried because the fingerprints found on the cash drawer were not his. Also, the quality of eyewitness identifications has been improved by defense attacks on suggestive pretrial identification procedures.[45]

Professor Lawrence H. Tribe has added that "procedure can serve a vital role as . . . a reminder to the community of the principles it holds important." He explains:

---

[40] *Id.* at 695.

[41] Fuller, *The Adversary System,*" in TALKS ON AMERICAN LAW 35 (H. Berman ed., 1960). In more down-to-earth language, John Condon, a Buffalo criminal defense lawyer, once commented that he is "an expert in quality control."

[42] John B. Mitchell, *The Ethics of the Criminal Defense Attorney,* 32 STANFORD L. REV. 293 (1980).

[43] *Id.* at 298.

[44] *Id.* at 306–307.

[45] *See* Daniel Wise, *Court Declines To Order Change In Lineup Rules,* N.Y.L.J., June 29, 2001, at 1 (reporting that, as a result of a motion by a Bronx public defender, a New York judge urged the police department and prosecutors to consider using a more accurate lineup procedure than the one routinely employed). *See also Motion for "Double Blind Sequential" Lineup Is Denied; Study of Sequential Lineups Suggested,* N.Y.L.J., July 5, 2001, at 17 (quoting court ruling urging such lineups to "enhanc[e] the accuracy and fairness of these very significant identification procedures.") Evelyn Apgar, *Police Lineups in New Jersey Herald for the Exit Line,* NJ LAWYER, p. 4, Aug. 6, 2001.

The presumption of innocence, the rights to counsel and confrontation, the privilege against self-incrimination, and a variety of other trial rights, matter not only as devices for achieving or avoiding certain kinds of trial outcomes, but also as affirmations of respect for the accused as a human being — affirmations that remind him and the public about the sort of society we want to become and, indeed, about the sort of society we are.[46]

These rights to which Professor Tribe refers are essential components of the adversary system as it has evolved in American constitutional law.

§ 2.05　THE FALSE METAPHOR OF WARFARE

A familiar device of those who denigrate the adversary system is the metaphor and rhetoric of war, complete with "battlefield," "weapons," "ammunition," and lawyer-mercenaries who "marshal the forces" for a "grimly combative" engagement.[47] "We set the parties fighting," says Marvin Frankel.[48]

The true picture is rather different from the physical violence and "bloodletting"[49] that is conjured up by that rhetoric. People who have grievances against one another come to lawyers as an alternative to fighting it out physically. "We" don't set the parties fighting. Rather, society, through the legal system, channels the grievances of people and groups into socially controlled, non-violent means of dispute resolution. We — the lawyers — play an indispensable part in that constructive social process.

A dramatic illustration of violence transformed into peaceable dispute resolution occurred in the 1960s, when a major social concern was to "get them out of the streets and into the courtrooms." The reference was to African-Americans and their serious and longstanding grievances against American society. Riots, with arson, looting, and serious assaults, took place in several cities, including our national capital. With remarkable efficiency, the adversary system was put to work to further the ideals of equal protection of the laws and other fundamental concepts of our constitutional democracy.[50]

We are sometimes told that other countries, like Japan, are superior to the United States because they have fewer lawyers and less litigation.[51] But in

---

[46] Tribe, *Trial by Mathematical Precision and Ritual in the Legal Process*, 84 HARV. L. REV. 1329, 1391–1392 (1971).

[47] FRANKEL, PARTISAN JUSTICE at 11. This kind of exaggeration runs through Frankel's discussion of partisan — that is, adversary — justice, e.g., "battles" (44), "battle" (69), "weaponry" (18), "weapons" (26), "a species of war" (26), "war" (44), "warriors" (46), "warrior" (47), "Making . . . War," (114), and even "bloodletting" (114).

[48] *Id.*, *quoting* C.P. Curtis, IT'S YOUR LAW 1 (1954). Curtis was sometimes careless in language and superficial in arguments in defense of adversarial ethics, which makes him a favorite target of critics. *See, e.g.*, Noonan, *Other People's Morals: The Lawyer's Conscience*, 48 TENN. L. REV. 227 (1981).

[49] *Id.* at 114.

[50] *See* Frank Michelman, *The Supreme Court and Litigation Access Fees*, 1973 DUKE L. JOUR. 1153, 1974 DUKE L. JOUR. 527.

[51] This was a recurrent theme of Vice President Dan Quayle; *see, e.g.*, his speech to the American Bar Association, August 13, 1991.

place of an American "litigation explosion" (which is a myth),[52] Japan has suffered a true explosion of violence. In addition to the usual illegal services, criminal organizations in Japan provide an extortion service known to the police there as "intervention in civil affairs."[53] As reported in *The New York Times*, a factor in the strength of the yakuza, or organizations of criminals, is that the number of lawyers is limited. "Thus, many people with grievances, like victims of traffic accidents, hire yakuza to obtain damage payments [in exchange for] a percentage of the payment." The yakuza offer their services openly, some from storefront offices. In effect, "the mob in Japan . . . fills a function played by lawyers in other societies."[54] In place of the metaphorical violence of American litigation, therefore, the paucity of lawyers in Japan has resulted in violence in fact.

§ 2.06   THE ADVERSARY SYSTEM IN CIVIL LITIGATION

The adversary system has also been instrumental, principally in civil litigation, in mitigating the grievances of minority groups, women, consumers, tenants, citizens concerned with health and safety in our environment, and others. Because we celebrate these advances in individual rights and liberties, we view with concern and some suspicion the calls for mitigation of adversarial zeal. Of course, it is preferable to negotiate a satisfactory resolution of a dispute. Experience teaches, however, that those in power do not ordinarily choose to negotiate unless there is a credible threat of successful litigation.

In a report to his Board of Overseers in 1983, Harvard President Derek Bok decried "the familiar tilt in the law curriculum toward preparing students for legal combat," and called instead for law schools to train their students "for the gentler arts of reconciliation and accommodation."[55] These are themes long associated with Chief Justice Warren Burger.[56]

In response to such critics, Professor Owen Fiss has observed that they see adjudication in essentially private terms. Viewing the purpose of civil lawsuits to be the resolution of discrete private disputes, the critics find the amount of litigation we encounter to be evidence of "the needlessly combative and quarrelsome character of Americans."[57] Fiss, on the other hand, sees

---

[52] *See, e.g.*, Galanter, *The Day After the Litigation Explosion*, 46 MD. L. REV. 3 (1986); Galanter, *Reading the Landscape of Disputes: What We Know and Don't Know (and Think We Know) about Our Allegedly Contentious and Litigious Society*, 31 U.C.L.A. L. REV. 4 (1983); Chesebro, *A Galileo's Retort: Peter Huber's Junk Scholarship*, 42 AMER. U. L. REV. 1637 (1993). Coyle & MacLachlan, *Business Cases Clog Courts*, NAT. L. JOUR. 1, Aug. 7, 1995 (Business cases, not tort cases, are crowding the federal court docket).

[53] Weisman, *Is Big Business Getting Too Cozy with the Mob?*, N.Y. TIMES, Aug. 29, 1991, at A4.

[54] *Id.*

[55] *See* Owen Fiss, *Against Settlement*, 93 YALE L.J. 1073 (1984), *citing* Derek Bok, *A Flawed System*, HARV. MAG. 45 (May-June, 1983), *reprinted*, N.Y. ST. B.J. 8 (Oct., 1983), N.Y. St. B.J. 31 (Nov., 1983); *excerpted*, 33 JOUR. LEG. ED. 579 (1983).

[56] *Id.*, *citing* Burger, *Isn't There a Better Way?* 68 A.B.A. JOUR. 274 (1982); Burger, *Agenda for 2000 A.D. — A Need for Systemic Anticipation*, 70 F.R.D. 83, 93–96 (1976).

[57] *Id.* at 1089–1090.

adjudication in more public terms. That is, civil litigation is "an institutional arrangement for using state power to bring a recalcitrant reality closer to our chosen ideals."[58] Thus, "we turn to courts not because of some quirk in our personalities, but because we need to, and we train our students in the tougher arts not because we take a special pleasure in combat, but to equip them to secure all that the law promises."[59] Fiss concludes:

> To conceive of the civil lawsuit in public terms as America does might be unique. I am willing to assume that no other country . . . has a case like *Brown v. Board of Education*, in which the judicial power is used to eradicate the caste structure. I am willing to assume that no other country conceives of law and uses law in quite the way we do. But this should be a source of pride rather than shame. What is unique is not the problem, that we live short of our ideals, but that we alone seem willing to do something about it. Adjudication American-style is not a reflection of our combativeness but rather a tribute to our inventiveness and perhaps even more to our commitment.[60]

Comparing "adjudication American-style" with that in England, Ralph Temple has noted that there are no lawsuits in Britain challenging the legality of an oppressive law, no injunctions against illegal government actions, and no class actions to protect civil liberties.[61] British law "has yet to discover the principle flowing from *Marbury v. Madison* . . . , that a healthy legal system requires that the courts have the power to declare unlawful those acts of the majority, through its legislature or its executive, which are abusive."[62]

Temple notes that there is no greater animosity between Irish Protestants and Catholics than there was between Southern whites and blacks. Nevertheless, the bitterness has been deeper and the violence greater in Ireland because the British legal system is "incapable of producing social revolution and justice through its legal system — incapable of producing a *Brown v. Board of Education*, a *Baker v. Carr*, or a *United States v. Richard Nixon*."[63] That is, through our constitutional adversary system, "[t]ime and again the heat of our social struggles has been effectively transmuted into courtroom battles, and our society is the stronger for it."[64]

As indicated by their citation of *Brown v. Board of Education* and other cases of national import, Fiss and Temple are directing their attention principally to civil litigation in which the outcome of the particular case is an expression of public policy that extends beyond the interests of the immediate parties. The point they make is of broader significance, however, and is not limited to the overtly "political" case or even to the leading case that establishes the new rule.

---

[58] *Id.*

[59] *Id.*

[60] *Id.*

[61] Ralph Temple, *In Defense of the Adversary System*, ABA LITIGATION, vol. 2, no. 2, 43, 47 (Winter, 1976).

[62] *Id.*

[63] *Id.*

[64] *Id.*

For example, a case might hold for the first time that a tenant has a right, apart from the express terms of her lease, to safe and habitable premises, or that a consumer can avoid an unconscionable sales-financing agreement, or that an employee under a contract terminable at will can sue for wrongful discharge, or that an insurance company can be held liable in punitive damages for arbitrarily withholding benefits due under a policy. Such a case, establishing new rights and deterrents against harmful conduct through civil litigation, is also "a tribute to our inventiveness," using "state power to bring a recalcitrant reality closer to our chosen ideals." If the leading case is to have meaning, however, it will come to fruition in the series of every-day cases that follow and apply it, cases that will truly make the ideal into reality.

In that sense, even ordinary personal injury litigation is an expression, procedurally and substantively, of important public policies. Through the adversary system we provide a social process through which a person with a grievance against another can petition the government for redress in a peaceable fashion. Echoing Fiss and Temple, therefore, the Supreme Court has noted that "[o]ver the course of centuries, our society has settled upon civil litigation as a means for redressing grievances, resolving disputes, and vindicating rights.[65] The Court added: "That our citizens have access to their civil courts is not an evil to be regretted; rather, it is an attribute of our system of justice in which we ought to take pride."[66]

§ 2.07 THE CIVIL TRIAL AND THE CONSTITUTION

Rights like trial by jury and the assistance of counsel — the cluster of rights that comprise constitutional due process of law — are most important when the individual stands alone against the state as an accused criminal. The fundamental characteristics of the adversary system also have a constitutional source, however, in our administration of civil justice. Just as a judge in criminal litigation must be impartial,[67] a judge in a civil trial "best serves the administration of justice by remaining detached from the conflict between the parties."[68] A judge who departs from the essentially passive role that is characteristic of the adversary system deprives civil litigants of due process of law.[69] Also, proper representation in civil as well as criminal cases demands that attorneys take an active role in investigating, analyzing, and advocating their clients' cases. This is "the historical and the necessary way in which lawyers act within the framework of our system of jurisprudence to promote justice and to protect their clients' interests."[70]

---

[65] *Zauderer v. Office of Disciplinary Counsel*, 105 S.Ct. 2265, 2278 (1985).

[66] *Id.*

[67] "[The trial judge] must not take on the role of a partisan; he must not enter the lists; he must not by his ardor induce the jury to join in a hue and cry against the accused. Prosecution and judgment are two quite separate functions in the administration of justice; they must not merge." *United States v. Marzano*, 149 F.2d 923, 926 (2d Cir. 1945) (L. Hand, J.).

[68] *Gardiner v. A.H. Robins Company, Inc.*, 747 F.2d 1180 (8th Cir., 1984), *quoting Reserve Mining Co. v. Lord*, 529 F.2d 181, 185–186 (8th Cir., 1976).

[69] *Id.* at 1191–1192.

[70] *Hickman v. Taylor*, 329 U.S. 495, 511 (1947) (Jackson, J., concurring).

The Supreme Court has held that the Due Process Clauses protect civil litigants who seek recourse in the courts, either as plaintiffs attempting to redress grievances or as defendants trying to maintain their rights.[71] Due process in civil cases is not identical, of course, to due process in serious criminal cases. For example, as in criminal cases not involving imprisonment, the individual's right to an opportunity to be heard does not necessarily mean that the state has an obligation to provide counsel to a civil litigant at state expense.[72] The Supreme Court has recognized, however, that in civil cases as well as criminal, due process would be denied if a court were arbitrarily to refuse to hear a party through retained counsel.[73] Also, the right to trial by jury in the traditional common law manner is guaranteed in civil actions at law by the Seventh Amendment[74] and by similar state constitutional provisions.

It is misleading to suggest, therefore, that the adversary system is part of our constitutional tradition in the administration of criminal but not civil justice. In fact, the adversary system in civil litigation has played a central role in fulfilling the constitutional goals to "establish Justice, insure domestic Tranquility, . . . promote the general Welfare, and secure the Blessings of Liberty . . . ."[75] The Supreme Court recognized these purposes in its holdings that civil litigation is part of the First Amendment right to petition, through the courts, for redress of grievances.[76] That right is not limited to political issues or litigation against the government, but embraces "any field of human interest" and any controversy, including even personal injury cases between private parties.[77]

The line of cases establishing the constitutional foundations of civil litigation begins, appropriately, with a civil rights case, *NAACP v. Button*.[78] The

---

[71] *Logan v. Zimmerman Rush Co.*, 102 S.Ct. 1148, 1154 (1982). *See also* Pielemeier, *Due Process Limitations on the Application of Collateral Estoppel Against Nonparties to Prior Litigation*, 63 B.U.L. REV. 383, 397–401 (1983).

[72] *Lassiter v. Department of Social Services*, 452 U.S. 18, 101 S.Ct. 2153 (1981); *cf. Santosky v. Kramer*, 102 S.Ct. 1388 (1982); *In Matter of the Appeal in Gila County Juvenile Action*, 637 P.2d 740 (Ariz. 1981).

[73] *Powell v. Alabama*, 287 U.S. 45, 69 (1932); *Goldberg v. Kelley*, 397 U.S. 254, 270 (1970).

A plurality opinion in *Walters v. National Association of Radiation Survivors*, 473 U.S. 305, 105 S.Ct. 3180 (1985), upheld a 120-year-old statute that put a $10 limit on lawyers' fees in applications for benefits before the Veterans Administration. The plurality found the procedures consistent with due process because veterans' groups make trained advocates available to veterans free of charge, the veterans' applications are unopposed by any adversary, and the veterans' burden of proof is less than a preponderance of the evidence.

Despite those unique factors, Justice Stevens was correct in concluding that the plurality opinion "does not appreciate the value of individual liberty." 105 S.Ct. at 3209, 3216 (Stevens, J., dissenting). *See also* Himelstein, *This Is One Court with a Shortage of Lawyers — Judge Lets It Be Known: Veterans Need Legal Help, Fast*, LEGAL TIMES, May 4, 1992, at p. 1.

Congress responded by repealing the statute limiting lawyers' fees.

[74] *Sartor v. Arkansas Natural Gas Co.*, 320 U.S. 620, 627 (1944); *Stevens v. Howard D. Johnson*, 181 F.2d 390, 394 (4th Cir., 1950).

[75] U.S. Const., Preamble.

[76] *Bill Johnson's Restaurants, Inc. v. NLRB*, 461 U.S. 731, 741 (1983); *United Mine Workers v. Illinois Bar Association*, 389 U.S. 217, 223 (1967).

[77] *United Mine Workers v. Illinois Bar Association*, 389 U.S. at 223, *quoting Thomas v. Collins*, 323 U.S. 516, 531 (1945).

[78] 371 U.S. 415, 83 S.Ct. 328 (1963).

State of Virginia had sought to prohibit NAACP lawyers from soliciting clients to litigate school desegregation cases. The state's position was that it had a legitimate, traditional interest in proscribing solicitation by lawyers who have a financial interest (as the NAACP lawyers did)[79] in stirring up litigation.

Significantly, even in dissenting in *Button*, Justice Harlan made the same point that Professor Fiss was later to make:

> We have passed the point where litigation is regarded as an evil that must be avoided if some accommodation short of a lawsuit can possibly be worked out. Litigation is often the desirable and orderly way of resolving disputes of broad public significance, and of obtaining vindication of fundamental rights.[80]

The majority also saw the case in terms of broad public policy. In the context of NAACP objectives, litigation is "not a technique of resolving private differences;" rather it is a "means for achieving the lawful objectives of equality of treatment by . . . government," and "a form of political expression" that may well be "the sole practical avenue open to a minority to petition for redress of grievances."[81]

Button was followed a year later by *Brotherhood of Railroad Trainmen v. Virginia*.[82] That case involved a union practice of soliciting job-related personal injury litigation on behalf of lawyers selected by the union. The two dissenting justices pointed out that, unlike *Button*, the *Brotherhood* case did not involve "a 'form of political expression' to secure, through court action, constitutionally protected civil rights."[83] On the contrary, they noted, "[p]ersonal injury litigation is not a form of political expression, but rather a procedure for the settlement of damage claims."[84] The Court nevertheless held, following *Button*, that "in regulating the practice of law a State cannot ignore the rights of individuals secured by the Constitution."[85] The Court recognized that the substantive (personal injury) rights involved had been conferred by Congress in the Safety Appliance Act and the Federal Employers' Liability Act, "statutory rights which would be vain and futile" if workers, through a selected spokesperson, could not receive counsel regarding civil litigation.[86]

The next case in the *Button* line is *United Mineworkers of America v. Illinois State Bar Association*,[87] where the union had employed a lawyer on salary to represent members in litigating workers' compensation claims. The state enjoined the union activity as unauthorized practice of law, distinguishing *Button* as being concerned chiefly with "litigation that can be characterized as a form of political expression."[88]

---

[79] *See id.*, 371 U.S. at 457 (Harlan, J., dissenting).

[80] *NAACP v. Button*, 371 U.S. at 453.

[81] *Id.* at 429.

[82] 377 U.S. 1, 84 S.Ct. 1113 (1964).

[83] *Id.* at 10 (Clark, J., dissenting), *quoting NAACP v. Button*, 371 U.S. at 429.

[84] *Id.* at 10 (Clark, J., dissenting).

[85] *Id.* at 6.

[86] *Id.* at 5–6.

[87] 389 U.S. 217, 88 S.Ct. 353 (1967).

[88] *Id.* at 221.

The Supreme Court responded, however, that its decisions in *Button* and *Brotherhood of Railroad Trainmen* cannot be so narrowly limited. Even though the litigation in question was not bound up with political matters of acute social moment, the First Amendment extends beyond political activity. "Great secular causes, with small ones," are protected, and are "not confined to any field of human interest."[89] Subsequently, in response to a further effort to limit the scope of these cases, the Supreme Court reiterated in *United Transportation Union v. State Bar of Michigan* that the union's activity "undertaken to obtain meaningful access to the courts [in personal injury cases] is a fundamental right within the protection of the First Amendment."[90]

The underlying substantive rights in the union cases had been established by federal statute, but that fact is not controlling. On the contrary, the right to petition for redress of grievances in a tort case in a state court is protected even if the state litigation has a chilling effect on federal statutory rights. For example, in *Bill Johnson's Restaurants v. NLRB*,[91] an employer had sued a waitress in state court for libel and other torts, demanding relief that included $500,000 in punitive damages. The alleged libel had been committed during efforts to organize a union. The employer had threatened to "get even" with the picketers "if it's the last thing I do," and he had warned the waitress' husband that he would hurt the couple financially.[92] After a four-day hearing, an NLRB administrative law judge found that the employer had filed the state civil action to retaliate against the employee's exercise of rights under the National Labor Relations Act, and also found that the allegedly libelous statements were truthful. Relying upon those findings, the NLRB enjoined the employer from prosecuting the state action, and the Ninth Circuit affirmed the Board's order.

The Supreme Court acknowledged that the broad, remedial provisions of the National Labor Relations Act were intended to guarantee employees the right to engage in concerted activity without fear of restraint or interference from the employer.[93] The Court also recognized the chilling effect on that right of a state lawsuit, particularly when filed against an hourly-wage waitress who lacks the backing of a union.[94] Nevertheless, the Court unanimously reinstated the state tort action.

In doing so, the Court relied in part on an earlier holding that the antitrust laws do not prohibit filing of a lawsuit, regardless of the plaintiff's anticompetitive motive in doing so, unless the suit is a "mere sham."[95] Thus, as long as litigation has a "reasonable basis," as distinguished from being "baseless litigation," the First Amendment right to petition for redress of grievances through civil litigation prevails over legislative policy.[96] Not only does the

---

[89] *Id.* at 233, *quoting Thomas v. Collins*, 323 U.S. 516, 531, 65 S.Ct. 315, 323 (1945).

[90] 401 U.S. 576, 585, 91 S.Ct. 1076, 1082 (1971).

[91] 461 U.S. 731, 103 S.Ct. 2161 (1983).

[92] *Id.* at 733, 2165.

[93] *Id.* at 470, 2168.

[94] *Id.* at 471, 2169.

[95] *California Motor Transport Co. v. Trucking Unlimited*, 404 U.S. 508, 511 (1972). This rule is often referred to as the *Noerr* doctrine, from *Eastern Railroad Presidents Conference v. Noerr Motor Freight, Inc.*, 365 U.S. 127 (1961).

[96] *Bill Johnson's Restaurants v. NLRB*, 103 S.Ct. at 2170.

party to a labor dispute have a constitutional right to seek local judicial protection from tortious conduct, but the state has "a compelling interest in maintaining domestic peace"[97] — a fundamental social goal that is fostered by civil litigation.

Bill Johnson's Restaurants was reaffirmed in *Professional Real Estate Investors, Inc. v. Columbia Pictures Industries, Inc.*[98] The Court explained that the First Amendment right to litigate cannot be overcome by the "sham" exception unless the lawsuit is "objectively baseless" or "objectively meritless."[99] To satisfy that test, the litigation must be "so baseless that no reasonable litigant could realistically expect to secure favorable relief."[100] All that is necessary is an objective "chance" that a claim "may" be held valid.[101] In that event, the First Amendment right is secure, even if the litigant has no subjective expectation of success and is acting maliciously.[102]

The union cases discussed earlier — *Brotherhood of Railroad Trainmen, United Mine Workers,* and *United Transportation Union* — involved associational activity. That is, union members had joined together to protect common interests, including the right to petition for redress of grievances through the courts. Those opinions therefore discuss both the right of association and the right to petition, each of which is separately protected by the First Amendment. The right to petition is, of course, granted to individuals and not solely to associations. Indeed, the Court in *Brotherhood of Railroad Trainmen* expressed its concern with "the rights of individuals" to petition for redress of grievances.[103] Moreover, it would be anomalous if an individual were to have a lesser right than a group to seek redress in the courts.[104]

§ 2.08   THE JURY AS AN ASPECT OF THE ADVERSARY SYSTEM

Another constitutional element of our adversary system is the jury. In criminal cases the right to trial by jury is guaranteed by Article III, section

---

[97] 461 U.S. at 741,103 S.Ct. at 2169.

[98] 508 U.S. 49, 113 S.Ct. 1920, 1927 (1993).

[99] *Id.* at 1928.

[100] *Id.* at 1929.

[101] *Id.*

[102] *Id.* at 1926, 1929.

[103] *Brotherhood of Railroad Trainmen v. Virginia,* 377 U.S. at 6. *See also Bill Johnson's Restaurants v. NLRB,* 461 U.S. 731 (1983).

[104] The fact that an association was involved cannot, therefore, have been the controlling factor. However, the plurality opinion in *Walters v. National Association of Radiation Survivors* says of the union cases that "the First Amendment interest at stake was *primarily* the right to associate." 473 U.S.305, 335 (1985) (emphasis added). The *Walters* plurality does not discuss the right to petition for redress of grievances, nor does it cite the Court's opinion in *Bill Johnson's Restaurants,* unanimously upholding the individual's right to petition. In the same year, moreover, the Supreme Court reiterated that "[f]iling a complaint is a form of petitioning activity." *McDonald v. Smith,* 472 U.S. 479 (1985).

The strongest argument for the defendant waitresses in *Bill Johnson's Restaurants* was that the state litigation had been brought by their employer for the purpose of chilling their constitutional and statutory rights to associate in a union; even so, it was the employer's right to petition, not the employees' right of association, that prevailed.

2, of the Constitution and by the Sixth Amendment; in civil cases at law, trial by jury is secured by the Seventh Amendment. State constitutions have similar provisions.

In criminal cases the jury serves to prevent oppression by the government.[105] As observed by Justice Lewis F. Powell, Jr. (who was neither a radical nor a cynic):

> Judges are employees of the state. They are usually dependent upon it for their livelihood. And the use of economic pressure to express displeasure with decisions unfavorable to those in power is not novel. Congress' exclusion of the Justices of the Supreme Court from the general pay increase for other federal judges [in 1965] is an unfortunate example . . . .[106]

Justice Powell went on to note that reprisals against jurors for verdicts disagreeable to those in power are less likely because they would involve far greater political risks.[107] As the Supreme Court has held, therefore, the jury provides "an inestimable safeguard against the . . . compliant, biased, or eccentric judge."[108]

Trial by jury is particularly important in criminal litigation, but its value in civil trials is considerable. As noted by Alexander Hamilton in The Federalist No. 83, the most effective argument against adoption of the Constitution without a Bill of Rights was the absence of a requirement of trial by jury in civil cases.[109] The Supreme Court has therefore recognized that the civil jury is "so fundamental and sacred" that it should be "jealously guarded" by the courts.[110]

One of our most respected federal trial judges, William G. Young, has emphasized the effect of the jury in democratizing the law:

> Without juries, the pursuit of justice becomes increasingly archaic, with elite professionals talking to others, equally elite, in jargon the elegance of which is in direct proportion to its unreality. Juries are the great leveling and democratizing element in the law. They give it its authority and generalized acceptance in ways the imposing buildings and sonorous openings cannot hope to match.[111]

Thus, the American jury system is "our most vital day-to-day expression of direct democracy," in which "citizens are themselves the government."[112] In

---

[105] *Duncan v. Louisiana*, 391 U.S. 145, 155 (1968).

[106] Lewis F. Powell, *Jury Trial of Crimes*, 23 WASH. & LEE L. REV. 1, 9–10 (1966).

[107] *Id.* at 10. *See* Robert D. McFadden, *U.S. Judge Retracts Criticism of a Juror*, N.Y. TIMES, Feb. 10, 1987. The judge publicly apologized for criticizing the sole juror who had held out for acquittal after a two-week trial, thereby causing a mistrial. On its editorial page the *Times* denounced the criticism of the juror as an "outrage." N.Y. TIMES, Feb. 12, 1987, at A30. On June 24, 2002, the U.S. Supreme Court ruled that only a jury may sentence a convicted murderer to death. *See Ring v. Arizona*, 2002 WL 1357257 (U.S.)

[108] *Duncan v. Louisiana*, 391 U.S. at 156.

[109] Cited in *In re U.S. Financial Securities Litigation*, 609 F.2d 411, 420 n.29 (9th Cir. 1979).

[110] *Jacob v. City of New York*, 315 U.S. 752, 752–753, 62 S.Ct. 854 (1942), *quoted in In re U.S. Financial Securities Litigation*, 609 F.2d at 421. *See also Dimick v. Schiedt*, 55 S.Ct. 296, 301 (1935); *Beacon Theatres v. Westover*, 79 S.Ct. 948 (1959).

[111] W.G. YOUNG, TRYING THE HIGH VISIBILITY CASE, text at note 26 (1984).

[112] *Id.*, text at note 20. *See also* Jeffrey Morausen, *We the Jury*.

this governmental role, juries have the power to nullify legislation — to "limit . . . the power of legislatures who eventually must countenance the nonenforceability of [criminal] laws which citizens are unwilling to enforce."[113] Similarly, jurors can bring the moral sense of the community to bear in civil cases in finding for plaintiffs or defendants and in assessing damages.

Also, as Chief Justice Rehnquist has reiterated, the "very inexperience [of jurors] is an asset because it secures a fresh perception of each trial, avoiding the stereotypes said to infect the judicial eye."[114] Professor Paul Carrington adds the pungent comment that juries are "a remedy for judicial megalomania, the occupational hazard of judging."[115]

§ 2.09 THE SEARCH FOR AN ALTERNATIVE SYSTEM

In both criminal and civil cases, therefore, the adversary system of justice comprises a constitutional system that includes the right to retained counsel, trial by jury, and other processes that are constitutionally due to one who seeks to redress a grievance through litigation. It is not surprising, therefore, that those who urge fundamental changes in the adversary system typically ignore the constitutional obstacles to their proposals.

As we have seen, for example, Marvin Frankel acknowledges that the adversary system is "cherished as an ideal of constitutional proportions" in part because "it embodies the fundamental right to be heard."[116] He acknowledges too that other cherished values, including privacy, personal dignity, security, and autonomy, are commonly found to outweigh the search for truth.[117] Accordingly, the Supreme Court has recognized the lawyer's obligation to suppress evidence that has been obtained in violation of those values.[118] Frankel adds, therefore, that "[t]he problem of how to weigh the competing values is, obviously, at the heart of the concerns to be addressed in these chapters."[119]

Nevertheless, Frankel's book includes barely a paragraph describing in positive terms the right to counsel,[120] refers only in passing to the privilege against self-incrimination,[121] and makes scant if any reference to privacy, personal dignity, autonomy, or other fundamental rights that gain vitality from the adversary system. Although the thesis of his book is that the adversary system too often sacrifices truth to "other values that are inferior, or even illusory,"[122] Frankel does not identify which of the competing values that he

---

[113] Paul Carrington, *Trial by Jury*, Duke L. Mag. 13 (vol. 5, no. 1, 1987) *See also* Scheflin, *Jury Nullification: The Right to Say No*, 45 S. Cal. L. Rev. 168 (1972); P. Devlin, Trial by Jury 160 (1956); N.J. Finkel, Commonsense Justice: Jurors' Notions of the Law (Harvard, 1995).

[114] *Parklane Hosiery Co., Inc. v. Shore*, 439 U.S. 322, 355 (1979) (Rehnquist, J., dissenting), *quoting* H. Kalven & H. Zeisel, The American Jury (1966).

[115] Paul Carrington, *Trial by Jury*, Duke L. Mag. 13 (vol. 5, no. 1, 1987).

[116] Frankel, Partisan Justice at 12.

[117] *Id.*

[118] *Id.*

[119] *Id.*

[120] *Id.* at 5–6.

[121] *Id.* at 76, 78 *et seq.*

[122] *Id.* at 12.

has identified are in fact inferior or illusory, nor does he suggest how those rights are to be subordinated without doing violence to the Constitution.

Those who would either replace or make substantial changes in the adversary system must ultimately sustain the burden of showing how their proposals can be reconciled with constitutional rights. Even before that point is reached, however, they must demonstrate, in their own utilitarian terms, that the adversary system is inferior to the proposed alternatives. To the contrary, the available evidence suggests that the adversary system is the method of dispute resolution that is most effective in determining truth, that gives the parties the greatest sense of having received justice, and that is most successful in fulfilling other social goals as well.

One system of justice that has recently received serious although brief consideration is the way in which trials are conducted under autocratic regimes like the Soviet Union and China, where lawyers are "servants of the state." For example, at the conference of "members of the country's professional elite" referred to earlier,[123] the discussants considered whether the United States should adopt "the system of adjudication used in the countries that describe themselves as socialist," including the (then Communist) Soviet Union.[124] Specifically, the advocate would not be chosen by and owe primary allegiance to a party to the litigation; rather, each lawyer would be a member of the court's staff, responsible to the court for investigating and presenting an "assigned" side of the case.[125] This proposed abandonment of the traditional ideal of the right to counsel was not limited to civil cases; indeed, it was being contemplated principally for criminal cases.[126] The discussants concluded, however, that despite the "perversions" of client-centered advocacy, "the detachment of advocate from client might beget worse."[127] It was on that "note of resignation" that the discussion of alternatives to the adversary system "died out."[128]

More sophisticated (and more persevering) critics have turned to the inquisitorial systems of continental European democracies for an alternative to the adversary system or for ideas for restructuring it.[129] The central characteristic of the inquisitorial model is the active role of the judge, who is given the principal responsibility for searching out the relevant facts. In an adversary system the evidence is presented in dialectical form by opposing lawyers; in an inquisitorial system the evidence is developed in a predominantly unilateral fashion by the judge, and the lawyers' role is minimal.[130]

One contention of those who favor the inquisitorial model is that the adversary system limits the fact-finder to two sources of data or to one of two

---

[123] HAZARD, *supra*, note 1.

[124] *Id.* at 125–126.

[125] *Id.*

[126] *Id.*

[127] *Id.* at 126.

[128] *Id.*

[129] *See, e.g.,* JOHN H. LANGBEIN, COMPARATIVE CRIMINAL PROCEDURE: GERMANY (1977); LLOYD L. WEINREB, DENIAL OF JUSTICE: CRIMINAL PROCESS IN THE UNITED STATES (1977).

[130] *See* MIRJAN H. DAMASKA, *Presentation of Evidence and Factfinding Precision*, 123 U. PA. L. REV. 1083, 1087–1090 (1975).

rival factual conclusions.[131] Frequently, of course, there is no need for more than two submissions, for example, if the sole issue is whether one car or the other ran the red light, or whether the defendant was the man who had the gun. In such a case, it is ordinarily appropriate for the factfinder to rely upon two sets of conflicting data, which may come, of course, from numerous sources.

Where there truly are more than two sides of a case, however, the adversary system provides a variety of devices for presenting them. Such procedures include joinder of plaintiffs and defendants, impleader, interpleader, intervention, class actions with more than one class representative and with sub-classes, and amicus presentations. To take a relatively simple illustration, a single adversary proceeding may involve the following diverse submissions of fact: (a) D1 was negligent in driving; (b) D2 was negligent in repairing the brakes; (c) D3 manufactured a car with a faulty brake-system design; (d) D4 supplied the car manufacturer with brakes that had a latent defect; (e) P was actually the only party at fault; and (f) P was contributorily negligent.

§ 2.10 EFFECTIVENESS IN THE SEARCH FOR TRUTH

Those who favor the inquisitorial model also contend that it produces a larger body of relevant information for the decision-maker than does an adversarial system. For example, Professor Peter Brett argues that the inquisitorial system is preferable because the judge is not limited to the material that the opposing parties choose to present.[132] Rather, the judge "may if he wishes" actively search out and incorporate in his decision materials that neither party wishes to present. All other considerations, Brett asserts, "pale into insignificance beside this one."[133]

Unfortunately, however, just as the inquisitorial system "allows the fact-finder free rein to follow all trails,"[134] it also allows the fact-finder to ignore all trails but the one that initially appears to be the most promising. It does so, moreover, without the corrective benefit of investigation and presentation of evidence by active adversaries.

This concern was expressed in a prominent thesis that was put forth by Professor Lon L. Fuller and adopted by a Joint Conference of the American Bar Association and the Association of American Law Schools:[135]

> What generally occurs in practice is that at some early point a familiar pattern will seem to emerge from the evidence; an accustomed label is waiting for the case and without awaiting further proofs, this label is promptly assigned to it. It is a mistake to suppose that this premature cataloguing must necessarily result from impatience,

---

[131] Peter Brett, *Legal Decisionmaking and Bias: A Critique of an "Experiment,"* 45 U. Colo. L. Rev. 1, 23 (1973).

[132] *Id.* at 9.

[133] *Id.* at 22.

[134] *Id.*

[135] Lon L. Fuller, *The Adversary System*, in Talks on American Law 34 (H. Berman ed., 1971); Joint Conference on Professional Responsibility, *Report*, 44 ABA Jour. 1159 (1958).

prejudice or mental sloth. Often it proceeds from a very understandable desire to bring the hearing into some order and coherence, for without some tentative theory of the case there is no standard of relevance by which testimony may be measured. But what starts as a preliminary diagnosis makes a strong imprint on the mind, while all that runs counter to it is received with diverted attention.

An adversary presentation seems the only effective means for combatting this natural human tendency to judge too swiftly in terms of the familiar that which is not yet fully known.

As suggested by its adoption by the Joint Conference, Professor Fuller's thesis is undoubtedly shared by the overwhelming majority of American lawyers and judges, on the basis of both intuition and practical experience.

The validity of the Fuller thesis can be considered in both theoretical and practical contexts. If the inquisitorial judge is to pursue the truth of a particular matter, where does she start? The "most sophisticated modern view" in Europe recognizes an inescapable "circularity" in the inquisitorial judge's role: "You cannot decide which facts matter unless you have already selected, at least tentatively, applicable decisional standards. But most of the time you cannot properly understand these legal standards without relating them to the factual situation of the case."[136] In addition, "[i]t stands to reason that there can be no meaningful interrogation [of witnesses by the judge] unless the examiner has at least some conception of the case and at least some knowledge about the role of the witnesses in it."[137]

In Europe the solution to the inquisitorial judge's "circularity" problem is the investigative file, or dossier. The dossier is prepared by the police, who, in theory, act under the close supervision of a skilled and impartial judge or examining magistrate. "The practice, however, is in striking contrast to [this] myth."[138] The examining magistrate's investigative and supervisory role is minimal. The dossier — on which the trial judge relies to decide what facts and law are relevant to the case — is little more than a file compiled by the police.[139] "The plain fact is that examining magistrates are no more likely than comparable American officials to leave their offices, conduct prompt interrogations of witnesses or of accused persons, or engage in searches or surveillance. For such tasks, they rely almost entirely upon the police."[140] The trial judge, in turn, tends to rely heavily upon the police-developed dossier.[141]

The prosecutorial bias that inevitably results from this process is confirmed by the personal experience of Bostjan M. Zupancic. Zupancic clerked for several investigating magistrates in the Circuit Court of Ljubljana,

---

[136] Damaska, 123 U. PA. L. REV. at 1087.

[137] Id. at 1089.

[138] Goldstein and Marcus, *The Myth of Judicial Supervision in Three 'Inquisitorial' Systems: France, Italy, and Germany*, 87 YALE L.J. 240, 248 (1997); *see also* Weigand, *Continental Cures for American Ailments*, 2 CRIME AND JUSTICE 381 (Morris & Tonry, eds., 1980); Edward Tomlinson, *Nonadversarial Justice: The French Experience*, 42 MD. L. REV. 131 (1983).

[139] Goldstein and Marcus, 87 YALE L.J. at 247–250, 259.

[140] Id. at 250.

[141] Id. at 166.

Yugoslavia. "One cannot start from the presumption of innocence" under an inquisitorial system, he writes.

> In purely practical terms, if one opens a file in which there is only a police report and the prosecutor's subsequent request for investigation and develops one's thought processes from this departing point — one cannot but be partial. A clear hypothesis is established as to somebody's guilt, and the investigating magistrate's job is to verify it. But just as a scientist cannot start from the premise that his hypothesis is wrong, so the investigating magistrate cannot start from the premise that the defendant is innocent.[142]

In Zupancic's experience, therefore, prosecutorial bias on the part of the inquisitorial judge is not a matter of probability; it is a certainty.[143]

Meanwhile, the prosecutor plays a distinctly secondary role to the police and the judge, and defense counsel is "particularly inactive."[144] "Rarely does [the defense attorney] conduct his own investigation in preparing for trial. Even if his client should suggest someone who he thinks will offer testimony favorable to the defense, he often passes the name on to the prosecutor or judge without even troubling first to interview the witness himself."[145] Very likely, European defense lawyers do not conduct the kind of thorough interview of a potential witness that is professionally required in the United States, because they could be charged with a criminal offense or with professional impropriety for obstructing justice if they did so.[146]

Only in the rare case in which the defense lawyer assumes an active — that is, an adversarial — role, is there an exception to the typical situation in which the inquisitorial judge follows the course plotted out by the police.[147] In those few cases, "genuine probing trials" do take place.[148] The European experience itself seems to confirm, therefore, that adversarial presentation by partisan advocates is more effective in developing relevant material than is unilateral investigation by a judge.

Our constitutional adversary system is based in part on the premise that the adversary system is more effective in the search for truth. As the Supreme Court has reiterated in an opinion by Justice Powell:

> The dual aim of our criminal justice system is "that guilt shall not escape or innocence suffer," . . . . To this end, we have placed our confidence in the adversary system, entrusting to it the primary responsibility for developing relevant facts on which a determination of guilt or innocence can be made.[149]

---

[142] Bostjan M. Zupancic, Criminal Law: The Conflict and the Rules 54, note 45.

[143] Id. See also id. at 54–63.

[144] Id. at 265.

[145] Id.

[146] Damaska, 123 U. Pa. L. Rev. at 1088–1089 and note 12.

[147] Goldstein and Marcus, 87 Yale L. Jour. at 265–266.

[148] Id. at 265.

[149] United States v. Nobles, 422 U.S. 225, 230, 95 S.Ct. 2160, 2166 (1975), quoting Berger v. United States, 295 U.S. 78, 88 (1935), and citing United States v. Nixon, 418 U.S. 683, 709 (1974); Williams v. Florida, 399 U.S. 78, 82 (1970); Elkins v. United States, 364 U.S. 206, 234 (1960) (Frankfurter, J., dissenting).

In the criminal process there are special rules, particularly the exclusionary rules, that recognize values that take precedence over truth. The adversary system should be even more effective in determining truth in the civil process, therefore, where such values are not ordinarily applicable. A study of civil litigation in Germany conducted by Professor Benjamin Kaplan (later a Justice in the Supreme Judicial Court of Massachusetts) found the judge-dominated search for facts in German civil practice to be neither broad nor vigorous, and "lamentably imprecise."[150] Professor Kaplan concluded that the adversary system in this country does succeed in presenting a greater amount of relevant evidence before the court than does the inquisitorial system.[151]

There is support for that conclusion in experiments conducted by members of the departments of psychology and law at the University of North Carolina.[152] One study[153] tested the thesis, which Professor Freedman had put forward, that the most effective means of determining truth is to place upon a skilled advocate for each side the responsibility of investigating and presenting the facts from a partisan perspective.[154] Although that proposition is related to the Fuller thesis, its focus is different. Professor Fuller was concerned with the fact-finder and with her mental processes in developing a working hypothesis and then unconsciously becoming committed to it prematurely. The second thesis focuses on the adversaries and on their incentive to search out and to present persuasively all material that is useful to each side, thereby providing the fact-finder with all parts of the whole.

The study produced conclusions that tend to confirm both Fuller's thesis regarding the judge's psychological risk of premature commitment to a theory, and Freedman's thesis regarding the adversaries' incentive to investigate diligently. First, as soon as they become confident of their assessment of the case, inquisitorial fact investigators tend to stop their search, even though all the available evidence is not yet in.[155] Second, with one exception of major importance, even adversary investigators have a similar but lesser tendency to judge prematurely.[156]

---

[150] Benjamin Kaplan, *Civil Procedure — Reflections on the Comparison of Systems*, 9 BUFF. L. REV. 409, 420–421 (1960).

[151] *Id.*

[152] The first of those studies purports to validate the Fuller thesis. John Thibault, Lauren S. Walker, & E. Allen Lind, *Adversary Bias in Legal Decisionmaking*, 86 HARV. L. REV. 386 (1972). The researchers conclude: "The adversary mode apparently counteracts judge or juror bias in favor of a given outcome and thus indeed seems to combat, in Fuller's words, a 'tendency to judge too swiftly in terms of the familiar that which is not yet fully known.'" *Id.*, at 401. However, the methodology of that study has been subjected to devastating criticism. *See* Mirjan H. Damaska, *Presentation of Evidence and Factfinding Precision*, 123 U. PA. L. REV. 1083 (1975); Peter Brett, *Legal Decisionmaking and Bias: A Critique of an Experiment*, 45 U. COLO. L. REV. 1 (1973). Although those criticisms destroy the usefulness of the study, they do not, of course, invalidate the Fuller thesis. Also, the subsequent studies, which are discussed below, have avoided the methodological errors of the first study.

[153] E. Allen Lind, John Thibault, & E. Allen Walker, *Discovery and Presentation of Evidence in Adversary and Nonadversary Proceedings*, 71 MICH. L. REV. 1129 (1973).

[154] The proposition was taken from Monroe H. Freedman, *Professional Responsibilities of the Civil Practitioner*, in EDUCATION IN THE PROFESSIONAL RESPONSIBILITIES OF THE LAWYER 151, 152 (D. Weckstein ed., 1970).

[155] Lind, Thibault, and Walker, 71 MICH. L. REV. at 1141.

[156] *Id.* at 1141–1143.

Third (the crucial exception), when adversary fact investigators find the initial evidence to be unfavorable to their clients, they are significantly more diligent than are inquisitorial investigators in seeking out additional evidence.[157] The researchers concluded, therefore, that the adversary system "does instigate significantly more thorough investigation by advocates initially confronted with plainly unfavorable evidence."[158] That is, in those situations of "great social and humanitarian concern" the adversary system maximizes the likelihood that all relevant facts will be ferreted out and placed before the ultimate fact-finder.[159]

Another finding, which surprised the researchers, is that the opponent of an adversarial lawyer transmits more facts that are unfavorable to her own client. Apparently, awareness that one has an adversary who is determined to expose any coverup is a significant inducement to candor.[160]

We do not mean to suggest that these studies are conclusive proof that the adversary system is preferable as a means to determine truth. Such experimental efforts to replicate real life and to quantify it statistically are limited in their usefulness. At the very least, however, the research that has been done provides no justification for preferring the inquisitorial search for truth or for undertaking radical changes in our adversary system.

§ 2.11   THE FLAWED ANALOGY TO NON-LITIGATION SETTINGS

Opponents of an adversarial model sometimes argue that "others searching after facts — in history, geography, medicine, whatever — do not emulate our adversary system."[161] That proposition, even if accurate, hardly demonstrates that an adversary system is not preferable when society seeks to resolve disputes that have arisen between contesting parties. There are inevitable differences between, say, a scientist seeking a cure for cancer, and two parties who blame each other for an automobile accident. The laboratory is not a courtroom, where each contesting party is asserting her truth as exclusive of the other's and each is demanding her due.

Moreover, in the case of the research scientist, truth is ultimately knowable in an absolute sense — either a cure works or it doesn't. In most litigation, however, we can rarely be certain that a verdict is synonymous with "truth." This is so, unhappily, even when the verdict is based on scientific evidence and/or a confession, and guilt has been determined beyond a reasonable doubt.[162] The modes of inquiry, therefore, tend to reflect the kind of "truth" that is being sought and the manner in which the issue has been presented for resolution.

---

[157] *Id.*

[158] *Id.* at 1143.

[159] *Id.*

[160] *Id.* at 1136.

[161] Marvin E. Frankel, *The Search for Truth: An Umpireal View*, 123 U. Pa. L. Rev. 1036 (1975). *See also* Peter Brett, 45 Colo. L. Rev. at 23.

[162] *See, e.g.*, Jim Dwyer, Peter Neufeld, & Barry Scheck, Actual Innocence: Five Days to Execution and Other Dispatches from the Wrongly Convicted (2000).

Also, the accuracy of the proposition that other disciplines do not follow some form of adversary process is highly doubtful, at least in the breadth in which it is stated.[163] Moreover, to the extent that other disciplines do not use adversarial or dialectical techniques in attempting to resolve disputed issues, they suffer for it.

Assume, for example, a historian trying to determine whether Richard III ordered the murder of the princes in the Tower, or whether it was militarily justifiable for the United States to drop the second atomic bomb on Nagasaki. Obviously, the historian's inquiry would not be conducted in a courtroom, nor would contesting advocates ordinarily be available to appear and present their cases. However, the conscientious historian's search for truth ideally would start from a position of neutrality and would necessarily include a careful evaluation of evidence marshaled in conflicting memoirs of those who were involved or by other historians and commentators strongly committed to differing views.

Unfortunately, though, even scholarly historians (like judges and magistrates) are not always neutral in their search for truth and are not always truthful in their use of research data. For example, the prominent military historian, S.L.A. Marshall, wrote a book purporting to show that 75 percent of infantrymen will not fire their weapons when engaging the enemy.[164] The book has been described as "fundamental" and has had a "profound influence" in military education.[165] Nevertheless, three historians have concluded, more than four decades later, that "[t]he systematic collection of data that made Marshall's ratio of fire so authoritative appears to have been an invention."[166]

Another scandal raising questions of methodology in historical research has related to the role of German industrialists in supporting Hitler. The controversy has involved charges and counter-charges of ideological bias, professional jealousy, and even fraudulent use of sources.[167] As a consequence of this fiercely adversarial debate, historians are "learning [a lesson] very fast . . . . [T]hey are checking their quotations and footnotes thrice over."[168] In short, historical research and analysis has gained in reliability as a result of adversarial challenge.

In medicine there is ordinarily less partisanship than in historical research, because there is less room for the play of political ideology. There is also less

---

[163] A professor of biological sciences and dean of Columbia College has explained "the process of scientific investigation" in part as follows:

> We scientists love to do experiments that show our colleagues to be wrong and, if they are any good, they love to show us to be wrong in turn. *By this adversarial process,* science reveals the way nature actually works.

Robert E. Pollack, *In Science, Error Isn't Fraud,* N.Y. TIMES, May 2, 1989, at A25 (emphasis added).

[164] S.L.A. MARSHALL, MEN AGAINST FIRE (1947).

[165] Halloran, *Pivotal S.L.A. Marshall Book on Warfare Assailed as False,* N.Y. TIMES, Feb. 19, 1989, at A1, A34.

[166] *Id.*

[167] Colin Campbell, *A Quarrel Over Weimar Book,* Dec. 23, 1984, at A1, A35; Colin Campbell, *Academic Fraud Inquiry Dropped,* N.Y. TIMES, Jan. 3, 1985, at C22.

[168] Volker R. Berghahn, *Book Review,* D. ABRAHAM, THE COLLAPSE OF THE WEIMAR REPUBLIC, *N.Y. Times Book Review,* Aug. 2, 1987, at 12, 13.

personal interest and bias than in the typical contested lawsuit. Nevertheless, anyone about to make an important medical decision for oneself or one's family would be well advised to get a second opinion. And if the first opinion has come from a doctor who is generally inclined to perform radical surgery, the second opinion might well be obtained from a doctor who is generally skeptical about the desirability of surgery. According to one study, for example, about 20 percent of surgical operations have been unnecessary.[169] A bit more adversariness in the decision-making process might well have saved a gall bladder here or a uterus there.[170]

Moreover, it is well established in our law that the extent of due process — meaning adversary procedures — properly varies depending upon what is at stake in the litigation.[171] In medical research, prior to World War II, the material rewards of biological research were small, and scientific chicanery was infrequent.[172] Since then, however, publication of discoveries has become essential to professional advancement and to obtaining large grants of money for research.[173] The resultant scandals in the search for scientific truth — including those at the Sloan-Kettering Institute, the University of Cincinnati, Emory University, the University of Utah, M.I.T., and Harvard University — have become sufficiently numerous[174] to warrant editorial comment in *The New York Times*.[175] One result is that scientists have come to recognize the need for an adversarial check by replication of research by a skeptical colleague.[176]

In response to repeated cases of fraud and document destruction — of a kind that critics of partisan justice assume to be unique to lawyers in an

---

[169] Nancy Hicks, *A Second Opinion Reduces surgery*, N.Y. Times, June 19, 1973, at 21.

[170] *See, e.g.*, Gina Kolata, *Rate of Hysterectomies Puzzles Experts*, Science Times, N.Y. Times, Sept. 20, 1988, at C1.

[171] Charles Black, Capital Punishment 32–35 (1974).

[172] Ernest Borek, *Cheating in Science*, N.Y. Times, Jan. 22, 1975, at 35. Nevertheless, recent scholarship has raised serious questions about the integrity of such figures as Louis Pasteur. A Princeton professor maintains, among other things, that Pasteur, to head off competitors, purposely withheld reporting a method he used to prepare the chicken cholera vaccine. Lawrence K. Altman, *Revisionist History Sees Pasteur As Liar Who Stole Rival's Ideas*, N.Y. Times, May 16, 1995, at C1 (discussing Gerald L. Geison, The Private Science of Louis Pasteur). *See also* Dinita Smith, *Scholar Who Says Jung Lied Is at War with Descendants*, N.Y. Times 1, June 3, 1995, at A1.

[173] *Id.*

[174] Philip J. Hilts, *Misconduct in Science Is Not Rare, a Survey Finds*, N.Y. Times, Nov. 12, 1993, at A22; *Scientist Fined for Killing Cells Created in Lab by a Colleague*, N.Y. Times, Aug. 31, 1994; Lawrence K. Altman, *Her Study Shattered the Myth that Fraud in Science is a Rarity*, N.Y. Times, Nov. 23, at C3; Ernest Borek, *Cheating in Science*, N.Y. Times, Jan. 22, 1975, at 35; *Harvard Scientists Retract Publications on Medical Findings*, N.Y. Times, Nov. 22, 1986, at 9, col. 1; Philip M. Boffey, *Study Accusing Researchers of Inaccuracies Is Published*, N.Y. Times, Jan. 15, 1987, at A18; Nicholas Wade, *Fraud and Garbage in Science*, N.Y. Times, Jan. 29, 1987, at A26; Lawrence K. Altman, *Cholesterol Researcher Is Censured for Misrepresenting Data in Article, N.Y. Times*, July 18, 1987, at 8; Malcolm W. Browne, *Physicists Debunk Claim of a New Kind of Fusion*, N.Y. Times, May 3, 1989, at A1; Warren E. Leary, *Inquiry to Reopen in Science Dispute*, N.Y. Times, Apr. 30, 1989, at 29. *See also*, Levine, *Scientific Method and the Adversary Model: Some Preliminary Thoughts*, 29 Am. Psychologist 661, 669–676 (1984).

[175] *Credit and Credibility in Science*, N.Y. Times, July 26, 1987, at D26.

[176] *Id.*

adversary system — the National Institutes of Health felt compelled to establish an Office of Scientific Integrity.[177] The office was originally designed by scientists "who wanted to keep lawyers and legal procedure out of their affairs."[178] But the methods of scientists proved to be a "recipe for disaster" when applied to adjudication.[179] The OSI unfairly and irreparably damaged reputations and careers.[180] As the scientist who first headed up the office acknowledged, he had had no notion of the importance of "fair play and all that."[181] The former director of NIH said that she was "horrified" by the results of nonadversarial justice. "I came full circle to thinking that an adversarial system was necessary," she said, to avoid "a hideous travesty of justice."[182]

In anthropology, "checks and balances" to "control subjectivity" are now recognized as essential.[183] The controversy over a book critical of Margaret Mead's work on Samoa illustrates the problem. Professor Derek Freeman has contradicted Mead's highly influential conclusions regarding childraising, sexual promiscuity, competitiveness, violent behavior, psychological disturbances, and jealousy. He attributes her alleged errors to factors familiar to any adversary cross-examiner: lack of opportunity to observe accurately (she was unfamiliar with the language and lived with expatriate Americans rather than in a Samoan household) and bias (she was intent upon proving that culture controls the character of individuals and societies).[184] Freeman, on the other hand, is known to have strong ideological biases of his own.[185]

As for the merits of the disputed issues, "anthropologists suspect that, as often turns out to be the case, neither [Mead nor Freeman] is totally right or totally wrong."[186] That is, Freeman's adversarial approach has corrected and supplemented Mead's work, which still provides correction and supplementation to his.

Even the field of fossil history — where political or social ideology would appear to have scant influence — has produced evidence that the inquisitorial system is a flawed one for seeking truth. Some of the most influential geological findings in the past quarter century have recently produced charges of "willfully tr[ying] to dupe the scientific community" and "the biggest paleontological fraud of all time." These charges have been met with counter-charges of "lies," "malicious bias," "professional jealousy," and "trying to cash in."[187]

---

[177] See Kolata, *Inquiry Lacking Due Process*, N.Y. TIMES, June 15, 1996, at C3.

[178] *Id.*

[179] *Id.*

[180] *Id.*

[181] *Id.*

[182] *Id.*

[183] N.Y. TIMES, Feb. 6, 1973, at E8, col. 1.

[184] Edwin McDowell, *New samoa book challenges Margaret Mead's Conclusion*, N.Y. TIMES, Jan. 31, 1983, at A1, C12.

[185] *Id.* at C12.

[186] *Id.* at A1.

[187] William K. Stevens, *Scientist Accused of Faking Findings*, N.Y. TIMES, Apr. 23, 1989 at A24.

In short, probably any search for truth can benefit from adversarial "checks and balances" to "control subjectivity." That is particularly true when, as in legal disputes, there are conflicting versions of fact, disagreements over policy, and uncertainty resulting from personal interest and bias.

§ 2.12   A PARADIGM OF THE INQUISITORIAL SEARCH FOR TRUTH

One final illustration. There is considerable concern with the broad, unsupervised prosecutorial discretion that pervades American criminal justice and that produces a large proportion of negotiated guilty pleas. Suppose, then, that we wanted to find out whether judicial supervision of prosecutions, which is characteristic of the inquisitorial systems in France, Italy, and Germany, successfully avoids the problems associated with prosecutorial discretion and plea bargaining.

If we followed an inquisitorial mode of investigation, we might seek out one of the country's leading authorities on criminal law and procedure, whose background includes experience in law practice, service as a consultant to a presidential crime commission, and scholarship in the field. In short, we might turn to Abraham S. Goldstein, Sterling Professor of Law at Yale University, and provide him with grants to employ the assistance of several qualified investigators. If we did, Professor Goldstein could be expected to produce a lengthy, scholarly, and carefully reasoned article in the Yale Law Journal titled, *The Myth of Judicial Supervision in Three 'Inquisitorial' Systems: France, Italy, and Germany.*[188]

We might also expect this paradigm of inquisitorial investigation and fact-finding to settle the issue, but we would be disappointed. In the best adversarial tradition, two other scholars, also with impressive credentials, would write a response to Professor Goldstein and his co-author. The response would charge that the authors had "misinterpreted the most important characteristics of the procedures they intended to describe" and that "their descriptions are substantially misleading," because they were "preoccupied with their own false model" and "captives of the myths they seek to explode."[189]

The irony, of course, is that the scholars who adopted an adversarial posture to challenge Professor Goldstein's inquisitorial findings are two of the leading proponents of the inquisitorial system as a means for determining truth. If we cannot trust that system successfully to seek out the truth in the ideal circumstances of Professor Goldstein's study, however, how much confidence can we have in the inquisitorial system in the courtroom?

The discussion thus far has focused principally on the relative effectiveness of the adversarial and inquisitorial systems in determining truth. The conclusion advanced is that the adversary system is superior, because it mitigates the decision-maker's tendency to judge prematurely and uses the incentive of the contesting parties to search out relevant facts, policies, and authorities.

---

[188] Goldstein and Marcus, 87 YALE L. J. 240.

[189] John H. Langbein and Lloyd L. Weinreb, *Continental Criminal Procedure: "Myth" and Reality*, 87 YALE L. J. 1549, 1550, 1552, 1567 (1978).

At the very least, however, we think it is fair to say that the proponents of an inquisitorial system have not made their case, on grounds of truth-seeking, for remodeling the adversary system in the image of the inquisitorial system.[190]

§ 2.13 INDIVIDUALIZED DECISION-MAKING VERSUS BUREAUCRACY

There is much more to the adversarial-inquisitorial dispute, however, than efficacy in the search for truth. There is also an underlying difference in basic attitudes towards official power and individual rights. The conservative political philosopher, Ernst van den Haag, once described the genius of American democracy, in which official power is subject to checks and balances, as "institutionalized mutual mistrust." It has been observed similarly that "a cornerstone of our adversary system . . . is distrust of bureaucratic and rigidly controlled decision-making."[191] That is, the adversary system reflects not only respect for the individual, but also a lesser respect for bureaucratic authority.

A tennis anecdote helps to illustrate the point. In the 1937 Wimbledon Tournament, the American Champion, Don Budge won a decisive break point in his semifinals match because an official called his opponent's ball out when, as Budge knew, it was in. Budge therefore gave back the point by making an obvious error in returning the next serve. After Budge had won the match, he was approached by Baron Gottfried von Cramm, the German star whom he was to play in the finals. To Budge's surprise, von Cramm criticized Budge for having engaged in unsportsmanlike conduct. It is preferable, von Cramm explained, for a player to suffer an injustice than for an official to be embarrassed by exposure of the erroneous call that caused the injustice.[192] As that anecdote suggests, there are political, social, and humanist values that

---

[190] Moreover, the proposals for adopting the inquisitorial system in this country seem so academic as to be out of touch with reality. An indefatigable proponent of the German system, Professor John H. Langbein, candidly admits that if he had to choose between the German procedure that he praises, and the American procedure that he denigrates, he might have qualms about choosing the German system. Langbein, *The German Advantage in Civil Procedure*, 52 CHI. L. REV. 823, 853 (1985). The reason is that he probably would be litigating in Cook County, Illinois, where "judges are selected by a process in which the criterion of professional competence is at best an incidental value." *Id*. Langbein then implies that he would take his chances with a random choice among federal judges, but he is not clear that he would. We, surely, would not.

To institute the inquisitorial system in this country, with a judiciary properly trained on the German model for its special functions, would require that we first restructure our educational system. Career judges would have several years of legal education, pass a first state examination, and apprentice for two and one-half years. *Id*. at 848–849. (With which judges in Cook County would they apprentice?) After a second examination, a judicial career would begin in the lowest courts; promotion would be based upon an "efficiency rating" determined by such criteria as caseload discharge rates, reversal rates, and evaluation by other judges. *Id*. at 850 (By which judges in Cook County would they be evaluated?) Entirely apart from the formidable constitutional difficulties, therefore, the institution of the inquisitorial system in the United States does not seem imminent for purely practical reasons.

[191] Stephen A. Saltzburg, *The Unnecessarily Expanding Role of the American Trial Judge*, 64 VA. L. REV. 1, 19 (1978).

[192] Bodo, *Whatever Happened to Sportsmanship?* EASTERN REV. 29 (Oct., 1983).

are expressed in the American preference for a system in which there is relatively greater regard for the individual litigant and less for the bureaucratic decision-maker.[193]

One of the ways in which our constitutionalized adversary system controls the bureaucratic tendencies of a professional judiciary is through trial by jury.[194] As discussed earlier, the jury system serves several crucial functions — preventing governmental oppression, countering compliant, biased, or eccentric judges, leveling and democratizing the law, bringing a fresh perspective to familiar fact patterns, and governing by direct democracy. Achievement of those goals requires an independent jury that could not exist under the judicial control that is characteristic of an inquisitorial judge.[195] The judge would investigate the facts; the judge would select the witnesses; the judge would conduct virtually all of the examination of witnesses; and, then, the judge would instruct the jury. In short, the trial would most closely resemble the presentation of evidence by a prosecutor to a grand jury. Although the grand jury was conceived as a safeguard against government abuse, it has become so dominated by the prosecutor that there are frequent suggestions that it be abolished as useless. In an inquisitorial system, we could expect a similar fate for the petit jury.

Damaska provides another perspective on the greater tolerance in continental Europe for bureaucratic justice. He has found in Anglo-American law a striving for "the just result" in the light of the particular circumstances of the individual case.[196] He contrasts this traditionally strong attachment to "individualized justice" with the relatively greater concern of continental decision-makers for "uniformity and predictability: they are much more ready than the common-law adjudicator to neglect the details of the case in order to organize the world of fluid social reality into a system."[197] For anyone trained in the American constitutional system, there is something chilling about a bureaucratic determination to organize the world of fluid social reality into a uniform and predictable system, without regard to the particular cases of individuals.

§ 2.14 THE SENSE OF HAVING BEEN TREATED FAIRLY

The concept of individualized justice embraces two related but distinct ideas. First, there is individualized justice in the sense of respect for the

---

[193] However, sportsmanship suffered a serious blow that year. Shortly after having lost to Budge, von Cramm refused to become a Nazi and publicly criticized the German regime. On his return home, he was arrested, charged with homosexual activities with a German Jew, and sentenced to a year in prison. Wimbledon officials then let it be known that they would not allow the Baron to play there again. Brad Bradford, *A Tennis Champ vs. the Nazis*, N.Y. Times, Letters to the Editor, Feb. 16, 2000, *citing* Alan Tregrove, The Story of the Davis Cup.

[194] W.G. Young, Trying the High Visibility Case, text at notes 18–26 (1984); Saltzburg, 64 Va. L. Rev. at 19.

[195] In fact, the "episodic" nature of investigation and of presenting evidence in Germany makes a jury a practical impossibility. Kaplan, 9 Buff. L. Rev. at 418–419.

[196] Damaska, *Presentation of Evidence and Factfinding Precision*, 123 U. Pa. L. Rev. 1083, 1103–1104 (1975).

[197] *Id.* at 1104.

individual in the light of his or her particular circumstances. Second, there is the idea of individual autonomy — that each of us should have the greatest possible involvement in, if not control over, those decisions that affect our lives in significant ways. With regard to the latter, the empirical studies that have been done suggest, again, a preference for the adversary system over the inquisitorial.

In one such study,[198] the experimenters sought to use the insight of John Rawls[199] that individuals who are ignorant of their own status of relative advantage or disadvantage will choose ideal principles of justice. Subjects in one experimental group were told the details of a dispute, which strongly favored one party, but they were not told which side they would ultimately have to assume. Thus, the subjects were kept behind a Rawlsian "veil of ignorance" regarding their tactical interest in the procedure that might be used to resolve the dispute. Subjects in another experimental group were told about the same dispute but were informed at the outset which side they would be on. The subjects of the study were thus in three groups — those who were ignorant of what their status would be, those who knew that they would have the advantageous position, and those who knew that they would be in the disadvantageous position.

Members of each group were next presented with various models of hearing procedures, ranging from inquisitorial to adversarial, with mixed procedures in between; that is, the procedural models were designed to provide dispute resolution choices ranging from maximum decision-maker control to maximum party control. The subjects were then asked to express their preferences among the procedural models.

"One of the clearest findings in our data," the researchers concluded, "is that the adversary procedure is judged by all of our subjects — both those in front of and behind the veil of ignorance — to be the most preferable and the fairest mode of dispute resolution."[200] More significantly, those subjects who were seeking the fairest procedural model in ignorance of what their own status would be were the most strongly in favor of the adversary system.[201]

Similar results were obtained in further studies conducted in the United States and Germany.[202] One conclusion of the experiment in Germany is that the results in the United States were not significantly affected by cultural bias.[203] Most important, when the ultimate decisional power is in a third party, "participants in both Hamburg and Chapel Hill prefer to use an

---

[198] John Thibault, Laurens Walker, Stephen LaTour, & Pauline Houlden, *Procedural Justice as Fairness*, 26 STAN. L. REV. 1271 (1974).

[199] JOHN RAWLS, A THEORY OF JUSTICE (1971).

[200] Thibault, Walker, LaTour & Houlden, 26 STAN. L. REV. at 1287–1288.

[201] *Id.* at 1288–1289.

[202] Stephen LaTour, Pauline Houlden, Laurens Walker, & John Thibault, *Procedure: Transnational Perspectives and Preferences*, 86 YALE L. J. 258 (1976).

[203] Assuming that there is a culturally determined bias in the United States in favor of an adversary system, that would be a reason to retain that system. Also, Professor Hazard has suggested another perspective on the cultural aspects of procedural models. In our political culture, he notes, "the interrogative system of trial could well turn out to resemble congressional hearings." G. HAZARD, ETHICS IN THE PRACTICE OF LAW 128.

adversary procedure," in which their control over the presentation of the case is highest.[204]

Researchers also have conducted studies to determine whether a litigant's acceptance of the fairness of the actual decision is affected by the litigation system used. They have concluded that "the perception of the fairness of an adversary procedure carries over to create a more favorable reaction to the verdict for persons who directly participate in the decision-making process."[205] This is true "regardless of the outcome."[206] Therefore, "the attorney should see himself as the agency through which the client exercises salutary control over the process. In this client-centered role, the attorney best functions as an officer of the court in the sense of serving the wider public interest."[207]

§ 2.15   THE PROBLEM OF SOCIO-ECONOMIC UNFAIRNESS

There is, nevertheless, a troubling question, about the fairness of a client-centered adversary system in which the wealth of the contending parties — and, therefore, the quality of the representation — may be seriously out of balance. "How much justice can you afford?" the lawyer in a *New Yorker* cartoon pointedly asked a client.[208]

One response is that unequal justice is one of the costs of the American economic system. How much food, housing, clothing, education, or other basic needs can one afford? Sadly, equal justice may be far down on the list for a major portion of our citizens. The criticism is not of an adversary system but of a capitalist one.

Yet an expressed purpose of the Constitution is to "establish Justice,"[209] the judiciary is one of the three branches of our constitutional structure, and due process of law and equal protection under the law are explicitly guaranteed to all persons.[210] If another system of justice were likely to reduce significantly the unfairness caused by an imbalance in litigation resources, without introducing comparable unfairness, one would have to embrace it.

There is no persuasive evidence, however, that the inquisitorial system does that job. At least in personal injury cases, the contingent fee is a great equalizer of legal resources between rich and poor.[211] Legal clinics and prepaid legal plans also mitigate the problem. Moreover, if we are sufficiently concerned about unequal advocacy that we are prepared to revolutionize our

---

[204] LaTour, Houlden, Walker, and Thibault, 86 YALE L. J. at 282.

[205] Walker, Lind, and Thibault, *The Relation Between Procedural and Distributive Justice*, 65 VA. L. REV. 1401, 1416 (1979).

[206] *Id.* at 1417.

[207] *Id.*

[208] THE NEW YORKER BOOK OF LAWYER CARTOONS 73 (2000).

[209] U.S. CONST., Preamble.

[210] U.S. CONST, Amend. V & XIV.

[211] For example, after thousands of people were killed and injured by the release of toxic gas in Bhopal, India, lawyers from the United States traveled half way around the world to take on a multinational corporation on behalf of impoverished victims who otherwise would have gone without effective representation or redress. *See* Ch. 13, *infra.*

system of justice, a more sensible course would be a genuine effort to equalize advocacy through a vastly expanded system of government-supported legal aid.[212]

In any event, it is doubtful that we would be better off with a system of inquisitorial judges instead of zealous advocates. As long as we maintain a capitalist society (or something approximating one) the judges will come predominantly from the upper socioeconomic classes. The judges will also be interested in advancing their careers. One need not be a Marxist to expect class, political favoritism, and other bias to play a significant part in inquisitorial judging.[213] Even in the face of superior resources, therefore, representation by one's own advocate before a jury of one's peers seems a safer choice.

§ 2.16 CONCLUSION

The adversary system, like any human effort to cope with important and complex issues, is sometimes seriously flawed in execution. It is both understandable and appropriate, therefore, that it be subjected to criticism and reform. The case for substantially restructuring it, however, has not been made. On the contrary, based upon reason, intuition, experience, and some experimental studies, there is good reason to believe that the adversary system is superior in determining truth when facts are in dispute between contesting parties.

Even if it were not the best method for determining the truth, however, the adversary system is an expression of some of our most precious rights. In a negative sense, it serves as a limitation on bureaucratic control. In a positive sense, it serves as a safeguard of personal autonomy and respect for each person's particular circumstances. The adversary system thereby gives both form and substance to the humanitarian ideal of the dignity of the individual. The central concern of a system of professional ethics, therefore, should be to strengthen the role of the lawyer in enhancing individual human dignity within the adversary system of justice.

---

[212] *See generally* DEBORAH RHODE, IN THE INTERESTS OF JUSTICE: REFORMING THE LEGAL PROFESSION (2000); FRANKEL, PARTISAN JUSTICE, Ch. 9; Roger C. Cramton, *The Future of the Legal profession: Delivery of Legal Services to Ordinary Americans*, 44 CASE W. RES. L. REV. 531, 587–601 (1994); EMERY A. BROWNELL, LEGAL AID IN THE UNITED STATES (1951).

[213] For example, inquisitorial judging by professional magistrates has not resulted in fair and impartial adjudication in Belgium. According to *The New York Times*, the vast majority of Belgians consider their judicial system to be thoroughly defective. Rosenberg, *Barbarity in Belgium*, Oct. 21, 1996, at A16. There is a "tradition of cronyism" in which "[political party] loyalty weighs more heavily than competence." Marlise Simons, *Sex, Lies and the Courts: A Fury Rises in Belgium*, Oct. 18, 1996. An editorial in the Belgian newspaper *De Morgen* said: "Incompetent magistrates are not punished, the promotion of cronies is not questioned, unsolved crimes are accepted as destiny, [and] investigations are shelved in dubious ways . . . . " *Id.*

Chapter 3

THE LAWYER'S VIRTUE AND THE CLIENT'S AUTONOMY[1]

§ 3.01 INTRODUCTION

Can you be a good lawyer and a good person at the same time? The question implies that serving your clients competently and zealously will require you to violate your personal morality in at least some instances.

At the heart of that issue is whether it is the lawyer or the client who should make the moral decisions that come up in the course of the representation. As it is frequently put: Is the lawyer just a "hired gun," or should the lawyer "obey his own conscience, not that of his client"?[2]

Note that we are not talking about doing things that are either unlawful or that are forbidden by ethical rules. Rather, the issue is whether a lawyer — having committed herself to represent a client — may then disregard the client's instructions to use lawful and ethical means in pursuit of a lawful end, on the ground that the lawyer disapproves of either the means or the end?

We will see later on that the Model Code of Professional Responsibility and the Model Rules of Professional Conduct take significantly different positions on this issue, while the Restatement of the Law Governing Lawyers makes some important refinements on both. It will be useful first, however, to consider some of the efforts to resolve the question of the good lawyer and the implications of those resolutions.

§ 3.02 THE LAWYER AS MORAL MASTER

Expressing a view that is common in the profession, lawyers sometimes use the phrase "client control" (that is, control of the client by the lawyer) to describe the proper professional relationship. In a law school commencement address titled *Professionalism in Lawyering*, Clement F. Haynsworth, Jr., then Chief Judge of the United States Court of Appeals for the Fourth Circuit, stressed the importance of professional competence in handling a client's affairs. Judge Haynsworth went on to say, however, that competence is not the highest professional value. Even more important than competence is that:

> [The lawyer] serves his clients without being their servant. He serves to further the lawful and proper objective of the client, but the lawyer must never forget that he is the master. He is not there to do the client's bidding. It is for the lawyer to decide what is morally and

---

[1] A substantial part of this chapter was presented in 1977 as the Thirteenth Annual Pope John XXIII Lecture at Catholic University Law School. *See* Monroe H. Freedman, *Personal Responsibility in a Professional System*, 27 CATH. UNIV. L. REV. 191 (1978).

[2] The last phrase is from ABA, Canons of Professional Ethics 15 (1908).

legally right, and, as a professional, he cannot give in to a client's attempt to persuade him to take some other stand . . . . [T]he lawyer must serve the client's legal needs as the lawyer sees them, not as the client sees them. During my years of practice, . . . I told [my clients] what would be done and firmly rejected suggestions that I do something else which I felt improper . . . .[3]

Those are striking phrases to describe the relationship of lawyer and client — the lawyer is the "master" who is to decide what is "morally . . . right," and who serves the client's needs only "as the lawyer sees them, not as the client sees them."

Thurman Arnold, who was a prominent practitioner and a federal appellate judge, held a philosophy similar to Haynsworth's. As described with approval by former Supreme Court Justice Abe Fortas, Arnold did not permit a client to dictate or determine the strategy or substance of the representation, even if the client insisted that his prescription for the litigation was necessary to serve the larger cause to which he was committed.[4]

There is significant sentiment within the bar, therefore, that a lawyer has both a moral and a professional duty to conduct a client's matter in accordance with the lawyer's views of right and wrong, even though the client wants to do something that is both lawful and ethical. Oddly enough, most critics of the legal profession argue not that such attitudes are paternalistic, elitist, and even arrogant; rather, they complain that not enough lawyers conduct themselves that way.[5]

§ 3.03   ROLE DIFFERENTIATION AND MORALITY

The phrase "role differentiation" is used by critics of zealous, client-centered lawyering to express the idea that lawyers will do things on behalf of their clients that the lawyers themselves would be unwilling to do if they were not acting in their role as lawyers. These critics contend that role differentiation causes lawyers to act in ways that are amoral and even immoral. Rejecting that criticism, the position taken here is that role differentiation is essential to any rational moral system and that it is entirely appropriate that lawyers' moral judgments take account of the fact that they have voluntarily assumed fiduciary responsibilities to their clients.

A leading critic of role differentiation is Professor Richard Wasserstrom. In an article that has been widely cited with approval,[6] Wasserstrom recalls John Dean's list of those involved in the Watergate coverup. Dean placed an asterisk next to the names of each of the lawyers on the list, because he had been struck by the fact that so many of those implicated in wrongdoing were lawyers. Wasserstrom concludes that the involvement of lawyers in Watergate was

---

[3] Haynsworth, *Professionalism in Lawyering*, 27 S.C.L.Q. 627, 628 (1976).

[4] Fortas, *Thurman Arnold and the Theatre of the Law*, 79 YALE L. JOUR. 988, 996 (1970).

[5] *See, e.g.*, JEROLD AUERBACH, UNEQUAL JUSTICE (1976); D. LUBAN, ed., THE GOOD LAWYER (1984); M. GREEN, THE OTHER GOVERNMENT (1975); WILLIAM SIMON, THE PRACTICE OF JUSTICE: A THEORY OF LAWYERS' ETHICS (1998).

[6] Richard Wasserstrom, *Lawyers as Professionals: Some Moral Issues*, 5 ABA Human Rights 1 (1975).

"natural, if not unavoidable," the "likely if not inevitable consequence of their legal acculturation." Indeed, on the basis of Wasserstrom's analysis the only matter of wonder is why so many of those on John Dean's list were *not* lawyers. What could possibly have corrupted the non-lawyers to such a degree as to have led them into what Wasserstrom sees as the uniquely amoral and immoral world of the lawyers? "For at best," Wasserstrom asserts, "the lawyer's world is a simplified moral world; often it is an amoral one; and more than occasionally perhaps, an overtly immoral one."[7]

Wasserstrom considers "role-differentiated behavior" to be the root of the problem. As he says, the "nature of role-differentiated behavior . . . often makes it both appropriate and desirable for the person in a particular role to put to one side considerations of various sorts — and especially various moral considerations — that would otherwise be relevant if not decisive."[8]

Illustrative of how Wasserstrom thinks lawyers should make moral considerations relevant is his suggestion that a lawyer should refuse to advise a wealthy client of a tax loophole provided by the legislature for only a few wealthy taxpayers.[9] If that case were to be generalized, it would mean that the legal profession can properly regard itself as an oligarchy, whose duty is to nullify decisions made by the people's duly elected representatives.[10] That is, if lawyers believed that particular clients (wealthy or poor) should not have been given certain rights, the lawyers would be morally (and professionally?) bound to circumvent the legislative process, and to forestall the judicial process, by the simple device of keeping their clients in ignorance of tempting rights.

Nor is that a caricature of Wasserstrom's position. The role-differentiated amorality of the lawyer is valid, he says, "only if the enormous degree of trust and confidence in the institutions themselves (that is, in the legislative and judicial processes) is itself justified." "[W]e are today," he asserts, "certainly entitled to be quite skeptical both of the fairness and of the capacity for self-correction of our larger institutional mechanisms, including the legal system."[11]

If that is so, it seems to be a *non sequitur* to suggest that we should place that same trust and confidence in the morality of lawyers, individually or collectively. A common complaint, implicit in much of what Wasserstrom says, is that lawyers have too much influence in our public life. In that view, lawyers should not be entrusted, or encouraged, to override democratic institutions as well as their clients' rights to self-governance.

Nevertheless, Wasserstrom suggests that lawyers should "see themselves less as subject to role-differentiated behavior and more as subject to the demands of *the* moral point of view."[12] Is it really that simple? Is there a single point of view that can be identified as "the" moral one? Indeed, there are

---

[7] *Id.* at 2.

[8] *Id.* at 3.

[9] *Id.* at 7–8.

[10] Wasserstrom acknowledges that concern but rejects it. *Id.* at 10–11.

[11] *Id.* at 13.

[12] *Id.* at 12 (emphasis added).

lawyers who believe that the principal moral evil of the tax laws is the progressive taxation of wealthy people. Should those lawyers be barred from doing tax work because they disagree with "the moral point of view"?

"There is something quite seductive," adds Wasserstrom, "about being able to turn aside so many ostensibly difficult moral dilemmas with the reply that my job is not to judge my client's cause, but to represent my client's interest."[13] Surely, though, it is at least as seductive to be able to say, "my moral judgement — or my professional responsibility — requires that I be your master. Therefore, you will conduct yourself as I direct you to do."

Another scholar who shares Wasserstrom's view that lawyers can properly nullify clients' rights in pursuit of a higher purpose is Professor William Simon. Simon argues that a lawyer ought to be more concerned with achieving what the lawyer considers to be justice in each case, rather than with serving the lawyer's traditional role of advancing or protecting the client's lawful rights.[14] Thus, he would have lawyers subordinate traditional ethical values such as loyalty, confidentiality, and zeal. Whatever one might think about Simon's idealism, its achievement would require not only renouncing the lawyer's traditional role, but also a thorough rewriting or abandonment of the law of malpractice[15] as well as the rules of lawyers' ethics.[16]

A more positive view of role-differentiated behavior was provided in an article in *The New York Times* about the former tennis star, Manuel Orantes:[17]

> He has astounded fans by applauding his opponent's good shots and by purposely missing a point when he felt that a wrong call by a linesman has hurt his opponent. "I like to win," he said in an interview, "but I don't feel that I have won a match if the calls were wrong. I think if you're playing Davis Cup or for your country it might be different, but if I'm playing for myself I want to know I have really won."[18]

---

[13] *Id.* at 9.

[14] WILLIAM H. SIMON, THE PRACTICE OF JUSTICE: A THEORY OF LAWYERS' ETHICS (1998).

[15] In a recent malpractice case, the Colorado Supreme Court rejected a "manifest injustice" exception to the lawyer-client privilege. *Wesp v. Everson*, 33 P.3d 191, 201 (Colo., 2001). Referring to the idea of a "manifest injustice" exception as both "far-reaching" and "unpredictable" the court found "neither legal precedent nor authority that supports the existence of any such exception." *Id.* Simon, of course, would impose such an exception much more broadly, on all ethical and fiduciary obligations that lawyers owe to clients.

[16] A variation on the theme of disregarding the law in the interests of justice is suggested by Professor Deborah Rhode in her book, IN THE INTERESTS OF JUSTICE: REFORMING THE LEGAL PROFESSION (2001). Rhode does not suggest overriding clients' rights in order to achieve justice; however, she does urge that lawyers for the poor and the oppressed develop "evasive strategies" to circumvent laws that frustrate what the lawyers believe to be justice for their clients. At the same time, however, Rhode is critical of lawyers representing clients of whom she disapproves when they use similar "evasive strategies" to advance their clients' interests. Rhode's proposal is criticized in Monroe H. Freedman, *How Lawyers Act in the Interests of Justice*, 70 FORDHAM L. REV. 1726 (2002).

[17] Deidre Camondy, N.Y. TIMES, Sept. 11, 1975, at 43.

[18] Orantes' attitude is unusual, but not unique. Mats Wilander refused a match point in the semifinals of the 1982 French Open tournament because the umpire had erroneously called Jose-Luis Clerc's ball long. Wilander told the umpire, "I can't win like this. The ball was good." Nick

That is, one's moral responsibilities may well be different if one undertakes special obligations to one's teammates or to one's country, rather than acting entirely for oneself.

Taking a different illustration, suppose that you are going about some pressing matter when your arm is suddenly seized by an old man with a long gray beard, a wild look in his eye, and what appears to be an enormous dead bird hanging around his neck, and the old man launches into a tale of a bizarre adventure at sea. If he is a stranger and you are alone on a poorly lighted street, you may well call the police. If he is a stranger, but you decide that he is harmless, you may simply go on to your other responsibilities. If he is a friend or member of your family, you may feel obligated to spend some time listening to the ancient mariner, or even to confer with others as to how to care for him. If you are a psychiatric social worker, you may act in yet some other way, and that action may depend upon whether you are on duty at your place of employment, or hurrying so that you will not be late to a wedding — and in the latter case, your decision may vary depending upon whether the wedding is someone else's or your own.

Surely there can be no moral objection to those radically different courses of conduct, or to the fact that they are governed substantially by personal, social, and professional context, that is, by role-differentiation. One simply cannot be expected, in any rational moral system, to react to every stranger in the same way in which one may be obligated to respond to a member of one's family or to a friend.

§ 3.04 CLIENT AUTONOMY

In an interesting and thought-provoking article, Professor Charles Fried has analogized the lawyer to a friend — a "special-purpose" or "limited-purpose" friend "in regard to the legal system."[19] The lawyer, thereby, is seen to be "someone who enters into a personal relation with you — not an abstract relation as under the concept of justice." That means, Fried says, that "like a friend [the lawyer] acts in your interests, not his own; or rather he adopts your interests as his own."[20]

The moral foundation upon which Fried justifies that special-purpose friendship is the sense of self, the moral concepts of "personality, identity, and liberty."[21] He notes that social institutions are so complex that without the assistance of an expert adviser, an ordinary lay person cannot exercise the personal autonomy to which he or she is morally and legally entitled within the system. "Without such an adviser, the law would impose constraints on the lay citizen (unequally at that) which it is not entitled to impose explicitly."

Stout, *Wilander Topples Clerc, Gains Final*, N.Y. TIMES, June 5, 1982, at 17. Martina Navratilova was also known for her exemplary sportsmanship, disputing bad line calls in her favor and giving the point to her opponent. She also routinely applauded her opponents when they hit good shots. *See* ADRIANNE BLUE, MARTINA: THE LIVES AND TIMES OF MARTINA NAVRATILOVA (1995).

[19] Fried, *The Lawyer as Friend: The Moral Foundations of the Lawyer-Client Relation,*" 85 YALE L. JOUR. 1060, 1071 (1976).

[20] *Id.*

[21] *Id.* at 1068.

The limited purpose of the lawyer's friendship, therefore, is "to preserve and foster the client's autonomy within the law."

Explaining the importance of client autonomy, Professor Sylvia A. Law has written:

> A lawyer has a special skill and power to enable individuals to know the options available to them in dealing with a particular problem, and to assist individuals in wending their way through bureaucratic, legislative or judicial channels to seek vindication for individual claims and interests. Hence lawyers have a special ability to enhance human autonomy and self-control. [22]

She adds, however, that:

> Far too often, professional attitude, rather than serving to enhance individual autonomy and self-control, serves to strip people of autonomy and power. Rather than encouraging clients and citizens to know and control their own options and lives, the legal profession discourages client participation and control of their own legal claims. [23]

The essence of Professor Fried's argument does not require the metaphor of friendship, other than as an analogy in justifying the lawyer's role-differentiation. It was inevitable, however, that Fried's critics would give the metaphor of friendship the same emphasis that Fried himself does. They have thereby missed his essential point that human autonomy is a fundamental moral concept that must determine, in substantial part, the answers that we give to some the most difficult issues regarding the lawyer's role.

Shortly after Fried's article was published, Professors Edward A. Dauer and Arthur Allen Leff made some perceptive and devastating comments about the limited-purpose logic of Fried's metaphor of friendship. [24] At the same time, however, Dauer and Leff expressed their own views of the lawyer's role and character, views which we consider to be both cynical and superficial. They see an "invariant element" of the lawyer-client relationship as follows:

> The client comes to a lawyer to be aided when he feels he is being treated, or wishes to treat someone else, not as a whole other person, but (at least in part) as a threat or hindrance to the client's satisfaction in life. The client has fallen, or wishes to thrust someone else, into the impersonal hands of a just and angry bureaucracy. When one desires help in those processes whereby and wherein people are treated as means and not as ends, then one comes to lawyers, to us. Thus, if you feel the need for a trope to express what a lawyer largely is, perhaps this will do: A lawyer is a person who on behalf of some people treats other people the way bureaucracies treat all people — as nonpeople. Most lawyers are free-lance bureaucrats
> . . . . [25]

---

[22] Sylvia Law, *Afterword: The Purpose of Professional Education,"* in LOOKING AT LAW SCHOOL 205, 212–213 (Gillers ed., 1977).

[23] *Id.*

[24] Edward Dauer and Arthur Leff, *The Lawyer as Friend,* 86 YALE L. JOUR. 573 (1977).

[25] *Id.* at 581.

Despite that caricature, Dauer and Leff manage to conclude that "a good lawyer can be a good person." They do so, however, by defining a "good person" in the following terms: "In our view the lawyer achieves his 'goodness' by being — professionally — no rottener than the generality of people acting, so to speak, as amateurs."[26] The best that can be said for that proposition, we believe, is that it is not likely to stop those with any moral sensitivity from continuing to ask whether it is indeed possible for a good lawyer to be a good person.

Other commentators have explored the question of client autonomy not so much from the perspective of "goodness" as from the perspective of power.[27] Professor Stephen Ellmann has argued that the disparity in socioeconomic status between most lawyers and clients encourages lawyers to assume and clients to cede decision-making power.[28] He points out that lawyers sometimes use coercion, threats, and manipulation to wield power over their clients. Ellmann argues that clients exercise their autonomy best when three conditions are met: first, they are aware a decision must be made and that they are entitled to make it; second they know the choices open to them and comprehend the extent and likelihood of the costs and benefits of various alternatives, and third, they are acting with as full an understanding of their own values and emotional needs as possible.[29]

Professor William Simon points out that even when lawyers think they are merely providing information for clients to consider in making their own decisions, the lawyers convey judgments in the information they choose to present and how they present it.[30] As Simon illustrates through a minor criminal case he undertook as a young lawyer,[31] clients tend to defer to the judgment of lawyers, no matter how inexperienced the lawyer.[32] Simon agrees that lawyers are not always very good at recognizing or accepting a client's autonomous choice, especially when the lawyer believes that the choice is not in the client's best interests.[33]

---

[26] *Id.* at 582. Other observations by Professors Dauer and Leff are less witty but more substantive and sensitive.

[27] Professor Thomas Shaffer has combined the two ideas. *See* Chapter 1, *supra.*

[28] *See* Stephen Ellmann, *Lawyers and Clients*, 34 UCLA L. REV. 717, 718 (1987).

[29] *See id.* at 727. Ellmann has also offered a critique of the "client-centered practice" as advanced by David Binder and Susan Price, which holds that the chief responsibility of a lawyer is to enable clients to make autonomous choices. *See* DAVID BINDER & SUSAN PRICE, LEGAL INTERVIEWING AND COUNSELING: A CLIENT-CENTERED APPROACH (1977); *see also* DAVID BINDER, ET AL., LAWYERS AS COUNSELORS: A CLIENT CENTERED APPROACH (1991). Binder and Price urge such techniques as "active listening" in order to facilitate "non-judgmental empathetic understanding" and thereby gain client trust and candor. Ellmann is suspicious of lawyers engaging in what he considers to be quasi-therapeutic methods, which he says can create a false sense of intimacy. *See* Ellmann, *Lawyers and Clients, supra* note 28, at 739; *see also* Stephen Ellmann, *Empathy and Approval*, 43 HASTINGS L.J. 991 (1992) (arguing against non-judgmental empathy because of its potential for manipulation).

[30] *See* William H. Simon, *Lawyer Advice and Client Autonomy*, 50 MD. L. REV. 213, 217 (1991).

[31] *See id.* at 214. Simon represented the housekeeper of a partner in his law firm. As Simon notes, this is the only criminal case that he ever handled.

[32] *See id.* at 215.

[33] *See id.* at 213.

§ 3.05 THE LAWYER'S AUTONOMY AND THE LAWYER'S MORAL RESPONSIBILITY

The most serious flaw in Fried's friendship metaphor is that it is misleading when the moral focus is on the point at which the lawyer-client relationship begins. Friendship, like love, seems simply to happen, or to grow, often in stages of which we may not be immediately conscious. Both in fact and in law, however, the relationship of lawyer and client is a contract, which is a significantly different relationship, formed in a significantly different way.[34]

Unlike friendship, a contract involves a deliberate choice by both parties at a particular time. Thus, when Professor Fried says that friendship is "an aspect of the moral liberty of self to enter into personal relations freely,"[35] the issue of the morality of the decision to enter the relationship is blurred by the amorphous nature in which friendships are formed. Since entering a lawyer-client contract is a more deliberate, conscious decision, that decision can justifiably be subjected to a more searching moral scrutiny.

In short, a lawyer should (and does) have the freedom to choose clients on any standard he or she deems appropriate.[36] As Fried points out, the choice of client is an aspect of the lawyer's free will, to be exercised within the realm of the lawyer's moral autonomy. Implicit in the exercise of that autonomy, however, is the lawyer's moral responsibility for the choices she makes. The question is not whether everyone is entitled to *a* lawyer; rather, for each of us, the question is whether a particular person is entitled to *me* as his lawyer. This means, contrary to Fried's view, that the lawyer's choice of client can properly be subjected to the moral scrutiny and criticism of others, particularly those who would seek on moral grounds to persuade the lawyer to use her professional training and skills in ways that the critics consider to be more consistent with personal, social, or professional ethics.[37]

Once the lawyer has chosen to accept responsibility to represent a client, however, the zealousness of that representation cannot be tempered by the lawyer's moral judgments of the client or of the client's cause.[38] That point is of importance in itself, and is worth stressing also because it is one of the

---

[34] Although the idea of contract plays such a major role in political theory and in jurisprudence, it has been neglected in discussions of lawyer-client relations. We hasten to add, however, that we are not suggesting "The Lawyer as Contractor" as an all-purpose analogy. It is relevant to the question of the lawyer's personal moral responsibility in selecting (and rejecting) clients, but it may well be useless in other contexts.

[35] Fried, 85 YALE L. JOUR. at 1078.

[36] RESTATEMENT, Introductory Note to Chapter 2 ("Except when appointed counsel by a tribunal, a lawyer need not accept representation of a client."); *accord*, Model Rules, Rule 6.2, Cmt.; Model Code, EC 2-26; Canons of Professional Ethics, Canon 31.

[37] This point is developed further in the next chapter, under "Moral Accountability in Choosing Clients." *See also* Appendix B, *infra*, (Freedman and Professor Michael Tigar debating whether a lawyer has a moral obligation to justify the decision to represent a client; Monroe H. Freedman, *The Lawyer's Moral Obligation of Justification*," 74 TEX. L. REV. 111 (1995); Abbe Smith, *Defending Defending: The Case for Unmitigated Zeal on Behalf of People Who Do Terrible Things*, 28 HOFSTRA L. REV. 925, 934–38 (2000) (discussing the moral significance of the decision to undertake the representation of a client and disclosing that the author would not represent police officers accused of crime).

[38] *See* Law, *supra* note 22, at 213–14.

considerations that a lawyer should take into account in making the initial decision whether to enter into a particular lawyer-client relationship.

Even after the lawyer has agreed to represent a client, the lawyer may still have some ability to avoid involvement in conduct that is morally offensive to the lawyer. The lawyer may limit the scope of the relationship, as long as the limitation is reasonable and the client knowingly consents. Also, she may withdraw from the representation if the client consents or if withdrawal can be accomplished with no significant harm to the client's interests.[39] In addition, we would allow the lawyer to withdraw in a matter other than criminal litigation, if the lawyer discovers that the client has knowingly induced the lawyer to take the case or to take action on the client's behalf on the basis of material misrepresentations about the facts of the case, and if withdrawal can be accomplished without direct divulgence of the client's confidences.[40]

§ 3.06 THE OBLIGATION OF MORAL CONSULTATION

Returning to our earlier disagreement with Professor Wasserstrom's criticism of role-differentiation, we did not mean to suggest that role differentiation has not produced a degree of amorality and even immorality in the practice of many lawyers. The problem is expressed in the news item regarding Manuel Orantes.[41] Playing for himself, Mr. Orantes has earned an enviable reputation, not only for his athletic prowess, but also for his good sportsmanship — that is, for his morality in his relations with his adversaries. Yet when he plays with teammates and for his country, he adopts different standards of conduct.

We think that Orantes is wrong in a way that many lawyers frequently are wrong. We do not mean that in Davis Cup play he is not bound by special, voluntarily-assumed obligations to others. On the contrary, he is bound by his role as teammate and countryman to accept the decision of his teammates, which may well be that each player should play to win, without relinquishing any advantage that the rules of the game and the calls of the judges allow. Where Orantes is wrong, however, is in preempting that decision, in presuming that their decision is, in fact, that winning is all. Perhaps if he actually put the choice to them, Orantes' teammates would decide that they would prefer to achieve, for themselves and for their country, the kind of character and reputation for decency and fairness that Orantes has earned for himself. Perhaps they would not decide that way. The choice, however, is theirs, and it is a denial of their humanity to assume the less noble choice and to act on that assumption without consultation.

In day-to-day law practice, the most common instances of amoral or immoral conduct by lawyers are those occasions in which lawyers preempt their clients' moral judgments. This occurs in two ways. Most often lawyers assume that

---

[39] Indeed, if the lawyer's sense of moral repugnance is so strong as to impair her ability to serve the client professionally, she would be required to withdraw. See MR 1.7(b); DR 5-101(A); Restatement § 32(2)(b).

[40] See Chapter 5, *infra*, under "Confidentiality Under the Model Rules."

[41] See *supra*, text at note 17.

the client wants her to maximize his material or tactical position in every way that is legally permissible, regardless of non-legal considerations. That is, lawyers tend to assume the worst regarding the client's desires, and act accordingly. Much less frequently, we believe, a lawyer will decide that a particular course of conduct is morally preferable, even though not required legally, and will follow that course on the client's behalf without consultation. In either event, the lawyer fails in her responsibility to maximize the client's autonomy by providing the client with the fullest advice and counsel, legal and moral, so that the client can make the most informed choice possible.[42]

An illustration of the former situation is the case of two experienced and conscientious lawyers who once asked Professor Freedman to help them to resolve an ethical problem. They represented a party for whom they were negotiating a complex contract involving voluminous legal documents. Opposing counsel had insisted upon eliminating a particular guarantee provision, and the lawyers who sought Freedman's advice had agreed to do so, having been authorized by their client to forgo the guarantee if necessary. However, the other attorneys had overlooked the fact that the same guarantee was provided elsewhere in the documents. Having agreed to eliminate the guarantee provision, with specific reference to a particular clause on a particular page, were the lawyers who sought advice obligated to call the attention of opposing counsel to the similar clause on a different page? Or, on the contrary, were they obligated, as one put it, "to represent our client, not to educate the lawyers on the other side?"[43]

Each of the lawyers was satisfied that, if he were negotiating for himself, he would unquestioningly point out the second guarantee clause to the other party. Moreover, each of them was more attentive to, and concerned about, questions of lawyers' ethics than most lawyers probably are. Nevertheless, it had not occurred to either of them that their professional responsibility was not to resolve the issue between themselves, but to present the issue to the client for resolution.[44]

---

[42] *Cf.* Anthony Alfieri, *Defending Racial Violence*, 95 COLUM. L. REV. 1301 (1995) (proposing an "ethic of race conscious responsibility" whereby criminal lawyers would reject trial strategies that perpetuate racial stereotypes). As indicated in the next chapter, we disagree with Alfieri's proposal, because criminal lawyers have a duty to zealously represent individual clients notwithstanding the effect on third parties, and because a defense lawyer should not unilaterally sacrifice the client's right to a lawful trial strategy to a principle about which the client may or may not care. However, we do not object to what he calls the "weak version" of his proposal — that lawyers advise clients to consider the impact of racially "loaded" defenses on the larger community. *Id.* at 1066–67. Although we do not believe that this conversation will be fruitful with many clients, we think that encouraging more talk between lawyers and clients is a good thing. *See* Abbe Smith, *Burdening the Least of Us: "Race-Conscious" Ethics in Criminal Defense*, 77 TEX. L. REV. 1585 (1999) (criticizing Alfieri's work as wrongly focused on criminal defense as the source of racism in the criminal justice system and as unduly hostile to zealous advocacy on behalf of an accused).

[43] A discussion/debate among experienced lawyers on the issue of taking advantage of an opposing lawyer's mistake is reproduced in App. C, *infra*.

[44] The attitude of the two lawyers does not appear to be the result of what Professor Wasserstrom calls the "acculturation" of legal training and practice. Freedman has used that illustration and others like it as classroom problems early in the first semester of the first-year Contracts course. Consistently, students who have had minimal exposure to the corrupting influence of law school, and no experience as practitioners, assume that the lawyer's proper function is to make the moral decision without consulting the client.

Another illustration of a lawyer's preemption of the client's moral decision is the case related by a law professor about an experience he had had in practice. Associated with a New York City law firm, the professor had been assigned to represent a corporate client in a series of mergers with other companies. In dealing with the lawyers for the other companies, the lawyer would educate less sophisticated lawyers on the other side regarding potential disadvantages to their clients in the transaction. Other lawyers in the firm considered him to be "something of a softy," but tolerated what he was doing. The reputation of the firm was not one of being "soft" with the opposition, however, and the client was not told what was happening and given a choice of hard or soft representation.

Ironically, the lawyer had felt an obligation to make sure that his client's adversaries were fully informed about their rights, but he had purposefully withheld from his own client the fact that he was acting in a way that was materially and adversely affecting the client's rights. In so doing, the lawyer had violated his fiduciary obligations to his client, including a failure to present the moral issue to the client.[45]

§ 3.07   OBJECTIVES VS. MEANS

Discussions of which decisions should be made by the client and which by the lawyer sometimes assume that there is a meaningful distinction between objectives and means. For example, Rule 1.2(a) of the Model Rules requires the lawyer to abide by the client's decisions regarding the "objectives" of the representation, but require the lawyer only to consult with the client regarding "the means by which they are to be pursued." In an understatement, the drafters then acknowledge that a "clear distinction between objectives and means sometimes cannot be drawn."[46] The distinction between objectives and means is not only unworkable but, as we will see later in this chapter, it is inconsistent with all other codifications, from the Canons of Professional Ethics (1908)[47] to the Model Code (1969)[48] and the Restatement (1998).[49]

One of the problems with an attempted distinction between objectives and means is that it ignores the fact that either one can involve the kind of moral decision that should be decided by the client (with, of course, the lawyer's advice).[50] Consider the case of Alger Hiss, who was accused in the 1950s of

---

As indicated by that response, and by other student responses to problems of lawyer's ethics, law teachers have a moral role to perform as an essential part of their professional responsibilities. *See* Monroe H. Freedman, *Professional Responsibility of the Civil Practitioner: Teaching Legal Ethics in the Contracts Course*, 21 JOUR. OF LEGAL ED. 569 (1969); MONROE H. FREEDMAN AND WENDY M. ROGOVIN, CONTRACTS: AN INTRODUCTION TO LAW AND LAWYERING, (2002).

[45] For illustrations of such counseling, *see* Thomas Shaffer, *Legal Ethics and the Good Client*, 36 CATH. U.L. REV. 319, 327–328 (1987). The next chapter considers further the question of what the lawyer should do when the client makes the "wrong" choice.

[46] MR 1.2, Cmt. [1].

[47] Canons 15 and 24.

[48] DR 7-101(A)(1).

[49] Sections 16(1) and 22.

[50] The discussion assumes that the moral decision relates to whether to use means or whether to pursue ends that are permitted by law and the ethical rules. *See, e.g.*, DR 7-101(A)(1).

being a member of a communist cell and of having violated espionage laws.[51] Assume that Hiss was innocent of the charges, but that Hiss' wife had been a party member and that exposure of her activities would explain away the most telling evidence against him. Imagine further Hiss' lawyer advising him that the only way to defend himself successfully would be to tell the truth about his wife's involvement, and Hiss replying that, in no way, directly or indirectly, was his wife to be brought into the case, even if it meant an erroneous conviction for himself. In those circumstances, we doubt that even Clement Haynsworth or Thurman Arnold would insist upon conducting the case in such a way as to implicate the client's wife.

A more dramatic case was the murder-kidnap trial of a group of Hanafi Muslims, who had invaded several public and private offices in the District of Columbia. According to the *Washington Post*, "the defendants were determined to share the guilt for crimes they may not have committed as a gesture of loyalty to their leader and belief in their faith." The *Post* quoted a defense attorney as saying, "They are willing to go down the tube for a principle."[52]

Despite their clients' strong desires, which were based in major part on religious conviction, the lawyers apparently decided to put on evidence adverse to the leader and to conduct hostile cross-examination of him. The *Post* further reported that the lawyers understood their decision to be in accordance with their "duty to provide what they think is the best defense possible," even though they would be acting contrary to their clients' instructions as well as their clients' religious beliefs. Further, the lawyers appeared to have been encouraged in that view by the Bar Counsel of the District of Columbia Bar.[53]

Professor Freedman once presented the Hanafi Muslim case to a group of judges, attorneys, and law professors at a conference on the ethics of advocacy. A majority of the conferees concluded that issues of "strategy" should be decided by the client, but that "tactics" should be decided by the lawyer. Strategy was defined as objectives, while tactics were defined as day-to-day issues, such as "whether to call or cross-examine a particular witness."[54] Nevertheless, on the specific case of the Hanafi Muslims the conferees voted overwhelmingly in support of the clients' right to control the decision regarding cross-examination of their leader. We think the decision would have been the same if the client in a matrimonial matter did not want her child to go through the trauma of being a witness, even if the child's testimony would be crucial to winning the case.

Arguably, however, the Hiss, Hanafi Muslim, and matrimonial cases all present moral rather than purely tactical decisions. Love, loyalty, and religious dedication are not the stuff of "tactics" or "means."[55]

---

[51] Hiss was convicted of having committed perjury in denying some of the charges against him.

[52] J.Y. Smith, *Hanafis Loyalty to Leader Seen as Defense Obstacle*, WASH. POST, July 10, 1977, at A1.

[53] *Id.*

[54] These distinctions between strategy and tactics are not recognized by dictionaries, and are no more useful than are objectives and means. *See, e.g.*, Random House Webster's Collegiate Dictionary (2nd ed., 1997), defining "strategy" as "a plan or method for achieving a specific goal," and "tactic" as "a plan, procedure, or expedient for promoting a desired end."

[55] Note, however, that the clients' desires raised the risk, first, of "wrong" decisions in those cases, and, second, of the possibility that false or misleading evidence would be presented to the court.

A case that would seem to come as close as possible to posing a decision about "means" uncomplicated by moral considerations is *State v. Pratts*.[56] In that case, the lawyer representing a criminal defendant had interviewed a witness who had given the lawyer a statement helpful to the defense. The lawyer learned, however, that shortly thereafter the witness had given the prosecutor a different statement, damaging to the defendant. Thus, the witness — and the defendant's entire case — could have been seriously embarrassed on cross-examination. The lawyer's decision, therefore, was that the witness should not be called. For similar reasons, the prosecutor also decided not to call the witness.

The defendant disagreed with his lawyer. Fully aware of the risks of calling the witness, the defendant decided that the witness was part of the case that he wanted presented on his behalf. Informed of the disagreement, the trial judge accepted the decision of the defense attorney, and the witness was not called. The defendant was convicted.

On appeal, the Superior Court of New Jersey affirmed. The court defined the issue as "who was responsible for the conduct of the defense," and held that "when a defendant accepts representation by counsel, that counsel has the authority to make the necessary decisions as to the management of the case."[57] Quoting a federal appeals decision, the court added that the defendant "has a right to be cautioned, advised, and served by [court-appointed] counsel so that he will not be a victim of his poverty. *But he has no right . . . to dictate the procedural course of his representation.*"[58]

We think the court was wrong. At issue was not the lawyer's day in court, but the defendant's — the defendant's constitutional rights to trial, to counsel, and to due process of law, and the defendant's rights to call and to confront witnesses. As the Supreme Court has noted, under the Sixth Amendment, "[t]he right to defend is given directly to the accused: for it is he who suffers the consequences if the defense fails."[59] Applying the right of confrontation, the Supreme Court has held that denial of cross-examination of a witness without a waiver by the client is "a constitutional error of the first magnitude and no amount of showing of want of prejudice would cure it."[60]

Indeed, we would put the *Pratts* case, too, in the realm of morality. In a society like ours, an essential purpose of a criminal trial is to manifest respect for the dignity of the individual. As Professor Zupancic has written, the defendant is not "an object of purposes and policies, but an equal partner in a legal dispute."[61] Further, as noted above, a fundamental aspect of human

---

[56] 145 N.J. Super. 79, 366 A.2d 1327 (1975), *aff'd per cur.*, 365 A.2d 928 (1976).

[57] 145 N.J. Super. at 88, 366 A.2d at 1333.

[58] *Rogers v. United States*, 325 F.2d 485, 488 (10th Cir., 1963) (emphasis by the New Jersey court).

[59] *Faretta v. California*, 422 U.S. 806, 819–820 (1975).

[60] *Brookhart v. Janis*, 384 U.S. 1, 3, 86 S.Ct. 1245, 1246 (1966). The decision of the United States Supreme Court in *Brookhart* was 8-1. Writing a separate opinion in which no other Justice concurred, Justice Harlan contended that "a lawyer may properly make a tactical determination of how to run a trial even in the face of his client's . . . explicit disapproval." Justice Harlan added, "The decision, for example, whether or not to cross-examine a specific witness is, I think, very clearly one for counsel alone." Again, all eight of the other Justices repudiated this view.

[61] Bostan M. Zupancic, *Truth and Impartiality in Criminal Process*, 7 JOUR. CONTEMP. L. 39, 133 (1982).

dignity is personal autonomy, which is especially precious in the kinds of matters in which lawyers are needed for assistance. In the words of Justice William J. Brennan, "[t]he role of the defense lawyer should be above all to function as the instrument and defender of the client's autonomy and dignity in all phases of the criminal process."[62]

Moreover, the "assistance" of counsel that is guaranteed by the Sixth Amendment is just that. As the Supreme Court held in *Faretta v. California*, "an assistant, however expert, is still an assistant. The language and spirit of the Sixth Amendment contemplate that counsel, like the other defense tools guaranteed by the Amendment, shall be an aid to a willing defendant . . . . "[63] Otherwise, "counsel is not an assistant, but a master,"[64] with the result that the right to make a defense is "stripped of the personal character upon which the Amendment insists."[65]

As we have seen, the client's "sense of self" has been identified in moral philosophy with such fundamental concepts as human identity and liberty.[66] It is not surprising, therefore, that in *Faretta* the Supreme Court found the client's right to control his own trial to be of constitutional significance.

Also, psychological studies suggest that client control of the case is a significant element in a litigant's perception that justice has been done, regardless of the outcome.[67] Accordingly, the researchers recommend that "civil and criminal processes should be designed to facilitate personal participation by the parties."[68] With specific reference to the lawyer-client relationship, the researchers interpret their data to mean that a case "ought to be regarded as belonging to the client, not to the lawyer," and that "the attorney

---

[62] *Jones v. Barnes*, 103 S.Ct. 3308, 3318–3319 (1983) (Brennan, J., dissenting).

[63] 422 U.S. at 820.

[64] Contrast Chief Judge Haynsworth's language at note 3, *supra*.

[65] *Id*. *Faretta* held that a defendant in a criminal case has a constitutional right to waive counsel and to proceed *pro se*. In *dictum*, the Court said, "It is true that when a defendant chooses to have a lawyer manage and present his case, law and tradition may allocate to the counsel the power to make binding decisions of trial strategy in many areas. . . . This allocation can only be justified, however, by the defendant's consent, at the outset, to accept counsel as his representative." *Id*. at 820–821.

This should not be understood to mean that the client, simply by exercising his right to counsel, has knowingly and voluntarily waived other constitutional rights like calling and confronting witnesses. See *Johnson v. Zerbst*, 58 S.Ct. 1019, 1023 (waiver of a constitutional right requires "intentional relinquishment" of a "known right"). Moreover, the cases cited by the Court in *Faretta* (as well as the reasoning of the case) indicate that counsel can make no trial decision of consequence over the express objection of the defendant. See *Brookhart v. Janis*, 384 U.S. 1, 4, 86 S.Ct. 1245, 1247 (1966); *Henry v. Mississippi*, 379 U.S. 443, 452 (1965). That conclusion is reinforced by "right of privacy" cases, which give constitutional status to each person's "independence in making certain kinds of important decisions." See *Whalen v. Roe*, 429 U.S. 589 (1977).

[66] Fried, *Lawyer or Friend*, 85 YALE L. JOUR. at 1068.

[67] John Thibault & Laurens Walker, *A Theory of Procedure*, 66 CAL. L. REV. 541, 551 (1978); Stephen LaTour, Pauline Houlden, Laurens Walker & John Thibault, *Procedure: Transnational Perspectives and Preferences*, 86 YALE L. JOUR. 258, 283 (1976); John Thibault, Laurens Walker, Stephen LaTour & Pauline Houlden, *Procedural Justice as Fairness*, 26 STAN. L. REV. 1271, 1287–1288 (1974).

[68] Laurens Walker, E.Allen Lind John Thibault, *The Relation between Procedural and Distributive Justice*, 65 VA. L. REV. 1401, 1417 (1979).

should see himself as the agency through which the client exercises salutary control over the process."[69] They conclude: "In this client-centered role, the attorney best functions as an officer of the court in the sense of serving the wider public interest."[70]

A vivid example of the difficulty that can arise in balancing client autonomy and lawyer responsibility is the "Unibomber" case in the late 1990s.[71] Confessed Unibomber Theodore Kaczynski was charged with capital murder arising out of his campaign against "technology," which he carried out by sending bombs through the mail to various academics and scientists.

Defense lawyers representing Kaczynski — experienced and skilled career public defenders Judy Clarke and Quin Denvir — believed that the only way to avoid the death penalty was to put forward a mental illness defense. However, Kaczynski steadfastly resisted being portrayed as mentally ill, because he did not believe he had a mental illness and found such a portrayal personally humiliating.[72] By all accounts, Clarke and Denver were devoted to their client and wanted only to act in his best interests. They believed that they would best serve their client's best interests by demonstrating that he was not in his right mind — thereby mitigating his wrongdoing in order to save his life. But Kaczynski cared more about the sanctity of his ideas than the sanctity of his life, and did not want his ideas to be depicted as those of a crazy man. The difficult question raised by this case is whether a client-centered defense lawyer must go along with a client-driven strategy that will likely lead to the client's execution.[73]

Although it is plainly proper for a lawyer to counsel a client about a legal strategy or decision, it is sometimes difficult to know how hard to press a client in the course of counseling. This is especially true when the lawyer believes there is a "right decision." The lawyer must balance respect for client autonomy against her professional responsibility to effectively advise the client.[74] This dilemma arises frequently in the context of advising criminal defendants about plea offers. Sometimes both respect for the client and professional duty will cause a criminal lawyer to lean extremely hard to

---

[69] Id.

[70] Id.

[71] For a fascinating and occasionally troubling account of the process of decision-making by lawyers and client in the Unibomber case, see William Finnegan, Defending the Unibomber, THE NEW YORKER, Mar. 6, 1998, at 52.

[72] The ethical system that is urged throughout this book assumes a rational, competent client who is able to assert his autonomous interests. Kaczynski had been found competent to stand trial.

[73] In the end, Kaczynski pled guilty to several charges, in exchange for which he was spared a death sentence.

[74] See Stephen Ellman, Lawyers and Clients, 34 UCLA L. REV. 717, 733–53 (1987) (discussing client autonomy and the lawyer's responsibility in view of the power imbalance between lawyers and clients); William H. Simon, The Ideology of Advocacy: Procedural Justice and Professional Ethics, 1978 WIS. L. REV. 29, 132–33, 139–42 (discussing client autonomy and lawyer responsibility in poverty law practice).

persuade a client to take a plea.[75] On the other hand, the final decision whether to plead guilty or go to trial is clearly the client's.[76]

In the Unibomber case, we would have pressed Kaczynski hard to pursue the legal strategy that would have allowed him to live, as urged by his lawyers Clarke and Denvir. However, if Kaczynski could not be moved, and insisted that we not put forward an insanity defense at trial and not argue mental illness as mitigation at the penalty phase, we would have proceeded as follows: If it would not have hurt the client, we would have suggested that the client seek other counsel and we would have withdrawn. If it was not possible for the client to obtain other counsel, or withdrawing would otherwise have hurt the client, we would have remained as counsel and put forward the client's chosen defense. However, if we believed that our client was urging something so untenable that no reasonable lawyer would do it — and we consider this to be a rare event and not the case with Kaczynski — we would ask the court to appoint a guardian.[77]

---

[75] See 1 ANTHONY AMSTERDAM ET AL., ALI/ABA COMMITTEE ON CONTINUING PROFESSIONAL EDUCATION, TRIAL MANUAL 5 FOR THE DEFENSE OF CRIMINAL CASES § 201, at 339 (1988):

> But counsel may and must give the client the benefit of counsel's professional advice on this crucial decision [of whether to plead guilty]; and often counsel can protect the client from disaster only by using a *considerable amount of persuasion* to convince the client that a plea which the client instinctively disfavors is, in fact, in his or her best interest. This persuasion is most often needed to convince the client that s/he should plead guilty in a case in which a not guilty plea would be destructive. *The limits of allowable persuasion are fixed by the lawyer's conscience.* [emphasis added].

See also David Luban, *Paternalism and the Legal Profession*, 1981 WIS. L. REV. 545 (arguing that lawyers should properly engage in paternalistic coercion when a client's goal fails to meet a minimal test of objective reasonableness); Abbe Smith, *Rosie O'Neill Goes to Law School: The Clinical Education*, 28 HARV. C.R.-C.L. L. REV. 1, 37 (1993) ("There are times when a criminal lawyer, if he or she is a caring and zealous advocate, must lean hard on a client to do the right thing. The clearer the right thing is . . . the stronger the advice.").

[76] MR 1.2(a); EC 7-7; ABA Standards for Criminal Justice, Std. 4-5.2; Restatement § 22.

Nevertheless, it is not always easy for lawyers to accept a client's decision. Lawyers often see the world in terms of costs and benefits (as evaluated "objectively" by the lawyer). Clients sometimes have their own interests and values. *See* Abbe Smith, *Defending the Innocent*, 32 CONN. L. REV. 485, 498–500 (2000) (discussing the decision of Patsy Kelly Jarrett, a woman sentenced to life in prison, to refuse a plea for time-served sentence, when she had already served ten years, because she could not admit to a crime she did not commit); Jim Dwyer, *Testimony of Priest and Lawyer Frees Man Jailed for '87 Murder*, N.Y. TIMES, July 25, 2001, at A1 (reporting that exonerated prisoner Jose Morales, who served thirteen years in prison, had "no regrets" about turning down a plea offer: " 'I would only have had to serve one and a half to three years. . . . If I had to do it all over again, I still would not take the plea. I had nothing to do with this.' ").

[77] See MR 1.14(b) ("A lawyer may seek the appointment of a guardian or take other protective action with respect to a client only when the lawyer reasonably believes that the client cannot adequately act in the client's own interests."); RESTATEMENT § 24(4) ("A lawyer representing a client with diminished capacity . . . may seek the appointment of a guardian or take other protective action within the scope of the representation when doing so is practical and will advance the client's objectives or interests. . . . ").

Note that the Model Rule allows the lawyer to seek a guardian "only when the lawyer reasonably believes that the client cannot adequately act in the client's own interests," while the Restatement turns on whether appointment of a guardian "will advance the client's objectives or interests." The Restatement clearly does not apply in the Unibomber case, and the Model Rule probably doesn't.

Of course, a legal guardian might then experience the same dilemma in determining whether to advance the client's wishes or what the guardian believes to be in the client's best interests.

For client-centered lawyers who are deeply opposed to the death penalty, the Unibomber case is a nightmare. Our view is that someone ought to be representing the client's desires. The problem with that however, is that important facts and legal issues may never be presented to the fact finder, and in this case that would likely result in the client's death. Kaczynski's lawyers might well have felt that if they refrained from putting forward a mental illness defense they would be engaging in "lawyer-assisted suicide" — and this would be no ordinary suicide, but suicide at the hands of the state. Still, how strongly should a lawyer fight to sustain life when the client is competent and clearly doesn't want that life?[78]

The constitutional dimension of client autonomy is, of course, of great importance in understanding the lawyer-client relationship. As explained in the preceding chapter, the adversary system is an expression of several fundamental rights embodied in the Constitution. We should note, however, that although the Constitution may prescribe the minimum requirements of lawyers' professional responsibilities, those responsibilities do not necessarily end where constitutional law leaves off. For example, the Constitution may not always require reversal of a conviction when a prosecutor has intentionally misstated the evidence or has urged the jury to draw impermissible inferences from the record;[79] nevertheless, it is unquestionably unprofessional conduct for a prosecutor to do so.[80]

Similarly, the Supreme Court held in *Jones v. Barnes* that the Sixth Amendment does not require court-appointed counsel to raise every point on appeal that the client wants raised. The majority reasoned in part that, unlike trial by jury, there is no constitutional right to an appeal.[81] Three years after *Barnes*, however, in a case dealing with the client's Sixth Amendment rights at trial, the Court held that counsel "must take all reasonable lawful means to attain the objectives of the client."[82]

Also, the Court noted, "the fact that the ABA may have chosen to recognize a given practice as desirable or appropriate [as an ethical matter] does not mean that that practice is required by the Constitution."[83] In his concurrence in *Jones*, Justice Harry A. Blackmun agreed that the ideal allocation of decision-making authority between client and lawyer does not necessarily require reversal of a conviction on constitutional grounds. He stressed, however, that "as an *ethical* matter," an attorney should defer to the client's wishes: "the lawyer, after giving his client his best opinion as to the course

---

[78] *See* Matthew Purdy, *Crime, Punishment and the Brothers K.*, N.Y. TIMES, Aug. 5, 2001, at A25 (quoting a letter from Kaczynski in which he states that he " 'would unhesitatingly chose death over incarceration' ").

[79] *See United States v. Hasting*, 461 U.S. 499, 103 S.Ct. 1974 (1983).

[80] ABA STANDARDS FOR CRIMINAL JUSTICE 3-5.8(a). *See also Donnelly v. De Christoforo*, 416 U.S 637, 648, n. 23, 94 S.Ct. 1868, 1873, n. 23 (1974).

[81] 103 S.Ct. at 3312. Despite the Court's distinction between trial and appeal, we agree with Justice Brennan's dissent in *Jones*.

[82] *Nix v. Whiteside*, 106 S.Ct. 988, 994 (1986). This echoes the language of DR 7-101(A)(1): "A lawyer shall not intentionally . . . [f]ail to seek the lawful objectives of his client through reasonably available means permitted by law and the Disciplinary Rules . . . ."

[83] *Jones v. Barnes*, 103 S.Ct. at 3313, note 6.

most likely to succeed, should acquiesce in the client's choice of which nonfrivolous claims to pursue."[84]

Against such weighty considerations of human dignity and autonomy, which find expression in moral philosophy, psychological studies, norms of professional ethics, and in the Constitution, what justification is there for the attorney to override a client's decision? In *Pratts* there was some saving of time at the trial. On the other hand, in a case in which the client prefers not to call a particular witness whom the lawyer wants to call, the client's decision would conserve time. In either event, the time element would not appear to be a compelling reason to deprive the client of the opportunity to make the decision in a matter of such importance to the client.

We suspect that the real reason lawyers prefer to make the final decision, and that judges are inclined to give it to them, is not professional duty, but professional pride. That is, the lawyer does not want the judge or any colleagues present to think that she is so unskilled as to put forward an unconvincing theory of the case, call a witness who is extremely vulnerable to cross-examination, or refrain from cross-examining a critical witness. Thus, the lawyer's sense of pride — the lawyer's ego, really — trumps the client's sense of self, and allows the lawyer to be the client's master rather than his servant. On the other hand, if the lawyer's response is that her real concern is with the client's welfare, this may be another instance of misplaced paternalism.

§ 3.08 SUMMARY OF LAWYER-CLIENT AUTONOMY

One of the essential values of a just society is respect for the dignity of each member of that society. Essential to each individual's dignity is the free exercise of his autonomy. Toward that end, each person is entitled to know his rights with respect to society and other individuals, and to decide whether to seek fulfillment of those rights through the due processes of law.

The lawyer, by virtue of her training and skills, has a legal and practical monopoly over access to the legal system and knowledge about the law. The lawyer's advice and assistance are often indispensable, therefore, to the effective exercise of individual autonomy.

Accordingly, the attorney acts both professionally and morally in assisting clients to maximize their autonomy, that is, by counseling clients candidly and fully regarding the clients' legal rights and moral responsibilities as the lawyer perceives them, and by assisting clients to carry out their lawful decisions. Further, the attorney acts unprofessionally and immorally by depriving clients of their autonomy, that is, by denying them information regarding their legal rights, by otherwise preempting their moral decisions, or by depriving them of the ability to carry out their lawful decisions.[85]

---

[84] *Id.* at 3314. *See* ABA Standards for Criminal Justice 21-3.2, Cmt. at 21–42 (2d ed., 1980).

[85] When we speak of denying clients information or depriving them of the ability to carry out lawful decisions, we mean it in an absolute sense. That is, a lawyer may decline to answer a client's question about the law as long as the lawyer doesn't mislead the client, and the client has a reasonable opportunity to seek the answer from another lawyer.

On the other hand, if we understand Professor Wasserstrom's tax case (the tempting loophole

Until the lawyer-client relationship is contracted, however — until, that is, the lawyer chooses to induce another to rely upon her professional knowledge and skills — the lawyer ordinarily acts entirely within the scope of her own autonomy. Barring extraordinary circumstances,[86] therefore, the attorney is free to exercise her personal judgment as to whether to represent a particular client. Since a moral choice is implicated in such a decision, however, others are entitled to judge and to criticize, on moral grounds, a lawyer's decision to represent a particular client or cause.[87]

§ 3.09   LAWYER-CLIENT DECISION-MAKING UNDER THE MODEL CODE

The Model Code of Professional Responsibility is generally in accord with these views. With regard to the lawyer's autonomy to accept or reject a client, the Model Code says flatly that "[a] lawyer is under no obligation to act as advisor or advocate for every person who may wish to become his client."[88]

After the lawyer has accepted a client, however, the Model Code sharply circumscribes the lawyer's autonomy. "In the final analysis, . . . the lawyer should always remember that the decision whether to [forgo] legally available objectives or methods because of non-legal factors is ultimately for the client and not for himself."[89] A lawyer is entitled to make decisions on his own, but only in areas "not affecting the merits of the cause or substantially prejudicing the rights of a client."[90] Otherwise, the authority to make decisions is "exclusively that of the client." As long as the client's decisions are made within the framework of the law, "such decisions are binding on his lawyer."[91]

Those unequivocal ethical considerations regarding client autonomy serve to resolve an element of circularity in the disciplinary rules. DR 7-101(A)(1)

---

for wealthy people), he would permit the lawyer to prepare the tax return, but without advising the client of the loophole. We consider that to be reprehensible. (We assume that if Professor Wasserstrom meant merely that lawyers can elect not to do tax work for wealthy people — a choice any lawyer is free to make — he would have said that. In his hypothetical, however, the lawyer *is* doing tax work for a wealthy client, which inevitably involves finding loopholes, or "tax avoidance.")

[86] In part because of the monopoly lawyers are given, the lawyer does undertake special responsibilities to society regarding the effective functioning of the legal system. To that extent, the lawyer's autonomy may be circumscribed, for example, by the obligation to represent someone who otherwise would be unrepresented. *See, e.g.*, Model Code, EC 2-29.

[87] *See* Freedman, *The Lawyer's Moral Obligation of Justification*," 74 TEX. L. REV. 111 (1995); *see also* App. B *infra*.

[88] EC 2-26. At the same time, the Model Code urges that "a lawyer should not lightly decline proffered employment" (EC 2-26), that he should accept his share of tendered employment that may be "unattractive both to him and the bar generally" (EC 2-26), and that he "should not decline representation because a client or a cause is unpopular or community reaction is adverse" (EC 2-27). *See also* EC 2-29.

[89] EC 7-8.

[90] EC 7-7.

[91] *Id.* Implicit in these ethical considerations is the power of the client to delegate to the lawyer the authority to make decisions affecting the client's rights. That is, the client has the right of ultimate decision-making in her own case, but she is not required to exercise that right if she would prefer to have the lawyer make decisions on her behalf. *See, e.g.*, D.C. Bar Legal Ethics Committee Opin. 103, quoted in text at note 94 *infra*.

says that a lawyer "shall not intentionally . . . [f]ail to seek the lawful objectives of his client through reasonably available means permitted by law and the Disciplinary Rules . . . . " That seems to reaffirm client autonomy, but the rule continues: "except as provided by DR 7-101(B)." When we turn to DR 7-101(B)(1), we find that a lawyer "may . . . exercise his professional judgment to waive or fail to assert a right or position of his client." DR 7-101(B)(1), therefore, would at first appear to swallow up all of the language that has gone before. That is, the lawyer is required to seek the client's lawful objectives through lawful means, but, nevertheless, the lawyer is given discretion to relinquish the client's rights.

However, DR 7-101(B)(1) actually begins with a qualifying phrase that refers back to the earlier provisions regarding client autonomy. The rule in full reads: "a lawyer may . . . *[w]here permissible*, exercise his professional judgment to waive or fail to assert a right or position of his client."[92] The phrase "[w]here permissible" is, of course, a significant limitation. As we have seen, "where [it is] permissible" for the lawyer to "make decisions on his own" is in those areas "not affecting the merits of the cause or substantially prejudicing the rights of a client."[93] In addition, "[w]here a lawyer fully informs a client of the client's ultimate authority and the client then chooses to delegate broad authority to the lawyer, it would be permissible for the lawyer to make fundamental litigation decisions."[94] Read in full context, therefore, DR 7-101(B)(1) is not inconsistent with the other provisions of the Model Code that protect the client's right to control her own case.[95]

Although the lawyer is required to abide by the client's lawful decisions, the lawyer's role in the decision-making process is not a passive one. On the contrary, the lawyer should "exert his best efforts to insure that decisions of his client are made only after the client has been informed of relevant considerations."[96] Moreover, the lawyer's advice need not be confined to purely legal considerations. "[I]t is often desirable for a lawyer to point out those factors which may lead to a decision that is morally just as well as legally permissible."[97] Specifically, "when an action in the best interest of his client seems to him to be unjust, [the lawyer] may ask his client for permission to [forgo] such action."[98]

In some circumstances, the lawyer may go further. When the lawyer believes that a particular course of conduct would be illegal, he may refuse to aid or participate in it, even though there is some support for an argument that the conduct is legal.[99] The lawyer's refusal to go along with the

---

[92] Emphasis added.

[93] EC 7-7.

[94] D.C. Bar Legal Ethics Committee, Opin. 103.

[95] That construction is supported by additional language in DR 7-101(A)(1) that a lawyer "does not violate this Disciplinary Rule . . . by acceding to reasonable requests of opposing counsel *which do not prejudice the rights of his client* . . . . " (Emphasis added). *See also* EC 7-38.

[96] EC 7-8.

[97] *Id.*

[98] EC 7-9. Of course, if the client "knowingly and freely assents" to termination of the lawyer's employment, the lawyer may withdraw. DR 4-110(C)(5).

[99] DR 7-101(B)(2).

questionable conduct might well result in his dismissal by the client, but conduct that is arguably legal would not justify the lawyer's outright withdrawal (or threat of withdrawal) from the representation. The lawyer is permitted to withdraw only if the client "[i]nsists that the lawyer pursue a course of conduct that *is* illegal or that is prohibited under the Disciplinary Rules."[100]

Paradoxically, however, the lawyer also is permitted to withdraw if the client "[i]nsists . . . that the lawyer engage in conduct that is contrary to the judgment and advice of the lawyer . . . ."[101] That is, of course, an extremely broad standard (which would appear to include cases in which the lawyer believes that a course of conduct would be illegal). However, that discretion to withdraw is significantly limited in its applicability to matters that are "not pending before a tribunal."

In addition, the lawyer is permitted to withdraw from any matter if the client "[p]ersonally seeks to pursue an illegal course of conduct."[102] Moreover, the lawyer is required (not just permitted) to withdraw if "[h]e knows or it is obvious that his continued employment will result in violation of a Disciplinary Rule."[103]

Even where the Model Code appears to permit or require withdrawal, however, withdrawal is subject to a significant limitation. "In any event, a lawyer shall not withdraw from employment until he has taken reasonable steps to avoid foreseeable prejudice to the rights of his client . . . ."[104] This provision does not appear to mean that the lawyer is forbidden to withdraw whenever foreseeable prejudice would result. Rather, the lawyer must "endeavor[] to minimize the possibility of harm."[105] Note, though, that the lawyer may not withdraw first, and then undertake to avoid foreseeable prejudice to the client. The Model Code says that the lawyer shall not withdraw "*until* he *has taken* reasonable steps to avoid foreseeable prejudice."[106]

Taken all in all, therefore, the Model Code is protective of the lawyer's autonomy in deciding what clients and causes to represent, and it is protective of the client's autonomy once the lawyer has made a commitment to represent the client.

§ 3.10   LAWYER-CLIENT DECISION-MAKING UNDER THE MODEL RULES

The Model Rules echo the Model Code in recognizing that "[t]he normal client-lawyer relationship is based on the assumption that the client, when properly advised and assisted, is capable of making decisions about important matters."[107] Nevertheless, there is language in the Model Rules that appears

---

[100] DR 2-110(C)(1)(c); emphasis added.

[101] DR 2-110(C)(1)(e).

[102] DR 2-110(C)(1)(b).

[103] DR 2-110(B)(2).

[104] DR 2-110(A)(2).

[105] EC 2-32.

[106] DR 2-110(A)(2); emphasis added.

[107] MR 1.14, Comment.

to be closer to the Haynsworth-Wasserstrom notion of the lawyer-client relationship than to that of the Model Code.

The principal provision allocating decision-making authority between lawyer and client is in MR 1.2(a): "A lawyer shall abide by a client's decisions concerning the objectives of representation . . . and shall consult with the client as to the means by which they are to be pursued." Thus, a distinction is drawn between the "objectives" of the representation and the "means" of pursuing them.[108] Objectives are for the client to decide,[109] while means are for the lawyer after consultation with the client.[110]

By contrast, the Model Code requires that the lawyer "seek the lawful objectives of his client through reasonably available means."[111] Also, the Model Code expressly gives the client authority over any decision "affecting the merits of the cause or substantially prejudicing the [client's] rights,"[112] including "the decision whether to [forgo] legally available . . . methods."[113] Under the Model Code, therefore, the distinction between objectives and means is not significant.[114] Under the Model Rules, however, the distinction between objectives and means could be critical, because the lawyer's decision appears to control with regard to "means" regardless of whether the client's legal rights would be substantially prejudiced by the lawyer's choice of action.[115] That result can and should be avoided, however, by reading "objectives" to include any decision "affecting the merits of the cause or substantially prejudicing the [client's] rights," including "the decision whether to [forgo] legally available . . . remedies."[116] In effect, that is the way it is interpreted by Professor Hazard, the Reporter for the Model Rules.[117]

---

[108] As discussed below, the distinction is a highly questionable one as a matter of both drafting and policy.

[109] *See* MR 1.4.

[110] The drafters of the Model Rules acknowledge that "[a] clear distinction between objectives and means sometimes cannot be drawn." Nor is other language in the Comment helpful in doing so. "Both lawyer and client have authority and responsibility in the objectives and means of representation . . . . [I]n many cases the client-lawyer relationship partakes of a joint undertaking." These general propositions do not serve to clarify the rule at all, and are useless for deciding particular cases.

[111] DR 7-101(A)(1).

[112] EC 7-7.

[113] EC 7-8.

[114] This is consistent with the Canons of Professional Ethics, which governed from 1908-1969. Canon 15 provided that "the client is entitled to the benefit of any and every remedy and defense that is authorized by the law of the land, and he may expect his lawyer to assert every such remedy or defense." One limitation on this was the lawyer's right, under Canon 24, to control "incidental matters . . . not affecting the merits of the cause, or working substantial prejudice to the rights of the client." The other limitation was in Canon 15, which told the lawyer to use his own conscience to avoid "violation of law or any manner of fraud or chicane."

[115] Also suggesting a different result from the Model Code is the Comment to MR 1.3, which says that "a lawyer is not bound to press for every advantage that might be realized for a client." However, the same comment says that "[a] lawyer should act with commitment and dedication to the interests of the client and with zeal in advocacy upon the client's behalf."

[116] *See* Model Code, EC 7-7 and 7-8.

[117] "[T]he client has authority to instruct the lawyer what course of action to pursue, so long as the course of action is within the limits of the law." Hazard, *My Station As a Lawyer*, 6 Geo. St. L. Rev. 1, 4–5 (1989), citing MR 1.2.

The Comment to MR 1.2 also says: "In questions of means, the lawyer should assume responsibility for technical and legal tactical issues, but should defer to the client regarding such issues as . . . concern for third persons who might be adversely affected." What if both those elements are present? That is, what if the issue is a "legal tactical" one but also would affect a third person?

In the Hanafi Muslim case, for example, the defendants objected to the legal tactic of putting principal responsibility on their religious leader through hostile cross-examination. Since the method of cross-examining a witness is perhaps the quintessential "technical and legal tactical issue," the lawyers' decision would appear to control under MR 1.2(a); also, there is no suggestion in the Model Rules that the clients' religious beliefs are sufficient to affect the result. On the other hand, the defendants' decision also related to their "concern" for their leader, a "third person who might be adversely affected." If viewed that way, the clients' decision would prevail regarding cross-examination. As indicated earlier, we think it must — as must their religious convictions alone.

Consider also the *Pratts* case, discussed above, in which the defendant wanted to call a particular witness, but his lawyer refused on tactical grounds. Under a literal reading of MR 1.2, the lawyer could ethically override the defendant's determination to exercise his Sixth Amendment right to call the witness.[118] Presumably, however, the drafters of the Model Rules did not intend to deprive a client of a fundamental right over the client's expressed objections. Indeed, the Constitution would preclude that result.[119]

The impossibility of making a meaningful distinction between objectives and means was recognized in the Restatement.[120] The lawyer is required "to proceed in a *manner* reasonably calculated to advance a client's lawful objectives, *as defined by the client* after consultation."[121] This phrasing is more like that of the 1908 Canons and the Model Code, than of the Model Rules. Most significant is the phrase, "as defined by the client." Also, the "manner" of proceeding toward that goal must be "reasonably calculated to advance [the] client's lawful objectives." The Restatement adds that "the client has general control over what the lawyer does," because "a representation concerns a client's affairs and is intended to advance the client's lawful objectives as the client defines them."[122]

By contrast, the "Authority Reserved to a Lawyer" by the Restatement includes only the authority to (1) refuse to participate in acts that the lawyer reasonably believes to be unlawful, and (2) make decisions or take action that

---

[118] There was no suggestion in *Pratts* that the lawyer knew that the witness was going to lie. The decision was a purely tactical one, on the ground that the witness had told inconsistent stories and was therefore subject to impeachment.

[119] A constitutional right cannot be waived unless it is "clearly established that there was 'an intentional relinquishment or abandonment of a known right or privilege.'" *Brookhart v. Janis*, 384 U.S. 1, 4, 86 S.Ct. 1245, 1247 (1966), *quoting Johnson v. Zerbst*, 58 S.Ct. 1019, 1023; *Henry v. Mississippi*, 379 U.S. 443, 451 (1965).

[120] The Restatement is particularly significant in interpreting the Model Rules because the Reporter for the Model Rules, Professor Geoffrey C. Hazard, Jr., was also the Director of the American Law Institute when the Restatement was drafted and adopted.

[121] RESTATEMENT § 16(1).

[122] *Id.*, § 22, Cmt. *b*.

the lawyer reasonably believes to be required by law or by an order of the court.[123]

Moreover, the Restatement lists five useful criteria for determining when the lawyer is required to defer to the client's "general control":[124]

(a) How important the decision is for the client;

(b) Whether the client can reach an informed decision on authorizing the lawyer;

(c) Whether reserving decision to the client would necessitate interrupting trials or constant consultations;

(d) Whether reasonable persons would disagree about how the decision should be made;

(e) Whether the lawyer's interests may conflict with the client's.

Another provision of the Model Rules that also might deprive the client of autonomy with regard to his own case is MR 1.16(b)(3). That rule says that the lawyer may withdraw from the representation, despite "material adverse effect" on the interests of the client, if the client insists upon pursuing an objective that the lawyer considers "repugnant or imprudent." If that language were construed broadly, the lawyer could threaten the client with withdrawal — and thereby coerce the client to change her objective — even if the lawyer's withdrawal would result in the client's imprisonment, deportation, or loss of custody of a child.[125]

The potential for harshness in a literal reading of MR 1.16(b)(3) is lessened by the Restatement.[126] First, the Restatement defines the word "imprudent" narrowly, as "so detrimental to the client that a reasonable lawyer could not in good conscience assist it."[127] The Restatement adds that "A client's intended action is not imprudent [nor, presumably, is it repugnant] simply because the lawyer disagrees with it."[128] Moreover, the Restatement applies a rule of proportionality regarding withdrawal on the ground of imprudence or repugnance. The lawyer is forbidden to withdraw in such a case "if the harm that withdrawal would cause significantly exceeds the harm to the lawyer or others in not withdrawing."[129]

---

[123] *Id.*, § 23.

[124] *Id.*, § 22, Cmt. *e.*

[125] In this regard, the Model Code is preferable. Under DR 2-110(C)(1)(e), the lawyer may withdraw if the client insists, "in a matter not pending before a tribunal," that the lawyer act in a way that is contrary to the judgment and advice of the lawyer. Since the Model Code provision does not apply in any matter that is pending before a tribunal, a major category of cases would be eliminated from its scope (*e.g.*, virtually all of those in which imprisonment, deportation, or loss of custody of a child would result).

A second significant difference is that DR 2-110(C)(1)(e) applies only to situations in which the lawyer herself would be required to "engage in" conduct that is contrary to the lawyer's judgment and advice. Under the MR 1.16(b)(3) there is no such limiting language. Arguably, the lawyer could withdraw, or use the coercive threat to withdraw, even if the client's "imprudent" objective could be achieved without the lawyer's direct participation.

[126] RESTATEMENT, § 32(3)(f).

[127] *Id.*, Comment *j.*

[128] *Id.*

[129] RESTATEMENT, § 32(4). This language was added after criticism of a previous draft in Monroe H. Freedman, *ALI to Clients: Drop Dead!*, LEGAL TIMES, May 31, 1993, at 26.

Earlier in this chapter, we noted Professor Sylvia Law's observation that "lawyers have a special ability to enhance human autonomy and self-control."[130] Recognizing that special ability, the Model Code obligates the lawyer to respect and enhance the client's autonomy by advising the client fully, by abiding by the client's lawful decisions, and by seeking the client's lawful objectives through reasonably available means. Similar ethical requirements span the past century, from the 1908 Canons of Professional Ethics to the 1998 Restatement. The Model Rules can and should be interpreted similarly, to preserve client autonomy in matters of importance to the client.

---

[130] Sylvia Law, *Afterword: The Purpose of Professional Education*, in LOOKING AT LAW SCHOOL 205, 212–213 (Gillers ed., 1977).

Chapter 4

ZEALOUS REPRESENTATION: THE
PERVASIVE ETHIC

§ 4.01 INTRODUCTION

Closely related to the concept of client autonomy is the lawyer's obligation to give "entire devotion to the interest of the client, warm zeal in the maintenance and defense of his rights and the exertion of [the lawyer's] utmost learning and ability."[1] This ethic of zeal is a "traditional aspiration"[2] that was already established in Abraham Lincoln's day,[3] and zealousness continues today to be "*the* fundamental principle of the law of lawyering"[4] and "the dominant standard of lawyerly excellence."[5]

Client autonomy refers to the client's right to decide what her own interests are. Zeal refers to the dedication with which the lawyer furthers the client's interests. The ethic of zeal is, therefore, pervasive in lawyers' professional responsibilities because it informs all of the lawyer's other ethical obligations with "entire devotion to the interest of the client."

The classic statement of that ideal is by Lord Henry Brougham in his representation of the Queen in *Queen Caroline's Case*. In an early instance of "graymail," Brougham threatened to defend his client on a ground that would have cost the King his crown and that might well have caused a revolution:[6]

> [A]n advocate, in the discharge of his duty, knows but one person in all the world, and that person is his client. To save that client by all means and expedients, and at all hazards and costs to other persons, and, amongst them, to himself, is his first and only duty; and in performing this duty he

---

[1] ABA Canons of Professional Ethics 15 (1908).

[2] RESTATEMENT THIRD OF THE LAW GOVERNING LAWYERS, § 16, Cmt. d (2000).

[3] CHARLES WOLFRAM, MODERN LEGAL ETHICS 578 n. 73 (1986); *citing* GEORGE SHARSWOOD, AN ESSAY ON PROFESSIONAL ETHICS 24 (2d ed., 1860); L. Ray Patterson, *Legal Ethics and the Lawyer's Duty of Loyalty*, 29 EMORY L. J. 909 (1980); Monroe Freedman, *Abraham Lincoln — Lawyer for the Twenty-First Century?*, LEGAL TIMES, Feb. 12, 1996, at 26 (discussing DAVID H. DONALD, LINCOLN (1995)).

[4] GEOFFREY C. HAZARD & WILLIAM W. HODES, THE LAW OF LAWYERING 17 (1988 Supp.) (emphasis in the original). The authors wrote this five years after the Model Rules were adopted. In their third edition the authors have changed the phrasing, but expressly equate "diligence" in MR 1.3 with zeal, for example, referring to "the basic duty of diligence (or zealousness)." *Id.*, § 6.2 (3d ed., 2001).

[5] V(1) REPORT FROM THE CENTER FOR PHILOSOPHY AND PUBLIC POLICY 1, 4 (Winter 1984). "The prevailing notion among lawyers seems to be that the lawyer's duty of loyalty to the client is the first, the foremost, and, on occasion, the only duty of the lawyer." Paterson, *supra* note 3, at 918, 947. *Accord*, WOLFRAM, *supra* note 3, at 580, *citing In re Griffiths*, 413 U.S. 717, 724 n. 14, 93 S.Ct. 2851, 2856 (1973).

[6] LORD HENRY BROUGHAM, TRIAL OF QUEEN CAROLINE 8 (1821).

71

must not regard the alarm, the torments, the destruction which he may bring upon others. Separating the duty of a patriot from that of an advocate, he must go on reckless of the consequences, though it should be his unhappy fate to involve his country in confusion.[7]

Let justice be done — that is, for my client let justice be done — though the heavens fall. That is the kind of representation that we would want as clients, and it is what we feel bound to provide as lawyers. The rest of the picture, however, should not be ignored. In an adversary system there is an advocate on the other side and an impartial judge over both.[8] Despite the advocate's argument, therefore, the heavens do not really have to fall — not unless justice requires that they do.

The obligation of "entire devotion to the interest of the client [and] warm zeal in the maintenance and defense of his rights" is not limited to the lawyer's role as advocate in the courtroom.[9] Undoubtedly, some of the most important, dramatic, and controversial issues of zealous representation arise in litigation, and these will be a principal focus of this chapter. It is important to remember, however, that any lawyer who counsels a client, negotiates on a client's behalf, or drafts a legal document for a client must do so with an actual or potential adversary in mind. When a contract is negotiated, there is a party on the other side. A contract, a will, or a form submitted to a government agency may well be read at some later date with an adversary's eye, and could become the subject of litigation. The advice given to a client and acted upon today may strengthen or weaken the client's position in contentious negotiations or in litigation next year. In short, it is not just the advocate in the courtroom who functions in an adversary system, and it is not just the client currently in litigation who may both require and be entitled to "warm zeal in the maintenance and defense of his rights."

§ 4.02 MORAL ACCOUNTABILITY IN CHOOSING CLIENTS

The obligation of zealous representation begins after the lawyer has decided to undertake responsibility for the client's cause. What obligation does the lawyer have to accept every client who comes in the door?

Discussions of the ethic of zeal frequently assert that the lawyer has no choice regarding the acceptance of a client or a cause. Consider, for example, David Dudley Field's defense of his representation of clients who have been called (with undue romanticism) robber barons. Field argued that he could not properly be criticized for his choice of clients because a lawyer is "bound

---

[7] The Queen was charged with adultery (of which, as Brougham knew, she was undoubtedly guilty). If convicted, she would have been divorced from the King and stripped of her title. Brougham's speech was a threat to reveal publicly that the King had been secretly married to a Roman Catholic, which, by statute, would have caused him to forfeit the crown "as if he were naturally dead." Moreover, Brougham's threat was particularly potent because of the dangerous social and political unrest at the time. The story is well told in FLORA FRASER, THE UNRULY QUEEN (1996).

[8] *See* Chapters Two and Nine.

[9] The ethic of zealous representation "is generally taken as a credo by lawyers in nonadvocate roles just as much as by courtroom lawyers." DAVID LUBAN, LAWYERS AND JUSTICE 11 (1988).

to represent any person who has any rights to be asserted or defended."[10] Similarly, Judge George Sharswood wrote that "[t]he lawyer, who refuses his professional assistance because in his judgment the case is unjust and indefensible, usurps the functions of both judge and jury."[11]

Although such statements are frequently accepted without criticism, they do not represent either professional practice or professional rules. Judge Sharswood's lectures on legal ethics were the principal source for the ABA's Canons of Professional Ethics (1908), but Canon 31 expressly rejected the view that a lawyer is bound to accept any client who requests his services:

> No lawyer is obliged to act either as adviser or advocate for every person who may wish to become his client. He has the right to decline employment. Every lawyer upon his own responsibility must decide what employment he will accept as counsel, what causes he will bring into Court for plaintiffs, [and] what cases he will contest in Court for defendants. . . .

Similarly, the Model Code states that "[a] lawyer is under no obligation to act as advisor or advocate for every person who may wish to become his client . . . ,"[12] and the Model Rules state that "[a] lawyer ordinarily is not obliged to accept a client whose character or cause the lawyer regards as repugnant."[13] In fact, lawyers in private practice refuse to represent people for a variety of reasons, most commonly because the would-be client cannot afford the lawyer's fees.[14]

If one begins with the erroneous notion that lawyers cannot exercise choice regarding clients, there is considerable compulsion to conclude that lawyers must have discretion regarding what rights are to be asserted. Otherwise, the lawyer's working life could be devoted to using means that the lawyer regards as repugnant in order to achieve ends that the lawyer regards as repugnant on behalf of clients with whom the lawyer does not want to be associated. In order to avoid that result, Sharswood held that the lawyer must not use lawful means that the lawyer believes would have unjust consequences. For example, Sharswood contended that a lawyer should refuse to plead the statute of limitations in defense of a debt that the client in fact owes.[15]

But Sharswood had it backwards. No lawyer is required to represent a client who owes a debt but who seeks to resist paying it solely on the ground that the statute of limitations has run. The lawyer who is offended by such a cause can simply decline to take it on. If a lawyer chooses to commit himself to serve that client, however, then the lawyer is duty-bound "to seek the lawful objectives of his client through reasonably available means permitted by

---

[10] Quoted in DAVID LUBAN, LAWYERS AND JUSTICE 7 (1988).

[11] GEORGE SHARSWOOD, AN ESSAY ON PROFESSIONAL ETHICS 83–84 (1854), quoted in DAVID LUBAN, LAWYERS AND JUSTICE 10 (1988).

[12] EC 2-26.

[13] MR 6.2, Cmt. [1]. The context is a rule that requires the lawyer to accept a court appointment "except for good cause."

[14] MR 6.1 urges the lawyer to "aspire" to provide at least 50 hours of pro bono services to people of limited means.

[15] SHARSWOOD, *supra*, note 3.

law. . . . "[16] It is not for the lawyer to unilaterally deprive the client of a right that the legislature has seen fit to provide and that the courts are prepared to enforce.

We want to emphasize, however, an argument made in the previous chapter. The lawyer's decision to accept or to reject a client is a moral decision for which the lawyer can properly be held morally accountable.[17] Indeed, there are few decisions that a lawyer makes that are more significantly moral than whether she will dedicate her intellect, training, and skills to a particular client or cause. Thus, even the "purely financial" decision to accept only clients who can afford a $500-an-hour fee, and to turn away all others no matter how just their causes might be, is inescapably a moral decision.

One of the most important considerations in deciding to accept or reject a client is that the lawyer, in representing the client, might be required to use tactics that the lawyer finds offensive. For example, a lawyer might choose not to accept a rape case because of the likelihood that defending the case would require the lawyer to attack the character of the rape victim in order to discredit her testimony.[18] The proper solution to the lawyer's moral objections to using such tactics, however, is not for the lawyer to take the case and deny the client his rights; rather, the lawyer should refuse to take the case.[19] Also, the lawyer who believes that certain rights should not be

---

[16] DR 7-101(A)(1). *But cf.* MR 1.2, Cmt. [1], which says, paradoxically: "The *client has ultimate authority to determine* the purposes to be served by legal representation, within the limits imposed by law. . . . At the same time, *a lawyer is not required to pursue objectives or employ means simply because a client may wish* that the lawyer do so." (Emphasis added).

A related issue, the practical impossibility of attempting to distinguish between objectives and means, is discussed in Chapter Three, *supra*.

[17] The importance of accountability has been expressed in the following way:

> Moral justification . . . cannot be exclusive or hidden; it has to be capable of being made public. . . . John Rawls has set it forth most explicitly, under the name of *publicity*, as a formal constraint on any moral principle worth considering. According to such a constraint, a moral principle must be capable of public statement and defense.

SISSELA BOK, LYING 92 (1978). For an illustration of moral accountability in this sense, *see* App. A, *infra*.

[18] *See* Ch. Eight, *infra*.

[19] Lawyers can and do avoid certain general areas of practice altogether because of the nature of the representation or the associations it requires. You will find, for example, that clients lie, steal, and even kill other people out of pure greed. If you don't want to be associated with such clients, you should not to go into corporate practice. *See, e.g.*, WILLIAM H. SHAW & VINCENT E. BARRY, MORAL ISSUES IN BUSINESS (4th ed. 1989).

Notwithstanding our belief that everyone is entitled to zealous representation, the authors would decline to undertake certain cases. Freedman stopped representing clients accused of rape, because he did not want to have to engage in the sort of advocacy to which those clients are entitled. For a similar view, *see* Cookie Ridolfi, *Statement on Representing Rape Defendants* in LEGAL ETHICS (Deborah L. Rhode & David Luban, eds. 3rd ed. 2002) (discussing her discomfort defending rape cases after obtaining an acquittal for a client who raped again). Smith would decline to represent police officers accused of crimes committed in the course of duty. *But see* Abbe Smith, *Defending Defending*, 28 HOFSTRA L. REV. 925, 934–38 (2000) (justifying zealous representation on behalf of a police officer who violently abused a suspect).

Both authors believe that public defenders ought not decline any cases, except on grounds of conflict of interest. The moral justification for public defenders representing all clients, no matter the charge or circumstance, is the right of the indigent accused to the same skill, zeal, and relationship of trust and confidence that fee-paying clients can expect. *See* Abbe Smith, *When Ideology and Duty Conflict*, in ETHICAL PROBLEMS FACING THE CRIMINAL DEFENSE LAWYER (Rodney J. Uphoff, ed. 1995).

recognized because they are morally unjustifiable, could be a persuasive voice in supporting legislation to change the applicable law.

In 1975 Freedman argued (contrary to the position expressed here) that it is wrong to criticize a lawyer for choosing to represent a particular client or cause. "[I]f lawyers were to be vilified for accepting unpopular clients or causes," he said, "then those individuals who are most in need of representation would find it difficult if not impossible to obtain counsel."[20] By the following year, however, he had rejected that position.[21]

It has done no good to write rules that attempt to insulate lawyers from criticism for the clients and causes they represent.[22] Lawyers who have represented unpopular clients and causes have in fact been vilified, even by other lawyers and judges.[23] Nevertheless, the concern that people and causes will go unrepresented because lawyers fear criticism has proved to be baseless.[24] Despite predictable public condemnation, lawyers have come forward to defend "the meanest man in New York,"[25] a Nazi death-camp guard,[26] and Osama bin Laden (within days of the destruction of the World Trade Center). Moreover, in the unlikely event that no lawyer is available to represent someone because of the repugnance of the client or cause, an available solution is the appointment of an attorney by the court.[27]

---

[20] MONROE FREEDMAN, LAWYERS ETHICS IN AN ADVERSARY SYSTEM 11 (1975). *Cf.* Model Rules of Prof'l Conduct 1.2(b) (1983), which appears to have a similar rationale.

[21] Monroe Freedman, *Are There Public Interest Limits on Lawyers' Advocacy?*, II SOC. RESP. 31, 34 (1976); Monroe Freedman, *Personal Responsibility in a Professional System*, 27 CATH. U. L. REV. 191, 199 (1978) (1977 Pope John XXIII Lecture, Catholic University Law School).

In 1971, Freedman debated Professor Michael Tigar on this issue, and believed over the years that he had won. After finding and reviewing a transcript of the debate, however, he discovered that, without realizing it, he had not only adopted Professor Tigar's position, but some of his phrasing as well. Tigar, on the other hand, appears to have adopted Professor Freedman's former position. *See* Appendix B. *See also* Monroe Freedman, *The Lawyer's Moral Obligation of Justification*, 74 TEX. L. REV. 111 (1995).

[22] *See, e.g.*, MR 1.2(b): "A lawyer's representation of a client . . . does not constitute an endorsement of the client's political, economic, social or moral views or activities." The Model Code Comparison that follows MR 1.2 says that paragraph (b) has no counterpart in the Model Code, but compare EC 2-27, 2-28, and 7-17.

As a practical matter a rule forbidding criticism of a lawyer for representing a particular client or cause could not be enforced against lawyers, much less against citizens in general. U.S. Constitution, First Amendment.

[23] *See, e.g.*, MONROE FREEDMAN, LAWYERS' ETHICS IN AN ADVERSARY SYSTEM 9-20 (1975); App. A, *infra*.

[24] Far more realistic, unfortunately, is the problem that justice is being denied to people for no better reason than that they cannot afford to pay lawyers' fees. *See, e.g.*, MARVIN FRANKEL, PARTISAN JUSTICE Chapter 9 (1980).

[25] See App. A, *infra*.

[26] See App. B, *infra*.

[27] *See, e.g.*, EC 2-29; MR 6.2; *Rubin v. State*, 490 So.2d 1001 (Fla. App. 3d Dist. 1986) (court-appointed defense attorney held in contempt for refusing to proceed after having been denied leave to withdraw); *Sanborn v. State*, 474 So.2d 309 (Fla. App. 3d Dist. 1985) (leave to withdraw denied to court-appointed defense attorney).

§ 4.03   THE NEED TO EARN A LIVING AS A MORAL CONSIDERATION

As the Supreme Court has noted, the "real-life fact [is] that lawyers earn their livelihood at the bar."[28] This is not a recent revelation nor a reason for embarrassment. More than a century earlier, Abraham Lincoln consistently referred to his law practice as a business rather than a profession.[29] Supporting oneself and one's family is a moral responsibility. Accordingly, any decision to turn down legal business for moral reasons has to be balanced against the effect that decision might have on one's ability to earning a living. To recognize that there are moral concerns on both sides of the issue serves to emphasize that the choice can be an extremely difficult one.

We celebrate the lawyers who take on unpopular clients and causes, and rightly so. But we should also celebrate the lawyers who turn down clients for reasons of conscience. One difference is that representing a notorious client can make a lawyer's reputation and career; turning down a client has never done so.

Ralph Temple was a partner in a law firm that was barely making enough money to stay in business. One day, one of the partners came in with an unusually lucrative client. In the midst of general jubilation, Temple raised the question of whether the firm really wanted to represent this client — the U.S. lobbyists for a dictator notorious for torture and murder of civilians. There was an extended and at times heated debate. Ultimately, the client was turned down. The firm broke up for financial reasons about a year later. Temple has never regretted his decision.

We do not believe that Temple's decision to turn down the lobbyists for the dictator was any less noble than, say, Clarence Darrow's decision to represent Leopold and Loeb, Edward Bennett Williams' decision to represent Senator Joseph McCarthy, or Michael Tigar's decision to represent the Nazi death-camp guard, John Demjanjuk.[30] Certainly, Temple's decision to turn down the lucrative client was more costly and contributed nothing to Temple's fame as a lawyer.[31]

---

[28] *Bates v. State Bar of Arizona*, 433 U.S. 350, 368, 97 S.Ct. 2691, 2701 (1977).

[29] *See* Monroe Freedman, *Abraham Lincoln — Lawyer for the Twenty-First Century?*, LEGAL TIMES, Feb. 12, 1996, at 26 (discussing DAVID H. DONALD, LINCOLN (1995)). Also, Henry Clay loved the law, and described his practice before the Supreme Court as "a very convenient and money getting business." MERRILL D. PETERSON, THE GREAT TRIUMVIRATE 18 (1987).

[30] Tigar has eloquently defended that representation. *See* App. B, *infra*; Michael Tigar, *Defending*, 74 TEX. L. REV. 101 (1995); *See also* Monroe Freedman, *The Lawyer's Moral Obligation of Justification*, 74 TEX. L. REV. 111 (1995).

[31] Another example of a lawyer exercising his autonomy in choosing a client, even at a financial sacrifice, is Professor Laurence Tribe's representation of the estate of Rose Cipollone, in a cigarette products-liability case. Arguing before the Supreme Court, Tribe won a ruling that the warning label on cigarettes does not bar smokers from suing for damages. Tribe represented Cipollone without a fee. Earlier, he had turned down a seven-figure fee to represent the cigarette industry in the case. Jeffrey Toobin, *Supreme Sacrifice*, THE NEW YORKER, July 8, 1996, at 43.

In contrast, Abraham Lincoln was indifferent to whether he represented a fugitive slave or a slaveholder. Years after he had begun to speak eloquently against the evils of slavery, Lincoln represented a slaveholder in an effort to recover run-away slaves. *See* Anton-Hermann Chroust, *Abraham Lincoln Argues a Pro-Slavery Case*, 5 Amer. Jour. Legal Hist. 299 (1961). In Lincoln's view, "his business was law, not morality." DAVID H. DONALD, LINCOLN 103–04 (1995).

Query: Which do you admire more?

Associates, of course, have less power than partners to make this kind of decision and are more vulnerable if they raise issues of conscience.[32] Nevertheless, even in a difficult job market, young lawyers have exercised significant discretion in avoiding firms that specialize in certain areas of practice. Also, even after joining firms, young lawyers have spoken out. On occasion, associates have requested that they not be assigned to particular cases. In a more dramatic instance, a group of associates at a major firm in Washington D.C. protested the firm's representation of the apartheid government of South Africa.[33] The fact that they were successful should not obscure the courage they showed in jeopardizing their advancement to partnerships.[34]

An associate can also bring moral considerations to a client's attention, sometimes at no personal risk at all. For example, as an associate in a large firm, Freedman was assigned to evict a tenant of a major real estate client. In reviewing the case, Freedman found that the tenant was a Korean War widow with a young child. The only reason for the eviction was that the child had had difficulty turning off her bath water one evening, the tub had overflowed, and the ceiling below had been damaged. Otherwise, there were no complaints about the tenant. "If you want to evict her, I'll do it," he said, "but I wasn't sure you'd want to, given the facts."[35] The client thought it over, and the next day told Freedman not to evict the woman.[36]

Turning down clients on moral grounds (as distinguished from suggesting moral considerations to a client) can be costly and therefore can require considerable courage. However, the decision of whether to represent a client is the point at which the lawyer has the most scope for exercising autonomy. Once you have committed yourself to serve as your client's zealous representative, your ability to act on conscientious grounds is, and should be, significantly limited.

---

[32] This point is made in Teresa Stanton Collett, *Understanding Freedman's Ethics*, 33 ARIZ. L. REV. 455, 457 (1991).

[33] *See* Ruth Marcus, *Covington & Burling Drops S. African Airline as Law Client*, WASH. POST, Oct. 5, 1985, at C3.

[34] A courageous but unsuccessful attempt to reject a client was made by twelve lawyers at Cravath, Swaine & Moore. The client, Credit Suisse, had been identified in U.S. government documents as the most frequent violator of rules against laundering looted Nazi gold. Some of the gold on deposit had been extracted from the teeth of European Jews and other victims of Nazi death camps. The firm had been retained to represent the bank to oppose claims of the victims' survivors. The lawyers wrote in part: "Credit Suisse earns through the Firm's involvement a legitimacy worth more to it than the wealth it has hoarded. In other words, the fee they pay the Firm buys them that which one is most obligated not to give those implicated in Nazi crimes." The Cravath firm nevertheless chose to represent Credit Suisse.

But see Carrie Johnson, *Arent Fox Rejects a Client*, LEGAL TIMES 14, April 14, 1997 (Law firm declined to represent insurance company which had been refusing for decades to honor insurance policies that had been taken out by people later killed in concentration camps.)

[35] To do this involved neither risk nor courage. Professor Shaffer argues that a lawyer should not avoid the risk by saying that she will follow the client's instructions even if the client decides to be ruthless. Thomas Shaffer, *Legal Ethics and the Good Client*, 36 CATH. U.L. REV. 319, 327–328 (1987).

[36] Shaffer gives another illustration of no-risk moral counseling, at *id.*

§ 4.04 ARE THERE MORAL LIMITS ON ZEALOUS REPRESENTATION?

Some critics of zeal argue that clients are not always entitled morally to everything that the law allows them, and that the proper solution is that zealous representation be rationed in the lawyer's discretion.[37] The most influential analysis of this kind is Professor Murray Schwartz's critique of what he calls the Principles of Professionalism and of Nonaccountability.[38] His Principle of Professionalism states:

> When acting as an advocate, a lawyer must, within the established constraints upon professional behavior, maximize the likelihood that the client will prevail.

Professor Schwartz's Principle of Nonaccountability states:

> When acting as an advocate for a client according to the Principle of Professionalism, a lawyer is neither legally, professionally, nor morally accountable for the means used or the ends achieved.

Our focus is on the reference to moral accountability. (If the lawyer is acting "within the established constraints upon professional behavior," then by definition she is neither legally nor professionally accountable for what she does.) In moral terms, Schwartz's principles posit that the lawyer "can properly refuse to be called to account with respect to the morality of *the means used or ends achieved* on behalf of the client."[39] In the next two sentences, however, Schwartz states the proposition differently: the lawyer, he says, "is beyond reproof *for acting on behalf of the client*," and the lawyer has become totally *"immune* from [moral] accountability."[40] Understandably, Schwartz disapproves of the idea that lawyers should be entirely free from any moral accountability whatsoever in their professional role.

As the quotations indicate, however, Schwartz confuses two issues that should be considered separately. It is one thing to say that a lawyer can properly be held morally accountable for choosing to "act[] on behalf of" a particular client. It is quite another to say that a lawyer can properly be subjected to moral censure for using lawful means to achieve a client's lawful ends. As discussed earlier, Schwartz is correct in concluding that a lawyer can be held morally accountable for accepting an immoral cause.[41] He is wrong, however, in suggesting that the advocate's zeal on behalf of a client

---

[37] *See, e.g.* William H. Simon, *"Thinking Like a Lawyer" About Ethical Questions*, 27 HOFSTRA L. REV. 1 (1998); WILLIAM H. SIMON, THE PRACTICE OF JUSTICE: A THEORY OF LAWYERS' ETHICS (1998); DAVID LUBAN, LAWYERS AND JUSTICE 159 (1988).

[38] Murray L. Schwartz, *The Zeal of the Civil Advocate, in* THE GOOD LAWYER 151 (David Luban, ed., 1984); Murray L. Schwartz, *The Professionalism and Accountability of Lawyers*, 66 CAL. L. REV. 669 (1978).

[39] Schwartz, *The Zeal of the Civil Advocate* at *id.* (emphasis added).

[40] *Id.* (emphasis added).

[41] To guard against the remote possibility that a client with a legal right to litigate might be denied that right altogether, Schwartz recognizes that "the last lawyer in town" should be required to take the case.

should be constricted by moral standards that have not been enacted into law by the legislature or recognized by the courts.[42]

Because Freedman's position has been misunderstood in the past,[43] let us reiterate it. Lawyers *are* morally accountable. A lawyer can be "called to account" and is not "beyond reproof" for the decision to accept a particular client or cause. Also, while representing a client, the lawyer should counsel the client regarding the moral aspects of the representation. If a lawyer chooses to represent a client, however, it would be immoral as well as unprofessional for the lawyer, either by concealment or coercion, to deprive the client of lawful rights that the client elects to pursue after appropriate counseling.

The O.J. Simpson case produced a new onslaught of criticism of zealous representation, focusing particularly on criminal defense advocacy.[44] Defense strategies and tactics that have traditionally been regarded as consistent with the ethic of zealous advocacy[45] are now being attacked as overly aggressive, immoral, or insensitive,[46] and defense lawyers find themselves repeatedly having to explain or justify their role.[47]

---

[42] Along the same line, Luban has argued that the ethical rules be redrafted "to allow lawyers to forgo immoral tactics or the pursuit of unjust ends without withdrawing, even if their clients insist that they use these tactics or pursue these ends." DAVID LUBAN, LAWYERS AND JUSTICE (1988). Professor William Simon has gone further, arguing that lawyers ought to pursue each lawyer's personal view of justice over the client's interest. *See generally* WILLIAM H. SIMON, THE PRACTICE OF JUSTICE: A THEORY OF LAWYERS' ETHICS (1998).

[43] These views have been in print at least since 1976. *See* note 21, *supra*. Nevertheless, critics purporting to analyze Professor Freedman's position on lawyers' ethics have failed to take them into account. *See, e.g.*, DAVID LUBAN, LAWYERS AND JUSTICE (1988); DAVID LUBAN, ed., THE GOOD LAWYER (1984).

[44] The critics include commentators who were once supporters of zealous criminal defense advocacy. *See, e.g.*, Albert W. Alschuler, *How to Win the Trial of the Century: The Ethics of Lord Brougham and the O.J. Simpson Defense Team*, 29 McGEORGE L. REV. 291, 321 (1998) (urging a return to "civility, trust, and fair dealing"). For an illustration of some of the trial tactics of the defense in the O.J. Simpson case, *see* JEFFREY TOOBIN, THE RUN OF HIS LIFE: THE PEOPLE VERSUS O.J. SIMPSON 144–57, 208–26, 419–21, 423–24 (1996).

[45] *See infra* Chapter 4.

[46] *See* William Simon, *The Ethics of Criminal Defense*, 91 MICH. L. REV. 1703, 1704–05 (1993) (asserting that criminal defense lawyers routinely engage in unscrupulous practices in the name of "aggressive defense"); Anthony Alfieri, *Defending Racial Violence*, 95 COLUM. L. REV. 1301 (1995) (arguing that criminal lawyers perpetuate racist stereotypes by putting forward "racialized" defense theories); DAVID LUBAN, LAWYERS AND JUSTICE 150-53 (1988) (arguing that defense lawyers should not cross-examine a rape complainant about her "sex life" even when the defense is consent). For a response to Luban's argument on the cross-examination of rape complainants, *see* Abbe Smith, *Rosie O'Neill Goes to Law School: The Clinical Education of The Sensitive New Age Public Defender*, 28 HARV. C.R.-C.L. L. REV. 1, 42–45 (1993).

Notwithstanding his own criticism of some defense practices, David Luban presents a forceful refutation to William Simon's argument for limits on defense advocacy. *See* David Luban, *Are Criminal Defenders Different?* 91 MICH. L. REV. 1729 (1993).

[47] *See, e.g.*, Abbe Smith, *Defending Defending: The Case for Unmitigated Zeal on Behalf of People Who Do Terrible Things*, 28 HOFSTRA L. REV. 925 (2000) (defending the ethics of defense tactics in the Abner Louima case in which Brooklyn police officers were accused of committing brutal assault a precinct bathroom); Michael E. Tigar, *Defending*, 74 TEX. L. REV. 101, 101 (1995) (defending his representation of Terry Nichols, accused of participating in the bombing of a federal building in Oklahoma City in 1995). For an incisive response to those who criticize defense lawyers as "overzealous," *see* ALAN DERSHOWITZ, THE BEST DEFENSE 410 (1982) ("I have been accused several times of overzealousness. I confess my guilt. In a world full of underzealous, lazy, and incompetent defense lawyers, I am proud to be regarded as overzealous on behalf of my clients.").

One recurring criticism is that the defense in Simpson's case "played the race card." They did this by stressing the virulent racism of Mark Fuhrman, the police detective who was a principal witness for the prosecution. For example, the defense showed that Fuhrman had lied when he had claimed that he did not use the word "nigger." The defense also revealed that Fuhrman had boasted of arresting African-American men who were accompanying white women. Although the defense did indeed "play the race card," it was the state that had dealt it, by knowingly employing and promoting an outspoken racist on the police force and by showcasing him as a witness for the prosecution.[48] For our own part, we would rather live in a society in which a guilty O.J. Simpson goes free than one that tolerates police officers like Mark Fuhrman.[49]

Two especially disturbing critiques of criminal defense advocacy have been offered by William Simon and Anthony Alfieri, both of whom are concerned with social justice.[50] In Simon's article, "The Ethics of Criminal Defense,"[51] he argues that defense lawyers routinely engage in overly aggressive and "ethically questionable" practices, such as delaying a case in order to frustrate government witnesses, presenting perjured testimony by defendants, and embarrassing or blaming alleged victims.[52] Simon concedes, however, that the tactics he refers to are not prohibited by either law or ethical rules.[53] Moreover, his portrayal of defense advocacy tends to overlook that defense lawyers have prosecutorial adversaries and that judges are rarely favorable (and are not infrequently hostile) to the defense.[54]

Simon also rejects the argument that criminal defense is "different" from other kinds of law practice, in a way that justifies a more aggressive level of advocacy.[55] He dismisses as empty rhetoric the suggestion that the state

---

[48] The phrase, "play the race card" belittles racism (as it is intended to do) when it is used to describe justified efforts by the defense to counter racism inherent in the prosecution's case. An interesting variation on this theme is recounted in Steven Lubet, *Storytelling and Trials: Playing the 'Race Card" in Nineteenth-Century Italy*, 48 U.C.L.A. L. REV. 49 (2001)(describing an effort to counter antisemitism in a prosecution).

[49] A senior Los Angeles police officer admitted: "Sure, they knew about Fuhrman; they had to know. Lots of people knew . . . and they turned the other way." Kenneth B. Noble, *Many Black Officers Say Bias Is Rampant in Los Angeles Police Force*, N.Y. TIMES, National Report, Sept. 4, 1995 at 6. A salutary result of the "race card" is that the L.A.P.D. Chief of Police is now "determined to root out racist cops, as urged [four years before] by the special commission headed by Warren Christopher." N.Y. TIMES, *Editorial*, Aug. 25, 1995. It is highly unlikely that this would ever have happened had it not been for Simpson's acquittal.

[50] Simon and Alfieri are both former poverty lawyers, now academics, who have written extensively on poverty law, lawyering, and legal ethics. Neither has ever been a criminal defense lawyer.

[51] SIMON, *supra* note 42.

[52] SIMON, *supra* note 42, at 1704–22.

[53] *See id.* at 1704.

[54] *See* Abbe Smith, *Defense Oriented Judges*, _____ HOFSTRA L. REV. _____ (forthcoming 2004) (discussing the hostility of judges towards criminal defenders and their clients); *see also* JAMES KUNEN, HOW CAN YOU DEFEND THOSE PEOPLE 256 ("I do think it's better to be overzealous than underzealous. Overzealousness can be corrected by the prosecution. . . . Underzealousness cannot be corrected by anyone.").

[55] *See United States v. Wade*, 388 U.S. 218, 256 (1967) (White, J., dissenting in part and concurring in part) (describing the defense lawyer's "different mission," which requires a defender to "put the State's case in the worst possible light, regardless of what he thinks or knows to be the

is powerful and potentially dangerous to individual liberties, by asserting that there is no "state," only "harassed, overworked bureaucrats."[56] Thus, with a few fatuous phrases, Simon minimizes the enormous resources of the prosecution, including police investigators and the backup facilities of the FBI, and he rejects the need for meaningful checks and balances in the administration of justice.[57]

Alfieri's critique is more limited than Simon's.[58] He has no objection to zealous advocacy on behalf of criminal defendants,[59] so long as the advocacy does not perpetuate "dominant narratives"[60] about race, or "exploit racial difference."[61] He acknowledges the high risk of "state violence"[62] in the criminal justice system, but is less concerned with the power of the state to prosecute and to abuse individuals than with the power of individuals to injure "the community."[63]

Alfieri illustrates what he considers to be the use of racism in criminal defense with a defense theory used by lawyers on behalf of two African-American men prosecuted for crimes arising out of the riots following the

---

truth"); *see also* Luban, *Are Criminal Defenders Different?*, *supra* note 46 (arguing that criminal defenders are different from civil lawyers); LUBAN, LAWYERS AND JUSTICE, *supra* note 42, at 58–66 (exempting criminal defense from a critique of adversary ethics); Deborah L. Rhode, *Ethical Perspectives on Legal Practice*, 37 STAN. L. REV. 589, 605 (1985) (acknowledging that "the case for undiluted partisanship is most compelling" in criminal defense); Richard Wasserstrom, *Lawyers as Professionals: Some Moral Issues*, 5 HUM. RTS. 1, 12 (1975) ("[I]t makes sense to charge the defense counsel with the job of making the best possible cause for the accused — without regard . . . for the merits. . . . But this does not, however, justify a comparable perspective on the part of lawyers generally.").

[56] SIMON, *supra* note 42, at 1707–78; *cf.* Luban, *Are Criminal Defenders Different? supra* note 46, at 1735 ("The state is not just a group of harassed, overworked bureaucrats in the D.A.'s office. It is a group of harassed, overworked bureaucrats, backed by the police and able in many cases to immobilize their adversaries in cold concrete.").

[57] *See* Luban, *Are Criminal Defenders Different?*, *supra* note 46, 1730–44, 1762–66 (discussing the prosecution advantage in resources, procedure, and legitimacy, and noting the "two worlds" of criminal defense, one for poor clients with overburdened public defenders and the other for the small minority of well-to-do clients with private lawyers).

[58] For a critique of Alfieri's views on criminal defense, *see* Abbe Smith, *Burdening the Least of Us: "Race-Conscious" Ethics in Criminal Defense*, 77 TEX. L. REV. 1585 (1999); *see also* Robin D. Barnes, *Interracial Violence and Racialized Narratives: Discovering the Road Less Traveled*, 96 COLUM. L. REV. 788 (1996).

[59] *See* Anthony V. Alfieri, *Defending Racial Violence*, *supra* note 46, at 1321 n. 149.

[60] *Id.* at 1305. Alfieri defines "narratives" as the "rhetorical structure of criminal defense stories." *Id.* at 1304. When he refers to "dominant narratives" about race, he means defense theories, or "stories," that comport with prevailing racial stereotypes. His essay "challenges criminal defense lawyers' freedom in story-telling," *id.* at 1306, by placing "race conscious" ethical limits on the theories defense lawyers may advance. *See id.* At 1331–1342. *See also* Anthony V. Alfieri, *Lynching Ethics: Toward a Theory of Racialized Defenses*, 95 MICH. L. REV. 1063 (1997) (continuing Alfieri's critical examination of race-based defense practices); Anthony V. Alfieri, *Race Trials*, 76 TEX. L. REV. 1293 (1998) (discussing the way in which "race trials" perpetuate racial status distinctions and hierarchies).

[61] Alfieri, *Defending Racial Violence*, *supra* note 46, at 1321. For a thoughtful discussion of the use of race and ethnic bias in criminal defense advocacy from a defense perspective, *see* Eva Nilsen, *The Criminal Defense Lawyer's Reliance on Bias and Prejudice*, 8 GEO. J. LEGAL ETHICS 1 (1994).

[62] Alfieri, *Defending Racial Violence*, *supra* note 46, at 1321.

[63] *Id.* at 1306, 1326–31.

Rodney King verdict in Los Angeles in 1992.[64] The defense lawyers maintained that their clients had had diminished capacity because they had been affected by the "group contagion" of mob violence."[65] Because the defendants were African-American, Alfieri contends that this defense strategy perpetuated racism, by reinforcing the stereotype of the deviant, out-of-control black man.[66]

Whatever one thinks of the group-contagion defense, it does not depend upon racist stereotypes, since it could just as well be used in a case of violence during rioting by whites.[67] In fact, that is precisely what Atticus Finch, the lawyer-hero of *To Kill a Mockingbird*, did when he portrayed Walter Cunningham, the leader of a white lynch gang, as "basically a good man." Finch justified Cunningham's attempted murder of Tom Robinson by saying that Cunningham had just been "part of a mob."[68]

Alfieri does want criminal defense lawyers to defend the "subordinated" from the powerful,[69] and acknowledges that this is a "great burden."[70] Nevertheless, he insists that defense lawyers not only carry this burden, but that they combat ignorance and advance racial harmony at the same time. Since defense lawyers inevitably fail this quixotic challenge,[71] Alfieri singles them out for blame[72] in a criminal justice system that is pervasively racist, from arrest to punishment.[73]

§ 4.05   ZEAL UNDER THE ETHICAL RULES

As we have seen, the 1969 Model Code of Professional Responsibility is more clearly protective of the client's autonomy than are the 1983 Model Rules of

---

[64] Police officers were acquitted of brutality charges in state court despite a videotape of them persistently beating a prostrate King.

[65] Alfieri, *Defending Racial Violence*, *supra*, note 46 at 1301–1303.

[66] *Id*. at 1301–06.

[67] *See generally* Patricia J. Falk, *Novel Theories of Criminal Defense Based on the Toxicity of the Social Environment: Urban Psychosis, Television Intoxication, and Black Rage*, 74 N.C. L. Rev. 731 (1996).

[68] Harper Lee, To Kill a Mockingbird 168 (1960). For critical views of Atticus Finch, *see* Monroe H. Freedman, *Atticus Finch — Right and Wrong*, 45 Ala. L. Rev. 473 (1994) (arguing that Finch is not an adequate model for today's lawyer because he participated in and minimized racism, and because he never voluntarily used his skills as a lawyer to ameliorate the pervasive racism in his community); Steven Lubet, *On Reconstructing Atticus Finch*, 97 Mich. L. Rev. 1339 (1999) (arguing that Finch used sexist tactics in his cross-examination of Mayella Ewell).

[69] Alfieri, *Defending Racial Violence*, *supra* note 46, at 1304.

[70] *Id*. at 1305.

[71] *Cf*. Curtis, *supra* note 24, at 5–6:

> A lawyer . . . has lower standards of conduct toward outsiders than he has toward his clients. . . . He is required to treat outsiders as if they were barbarians and enemies. The more good faith and devotion the lawyer owes to his client, the less he owes to others when he is acting for his client. It is as if a man had only so much virtue, and the more he gives to one, the less he has available for anyone else."

[72] Alfieri, *Defending Racial Violence*, *supra*, note 46, at 1342.

[73] *See generally* Randall Kennedy, Race, Crime, and the Law 286–92 (1997); David Cole, The Uses of Inequality: Race, Class and American Criminal Justice (2000).

Professional Conduct. Similarly, the Model Code maintains a broader and clearer obligation of zeal on the lawyer's part than do the Model Rules.

Canon 7 of the Model Code expresses the axiomatic professional norm[74] of zeal: "A Lawyer Should Represent a Client Zealously Within the Bounds of Law." Moreover, the Model Code recognizes that the lawyer's duty of zealous representation of clients is owed not simply to individual clients but to the legal system itself.[75] As explained in EC 7-1: "In our government of laws . . . each member of our society is entitled to have his conduct judged and regulated in accordance with the law; to seek any lawful objective through legally permissible means; and to present for adjudication any lawful claim, issue, or defense." Thus, in serving individual clients, the lawyer serves the interests of justice in a free society.

For a lawyer to represent her client less than zealously would therefore warrant professional discipline. Under DR 7-101(A)(1) of the Model Code, a lawyer "shall not intentionally . . . [f]ail to seek the lawful objectives of his client through reasonably available means permitted by law and the Disciplinary Rules." Note too that DR 7-101 is not limited to the lawyer as advocate; the rule is headed in general terms: "Representing a Client Zealously." The message of the Model Code is, therefore, "clear: loyalty to the client, regardless of . . . other restraints, is the all-encompassing duty."[76]

The contrast in the Model Rules is striking. There is no specific Rule that enjoins the lawyer to zealous representation.[77] Zeal is mentioned twice in the Preamble, each time expressly limited to the lawyer as advocate. The other reference to zeal is in Comment [1] to Rule 1.3, which also refers to the lawyer as advocate.

Rule 1.3 itself says simply that, "[a] lawyer shall act with reasonable diligence and promptness in representing a client." That is a salutary standard for waiters, file clerks, and dry cleaners, but it somehow lacks the fervor of Lord Brougham's famous statement of the lawyer's fiduciary duty. In addition, the comment says: "a lawyer is not bound to press for every advantage that might be realized for a client." Comment [1] adds, however, that "[a] lawyer should act with commitment and dedication to the interests of the client and with zeal in advocacy upon the client's behalf."

Despite tepid endorsement of zealous representation in the Model Rules, there is reason to believe that they will be interpreted to include the pervasive obligation of zealous representation. As we have seen, the ethic of zeal has a long tradition in the bar, and continues to be the dominant ethic of lawyers today. Also, the Reporter to the Model Rules has acknowledged that the ethic of zealous representation continues to be *the* fundamental principle of the law of lawyering," and has explained that although "[t]he Model Rules contain no single Rule that *explicitly* posits the lawyer's duty to the client in such

---

[74] The Preliminary Statement to the Model Code describes the canons that head each of its divisions as "axiomatic norms."

[75] EC 7-1.

[76] Patterson, *supra* note 3, at 947.

[77] Note, too, that there is little mention of zealous representation in the Restatement. Nevertheless, RESTATEMENT § 16, Cmt. d, recognizes that zealous representation is a "traditional aspiration" of the bar.

sharp terms [as in DR 7-101], . . . the overall approach has not changed."[78] Moreover, the Supreme Court in a criminal case has held that counsel "must take all reasonable lawful means to attain the objectives of the client."[79] It appears, therefore, that the inadequacies in the drafting of the Model Rules will be overcome by tradition and corrected by interpretation.

§ 4.06   ZEAL IN THE COURTROOM

Consider *Re McAlevy*:[80]

He sprang from his chair screaming, grabbed opposing counsel by the throat and began to choke him. The judge and the law clerk tried to separate the two men who were now locked in combat, and at one point all four persons — the judge, his law clerk and the two attorneys — were rolling on the floor. The judge suffered minor injuries before the two combatants could be separated.

The New Jersey Supreme Court was more than justified in issuing a "severe reprimand" to the lawyer responsible for this unseemly courtroom fracas. Clearly, there are some limits to lawyerly zeal.

Indeed, Canon 7 of the Model Code, which requires the lawyer to represent her client zealously, expressly limits zealous representation to means that are "permitted by law and the Disciplinary Rules."[81] In particular, a lawyer appearing before a tribunal is forbidden to engage in "undignified or discourteous conduct which is degrading to [the] tribunal."[82] However, as the Supreme Court has held (with regard to offensive speech), "one man's vulgarity is another's lyric."[83] Or, as another court has put it, a "trial is not a minuet."[84] What may appear to a judge to be undignified, discourteous, or degrading may seem to the lawyer to be essential to the effective representation of her client.

The problem is, in part, one of perspective. Along with a great deal of mutual respect between judges and the lawyers who appear before them, there is also a considerable amount of tension between them. One probable reason for that tension is the fact that the judge and the advocates have different functions. The lawyers are committed to seek justice as defined by the interests of their clients, while the judge is dedicated to doing justice between the parties. From the perspective of the judge, therefore, at least one lawyer in each case is attempting to achieve something to which her client is *not* entitled. From the perspective of the lawyer, however, the judge is always poised to deprive her client of something to which the client *is* entitled. Also, in the words of Professor Louis Raveson, "some level of emotional reaction, some degree of

---

[78] GEOFFREY C. HAZARD & WILLIAM W. HODES, THE LAW OF LAWYERING 17 (1986) (emphasis in the original). Regarding the author's change in phrasing in the Third Edition, *see* note 4, *supra*.

[79] *Nix v. Whiteside*, 475 U.S. 1157, 166, 106 S.Ct. 988, 994 (1986).

[80] *In Re McAlevy*, 69 N.J. 349, 354 A.2d 289, 290 (1976), quoted in Francis D. Doucette, *Advocacy and Chivalry*, CASE & COMMENT 43 (July-August 1987).

[81] DR 7-101(A)(1); DR 7-102(A)(8).

[82] DR 7-106(C)(6).

[83] *Cohen v. California*, 403 U.S. 15, 25 (1971).

[84] *Taylor v. United States*, 134 U.S. App. D.C. 188, 189, 413 F.2d 1095, 1096 (1969).

temporary animosity, and a measure of turmoil, are part of the natural processes of trial advocacy."[85]

Moreover, a judge's concern with moving the court's calendar expeditiously is not always compatible with what a litigant considers to be necessary for a full and fair hearing. Frequently, therefore, judges and advocates have differing views about how much process is due in a particular matter.

How far, then, should an advocate go in pressing a point before a judge who would prefer not to hear more? Ordinarily, the answer is tactical rather than ethical. The purpose of argument is to persuade, and tactics that are offensive to the judge are not likely to aid in persuasion. In addition, judges have the power to hold lawyers in contempt, and some judges have abused that power to punish even "minor excesses of advocacy."[86]

There are occasions, however, when a judge appears to have decided an issue without a full appreciation of the facts or law, or when there is no hope of changing a judge's ruling but when it is necessary to establish an adequate record for purposes of appeal. In such cases, the advocate's responsibility is to represent the client's interests effectively, even in the face of improper judicial efforts to pressure the lawyer to forbear. As Chief Justice Warren Burger has emphasized, the advocate, although an "officer of the court," must nevertheless "repudiate any external effort to direct how the obligations to the client are to be carried out."[87] It is "crucial," the Chief Justice noted, that a professionally qualified advocate be "wholly independent of the government."[88]

Chief Justice Burger has also pointed to an important source for guidance as to the appropriate limits of deference to the court. In *In re Snyder*,[89] a lawyer was suspended from practice for six months for conduct that was "unbecoming a member of the bar"[90] and "prejudicial to the administration of justice."[91] The substance of the charge was that Snyder had written a letter to a judge that was "totally disrespectful to the federal courts and to the judicial system" and that "demonstrate[d] a total lack of respect for the legal

---

[85] Louis Raveson, *Advocacy and Contempt: Constitutional Limitations on the Judicial Contempt Power, Part One: The Conflict Between Advocacy and Contempt*," 65 WASH. L. REV. 477, 514 (1990).

[86] *Id*. at 593. Professor Raveson illustrates his point in part with *In re Buckley*, 10 Cal.3d 237, 110 Cal. Rptr. 121, 514 P.2d 1201 (1973) (attorney stated to judge, "This court obviously doesn't want to apply the law"); *In re Cohen*, 370 F.Supp. 1166, 1171–72 (1973) (attorney made sarcastic, mocking, and disrespectful comments about witness' testimony, engaged in a shouting match with witness, and yelled, "You are not telling the truth now, Mrs. Brown"); and *In re Burns*, 19 Mich. App. 525, 173 N.W. 1 (1969) (attorney continued to argue after trial judge advised him not to do so during court's instructions and judge banged gavel three times but attorney failed to comply). Nevertheless, contempt depends upon actual obstruction of justice. "The opinions reveal repeated caution that a judge's overreaction to the unavoidable contentiousness of trial advocacy — the confusion of 'offenses to their sensibilities' with 'obstruction to the administration of justice' — does not define contempt." Raveson, *id*. at 514.

[87] *Polk County v. Dodson*, 454 U.S. 312, 327, 102 S.Ct. 445, 454 (1981) (Burger, C.J., concurring).

[88] *Id*.

[89] 472 U.S. 634, 105 S.Ct. 2874 (1985).

[90] FED. R. APP. P. 46.

[91] *See* DR 1-102(A)(5); MR 8.4(d).

process and the courts."[92] In an opinion by the Chief Justice, the Supreme Court unanimously reversed the disciplinary action against Snyder.[93]

The Court held that phrases like "unbecoming a member of the bar" and "prejudicial to the administration of justice," must be read in the light of "traditional duties imposed on an attorney."[94] "More specific guidance," the Court said, "is provided by case law, applicable court rules, and 'the lore of the profession,' as embodied in codes of professional conduct."[95] Insofar as the codes of professional conduct embody the "lore of the profession," it is worth relating some of that lore in seeking to understand the rules of ethics, including the ethic of zeal.

Consider, for example, the following exchange between court and counsel:

> JUDGE: . . . You know that is a most improper question to ask.
>
> ATTORNEY: I know when a person has his mind made up, it is not easy to change it.
>
> JUDGE: I do not want you to make a speech now.
>
> ATTORNEY: I am going to make a speech — that is what I am paid for.

In another transcript excerpt, the dialogue between attorney and judge went this way:

> ATTORNEY: I stand here as an advocate for a brother citizen, and I desire that the [record in this case be complete and accurate].
>
> JUDGE: Sit down, Sir! Remember your duty or I shall be obliged to proceed in another manner [*i.e.*, referring to disciplinary proceedings against the lawyer].
>
> ATTORNEY: Your [Honor] may proceed in any manner you think fit. I know my duty as well as Your [Honor] knows yours. I shall not alter my conduct.

Each of those incidents has come down in our professional lore from the tradition of the English barrister. Neither case resulted in disciplinary action. On the contrary, each episode has been cited as representing the ideal of an independent bar. For example, the advocate who insisted upon making a speech was Sir Marshall Hall, a noted barrister of the earlier part of the

---

[92] *Synder*, 472 U.S. at 637, 105 S.Ct. at 2877.

[93] *See also, Lawyer's Profane Remarks About Judge In Personal Matter Don't Constitute Contempt*, 18 ABA/BNA Lawyers' Manual on Professional Conduct, No. 1, p. 10 (Jan. 2, 2002) (Following criticism of the lawyer by the judge in court, the lawyer told the judge's law clerk that the judge was "a f**king bitch and that she should not be on the bench"). *In re Conway*, Ohio Ct. App. 8th Dist., No. 79615, 12/13/01.

[94] *Synder*, 472 U.S. at 645, 105 S.Ct. at 2881. Phrases like "unbecoming a member of the bar" and "prejudicial to the administration of justice" are inherently vague and are subject to abusive enforcement. Unless they are narrowly and clearly defined in advance, they do not give the kind of notice required by due process. *See, e.g., Gentile v. State Bar of Nevada*, 501 U.S. 1030, 111 S.Ct. 2720 (1991). The Court in *Snyder* did not reach this constitutional issue. 472 U.S. at 642, 105 S.Ct. at 2880.

[95] *Id.*

twentieth century. His biographer relates that Sir Marshall not only made his speech but "won the day."[96]

The lawyer in the second instance was no less a figure in English law than Lord Erskine (later to become Lord Chancellor of England). According to Lord Campbell, Erskine's defiance of the court was "a noble stand for the independence of the bar."[97] Professors David Louisell and Geoffrey Hazard introduced the episode in their casebook with the comment: "So much emphasis is currently placed upon avoidance of improper argument that it seems amiss not to remind today's young lawyer of his duty of effective representation of his client in an adversary system."[98]

Similarly, one of the most highly regarded of American jurists, Chief Justice Roger J. Traynor of the California Supreme Court,[99] cited Lord Erskine's defiance of the court to illustrate the attorney's "duty to protect the interests of his client" and his "right to press legitimate argument and to protest an erroneous ruling."[100]

Recall, too, Lord Brougham's classic graymail threat, quoted at the beginning of this chapter. It came during his opening statement in the trial of Queen Caroline for adultery. According to Fraser, Lord Brougham's opening was "a masterly performance."[101] As he finished, "the aged Lord Erskine, former Lord Chancellor, [was so moved that he] rushed from the chamber in tears."[102] Another barrister declared that Lord Brougham's opening statement was "one of the most powerful orations that ever proceeded from human lips."[103]

Although Brougham's client, Queen Caroline, was undoubtedly guilty as charged (and was widely believed to be guilty), she was ultimately exonerated. Nor was everyone favorably impressed with Brougham's performance. Lord Chancellor Eldon later "rebuked Brougham most weightily for his threats to the House"[104] — that is, for what Eldon saw as Brougham's overzealousness on behalf of his client. Nevertheless, Brougham was "the hero of the hour,"[105] and he subsequently succeeded Eldon as Lord Chancellor of England.[106]

A more recent American version of Hall's and Erskine's insistence on zealous representation was reported in the *New York Times*.[107] The lawyer

---

[96] EDWARD MARJORIBANKS, FOR THE DEFENSE: THE LIFE OF SIR EDWARD MARSHALL HALL 45 (1931).

[97] JAMES F. OSWALD, CONTEMPT OF COURT 51–52 (3d ed. 1910), *quoted in Gallagher v. Municipal Court*, 192 P.2d 905, 913 (Cal. Sup. Ct., 1948).

[98] DAVID LOUISELL & GOEFFREY C. HAZARD, CASES AND MATERIAL ON PLEADING AND PROCEDURE, STATE AND FEDERAL (2d ed. 1968).

[99] Chief Justice Traynor was Chairman of the Special Committee that drafted the ABA CODE OF JUDICIAL CONDUCT (1972).

[100] *Gallagher v. Municipal Court*, 192 P.2d 905, 913 (Cal. Sup. Ct. 1948).

[101] FRASER, THE UNRULY QUEEN 433 (1996).

[102] *Id.*

[103] *Id.*

[104] *Id.* at 438.

[105] *Id.* at 443.

[106] *Id.* at 465.

[107] NEW YORK TIMES, p. 33, 36, May 16, 1987.

was Barry Slotnick, whom the *Times* characterized as a conservative Republican. Slotnick was representing Bernard Goetz, a vigilante who had shot three young men who had been harassing him on a subway. The judge admonished Slotnick, first in front of the jury and later at a bench conference, for asking questions that included facts that were not supported by the evidence. The following colloquy then occurred at the bench after the prosecutor's objection to another question:

> Slotnick: Judge, you can speak a little louder and the jury can hear you.
>
> Judge: I'm upset with your conduct.
>
> Slotnick: I'm upset with your conduct.
>
> Judge: You know where you can go with that.

But Mr. Slotnick continued arguing, the *Times* reported, and eventually the judge came around to Slotnick's position, and permitted him to ask the question.

Consistent with this tradition of zealous representation, a lawyer cannot constitutionally be held in contempt of court so long as she does not create an obstruction that "blocks the judge in the performance of his judicial duty."[108] As Raveson has found, "The opinions reveal repeated caution that a judge's overreaction to the unavoidable contentiousness of trial advocacy — the confusion of 'offenses to their sensibilities' with 'obstruction to the administration of justice' — does not define contempt."[109]

Unquestionably, however, a judge must be able to protect against "actual obstruction," either in the courtroom or so nearby as "actually to obstruct justice."[110] Moreover, obstruction can include deliberately frustrating a legitimate ruling of the court, as by putting information before a jury that the judge has ruled inadmissible.[111]

"Actual obstruction" did not occur, however, when counsel, having been ordered to stop asking questions, replied: " . . . [W]e have a right to ask the questions, and we propose to do so unless some bailiff stops us."[112] In that case the Supreme Court held that it is "essential to a fair administration of justice that lawyers be able to make honest good-faith efforts to present their clients' cases."[113] The Court added that "[a]n independent judiciary and a vigorous, independent bar are both indispensable parts of our system of justice."[114]

---

[108] *In re McConnell*, 370 U.S. 230, 236, 82 S.Ct. 1288, 1292 (1962).

[109] Raveson, *supra* note 85, at 514.

[110] *In re McConnell*, 370 U.S. at 236, 82 S.Ct. at 1292.

[111] *Fisher v Pace*, 336 U.S. 155, 69 S.Ct. 425 (1949). *But cf., People v. Romanski*, 507 N.E.2d 887 (Ill. App.), *cert. denied*, 116 Ill.2d 572 (1987)("Romanski's remarks constituted a good faith attempt to represent his client and cannot fairly be seen as a violation of the court's order. . . . "); In the *Matter of Sullivan*, 586 N.Y.S.2d 322 (App. Div. 3d Dept. 1992).

[112] *In re McConnell*, 82 S.Ct. at 1292.

[113] *Id.*

[114] *Id.*

§ 4.07 LAWYERS' SPEECH — CRITICIZING JUDGES[115]

The problem is not that too many lawyers are publicly criticizing judges. Unfortunately, too few lawyers are willing to do so, even when a judge has committed serious ethical violations and should be held accountable.

For example, the New York State Bar Association not long ago debated a committee proposal to amend the state's ethical rules to require lawyers to report serious misconduct of judges. You might expect lawyers to welcome such a rule. For one thing, establishing an ethical duty to report would make it clear that the complaining lawyer is not a volunteer, but is acting in part because she would herself be violating a disciplinary rule if she failed to complain. Also, lawyers have a "special responsibility for the quality of justice."[116] The proposed rule was voted down, however, on the expressed concern that "a judge who knows that a lawyer has reported misconduct could hold it against the lawyer in current or future cases."[117] Also, some judges forget about the First Amendment when free speech is directed at them, and take disciplinary action against the lawyer.[118]

Unlike New York, most jurisdictions have adopted MR 8.3(b), which requires a lawyer to volunteer knowledge about serious violations of judicial ethics to the appropriate authority.[119] With regard to public criticism of judges, MR 8.2(a) forbids a lawyer to make a statement about a judge that the lawyer "knows to be false or with reckless disregard as to its truth or falsity." That is, lawyers are properly subject to a *New York Times v. Sullivan*[120] "actual malice" standard in their public criticism of judges.

Lawyers, of course, are particularly knowledgeable about judges' conduct, and are therefore in a position to inform the public about abuses of judicial power. Moreover, as the Supreme Court has held, judges are not "annointed priests," entitled to special protection from the "public clamor" of democratic society. The law gives judges and the institutional reputation of courts "no greater immunity from criticism than other persons or institutions." Those First Amendment truths were reiterated by the Supreme Court in an opinion

---

[115] This topic is relevant to zealous representation because effective representation of the client may require the lawyer to criticize the conduct of a judge. Also, a lawyer may be required to report seriously unethical conduct by a judge even though the lawyer might be justifiably concerned that the judge might retaliate by rulings that are contrary to the interests of future clients.

[116] Model Rules of Prof'l Conduct, Preamble: A Lawyer's Responsibilities (1983).

[117] *House Approves Proposed Amendments to Code*, STATE BAR NEWS, July/Aug. 1996, at 1, 6.

A rule requiring lawyers to report such conduct would make it clear that zealous representation does not require tolerance of judges who commit serious violations of judicial ethics. Note, however, that confidentiality would still override an obligation to report judicial misconduct. As stated in Model Rule 8.3(c), reporting is forbidden if doing so would require the lawyer to reveal client information protected by MR 1.6.

[118] *See, e.g., In re Robert J. Snyder*, 734 F.2d 334 (1984), *rev'd.*, 472 U.S. 634, 105 S.Ct. 2874 (1985).

[119] New York does require a lawyer to reveal knowledge of judicial misconduct, but only "upon proper request of a tribunal or other authority empowered to investigate or act upon" the conduct of judges. DR 1-103(B).

[120] 376 U.S. 254 (1964).

by Chief Justice Warren Burger.[121] Judges, after all, are not "flabby creatures."[122] Rather, they are expected to be "[people] of fortitude, able to thrive in a hardy climate."[123] Thus, we have a practice, "familiar in the long history of Anglo-American litigation, whereby unsuccessful . . . lawyers give vent to their disappointment in tavern or press."[124]

Consider, then, the following cases.

Case One. The judge's opinion is "irrational" and "cannot be taken seriously."

Case Two. "This judge sitting on the bench is a danger to the people of this city."

Case Three. "I have had more than enough of judicial opinions that . . . falsify the facts of the cases that have been argued, . . . that make disingenuous use or omission of material authorities, . . . that cover up these things. . . . "

Case Four. The state's appellate judges are "whores who became madams. I would like to [be a judge]. . . . But the only way you can get it is to be in politics or buy it — and I don't even know the going price."

Case Five. The judge's decision is "overt racism," and the defendants "have no more chance of having a fair hearing in front of [the judge] than they would being judged by the Ku Klux Klan."

Case Six. The judge is "dishonest," "ignorant," a "buffoon," a "bully," "drunk on the bench," and shows "evidence of anti-Semitism."

Do any of those criticisms warrant professional discipline of the lawyer?

The quotation in Case One will be familiar to most readers as what passes for civil discourse among Supreme Court Justices. The particular quotation ("irrational," "cannot be taken seriously") was directed against Justice Sandra Day O'Connor by Justice Antonia Scalia.[125] No professional disciplinary action has been reported against Scalia, or any other justice, for these or other uncivil remarks.[126]

The second quotation (the judge is a "danger to the people") is a criticism of a New York City criminal court judge by Mayor Rudy Giuliani (a lawyer).[127] It is similar to other remarks about the judge by Governor George Pataki (also a lawyer).[128] The Mayor and the Governor were castigating the judge on the basis of two decisions. Similarly, former New York criminal court judge Harold Rothwax used to tell his students at Columbia Law School, "The court of

---

[121] *Landmark Communications, Inc. v. Virginia*, 435 U.S. 829, 837, 843, 98 S.Ct. 1535, 1541, 1543 (1978).

[122] *U.S. v. Morgan*, 331 U.S. 409, 421, 61 S.Ct. 999, 1004 (1941).

[123] *Craig v. Harley*, 331 U.S. 367, 376, 67 S.Ct. 1249, 1255 (1947).

[124] 313 U.S. at 421, 61 S.Ct. at 1004.

[125] *Webster v. Reproductive Health Services*, 492 U.S. 490, 536, 109 S.Ct. 3040, 3067 (1989) (Scalia, J., dissenting).

[126] *See* Edward McGlynn Gaffney, Jr., *The Importance of Dissent and the Imperative of Judicial Civility*, 28 VAL. L. REV. 583 (1994).

[127] *Mayor Presses Ouster of Abuse Case Judge*, N.Y. TIMES, Feb. 17, 1996, at A29.

[128] Don Van Natta, *Judge Rebuked After a Woman Is Slain*, N.Y. TIMES, Feb. 15, 1996, at B3.

appeals is in session; we are all in danger."[129] Further ridiculing the administration of justice, Rothwax wrote that a jury trial is a "crapshoot"[130] and that New York's highest court is a "lottery."[131] No professional disciplinary action was ever reported against Giuliani, Pataki, or Rothwax for these public attacks on judges and the judicial system.

The intemperate and broad-scale attack on the integrity of judges in Case Three (complaining that judges too often falsify facts and use authorities dishonestly) is from a talk that Professor Freedman gave to the Judicial Conference for the Federal Circuit.[132] Fortunately, no disciplinary action was taken on that occasion.

Case Four (whores, madams, and the going price for a judgeship) is from a *Life* magazine article about a New York public defender named Martin Erdmann. Erdmann was subjected to disciplinary proceedings and censured for his comments, but the discipline was reversed by the New York Court of Appeals.[133] Yet, as pointed out by a dissenting judge, Erdmann's comments had been published in a magazine with a circulation of several million copies, and "[i]t is difficult to read the article . . . without coming to the conclusion that neither the legal system nor the legal profession possesses integrity. . . . "[134] Nevertheless, New York's highest court held 5-2 that "isolated instances of disrespect for the law, judges, and courts expressed by vulgar and insulting words or other incivility . . . committed outside the precincts of a court are not subject to professional discipline."[135] "Nor is the matter substantially altered," the court added, "if there is hyperbole expressed in the impoverished vocabulary of the streets."[136]

The quotation in Case Five (comparing the judge to the Ku Klux Klan) was by Ronald I. Kuby. The disciplinary committee dismissed a complaint against Kuby, and the United States District Court for the District of Connecticut affirmed. The court said that Kuby's statement "concerning a highly respected judge . . . was, to be charitable, intemperate, incivil and immature. It was not, however, actionable under the Disciplinary Rules . . . and First Amendment jurisprudence."[137]

The charge in Case Six (dishonest, buffoon, drunk, etc.) resulted, initially, in suspension of the lawyer from practice before the federal district court for two years. The grounds were that the lawyer, Stephen Yagman, had violated local rules forbidding a lawyer to engage in conduct that "degrades or impugns the integrity of the Court" and that "interferes with the administration of

---

[129] HAROLD J. ROTHWAX, GUILTY 31 (1996). Not everyone finds Judge Rothwax's commentaries to be either amusing or accurate. *See, e.g.,* Steven Duke, *Crime and Punishment*, N.Y. TIMES BOOK REVIEW, Mar. 31, 1996, at 8 (The book is "deeply misleading about the system as a whole.").

[130] *Id.* at 162.

[131] *Id.* at 31.

[132] 128 F.R.D. 437, 439 (1990); *see also* Monroe Freedman, *When Judges Tamper with the Evidence*, LEGAL TIMES, Nov. 19, 1990, at 22.

[133] *Matter of the Justices v. Erdmann*, 301 N.E.2d 426 (1973).

[134] *Id.* at 428.

[135] *Id.* at 426.

[136] *Id.*

[137] *In re Ronald L. Kuby*, G.P.-86-10, Order dated Aug. 18, 1993.

justice." But that disciplinary action was reversed in an opinion by Judge Alex Kozinski.[138]

Bound by prior authority in the Ninth Circuit, Judge Kozinski was not able to apply *New York Times v. Sullivan*.[139] The *New York Times* "actual malice" standard protects even false charges against a public official unless made with knowledge of falsity or in reckless disregard of the truth. As applied by the Ninth Circuit in disciplinary cases against lawyers, however, recklessness is determined objectively, by reference to the kind of investigation that would be made by "a reasonable attorney, considered in the light of all his professional functions . . . in the same or similar circumstances." The court's inquiry focuses on whether the attorney had a "reasonable factual basis for making the statements, considering their nature and the context in which they were made," including whether the attorney "pursued readily available avenues of investigation." Truth is, of course, an absolute defense, and the burden of proving falsity is on the disciplinary committee.[140]

As Judge Kozinski noted, that standard is consistent with cases like *In re Holtzman*.[141] There, Queens District Attorney Elizabeth Holtzman was reprimanded for issuing a press release that falsely accused a judge of requiring the victim of a sexual assault to demonstrate the position she had been in at the time of the assault. Before making her charges public, Holtzman had not obtained the minutes of the proceedings, had not made any effort to speak to court officers, the court reporter, defense counsel, or any other person present during the alleged misconduct, including the trial assistant in her office who had originally reported it. Thus, she had been reckless in not "pursu[ing] readily available avenues of investigation" before making false charges against the judge.[142]

Unlike allegations of fact, opinions are not subject to proof or disproof. This means, Judge Kozinski noted, that an expression of opinion (like an allegation of intellectual dishonesty, or being the worst judge on the bench) cannot be punished unless it implies a false assertion of fact.[143] "[I]f it is plain that the speaker is expressing a subjective view, an interpretation, a theory, conjecture, or surmise, rather than claiming to be in possession of objectively verifiable facts, the statement is not actionable."[144]

---

[138] *Standing Committee on Discipline v. Yagman*, 55 F.3d 1430 (1995).

[139] 376 U.S. 254, 84 S.Ct. 710 (1964).

[140] *Yagman*, 55 F.3d at 1437–38.

[141] 577 N.E.2d 30 (N.Y. 1991).

[142] Holtzman's lawyer, Norman Redlich, has noted, however, that she acted only after she had a sworn statement from the prosecutor who had been present at the hearing. Letter from Norman Redlich to Monroe Freedman (Apr. 19, 1996). This fact does not appear in the court's opinion. *See* Case Three, *supra*.

[143] With regard to anti-Semitism, Yagman had said that the judge "has a penchant for sanctioning Jewish lawyers: me, David Kenner and Hugh Manes. I find this to be evidence of anti-Semitism."

In rejecting the charge against Yagman on this count, Kozinski relied in part on the RESTATEMENT (SECOND) OF TORTS, § 566, Cmt. c: "A simple expression of opinion based on disclosed . . . nondefamatory facts is not itself sufficient for an action of defamation, no matter how unjustified and unreasonable the opinion may be or how derogatory it is."

[144] *Yagman*, 55 F.3d at 1441, *quoting Haynes v. Alfred A. Knopf*, Inc., 8 F.3d 1222, 1227 (7th Cir. 1993).

Yagman's statement that the judge had been "drunk on the bench," however, "could be interpreted as suggesting that [the judge] had actually, on at least one occasion, taken the bench while intoxicated." It therefore implies facts that are capable of objective verification.[145] However, the committee presenting disciplinary charges against Yagman had the burden to prove the falsity of Yagman's statement about the judge's drunkenness, and it failed to present any evidence at all on that issue. Accordingly, Yagman could not be disciplined for that statement either.[146]

Those who argue that lawyers are entitled to less freedom of speech than other citizens rely principally on two Supreme Court decisions. One case, *Florida Bar v. Went For It*,[147] involved solicitation of clients, which is commercial speech, and therefore receives only "a limited measure of protection, commensurate with its subordinate position in the scale of First Amendment values."[148] By contrast, criticism of a public official is core First Amendment speech.

The other Supreme Court case limiting lawyer's speech is *Gentile v. State Bar of Nevada*.[149] The five-member majority there emphasized that the case involved not only speech, but the conflicting right to a fair trial. In that context, the majority held: "The regulation of attorneys' speech is limited — it applies only to speech that is substantially likely to have a materially prejudicial effect [on a fair trial]."[150]

Judge Kozinski concluded his opinion in *Yagman* with a quotation from Justice Hugo Black:[151]

> The assumption that respect for the judiciary can be won by shielding judges from published criticism wrongly appraises the character of American public opinion. For it is a prized American privilege to speak one's mind, although not always with perfect good taste, on all public institutions. And an enforced silence, however limited, solely in the name of preserving the dignity of the bench, would probably engender resentment, suspicion, and contempt much more than it would enhance respect.

Like Justice Scalia, Judge Rothwax, Governor Pataki, and Mayor Giuliani, therefore, lawyers in general do not forfeit their First Amendment rights when they become members of the bar.[152]

---

[145] *Id.* at 1441.

[146] *Id.* at 1441–42.

[147] 515 U.S. 618, 115 S.Ct. 2371 (1995).

[148] *Id.* at 623, 115 S.Ct at 2375. *See* Ch. 12, *infra*.

[149] 501 U.S. 1030, 111 S.Ct. 2720 (1991).

[150] *Id.* at 1075, 111 S.Ct at 2745.

[151] *Bridges v. California*, 314 U.S. 252, 270–71, 62 S.Ct. 190, 197–98 (1941).

[152] Nor do judges forfeit their right to respond to public criticism of themselves or each other, although it is frequently said that they are forbidden to do so. In fact, "[a] judge may speak, write, lecture, teach and participate in other extra-judicial activities concerning the law, the legal system, [and] the administration of justice. . . ." Canons of Judicial Conduct, Canon 4B (1990). The pertinent limitation is that a judge may not make a public comment "while a proceeding is pending or impending in any court," but even that limitation applies only if the comment "might

§ 4.08   FRIVOLOUS ARGUMENTS

Lawyers are generally familiar with the ethical rule forbidding frivolous arguments,[153] principally because of sanctions imposed under rules of civil procedure for making such arguments.[154] Not all lawyers are aware, however, of two ways in which the prohibitions of frivolous arguments are restricted in both the rules themselves and in their enforcement. First, the term "frivolous" is narrowed by the way it is defined and explained in the ethical rules and in court decisions. Second, the ethical rules have express limitations with respect to arguments made on behalf of criminal defendants,[155] and courts are generally loath to sanction criminal defense lawyers.[156]

[1]   Sanctions in Civil Cases Under Rule 11 and Similar Rules

During the decade after the 1983 amendments to Rule 11 of the Federal Rules of Civil Procedure, a dangerous tendency developed to impose severe sanctions against lawyers under various federal and state rules.[157] This excessive use of sanctions for allegedly frivolous filings prior to the 1993 amendment of Rule 11 has left a misleadingly broad impression of the meaning of "frivolous."

Rule 11 is similar to the ethical codes (discussed below) in permitting a claim or defense that is "warranted by existing law or by a nonfrivolous argument for the extension, modification, *or reversal of existing law or the establishment of new law*."[158] Giving added emphasis to the italicized language, the Advisory

---

reasonably be expected to affect [the proceeding's] outcome or impair its fairness." *Id.* Canon 3B(9). *See also Republican Party v. White*, 536 U.S. 765 (2002).

In a highly publicized case, President Bill Clinton, Senate Majority Leader Robert Dole, and members of Congress attacked Federal District Judge Harold Baer, threatening him with impeachment because of a decision to suppress evidence in a drug case. In response to those attacks, and while the proceeding was still pending before Judge Baer, The Chief Judge and three other judges of the Second Circuit Court of Appeals published a defense of the judge. Acknowledging Canon 3B(9), the judges said: "the Code also places on judges an affirmative duty to uphold the integrity and independence of the judiciary. In this instance, we believe our duty under this latter provision overrides whatever indirect comment on a pending case might be inferred from this statement (and we intend none)." Don Van Natta, *Judges Defend a Colleague from Attacks*, N.Y. TIMES, Mar. 29, 1996, at B1. *See also* James Dao, *Pataki, in High Court, Exchanges Barbs With Top Judge*, N.Y. TIMES, May 2, 1996, B3; Editorial, *An Alert From the Chief Justice*, N.Y. TIMES, Apr. 11, 1996, at A24; Cylde Haberman, *Under Fire, Judge Decides to Fire Back*, N.Y. TIMES, Feb. 27, 1996, at B1.

In addition, Second Circuit Judge (and former Yale Law School Dean) Guido Calabresi said in a speech at a circuit conference that if a suggestion is made that a judge should resign or be impeached because of an unpopular ruling, it is "perfectly appropriate" for judges to make a statement in response. ABA JOURNAL, June 1996, at 110, 112.

[153] MR 3.1; DR 7-102(A)(2), EC 7-4; ALI Restatement of the Law Governing Lawyers 3d, § 110.

[154] *E.g.*, F.R. Civ. Proc., Rule 11; see also 28 U.S.C. § 1927 (applying to all proceedings), and F.R.App.Proc.,Rule 38 (applying to all appeals). See generally, GREGORY P. JOSEPH, SANCTIONS: THE FEDERAL LAW OF LITIGATION ABUSE (3d ed., 2000; Supp. 2003).

[155] See MR 3.1 and cmt. [3]; Restatement § 110, cmt. *f.*

[156] See notes 204-211, *infra*.

[157] *See, e.g.*, FED. R. CIV. P. 11; FED. R. APP. P. 38, 46; 28 U.S.C. § 1912, 1927.

[158] Emphasis added.

Committee's Notes to the 1983 version of Rule 11 cautioned that the rule is "not intended to chill an attorney's enthusiasm or creativity in pursuing factual or legal theories."[159] Nevertheless, there is significant evidence that creativity has been chilled by sanctions under Rule 11. In addition, judicial enforcement of the rule has had a disproportionate impact on plaintiffs' attorneys in civil rights cases, impaired lawyer-client confidentiality, and caused serious conflicts of interest between lawyers and clients.[160]

In an important article, "Rule 11 in the Real World," Mark Stein explained, from his experience as a litigator, that lawyers were most inclined to threaten sanctions when an adversary's position is "not frivolous, but [rather, when it] is simultaneously dangerous and vulnerable."[161] That is, the unwarranted charge that an argument is frivolous has been used to distract the court from the merits of the argument. Moreover, even if the adversary lawyer is aware that his position is meritorious, "he may still be cowed by the threat of sanctions because of the unpredictable way in which courts award them."[162]

In response to broad criticism of the 1983 version of Rule 11, the rule was amended in 1993.[163] Since then, the volume of cases involving charges of frivolous filings has been substantially reduced. However, the reason for that decrease is not clear. One reason could be that the amendment made imposition of sanctions discretionary with the judge, rather than mandatory. Another possible reason is that a motion for sanctions can no longer be simply an afterthought to another motion (e.g., a motion for summary judgment), but must be made and supported in a separate pleading. Also, the 1993 Rule 11 has a "safe harbor" provision, under which a lawyer whose filing is challenged as frivolous has twenty-one days to withdraw the filing without sanction. In one respect, this "safe-harbor" can be a potent threat, coercing withdrawal

---

[159] 97 F.R.D. 165 (1983).

[160] See JEROLD S. SOLOVY ET AL., SANCTIONS UNDER FEDERAL RULE OF CIVIL PROCEDURE 11 (1996); GREGORY P. JOSEPH, SANCTIONS: THE FEDERAL LAW OF LITIGATIONS ABUSE (2d ed. 1994); *Developments in the Law — Lawyers' Responsibilities and Lawyers' Responses*, 107 HARV. L. REV. 1547, 1642–1644 (More than 20 percent of lawyers interviewed "did not assert a potentially meritorious claim"); George Cochran, *Rule 11: The road to Amendment*, 61 MISS. L.J. 5 (1991); Carl B. Rubin & Laura Ringenbach, *Preliminary Draft of Proposed Amendments to the Federal Rules of Civil Procedure and the Federal Rules of Evidence*, 137 F.R.D. 53, 64 (1991); Jeffrey M. Stempel, *Sanctions, Symmetry, and Safe Harbors: Limiting Misapplication of Rule 11 by Harmonizing It with Pre-Verdict Dismissal Devices*, 60 FORDHAM L. REV. 257, 259 (1991) (Rule 11 "discouraged innovative lawyering"); Georgene M. Vairo, *Rule 11: Where We Are and Where We Are Going*, 60 FORDHAM L. REV. 475, 483–486 (1991) (Rule 11 is being used to chill plaintiffs' access to courts); STEPHEN B. BURBANK, RULE 11 IN TRANSITION: THE REPORT OF THE THIRD CIRCUIT TASK FORCE ON FEDERAL RULE OF CIVIL PROCEDURE 11 (1989); Paul Rothstein & Richard Wolfe, *Innovative Attorneys Starting to Feel Chill from New Rule 11*, LEGAL TIMES, Feb. 23, 1978, at 18; Melissa Nelken, *Sanctions Under Amended Federal Rule 11: Some "Chilling" Problems in the Struggle Between Compensation and Punishment,"* 74 GEO. L. J. 1313 (1986); THOMAS E. WILLGING, THE RULE 11 SANCTIONING PROCESS (1988).

[161] Mark S. Stein, *Rule 11 in the Real World: How the Dynamics of Litigation Defeat the Purpose of Imposing Attorney Fee Sanctions for the Assertion of Frivolous Legal Arguments*, 132 F.R.D. 309, 313 (1990). Another lawyer has commented that sanctions aren't needed for claims that are truly frivolous, because "there has always been a sanction for frivolous claims — it's called losing." Another lawyer has observed that "good judges don't need Rule 11, and bad judges shouldn't have it."

[162] *Id.*

[163] See JOSEPH, n. 160, *supra*, at 21-34.

of arguments that Stein characterizes as "'not frivolous, but . . . simultaneously dangerous and vulnerable."[164] A positive effect of the safe-harbor amendment, however, is that a motion for sanctions cannot be filed at the end of litigation, because at that point it is no longer possible to make use of the safe-harbor withdrawal.

There is still reason for concern, therefore, that Rule 11, and similar rules in state courts, are continuing to have a deleterious effect on creative lawyering in civil cases. This is so in part because of the abuse of the rule by some judges, especially prior to the 1993 amendments, and because of the continuing *in terrorem* effect of possible sanctions under Rule 11 and similar rules. Nevertheless, the reduction in Rule 11 sanctions in federal courts since 1993 is a salutary development.

[2] Defining "Frivolous"

Despite the abuses under Rule 11 and similar rules, the definition of "frivolous" has been an extremely narrow one. The traditional legal definition of frivolous is "obviously false on the face of the pleading," as when something was pleaded that "conflicted with a judicially noticeable fact or was logically impossible, such as a plea of judgment recovered before the accrual of the cause of action."[165] Surely, a lawyer could properly be subjected to sanctions for filing a pleading that is frivolous in the sense of being "obviously false on [its] face." Moreover, lawyers can properly be punished for filing or maintaining pleadings that are "sham" or "baseless," that is, those that appear to state proper claims or defenses, but that are known to the lawyer to be false in fact.[166]

The Supreme Court has gone somewhat further, by unanimously defining a "frivolous" claim as one based on an "indisputably meritless" or "outlandish" legal theory, or one whose factual contentions are "clearly baseless," such as a claim describing "fantastic or delusional scenarios."[167] Elaborating on that definition, the Court held that frivolousness can be found when the facts alleged "rise to the level of the irrational or the wholly incredible."[168]

In addition to establishing this highly restrictive definition, the Supreme Court has cautioned judges against finding arguments to be frivolous. "Some improbable allegations might properly be disposed of on summary judgment," the Court explained, "but to dismiss them as frivolous without any factual development is to disregard the age-old insight that many allegations might be 'strange, but true; for truth is always strange, Stranger than fiction.' "[169]

---

[164] *Supra*, n. 161.

[165] Risinger, *Honesty in Pleading and Its Enforcement: Some 'Striking' Problems with Federal Rule of Civil Procedure 11*, 61 MINN. L. REV. 1, 18 (1976).

[166] *Id.* at 26–29.

[167] *Neitzke v. Williams*, 490 U.S. 319, 32–28, 109 S.Ct. 1827, 1832, 1833 (1989)(construing 28 U.S.C. § 1915(d)) (1948).

[168] *Denton v. Hernandez*, 504 U.S. 25. 33, 112 S.Ct. 1728, 1733 (1992).

[169] *Id.* at 1733–34, *quoting* LORD BYRON, DON JUAN, Canto XIV, stanza 101 (Truman Steffan, Esther Steffand, & Willis Pratt eds., 1977).

[3] The Chilling Effect of Sanctions on Creative Lawyering

Some judges have tended to ignore the narrow definition of what constitutes a frivolous argument, and have imposed sanctions against lawyers who file pleadings or make arguments that have proven to be unavailing. When that happens, zealous advocacy is not the only value that is placed at risk. The genius of our common law is also jeopardized.

For example, Justice Cardozo noted that nine out of ten, and perhaps even more, of the cases taken to the New York Court of Appeals during his time on that bench were "predetermined," their fate "preestablished" by "inevitable laws" from the moment of their filing. *MacPherson v. Buick Motor Co.* appears to be a perfect example. [170] In 1908, the Court of Appeals of New York had reaffirmed the long-established rule that a consumer cannot recover against the manufacturer of a product for negligence. [171] Not long thereafter, Mac-Pherson, who had been injured while driving a car with a defective wheel, sued the Buick Motor Company for negligent manufacture. Surely, MacPherson's case was one of those that Cardozo called "predetermined." [172] The result of MacPherson's appeal, however, was Cardozo's most celebrated torts opinion, reversing long-established law by allowing a consumer to sue a manufacturer for a defective product, and demonstrating the creative common-law judging for which he has been so highly regarded. [173]

As Professor Grant Gilmore observed, the *MacPherson* decision "imposed liability on [a defendant] who would almost certainly . . . not have been liable if anyone but Cardozo had been stating and analyzing the prior case law." [174] At the time of filing the complaint, however, MacPherson's lawyer could not have known that Cardozo would choose to reverse a century of unbroken precedent that had only recently been reaffirmed. Much less could he have known that Cardozo would be able to carry a majority of the court with him. Without that frivolous-appearing complaint, however, Cardozo could not have changed the common law of manufacturer's liability as he did.

Even Cardozo, the great innovator, observed that "the range of free activity for judges is relatively small," [175] in part because judges are limited to the issues that are brought before them by counsel. Behind every innovative judge, therefore, is a lawyer whose creative (and, arguably, frivolous) litigating opened up that small range of judicial opportunity, thereby making the precedent-shattering decision possible.

Innovative judging (and lawyering) is not restricted to common law cases. Depending on how one counts the cases, the Supreme Court has overruled its own decisions 200 to more than 300 times. On at least 16 occasions, this

---

[170] 217 N.Y. 382 (1916).

[171] *Torgesen v. Schultz*, 192 N.Y. 156 (1908).

[172] The point is underscored by *Cadillac Motor Co. v. Johnson*, 221 Fed. 801, 261 Fed. Rep. 878 (1915).

[173] *See* G. Edward White, Tort Law in America 210 (1980).

[174] Grant Gilmore, The Ages of American Law 75 (1977), *quoted in* G.E. White, Tort Law in America 120 (1980).

[175] Benjamin Cardozo, The Growth of the Law 60 (1924).

has happened within three years.[176] At other times, the most venerable of precedents have fallen, including at least ten cases that were overruled after as many as 94 to 126 years.[177] For example, in *Erie Railroad v. Tompkins*,[178] the Supreme Court overruled a precedent that had been applied every day in every federal trial court for nearly a century.[179] On the occasion of one about-face by the Court, Justice Roberts protested that "[n]ot a fact differentiates [the overruled case] from this [one] except the names of the parties."[180] Indeed, the majority itself acknowledged in that case, "The District Court denied the relief sought and the Circuit Court of Appeals quite properly affirmed its action on the authority of *Grovey v. Townsend*," which the Court then proceeded to overrule.[181]

The Rehnquist Court has overruled prior authority in over forty cases.[182] Most recently, in *Lawrence v. Texas*,[183] the Court struck down state legislation outlawing private, consensual homosexual conduct. In doing so, the Court overturned *Bowers v. Hardwick*,[184] decided seventeen years before. In *Bowers*, a majority of the Court had described the legal argument that ultimately prevailed in *Lawrence* as "at best, facetious."[185] Since the dictionary definition of "facetious" is "not meant to be taken seriously or literally . . . ,"[186] the Court was characterizing that argument in a way that was perhaps even more pejorative than the word "frivolous."

Established precedents are now especially vulnerable in death penalty cases. In *Atkins v. Virginia*,[187] holding that the Eighth Amendment forbids

---

[176] *Rose v. Himley* (decided, 1808; overruled, 1810); *Kansas Pac. R. Co. v. Prescott* (decided, 1873; overruled in part, 1874); *Harshman v. Bates* (decided, 1875; overruled, 1877); *Jones v. Opelika* (decided, 1942; overruled, 1943); *Minersville District v. Gobitis* (decided, 1940; overruled, 1943); *Hust v. Moore-McCormack Lines* (decided, 1946; overruled, 1949); *Trupiano v. U.S./ McDonald v. U.S.* (decided, 1948; overruled, 1950; *Kinsella v. Krueger/Reid v. Covert* (decided, 1956; overruled, 1957); *Ladner v. U.S.* (decided, 1958; overruled, 1958); *Kesler v. Dept. of Public Safety* (decided, 1962; overruled, 1965); *Rehabilitation Services v. Zarate* (decided, 1972; overruled, 1974); *Sterett v. Mothers' & Children's Rights Organization* (decided 1972; overruled, 1974); *Fuentes v. Stevin* (decided, 1972; overruled, 1974); *Bonelli Cattle v. Arizona* (decided, 1973; overruled 1976); *U.S. v. Jenkins* (decided, 1975; overruled, 1978); *South Carolina v. Gathers* (decided, 1989; overruled, 1991).

[177] *Stein v. Bowman* (decided, 1839; overruled in part, 1933); *Swift v. Tyson* (decided, 1842; overruled, 1938); *Schooner Catherine v. Dickinson* (decided, 1854; overruled, 1975); *Pennoyer v. Neff* (decided, 1878; overruled, 1977); *Rolston v. Missouri Fund Comm'rs* (decided, 1887; overruled in part, 1984); *Coffey v. U.S.* (decided, 1886; overruled, 1984); *Ex Parte Bain* (decided, 1887; overruled in part, 1985); *Kentucky v. Dennison* (decided, 1861; overruled, 1987); *Kring v. Missouri* (decided, 1883; overruled, 1990); *Ex Parte Bain* (decided 1887; overruled, 1985).

[178] 304 U.S. 64 (1938).

[179] *Swift v. Tyson*, 41 U.S. (16 Pet.) 1 (1842).

[180] *Smith v. Allwright*, 321 U.S. 649, 669, 64 S.Ct. 757, 768 (1942), citing *Grovey v. Townsend*, 295 U.S. 45, 55 S.Ct. 622.

[181] *Id.* at 652.

[182] THE CONSTITUTION OF THE UNITED STATES OF AMERICA: ANALYSIS AND INTERPRETATION 2245–2256 (eds., Johnny H. Killian & George A. Costello) (1996); *id.* at 171 (2000 Supp.); L. EPSTEIN, J.A. SEGAL, H.J. SPAETH, & T.G. WALKER, THE SUPREME COURT COMPENDIUM 194–206 (3d ed.); *Major Decisions of the Court, 1790–2002*: CONGRESSIONAL QUARTERLY 87-141.

[183] 123 S.Ct. 2472 (2003).

[184] 478 U.S. 186, 106 S.Ct. 2841 (1986).

[185] *Id.* at 194, 2844.

[186] WEBSTER'S COLLEGE DICTIONARY (Random House, 1991).

[187] 536 U.S. 304, 122 S.Ct. 2242 (2002).

the execution of a mentally retarded person, the Rehnquist Court overturned *Penry v. Lynaugh*,[188] decided thirteen years before. In the same term, the Court held in *Ring v. Arizona*[189] that the Sixth Amendment requires that a jury, not a judge, make the finding of any fact on which the death penalty depends; in doing so, the Court overruled *Walton v. Arizona*,[190] decided twelve years before. In *Ring*, the Court candidly acknowledged that "[o]ur precedents are not sacrosanct."[191] As explained by Justice Scalia, concurring in *Ring*, "I have acquired new wisdom . . . or, to put it more critically, have discarded old ignorance."[192]

[4] Frivolous Arguments Under the Ethical Rules

Recognizing how creative lawyering can dispel "old ignorance" and impart "new wisdom" to judges, the American Bar Association has taken care in its ethical rules not to discourage lawyers from challenging established precedent or otherwise seeking to make new law on behalf of their clients. For example, Model Rule 3.1 provides that "[a] lawyer shall not bring or defend a proceeding, or assert or controvert an issue therein, unless there is a basis for doing so that is not frivolous." Under such a rule, of course, MacPherson's lawyer would be subject to professional discipline, along with countless other lawyers whose creative litigating helped to shape our law. However, a contention is not frivolous within the rule if it is made as "a good faith argument for an extension, modification or reversal of existing law." Also, the Comment notes that "the law is not always clear and never is static." Accordingly, "in determining the proper scope of advocacy, account must be taken of the law's ambiguities and potential for change." Moreover, filing an action or defense is not frivolous under the Model Rules "even though the lawyer believes that the client's position ultimately will not prevail."[193]

Similarly, DR 7-102(A)(2) of the Model Code begins by forbidding a lawyer to "[k]nowingly advance a claim or defense that is unwarranted under existing law." Again, however, the exception to the rule is crucial: the lawyer is

---

[188] 492 U.S. 302, 109 S.Ct. 2934 (1989).

[189] 536 U.S. 584, 122 S.Ct. 2428 (2002).

[190] 497 U.S. 639, 110 S.Ct. 3047 (1990).

[191] 536 U.S. at 608, 122 S.Ct. at 2442–2443.

[192] 536 U.S. at 611, 122 S.Ct. at 2444.

[193] A related provision in the Model Code is DR 7-102(A)(1). In the Model Rules, the Model Code Comparison to MR 3.1 suggests that there are three noteworthy differences between MR 3.1 and DR 7-102(A)(1). However, these differences do not appear to be significant.

Conduct is improper under DR 7-102(A)(1) if the purpose is "merely" to harass or maliciously injure another. Under MR 3.1 there must be "a" basis that is not frivolous (and frivolous is defined the same as under the Model Code), but if there is a non-frivolous basis, then there is ground for a good faith argument, and if there is ground for a good faith argument, then the purpose is not merely to harass or injure another

The comparison also says that the test under MR 3.1, unlike DR 7-102(A)(1), is an objective one. However, DR 7-102(A)(1) applies if the lawyer "knows *or it is obvious*" that the litigation is frivolous. The emphasized language is an objective standard.

MR 3.1 does say expressly that in criminal cases the defense can always put the prosecution to its proof. This is worth reiterating, although we are not aware that there has ever been any confusion about the point under the Model Code.

permitted to advance a claim that is unwarranted under existing law "if it can be supported by good faith argument for an extension, modification, or reversal of existing law." EC 7-4 adds that "a lawyer is not justified in asserting a position in litigation that is frivolous." The same Ethical Consideration says, however, that the advocate may urge any permissible construction of the law that is favorable to his client "without regard to his professional opinion as to the likelihood that the construction will ultimately prevail."

Further, if the advocate has doubts about the bounds of the law, she should resolve them in favor of the client's interests.[194] Thus, a lawyer contemplating a novel legal argument, or even one that has been rejected by the court in previous litigation, can nevertheless act ethically in presenting that argument despite her own professional opinion that the argument will be rejected. In other words, a lawyer can make an argument in "good faith" under DR 7-102(A)(2) even if the lawyer has no faith that the argument will prevail.

Thus, the Model Code encourages the litigating lawyer to foster growth and change in the law, urging the lawyer, "with courage and foresight," to be "able and ready to shape the body of the law to the ever-changing relationships of society."[195]

The Restatement of the Law Governing Lawyers has almost identical language to the Model Rules and Model Code.[196] In addition, the Comment to Section 110 urges judges to exercise restraint in disciplining lawyers for frivolous advocacy, noting that "[a]dministration and interpretation of prohibitions against frivolous litigation should be tempered by concern to avoid over-enforcement."[197]

[5] Constitutional Limits on Sanctions for Frivolous Law Suits

Moreover, judges who have imposed sanctions against lawyers have typically ignored the constitutional limitations on sanctioning lawyers for filing frivolous pleadings.[198] As the Supreme Court has reiterated in *Professional Real Estate Investors, Inc. v. Columbia Pictures Industries, Inc.*,[199] there is a First Amendment right to petition for redress of grievances by litigating civil cases. That right has, of course, been purposefully chilled by sanctions intended to discourage litigation.

A "sham" lawsuit is an exception to the constitutional right to petition through the courts. However, the "sham" exception does not apply unless the

---

[194] EC 7-3. In counseling a client, however, the lawyer should be candid regarding the probable outcome of the issue in litigation. *Id.*

[195] Model Code, Preamble.

[196] *See* RESTATEMENT § 110 (1) ("A lawyer may not bring or defend a proceeding or assert or controvert an issue therein, unless there is a basis for doing so that is not frivolous, which includes a good-faith argument for an extension, modification, or reversal of existing law.").

[197] RESTATEMENT § 110, Cmt. b.

[198] *See, e.g.*, Stephen B. Burbank, *Sanctions in the Proposed Amendments to the Federal Rules of Civil Procedure: Some Questions About Power*, 11 HOFSTRA L. REV. 997 (1983); discussion, Chapter 2, *supra*, under *The Civil Trial and the Constitution*.

[199] 508 U.S. 49, 113 S.Ct. 1920, 1927 (1993).

suit is "objectively baseless" or "objectively meritless."[200] To satisfy that test, the litigation must be "so baseless that no reasonable litigant could realistically expect to secure favorable relief."[201] All that is necessary to establish the constitutional right is an objective "chance" that a claim "may" be held valid.[202] In that event, the First Amendment right is secure, even if the litigant has no subjective expectation of success and has a malicious motive for pursuing the claim.[203]

[6]   The Rarity of Sanctions for Frivolous Arguments in Criminal Cases

Criminal defense lawyers are rarely disciplined or otherwise sanctioned for asserting frivolous positions in advocacy.[204] One reason is that criminal defense is different from other types of advocacy. As stated in the comment to Model Rule 3.1, which relates to frivolous arguments:

> The lawyer's obligations under this Rule are subordinate to federal or state constitutional law that entitles a defendant in a criminal matter to the assistance of counsel in presenting a claim or contention *that otherwise would be prohibited by the Rule.*[205]

Also, a comment in the Restatement of the Law Governing Lawyers notes that while the section on frivolous arguments applies "generally" to criminal defense lawyers, they may nevertheless take "any step" that is either "required or permitted" by the constitutional guarantee of the effective assistance of counsel.[206]

Illustrating the rare cases in which criminal defense counsel have been sanctioned, the Restatement[207] cites *In re Becraft.*[208] There the Ninth Circuit imposed a sanction against a lawyer in a criminal appeal who had repeatedly raised an argument that the court characterized as a "patent absurdity" and that the Eleventh Circuit had previously found to be "utterly without merit."[209] Even in such a case, however, the *Becraft* court emphasized its

---

[200] *Id.* at 60, 113 S.Ct. at 1928.

[201] *Id.* at 62, 113 S.Ct. at 1929.

[202] *Id.*

[203] *Id.* at 56, 61, 113 S.Ct. at 1926, 1929.

[204] Restatement § 110, Reporter's Note to cmt. *f*, "Advocacy in a criminal-defense representation." See also *In re Becraft*, 885 F.2d 547, 550 (9th Cir. 1989), noting "the absence of authority imposing sanctions against defense counsel."

[205] Emphasis added.

[206] *Id.*, cmt. *f.*

[207] *Id.*, Reporter's Note to cmt. *f.*

[208] 885 F.2d 547 (9th Cir. 1989).

[209] *Id.* at 548, 549. In a number of tax evasion cases, Becraft had unsuccessfully contended that the Sixteenth Amendment does not authorize a direct nonapportioned income tax on resident United States citizens, and thus the federal income tax laws are unconstitutional with respect to such citizens. *Id.* at 548. It is difficult to contemplate the national chaos that would follow a decision that the collection of income taxes from resident citizens is unconstitutional, and that it has been so for almost a century.

Becraft had also argued that state citizens are not subject to federal jurisdiction, on the ground that federal authority is limited to the United States territories and the District of Columbia (*id.* at 549) — an argument that makes one wonder how prescient Becraft was with respect to the Rehnquist Court's views on federalism.

reluctance to sanction a criminal defense lawyer:[210]

> [W]e are hesitant to exercise our power to sanction under Rule 38
> against criminal defendants and their counsel. With respect to coun-
> sel, such reluctance, as evidenced by the lack of authority imposing
> sanctions against defense counsel, primarily stems from our concern
> that the threat of sanctions may chill a defense counsel's willingness
> to advance novel positions of first impression. Our constitutionally
> mandated adversary system of criminal justice cannot function prop-
> erly unless defense counsel feels at liberty to press all claims that
> could conceivably invalidate his client's conviction. Indeed, whether
> or not the prosecution's case is forced to survive the "crucible of
> meaningful adversarial testing" may often depend upon defense
> counsel's willingness and ability to press forward with a claim of first
> impression.

The court added that because significant deprivation of liberty is often at stake
in a criminal prosecution, "courts generally tolerate arguments on behalf of
criminal defendants that would likely be met with sanctions if advanced in
a civil proceeding."[211]

[7] The Necessity to Make "Frivolous" Arguments in Death Penalty Cases

As we have seen, even in civil cases, lawyers have considerable range, both
ethically and constitutionally, in raising issues that are arguably frivolous.
With respect to criminal defense, moreover, courts are loath to impose
sanctions against lawyers in any case in which the defendant's liberty is at
stake.[212]

Furthermore, as serious as is loss of liberty, our jurisprudence recognizes
that death is different.[213] This is so not only as a fact of life and death, but
also for the practical reason that appellate and post-conviction remedies are
pursued in almost 100% of cases in which the death penalty is imposed.[214]
It is therefore crucial that in any capital case, "any and all conceivable errors"
be preserved for review.[215] The alternative is that a client may be put to death
by the state, despite reversible error, because counsel has waived the issue
or defaulted on it.

An example is *Smith v. Kemp*.[216] This was one of two prosecutions for the
same murder. In the case involving codefendant Machetti, who was the

---

[210] *Id.* at 550, *citing United States v. Cronic*, 466 U.S. 648, 656, 104 S.Ct 2039, 2045 (1984).

[211] *Id.*

[212] *In re Becraft*, 885 F.2d at 550.

[213] See, e.g., *California v. Ramos*, 463 U.S. 992, 998–999 (1983). See also *Atkins v. Virginia*, 536 U.S. 304, 337, 122 S.Ct. 2242, 2259 (2002) (Scalia, J., disapproving but recognizing the Court's "death-is-different jurisprudence.").

[214] ABA Guidelines for the Appointment and Performance of Defense Counsel in Death Penalty Cases, Guideline 10.8, History of Guideline (Feb., 2003).

[215] *Id.*, Commentary, quoting Steven B.Bright, *Preserving Error at Capital Trials*, THE CHAMPION, Apr. 1997, at 42–43.

[216] 715 F.2d 1459 (1983).

"mastermind" in the crime,[217] the lawyers timely raise the issue that women had been unconstitutionally under-represented in the jury pool.[218] As a result, Machetti's conviction and death sentence were overturned, resulting in a new trial and a sentence of life in prison.[219]

Codefendant John Eldon Smith was tried in the same county, by a jury drawn from the same jury pool. However, Smith's lawyers did not timely raise the constitutional issue, because they had overlooked authority that gave support to the argument.[220] Since his lawyers' failure to raise the issue was not adequate to overcome nonconstitutional reasons of comity, finality, and agency, Smith was electrocuted.

The agency issue is an essential part of the jurisprudence of death. The Supreme Court, in an opinion by Justice O'Connor, expressly relied upon the Restatement of Agency § 242, for the "well-settled principle of agency law" that a master is subject to liability for harm caused by the negligent conduct of a servant within the scope of the employment.[221] Thus, the Court could "discern no inequity" in requiring a criminal defendant ("the master") to "bear the risk of attorney error."[222] The error in that case was that the attorney ("the servant") was 72 hours late in filing a "purely ministerial" notice of appeal in the state court.[223] Accordingly, Roger Coleman was precluded from raising eleven constitutional challenges to his conviction, and he too was put to death by the state.[224]

A similar agency problem arises when a lawyer makes the tactical decision to omit an argument that appears to be weak (or when a lawyer claims to have done so when challenged with ineffective assistance of counsel). An illustration of that is *Smith v. Murray*.[225] There the lawyer chose to forgo an argument that was contrary to an opinion that the Virginia Supreme Court had handed down only two years before. Writing for the United States Supreme Court, Justice O'Connor praised the lawyer for "winnowing out" the weak argument and focusing on those more likely to prevail, and lauded this practice as the "hallmark of effective appellate advocacy."[226]

---

[217] *Id.* at 1476 (Hatchett, J., concurring in part and dissenting in part).

[218] *Machetti v. Linahan*, 679 F.2d 236 (11th Cir. 1982).

[219] *Smith v. Kemp* at 1476 (Hatchett, J., concurring in part and dissenting in part).

[220] *Id.* at 1470–1471, *citing Taylor v. Louisiana*, 419 U.S. 522 (1975); *Duren v. Missouri*, 439 U.S. 357 (1979).

[221] *Coleman v. Thompson*, 501 U.S. 722.

[222] *Id.* at 2567.

[223] *Id.* 742.

[224] Justice O'Connor also relied on federalism to support her opinion. Indeed, the first words of her opinion, in a case involving whether a person will live or die, are: "This is a case about federalism." *Id.* at 726. But see *Davis v. Monroe County Board of Education*, 119 S.Ct. 1661 (1991), where Justice O'Connor chose to ignore the federalism issue (raised by her dissenting colleagues) to allow a cause of action for sexist harassment of a schoolgirl — an important issue, but not one as compelling as death by electrocution.

[225] 477 U.S. 527, 106 S.Ct. 2661 (1986).

[226] *Id.* at 536, 2667, *quoting Jones v. Barnes*, 463 U.S. 745, 751–752, 103 S.Ct. 3300, 3312–3313 (1983). This position is not universally accepted. See, e.g., Freedman, *Book Review*: WIENER, BRIEFING AND ARGUING FEDERAL APPEALS, 30 GEO. WASH. L. REV. 146 (1961) (arguing that effective advocacy requires that the lawyer raise every issue that might conceivably attract even one vote on a multi-judge panel).

As a result of this model of effective appellate advocacy in the state court, however, the lawyer's client was precluded from raising a winning constitutional issue in the federal courts.[227] As Justice O'Connor held, the lawyer's "deliberate, tactical decision" to winnow out what appeared to him to have been a weak argument in the state appeal, made it "self-evident" that the lawyer's *client* had given up his right to have the argument heard on federal habeas corpus.[228]

The conclusion is therefore clear. Counsel in a capital case must, as a matter of professional responsibility, raise every issue at every level of the proceedings that might conceivably persuade even one judge in an appeals court or in the Supreme Court, in direct appeal or in a collateral attack on a conviction or sentence. This is the essence of the ABA's Guideline 10.8 in its new Guidelines for the Appointment and Performance of Defense Counsel in Death Penalty Cases (February, 2003). In addition, as noted in the Commentary to Guideline 10.8(A)(3)(d), assertion of a claim (even a "frivolous" one) might increase the chances of a desirable plea agreement or might favorably influence a governor or other official in making a decision regarding clemency.

In short, particularly in a capital case, the lawyer for the accused has a professional obligation to assert at every level of the proceedings what otherwise might be deemed a frivolous claim. Moreover, the same is true in any case involving potential deprivation of liberty in which an appeal or collateral attack might be contemplated.

§ 4.09 LAWYERS' SPEECH — TRIAL PUBLICITY[229]

The First Amendment right to freedom of speech is never more important to an individual than when he or she has been publicly accused of wrongful conduct in a criminal prosecution or a civil complaint. A prosecutor or civil litigant is privileged to publish to the world — including one's family, friends, neighbors, business associates, and potential customers — what in most other circumstances would be grounds for a libel action. In a criminal case, "the scales of justice in the eyes of the public are weighed extraordinarily heavy against an accused after his indictment."[230] In a civil case it may be no less urgent to respond publicly to allegations of shameful conduct like fraud, malpractice, spousal or child abuse, or selling products that can maim or kill. Also, the delay before ultimate vindication may be many months, if not years,[231] and the good name earned during a lifetime can be destroyed.[232]

---

[227] *See id.* at 551–553, 2675–2676 (Stevens, J., dissenting).

[228] *Id.* at 533, 534, and 2666. Justice O'Connor also noted "the profound societal costs that attend the exercise of habeas jurisdiction," but had nothing to say about the costs to society and to the individual when a hearing on a legitimate constitutional claim is denied in a death case. *Id.* at 539, 2668.

[229] Trial publicity by prosecutors is treated separately, in Chapter 11 on Prosecutors' Ethics.

[230] *Chicago Council of Lawyers v. Bauer*, 522 F.2d 242, 250 (7th Cir., 1973), *cert. denied*, 96 S.Ct. 3201 (1976). *See also* ALFRED FRIENDLY & RONALD GOLDFARB, CRIME AND PUBLICITY 135–36 (1968), cited in Max D. Stern, *The Right of the Accused to a Public Defense*, 18 HARV. C.R.-C.L. L. REV. 53, 83 (1983).

[231] *See, e.g.*, App. A, *infra*. Two years after extensive condemnation of Dr. Bernard Bergman in the news media, in which he was described as "The Meanest Man in New York," the federal

There can be no more pressing occasion, therefore, for immediate, effective public rebuttal.[233] Moreover, the ordinary citizen can gain access to the news media only when the allegations have first been made public or a trial has begun, because only then is "the full spotlight of media attention . . . focused upon him."[234]

It could be disastrous, however, for an unskilled defendant to confront the cacophony and confusion of a press conference.[235] Even sophisticated and articulate people have been known to founder in the face of a press corps eager for an embarrassing sound bite or an unflattering photo opportunity. Also, as Justice Brennan has noted, public statements by the defendant that appeared to be incriminatory could be admissible at trial.[236] Defense counsel, by virtue of her knowledge about the case and her training as an advocate, is frequently the most appropriate person to speak publicly on behalf of the defendant.

As Congressman (later President) James Buchanan said, in a case involving the imprisonment of a lawyer for criticizing a judge, it is "the imperative duty of an attorney to protect the interests of his client out of court as well as in court."[237] More recently, Leonard Garment (former White House counsel, and

---

judge who heard the case said: "[I]t appears to be undisputed that the media (and people desiring to be featured in the media) have vilified him for many kinds of evildoing of which he has in fact been innocent." *United States v. Bergman*, 416 F.Supp. 496, 502 (S.D.N.Y. 1976) (Sentencing Memorandum).

232 After he was acquitted of criminal charges involving dishonesty, former Secretary of Labor Ray Donovan bitterly commented, "Now tell me where I can go to get my good name back." *See How Do I Repair Reputation? Donovan After his Trial*, CHI. TRIB., May 27, 1987, at C4. The same can be said about Captain James J. Yee, a former Muslim chaplain at the U.S. Naval Base in Guantanamo Bay, Cuba. Captain Yee was initially charged with espionage and aiding the enemy, which resulted in him being held for 76 days in the naval brig, much of the time in leg irons. Although these charges were dropped, Captain Yee was then charged with adultery and downloading pornography. Those charges were ultimately thrown out on appeal. *See* Reuters, *Convictions Dropped for Muslim Chaplain at Guantanamo Bay*, N.Y. TIMES, April 15, 2004, at A24; Editorial, *Military Injustice*, N.Y. TIMES, March 24, 2004, at A20.

233 "I . . . would shudder at the prospect of being charged with some crime, especially one of moral turpitude, and being condemned to suffer silence until some distant day when even an acquittal would not be recompense." Vermont Royster, *The Free Press and a Fair Trial*, 43 N.C.L. REV. 364, 369 (1965).

234 *United States v. Ford*, 830 F.2d 596, 599 (6th Cir. 1987). The court continued:

> The defendant's interest in replying to the charges and to the associated adverse publicity, thus, is at a peak. So is the public's interest in the proper functioning of the judicial machinery. The "accused has a first Amendment right to reply publicly to the prosecutor's charges, and the public has a right to hear that reply, because of its ongoing concern for the integrity of the criminal justice system and the need to hear from those most directly affected by it."

Id., quoting Monroe H. Freedman & Janet Starwood, *Prior Restraints on Freedom of Expression by Defendants and Defense Attorneys: Ratio Decidendi v. Obiter Dictum*, 29 STAN. L. REV. 607, 618 (1977).

235 Also, in a criminal case, the defendant may be held without bail and unable to speak out effectively.

236 *Nebraska Press Ass'n v. Stuart*, 427 U.S. 539, 600, 96 S.Ct. 2791, 2822, n. 25 (1976) (Brennan, J., concurring).

237 Quoted in LAURENCE TRIBE, AMERICAN CONSTITUTIONAL LAW 628, n. 26 (1978).

attorney for several public figures) has commented on his duty to represent his clients in the court of public opinion as well as in the courtroom.[238] Moreover, the defense lawyer's public explanation of what is at stake in the case can be important to raising the funds that are necessary to mounting an effective defense.[239] Thus, zealous representation may well require the lawyer to speak out publicly on the client's behalf.[240]

The principal reason given for restricting trial publicity is that it can interfere with the constitutional right to a fair trial. But the Supreme Court has made it clear that it is virtually impossible to make a trial constitutionally unfair by trial publicity, even by pervasive prejudicial publicity that has been purposefully instigated by the prosecution.

During a brief five-year period during the 1960s, the Supreme Court did overturn four criminal convictions on grounds of prejudicial trial publicity.[241] However, in *Murphy v. Florida*[242] the Supreme Court distinguished those cases away, describing the trials with phrases like "circus atmosphere," "carnival," "utterly corrupted by press coverage," and "the verdict of a mob."[243] Further, the Court held that even a showing that a juror had a "preconceived notion as to the guilt . . . of an accused" because of pretrial publicity is not sufficient to establish that a trial is constitutionally unfair.[244] Thus, after *Murphy*, no trial can be found unfair unless it has been "utterly corrupted" by publicity.[245]

The virtual impossibility of meeting the "utterly corrupted" or "verdict of a mob" standard is illustrated by *Murphy* itself. Before the trial, the jurors were exposed to extensive prejudicial publicity about Murphy and his criminal record. Murphy's record included the theft of the Star of India sapphire and a conviction for murder. This was known to all members of the jury, one of whom "freely admitted that he was predisposed to convict" Murphy.[246] Also, the trial court denied a motion for a change of venue. Even Chief Justice Burger characterized the media coverage as "bizarre" and criticized the trial

---

[238] Barbara Cottman Becnel, *Seeking Publicity Increasingly Seen as Trial Tactic: Lawyers Unabashedly Try to Win in Court of Public Opinion*, L.A. DAILY J., July 28, 1987, at 1. *See also,* Robert S. Bennett, *Press Advocacy and the High-Profile Client*, 30 LOYOLA L.A. L. REV. 13 (1996); Stanley S. Arkin, *Self Defense by the Defense* — *Publicity, Fair Trial*, N.Y.L. JOUR., p. 1, June 11, 1987.

Another compelling reason for the defense lawyer to exercise his or her right of free speech about the case is that the lawyer might be the target of news media criticism relating to the case. *See, e.g.,* App. A, *infra.*

[239] A case in point is given in Stern, *supra* note 230, at 80.

[240] The decision for the lawyer to do so is the client's, after proper counseling by the lawyer. *See* Chapter 3, *supra.* But compare MR 1.2(a), which would appear to allow the lawyer to engage in publicity over the client's objections, on the ground that trial publicity is a "means" or "tactic" rather than an "objective."

[241] *Irvin v. Dowd*, 366 U.S. 717, 81 S.Ct. 1639 (1961); *Rideau v. Louisiana*, 373 U.S. 723, 83 S.Ct. 1417 (1963); *Estes v. Texas*, 381 U.S 532, 85 S.Ct. 1628 (1965); and *Sheppard v. Maxwell*, 384 U.S. 333, 86 S.Ct. 1507 (1966).

[242] 421 U.S. at 794, 95 S.Ct. 2031 (1975).

[243] *Id.* at 797–181, 95 S.Ct. at 2035–2036.

[244] *Id.* at 800, 95 S.Ct. at 2036.

[245] *Id.* at 798, 95 S.Ct. at 2035.

[246] *Id.* at 804, 95 S.Ct. at 2038 (Brennan, J., dissenting).

judge for having failed to prevent pretrial discussion of the prejudicial publicity among the jurors.[247] Nevertheless, the Court rejected Murphy's claim that his trial had been prejudiced. Thereafter, in *Mu'Min v. Virginia*,[248] the Court found no prejudice in a capital murder case where the publicity included numerous references to evidence that was both inflammatory and inadmissible.

In light of *Murphy*, *Mu'Min*, and others,[249] it seems fanciful to suggest that the defense could so taint a trial with pretrial publicity as to deny the government a fair trial. Consider, for example, *Gentile v. State Bar of Nevada*, a disciplinary matter arising out of a criminal prosecution.[250] The underlying case involved the prosecution of Grady Sanders for theft of nearly $300,000 and nine pounds of cocaine from a safety deposit box being used by undercover police officers for sting operations. Early suspects were two police officers who had had access to the box. Almost immediately, however, law enforcement officials announced that the officers had been cleared, and identified Sanders, who owned the safety deposit company, as the prime suspect.

The prosecution then issued extensive praise for the officers and condemnation of Sanders. Prosecutors announced that the officers were cooperating with the investigation but that Sanders was not. They described the officers as "two of the most daring and respected cops on the force," while Sanders was accused of being linked to organized crime. This kind of prejudicial publicity, orchestrated by the prosecution, went on for a year before Sanders was indicted.

Oddly enough, the *Gentile* case was not a disciplinary action against the Sanders prosecutors for engaging in pretrial publicity in violation of Model Rule 3.6. Instead, the target was Sanders' defense lawyer, Dominic Gentile (pronounced Jen-TEEL). Just after his client's indictment, and following the year of prejudicial publicity about his client, Gentile had held a short press conference to offer Sanders' side of the case. If he had not done so, there would have been another six months of unanswered attacks before Sanders' trial. Gentile said that Sanders was innocent, that four of the witnesses against him were known drug-dealers and convicted money-launderers, that the likely thief was one of the undercover officers, and that Sanders was a scapegoat. Six months later, the jury agreed.

The Nevada Supreme Court, in upholding the disciplinary action against Gentile, specifically found that he had not prejudiced the case. Moreover, the

---

[247] *Id.* at 803, 95 S.Ct. at 2038 (Burger, C.J., concurring).

[248] 500 U.S. 415, 111 S.Ct. 1899 (1991).

[249] Another extreme case in which no prejudice was found is *Patton v. Yount*, 467 U.S. 1025, 104 S.Ct. 2885 (1984). *See also Beck v. Washington*, 369 U.S. 541 (1962) (extensive reporting of a U.S. Senate investigation and of the grand jury indictment of the accused did not deprive defendant of fair trial); *United States v. Haldeman*, 559 F.2d 31, 59–71 (D.C. Cir.), *reh. denied* (1976), *cert. denied*, 97 S.Ct. 2641 (1977) (the "extraordinarily heavy coverage" of the Watergate conspiracy did not deprive the defendants of a fair trial).

For an earlier case in which the Court found no prejudice despite pervasive adverse publicity that was actively promoted by the prosecution, *see Stroble v. California*, 343 U.S. 181 (1951). The pretrial publicity in *Stroble* included the defendant's confession to the sexual molestation and murder of a six-year-old girl. It was published along with headlined descriptions of the defendant as a "werewolf," a "fiend," and a "sex-mad killer."

[250] 501 U.S. 1030, 111 S.Ct. 2720 (1991).

U.S. Supreme Court has been unable to find prejudice even in cases like *Murphy* and *Mu'Min*. With striking inconsistency, however, a majority of five justices, in an opinion by Chief Justice Rehnquist, held that Gentile had violated what was then MR 3.6 by creating a "substantial likelihood of materially prejudicing the trial."[251] Also, the Rehnquist majority of five upheld the constitutionality of the "substantial likelihood of material prejudice" standard for lawyer discipline, even though the Nevada court had interpreted this clause to be less stringent than a "clear and present danger" standard.

A different majority of the Supreme Court reversed the disciplinary action against Gentile, however, on the ground that MR 3.6 was void for vagueness under the due process clause. On this issue, Justice Sandra Day O'Connor broke from the Rehnquist opinion, giving Justice Anthony Kennedy a majority of five. The Court's focus in dealing with the vagueness issue was MR 3.6(c), the "safe harbor" provision. This provision says that even though the lawyer's speech has a substantial likelihood of materially prejudicing the trial, he may nevertheless state, "without elaboration," the "general" nature of the defense. The Kennedy majority held that the words "elaboration" and "general" are "classic terms of degree" which, in the context of MR 3.6, "have no settled usage or tradition of interpretation." For those reasons, lawyers could only "guess at its contours." Accordingly, the rule was unconstitutionally void for vagueness.

The ABA responded to *Gentile* with an amended MR 3.6.[252] Subsection (a) again forbids a lawyer to make an out-of-court statement if the lawyer "knows or reasonably should know that it will have a substantial likelihood of materially prejudicing an adjudicative proceeding in the matter."[253] However, adopting the position recommended in the first edition of this book,[254] the new rule has a subsection that renders the proscription almost entirely ineffective. MR 3.6(c) says that notwithstanding subsection (a), a lawyer may make a statement that a reasonable lawyer would believe is required to protect a client from the "substantial undue prejudicial effect of recent publicity not initiated by the lawyer or the lawyer's client."

That means that the lawyer may, with impunity, defend her client's reputation, regardless of whether the harmful statements about the client have been made by the other side or by third persons.[255] Moreover, a lawyer for a criminal defendant is permitted to respond publicly to the indictment whenever the the charges have been publicized.

---

[251] The Rehnquist majority found this potential prejudice in Gentile's statement of his client's innocence and the detective's guilt, and in his reference to the character, credibility, and criminal records of witnesses against Sanders. In short, they found that Gentile had prejudiced a fair trial by responding directly to the publicity that had already been broadcast by the prosecution.

[252] MR 3.8, which relates to prosecutors' ethics, was also amended with regard to trial publicity. *See* Chapter 11, *infra*.

[253] The restriction applies, of course, only to a lawyer who is "participating or has participated in the investigation or litigation of [the] matter." MR 3.6(a).

[254] MONROE FREEDMAN, UNDERSTANDING LAWYERS' ETHICS 228–236 (1st ed., 1990). *See also* Monroe Freedman, *Muzzling Trial Publicity*, LEGAL TIMES, Apr. 15, 1993, at 24; Monroe Freedman, *Silencing Defense Lawyers*, LEGAL TIMES, May 6, 1991, at 22.

[255] This is clear from a plain reading of MR 3.6(c) and from Comment [7].

In addition, notwithstanding subsection MR 3.6(a), MR 3.6(b)(2) permits the lawyer to state publicly any information "contained in a public record."[256] For many years, prosecutors have created a fulsome public record with a "speaking indictment," which details the charges and any other defamatory information that the prosecutor wants to trumpet in press conferences.[257] Although criminal defense lawyers and civil lawyers have been slow to realize it, they too can create public records that can effectively exempt them from MR 3.6(a). For example, criminal defense lawyers can file bail applications, motions to dismiss the indictment, motions *in limine*, and motions to suppress evidence, all of which can include information that the lawyer wants to discuss publicly. Similarly, lawyers in civil cases can freely discuss any information contained in complaints, answers, motions to dismiss, motions for summary judgment, and any other pleadings or discovery documents that have been filed with the court and that are not subject to a protective order.

For practical purposes, therefore, MR 3.6 does not restrict criminal defense lawyers or civil lawyers from zealously representing their clients in the public forum as well as in court. Indeed, for a lawyer to do so, as noted by Justice Anthony Kennedy, is not just permitted but can be a lawyer's duty:[258]

> An attorney's duties do not begin inside the courtroom door. He or she cannot ignore the practical implications of a legal proceeding for the client . . . . [A]n attorney may take reasonable steps to defend a client's reputation and reduce the adverse consequences of indictment . . . . A defense attorney may pursue lawful strategies . . . including an attempt to demonstrate in the court of public opinion that the client does not deserve to be tried."

§ 4.10   COMMUNICATING WITH OTHER PERSONS ON BEHALF OF A CLIENT

A premise of the adversary system is that anyone who is or may be involved in a legal matter is entitled to have the benefit of a trained and skilled lawyer. Ethical rules therefore limit lawyers in their communications with non-lawyers representing clients. The underlying concern is that the non-lawyer could be at a significant disadvantage because of ignorance of the law and of lawyering skills. In addition, there are rules forbidding lawyers to mislead third parties.

The rules deal with two categories of cases, those in which the person with whom the lawyer communicates is unrepresented, and those in which the person is represented by another lawyer. These rules are often thought of as protecting persons whose interests are "adverse" to those of a lawyer's client, but they are not limited to protecting the interests of parties who are opposed to each other in litigation or across a bargaining table.[259] For example, the

---

[256] An exception, of course, would be a document that is subject to a protective order.

[257] *See* § 11.10, *infra* (on "Trial Publicity by Prosecutors"). We use the word "fulsome" intending both dictionary meanings.

[258] *Gentile v. State Bar of Nevada*, 501 U.S. 1030, 1043 (1991) (Kennedy, J., concurring).

[259] DR 7-104 is the only relevant rule that refers to communicating with one of "adverse inter-

rules protect potential witnesses from being misled regarding the lawyer's partisan role in a matter that the lawyer is investigating.

[1] Communicating with Unrepresented Persons

We begin with lawyers who communicate with non-lawyers who have no legal representation. DR 7-104(A)(2) of the Model Code forbids a lawyer to "give advice" to a person who is not represented by a lawyer, "other than the advice to secure counsel," if that person's interests "are or have a reasonable possibility of being in conflict with the interests of the lawyer's client."

If an adverse party chooses self-representation, this provision does not prevent a lawyer from acting on her client's behalf in negotiations or litigation. Also, in any case, the rule permits a lawyer to investigate a matter by getting information from an unrepresented person with adverse interests. Nor under DR 7-104(A)(2) is a lawyer who is investigating required to make clear to the unrepresented person that the lawyer is representing a client with adverse interests. However, DR 7-102(A)(5) forbids a lawyer who is representing a client to make a false statement of law or fact to anyone, and DR 1-102(A)(4) forbids conduct involving dishonesty, fraud, deceit, or misrepresentation. The lawyer would therefore be forbidden to do anything that would affirmatively mislead the unrepresented person about the lawyer's role. Also, since DR 1-102(A)(6) forbids a lawyer to circumvent a disciplinary rule through another person, a lawyer would be forbidden to direct or to condone an investigator's misrepresentations to an unrepresented person.

The Model Rules are similar, but not identical. Under MR 4.3 a lawyer dealing on behalf of a client with an unrepresented person is forbidden to state or imply that the lawyer is disinterested. In addition, if the lawyer knows or reasonably should know that the unrepresented person misunderstands the lawyer's role, the lawyer must make reasonable efforts to correct the misunderstanding. Here, too, the lawyer is permitted to interview the unrepresented person to investigate the matter, but she may be under an affirmative obligation to clarify her role even if she has done nothing affirmatively to mislead the person.

Unlike DR 7-104(A)(2), the text of MR 4.3 does not forbid a lawyer to give legal advice to an unrepresented person, but the comment includes this proscription. Regardless of a specific rule, lawyers should be cautious about giving legal advice to anyone whom they do not represent. The Scope section of the Model Rules notes that the existence of a lawyer-client relationship depends on state substantive law, which will turn on the facts of particular cases.[260] If a lawyer does give legal advice to an unrepresented person, therefore, the lawyer runs the risk of a finding that the person has reasonably understood that the lawyer has become that person's lawyer.[261] This can

---

est" or whose interests may be "in conflict" with those of the lawyer's client. No Model Rule uses the phrase "adverse interest" or its equivalent. One of the rules we will be discussing, MR 4.2, originally referred to a lawyer's communications with a represented "party." In 1995, MR 4.2 was amended to refer instead to a represented "person."

[260] Model Rules, Scope, para. [3].

[261] Such a finding would be based on the formation of a contract implied in fact.

expose the lawyer to malpractice liability to that person, based, *e.g.*, on a charge of incompetent representation and/or of a conflict of interest.[262]

In addition, as under the Model Code, the lawyer is forbidden by MR 4.1(a) to make a false statement of material fact or law to a third person, and by MR 8.4(c) to engage in conduct involving dishonesty, fraud, deceit, or misrepresentation.[263] Also, under MR 8.4(a), the lawyer may not violate a rule through the acts of another. MR 5.3 goes further, requiring lawyers to "make reasonable efforts" to ensure that non-lawyers who are associated with them act in ways consistent with the lawyers' professional responsibilities. Moreover, MR 5.3(c) expressly makes a lawyer responsible for conduct by a non-lawyer that the lawyer ratifies.

These results seem sensible and desirable, but can have undesirable consequences. In the 1960s, Freedman was involved in efforts on behalf of a fair housing group to enforce the District of Columbia's rules against racial discrimination in housing. The only way to make a case of discrimination was through "testers." An African-American couple would purport to be interested in buying or renting a house in a particular neighborhood. They would claim to be married and to have two children and a particular income level. Immediately after they were told that no houses were available for sale or rent in the neighborhood, a white couple purporting to have the same family and income would apply for a house. When the white couple were then shown two or three available houses, there would be persuasive evidence of racial discrimination.

This was a reasonable way — in fact, a necessary way — to carry the burden of proving discrimination. The problem is that under either the Model Code or the Model Rules, Freedman's conduct would have been unethical. Acting through others (the testers), he made material misrepresentations of fact to the real estate brokers and engaged in conduct involving dishonesty, fraud, deceit, and misrepresentation.[264]

The same issue can arise, of course, in any litigation. In a case involving a coverage dispute between an insurer (Aetna) and its insured (Monsanto), Aetna's lawyers sent out investigators to interview former employees of Monsanto.[265] Affidavits of the former employees (which the judge credited) included a variety of ways in which Aetna investigators had misled them. For example, some said that investigators had told them that they represented Monsanto's insurance company but had not said that Monsanto was suing the insurance company; the investigators thereby gave the impression that they were aligned with Monsanto. Other affidavits related more direct forms of misrepresentation.

---

[262] With regard to conflicts of interest, *see* Ch. Ten, *infra*.

[263] MR 4.1, Cmt. [1] says that a lawyer is "required to be truthful when dealing with others on a client's behalf, but generally has no affirmative duty to inform an opposing party of relevant facts." The comment adds, however, that a misrepresentation can occur by "failure to act."

[264] The same was true then under Canon 15 of Canons of Professional Ethics, which proscribed "any manner of fraud or chicane."

[265] *Monsanto Company v. Aetna Casualty and Surety Company*, 593 A.2d 1013 (Del. Super. Ct., 1990). The defendants were not just Aetna but several insurers, and related to their liability for environmental pollution litigation against Monsanto across the country.

The court's opinion is headed with a quotation from oral argument by Aetna's counsel:[266]

> [Telling the truth in civil litigation] is, of course, a very attractive proposition. But, I would like to visit with your Honor further examination of that proposition, because while that might be nice in a perfect world, it is not the way the system operates in litigation in this country.

That was a questionable way to argue the issue that was before the court, and it gave rise to a questionable response from an angry judge: "one who is in search of the truth must tell the truth."[267] If the judge's proposition were accepted, no undercover or sting operation would be permitted, and much activity that is more seriously antisocial than misrepresenting one's true role in an investigation would be virtually impossible to uncover and to prove.[268] Nevertheless, on the facts as found by the judge, he was correct in concluding that the conduct had violated the Model Rules.[269]

Some commentators have contended, though, that the Model Rules do not in any case preclude "undercover investigators," *i.e.*, those who "disguise identity or purpose" in dealing with others.[270] Others argue that the rules of lawyers' ethics take the categorical position, in effect, that "lying is never justified," and these commentators recommend appropriate amendments to take account of cases where deception is morally justifiable.[271]

David B. Isbell and Lucantonio N. Salvi contend that the Model Rules, "properly read, . . . do not prohibit the use of misrepresentations solely with regard to identity and purpose, and solely for evidence-gathering purposes, by investigators and testers acting under the direction of lawyers."[272]

---

[266] *Id.* at 1015.

[267] *Id.* at 1016. The judge's direct response was "in the strongest way possible to reject counsel's observations as being so repugnant and so odious to fair minded people that it can only be considered as anathema to any system of civil justice under law." *Id.* at 1015.

Finding that the investigators' misleading conduct had tainted the trial, the judge issued an order scripting the information investigators would have to provide to any other potential witnesses in the case. *Id.* at 1021.

[268] *See, e.g., Richardson v. Howard*, 712 F.2d 319, 321 (7th Cir., 1983):

> This court and others have repeatedly approved and sanctioned the role of "testers" in racial discrimination cases. [Citing cases]. It is frequently difficult to develop proof in discrimination cases and the evidence provided by testers is frequently valuable, if not indispensable . . . . [W]e have long ago recognized that this requirement of deception was a relatively small price to pay to defeat racial discrimination.

See also David B. Isbell & Lucantionio N. Salvi, *Ethical Responsibility of Lawyers for Deception by Undercover Investigators and Discrimination Testers: An Analysis of the Provisions Prohibiting Misrepresentation Under the Model Rules of Professional Conduct*, 8 GEO. J. LEGAL ETHICS 791, 795 (1995): "[I]nvestigators and testers serve socially desirable purposes, whose value to society outweighs the costs of the deception involved."

[269] *Monsanto*, 593 A.2d at 1020–1021. The conduct would also have violated the Model Code; *see* discussion, *supra*.

[270] Isbell & Salvi, *supra* note 268, at 795.

[271] *See, e.g.,* Christopher J. Shine, Note, *Deception and Lawyers: Away From a Dogmatic Principle and Toward a Moral Understanding of Deception*, 64 NOTRE DAME L. REV. 722 (1989).

[272] Isbell & Salvi, *supra* note 268, at 796.

Here is the central part of their analysis.[273] Rule 4.1(a) does forbid a lawyer to "make a false statement of material fact" to a third person. However, the rule is prefaced by the phrase, "In the course of representing a client." This phrase does not refer, they say, to the existence of a lawyer-client relationship, but means that the lawyer must be "functioning as a lawyer," and not as a "private citizen" in the activity in question. But, they assert, "[i]nvestigators and testers are not ordinarily lawyers and in any event do not function as such." Accordingly, if a lawyer were to act as an investigator, she would not be "functioning as a lawyer" and therefore would not be "in the course of representing a client." Moreover, a lawyer supervising or ratifying the conduct of the investigator would not be acting improperly under MR 5.3 for the same reason, that is, the conduct that is being supervised or ratified would not be unethical if engaged in by the lawyer.[274]

As much as we would like to reach the same conclusion, we cannot reconcile the analysis with the text. In ordinary usage, the phrase "in representing a client" clearly refers to activity on behalf of a client in the course of a lawyer-client relationship. This is so even if the activity is something that can be done by a private citizen, like reading a book, or writing a letter, or, for that matter, interviewing a potential witness.[275] Not surprisingly, therefore, ABA Formal Opinion 95-396 says flatly, "if the investigator acts as the lawyer's 'alter ego,' the lawyer is ethically responsible for the investigator's conduct."[276]

Moreover, in commercial cases, we are confident that lawyers charge their clients fees for the lawyers' "professional services" for time that is devoted to supervising undercover or sting operations. Also, we would expect that, in appropriate circumstances, lawyers would assert a work-product privilege for communications with their investigators/testers. Finally, a decisive refutation of the Isbell-Salvi position is that it is irrelevant whether the lawyer who engages in conduct involving dishonesty, fraud, deceit, or misrepresentation is acting "as a private citizen," rather than on behalf of a client. As properly noted in ABA Formal Opinion 336, the ethical rules forbidding such conduct are not limited to acts by lawyers in their capacity as lawyers.

---

[273] *Id*. at 814–815.

[274] *Id*. at 818–819.

[275] Also, the authors assert that a distinction cannot properly be drawn that would allow prosecutors but not civil practitioners to conduct undercover activities. Such a distinction, they say, "would find no anchor in the text of the rule." *Id*. at 796.

Yet one might well focus on the same language, *i.e.*, "in the course of representing a client" and reach that result. Lawyers in private practice "represent clients," within the meaning of MR 4.1. One of the distinctive features of a prosecutor, however, is that she has no client in the ordinary sense. Therefore, consistent with the text, one might say that prosecutors, unlike private practitioners, are not covered by MR 4.1. *See* F. Dennis Saylor, IV & J. Douglas Wilson, *Putting a Square Peg in a Round Hole: The Application of Model Rule 4.2 to Federal Prosecutors*, 53 U. PITT. L. REV. 459 (1992).

No, we are not persuaded by this argument either, and it has been expressly rejected by ABA Opin. 95-396, at notes 9 and 10. However, it works as well (or as poorly) as Isbell and Salvi's.

[276] *See also* MR 5.3, which requires lawyers to "make reasonable efforts" to ensure that non-lawyers who are associated with them act in ways consistent with the lawyers' professional responsibilities. In addition, MR 5.3(c) expressly makes a lawyer responsible for conduct by a non-lawyer that the lawyer ratifies.

We agree, therefore, with those who urge that the Model Rules be amended to permit deception when the certain criteria have been met.[277] We propose the following criteria: (1) there must be a good faith reason, consistent with truth-seeking, to perpetrate the deception; (2) there must be no alternative means reasonably available to achieve the result;[278] (3) if the deception involves a tribunal, it must be revealed within a reasonable time after it has occurred;[279] and (4) no person may be caused to suffer significant and irreparable injury (other than exposure of wrongful conduct) by the deception.[280]

In an important development that is likely to be emulated in other states, the Supreme Court of Oregon has amended its DR 1-102 (the parallel provision to MR 8.4) to allow covert investigations.[281] Oregon's new DR 1-102(D)[282] expressly permits lawyers "to advise clients or others about or to supervise lawful covert activity in the investigation of violations of civil or criminal law or constitutional rights." "Covert activity" is defined as "an effort to obtain information on unlawful activity through the use of misrepresentations or other subterfuge." There are two provisos. The first is that the lawyer's conduct must be "otherwise in compliance with these disciplinary rules."[283] The second is that the lawyer, in beginning the covert activity, must "in good faith believe that there is a reasonable possibility that unlawful activity has taken place or will take place in the foreseeable future."

---

[277] *See, e.g.*, Christopher, *supra* note 271, at 750. Our criteria are similar in some respects to Christopher's, but are significantly different overall.

[278] This would involve consideration of the expense and delay required by formal discovery. Also, it recognizes that before litigation is filed, formal discovery is unavailable; yet a potential plaintiff is under an obligation to have some factual basis before filing an action or else to risk sanctions, as under Rule 11.

[279] *See, e.g.*, discussion of *In re Friedman, infra*, note 280.

[280] *In re Friedman*, 392 N.E.2d 1333 (Ill., 1979), was a disciplinary action against a prosecutor. The case illustrates the four criteria, but we also believe that Freedman's analysis of the applicable rules (discussed below) was correct on the facts of the case.

A police officer had told the prosecutor that the officer had been offered a bribe by a defense lawyer if the officer testified falsely that the victim of an assault was unwilling to come to court. The only way to make a case against the corrupt lawyer was to go forward with the scheme so that the bribe would be paid. The prosecutor was subjected to discipline for presenting the officer's perjury and related violations.

Professor Freedman submitted an affidavit in the case saying, in part, that the prosecutor had not committed a disciplinary violation because his compelling motive had been to expose corruption in the administration of justice, and because the relevant rules contemplate cases in which there is no intention to reveal the deception to the tribunal (as the prosecutor had promptly done). *See Id.* at 399–400 (Underwood, J., concurring). Freedman analogized the case to a firefighter setting a backfire to stop a conflagration that threatens to destroy a city, and then being prosecuted for arson.

The Illinois Supreme Court split three ways, with a majority holding that the prosecutor had violated the rules, but a different majority holding that he should not be disciplined.

[281] Reported in Lawyers' Manual on Professional Conduct, 18 *Current Reports* 94–96 (Feb. 13, 2002).

[282] Quoted, *id.* at 95.

[283] That appears to mean that, although the investigators and testers may use deception, the lawyer herself may not do so.

[2] Communicating with Represented Persons (Civil)

MR 4.2 and DR 7-104(A)(1) are virtually identical. They forbid a lawyer to communicate about the representation with a person the lawyer knows to be represented by another attorney in the matter. The two exceptions are when the person's attorney has authorized the lawyer to make the contact, or when the lawyer is authorized by law.

In civil cases, controversy over these rules has centered around the issue of which employees of a represented corporate party are included in the ban. The issue is important because of the importance of fact investigation and the considerable expense of formal discovery, which can be prohibitive for many plaintiffs. This is particularly true of depositions, which are the formal counterpart to informal interviewing, and which can be made extremely expensive by defendants who have the resources to prolong them.

First, with regard to *former* employees, ABA Formal Opinion 91-359 has held them to be outside MR 4.2, noting that "[n]either the Rule nor its comment purports to deal with *former* employees of a corporate party."[284] The committee reasoned that "the effect of the Rule is to inhibit the acquisition of information about one's case," and therefore "the Committee is loathe . . . to expand [the Rule's] coverage to former employees by means of liberal interpretation."

With regard to current employees, Comment [4] to MR 4.2 says that the prohibition extends to (1) "persons having managerial responsibility on behalf of the organization;" (2) any person "whose act or omission in connection with that matter may be imputed to the organization for purposes of civil or criminal liability;" and (3) one "whose statement may constitute an admission on the part of the organization."

The part of Comment [4] to MR 4.2 that has caused particular confusion is the reference to employees whose statement "may constitute an admission on the part of the organization." An "admission" can refer to the hearsay exception (admission of a party, which is admissible as evidence, but subject to rebuttal), or it can refer to an admission in the sense of binding a party, as in a stipulation, which is not subject to rebuttal).

A Superior Court decision in Massachusetts, *Messing, Rudavsky & Weliky, P.C. v. President and Fellows of Harvard College,*[285] used the former interpretation, banning informal interviews of any corporate employee whose statement would be admissible in evidence as an exception to the hearsay rule. This bars informal interviews with any employee who might make a statement within the scope of his employment, which effectively forbids useful informal discovery from any employee.

Fifty-four teachers and scholars joined an amicus brief prepared by Professors John Leubsdorf, Stephen Gillers, and Susan Koniak, opposing that interpretation.[286] The brief maintains that the comment refers to "admissions

---

[284] Emphasis in the original.

[285] On appeal, No. SJC-08592 (2001).

[286] Other signers included Professors Roger Cramton, Monroe Freedman, Bruce Green, Steven Lubet, Carrie Menkel-Meadow, Nancy Moore, Thomas Morgan, Deborah Rhode, Ronald Rotunda, Ted Schneyer, and Thomas Shaffer. This is a rare unanimity of people among whom there are frequent disagreements on important issues of lawyers' ethics.

that bind the organization, not statements admissible against it that it remains free to rebut." Under this reading, the party conducting the informal interview is free to conduct important fact investigation of most employees, but may not interview anyone whose statement "would have the effect of binding the organization with respect to proof of the matter."[287]

The amicus brief in effect adopted the dominant interpretation of DR 7-104(A)(1) and MR 4.2, which comes from the New York Court of Appeals decision in *Niesig v. Team I*[288] and is referred to as the "alter-ego/speaking authority" test.[289] This test is best summarized in Restatement § 100(2) as including an employee or agent (a) who supervises, directs, or regularly consults with the lawyer concerning the matter, or who has power to compromise or settle the matter; (b) whose acts or admissions may be imputed to the organization for purposes of civil or criminal liability in the matter; and (c) whose statement, under applicable rules of evidence, would have the effect of binding the organization with respect to proof of the matter.

[3] Communicating with Represented Persons (Criminal)

As noted above, MR 4.2 and DR 7-104(A)(1) both forbid a lawyer to communicate about the representation with a person the lawyer knows to be represented by an attorney in the matter. The two exceptions are when the lawyer has been authorized by the person's attorney to make the contact, or when the lawyer is authorized to do so by law.

For several years there has been a heated controversy over whether prosecutors are bound by the no-contact rule of MR 4.2.[290] For example, prior

---

287 The quoted phrase is from Restatement § 100(2)(c).

A major part of the problem with Comment [4] to MR 4.2 is that it confuses an ethical rule with an evidentiary rule. A wiser course would be to allow informal interviewing regardless of whether a statement might otherwise constitute a binding admission (thereby maximizing truth-seeking and avoiding uncertainty about who can properly be interviewed), but to deny binding effect to any statement made by any corporate officer in informal interviewing (thereby eliminating the unfair advantage from the informal interview).

288 559 N.Y.S.2d 493 (1990). The court was interpreting DR 7-104(A)(1) of the New York Code of Professional Responsibility.

289 The court explained that those employees who are insulated by the rule are those "whose acts or omissions in the matter . . . are binding on the corporation (in effect, the corporation's 'alter egos') or imputed to the corporation for purposes of its liability, or employees implementing the advice of counsel." Those who will "bind" the corporation are those with "speaking authority" for the corporation and those "who are so closely identified with the interests of the corporate party as to be indistinguishable from it." "In practical application," the court explained further, the prohibited group includes only "those officials . . . who have the legal power to bind the corporation in the matter or who are responsible for implementing the advice of the corporation's lawyer, or any member of the organization whose own interests are directly at stake in the a representation." *Id.* at 498; the last quote is taken by the court from CHARLES W. WOLFRAM, MODERN LEGAL ETHICS § 11.6 (Practitioner's Ed., 1886).

290 *See, e.g.,* Alafair S.R. Burke, *Reconciling Professional Ethics and Prosecutorial Power: The Non-Contact Rule Debate,* 46 STAN. L. REV. 1635 (1994); Roger C. Cramton & Lisa K. Udell, *State Ethics Rules and Federal Prosecutors: The Controversies Over the Anti-Contact and Subpoena Rules,* 53 U. PITT. L. REV. 291 (1992); ABA Opin. 95-396; Monroe H. Freedman, *End Run at the Justice Department,* LEGAL TIMES, June 3, 1991.

to 1995 MR 4.3 forbad contact only with a represented "party." The argument was made, therefore, that prosecutors could freely contact a criminal suspect through an undercover agent — even if the suspect had a lawyer with regard to that matter — because until there was an indictment, there was no case, and the suspect was therefore not a "party" within the rule.[291] Only by amending the rule to change "party" to "person," it was argued, could pre-indictment contacts be included in the rule.[292] In 1995 that argument was eliminated by amendment of MR 4.2, which changed "party" to "person." That, however, did not end the debate.

There has always been general agreement that prosecutors are governed by ethical codes applicable to other lawyers. Any doubt about whether that includes federal prosecutors acting within particular states was answered by Congress in 1998 by the Ethical Standards for Attorneys for the Government Act (The McDade Amendment).[293] The Act provides that government attorneys are subject to the ethics rules of "each state where such attorneys engage in their duties, to the same extent and in the same manner as other attorneys in that State."

That does not end the debate over the applicability of MR 4.2 to federal prosecutors, because of the exception for contacts with represented parties that are "authorized by law." Unfortunately, that phrase is ambiguous (perhaps intentionally so), and commentators tend to find whatever meaning they look for.

One argument in support of prosecutors' contacts with represented persons is that courts have held that a wide range of such contacts do not violate constitutional protections relating to the right to counsel, self-incrimination, and due process. The contention is that those holdings mean that the courts have given "authorization by law" to prosecutors to engage in such contacts. However, holding that particular prosecutorial conduct does not violate the Constitution is not the same as holding that it is "authorized by law" for purposes of state ethical requirements.

The Supreme Court has emphasized this point. In *Mabry v. Johnson*, for example, a unanimous court noted that the concern of the Due Process clause is with "the manner in which persons are deprived of their liberty," and is not "a code of ethics for prosecutors."[294] Also, in *Nix v. Whiteside*, Chief Justice Warren Burger cautioned that courts must be careful not to "constitutionalize particular standards of professional conduct and thereby intrude into the State's proper authority."[295] Burger thereafter emphasized and elaborated on that point, saying, "[t]he fact that the Constitution permits particular conduct does not mean that it's professionally appropriate to engage in that conduct."[296]

---

[291] *See, e.g.*, ABA Opin. 95-396 (dissent by Ralph B. Elliot).

[292] *Id.*

[293] 28 U.S.C. § 530B(a) (Supp. IV 1998).

[294] 467 U.S. 504, 511, 104 S.Ct. 2543, 2547 (1984). *See also United States v. Agurs*, 427 U.S. 97, 110 (1986) ("Nor do we believe the constitutional obligation [of a prosecutor] is measured by the moral culpability . . . of the prosecutor.")

[295] 475 U.S. 157, 165, 106 S.Ct. at 994 (1986).

[296] ABA JOUR., Aug., 1990.

That is, when a court says, "[i]t's not unconstitutional," the court does not mean, "[i]t's ethical," or "[w]e think you ought to do it."[297]

Those Supreme Court authorities are consistent with the explanation of MR 4.2 in its Comment [2]. Defining the "authorized by law" exception, the comment says that it includes: (1) investigative activities by government lawyer themselves "or through investigative agents;" (2) "prior to the commencement of criminal or civil enforcement proceedings;" and (3) when there is judicial precedent that either (a) has "found the activity *permissible under this Rule*," or (b) has "found *this Rule inapplicable*."[298] Unless all three of those conditions are met, the prosecutor is forbidden to contact the represented person directly or through investigative agents. Moreover, echoing the holdings of the Supreme Court quoted above, the comment expressly concludes that MR 4.2 "imposes ethical restraints that go beyond those imposed by constitutional provisions."

One final point addressed by ABA Opinion 95-396 deserves mention here. There are situations in which a criminal defendant's lawyer is selected and paid by the defendant's employer. When that happens, there is a significant and plausible risk that the lawyer's loyalty is more to the employer than to the defendant. In short, there is a conflict of interest.[299] In such cases, the defendant is "represented," but not necessarily as he wants to be. Nevertheless, the defendant may be reluctant to discharge the lawyer and obtain independent representation. It would be improper, even in such a case, for a prosecutor to bypass the lawyer and communicate directly with the defendant.[300] On occasion, though, a defendant will initiate contact with the prosecutor. What then?

Because of our emphasis on client autonomy,[301] we are concerned that no criminal defendant have a lawyer imposed on him by others. We agree with Opinion 95-396, therefore, that an appropriate course of action would be for the prosecutor to request a court (if there is one with jurisdiction) to speak with the defendant on the record, but without either defense counsel or a prosecutor present. The purpose of this hearing would be to determine whether the defendant is satisfied with his lawyer or wants independent counsel and, if he does want independent counsel, to appoint a lawyer for him. As also noted in Opinion 95-396, the prosecutor, even though she has been approached by the defendant, should refrain from offering any advice or engaging in any substantive discussions with him.[302]

---

[297] *Id. See also* ABA Opin. 95-396 at notes 33 and 34. (Constitutional protections establish only "minimal historic standards" that defendants must receive, while ethics rules "seek to regulate the conduct of lawyers according to the standards of professionalism.")

[298] Emphasis added.

[299] *See* Ch. Ten, *infra*, on Conflicts of Interest, esp. the section headed "The Preventive Rationale" and note 18.

[300] However, it would be appropriate for a judge, *sua sponte*, to assure herself that the defendant has voluntarily waived the conflict of interest.

[301] *See* Ch. Three, *supra*.

[302] *See* Opin. 95-396 at notes 51 and 52. We have modified the language in the opinion to make it clear that neither a prosecutor nor the defense lawyer should be present at the hearing. Also, we disagree with the suggestion in the opinion that the court might authorize the prosecutor to communicate directly with the defendant rather than appoint new defense counsel. In order to assure an informed waiver, a defendant should have the advice of counsel before waiving counsel and dealing directly with the prosecutor.

§ 4.11   DOES ZEAL EVER JUSTIFY BREAKING OTHER ETHICAL RULES?

The outer limit of zealous representation is clear. Zealous representation must be carried out only "within the bounds of the law, which includes Disciplinary Rules."[303] We would not advise a lawyer-client, much less a law student, therefore, to risk professional discipline by violating a disciplinary rule, even if our personal view was that particular circumstances warranted doing so. The fiduciary obligations of a lawyer to a client, and of a professor to a student, would trump any personal views we might have about the undesirability of following a particular rule.

Nevertheless, some of the preceding discussions in this chapter, and specifically the discussion relating to undercover operations,[304] raise a question that is seldom if ever addressed in discussions of lawyers' ethics. Does zealous representation ever justify breaking the ethical rules?

[1]   Breaking Rules in Civil Cases

We have mentioned that Professor Freedman, in preparing litigation in housing discrimination cases, sent out investigators/testers, who were told to misrepresent their identities and their desire to buy a house. This would violate ethical rules forbidding a lawyer to make a false statement of material fact to another person, and forbidding conduct involving dishonesty, fraud, deceit, or misrepresentation.[305] In similar circumstances, we would do so again.

Would this be unethical? On a plain-meaning reading of the rules, clearly yes.[306] As recognized by Second Circuit Judge James L. Oakes, in an opinion cited with apparent approval by the ABA Center for Professional Responsibility, "the private lawyer who participates in a sting operation almost necessarily runs afoul of the canons of legal ethics."[307] Oakes went on to explain that a lawyer is forbidden to "[e]ngage in conduct involving dishonesty, fraud, deceit, or misrepresentation,"[308] and that lawyers are subject to this duty even when they are not acting in their capacity as lawyers.[309]

Despite the plain meaning of the ethical rules, however, courts regularly accept evidence that is produced by undercover or sting operations. For

---

[303] Model Code EC 7-1, DR 7-101.

[304] *See* § 4.10[1], *supra*.

[305] MR 4.1(a), 4.3, 8.4(a) and (c), 5.3; DR 7-102(a)(4)-(6).

[306] We are using the word "unethical" here to refer to a violation of one or more disciplinary rules, and not to refer more generally to conduct that we would consider to be wrongful in a moral sense.

[307] *United States ex rel. Vuitton et Fils S.A. v. Klayminc*, 780 F.2d 179, 186, 187–188 (2d Cir., 1985) (Oakes, J. dissenting), *rev'd sub nom. Young v. United States ex rel. Vuitton et Fils S.A.*, 481 U.S. 787 (1987). Judge Oakes objected to privately run sting operations that do not have prior judicial approval from a court; this issue was not reached by the Supreme Court, which reversed the majority decision on broader grounds.

[308] *Id., citing* DR 1-102(A)(4) (1980); MR 8.4(c) (1983).

[309] *Id., citing* ABA Formal Op. 336 (1974).

example, two years before Judge Oakes' observations, the Seventh Circuit was able to say:[310]

> This court and others have repeatedly approved and sanctioned the role of "testers" in racial discrimination cases . . . . It is frequently difficult to develop proof in discrimination cases and the evidence provided by testers is frequently valuable, if not indispensable . . . . [W]e have long ago recognized that this requirement of deception was a relatively small price to pay to defeat racial discrimination.

This judicial disposition to admit the fruits of sting operations is not restricted to cases of racial discrimination, but extends to commercial cases as well. For example, in a case involving testers who misrepresented themselves in order to expose trademark violations by a client's competitor, the court held that excluding the evidence that had been obtained by the testers "would not serve the public interest or promote the goals of the disciplinary rules."[311] Also, in another unfair trade case, the court relied on an affidavit of Professor Bruce Green, who stated that "[t]he prevailing understanding in the legal profession is that a public or private lawyer's use of an undercover investigator to detect ongoing violations of the law is not ethically proscribed, especially where it would be difficult to discover the violations by other means."[312] Again, the court admitted the evidence developed through a sting operation involving misrepresentations.

What, then, is a conscientious lawyer to do?[313] Can she, consistent with zealous (or even diligent) representation, fail to develop essential evidence that is only available through a sting operation? Indeed, if "the prevailing view in the legal profession" is that such conduct is not ethically proscribed, can a lawyer *competently* fail to conduct the sting?[314]

A similar issue has arisen regarding a lawyer's tape recording of a conversation without disclosing to the other person that the taping is going on (a practice that frequently accompanies sting operations). In 1974, the ABA Ethics Committee held that such taping was a violation of DR 1-102(A)(4), as conduct involving dishonesty, fraud, deceit, or misrepresentation.[315]

There are good reasons for such a restriction: (1) people tend to choose their words with greater care when a recording is being made; (2) the person who knows a recording is being made has an unfair advantage in choosing how to control the conversation and even in creating misleading impressions;[316] (3) the person who knows a recording is being made has an unfair advantage in being able to decide, unilaterally, not to use the recording at all; and (4)

---

[310] *Richardson v. Howard*, 712 F.2d 319, 321 (7th Cir., 1983).

[311] *Gidatex v. Campaniello*, 82 F.Supp.2d 119 (1999). The court relied in part on the article by Isbell and Salvi, which is criticized in § 4.10, *supra*.

[312] *Apple Corps Limited v. Lennon*, 15 F.Supp.2d 456, 475 (1998).

[313] *See* § 1.07, *supra*.

[314] Competence requires "the legal . . . preparation reasonably necessary for the representation." MR 1.1. A lawyer "shall not . . . [h]andle a legal matter without preparation adequate in the circumstances." DR 6-101(A)(2).

[315] ABA Formal Opin. 337. The committee also cited other ethical rules.

[316] *See, e.g.*, Monroe Freedman, *Keystone Kops in Jackboots*, LEGAL TIMES, June 12, 1995 (illustrating undercover operative's success in creating misleading impressions of taped conversations).

some people would prefer not to speak under such circumstances, but are denied the choice.[317] Nevertheless, twenty-five years later the ABA committee overruled itself, holding that surreptitious taping does not violate ethical rules, as long as doing so is not illegal in the jurisdiction.[318]

This raises the question of whether lawyers who conducted surreptitious taping before the ABA committee changed its opinion about the meaning of the ethical rules were acting unethically. It would appear, on the contrary, that those lawyers were properly engaged in zealous and competent representation, since courts were regularly admitting evidence obtained in violation of ethical rules.[319]

[2] Breaking Rules in Criminal Cases

The Supreme Court has sanctioned admission of evidence obtained by prosecution conduct that was admittedly "objectionable as a matter of ethics."[320] In *Moran v. Burbine*, the police lied to the defendant's lawyer, assuring her that she need not come to the police station that night because her client would not be interrogated. Less than an hour later, however, the police began a series of interrogations that resulted in a confession. Writing for the Court, Justice O'Connor expressed distaste for the "deliberate deception" of "an officer of the court."[321] Nevertheless, the Court rejected claims under the *Miranda* rule, the privilege against self-incrimination, the right to counsel, and due process, and admitted the evidence that the prosecution had wrongfully obtained. Thus, the Supreme Court has condoned what it has explicitly recognized to be unethical prosecutorial conduct.

Further, the Supreme Court has held that prosecutors are forbidden to use peremptory challenges to exclude jurors on grounds of race or gender.[322] But if a prosecutor is challenged for doing so, his justification on race-neutral grounds can suffice regardless of whether it is "persuasive, or even plausible."[323] Indeed, a judge is permitted to accept a prosecutor's justification even if it is "fantastic . . . , silly, or superstitious."[324] Moreover, the prosecutor is

---

[317] *See* Ass'n of the Bar of the City of N.Y., Formal Opin. 2003–02. Also, although taping of conversations has become common in many business contexts, we are accustomed to being given an automatic announcement when it is being done.

[318] Formal Opin. 01-422. *See also* Ass'n of the Bar of the City of N.Y., Formal Opin. 2003-02, modifying Opins. 1980-95 and 1995-10.

[319] *See, e.g., Stagg v. N.Y.C. Health and Hospitals Corporation*, 162 A.S.2d 595, 556 N.Y.S.2d 779 (2d Dept., 1990) ("New York follows the common-law rule that the admissibility of evidence is not affected by the means through which it is obtained. Hence, absent some constitutional, statutory, or overriding policy basis requiring a departure from the common-law rule in this case, we would discern no error in the admission of the challenged testimony even if an ethical violation were established."); *Tabbi v. Town of Tonawanda*, 111 Misc.2d 641, 444 N.Y.S.2d 560 (1981) (same).

[320] 475 U.S. 412, 423–424 (1986).

[321] *Id.* at 423, 424.

[322] *Batson v. Kentucky*, 476 U.S. 79 (1986) (race); *J.E.B. v. Alabama ex rel. T.B.*, 511 U.S. 127 (1994) (gender).

[323] *Purkett v. Elem*, 514 U.S. 765, 768, 115 S.Ct. 1769, 1771 (1995).

[324] *Id.*

permitted to use both race and gender as grounds for disqualifying jurors, as long as he can assert "legitimate reasons tangentially connected with their race."[325] In *Galbert v. Merkle*,[326] for example, the prosecutor asserted that he had excluded black women who were young and obese (the only African-Americans on the jury panel), because they are "really dangerous to me."[327] Because the prosecutor claimed to have used youth and obesity along with race and gender, his peremptory challenges were upheld.

The same prohibition against using race or gender as a basis for peremptory challenges applies to defense counsel.[328] Professor Smith has maintained, however, that the obligation of zealous advocacy ought to trump the prohibition against race-based jury selection by criminal defendants.[329] She takes this position notwithstanding her personal dislike of racial and gender stereotyping, and her concern that, in the name of effective advocacy, she may be teaching students to think in bigoted ways. Smith believes that her ethical obligation to defend the accused[330] means that she must make use of research regarding race and gender in jurors' decision-making, even if doing so results in excluding prospective jurors because of their race or gender. It is not that she believes that racial or demographic stereotypes are an accurate proxy for the attitudes and life experience of prospective jurors.[331] Rather, in view of limited voir dire in most criminal trials,[332] it would be less than diligent lawyering to disregard what is known about the influence of race and gender on jurors' attitudes.

At the beginning of this section, we raised the question of whether zealous representation ever justifies breaking other ethical rules. We do not advise others to do so. For ourselves, however, we accept the conclusion of the Supreme Court and numerous other courts that the answer is yes.

---

[325] *U.S. v. Brown*, 817 F.2d 674, 676 (10th Cir., 1987).

[326] 1997 WL 85012 (N.D. Cal., 1997).

[327] *Id.* at *3.

[328] *Georgia v. McCollum*, 505 U.S. 42 (1992).

[329] *See generally* Abbe Smith, *"Nice Work If You Can Get It": "Ethical" Jury Selection in Criminal Defense*, 67 FORDHAM L. REV. 523 (1998).

[330] *See* Deborah L. Rhode, *Ethical Perspectives on Legal Practice*, 37 STAN. L. REV. 589, 605 (1985) (acknowledging that "the case for undiluted partisanship is most compelling" in criminal defense).

[331] *See* JEFFREY ABRAMSON, WE THE JURY 171 (1994) ("[Social science data] generates probabilistic statements about the attitudes or biases of a specific group. Within limits, probabilistic theorems may be of use to lawyers, enabling them to play the odds or make educated bets.").

[332] *See* RANDALL KENNEDY, RACE, CRIME, AND THE LAW 220–27 (1997) (discussing the deficiencies of voir dire as it is typically conducted); *see also* Nancy Gertner, *Is the Jury Worth Saving?* 75 B.U. L. REV. 923, 930 (1995) (reviewing STEPHEN J. ADLER, THE JURY: TRIAL AND ERROR IN THE AMERICAN COURTROOM (1994)) ("As long as voir dire is limited and counsel is prevented from exploring juror predispositions in a meaningful way, peremptory challenges are an important safety valve.").

§ 4.12 THE CIVILITY/COURTESY/PROFESSIONALISM MOVEMENT

One of the most serious attacks on the traditional ethic of zeal goes under the deceptively benign banner of increasing civility, courtesy, and professionalism among lawyers.[333] The proponents of these notions mean a variety of very different things, but the end result is the subordination of zealous representation to vague and sometimes unethical notions of civility.[334] In addition, the enormous amounts of time and resources that have gone into the civility movement have distracted the profession from dealing with the severe ethical and constitutional problems resulting from the underfunding and overloading of public defenders' and prosecutors' offices and of the administration of justice in general.[335]

The civility movement began in hysteria in the early 1970s in a series of speeches by then Chief Justice Warren Burger. His immediate targets were lawyers representing unpopular clients in civil rights, civil liberties, and criminal cases. Chief Justice Burger charged that "adrenalin-fueled lawyers" were engaged in wide-ranging improprieties, from disruption of court proceedings to seeing how loud they could shout or how many people, including judges, they could insult. As a result, Burger claimed, "rules of evidence, canons of ethics and codes of professional conduct — the necessity for civility — all become irrelevant."[336]

The facts were otherwise. In 1971, the *New York Times* conducted a survey and interviews with legal authorities around the country. It found that courtroom disorder was "not a serious or growing problem."[337] Similarly, an extensive study sponsored by the Association of the Bar of the City of New York concluded that "there is no serious quantitative problem of disruption in American Courts."[338] But the facts did not matter. Chief Justice Burger continued his crusade and by 1984 was successful in promoting an ABA Commission on Professionalism. As a result, we now have an ABA Creed of Professionalism and about 100 similar courtesy codes and civility guidelines throughout the country.

---

[333] Typically, proponents hark back nostalgically to a golden age when, they say, lawyers were universally respected and law was an honored profession. The golden age, however, is a myth. *See* Marc Galanter, *Lawyers in the Mist: The Golden Age of Legal Nostalgia*, 100 DICK. L. REV. 549 (1996); Monroe Freedman, *A Brief "Professional" History*, LEGAL TIMES, Dec. 17, 1990, at 22; Monroe Freedman, *The Good Old Days, for Good Old Boys*, LEGAL TIMES, Feb. 28, 1994, at 31; Monroe Freedman, *Abraham Lincoln: Lawyer for the Twenty-First Century?* LEGAL TIMES, Feb. 12, 1996, at 26.

[334] For example, in a panel discussion among four lawyers, two law professors, and a judge, Professor Freedman was "the only one who believed that zealous client advocacy is more important than being civil." Amy Travison, *Zealousness May Be Too Rampant in the Legal Profession*, N.Y. STATE BAR NEWS, March/April 1996, at 22, *See also* Abbe Smith, *Burdening the Least of Us: "Race-Conscious" Ethics in Criminal Defense*, 77 TEX. L. REV. 1599-1601 (1999) (lamenting the call for restraint over passion in criminal defense advocacy).

[335] *See, e.g.*, MICHAEL MCCONVILLE & CHESTER L. MIRSKY, CRIMINAL DEFENSE OF THE POOR IN NEW YORK CITY (Center for Research in Crime and Justice at N.Y.U. Law School, 1989); Monroe Freedman, *Third World Justice*, LEGAL TIMES, Feb. 11, 1991, at 34.

[336] *See, e.g.*, Warren E. Burger, *The Necessity for Civility*, 52 F.R.D. 211, 212–14 (1971).

[337] N.Y. TIMES, Aug. 9, 1971, at p. 1.

[338] NORMAN DORSEN & LEON FRIEDMAN, DISORDER IN THE COURT 6 (1974).

The supporters of these creeds, codes, and guidelines insist that they simply exhort lawyers to behave with civility and that they are not intended to be enforced. Increasingly, however, judges are enforcing civility with a variety of sanctions against both lawyers and clients. [339] For example, judges have explicitly threatened sanctions against lawyers who violate civility codes. [340] Judges have also censured lawyers, by name, for conduct that is required by ethical rules but that the judges nevertheless consider to be "unprofessional." [341]

The most pernicious sanction, and the one calculated most effectively to chill zealous advocacy, was described by Chief Judge Marvin Aspen of the United States District Court for the Northern District of Illinois. [342] If a lawyer does something "unseemly" in court, the judge will gossip about it over lunch with other judges, identifying the lawyer by name. As a result, Aspen has said, the lawyer's reputation will be "tremendously" and "irreparably" damaged — and thereafter all the judges will take the opportunity to decide against the lawyer's clients any time a "close question" arises. [343] There is, of course, no due process for either the lawyer or her clients when judges engage in this kind of lunchroom Star Chamber.

Nor are the standards clear for what Judge Aspen calls "unseemly" conduct. In a survey on civility conducted by a Seventh Circuit committee chaired by Judge Aspen, civility was defined expansively as "professional conduct in litigating proceedings," and expressly included "good manners or social grace." [344] Thus, a lawyer responding that she had seen incivility in litigation could be referring to anything from incompetence to loud ties or garish lipstick. [345]

Just how misguided and misleading the rules of civility can be is illustrated by a panel discussion before the Chicago Bar Association. [346] The moderator, Robert Cummins, posed the following hypothetical: Opposing counsel calls you to request a short extension of time to file a pleading so that he can attend his son's graduation. It would not prejudice your client in any material way to grant the extension. Would you grant it to him?

Five members of the panel agreed that they would refuse to grant the extension. The five included not only the then current and past presidents of the Bar, but also Judge Aspen — the leading proponent of civility. Professor Freedman was the only dissenter, explaining that because the extension

---

[339] Federal District Court Chief Judge Marvin Aspen, a leader in the civility movement, has acknowledged that "moral exhortations are not going to be enough" to ensure civility. Jeffrey Cole, *Searching for Collegiality: An Interview with Judge Aspen*, 22 ABA LITIGATION 34, 37 (1996).

[340] *See Dondi Properties v. Commerce Savings & Loan Ass'n*, 121 F.R.D. 284 (1988).

[341] *See Sprung v. Negwer Materials*, Inc., 727 S.W.2d 883 (1987), *aff'd by* 775 S.W.2d 97 (1989).

[342] Jeffrey Cole, *Searching for Collegiality: An Interview with Judge Aspen*, 22 LITIGATION 34, 36 (1996).

[343] *Id.* at 36. Aspen repeated these threats at an ABA conference in Chicago on May 31, 1996.

[344] 143 F.R.D. 441, n.1 (1992).

[345] In a series of exchanges on Lexis/Counsel Connect, for example, definitions of civility ranged widely, from fraud and deceit to not returning telephone calls. In between were: being a junk-yard dog; being sneaky, mean or misleading; not being ethical; failing to provide discovery; obstructing discovery; badgering witnesses; ignoring deadlines; being rude; and being a jerk.

[346] Feb. 2, 2000.

would not prejudice the client, there was no reason to deprive opposing counsel and his son of sharing an important event in their lives. Judge Aspen and the other panelists offered no cogent reason for saying that they would refuse the extension.

Unfortunately, however, incivility can also mean representing one's client competently and zealously. Consider, for example, the remarks of Federal District Judge William Schwartzer, then Director of the Federal Judicial center. At an ABA conference,[347] Judge Schwartzer illustrated professionalism by recalling that, when he was a young lawyer, his research revealed that his client could win a case because the lawyer on the other side had missed a statute of limitations. When he reported the good news to the partner in charge of the case, however, the older lawyer sternly admonished the neophyte that "we don't practice law like that in this office." That is, the firm would not rely on the statute on its client's behalf because it would embarrass the lawyers on the other side to do so. The judge concluded the anecdote with the approving comment: "That made a great impression on me."[348]

The leading case on enforcing courtesy codes is *Dondi Properties v. Commerce Savings & Loan Assn.*[349] There, the U.S. District Court for the Northern District of Texas, sitting *en banc*, announced its intention to impose sanctions against lawyers who failed to abide by an aspirational courtesy code adopted by the bar. In one of the cases under *Dondi*, the plaintiff was suing for the defendant's alleged bad faith refusal to pay off an insurance claim. The defense lawyers were apparently emulating their client in using delay to avoid their client's legal obligation. They not only filed an untimely reply brief, but they failed to get consent of the plaintiff and failed to get leave of the court — both required by court rules. In responding to a motion to dismiss the improper reply brief, therefore, the court expressed its concern that justice delayed is justice denied, and it criticized the "sharp practices" of counsel.[350]

Who could disagree with that understandable judicial response? The court went on, however, to express its intention to impose sanctions against lawyers, like the *plaintiff's* lawyer, who had "failed to cooperate [with defendant's lawyers] when he filed the motion to strike the reply."[351] That is, by asserting his client's right under the rules of the court to move to strike the untimely brief, the plaintiff's lawyer had invited sanctions against himself under the courtesy code. A particular irony is that a principal target of courtesy codes are lawyers who ignore deadlines and delay cases.

A Missouri case echoes Judge Schwartzer's understanding of professionalism. In *Sprung v. Negwer Materials, Inc.*,[352] the plaintiff had suffered severe back and leg injuries when a cart supplied by the defendant tipped over, throwing a load of dry wall on him. After receiving service of a complaint, the defendant's lawyer negligently failed to serve or file an answer. At the

---

[347] ABA conference in Tucson, Arizona, February 24, 1995.

[348] For a pro-and-con discussion of taking advantage of an adversary's mistake, *see* App. C, *infra*.

[349] 121 F.R.D. 284 (1988).

[350] *Id.* at 286.

[351] *Id.* at 291.

[352] 727 S.W.2d 883 (1987), *aff'd by* 775 S.W.2d 97 (1989).

appropriate time, the plaintiff's lawyer moved for a default judgment, which was granted.

Fourteen days after the default, the defendant's lawyer filed an untimely answer to the complaint. The plaintiff asked his lawyer what that meant. The lawyer explained that the answer was too late to affect the default, that the default would become final within thirty days after its entry, and that there was no legal obligation to inform the defense about the default. The plaintiff then instructed his lawyer not to tell the defendant's lawyer about the default until after the thirty days had run, and the lawyer obeyed his client's instructions, as he was ethically required to do.[353]

The court could have vacated the judgment, of course, but declined to do so, on the ground that the defendant's lawyer had been negligent. Nevertheless, the Chief Judge and three other judges on the Missouri Supreme Court castigated the plaintiff's lawyer (who was identified by name[354]) for his lack of professionalism in giving his client the lawful benefit of the default. These opinions make it clear that the judges expected the lawyer to place courtesy to his "brother lawyer"[355] over the rights of his client. One opinion refers to ethical rules, like zealous representation, as "jargon"[356] that should not supersede "courtesy and consideration" to opposing counsel.[357] Another opinion refers to the plaintiff's lawyer as a "sharp practitioner"[358] whose conduct "should shock all right-thinking lawyers."[359] The judges conclude: "There are members of the bench and bar who can remember when [professional courtesy] would have included advance warning to a dilatory attorney adversary of intent to seek a default and immediate notice that one had been obtained."[360]

There are two ironies in these opinions. One is that the judges expected the plaintiff's lawyer to give the defendant greater rights than the court itself was willing to give.[361] The second is that the judges had no problem with a lawyer's enforcing the default against an unrepresented defendant; it was only when a "brother lawyer" entered the picture that counsel's conduct became shocking, dishonorable, and unprofessional.[362]

---

[353] MR 1.6; DR 4-101.

[354] *Sprung*, 727 S.W.2d at 895.

[355] *Id.* at 894.

[356] *Id.*

[357] *Id.* at 893.

[358] *Sprung*, 775 S.W.2d at 110.

[359] *Id.* at 109.

[360] *Id.* at 111.

[361] The opposite result was reached in *Kleinecke v. Montecito Water Dist.*, 147 Cal. App.3d 240 (1983)(Arthur Gilbert, J.)(The court tolled a statute of limitations to correct an error by plaintiff's lawyer, but said: "Our holding is not an indictment of defense counsel who by fortuitous circumstances had the opportunity to represent his client in a manner sanctioned by [prior case law].")

[362] *Accord*, Final Report of the Committee on Civility of the Seventh Federal Judicial Circuit, Proposed Standards, ¶ 18, 143 F.R.D. 441 (1992): "We will not cause any default or dismissal to be entered without first notifying *opposing counsel, when we know his or her identity*." (emphasis added).

Other jurisdictions where judges are attempting to subordinate zealous representation to notions of professionalism and courtesy include Georgia.[363] As one Georgia judge has acknowledged, enforcement of ethical rules requiring zealous advocacy could leave the professionalism movement "dead in the water."[364] And it follows, of course, that the success of the professionalism movement would leave zealous advocacy no less dead.

There are lawyers we respect who are promoting creeds of professionalism and civility. They assume that these creeds are harmless. Perhaps they are relying on the clause in the ABA model that says, "nothing in such a creed shall be deemed to supersede or in any way amend the Model Rules of Professional conduct or other disciplinary codes." But "aspirational" creeds are increasingly being given the force of law by judges who value courtesy to "brother lawyers" above "entire devotion to the interests of the client [and] warm zeal in the maintenance and defense of his rights."[365]

---

[363] *See Allen v. Lefkoff, Duncan, Grimes & Dermer*, 453 S.E.2d 719 (1995); *Green v. Green*, 437 S.E.2d 457 (1993); *Evanoff v. Evanoff*, 418 S.E.2d 62 (1992).

[364] *Allen v. Lefkoff, Duncan, Grimes & Dermer*, 453 S.E.2d 719, 725 (1995).

[365] For an interesting and important critique of civility codes, *see* Amy R. Mashburn, *Professionalism as Class Ideology: Civility Codes and Bar Hierarchy*, 28 VALPARAISO L. REV. 657 (1994).

Chapter 5

LAWYER-CLIENT TRUST AND CONFIDENCE

§ 5.01 INTRODUCTION

Competent representation requires that a lawyer be "fully informed of all the facts of the matter he is handling."[1] A client is not likely to give her lawyer facts that could be incriminating or embarrassing, however, unless she is assured that the lawyer will keep the information confidential.[2] Trust between lawyer and client is, therefore, the "cornerstone of the adversary system and effective assistance of counsel,"[3] and fidelity to that trust is "the glory of our profession."[4]

§ 5.02 THE BENEFITS OF LAWYER-CLIENT TRUST

The ethic of lawyer-client trust and confidence emphasizes the need of the individual client for effective representation. Thus, like other essential aspects of the adversary system such as client autonomy and zealous representation, the ethic of trust and confidence is client-centered. As we have seen, however, in a free society the public interest is served when individual dignity is

---

[1] *Upjohn v. United States*, 449 U.S. 383, 391, 101 S.Ct. 677, 683 (1981), *quoting* Model Code EC 4-1.

The renowned trial lawyer, Edward Bennett Williams said: "Any lawyer surprised by facts at trial has failed in the preparation. It's that simple." Accordingly, "I demand complete candor and honesty from the client — no holding back." Schwab, *Interview with Edward Bennett Williams*, in ABA, THE LITIGATION MANUAL: A PRIMER FOR TRIAL LAWYERS 1178, 1180, 1182 (J.G. Koeltl, ed., 1989). In the same primer, Irving Younger wrote: "Nothing [should] come as a surprise . . . . Everything must be anticipated . . . . If a lawyer doesn't . . . know what the case is all about, he shouldn't be trying it." Irving Younger, *Cicero on Cross-Examination*, ABA, THE LITIGATION MANUAL: A PRIMER FOR TRIAL LAWYERS 532, 533, 535 (J.E. Koelh. ed. 19

See also Model Code of Professional Responsibility EC 4-1 (1969); ABA STANDARDS FOR CRIMINAL JUSTICE, Commentary to § 4-4.1 (2d ed. 1980); RESTATEMENT, Introductory Note to Chapter 5.

[2] *Upjohn Co. v. United States*, 449 U.S. 383, 389, 391, 101 S.Ct. 677, 682, 683 (1981); *Hunt v. Blackburn*, 128 U.S. 464, 470, 9 S.Ct. 125, 127 (1888). *See also*, GEOFFREY C. HAZARD, JR. & W. WM. HODES, THE LAW AND ETHICS OF LAWYERING 268–69 (3d ed. 1999).

[3] *Linton v. Perrini*, 656 F.2d 207, 212 (6th Cir. 1981), quoted with approval, *Morris v. Slappy*, 461 U.S. 1, 21, 103 S.Ct. 1610, 1621 n.4 (1983)(Brennan, J., concurring). The ethical imperative to the lawyer is clear although, of course, "[n]o court could possibly guarantee . . . a 'meaningful relationship' between an accused and his counsel." 103 S.Ct. at 1617.

[4] *United States v. Costen*, 38 Fed. 24 (1889) (upholding the disbarment of a lawyer for violating his client's confidences). The author of the opinion, Justice David J. Brewer, was appointed to the Supreme Court shortly thereafter, and later served as a member of the committee that drafted the ABA's Canons of Professional Ethics (1908).

Justice Brewer went on to say that the profession and the community can tolerate overzealousness by a lawyer on behalf of a client but "cannot tolerate for a moment . . . disloyalty on the part of a lawyer to his client." *Id.*

respected, when autonomy is fostered, and when equal protection before the law is enhanced through professional assistance.

Also, when a lawyer succeeds in establishing a relationship of trust and confidence with a client, she is in a position to give advice that is not only important to the client but that is socially desirable. In the aphorism attributed to Elihu Root, "About half the practice of a decent lawyer consists in telling would-be clients that they are damned fools and should stop."[5] The lawyer is in a position to offer that good counsel, however, only if the client is willing to entrust the lawyer with information that might be embarrassing or incriminating. Moreover, the client who views the lawyer as deserving of trust will be more inclined to accept the lawyer's advice to do the right thing.

That important aspect of the lawyer's function is, of course, virtually invisible. Having persuaded the client not to commit a crime, a fraud, or some other wrongful act, the lawyer is not in a position to publicize her achievement, nor is the client likely to do so. Nevertheless, there is significant evidence of the success of lawyers in inducing their clients to act legally and morally. In the Model Rules, for example, the American Bar Association has recently affirmed that "[b]ased upon experience, lawyers know that almost all clients follow the advice given, and the law is upheld."[6] Similarly, with reference to perjury in criminal cases, "experienced defense lawyers have pointed out time and again that, permitted to continue to counsel with their criminal clients up to the very hour of the client's proposed testimony, they almost always were successful in persuading the client not to take the stand to testify falsely."[7]

§ 5.03 THE TRADITION OF CLIENT CONFIDENTIALITY

No rule of law, no matter how fundamental and explicit, has ever been unwavering or free of ambiguities, and the protection of lawyer-client confidentiality is no exception. Nevertheless, the professional ideal of confidentiality is clear, and the ethical mandate was recognized at least by the middle of the nineteenth century.[8] Thus, well over a century ago, "the duty to the

---

[5] Warren Lehman, *The Pursuit of a Client's Interest*, 77 MICH. L. REV. 1078, 1082 (1979). Dean Lehman adds that people "widely look to lawyers as worthy advisers and take seriously what they have to say. Surely every lawyer has at some time dissuaded a client from some wasteful or destructive pursuit." *Id.*

[6] Comment to MR 1.6.

[7] James G. Exum, Jr., *The Perjurious Criminal Defendant: A Solution to His Lawyer's Dilemma*, VI SOC. RESP 16, 20 (1980). The author, James G. Exum, Jr., is a judge in the North Carolina Supreme Court.

[8] L. Ray Patterson, *Legal Ethics and the Lawyer's Duty of Loyalty*, 29 EMORY L. J. 909 (1980). Oddly, Patterson refers to the ethic throughout his article as a "new" one, despite the fact that his own research demonstrates that strict confidentiality was firmly established at least a century ago.

Patterson interprets the writings of David Hoffman (1836) and George Sharswood (1854) as subordinating confidentiality to candor to courts and the interests of third parties, but his analysis is highly questionable. He achieves that tour de force in part by inferring from their writings a novel notion of "reciprocal agency" between lawyer and client, which he concedes "they did not articulate." *Id.* at 913. Patterson concedes, too, that his theory is "completely contrary to traditional notions" of the lawyer-client relationship. *Id.* at 917.

client began to predominate over the duties to the court and to opposing counsel."[9]

Under the Field Code, adopted in New York in 1848, the lawyer was required to "maintain inviolate the confidence, and, at every peril to himself, to preserve the secrets, of his clients."[10] Other states enacted similar provisions, at about the same time, that continue to stand today.[11] The first formally adopted body of ethical rules was the Alabama Code of Ethics of 1887. The Alabama Code mandated that the lawyer had "not only a legal duty to maintain the client's confidences under the attorney-client privilege, but that he had an absolute duty to maintain the secrets and confidences of the client at all costs as a matter of professional ethics."[12]

Note the distinction that was made early on between "confidences" and "secrets." There is a "legal duty" to maintain the client's "confidences" under the "attorney-client privilege," and there is a related but broader duty to maintain the client's "secrets" as a matter of "professional ethics." The word "confidence" refers to information protected by the attorney-client testimonial privilege under the law of evidence. That is, a lawyer is forbidden to testify in court about lawyer-client communications, unless the client waives the privilege or the court finds that the information is not protected by the lawyer-client privilege.[13] However, the word "secret" embraces confidences and much more. It includes any information that relates to the representation which the client has asked the lawyer to keep confidential, or disclosure of which would be embarrassing or detrimental to the client.[14]

Even if Patterson were correct in his analysis of Hoffman and Sharswood, however, he acknowledges that under the seminal FIELD CODE OF PROCEDURE (1848) and the influential ALABAMA CODE OF ETHICS (1887) "the lawyer had not only a legal duty to maintain the client's confidences under the attorney-client privilege, but that he had an absolute duty to maintain the secrets and confidences of the client at all costs as a matter of professional ethics." *Id.* at 911, 935.

Patterson's article is an interesting illustration, therefore, of a writer's ideology at war with his scholarship.

[9] *Id.* at 938.

[10] *Id.* at 911 n. 6.

[11] *Id.*

[12] *Id.* at 935.

[13] The testimonial privilege is universally recognized in the United States, but with variations from one jurisdiction to another. Generally, to the extent that a client has sought legal assistance from an attorney, in confidence, neither of them can be compelled to testify about the communications between them unless the client waives the privilege. There are, of course, limitations and exceptions. For example, the communications are not protected when the purpose of the representation is to help the client carry out a crime or fraud. Also, the privilege does not apply if an unprivileged third party was present during the communication, and it is lost if the client authorizes the lawyer to make disclosure to an unprivileged third party.

[14] Including both confidences and secrets in its definition of "confidential client information," RESTATEMENT § 59, Cmt. b, says:

This definition covers all information relating to representation of a client, whether in oral, documentary, electronic, photographic, or sources such as third persons whose communications are not protected by the attorney-client privilege. . . . It includes work product that the lawyer develops in representing the client, such as the lawyer's notes to a personal file, whether or not the information is immune from discovery as lawyer work product. . . . It includes information acquired by a lawyer in all client-lawyer

Despite these important distinctions between confidences and secrets, the word "confidences" is frequently used to embrace both confidences and secrets. Also, as we will see, the phrase "privileged communication," which appears to relate only to confidences in the narrower sense, may be used to include secrets as well.

The ABA's Canons of Professional Ethics, as adopted in 1908, expressly protected clients' "secrets or confidences" in Canon 6. In 1928, Canon 37 was added to explain the lawyer's "duty to preserve his client's confidences,"[15] and that provision was made even more emphatic in 1937.[16] The Canons, however, were ambiguous, if not self-contradictory.[17] Along with express protection of confidences and secrets, they included a future crime exception,[18] proscribed "any manner of fraud or chicane,"[19] required candor to the court,[20] and required the attorney to reveal fraud to the other party[21] and perjury to the prosecuting authorities.[22]

What, then, was the lawyer's obligation if a client was a fugitive from justice,[23] jumped bail,[24] violated parole,[25] or committed perjury?[26] The Formal Opinions of the ABA Committee on Professional Ethics that attempted to resolve those issues were in conflict for some time. For example, in Opinion 23 (1930), the Committee held that an attorney representing a fugitive from justice should not disclose the client's hiding place to the authorities, even when she learns of it not from the client but from the client's relatives. "It is in the public interest," said the Committee, "that even the worst criminal should have counsel, and counsel cannot perform their duties without knowing the truth." To hold that an attorney should reveal such a confidence, even when received from third parties, "would prevent such frank disclosure as might be necessary to a proper protection of the client's interest." Nevertheless, the Committee held in Opinions 155 and 156 (1936) that if a client has violated bail or parole, the attorney must reveal knowledge of the client's whereabouts.

---

relationships . . . including functioning as inside or outside legal counsel, government or private-practice lawyer, counselor or litigator, advocate or intermediary. It applies whether or not the client paid a fee, and whether a lawyer learns the information personally or through an agent, for example information acquired by a lawyer's secretary. Information acquired by an agent is protected even if it was not thereafter communicated to the lawyer, such as material acquired by an investigator and kept in the investigator's files.

[15] 53 ABA REPORTS 130 (1928).

[16] 62 ABA REPORTS 352, 765 (1937).

[17] See Monroe Freedman, *Professional Responsibility of the Criminal Defense Lawyer: The Three Hardest Questions*, 64 MICH. L. REV. 1469 (1966).

[18] Canon 37.

[19] Canon 15.

[20] Canon 22.

[21] Canon 41.

[22] Canon 29.

[23] ABA Opin. 23 (1930).

[24] ABA Opin. 155 (1936).

[25] ABA Opin. 156 (1936).

[26] ABA Opin. 268, 287 (1953).

The Committee expressly resolved those and other inconsistent rulings in Opinion 287 (1953). That opinion dealt with two situations. In one a lawyer who had obtained a divorce for a client learned from the client that the client had secured the divorce through perjury. In the other, a judge was about to impose sentence upon the client based upon misinformation that the client had no previous criminal record, while the lawyer knew from the client that he had a criminal record. The Committee held that in both those cases, the lawyer's obligation was to urge the client to disclose the truth, but to remain silent if the client did not do so.[27]

The Committee recognized a direct conflict within the Canons of Professional Ethics. Although Canon 37 imposed a general duty to preserve the client's confidences, Canon 29 required the lawyer to inform the prosecuting authorities of perjury. In addition, the Committee acknowledged that the attorney is an "officer of the court." The Committee explained the question-begging nature of that phrase, however, in the following way:

> We yield to none in our insistence on the lawyer's loyalty to the court of which he is an officer. Such loyalty does not, however, consist merely in respect for the judicial office and candor and frankness to the judge. It involves also the steadfast maintenance of the principles which the courts themselves have evolved for the effective administration of justice, one of the most firmly established of which is the preservation undisclosed of the confidences communicated by his clients to the lawyer in his professional capacity.

That is, precisely because the lawyer *is* an officer of the court, he is bound to further the effective administration of justice by maintaining his client's confidences, even in the face of the client's perjury.[28]

The Committee distinguished communications received from the client, and those received from other sources, holding that only the former would override a duty to reveal the truth. William B. Jones (later Chief Judge in the United States District Court for the District of Columbia) dissented on that point, maintaining that when the lawyer receives the information "as a result of his professional work for the client, . . . such information is a confidence or secret of the client that the lawyer is bound to preserve."[29]

---

[27] This was consistent with Opinion 268 (1945), in which the Committee had held that the lawyer's duty to preserve her client's confidences is superior to her duty to reveal a client's fraud on the court.

[28] The reasoning of Opinion 287 (1953) was applied to the issue of a client's fraud on a third party in Informal Opinion 778 (1964). The opinion related to a lawyer who represented a court-appointed guardian of the person and property of a minor. The guardian revealed to the lawyer that he had misappropriated a substantial part of the ward's estate. Recognizing that the lawyer was an officer of the court, that the guardian had been appointed by the court, and that the ward was under the special protection of the court, the committee nevertheless held that the lawyer was forbidden to reveal the guardian's fraud to the court, the ward, or the bonding company.

[29] Like Judge Jones, both the Model Code and the Model Rules make no distinction based on the source of the information in defining the information that is protected. The Model Code protects "information gained in the professional relationship." DR 4-101(A). The Model Rules protect "information relating to the representation." MR 1.6(a). Each is intended to be broadly inclusive.

An issue touched upon but not resolved in Opinion 287 is whether the lawyer is required to withdraw from representing the client who refuses to disclose the truth to the court. Opinion 287 says that the lawyer should "have nothing further to do" with the client in that event. However, neither client in the cases considered in that opinion would have been harmed by termination of the relationship, because both cases were at an end. What if the circumstances were such that the lawyer's withdrawal would amount to "waving a red flag" — *i.e.*, a signal from the lawyer that the client had lied?

That issue was considered by the ABA Committee on Professional Ethics in Opinion 314 (1965). In that case, the lawyer learned that his client had made false statements to the Internal Revenue Service.[30] The Committee held that when the lawyer discovers the client's fraud, the lawyer must advise the client to correct the statement. If the client refuses to do so, "the lawyer's obligation depends on all the circumstances." The most difficult of such circumstances, of course, is where the lawyer realizes that the IRS is relying upon his silence as corroborating the client's false statements. In that event, the lawyer "may" have a duty to withdraw from the representation, or may have a duty otherwise to dissociate himself from such reliance — "unless it is obvious that the very act of disassociation would have the effect of violating Canon 37" by indirectly revealing the client's confidences.

Thus, Opinion 287 held that the lawyer should not blow the whistle on the client's false statements, and Opinion 314 held that the lawyer is similarly forbidden to wave a red flag.[31]

§ 5.04   CLIENT CONFIDENCES UNDER THE MODEL CODE [32]

The professional ethic of strict maintenance of client confidences had been firmly established when a completely new Model Code of Professional Responsibility was promulgated by the ABA in 1969 to replace the 1908 Canons.

The Model Code, as originally drafted, appeared to revive the ambiguities regarding confidentiality that had existed under the Canons prior to Opinion 287. The Model Code recognizes that full knowledge of the facts by the lawyer is "essential to proper representation," and that such knowledge is facilitated by the "observance of the ethical obligation of the lawyer to hold inviolate the confidences and secrets of his client."[33] Nevertheless, the original version of DR 7-102(B)(1) of the Model Code also appeared to require the lawyer to reveal

---

[30] The client's false statement would be a felony under 18 U.S.C. § 1001 (1995), and, if made in a document, under § 7206 of the Internal Revenue Code.

[31] This issue resurfaces, *infra*, in the discussion of MR 1.6 (which forbids the lawyer to blow the whistle), and the comment to MR 1.6 (which seems to allow the lawyer to wave a red flag).

[32] DR 7-102(B)(1), which is discussed in this section, as well as Opinions 287 (1953) and 314 (1965), involve situations in which the lawyer learns of the perjury after it has been committed. The more difficult case, in which the lawyer has foreknowledge of the perjury, is discussed in the next chapter.

[33] EC 4-1.

a fraud by the client upon a tribunal or a third party, just as some provisions of the Canons had appeared to do prior to Opinion 287.[34]

DR 7-102(B)(1) had two operative clauses in the event of client fraud. The first required that the lawyer "promptly call upon the client to rectify the [fraud]." The second clause — the "and if" clause — provided: "and if his client refuses or is unable to do so, [the lawyer] shall reveal the fraud to the affected person or tribunal."[35]

The District of Columbia was the first jurisdiction in which the practicing bar focused on that provision. When the Model Code was adopted in the District, the bar, by a seventy-five percent vote by mail ballot, amended DR 7-102(B)(1) to delete the "and if" clause. Thus, the lawyer is to call upon the client to rectify the fraud — period.

In addition, the ABA acted promptly to significantly limit the effect of DR 7-102(B)(1). In 1971, the House of Delegates approved the ABA *Standards Relating to the Defense Function*, in which the ABA explained that the lawyer's obligation to reveal client fraud under the "and if" clause of DR 7-102(B)(1) did not relate to false testimony in a criminal case.[36]

In 1974, the ABA added a new clause, following the "and if" clause of DR 7-102(B)(1). As a result of that amendment, the attorney is required to reveal the client's fraud on a court or a third party, "except when the information is protected as a privileged communication." As we have seen, the phrase "privileged communication" appears to mean only "confidences" — information protected by the lawyer-client testimonial privilege. If construed broadly, however, it could mean "secrets" as well, thereby including information that would be embarrassing to the client. If read that way, the "except" clause (forbidding disclosure) would swallow up the "and if" clause (which appears to require disclosure). That is, the ABA's amendment could be read to have the same effect as the earlier amendment in the District of Columbia, which simply excised the "and if" clause.

That is what happened. In Opinion 341 (1975), the ABA Committee on Professional Ethics considered whether the phrase "privileged communication" in the new "except" clause refers only to clients' "confidences" or to clients' "secrets" as well. The Committee held that the "except" clause includes

---

[34] Second Circuit Judge Ellsworth Alfred Van Graafeiland has expressed the opinion that the phrase "fraud on a . . . tribunal" in DR 7-102(B)(1) does not include perjury. Judge Van Graafeiland points out that perjury is not included in the similar phrase, "fraud on the court" in FED. R. CIV. PROC. 60(b)(3). *Doe v. Federal Grievance Committee*, 847 F.2d 57, 64 (2d Cir. 1988) (Van Graafeiland, J., concurring). Under Rule 60(b)(3), "fraud on the court" is limited to "subversion of the legal process," as by "bribery of a judge or juror . . . ," in which the integrity of the court and its ability to function impartially is directly impinged." *Great Coastal Express, Inc. v. International Brotherhood of Teamsters*, 675 F.2d 1349, 1356 (4th Cir. 1982). In contrast to these "more egregious forms" of "fraud on the court," we can expect perjury to be "exposed by the normal adversary process." *Id.* at 1357.

[35] At the same time, EC 8-5 says that the lawyer should reveal any knowledge of "[f]raudulent, deceptive, or otherwise illegal conduct by a participant in a proceeding before a tribunal . . . *[u]nless constrained by his obligation to preserve the confidences and secrets of his client.*" (Emphasis added.)

[36] ABA STANDARDS RELATING TO THE PROSECUTION AND DEFENSE FUNCTION, SUPPLEMENT, 18 (1971).

secrets — that is, it forbids the lawyer to reveal the client's fraud on a tribunal or third party if doing so would be "embarrassing" to the client. As Professor Hazard has wryly remarked, "fraud is always embarrassing," and the ABA's amendment to DR 7-102(B)(1) therefore "eviscerated the duty to report fraud."[37]

As explained in Opinion 341, the apparent requirement of unamended DR 7-102(B)(1), that a lawyer disclose client fraud on the court or third parties, was "unthinkable," and resulted from an oversight in drafting.[38] The effect of the amendment was to "reinstate the essence of Opinion 287." That is, client confidentiality is "so important that it should take precedence in all but the most serious cases." Opinion 341 acknowledges that "the conflicting duties to reveal fraud and to preserve confidences have existed side-by-side for some time." The opinion adds, however, that "it is clear that there has long been an accommodation in favor of preserving confidences either through practice or interpretation." Relying upon "tradition . . . backed by substantial policy considerations," therefore, Opinion 341 reaffirmed the ethic of strict confidentiality.[39]

§ 5.05   THE ASSAULT ON CONFIDENTIALITY

As we have seen, the ethic of lawyer-client trust and confidence goes back at least to the middle of the nineteenth century, and was articulated with increasing clarity and force under the Canons of Professional Ethics and the Model Code of Professional Responsibility. In Patterson's words, the message of the Model Code is "clear: loyalty to the client, regardless of other constraints, is the all-encompassing duty. And to maintain this duty, confidentiality is essential."[40]

However, by the time the Model Rules of Professional Conduct were being drafted in the late seventies and early eighties, several critics had begun to challenge the client-centered ethics of the Model Code and the civil-libertarian

---

[37] GEOFFREY C. HAZARD, ETHICS IN THE PRACTICE OF LAW 27 (1978).

[38] "When DR 7-102(B)(1) was added to the Code of Professional Responsibility . . . , the full significance of DR 4-101(C) apparently was not appreciated. . . . " ABA Opin. 341 (1975). The reference appears to be to ABA, ANNOTATED CODE OF PROFESSIONAL RESPONSIBILITY 307 (1979), where the Reporter for the Model Code and a member of the drafting committee referred to the original version of DR 7-102(B)(1) as an "oversight" and a "drafting error."

DR 7-102(B)(1) was added very late in the drafting of the Model Code. DR 4-101(B)(1) and (2) had already stated flatly that a lawyer "shall not knowingly . . . [r]eveal a confidence or secret of his client . . . [or] [u]se a confidence or secret of his client to the disadvantage of the client." Applying the philosophy and analysis of Opinion 287, therefore, DR 4-101 would have trumped DR 7-102(B)(1), barring its application in cases involving confidences or secrets. What was overlooked, however, was the potential effect of DR 4-101(C)(2), which permits the lawyer to reveal confidences or secrets "when permitted under Disciplinary Rules." This language raises a strong argument that the balance was deliberately tipped in favor of divulgence by the original draft of DR 7-102(B)(1). Opinion 341 explains, however, that the addition of DR 7-102(B)(1) was not intended to have that effect. For that reason, the 1974 amendment, adding the "except" clause to DR 7-102(B)(1), was a clarifying amendment and not a change in substance.

[39] Also, Opinion 349 (1984) withdrew Opinions 155 (1936) and 156 (1936), which had required disclosure in cases in which the client had jumped bail or violated parole. The Committee found those opinions to be inconsistent with both the Model Code and the Model Rules.

[40] Patterson, *supra* note 8, at 947.

values of the adversary system that the Model Code expresses.[41] The most eloquent and influential of those critics was Marvin E. Frankel,[42] who wrote a series of articles[43] and a book[44] attacking the adversary system and proposing far-reaching changes in the ethic of confidentiality. Frankel's views are of particular importance because he was a member of the Kutak Commission, which drafted the Model Rules. Since the members of the commission had limited scholarly background or direct professional involvement in the field of lawyers' ethics, and none of them represented a different point of view, Frankel was a particularly influential member of the commission. His analysis is, therefore, of considerable importance in understanding the Model Rules as they finally evolved.

Frankel began his analysis by identifying "the vital premise" of the adversary system to be that partisan advocacy on both sides is the best way to discover truth.[45] While that is an important premise of the adversary system (and probably an accurate one),[46] it is neither the only premise nor the vital one. Indeed, Frankel himself noted that "a simplistic preference for truth may not comport with more fundamental ideals — including notably the ideal that generally values individual freedom and dignity above order and efficiency in government."[47]

Having identified the search for truth, rather than individual dignity and autonomy, as the vital premise, Frankel directed his attention almost exclusively to the <u>lawyer's role in the search for truth</u>, giving almost no attention to those other values and to the impact that his proposals would have upon them. He candidly acknowledged, however, that his recommended changes in lawyers' ethics were "radical,"[48] that they were directed to "breaking the adversary mold,"[49] and that they would therefore effect an "appreciable revolution"[50] in the traditional lawyer-client relationship. Frankel added that

---

[41] Ironically, Freedman was the first to argue that the Model Code should be replaced with entirely new "rules of professional conduct." Freedman's concerns, however, were with ambiguities and inconsistencies in the Model Code, its failure to deal adequately with important issues like prosecutors' ethics, and its unconstitutional provisions, particularly with regard to advertising and solicitation. In 1976, Freedman expressed those views at an annual meeting of the American Bar Association. An ABA commission was appointed the following year to reconsider the Model Code. Shortly thereafter, Robert J. Kutak, the chairman of the commission, announced the need for entirely new rules of professional conduct, quoting from Freedman's speech.

[42] Marvin Frankel was a Federal District Court Judge from 1965 to 1978, when he resigned from the bench to return to private practice.

[43] Marvin Frankel, *The Search for Truth: An Umpiral View*, 123 U. PA. L. REV. 1031 (1975); Frankel, *The Adversary Judge*, 54 TEX. L. REV. 465 (1976); Marvin Frankel, *From Private Fights Toward Public Justice*, 51 N.Y.U.L. REV. 516 (1976). *Cf.*, Monroe Freedman, *Judge Frankel's Search for Truth*, 123 U. PA. L. REV. 1060 (1975).

[44] MARVIN FRANKEL, PARTISAN JUSTICE (1980). *Cf.* Monroe Freedman, *Lawyer-Client Confidences and the Constitution*, 90 YALE L. J. 1486 (1981).

[45] FRANKEL, PARTISAN JUSTICE, *supra* note 44, at 12.

[46] Chapter 2, *supra*.

[47] Frankel, *The Search for Truth*, *supra* note 43, at 1056–57.

[48] FRANKEL, PARTISAN JUSTICE, *supra* note 54, at 83. Frankel puts the word in quotes, but not, apparently, by way of disclaimer.

[49] *Id.* at 100.

[50] *Id.* at 83.

a "volume could be written on the consequent changes in procedure, in client-lawyer relations, and on the lawyer's self-image" if his views were adopted.[51]

Frankel directed his attack on the adversary system principally against lawyer-client confidences. He recommended "a pervasive broadening of the [lawyer's] duty to reveal truth, even when it hurts" the client.[52] That is, having induced the client to confide in her, the lawyer is to use the information to the client's detriment. If the lawyer learns that the client has testified falsely, for example, she must divulge the client's confidences in order to rectify the falsehood.[53] If the client does not testify at all, but has confidentially revealed to the lawyer facts that would probably have a substantial effect on the determination of a material issue, the lawyer must give the information to the court, even though doing so is adverse to the client's interests and contrary to the client's instructions.[54]

Apart from the impact on fundamental values, the practical consequences of Frankel's proposals were formidable. We have noted, for example, the substantial agreement among practicing lawyers that the lawyer who knows the truth about the client's intentions is frequently able to dissuade the client from illegal or immoral conduct, and Frankel does not dissent from that professional consensus.[55] Moreover, the Supreme Court has more than once made the common sense observation that the "apprehension of disclosure" of confidences by the client will impair the full and frank communication that the lawyer needs to give sound advice to the client.[56] As Justice Byron White wrote for the Court:[57]

> As a practical matter, if the client knows that damaging information could more readily be obtained from the attorney following disclosure than from himself in the absence of disclosure, the client would be reluctant to confide in his lawyer and it would be difficult to obtain fully informed legal advice.

The fallacy of Frankel's proposals, therefore, is that the means chosen to promote more truth in the legal system — divulgence of client confidences — would be self-defeating. Certainly it is correct to say that lawyers know a good deal of truth. They do so, however, because clients feel secure in entrusting their lawyers with damaging truths. As the Supreme Court has recognized, in upholding an evidentiary privilege for therapists, "[w]ithout a privilege, much of the desirable evidence to which litigants . . . seek access — for example, admissions against interest by a party — is unlikely to come into being."[58] To deny the privilege would therefore fail to serve a "greater

---

[51] Id.

[52] Id. at 81.

[53] Id.

[54] Id. at 83.

[55] Marvin Frankel, *The Search for Truth Continued: More Disclosure, Less Privilege*, 54 U. COLO. L. REV. 51, 63 (1982).

[56] See, e.g., *Upjohn Company v. United States*, 4449 U.S. 383, 389, 101 S.Ct. 677, 682 (1981), quoting *Hunt v. Blackburn*, 128 U.S. 464, 470 (1880).

[57] *Fisher v. United States*, 425 U.S. 391, 403 (1976).

[58] *Jaffee v. Redmond*, 116 S.Ct. 1923, 1929 (1996); see also Salzburg, *Privileges and Professionals: Lawyers and Psychiatrists*, 66 VA. L. REV. 597, 610 (1980) ("The privilege creates a zone of privacy in which an attorney and client can create information that did not exist before and might not exist otherwise.")

truth-seeking function."[59] In short, once we required lawyers to betray their clients' confidences, lawyers would seldom have truths of any importance to reveal.[60]

§ 5.06 DOES CONFIDENTIALITY NEED RETHINKING?

Conventional wisdom is often valid. We have quoted the conventional wisdom on the importance of confidentiality in the preceding section — the consensus of judges and lawyers that confidentiality is essential to ensure candid disclosure of embarrassing and potentially harmful truths from clients. This consensus is based upon the most extensive kind of empirical evidence — the day-by-day, year-by-year, century-by-century experience of judges and lawyers.[61] It is not readily susceptible, however, to scientific empirical research. How would one determine scientifically how many clients in fact gave sensitive information to their lawyers which they would not have given but for assurance of confidentiality?[62]

In the absence of scientific empirical data, some academics have questioned whether confidentiality is important to obtaining sensitive information from clients. The principal citation is to an article by Professor Fred C. Zacharias titled, *Rethinking Confidentiality*.[63] Zacharias' article, however, does not claim to be more than a proposal to rethink confidentiality; it does not purport to be an accomplished fact. As Zacharias candidly acknowledges about his own empirical study, which is reported in the article, its sample was limited and its methodology was "somewhat unscientific."[64] He concludes, "I would be the first to caution against overreliance on [this] study."[65] Nevertheless,

---

[59] *Id.*

[60] As discussed in the next chapter, Frankel has abandoned his earlier position. Others, however, have picked up where Marvin Frankel left off, insisting upon truth above all other values in the adversary system. *See* Jeffrey Toobin, *Ito and the Truth School*, THE NEW YORKER, Mar. 27, 1995, at 42. (examining the philosophy of scholars and judges in the "truth school"). There is a small number of legal scholars who argue — especially in the criminal context — that the purpose of a criminal trial should be to uncover the truth, with a corresponding lessening of the rights of the accused. *See, e.g.*, Akhil Reed Amar, *Fourth Amendment First Principles*, 107 HARV. L. REV. 757 (1994); Harry I. Subin, *The Criminal Lawyer's "Different Mission": Reflections on the "Right" to Present a False Case*, 1 GEO. J. LEGAL ETHICS 125 (1987); William Simon, *The Ethics of Criminal Defense*, 91 MICH. L. REV. 1703, 1704–05 (1993) (asserting that criminal defense lawyers routinely engage in unscrupulous practices including subverting the truth). For an excellent response to Professor Harry Subin's position, *see* John B. Mitchell, *Reasonable Doubts Are Where You Find Them: A Response to Professor Subin's Position on the Criminal Lawyer's "Different Mission"*, 1 GEO. J. LEGAL ETHICS 339 (1987). *See also United States v. Wade*, 388 U.S. 218, 256 (1967) (White, J., dissenting in part and concurring in part) (describing the defense lawyer's "different mission," which requires a defender to "put the State's case in the worst possible light, regardless of what he thinks or knows to be the truth").

[61] A Harvard University scientist has observed: "Every human being is a behavioral scientist . . . . Scientists and non-scientists alike, we take our concepts from the common sense of our culture and language, and put them to the test in our day-to-day experience." Calvin Simonds, *Vigil*, 87 HARV. MAG. 4, 6 (Mar.-Apr., 1985).

[62] The question is rhetorical, but the answer appears to be: only in a survey that guaranteed confidentiality.

[63] 74 IOWA L. REV. 351 (1989).

[64] *Id.* at 396.

[65] *Id.*

Zacharias' article is frequently cited, misleadingly, as authority that confidentiality is not important to candid disclosure by clients to lawyers.[66]

There are, though, some studies that have been done by behavioral scientists, who are understandably concerned with the validity of responses to their own surveys about sensitive information. These are discussed in a book chapter by Robert F. Boruch titled, "On the Need to Assure Confidentiality and Privacy."[67] One study found respondents about five times more likely to admit to corporal punishment of their children when confidentiality was clear.[68] Another study, which involved over three thousand servicemen, related to use of illicit drugs, racial attitudes, and racist behavior. Respondents were more than twice as likely to admit to undesirable behavior when the methodology assured confidentiality.[69] In a Canadian study on the incidence of abortions, both legal and illegal, the authors concluded that less persuasive promises of confidentiality "could not obtain admissions of even all legal abortions."[70] Yet another study, of "leisure activities, including . . . intercourse, masturbation, and marijuana use," found that "absolute assurance [of confidentiality] clearly increased the likelihood of response to sensitive, rather than innocuous, questions, relative to groups receiving qualified assurance or no assurance."[71]

There is reason to believe, therefore, that the conventional wisdom of the legal profession regarding confidentiality, based on the innumerable experiences of countless judges and lawyers, is indeed valid, and that it does not need rethinking.

---

[66] *See, e.g.*, DEBORAH RHODE, IN THE INTERESTS OF JUSTICE (2000), which illustrates both the misplaced reliance on Zacharias' article and the flawed methodology of his work. Rhode erroneously refers to the article as an example of "[t]he most systematic research available," and cites it for the proposition that "only about a third [of clients surveyed] reported giving information to their lawyers that they would not have given without a guarantee of confidentiality." *Id*. at 111.

Even if only one-third of clients would have withheld information from their own lawyers without a guarantee of confidentiality, that would be sufficient to justify lawyer-client confidentiality. More important, imagine the reaction of a person asked by a stranger whether there was any personal information that she would not be willing to reveal without confidentiality. The clear implication of the question is: Have you done something that is harmful or embarrassing for you to reveal? What is surprising is that one-third were willing to answer yes.

Also, one wonders whether Zacharias gave convincing assurances of confidentiality to those surveyed. If he did give credible assurances of confidentiality, that would suggest his own recognition of the importance of confidentiality. And if he did not give such assurances, how can we be sure that the clients (with no benefit to themselves) would answer his intrusive questions candidly?

[67] ROBERT F. BORUCH & JOE S. CECIL, ASSURING THE CONFIDENTIALITY OF SOCIAL RESEARCH DATA (1979). Boruch, who wrote the chapter, based it on material he prepared for the National Academy of Sciences Panel on Privacy and Confidentiality, a subcommittee of the NAS Committee on Federal Statistics, and for the American Psychological Association's Task Force on Privacy. *Id*. at 60.

[68] *Id*. at 70.

[69] *Id*. at 71.

[70] *Id*. at 75.

[71] *Id*. at 73.

§ 5.07 CONFIDENTIALITY UNDER THE MODEL RULES

The impact of Marvin Frankel's unconventional views on the Kutak Commission was considerable. In its first public Discussion Draft, in 1980, the Commission proposed a reversal of Opinions 287 and 341 by requiring the lawyer to reveal client perjury to the court in civil cases [72] and permitting the lawyer to do so in criminal cases [73] "even if doing so requires disclosure of a confidence of the client or disclosure that the client is implicated in the falsification." The Discussion Draft also permitted the lawyer, in both civil and criminal cases, to reveal the client's confidences and secrets to the other side if the information would be favorable to that side. [74]

The Commission's Proposed Final Draft was published the following year. The lawyer was no longer permitted to turn over a client's confidences and secrets to the other side. However, other proposals relating to confidentiality became the most hotly contested issues in the debates that followed. Proposed MR 1.6 *permitted* the lawyer to reveal information [75] to prevent the client from committing a criminal act that the lawyer believes is likely to result in "death or substantial bodily harm." It also *permitted* the lawyer to reveal information to prevent "substantial injury to the financial interest or property of another" or to "rectify the consequences of a client's criminal or fraudulent act in the furtherance of which the lawyer's services [have] been used." In addition, proposed MR 3.3 appeared to *require* disclosure to the court if a lawyer learns that she has offered material evidence that is false and also if the client makes a false statement and the court is relying upon the lawyer's silence as corroboration. Further, proposed MR 4.1(b) *required* the lawyer to disclose information necessary to prevent assisting a client in any fraudulent or criminal act.

The House of Delegates adopted MR 3.3(a)(4), which appears to require the lawyer to inform the court if she learns that she has offered false evidence; it also adopted MR 3.3(a)2), which appears to require the lawyer to contradict the client if the court is relying upon the lawyer's silence as corroboration. As we will see in the next chapter, however, MR 3.3 does not mean, and was not intended to mean, what it appears to say.

The provisions in proposed MR 1.6 relating to divulging client fraud on third parties were rejected by the ABA House of Delegates by a substantial margin of 207–129. [76] Also, with regard to proposed MR 4.1(b), which would have required the lawyer to disclose information necessary to prevent assisting a client in any fraudulent or criminal act, the House of Delegates voted 188-127 to add the words "unless disclosure is prohibited by Rule 1.6." As a result of

---

[72] MR 3.1(b) (Discussion Draft, 1980).

[73] MR 3.1(f)(1) (Discussion Draft, 1980).

[74] MR 3.1(e) (Discussion Draft, 1980).

[75] The Model Rules have discarded the Model Code's reference to "confidences" and "secrets." Instead, what is protected under MR 1.6 is all "information relating to representation of a client."

[76] However, several jurisdictions that have adopted the Model Rules have added provisions regarding frauds and/or crimes against third parties. *See* STEPHEN GILLERS & ROY D. SIMON, REGULATION OF LAWYERS: STATUTES AND STANDARDS 83–87 (2002).

that limitation, MR 4.1(b) has no practical effect on confidentiality, and its inclusion in the Model Rules is "largely a matter of archeological interest."[77]

The lawyer's responsibility with regard to client fraud is therefore governed directly by MR 1.6(a), which says flatly that the lawyer "shall not reveal information relating to representation of a client. . . . " All proposed exceptions for cases of client fraud were overwhelmingly defeated by the House of Delegates when the Model Rules were adopted in 1983. Moreover, by similar strong votes, the House of Delegates rebuffed efforts in 1991 and in 2001 to amend MR 1.6 to allow lawyers to prevent or rectify client fraud on third parties. But don't stop reading here because, in the name of enforcing candor and preventing fraud, those who favor the interests of third parties over client confidentiality have come up with three disingenuous sequels.[78]

§ 5.08   THE "HIDDEN EXCEPTION" TO CONFIDENTIALITY IN THE COMMENT TO MR 1.6

The first disingenuous sequel regarding fraud on third parties was in 1983. The Reporter for the Model Rules, Professor Hazard, has described how he and a small group of ABA members "buried disingenuously" a "brief and cryptic" exception in the comment to MR 1.6.[79] The result, in Hazard's words, is that "some fools may not understand that Rule 1.6 does not mean what it seems to mean."[80] This is not surprising, since it is "doubtful whether many lawyers understood that hidden meaning" when it was promulgated.[81]

As Hazard has acknowledged, the ABA debate on divulgence of client fraud on third parties was "both exhaustive and indicative of House sentiment" in favor of confidentiality and against revealing the fraud.[82] However, the House of Delegates did not at that time address the comments to the rules it adopted. The comments were left to a subsequent meeting, when they were adopted without the same close attention and debate. As a result, Hazard and a small group of ABA members were able to create an exception that could be even "broader than any proposed by the Kutak Commission and rejected by the House of Delegates."[83] Indeed, "if given full scope, the overall thrust of Model Rule 1.6 will be altered dramatically."[84]

This "hidden" exception,[85] which threatened to vitiate the rule that had been adopted by such a heavy vote of the House of Delegates, was appended

---

[77] CHARLES WOLFRAM, MODERN LEGAL ETHICS 672 n.44. But note the effect of the 2003 amendment to MR 1.6, *infra*, § 5.10.

[78] The ABA's 2003 adoption of fraud exceptions to MR 1.6 is discussed in § 5.10, *infra*.

[79] 1 GEOFFREY C. HAZARD & W.WILLIAM HODES, THE LAW OF LAWYERING § 9.30 (3d ed., 2001).

[80] Geoffrey C. Hazard, Jr., *Rectification of Client Fraud: Death and Revival of a Professional Norm*, 33 EMORY L. J. 271, 306 (1984).

[81] 1 HAZARD & HODES, *supra*, note 79.

[82] HAZARD, *supra*, note 79, at 302.

[83] 1 HAZARD & HODES, *supra*, note 79.

[84] *Id. See also* Rotunda, *The Notice of Withdrawal and the New Model Rules of Professional Conduct: Blowing the Whistle and Waving the Red Flag*, 63 ORE. L. REV. 455, 481 (1984): "In some respects the decision to file a noisy notice of withdrawal may hurt clients more than open disclosure."

[85] HAZARD & HODES, *supra* note 79.

to MR 1.6 in a comment headed "Withdrawal." This new comment to MR 1.6 provides that "[i]f the lawyer's services will be used by the client in materially furthering a course of criminal or fraudulent conduct, the lawyer must withdraw. . . . "[86] Then, after withdrawing, the lawyer may "giv[e] notice of the fact of withdrawal, and . . . may also withdraw or disaffirm any opinion, document, affirmation, or the like."[87]

As it has been said, therefore, the rule forbids the lawyer to blow the whistle on client fraud, but the comment allows the lawyer to wave a red flag.[88] Hazard and Hodes have explained the effect of the comment this way:[89]

> Thus, for example, the "Withdrawal" comment would allow a lawyer who has closed a real estate deal, and who then finds that the deal was fraudulent, to terminate his representation and to notify the other party that the deed he prepared is "withdrawn." Similarly, he may "withdraw" an SEC filing, or a document that has come into the hands of successor counsel. In each case, the third party can consider what the withdrawal might mean and act accordingly.

There are, however, a number of problems with that conclusion.

One problem is that some among us might turn on those who tried to dupe us, and read the rule to mean exactly what it "seems to mean." In doing so, we would be supported by the Model Rules' own rule of construction, which is that the comments are merely "guides," while the text of the rule is "authoritative."[90] Particularly in light of the admittedly disingenuous way in which the comment was added to change the meaning of the text, we would be more than justified in following the clear meaning of MR 1.6 itself.

Another problem is revealed in Hazard and Hodes' explanation in the indented quote. "*In each case*," they say, "the third party *can consider what the withdrawal might mean*, and act accordingly." A serious difficulty with that is that lawyers withdraw from cases for a variety of reasons,[91] including ill health, inability to work with co-counsel, or the client's inability to continue paying the lawyer's fees. Nevertheless, as Hazard and Hodes suggest, third parties could assume the worst about what withdrawal might mean in every case, thereby presenting serious consequences for innocent clients. As Hazard and Hodes have acknowledged, withdrawal could become "a euphemism for client fraud," with the result that "lawyers and clients alike may suffer embarrassment in terminating a relationship for perfectly innocent reasons."[92]

---

[86] MR 1.6, cmt. [15].

[87] *Id.*, cmt. [16].

[88] Ronald D. Rotunda, *The Notice of Withdrawal and the New Model Rules of Professional Conduct: Blowing the Whistle and Waving the Red Flag*, 63 ORE. L. REV. 455 (1984).

[89] 1 HAZARD & HODES, THE LAW OF LAWYERING 109 (Supp., 1988). This illustration is not in the Third Edition; there is no indication of why not.

[90] Model Rules, Scope.

[91] *See, e.g.*, DR 2-110, MR 1.16.

[92] 1 HAZARD & HODES, *supra* note 89, at 109. Nor would it be an adequate solution to have lawyers explain to all relevant third parties their true reasons for withdrawing in all cases. For example, the nature of the lawyer's illness, or even the fact of the illness, might be something the lawyer might want to remain private.

Yet another problem with Hazard and Hodes' illustration of the comment to MR 1.6 is that the illustration goes significantly beyond the comment itself[93] (which in turn goes far beyond the rule). Note that the illustration relates to a case in which the lawyer "has closed" a real estate transaction that "was" fraudulent. The comment, however, refers only to a case in which the lawyer is required to withdraw because the lawyer's services "will be used" in materially "furthering" a course of criminal or fraudulent conduct. Moreover, the comment cites MR 1.16(a)(1), which deals expressly with withdrawing to avoid a *future* violation of law or disciplinary rules. By contrast, the comment makes no reference to MR 1.16(b)(2), which permits the lawyer to withdraw when the client "has used" the lawyer's services to perpetrate a crime or fraud.

Thus, although the comment does allow the lawyer to "withdraw or disaffirm any opinion, document, affirmation, or the like," that can happen only when the lawyer's withdrawal from the representation has been required in order to avoid *furthering* a crime or fraud that has *not yet been completed*. In the real estate case that Hazard uses in his illustration, the fraud has been completed, and the lawyer, therefore, can no longer withdraw or disaffirm the deed under the "Withdrawal" comment.

When limited to preventing future crimes or frauds, the exception in the comment makes sense. If a client has fraudulently induced a lawyer to help the client in perpetrating a crime or fraud, the lawyer should be permitted to withdraw the lawyer's own unwitting misrepresentation, but only when the lawyer's document is still capable of inducing material reliance by the third party. That is, the lawyer would not be permitted to call back a document to expose a fraud that has been completed, but the lawyer would be permitted to call back her own words when those words are false and are still capable of causing future harm.

As we said, that rule would make sense. It assumes a situation in which the client has rejected a relationship of trust and confidence, and has betrayed the lawyer into unwittingly furthering a crime or fraud.[94] It is not the rule,

---

[93] In the light of history, one has to wonder whether this a further instance of disingenuous rewriting of MR 1.6.

[94] *Compare*, AMERICAN LAWYER'S CODE OF CONDUCT Rule 6.5 (Reporter's Draft, 1980):

> In any matter other than criminal litigation, a lawyer may withdraw from representing a client if the lawyer comes to know that the client has knowingly induced the lawyer to take the case or to take action on behalf of the client on the basis of a material misrepresentation about the facts of the case, and if withdrawal can be accomplished without express divulgence of the client's confidences. The lawyer may also retract or disaffirm any opinion or statement of fact made by the lawyer as a result of the client's misrepresentation, if the lawyer reasonably believes that the opinion or statement is likely to be relied upon by others to their detriment.

A similar provision was subsequently adopted in New York as DR 4-101(c)(5). An important difference, however, is that New York omitted the ALCC's limitation, "In any matter other than criminal litigation."

The RESTATEMENT goes substantially further. *See* § 67(1) and (2), which permit a lawyer to disclose confidential client information to prevent a client's crime or fraud when it involves the lawyer's services and when it threatens substantial financial loss, and also permits disclosure to "prevent, rectify, or mitigate" such loss if the crime or fraud has already occurred.

[Handwritten marginal note: ONCE CRIME COMPLETED LAWYER MAY NOT WITHDRAW (IF COMMITTED W/ LAWYER ASSISTANCE)]

however, that the House of Delegates adopted in MR 1.6 in 1983[95] and reaffirmed in 1991 and 2001.

§ 5.09   THE SURPRISE EXCEPTION TO CONFIDENTIALITY IN FORMAL OPINION 366

The second disingenuous episode regarding fraud on third parties took place in the decade after the 1983 effort to improve MR 1.6 by inserting the comment on withdrawal. In 1991, the ABA Committee on Ethics and Professional Responsibility urged adoption of the previously rejected Kutak exception permitting disclosure of client confidences to prevent or rectify client fraud. As we have seen, the ABA House of Delegates again rejected the proposal, this time by a vote of 251-158. That would seem to have ended the matter, at least for another decade, because the Committee's argument in support of its proposal had asserted that unless the proposed amendment were adopted, a lawyer could not ethically do anything to warn a third party of client fraud.

Within a year, however, the committee found to its surprise that it, and everyone else, had been wrong about the true meaning of MR 1.6. In Formal Opinion 92-366, the committee considered what the Model Rules permit, and what they require, when a lawyer learns that her client has used her work product to perpetrate a fraud, is continuing to do so, or plans to do so in the future. The committee began by solemnly declaring that the answers to those question require a "somewhat difficult reconciliation" of the text and commentary of three rules — Rule 1.6, which admittedly imposes "a broad requirement of confidentiality"; Rule 1.2(d), which prohibits a lawyer from assisting client crime or fraud; and Rule 1.16(a)(1), which requires withdrawal from a representation where continued representation would result in a violation of any other rule.

With regard to a case where the lawyer learns of the client's fraudulent conduct before it has been completed, the committee concluded that the lawyer is not only permitted to disavow her work product upon withdrawal, but that doing so might be "necessary" in order to make the withdrawal effective.[96] In short, having failed to persuade the House of Delegates to adopt a *permissive* exception for client fraud, the committee managed to find that there had been a *required* exception there all the time. As the committee acknowledged, in a wry understatement, "the conclusion of this opinion has not been easily reached."[97]

---

[95] Indeed, it is similar to the original version of MR 4.1(b), which would have required the lawyer to reveal information necessary to prevent assisting the client in any fraudulent or criminal act. As we have seen, the House of Delegates vitiated MR 4.1(b) by amending it.

[96] ABA Formal Opinion 92-366, p. 12.

[97] *Id.*, p. 13. As observed by three dissenting committee members: "It is not the role of this Committee, however laudable the goal, so to torture the plain meaning and obvious intent of the Rules reflected in their language and legislative history as to supply by interpretation a result clearly and repeatedly rejected in enactment." *Id.*, at 22.

§ 5.10 THE 2003 AMENDMENTS TO MR 1.6 AND 1.13 REGARDING CLIENT FRAUD ON THIRD PARTIES

As discussed earlier in this chapter, the ABA House of Delegates has repeatedly rejected client-fraud exceptions to lawyer-client confidentiality.[98] In recent years, however, Enron and other corporate-fraud scandals have exploded in the news. The ethical rules already forbade lawyers to assist their clients in illegal or fraudulent activities.[99] Nevertheless, because of the alleged complicity of lawyers in some of the fraudulent activities of major corporations, the ABA came under considerable pressure from Congress, the SEC, and the public to make client fraud an exception to lawyer-client confidentiality. In response, in 2003, by a close vote of 218–201, the ABA amended the Model Rules to provide unduly broad fraud exceptions to confidentiality for *individual* (non-corporate) clients. Purposefully, however, those exceptions have no impact on lawyer-client confidentiality in the kinds of *corporate* fraud that gave rise to the exception.

[1] The Unduly Broad Fraud Exceptions to MR 1.6

We have three objections to the ABA's fraud exceptions to MR 1.6, which are MR 1.6(2)[100] and (3).[101]

First, as we have seen, those exceptions are not necessary to prevent lawyers from knowingly assisting clients in committing frauds on third parties. That problem had been dealt with in ethical rules long before the 2003 amendments.[102]

Second, the new exceptions go further than necessary or desirable either (a) to prevent a lawyer from knowingly participating in fraud on third parties or (b) to allow a lawyer to "wave a red flag" when she has unwittingly made misrepresentations that could result in defrauding third parties. Proposals for permitting lawyers to withdraw representations made by the lawyer that threaten to defraud third parties are provided in the American Lawyer's Code of Conduct, Rule 6.5, and in New York's DR 4-101(c)(5).[103] Each of these

---

[98] *See* § 5.07, *supra.*

[99] MR 1.2(d); DR 7-102(A)(7). *See also* MR 1.16(a)(1) and DR 2-110(B)(2) (mandatory withdrawal if the representation will result in violation of the rules of professional conduct or other law).

[100] Permitting a lawyer to reveal client information "to prevent the client from committing a crime or fraud that is reasonably certain to result in substantial injury to the financial interests or property of another and in furtherance of which the client has used or is using the lawyer's services." Consider also the effect of this amendment on MR 4.1(b).

[101] Permitting a lawyer to reveal client information "to prevent, mitigate or rectify substantial injury to the financial interests or property of another that is reasonably certain to result or has resulted from the client's commission of a crime or fraud in furtherance of which the client has used the lawyer's services."

[102] MR 1.2(d); DR 7-102(A)(7). *See also* MR 1.16(a)(1) and DR 2-110(B)(2) (mandatory withdrawal if the representation will result in violation of the rules of professional conduct or other law).

[103] *See* § 5.08, *supra*, n. 92.

proposals would accomplish the desired result without going as far as the amendments to MR 1.6.

The first of the ABA's 2003 amendments to MR 1.6, which is in 1.6(b)(2), is not unreasonable. It permits the lawyer to reveal client confidences "to the extent the lawyer reasonably believes necessary" to "prevent" the client from committing a crime or fraud that is "reasonably certain" to result in substantial injury to the financial interests or property of another "and in furtherance of which the client has used or is using the lawyer's services." This allows the lawyer to avoid being the unwilling instrument of a *fraud in progress*. In such a case, a lawyer could wave a red flag in the same way that is permitted under ALCC Rule 6.5 and N.Y. DR 4-101(c)(5).

However, the second amendment to MR 1.6, which is in subsection (b)(3), is both unnecessary and undesirable. It permits the lawyer to "mitigate or rectify" substantial injury to the financial or property interests of another when the injury already "has resulted." This is an extreme form of blowing the whistle on a client. Even though the lawyer's services are no longer being used to defraud a third party, the lawyer is allowed to go to the third party, volunteer information about the client's fraud, and offer to mitigate or rectify the fraud by testifying in a legal action on behalf of the third party against the lawyer's own client.

Such testimony by the lawyer would be permitted under the law of *evidence* by the traditional crime-fraud exception to the lawyer-client evidentiary privilege. But *ethical rules* permitting a lawyer to *volunteer* client information, even regarding a crime, have traditionally been limited to the information necessary to *prevent* the crime.[104] Compare, for example, MR 1.6(b)(1), which permits a lawyer to reveal information to *prevent* death or substantial bodily harm to a third person, but does not permit the lawyer to volunteer client information to someone who has *already* been physically harmed by the client. Thus, under amended MR 1.6, the ABA has cut back on confidentiality to provide greater protection to someone who has lost money to the client through fraud, than to a person who has been intentionally maimed by the client or to the spouse of someone who has been murdered by the client.

[2]   The Bogus Amendment to MR 1.13 — Still Protecting Corporate Fraud

Those who have long lobbied for exceptions to lawyer-client confidentiality to protect third parties from client fraud won a major victory in the ABA's 2003 amendments to MR 1.6. How much of a victory would it have been, however, if those amendments had included the following condition on disclosure of client fraud on third parties: "provided, however, that the lawyer shall not act to prevent, mitigate, or rectify client fraud *unless it is in the interests of the client* to do so." Obviously, such a proviso would nullify the disclosure of client fraud, since it would rarely if ever be in the interests of the client to have the lawyer blow the whistle on the client's fraud.

---

[104] *See, e.g.,* N.Y. DR 4-101(c)(3).

When the fraud is that of a corporate client, however, that proviso, nullifying disclosure of the client's fraud, is precisely what the ABA has written into MR 1.13.

To understand how corporate fraud is protected under MR 1.13, look first at the language of MR 1.6. Repeatedly, the expressed concern is with substantial injury to the financial or property interests of "another" — *not* with the best interests of the client. Indeed, the whole point of the amendments to MR 1.6 is to make the interests of third parties superior to those of the client in cases of client fraud.

In MR 1.13, however, which relates specifically to corporations (referred to as "the organization"), there is no language about the interests of anyone other than the corporate client. On the contrary, the expressed concern in MR 1.13 is solely and repeatedly with preventing "substantial injury to the organization" itself.[105] Moreover, in every situation in which the lawyer might reveal corporate-client information regarding fraud, the lawyer is expressly restricted by an overriding obligation to protect "the best interest" of the corporate client.[106]

This was not simply an oversight in drafting, and it is not a new issue. Since the early 1980s, similar preferential treatment for corporate clients in the original, unamended version of MR 1.13 has been pointed out, but ignored.[107] The short of it is that MR 1.13 was designed from the outset by the corporate bar to give special protection to corporate clients, and this preferential treatment was accepted by the Kutak Commission in order to get the endorsement of the Model Rules from the ABA's powerful Corporate Section.[108]

[a] An Illustrative Case of Corporate Fraud

We can illustrate the way the corporate sham works with a hypothetical taken from the first edition of this book, which was written thirteen years before the 2003 amendments to MR 1.6 and MR 1.13.[109] Assume that the CEO

---

[105] MR 1.13(b) (one reference); MR 1.13(c)(2) (two references).

[106] MR 1.13(b) (two references).

[107] *See, e.g.*, Monroe Freedman, *Lawyer-Client Confidences: The Model Rules' Radical Assault on Confidentiality*, 68 A.B.A. Jour. 428, 432 (April, 1982):

> . . . The proponents of whistle-blowing . . . insist that the whistle-blowing requirement should be imposed only on lawyers for corporations, as distinguished from lawyers representing individuals.
>
> Ironically, the Kutak commission has turned that notion upside-down. While lawyers representing individuals are required to make disclosures in many instances and permitted to make them in many more, lawyers representing business organizations are absolutely forbidden under Rule 1.13(b) and (c), in virtually all circumstances, to reveal even ongoing and future crimes.

See also, Schneyer, *Professionalism as Bar Politics: The Making of the Model Rules of Professional Conduct*, 14 Law & Soc. Inquiry 677 (1989); Freedman, Understanding Lawyers' ethics, Ch. 10 ("Corporate Lawyers and Their Clients: Some Special Ethical Rules") (1st ed., 1990); Freedman, *The Corporate Bar Protects Its Own*, Legal Times, June 15, 1992.

[108] *Id.*

[109] At pp. 202–205. In the earlier edition, the issue was whether the lawyer could withdraw from the representation, even though withdrawal might wave a red flag.

of a corporate client has devised and is carrying out a billing scheme that appears to be defrauding the corporation's customers. Assume also that (1) the CEO persists in the billing scheme despite the lawyer's urging him to stop, (2) the scheme involves the lawyer's services, (3) the lawyer reasonably believes that the scheme is both criminal and fraudulent, and (4) no one other than the lawyer has caught on to the scheme or is likely to catch on.

If the same fraud were being carried out by an individual businessman (not a corporate officer), the lawyer's concern, under MR 1.6, would be with preventing the "substantial injury to the financial interests" of the defrauded customers. In order to prevent that injury to others, the lawyer would be permitted to reveal her client's confidences both to prevent the fraud[110] and to mitigate or rectify it.[111] And in making the decision to breach the client's confidentiality, the lawyer would not be constrained by any language in MR 1.6 or its Comment about avoiding injury to the client or protecting the best interest of the client. Moreover, because no one but the lawyer has detected the fraud or is likely to do so, the lawyer "reasonably believes [it to be] necessary" that she blow the whistle in order to protect the defrauded customers.

But because the client in our hypothetical case is a corporation, the controlling rule becomes MR 1.13, and the lawyer's concern is shifted away from the substantial injury to the defrauded customers, and is refocused exclusively on the "best interest of the organization." As stated (or understated) in Comment [7] to MR 1.6, "where the client is an organization," the lawyer is permitted to reveal client information only "in limited circumstances." Let's take a look now at how MR 1.13 limits those circumstances.

[b] Going "Up the Ladder"

There is a lot of approving talk about how amended MR 1.13 requires the lawyer to report "up the ladder" to the highest authority in the corporation (ultimately to the board of directors) to forestall corporate fraud. This is <u>nonsense</u> for a number of reasons.

First, references to going up the ladder to higher authority in the corporation has been in MR 1.13 all along.[112] That much-acclaimed amendment in 2003 is not a significant amendment at all.[113]

More important, the lawyer is not required by MR 1.13 to go up the ladder. Indeed, she is required *not* to refer the matter to higher authority unless the fraud "is likely to result in substantial injury to the organization."[114] In our

---

[110] MR 1.6(b)(2).

[111] MR 1.6(b)(3).

[112] The ABA's ANNOTATED MODEL RULES OF PROFESSIONAL CONDUCT 203 (4th ed., 1999) refers to the original MR 1.13 as providing for "loyal disclosure," distinguishing this from the "more common . . . adverse disclosure." *Citing* Harris, *Taking the Entity Seriously: Lawyer Liability for Failure to Prevent Harm to Organizational Clients through Disclosure of Constituent Wrongdoing*, 11 GEO. J. LEGAL ETHICS 597 (1998).

[113] Nor, of course, does the lawyer need permission from MR 1.13 to inform the board of directors of information that is material to the representation. Under MR 1.4(a)(3) the lawyer has always been *required* to "keep the client reasonably informed about the status of the matter."

[114] MR 1.13(b) (first sentence).

hypothetical case, the fraud is not likely to be detected, so there is not likely to be substantial injury to the corporation if the lawyer remains silent. Accordingly, the lawyer is not required to go up the ladder.

In fact, the lawyer is expressly directed to act "in the best interest of the organization,"[115] and she is further told *not* to go up the ladder if she reasonably believes that doing so is not "necessary in the best interest of the organization."[116] (Note that there is not a word here about the best interests — or any interest — of those who are being defrauded.) Since the CEO's fraud is not likely to be detected, the lawyer could reasonably believe it to be in the best interest of the corporation that the fewer people who know about the fraud, the better for the corporation. In that event, it would not be "necessary in the best interest of the organization" to go up the ladder to the board of directors, and the lawyer would be forbidden to do so.

[c] "Reporting Out": Blowing the Whistle Outside the Corporation

So far, our discussion of MR 1.13 has referred only to revealing the CEO's fraud *within* the organization, by going "up the ladder." As we have seen, even reporting within the corporation is carefully restricted under MR 1.13(b). Subsection (c) then deals with what the lawyer should do, or not do, if the board of directors fails to put a stop to the CEO's fraud. Yes, MR 1.13(c)(2) does use the words, "the lawyer may reveal information relating to the representation whether or not Rule 1.6 permits such disclosure." But here are the critical restrictions on that language.

First, the board's failure to act appropriately regarding the fraud must itself be "clearly" a violation of law (that is, not just condoning fraud, but criminal).[117] In addition, the lawyer must reasonably believe that this criminal act by the board is "reasonably certain" to result in substantial injury to the company.[118] That quoted language is actually a *more restrictive* condition on the lawyer than that in the original version of MR 1.13, which required only that the board's criminal act be "likely" to result in substantial injury to the organization. (Note again, the exclusive emphasis on injury to the organization, not to the defrauded customers.) Thus, if the lawyer reasonably believes that the board's inaction is not "reasonably certain" to harm the company, the lawyer in our hypothetical case is forbidden to blow the whistle.

After those limitations comes the language appearing to permit reporting out — but with an even more stringent condition:[119]

> . . . the lawyer may reveal information relating to the representation whether or not Rule 1.6 permits such disclosure, *but only if and to the extent the lawyer reasonably believes necessary to prevent substantial injury to the organization.*

---

[115] *Id.*

[116] *Id.* (second sentence).

[117] MR 1.13(c)(1).

[118] MR 1.13(c)(2).

[119] *Id.* (emphasis added).

As we suggested earlier, imagine if the fraud exception to MR 1.6 contained that express proviso: "but only if and to the extent the lawyer reasonably believes necessary to prevent substantial injury to the client." Wouldn't everyone recognize that this "but only if" clause had nullified the fraud exception?

[3]   Summary of the Effect of the 2003 Amendments

Here, then, is the decision for the lawyer in our hypothetical case. She reasonably believes that (a) the CEO's fraud is not likely to be found out, (b) the board's inaction is not clearly criminal, (c) the board's inaction is not reasonably certain to result in substantial injury to the company, (d) revealing the fraud outside the company (*e.g.*, to the customers or to a prosecutor) is likely to cause substantial injury to the company, and (e) reporting out is not necessary to prevent substantial injury to the company. If the lawyer believes any one of those things, she is <u>forbidden</u> under MR 1.13 to take any action, directly or indirectly, to reveal the company's fraud outside the company.[120]

In short, amended MR 1.6 permits a lawyer to blow the whistle on an individual client's fraud, but MR 1.13 forbids it when the client is a corporation. This is accomplished by making injury to the interests of third parties the paramount concern of MR 1.6, and making the interests of the corporation the paramount concern of MR 1.13.

In our hypothetical case, for example, it is likely that the client will get away with defrauding third parties unless the lawyer reveals it. Under MR 1.6, the lawyer would be able to reveal an individual client's fraud because doing so is reasonably necessary to protect the paramount interests of the defrauded third parties. But under MR 1.13, on the same facts, the lawyer would be forbidden to reveal the corporate client's fraud, because revealing the fraud is contrary to protecting the paramount interest of the corporation. Put otherwise, the lawyer for the corporation is expressly forbidden to reveal the client's fraud outside the company unless the fraud is "reasonably certain" to come out anyway.

Thus, as it has all along under the Model Rules, the ABA has given the interests of corporate clients far greater protection than those of individual clients.

§ 5.11   THE ABA'S INCONGRUOUS EXCEPTIONS TO CONFIDENTIALITY

Some of the ABA's exceptions to lawyer-client confidentiality are a mockery of an ideal that has been characterized as "a sacred trust"[121] that "touch[es]

---

[120] Comment [6] to MR 1.13 does not change this result. Indeed, if it did, the text of the rule would control. "The Comments are intended as guides to interpretation, but the text of each rule is authoritative." Model Rules, Scope. However, Comment [6] reiterates the restrictive language of the rule itself:

> Under Paragraph (c) the lawyer may reveal such information *only when* the organization's highest authority insists upon or fails to address threatened or ongoing action that is *clearly* a violation of law, *and then only* to the extent the lawyer reasonably believes necessary to prevent *reasonably certain* substantial injury *to the organization*. [Emphasis added].

[121] *State v. Land*, 372 A.2d 297, 300 (N.J., 1977); 2 MEECHAM, AGENCY § 2297 (2d ed. 1914).

the very soul of lawyering."[122] For example, a lawyer is permitted to reveal client confidences in suing a client to collect the lawyer's fee.[123] Until 2001, however, the ABA has given inadequate importance to the most compelling reason for revealing confidences — to save human life.

[1] The Exception for Saving Human Life

There are two reasons to permit the lawyer to disclose client information in such a case. First, the value at stake, human life, is of unique importance. As the Supreme Court has recognized, death is different and deserves special consideration in our law.[124] Second, the occasions on which a lawyer's disclosure of a client's confidence is the only thing that stands between life and death are so rare that divulgence would pose no threat to the systemic value of lawyer-client trust. (Neither of these is true, of course, with regard to client fraud on third parties.)[125]

Freedman argued for many years, therefore, that a lawyer should be *required* to reveal confidences to the minimum extent necessary to avoid death or serious (*i.e.*, life-threatening) bodily harm.[126] Some years ago, however, he modified that position to favor *permitted* disclosure in such cases.[127] One case that persuaded him to change his view is where the lawyer learns that her client has agreed with a loved one who is terminally ill and in great pain to assist that person to commit suicide.[128]

Freedman has raised three objections to both DR 4-101(C)(3) and to MR 1.6(b)(1). Under DR 4-101(C)(3), a lawyer is permitted to reveal confidences or secrets relating to "[t]he intention of his client to commit a crime and the information necessary to prevent the crime." Under MR 1.6(b)(1), a lawyer was similarly permitted to reveal information relating to the representation "to prevent the client from committing a criminal act that the lawyer believes is likely to result in imminent death or substantial bodily harm." Under both these provisions, therefore, the lawyer is forbidden to reveal information to

---

[122] *Fred Weber, Inc. v. Shell Oil Co.*, 566 F.2d 602, 607 (1977).

[123] MR 1.6(b)(2); DR 4-101(C)(4).

[124] *California v. Ramos*, 463 U.S. 992, 998–999, 103 S.Ct. 3446, 3452 (1983): *see also*, *Atkins v. Virginia*, 2002 Lexis 4648 (holding that executing the mentally retarded violates the Eighth Amendment).

[125] This is why we disagree with RESTATEMENT § 67(1), which permits a lawyer to disclose confidential client information to prevent a client's crime or fraud that involves the lawyer's services and that threatens substantial financial loss, and with § 67(2), which permits the lawyer to disclose information to "prevent, rectify, or mitigate the loss" if the crime or fraud has already occurred.

[126] *See, e.g.*, Monroe Freedman, *Lawyer-Client Confidences Under the A.B.A. Model Rules: Ethical Rules Without Ethical Reason*, CRIM. JUST. ETHICS 3 (1984); Freedman, *Are There Public Interest Limits on Lawyers' Advocacy?* II Soc. RESP. 31, 36 (1976), *reprinted*, 2 J. LEGAL PROF. 47 (1977). *See also* M. FREEDMAN, LAWYERS' ETHICS IN AN ADVERSARY SYSTEM 6 (1975).

[127] Monroe Freedman, *The Life-Saving Exception to Confidentiality: Restating the Law Without the Was, the Will Be, or the Ought to Be*, 29 LOYOLA (L.A.) L. REV. 19 (1996).

[128] *See also* Michael K. McChrystal, *Lawyers and Loyalty*, 33 WM. & MARY L. REV. 367, 388 (1992) (suggesting a case where, to prevent a death, the lawyer must put her client's life at risk, *e.g.*, the client is an undercover police officer): "[E]ven the most clear-cut moral priorities can lose their force in unanticipated and extraordinary circumstances."

save life unless (1) the *client* is going to (2) commit an *act in the future* that is (3) *a crime*.[129]

Consider, for example, *Spaulding v. Zimmerman*.[130] The case began as a personal injury action arising from an automobile accident. When the defendant's medical expert examined the plaintiff, the doctor discovered that the plaintiff had a life-threatening aortic aneurysm which probably had been caused by the accident. The plaintiff was unaware of his condition, the defense lawyer did not tell him that he was in imminent danger of dying, and the case was settled for $6,500.[131] Under a rule that permits divulgence only when death would result from a client's criminal conduct, the lawyer would be forbidden to inform the plaintiff of his condition. The client is committing no act, and remaining silent is not a crime. The same would be true in the case in which a client confesses to his lawyer that he has committed the crime for which an innocent person is about to be executed.[132]

Also, DR 4-101(C)(3) permits the lawyer to reveal a client's confidence or secret to save a life only if it is *the client* who is going to commit the crime. Thus, the rule is so badly drafted that, if the client informed the lawyer that someone else is going to commit a murder, the lawyer would be forbidden to prevent it.[133]

A further objection to MR 1.6(b) is that the threat of death must be "imminent." This should be understood to mean that the lawyer could reveal the necessary information if death is reasonably likely to result in the foreseeable future unless the lawyer takes action. It has been contended, however, that the lawyer would be forbidden to say anything unless death was likely to occur right away. Under that view, if a corporate client was marketing jumbo jets with defective brakes or cars with exploding gas tanks, the lawyer would be forbidden to take action because the harm, though inevitable, might not occur for a significant period of time.

After repeated and lengthy debates in the American Law Institute, Freedman was successful in sponsoring what became § 66(1) of the Restatement of the Law Governing Lawyers.[134] That section allows a lawyer to use or disclose confidential client information when the lawyer "reasonably believes that its use or disclosure is necessary to prevent reasonably certain death or serious bodily harm to a person." Thereafter, in the summer of 2001, the ABA

---

[129] An additional objection to DR 4-101(C)(3) is that it lumps all crimes in the same category — hiding a bomb in a train station, set to go off at rush hour, is treated no differently from opening a shop in violation of Sunday closing laws.

[130] 116 N.W.2d 704 (Minn.1962).

[131] The court in *Spaulding v. Zimmerman* held that the lawyer had done nothing unethical, and Luban erroneously presumes that Freedman's position favors that result. DAVID LUBAN, LAWYERS AND JUSTICE 150 (1988).

[132] After the execution of the innocent person, however, if the client were prosecuted for complicity in the murder, and the lawyer knew that the client had testified falsely to deny involvement, MR 3.3(a)(4) would require the lawyer to reveal the perjury.

[133] This case presents another reason, however, for making disclosure permissive rather than mandatory. Disclosing the information necessary to save the life of a third party could put the *client's* life at serious risk from the murderer.

[134] *See* Monroe Freedman, *The Life-Saving Exception to Confidentiality: Restating the Law Without the Was, the Will Be, or the Ought to Be*, 29 LOYOLA (L.A.) L. REV. 19 (1996).

voted similarly to amend MR 1.6 to allow lawyers to reveal client information "to the extent the lawyer reasonably believes necessary . . . to prevent reasonably certain death or substantial bodily harm."

Smith disagrees with Freedman on this issue, preferring a strict principle that client secrets and confidences are sacrosanct and lawyers should not divulge them under any circumstances. Smith believes that in the rare case where it is truly necessary to disclose information obtained through the lawyer-client relationship (to stop the wrong person from being executed, to prevent premeditated murder, to prevent mayhem), a lawyer will do so not-withstanding the principle, and that the lawyer will not be disciplined for it. Smith believes it is more important to maintain and preserve the principle of confidentiality — no matter how difficult the circumstance — than it is to affirm individual lawyer morality.[135]

Smith also worries that lawyers will be more likely to use or disclose a client's confidential information to prevent "reasonably certain death or serious bodily harm" when the client is an indigent accused of crime — or an indigent who threatens to commit crime[136] — than any other client. Hence, there will be an even greater divide between the kind of legal services — and loyalty — provided to some clients than that provided to others.[137]

[2] The Exception for Preventing Perjury

Freedman and Smith agree, however, that the ABA makes an irrational distinction between preventing death and preventing perjury. Disclosing confidences to save life is a permitted exception, and the Model Rules take pains to caution the lawyer about exercising that discretion: "It is very difficult for a lawyer to 'know' when such a heinous purpose will actually be carried out, for the client may have a change of mind."[138] The drafters of the Model Rules showed no such restraint, however, regarding disclosure of client perjury (a subject that will be discussed at length in the next chapter). Under MR 3.3(a)(4), a lawyer is required (not just permitted) to reveal a client's confidences if necessary to prevent perjury or to correct materially false evidence that the lawyer has offered.

---

[135] Freedman believes that if lawyers will act that way in those rare cases, and if their actions will be condoned by disciplinary authorities, then the rules should comport with reality. It does not promote respect for law to promulgate rules with no expectation of either obedience or enforcement.

[136] *See Purcell v. District Attorney for the Suffolk District,* 676 N.E.2d 436 (1997). A legal services lawyer advised the police that his client planned to burn down an apartment building. The police were able to prevent the crime, saving the lives of the people in the building. The Supreme Judicial Court approved the lawyer's conduct, but ruled that the prosecutor could not call the lawyer as a witness against the client in the attempted arson case. Freedman considers this to be the right result in both respects. Nevertheless, he shares Smith's concern that lawyer's will exercise their discretion to save life more frequently when the clients are indigent.

[137] Smith worries as well that there will be spillover from lawyers who too readily disclose client information in the name of third parties. There is already a prevalent view among indigent defendants that court-appointed lawyers are not to be trusted, that they don't care about their clients. Poor clients will soon stop disclosing information to lawyers altogether — and perhaps they would be wise to do so.

[138] Comment to MR 1.6.

[3] The Exception for Collecting the Lawyer's Fee

Two other exceptions in the Model Rules are given lesser status than preventing perjury (lawyer is *required* to disclose) but are put on the same level as saving life (lawyer is *permitted* to disclose). One of these, carried over from the Model Code,[139] permits the lawyer to divulge client confidences in order to collect the lawyer's fee.[140] This, of course, is sanction for blackmail, and Freedman has actually seen a letter from a lawyer warning a client that if the client made it necessary for the lawyer to sue for his fee, the client's "questionable tax practices" would be exposed.

[4] The Exception for Establishing a Defense Against Charges and Claims

Another exception carried over from the Model Code[141] permits the lawyer to reveal information necessary "to establish a defense to a criminal charge or civil claim against the lawyer based upon conduct in which the client was involved, or to respond to allegations in any proceeding concerning the lawyer's representation of the client."[142] It is reasonable to permit the lawyer to protect herself against accusations of wrongdoing. By analogy to the privilege against self-incrimination, it is too much to demand self-destruction by remaining silent in the face of false accusations.[143] However, the rule should be understood to take effect only when charges have been instituted against the lawyer in a proceeding (as indicated by the phrases "establish a defense" and "in any proceeding").

Here again, however, the comment to the rule goes further than the rule itself:

> The lawyer's right to respond arises when an assertion of such complicity has been made. Paragraph (b)(2) does not require the lawyer to await the commencement of an action or proceeding that charges such complicity, so that the defense may be established by responding directly to a third party who has made such an assertion.

If that comment were allowed to change the plain meaning of the rule, a lawyer could ethically reveal incriminating client confidences in response to an "assertion" by a prosecutor or a reporter.

[5] The Exception for Obeying the Law or a Court Order

Another exception of some importance was left unclear in the Model Rules. What is a lawyer's obligation when a law or a court order requires the lawyer to reveal a client's confidence or secret? The Model Code provision on this point

---

[139] DR 4-101(C)(4).

[140] MR 1.6(b)(2).

[141] DR 4-101(C)(4).

[142] MR 1.6(b)(4).

[143] However, although the lawyer is not required to be heroic by remaining silent, she is permitted to do so.

is our favorite among ethical rules. Under DR 4-101(C)(2) a lawyer is ethically *permitted* to reveal a client's confidence or secret if she is *required* to do so by law or court order. That is, the lawyer who is facing conviction and a jail sentence for contempt of court is permitted to obey the court and reveal the client's confidence, but if she prefers to be heroic and protect the client, she will not face professional discipline for defying the court to protect her client. [144]

The Model Rules originally confused the issue. MR 1.6 had no exception either permitting or requiring disclosure of client information to comply with law or a court order. Nevertheless, the comment to MR 1.6(a), in contradiction to the rule, said that "the lawyer *must comply* with the final orders of a court or other tribunal of competent jurisdiction requiring the lawyer to give information about the client." Once again, the Model Rules' rule of construction would seem to preclude such a reading. As stated in the Scope note, the comments "provide guidance" but they do not "add obligations to the Rules," which are "authoritative." [145] Consistent with this criticism, the ABA in 2002 added what is now MR 1.6(b)(6), permitting the lawyer to reveal confidences to comply with law or a court order, and eliminating the mandatory comment. However, many jurisdictions have not yet adopted this amendment, leaving the problem unresolved.

[6] The Exception for Revealing Harmful Legal Authority

One other issue is worth noting, particularly in view of the serious inconsistencies we have seen between some important rules and the related comments in the Model Rules. In at least one of those instances — the "wave the red flag" comment to MR 1.6 — there was an admittedly disingenuous attempt to materially change the rule. In the other instances, we do not know whether the inconsistencies were disingenuous or were simply the result of sloppy drafting. With regard to the issue to which we turn now, the comment is consistent with the rule; however, the Reporter for the Model Rules, Professor Hazard, has published an interpretation of the rule that would, in effect, rewrite it to comport with a rejected version in the Kutak Commission's Discussion Draft of 1980.

What is the lawyer's obligation if her research discloses a case, statute, or rule that is harmful to her client's position, and that the other side has failed

---

[144] *See* Monroe Freedman, *Your Client or Your Freedom*, LEGAL TIMES, Jan. 14, 1991(discussing the case of attorney Linda Bakiel, who went to prison for several months for refusing to give incriminating information to a grand jury about her client).

[145] Another possibility is to read MR 3.4(c) as overriding MR 1.6. However, MR 3.4 is limited in its scope to "Fairness to Opposing Party and Counsel." Also, four other rules are cross-referenced in the comment to MR 1.6 as possibly superseding confidentiality, but MR 3.4 is not mentioned in that regard. In addition, the comment to MR 1.6 says that "a presumption should exist against . . . supersession" of MR 1.6 by other rules.

Yet another resolution of the difficulty would be to give an expansive reading to MR 1.6(b)(2), which says that the lawyer may reveal information to establish a defense to a criminal charge or a civil claim against the lawyer based upon conduct in which the client was involved. However, that reading goes beyond the text of MR 1.6(b)(2) as well as its history and its comment.

to cite?[146] For the most part, the question is academic because, before any ethical issue is reached, tactical reasons will almost always impel the advocate to cite the authority and to respond to it. The alternative is to risk discovery of the authority by the judge, with no chance for the advocate to be heard as to why it is distinguishable or wrong. Nevertheless, the issue unquestionably arises.[147]

The test established by ABA Opinion 280 in 1957 was whether the uncited authority was one "which the court should obviously consider in deciding the case." In DR 7-106(B)(1) of the Model Code, however, the ABA adopted a significantly different standard, requiring the lawyer to disclose "[l]egal authority in the controlling jurisdiction known to him to be directly adverse to the position of his client."[148] Thus, the standard became subjective and limited to authority that is both "controlling" and "directly" adverse. Not surprisingly, therefore, DR 7-106(B)(1) has rarely been applied.

In its 1980 Discussion Draft, the Kutak Commission proposed a standard similar to that in Opinion 280, requiring disclosure of any authority that "would probably have a substantial effect on the determination of a material issue."[149] That proposal did not survive. Instead, the ABA adopted MR 3.3(a)(3), which tracks DR 7-106(B)(1).[150]

Hazard has acknowledged that DR 7-106(B)(1) has been "rarely operative"[151] — a fact that was known to those who adopted it in MR 3.3(a)(3). Nevertheless, the discussion of MR 3.3(a)(3) in Hazard & Hodes' treatise on the Model Rules begins by saying that "[t]he duty to reveal adverse legal authority . . . is well established."[152] Then, without reference to the fact that a provision similar to that in Opinion 280 ("would be considered important by the judge sitting on the case") had been proposed by the Kutak Commission and rejected by the House of Delegates, the authors conclude by suggesting that MR 3.3(a)(3) be interpreted as if it had used the language of Opinion 280.[153]

---

[146] The issue is debated in Geoffrey Hazard, *Arguing the Law: The Advocate's Duty and Opportunity*, 16 GA. L. REV. 821 (1982), and Monroe Freedman, *Arguing the Law in an Adversary System*, 16 GA. L. REV. 833 (1982). *See also*, Richard Uviller, *Zeal and Frivolity: The Ethical Duty of the Appellate Advocate to Tell the Truth about the Law*, 6 HOFSTRA L. REV. 729 (1977); Roger Miner, *Professional Responsibility in Appellate Practice: A View from the Bench*, 19 PACE L. REV. 323 (1999) (criticizing Freedman's position).

[147] In a survey in the District of Columbia in 1972, ninety-three percent responded that they would not disclose adverse authority that was not cited by opposing counsel. Steve Allen Friedman, *Professional Responsibility in D.C.: A Survey*, 1972 RES IPSA LOQUITUR 60.

[148] DR 7-106((B)(1).

[149] Discussion Draft MR 3.1(c) (1980).

[150] RESTATEMENT § 111(2) does the same.

[151] Hazard, *Arguing the Law, supra* note 146, at 828.

[152] 1 HAZARD & HODES, THE LAW GOVERNING LAWYERS § 29.11 (3d ed., 2001).

[153] *Id.* There is some irony in the fact that the subject of the section is candor about authority adverse to one's position.

§ 5.12   THE ABA'S ETHICAL PROFILE

In the first chapter, we suggested that in writing rules of ethics, we make choices that establish our ethical priorities and thereby create an ethical profile.

On the basis of the ABA's ethical choices in its exceptions to lawyer-client confidentiality in the Model Rules, the ABA's ethical profile is not a flattering one. The ABA's most important value is preventing perjury (lawyer required to disclose client confidences). Next, in order of rank, are defending the lawyer against charges of wrongdoing; collecting the lawyer's fee (lawyer permitted to disclose, with no caveat); protecting third parties from fraud (except fraud by a corporation); and saving human life (lawyer permitted to disclose, but a caveat against doing it).

In addition, we have seen at least one example of a disingenuous comment created for the purpose of changing the meaning of a rule that had been adopted by a substantial majority vote. We have also seen an ethics committee opinion reaching a conclusion that the committee had previously conceded was an impossible interpretation. Further, we have seen what is, at best, some extremely poor drafting of important rules and comments, and, at worst, additional efforts at disingenuous manipulation.

§ 5.13   YOUR OWN ETHICAL PROFILE

Because we take note of cynicism and hypocrisy does not mean that we have to be cynical or hypocritical, and because ideals can be corrupted is not a sufficient reason to reject idealism.

The ideal of lawyer-client trust and confidence has a long and honorable tradition. It remains the "cornerstone of the adversary system and effective assistance of counsel," and fidelity to that trust is, indeed, "the glory of our profession."

As a member of the profession, you will be in a position to help to maintain that ideal.

Chapter 6

THE PERJURY TRILEMMA

Is it ever proper for a criminal defense lawyer to present testimony that she knows is perjurious? Our answer is yes.[1] This chapter explains why and analyzes the alternatives that have been proposed.

§ 6.01 THE MODEL OF INTENTIONAL OR SELECTIVE IGNORANCE

Underlying proposed solutions to the problem of client perjury are two sharply different models of the lawyer-client relationship. The traditional model, as we have seen, is one of trust and confidence between lawyer and client. The client is urged to confide in the lawyer and is encouraged to do so by a pledge of confidentiality.[2]

The other model is referred to in the literature as intentional ignorance (or, sometimes, selective ignorance). That is, the lawyer puts the client on notice that the lawyer would prefer not to know certain kinds of facts and/or that the lawyer can be expected to pass on to the judge or the other party information that the client would prefer to keep confidential. The burden is then on the uncounseled client to speculate about whether to entrust potentially harmful facts to the lawyer — to decide, that is, what is relevant and what is irrelevant, what is incriminating and what is exculpatory. That kind of decision is, of course, uniquely the lawyer's responsibility by virtue of her special training and skills.[3]

---

[1] An overwhelming proportion of trial lawyers agree. *See, e.g.*, Steven Allen Friedman, *Professional Responsibility in D.C.: A Survey*, 1972 RES IPSA LOQUITUR 60. Similar results were reported at the Sixth Annual Judicial Conference of the District of Columbia, held in June, 1981. The conclusion is also confirmed by extensive discussions we have had at innumerable professional meetings around the country.

However, several law professors disagree with this answer. We think it is significant that law professors have made a career choice that removes them from service to clients. A former dean of the Yale Law School has found law professors to be increasingly "less professionally oriented." Harry H. Wellington, *Challenges to Legal Education: The "Two Cultures" Phenomenon*, 37 J. LEGAL EDUC. 327 (1987). Also, a distinguished federal appellate judge has expressed concern that law professors are "indifferent to or hopelessly naive about the problems of legal practice." Harry T. Edwards, *The Role of Legal Education in Shaping the Profession*, 38 J. LEG. EDUC. 285 (1988).

Although the views of lawyers and law professors are relevant, we do not mean to suggest that one's own ethical judgments should be bound by them, ours or anyone else's.

[2] "A client must feel free to discuss anything with his or her lawyer . . . . It is for the lawyer in the exercise of independent professional judgment to separate the relevant and important from the irrelevant and unimportant." EC 4-1; *Upjohn v. U.S.*, 449 U.S. 387, 390–391 (1981).

[3] *See Hickman v. Taylor*, 329 U.S. 495, 511 (1947); *Upjohn v. United States*, 449 U.S. 387, 390–91 (1981). "Even the intelligent and educated layman has small and sometimes no skill in the science of law." *Powell v. Alabama*, 287 U.S. 45, 69, 53 S.Ct. 55, 64 (1932).

The problem for the client is illustrated by a case related by a lawyer who practiced intentional ignorance. The client was accused of stabbing her husband to death with a kitchen knife. In conferences with her lawyer, she consistently denied committing the crime. The facts, however, were damning. The killing had taken place in the couple's kitchen; only her fingerprints were on the knife; she was in the apartment at the time; and she had no other suspect to offer. An investigator informed the lawyer, however, of reports from neighbors that the husband had had a habit of getting drunk and brutalizing his wife. Confronted with this information by her lawyer, the defendant broke down and "confessed." Her husband had been drunk and was about to attack her again. As she backed away, her hand fell upon the knife and, in her terror, she stabbed him.

Why, expostulated the lawyer, had she not volunteered the information to him in the first place? Because, explained his client — who was unsophisticated about the law of self-defense — "it proved I did it."

Apart from the practical problems of requiring clients to do their own lawyering, we might question whether intentional ignorance is a moral resolution of the lawyer's ethical problem. Certainly, lawyers who practice intentional ignorance have the comfort of saying that they have never knowingly presented a client's perjury. On the other hand, by remaining ignorant, these same lawyers have disabled themselves from being in a position to dissuade their clients from committing the perjury. Lawyers can remain aloof from client perjury, but that does not prevent perjury from happening. Indeed, there is good reason to believe that there would be more perjury, not less, if lawyers did not know about it and were not in a position to discourage it.[4]

The ABA has taken a firm position against intentional ignorance, using unusually strong rhetoric in doing so. To advise the client at the outset not to admit anything that might "handicap the lawyer's freedom in calling witnesses or in otherwise making a defense" is "most egregious" and is advocated only by "unscrupulous" lawyers.[5] Intentional ignorance is also disapproved in ABA Formal Opinion 87-353. Nevertheless, as we will see, the ABA appears to have adopted the solution of intentional ignorance in as a solution to client perjury its Model Rules of Professional Conduct.

§ 6.02 THE TRILEMMA

The lawyer's ethical difficulty has been called a trilemma[6] because it derives

---

[4] "[E]xperienced defense lawyers have pointed out time and again, that, permitted to continue to counsel with their criminal clients up to the very hour of the client's proposed testimony, they almost always were successful in persuading the client not to take the stand to testify falsely." Chief Judge James Exum, *The Perjurious Criminal Defendant: A Solution to His Lawyer's Dilemma*, VI Soc. Resp. 16, 20 (1980). "Based upon experience, lawyers know that almost all clients follow the advice given, and the law is upheld." Comment to MR 1.6.

[5] ABA Standards Relating to the Defense Function, Commentary to sec. 3.2 (1971); *see also* ABA Standards Relating to the Defense Function 4-3.2(b) (1991) (Defense counsel should not . . . intimate to the client in any way that the client should not be candid in revealing facts so as to afford defense counsel free rein to take action which would be precluded by counsel's knowing of such facts.").

[6] *See* Monroe H. Freedman, *Professional Responsibility of the Criminal Defense Lawyer: The Three Hardest Questions*, 64 Mich. L. Rev. 1469 (1966).

from three obligations. First, in order to give clients the effective assistance of counsel to which they are entitled, lawyers are required to seek out all relevant facts.[7] Second, in order to encourage clients to entrust their lawyers with embarrassing or possibly harmful information, lawyers are under a duty of confidentiality with regard to information obtained in professional relationships.[8] Third, lawyers are expected to be candid with the court.[9]

A moment's reflection makes it clear, however, that a lawyer cannot do all of those things — know everything, keep it in confidence, and reveal it to the court over the client's objections. To resolve this trilemma, therefore, one of the three duties must give way.

If we forgo the first duty (seeking all relevant information), we would be adopting the model of intentional ignorance. If we sacrifice the second duty (maintaining confidentiality), clients would quickly learn that their lawyers could not be trusted and would withhold damaging information; again, the result is intentional ignorance. Only by limiting the third duty — by allowing lawyers to be less than candid with the court when necessary to protect clients' confidences — can we maintain the traditional lawyer-client model.

§ 6.03 FOCUSING ON THE INITIAL INTERVIEW

The critical focus of our concern in resolving the problem of client perjury is the initial interview with the client. That is, depending upon how the lawyer resolves the trilemma, she will act upon that decision at the outset of the relationship. In order to minimize the importance of the issue of how to deal with client perjury, it is sometimes said that the problem arises in relatively few cases. Regardless of whether that is true, however, every case involves an initial interview. Thus, every case requires the lawyer to decide which model of the lawyer-client relationship she will adopt.

Under the traditional model, she will impress upon her client how important it is that she know everything, and she will assure the client of confidentiality. On the other hand, under the model of intentional ignorance, she will, in one form or another, give the client a "lawyer-client Miranda warning."[10]

Obviously, such a warning is going to impede, if not wholly frustrate, the already difficult task of establishing a relationship of trust and confidence with the client. This problem is particularly acute for the public defender or court-appointed lawyer, who typically meets her client for the first time in jail. The defendant has not chosen the lawyer. On the contrary, the lawyer has been sent by the judge and is part of the system that is trying to convict and punish him. It is no easy matter to persuade this client that he can talk freely to his lawyer without fear of prejudice. The question in the client's mind is, "Can I really trust you?" And the client will not be reassured by a lawyer

---

[7] *See* Ch. 5, *supra.*

[8] *Id.*

[9] *See, e.g.,* ABA Canons of Professional Ethics 22 (1908).

[10] Professor Geoffrey Hazard was the first to use the phrase. GEOFFREY C. HAZARD, ETHICS IN THE PRACTICE OF LAW 50 (1978).

who invites full disclosure and at the same time cautions the client about the possible betrayal of his confidences.[11]

However, the reluctance to impart embarrassing or harmful information to one's lawyer is not unique to the indigent client or to the criminal defendant. Randolph Paul observed a similar phenomenon among a wealthier class in a far more congenial atmosphere:

> The tax adviser will sometimes have to dynamite the facts of his case out of the unwilling witnesses on his own side — witnesses who are nervous, witnesses who are confused about their own interest, witnesses who try to be too smart for their own good, and witnesses who subconsciously do not want to understand what has happened despite the fact that they must if they are to testify coherently.[12]

Paul goes on to explain that the truth can be obtained only by persuading the client that it would be a violation of a sacred obligation for the lawyer to reveal a client's confidence.

Perhaps, though, we are being unduly sympathetic towards a client who does not want to reveal his guilt to his lawyer. One might argue that if it is the client's knowing and voluntary choice, it is on his own head. Our response has been given in the previous chapters, particularly in the discussion of the role of the lawyer in fulfilling our society's regard for the dignity of the individual. The lawyer who gives a Miranda warning is not the client's champion against a hostile world; on the contrary, she presents herself at the outset as an agent of that hostile world. As Professor Geoffrey Hazard succinctly put it, "[t]o give the warning is to treat the [client] as a non-client.[13]

Nor is it accurate or fair to characterize the client's choice to withhold information from his lawyer as a knowing and voluntary one. Particularly when the client is alone against that hostile world, he may be frightened and confused — even, as Paul has indicated, unable to comprehend fully what is happening to him. What he needs is the wise counsel of his lawyer based upon the facts as they are, not as he would wish them to be. Until the client has had his lawyer's guidance about the case as it really is, the client is not in a position to make a truly knowing and voluntary choice about what to withhold. Put otherwise, to deprive the client of his right to the "guiding hand of counsel"[14] at the outset of the representation is too heavy a penalty to exact, even against the client who might be trying, without the benefit of counsel, to be "too smart for his own good."

It is true that most people who are formally accused of crimes in our system are guilty. Often, however, they are guilty of a lesser offense than what has been charged.[15] Moreover, sometimes they are innocent despite overwhelming

---

[11] At the Harvard Trial Advocacy Workshop in January, 1989, Professor Andrew Kaufman and Professor Freedman demonstrated client interviews under the two models. Although Federal District Judge William Young indicated that he had serious reservations about Freedman's resolution of the trilemma, he said that he found Kaufman's lawyer-client Miranda warning to be "spooky." (Videotape on file with the authors.)

[12] Randolph Paul, *The Responsibilities of the Tax Adviser*, 63 HARV. L. REV. 377, 383 (1950).

[13] HAZARD, *supra* note 10, at 51.

[14] *Powell v. Alabama*, 287 U.S. 45, 69, 53 S.Ct. 55, 64 (1932).

[15] "Overcharging" is a common practice of many prosecutors as part of the coercive process of plea bargaining.

evidence to the contrary, including their own confessions.[16] We know that innocent people have been sentenced to death, on guilt determined beyond a reasonable doubt.[17]

Particularly in a society that respects the dignity of the individual, it is important to recognize that the frightened and confused client who is given a lawyer-client Miranda warning may well be innocent. As Professor Stephen A. Saltzburg has observed, "Good persons (or persons with good claims) may shrink from the attorney who gives Miranda warnings as quickly as bad persons (or persons with bad claims)."[18] Note too that the lawyer-client Miranda warning must be given before any serious lawyer-client discussions can begin — that is, before the lawyer can possibly make an informed judgment about the client's guilt or innocence.

§ 6.04 A CASE IN POINT

Consider the woman with the kitchen knife, who had been fearful of telling her lawyer facts that she thought incriminating but which were actually exculpatory. In that case, the lawyer discovered the information through other sources, but that is not ordinarily likely or even feasible. Consider also the following case, in which an innocent client proposes to commit perjury.

Your client has been erroneously accused of a robbery committed at 16th and P Streets at 11:00 p.m. He tells you at first that at no time on the evening of the crime was he within six blocks of that location. You are able to persuade him, though, that he must tell you the truth and that doing so will in no way prejudice him. He then reveals to you that he was at 15th and P Streets, one block away from the scene of the crime, at 10:55 that evening; however, he was going east, away from the scene of the crime, and by 11:00 p.m. he was six blocks away.

There are two prosecution witnesses. The first mistakenly, but with some degree of persuasion, identifies your client as the criminal. The second witness is an elderly woman who is somewhat nervous and wears glasses. She testifies truthfully and accurately that she saw your client at 15th and P Streets at 10:55 p.m. She has corroborated the erroneous testimony of the first witness and made conviction seem virtually certain. On cross-examination, however, you are able to show that she is easily confused and has poor eyesight.[19] At that point, the prosecution's case rests, in effect, on the first witness, and your successful cross-examination of the second witness may have cast doubt on the prosecution's entire case.

---

[16] *See, e.g., Brown v. Mississippi*, 297 U.S. 278 (1936), and the Scottsboro cases, *Weem v. State*, 224 Ala. 524, 141 So. 215 (1932); *Patterson v. State*, 224 Ala. 531, 141 So. 195 (1932); *Powell v. State*, 224 Ala. 540, 141 So. 201 (1932).

[17] JIM DWYER, PETER NEUFELD, BARRY SCHECK, ACTUAL INNOCENCE: FIVE DAYS TO EXECUTION AND OTHER DISPATCHES FROM THE WRONGLY CONVICTED (2000); Hugo Bedau & Michael Radelet, *Miscarriages of Justice in Potentially Capital Cases*, 40 STAN. L. REV. 21 (1987).

[18] Stephen A. Saltzburg, *Privileges and Professionals: Lawyers and Psychiatrists*, 66 VA. L. REV. 597, 608 (1980).

[19] With regard to the question of whether the lawyer should cross-examine a witness she knows to be testifying truthfully and accurately, in order to make the witness appear to be mistaken or lying, *see* Chapter 8, *infra*.

Your client insists upon testifying, which is his right as a matter of due process. [20] He believes that he is more likely to be found not guilty if he takes the stand to testify, truthfully, that he is innocent of the crime, and he also wants to tell the jury, truthfully, where he was at 11:00 p.m. [21] However, he is convinced that he cannot afford to admit that the second prosecution witness correctly placed him one block from the scene of the crime at 10:55 p.m., because that would rehabilitate both the elderly witness and the prosecution's case against him. You try to dissuade him from testifying perjuriously, but he is adamant. What should you do?

§ 6.05   THE WITHDRAWAL SOLUTIONS

The most obvious way to avoid the ethical difficulty appears to be withdrawal from the case, if that can be done without prejudice to the client. The client will then find another lawyer and will probably withhold the incriminating information from her. In systemic terms, withdrawal under such circumstances is difficult to defend, since the new lawyer will be in no position to attempt to dissuade the client from presenting it. Only the original attorney, who knows the truth, has that opportunity, but she loses it in the very act of evading the ethical problem. [22] For that reason, we would not require the lawyer to withdraw as long as there is opportunity to dissuade the client.

Moreover, the lawyer should be forbidden to withdraw if doing so would prejudice the client in any way. Prejudice cannot ordinarily be avoided if the case is near to trial or the trial has begun. Replacing the lawyer in those circumstances will delay the calendar, a major concern of all judges and the overriding concern of too many. The court will require the lawyer to give

---

[20] *Rock v. Arkansas*, 483 U.S. 44, 107 S.Ct. 2704 (1987). *But see Nix v. Whiteside*, 475 U.S. 157, 173 (1980): "Whatever the scope of a constitutional right to testify, it is elementary that such a right does not extend to testifying falsely." The Court did not explain, however, whether this means that the defendant can be restrained from testifying if he insists upon doing so, or simply that there is no "right" to commit perjury in the sense that the defendant can be subjected to sanctions like an enhanced sentence or prosecution for perjury. *United States v. Henkel*, 799 F.2d 369 (7th Cir. 1986) takes the former view. *But cf. New Jersey v. Portash*, 440 U.S. 450 (1979) (prosecutor cannot expose defendant's perjury in violation of his privilege against self-incrimination).

[21] The client's assessment is correct. Cases have been won when the defendant has not testified (O.J. Simpson's case is a dramatic example), but they are a small minority.

> "In 99 percent . . . of all the criminal cases tried in the eighty-six judicial districts of the federal level [in 1956] defendants who did not take the stand were convicted by juries. . . . The fact of the matter is that a defendant who does not take the stand does not in reality enjoy any longer the presumption of innocence."

Edward Bennett Williams, *The Trial of a Criminal Case*, 29 N.Y. ST. BAR J. 36, 42 (1957), quoted in *State v. Albright*, 291 N.W.2d 487, 492 n.7 (Wis. 1980). Moreover, this is not one of those cases in which there are strong reasons for the defendant not to testify, such as impeachment with prior convictions.

[22] In Judge Exum's words:

> [Withdrawal represents] the disengagement of the profession from the problem of perjury at the expense of the profession's duty to do what it can to prevent the perjury from occurring. It tends to negate the importance of the lawyer's role as counselor and advisor.

Exum, *supra* note 4, at 16, 19.

extraordinary reasons for withdrawal, which would require the lawyer to reveal to the judge that the client intends to commit perjury. In addition, the new lawyer might well face the same problem. Indeed, the client might force disqualification of a series of lawyers in the same way, ultimately forcing the judge to try the case without a defense lawyer. That is likely to be an awkward and unsatisfactory procedure.

In most cases, therefore, the attorney can withdraw only by revealing the client's confidences to the judge — that is, by telling the judge that the client has admitted incriminating evidence to the lawyer and intends to try to lie his way out of it.[23] Since the judge will be imposing sentence on the client in the event of a conviction, the prejudice to the client would be severe. The same kind of prejudice might also affect the defendant's appeal.[24]

Even when the lawyer reveals the client's intended perjury to the judge, the motion to withdraw is likely to be denied. Again, the judge can anticipate a series of such motions. A common judicial response, therefore, is to tell the lawyer, "I understand your problem, but the next lawyer might have the same difficulty. You'll just have to go forward as best you can."

This has led to a sophisticated (or disingenuous) variation on withdrawal that is particularly unsatisfactory. The lawyer, well aware that her motion for leave to withdraw "for ethical reasons" will be denied, makes it anyway.[25]

---

[23] One convention for doing this is for the lawyer to tell the judge that she has "an ethical problem." Another is to say, "My client and I do not see eye to eye." Regardless of the formula, judges have no difficulty in understanding the lawyers to be saying that the client is insisting upon committing perjury.

In *Lowery v. Cardwell*, 575 F.2d 727 (9th Cir. 1978), for example, the lawyer said simply, "I cannot state the reason." 575 F.2d at 729. The Ninth Circuit recognized this to be an "unequivocal announcement" of the defendant's perjury. 575 F.2d at 730. *See also United States v. Henkel*, 799 F.2d 369 (7th Cir.1986) (Court inferred client perjury when the defense lawyer said simply that he could not "professionally . . . proceed." *Id.* at 370.); *People v. Johnson*, 62 Cal. App. 4th 608, 72 Cal. Rptr.2d 805 (1998) (Lawyer said he had an "ethical conflict," and the court was unable to hypothesize any other ethical conflict than perjury by the client. *Id.* at n. 6.)

[24] *See Holmes v. United States*, 370 F.2d 209, (D.C. Cir., 1966). A majority voted to remand the case to determine whether the defendant had been denied certain due process rights. One judge dissented, however, expressly basing his opinion in part on incriminating information that had been put into the record by the defendant's own lawyer.

> Finding the Holmes testimony at variance from the opening statement made by his trial attorney, the latter in the absence of the jury addressed the court: "For purposes of the record, Your Honor, about half of what the defendant said on the stand was a complete surprise to me." [continued]
>
> He added that in the course of "numerous interviews" the appellant had "consistently told me" a different story. The attorney asked Holmes no further questions.
>
> *From the foregoing, some idea can be gleaned as to why I do not join my colleagues in thinking there even possibly could have been "prejudice."*

370 F.2d at 212 (emphasis added).

[25] As Judge Exum has noted:

> The truth, of course, is that almost all judges know why counsel makes such a motion immediately upon being advised that counsel cannot reveal the reason, or that the reason is because of "ethical conflicts" which have arisen between lawyer and client. . . . Nevertheless the motion is generally denied.

Exum, *supra* note 4, at 16, 19.

Then, having attempted to protect herself from charges of complicity in her client's perjury,[26] she can elicit the client's perjury and argue it to the jury. She has protected herself, however, by engaging in a charade that betrays the client.[27] Again, when it comes time for sentencing and appeal, the judges will know from the defendant's own lawyer that he has committed perjury.

We agree, therefore, with Professor Norman Lefstein that "withdrawal from a defendant's case should never be viewed as a solution to the perjury dilemma."[28]

§ 6.06   TESTIFYING IN NARRATIVE — THE 7.7 SOLUTION

Another effort to deal with the trilemma first appeared as a proposal in Section 7.7 of the 1971 version of the ABA Standards Relating to the Defense Function. Under this "narrative" solution, the lawyer is required to "confine his examination to identifying the witness as the defendant and permitting him to make his statement." (Sometimes this is referred to, oxymoronically, as "passive representation.") That is, the lawyer has the client present his testimony in narrative form, rather than in the normal question-and-answer format. Then, in closing argument, the lawyer is to make no reference to what the lawyer has learned from the client to be false testimony.

Beyond any question, this procedure divulges the client's confidences. The judge is certain to understand what is going on, and it is generally agreed that the jury usually will as well.[29] Even if the jury does not realize the significance of the unusual manner in which the defendant is testifying, the jury is sure to catch on when the defense lawyer in closing argument makes no reference to the defendant's exculpatory testimony.

Ironically, Freedman originally argued that the narrative solution would never work, because prosecutors would object to the presentation of the defendant's testimony in narrative form.[30] That objection is virtually always sustained, because it deprives the adversary of the opportunity to object when a question is asked rather than after the jury has already heard the testimony. Freedman was, of course, wrong. Neither of us has ever heard of a case in which the prosecutor objected to a defense lawyer's asking a defendant to testify in narrative. Why should the prosecutor object, when the defendant's

---

[26] It is entirely possible, of course, that a lawyer who disingenuously moves for leave to withdraw has nevertheless prompted the client to commit perjury.

[27] See notes 23–25, supra.

[28] Norman Lefstein, Client Perjury in Criminal Cases: Still in Search of an Answer, 1 Geo. J. Legal Ethics 521, 525 (1988). Lefstein was the Director of the Public Defender Service in Washington, D.C., and chaired the ABA Criminal Justice Standards Committee.

[29] See, e.g., State v. Robinson, 290 N.C. 56, 224 S.E.2d 174 (1976). Juries would become increasingly aware of the significance of narrative testimony if it were to become institutionalized. Among other things, it would provide some dramatic material for television and movie treatment, and the public would not long remain ignorant of the reason for the lawyer's unusual conduct. For example, the popular television show, The Practice, has dramatized the narrative solution in an episode involving client perjury.

[30] Monroe Freedman, Lawyers' Ethics in an Adversary System 37 (1975).

own lawyer is signaling to everyone in the courtroom that the defendant is guilty and trying to lie his way out of it?

The narrative solution was never approved by the ABA, which deleted it from the Standards in 1979, with a reference to the emerging Model Rules. Then, in 1983, the Model Rules rejected it, explaining that it "compromises both contending principles; it exempts the lawyer from the duty to disclose false evidence but subjects the client to an implicit disclosure of information imparted to counsel." Also, Chief Justice Burger, who was its principal supporter, repudiated the narrative solution in *Nix v. Whiteside*. [31]

Nevertheless, the narrative solution still has its advocates, [32] and it has been adopted as part of Rule 3.3 in Massachusetts and in the District of Columbia. [33] Also, some courts have approved its use in decisions. A New York case, *People v. DePallo*, [34] is particularly shocking because of the lengths to which the defense lawyer went to betray his client. [35] In *DePallo*, the defense lawyer took four steps regarding his client's testimony. First, early in the trial, the lawyer informed the judge at a sidebar that "the defendant was going to take the witness stand, and that he had previously told me he was involved in this homicide . . . . " [36] The defendant's lawyer also told the judge that he had told the defendant that "he did not have to testify and should not testify, but if he did, he should do so truthfully." [37] Second, counsel had the defendant testify in narrative form. Third, after the defendant had testified, defense counsel told the judge in chambers — without the defendant present — that his client "never told me what he was going to say, but I knew it was not going to be the truth, at least to the extent of him denying participation." [38] Fourth,

---

[31] 475 U.S. 157, 170, n.6, 106 S.Ct. 988, 996 n.6 (1986). The Chief Justice chaired the committee that originally drafted section 7.7, and he wrote approving *dicta* about it in Supreme Court opinions. *See, e.g., United States v. Grayson*, 438 U.S. 41, 54 (1978). These *dicta* are not referred to in *Nix*.

[32] The most eloquent is Lefstein, *supra* note 28.

[33] In the District of Columbia, this was done by the Court of Appeals despite the fact that both the Jordan Committee, which drafted the District's version of the Model rules, and the D.C. Bar's Board of Governors, favored "a rule similar to that advocated by Professor Freedman." D.C. Bar Legal Ethics Comm., Opin. 234 (1993).

[34] 96 N.Y.2d 437, 754 N.E.2d 751, 729 N.Y.S.2d 649 (2001).

[35] During voir dire, the lawyer questioned his client to show the judge that the client was insisting on going to trial against the advice of the lawyer:

Q: MR. LAMATTINA: Mr. DePallo, is it true that I told you . . . that I think we should take a plea?

A: THE DEFENDANT: Yeah.

Q: MR LAMATTINA: You don't wish to take a plea?

A: THE DEFENDANT: No.

Q: MR. LAMATTINA: I just wanted to place that on the record.

A lawyer who takes cases to trial is not likely to be appointed to represent indigent defendants. The apparent purpose of this interrogation, therefore, was to make it clear to the judge that the lawyer, who was court-appointed, was not responsible for the case being tried and thereby delaying the court's calendar.

[36] 96 N.Y.2d at 439, 754 N.E.2d at 752, 729 N.Y.S.2d at 650.

[37] *Id.*

[38] *Id.* at 440, 752–753, 650.

in summing up the evidence in the case in his closing argument for the defense, counsel did not refer to the defendant's own testimony.

Thus, even if the jury had missed the significance of counsel's distancing himself from the defendant during the defendant's testimony, counsel's failure to argue the defendant's testimony clearly signaled that he believed his client to be guilty. In addition, counsel expressly informed the judge, who was later to sentence his client, that the client had been involved in the homicide and that he had compounded his crime by committing perjury.[39] Moreover, the communications to the judge were made without the defendant present, thereby denying the defendant his constitutional right to confront the chief witness against him — his own lawyer.[40] In its unanimous opinion affirming the conviction, the New York Court of Appeals held that defense counsel's multiple betrayals of his client had been "professionally responsible and acceptable."[41]

Since *DePallo*, New York courts have attempted to narrow its scope.[42] Nevertheless, the addition of New York to jurisdictions permitting the narrative

---

[39] The legal fiction is that judges are not improperly influenced by being told incriminating information about the defendant by defense counsel. Occasionally, however, the prejudicial effect is revealed. Here, for example, is how one judge showed at sentencing how defense counsel had prejudiced her client:

> How do I know that [you committed perjury]? It's hardly presumptuous on my part when your own attorney had to come to me in camera and inform me that she didn't want to stay on your case anymore as a matter of ethics because you perjured yourself and she knew you were perjuring yourself.

People v. Darrett, 2003 N.Y. App.Div. LEXIS 12935 at *15–16.

[40] The court did not consider the defendant's constitutional right to confront witnesses against him, nor did it address the privilege against self-incrimination, discussed *infra*, §§ 6.17–6.19. The court stated that the defendant had properly been excluded from participation in the session in chambers, on the ground that defense counsel's incriminating statements to the judge had been "simply procedural" and related to "counsel's professional ethical obligations" — as if the substance of it were not the defendant's alleged admission of guilt. Indeed, the court presumed that the defendant could have had no "meaningful input" regarding the accusations against him by his lawyer. *But see* n. 35, *supra*, indicating that the lawyer's only concern was not his client, but ingratiating himself with the judge to assure future appointments.

[41] *People v. DePallo*, 96 N.Y.2d at 441, 754 N.E.2d at 753,729 N.Y.S.2d at 651, *quoting* dictum in *Nix v. Whiteside*, 475 U.S. 157, 170 (1986). Ironically, *Nix* expressly repudiated the narrative solution on the same page. *See* n. 31, *supra*.

[42] *See, e.g.*: *People v. Berroa*, 99 N.Y.2d 134, 782 N.E.2d 1148, 753 N.Y.S.2d 12 (2002) (Defense counsel stipulated that defendant and two witnesses had not raised alibi defense in interviews with her, and directed jury's attention to her stipulation in closing argument, suggesting that jury could disregard the alibi testimony. New trial ordered because "defense counsel's credibility was directly and necessarily pitted against that of the defense witnesses." At 142, 1154, 18. *See also, People v. Darrett*, 2003 N.Y. App.Div. LEXIS 12935 (Suggesting ways to mitigate acknowledged prejudice in narrative solution); *DePallo v. Burge*, 2003 WL 22946152 (E.D.N.Y.) (criticizing exclusion of defendant from conference between lawyer and judge where lawyer accused client of perjury); *People v. Lewis*, 2004 WL 728245 (NY) (Sixth Amendment violated where defense attorney "undermined the defendants other witnesses").

One benefit to the defendant to be present at a conference with the judge in which the lawyer incriminates the client, is that the client might then elect to proceed pro se, rather than go forward with a "champion" who is going to sabotage his defense in closing argument. This kind of prejudice is illustrated in *People v. Gomez*, 761 N.Y.S.2d 156 (App.Div. 1st Dept., 2003), where the defendant testified to an alibi, but his lawyer argued an intoxication defense. The defendant's inevitable conviction was upheld.

solution is a dismaying development for indigent defendants. This is so because in virtually every case in which lawyers have revealed perjury, through the narrative solution or otherwise, the defendants have been poor and members of minority groups. This has produced a "race and class based double standard" that raises serious questions of denial of equal protection of the laws.[43] As Professor Deborah Rhode has said in a related context, "rich clients get richer while the poor get moral oversight."[44]

§ 6.07 KNOWING WHILE NOT KNOWING — THE ROY COHN SOLUTION

If intentionally remaining ignorant precludes effective representation, and knowing the truth presents an insoluble dilemma, why not choose a solution that avoids both evils? Speaking before a bar group, Roy Cohn gave his method for dealing with the guilty client who wants to commit perjury:

> Before a client could get three words out, any lawyer with half a brain would say, "You probably don't know whether you're guilty or not, because you don't know the elements of the crime you're charged with.
>
> [Then, to avoid hearing what I'm not supposed to hear, I ask the client:] "If someone was going to get up on the stand and lie about you, who would it be? And what would they lie about?" And if the client's got any brains, he'll know what I'm talking about.[45]

Under Cohn's solution, therefore, the lawyer has it both ways. For tactical purposes, he knows what he has to know. For purposes of any ethical obligation, however, he does not know either that the client is guilty or that the client is going to commit perjury when he denies the "lies" about him. Thus, the lawyer in Cohn's scenario would not attempt to dissuade the client from committing perjury (except perhaps for tactical reasons) because the lawyer does not "know" about it.

The knot of the perjury trilemma, therefore, like that of Gordius, is simply severed rather than untied. You might question, though, whether the Cohn solution — knowing enough for tactical purposes but not enough for ethical purposes — can properly be called an ethical one.

§ 6.08 MAINTAINING THE TRADITIONAL LAWYER-CLIENT MODEL

There is only one method of anticipating and dealing with client perjury that will maintain the traditional model of lawyer-client trust and confidence, protect the fundamental rights to which that relationship gives expression, and put lawyers in a position to dissuade the client from committing perjury.[46]

---

[43] See Silver, *Truth, Justice, and the American Way: The Case Against Client Perjury Rules*, 47 VAND. L. REV. 339, 358 (1994).

[44] Rhode, *Why the ABA Bothers: A Functional Perspective on Professional Codes*, 59 TEX. L. REV. 689, 713 (1981).

[45] David Berreby, *The Cohn/Dershowitz Debate*, NATL. L. J., June 7, 1982, at 15.

[46] See Chapters 2, 3, and 5 *supra*, which explain the adversary system, client autonomy, and lawyer-client trust and confidence.

At the initial client interview, the lawyer impresses upon the client that it is essential that the lawyer know everything there is to know about the client's case. The lawyer also explains to the client that she will maintain the client's confidences and secrets in strict confidence.

If the lawyer learns that the client is contemplating perjury, she should make continuing, good faith efforts to dissuade the client from that course. The lawyer is permitted to withdraw, as long as withdrawal would not prejudice the client; it is preferable, however, that the lawyer not withdraw, but that she continue to use her relationship of trust and confidence with the client, "up to the very hour of the client's . . . testimony,"[47] to dissuade the client from committing the perjury.

The client, faced with the threat of prison, may or may not be impressed with the fact that perjury is immoral and illegal, but may well be persuaded by the fact that the judge has the power to increase the sentence if she concludes that the defendant has given false testimony.[48] In any event, there is a professional consensus that lawyers are frequently successful in dissuading client perjury.[49] Note again, however, that lawyers can serve this function — to the benefit of society as well as their clients — only if their clients are willing to entrust them with their confidences and to accept their advice. That is not going to happen under the model of intentional ignorance.[50]

In the relatively small number of cases in which the client who has contemplated perjury rejects the lawyer's advice and decides to proceed to trial, to take the stand, and to give false testimony, the lawyer should go forward in the ordinary way. That is, the lawyer should examine the client in a normal professional manner and should argue the client's testimony to the jury in summation to the extent that sound tactics justify doing so.

This position was adopted by the Jordan Committee, which drafted the District of Columbia's version of the Model Rules, and also by the D.C. Bar's Board of Governors;[51] however, the D.C. Court of Appeals substituted a Rule 3.3 requiring client perjury to be presented by narrative testimony. The position proposed here has also been adopted by the National Association of Criminal Defense Lawyers in its Opinion 92-2. In addition, as discussed below, it has been endorsed by Professor Hazard, who was the Reporter for the Model Rules and who originally favored the disclosure requirement of MR 3.3.

---

[47] *See* Exum, *supra* note 4.

[48] *United States v. Grayson*, 438 U.S. 41 (1978). Prosecution for perjury is also possible. However, it is extremely unusual, perhaps in tacit acceptance of the idea that a criminal defendant has "a right to tell his story." *See* MONROE FREEDMAN, LAWYERS' ETHICS IN AN ADVERSARY SYSTEM 31 (1975).

[49] *See supra* note 4.

[50] Because the lawyer will be ignorant of the incriminating facts, there will be no occasion for the lawyer to attempt to dissuade the client from committing perjury, the client will give the perjurious testimony, the lawyer will elicit it in the ordinary way, and the lawyer will argue it to the jury. In systemic terms, therefore, there will be more perjury than under the traditional model, but lawyers will be able to say that they have not knowingly presented it.

[51] D.C. Bar Legal Ethics Comm., Opin. 234 (1993).

§ 6.09 THE OBJECTION ON GROUNDS OF PERSONAL MORALITY

We are not completely comfortable with this position. Indeed, one of the reasons that client perjury has produced such a substantial body of literature since 1966[52] is that no one has been able to resolve the trilemma in a way that is wholly consistent either with general norms of morality or with professional standards of ethics.[53] In the chapters on the adversary system, client autonomy, and the relationship of trust and confidence, as well as in this chapter, we have tried to present the reasons that have persuaded us to adopt the position we have. It is appropriate, however, to consider the reasons that leave us less than wholly satisfied.

The most troubling objection to presenting client perjury is that it is inconsistent with one's personal standards of morality. We like to think that we would not lie on our own behalf, even if five or ten years of freedom depended upon it. We cannot know, however, what we would do under those circumstances. That is not a reason in itself to help a client to present false testimony, but it does give us a sense of compassion for the person who feels driven to that course.

Beyond that, we cannot find — in terms of personal morality — a more acceptable course. We find deep moral significance in the dignity of the individual and in the way that dignity is respected in the American constitutional adversary system. Also, as we have seen, our analysis must focus on the first interview with the client. A lawyer is in no position at that point to make an informed judgment as to whether a client is guilty or innocent, what defenses he might have, or what his degree of culpability might be. The lawyer must act, therefore, upon a presumption of innocence. The lawyer cannot serve the client as he deserves to be served if she does not know everything there is to know about the client's case. Accordingly, the lawyer must urge him to tell her everything, and the lawyer must pledge confidentiality. Having given that pledge, we would be morally bound to keep it.

Would we never break our pledge? As we have indicated in the previous chapter, there are moral values that, for us, may take precedence over truthfulness. One is human life, for example, the innocent person on death row. In addition to the value at stake, the situation will occur so infrequently as to create no systemic threat; that is, there is no significant likelihood that the existence of this exception would make clients fearful of confiding in their lawyers.

---

[52] *See* Monroe Freedman, *Professional Responsibility of the Criminal Defense Lawyer: The Three Hardest Questions*, 64 MICH. L. REV. 1469 (1966).

[53] llustrative is the fact that twenty-two years later — after the Model Rules, *Nix v. Whiteside*, and ABA Opinion 87-353 — Norman Lefstein found it necessary to write an article titled, *Client Perjury in Criminal Cases: Still in Search of an Answer*, 1 GEO. J. LEGAL ETHICS 521, 525 (1988). *See also* MR 3.3, Cmt. on *Perjury by a Criminal Defendant* (1992):

> Whether an advocate for a criminally accused has the same duty of disclosure has been intensely debated. While it is agreed that the lawyer should seek to persuade the client to refrain from perjurious testimony, there has been dispute concerning the lawyer's duty when that persuasion fails.

We would also withdraw, despite prejudice to the client, to avoid having to go to trial before a corrupted judge or jury.[54] Again, the situation is so unlikely that there is no significant systemic threat. With respect to client perjury, the adversary system is designed, through cross-examination and otherwise, to take it into account. By contrast, a corrupted judge or juror subverts the adversary system itself.

Finally, we would violate confidentiality to the minimum extent necessary to defend ourselves against formalized charges of unlawful or unprofessional conduct. Admittedly, the morality of this exception is more difficult to defend than the first two.[55] It is analogous, however, to the privilege against self-incrimination, which recognizes the fundamental unfairness of requiring one to be self-destructive. Also, it seems implicit in the situation that the client, in one way or another, is prepared to betray the lawyer. In addition, although this contingency may not be as extraordinary as a threat to life or the corruption of a judge or juror, it is sufficiently uncommon to permit an exception without significant systemic threat.

We doubt that there is a criminal defense lawyer (or prosecutor, or civil litigator) who has not more than once faced the problem of perjury in some form,[56] but there are few who have ever had occasion to divulge client confidences in the areas in which we would allow exceptions.

Would we, then, give the client a Miranda warning about these exceptions? No, we would not. The life-and-death exception is the easy one — we put a higher value on being able to save a life than on warning a client (who is hypothetically going to be responsible for a death) that he should keep that particular truth from us. The other two exceptions are, unquestionably, less morally compelling than life and death, but sufficiently important in our scale of values. Again, the likelihood of these contingencies occurring is so slight that the harm that would be done to the lawyer-client relationship by a Miranda warning on these particular issues far outweighs the marginal value of fairness to the exceptional client to whom the warning would be relevant.

§ 6.10 THE OBJECTION OF SUBORNING PERJURY

The argument is sometimes raised that a lawyer who knowingly presents perjured testimony is suborning perjury. Subornation of perjury consists, however, in the corrupt inducement of perjury. Subornation is "the crime of procuring another to commit perjury by inciting, instigating, or persuading

---

[54] *See* AMERICAN LAWYER'S CODE OF CONDUCT, Rule 1.5 (Alternative A) (1980):

> A lawyer may reveal a client's confidence when the lawyer knows that a judge or juror in a pending proceeding in which the lawyer is involved has been bribed or subjected to extortion. In such a case, the lawyer shall use all reasonable means to protect the client, consistent with preventing the case from going forward with a corrupted judge or juror.

See also District of Columbia Rules of Professional Conduct, Rule 1.6(c)(2).

[55] On the other hand, breaching confidentiality to defend oneself against charges is far easier to defend than breaching confidentiality for the purely financial self-interest of collecting one's fee, which we would not permit, but which is permitted in DR 4-101(C)(4) and in MR 1.6(b)(2).

[56] Courts would be "inundated" with reports of perjury if lawyers told the court each time they "strongly suspected" it. *Doe v. Federal Grievance Committee*, 847 F.2d 57, 63 (1988).

the guilty party to do so."[57] Clearly, that is not what happens when the idea of perjury originates with the client, the lawyer uses her knowledge of the perjury to make ongoing, good faith efforts to dissuade the client from committing it, and the lawyer then proceeds with the perjury only if necessary under the compulsion of her role in our constitutionalized adversary system.[58]

A related objection is that the lawyer who examines the client in the ordinary way will coach the client in making the perjury more effective.[59] That is a *non sequitur*. Because the lawyer elicits the false testimony in the normal question-and-answer format in court does not mean that the lawyer either must or will help the client to improve upon his lies. It would be a violation of the plain meaning of a disciplinary rule[60] (and very likely unlawful) to do so; it would go beyond the necessities of confidentiality; and it would undercut the lawyer's efforts to dissuade the client by giving the client what would be, at best, a mixed message.

§ 6.11 THE OBJECTION OF LINE-DRAWING — THE NON-CLIENT WITNESS

If you are prepared to put the perjurious client on the stand, where do you draw the line? What if the client wants to support his false alibi with the corroborative perjury of another witness?

The simplest, and perhaps best, answer is that the line should be drawn at the defendant himself. In our view, however, it depends upon the witness' relationship to the defendant. In one case, for example, a new trial was ordered when the court learned that the defense attorney had refused to put on the defendant's mother and sister, who were prepared to corroborate the defendant's false testimony.[61] Certainly a spouse/partner or parent would be acting under the same human compulsion as the defendant. As Charles Fried has said:[62]

> Charles Curtis made the perspicacious remark that a lawyer may be privileged to lie for his client in a way that one might lie to save one's friends or close relatives.[63] I do not want to underwrite the notion that it is justifiable to lie even in those situations, but there is a great deal to the point that in those relations — friendship, kinship — we

---

[57] Lefstein, *supra* note 28, at 521, 548, *citing* 68 AM. JUR. 2d, *Perjury* § 67 (1972).

[58] *Accord*, Exum, *supra* note 4, at 24–25: "[I]f the defendant testifies at his own insistence and against the advice of counsel, counsel himself cannot be said to have suborned perjury. . . . Counsel, himself, has not violated the law."

[59] Kaufman makes this argument in the Harvard Trial Advocacy videotape referred to in note 11, *supra*.

[60] *See* DR 7-102(A)(6): "[A] lawyer shall not . . . [p]articipate in the creation . . . of evidence when he knows or it is obvious that the evidence is false."

[61] *See* Edward *Walsh, Lawyer's Dilemma: Must He call a Witness He Thinks Will Lie?*, WASH. POST, Oct. 31, 1971, at D3.

[62] Charles Fried, *The Lawyer as Friend: The Moral Foundations of the Lawyer-Client Relationship*, 85 YALE L. J. 1060, 1066 (1976). Fried, who is a professor at Harvard Law School, has served as U.S. Solicitor General and as a justice in the Massachusetts Supreme Judicial Court.

[63] *Citing* Charles Curtis, *The Ethics of Advocacy*, 4 STAN. L. REV. 3 (1951).

recognize an authorization to take the interests of particular concrete persons more seriously and to give them priority over the interests of the wider collectivity.

For that reason, we would present the testimony of a spouse/partner or parent if we could not succeed in dissuading them. Note, too, that the spouse/partner or parent might become the lawyer's strong and effective ally in the lawyer's efforts to dissuade the client from engaging in a perjurious defense.

A survey of lawyers in the District of Columbia reflected ambivalence on the issue of calling a collateral witness who you know will commit perjury, perhaps in part because the survey did not indicate whether the witness was a spouse or a casual acquaintance. When asked whether they would call the defendant himself when he intends to commit perjury, ninety-five percent responded that they would call the defendant, and ninety percent of those said that they would conduct the direct examination in the normal manner.[64] When asked, however, about offering perjury by a witness other than the defendant, only a bare majority (fifty-two percent) answered in the affirmative.[65]

In the final analysis, however, the question of drawing the line need not control the decision of whether to present the defendant's own false testimony. The decision that one should call the defendant does not preclude drawing the line at that point.[66]

§ 6.12   THE TRILEMMA UNDER THE MODEL CODE

The applicable rule in the Model Code appears to be unequivocal. DR 7-102(A)(4) says flatly that "a lawyer shall not . . . [k]nowingly use perjured testimony or false evidence."[67] The meaning of the rule appears to be plain. What the rule does not say, however, is how the lawyer is to fulfill that obligation. As we have seen, none of the possible solutions works in practice in a wholly satisfactory way.

For more than a decade, the only guidance provided by the ABA Committee on Ethics and Professional Responsibility was in Informal[68] Opinion 1314

---

64 Steven Allen Friedman, *Professional Responsibility in D.C.: A Survey*, 1972 RES IPSA LOQUI-TUR 60 (1972). Similar results were reported at the Sixth Annual Judicial Conference of the District of Columbia, held in June, 1981.

65 *Id.* A substantial number of those who answered in the negative gave tactical, not ethical, reasons.

66 As illustrated in the Harvard Trial Advocacy Workshop videotape (*see* note 11, *supra*), the lawyer can reserve the power to refuse to call collateral witnesses without turning it into a Miranda warning.

67 *See also* DR 7-102(A)(5) and (6).

68 Formal opinions are those dealing with issues of broad general interest. Informal opinions relate to issues that are "comparatively narrow in scope and arise infrequently." ABA, OPINIONS ON PROFESSIONAL ETHICS 6 (1967). Informal opinions appear to be written with less care and are generally understood to carry less weight than formal opinions.

It is not clear why the Committee understood the issue of client perjury to be one of narrow scope that arises infrequently. Even if it were true that clients infrequently contemplate perjury, the fact remains that the lawyer's solution to the problem must affect the initial interview with every client.

(1975).[69] The opinion is brief and conclusory, with no analysis of the underlying difficulties or conflicting policies. The conclusion states that the lawyer faced with client perjury must take one of two courses of action — withdraw, or disclose the perjury to the court.

As we have seen, withdrawal is almost certain to require disclosure to the court, and the motion for leave to withdraw is almost certain to be denied. The alternative mandate of Informal Opinion 1314, reporting the perjury to the court, has been discussed above in the context of the solution of withdrawal. The prejudice to the client through such a course is manifest, both in sentencing and on appeal.

Moreover, in holding that DR 7-102(A)(4) requires divulgence to the court, the opinion clearly went beyond the plain meaning of that rule. The rule does say, Thou shalt not "use" perjury; it does not say, Thou shalt reveal perjury. As the ABA subsequently recognized in Formal Opinion 87-353 (expressly disapproving IO 1314), "none of these prohibitions [DR 7-102(A)(4), (5) or (6)] *requires* disclosure to the tribunal of any information otherwise protected by DR 4-101."[70] At most, therefore, DR 7-102(A)(4) *permits* disclosure of the client's perjurious intent.[71]

Is it correct, however, to say that the lawyer is even *permitted* by DR 7-102(A)(4) to divulge confidences otherwise protected by DR 4-101? Again, to find that language in DR 7-102(A)(4) itself requires a good deal more than a plain meaning reading. That provision says only that the lawyer shall not "use" perjury. It does not say that the lawyer may violate DR 4-101 in order to accomplish that end.

Perhaps, though, we would not be violating DR 4-101, since that rule includes exceptions. One of those exceptions, DR 4-101(C)(2), simply begs the question. It says that a lawyer "may reveal . . . [c]onfidences or secrets *when permitted* under Disciplinary Rules. . . . " Since DR 7-102(A)(4) does not say anything about permitting the lawyer to reveal confidences or secrets, however, DR 4-101(C)(2), by its own terms, would not come into play.

The express language of DR 7-102(B)(1), prior to its amendment in 1974, did appear to require divulgence of confidences to prevent a fraud on the court (the lawyer "shall reveal the fraud to the affected . . . tribunal"). As we have seen, however, that conclusion was found to be contrary to "tradition . . . backed by substantial policy considerations," and to have been caused by an oversight in drafting.[72] The amendment to DR7-102(B)(1), therefore, simply clarified the original intention by "reinstat[ing] the essence of Opinion 287," which required the lawyer to protect client confidences.[73]

---

[69] *Disapproved*, Opin. 87-353 (1987).

[70] ABA Opin. 87-353 (1987) (emphasis in original).

[71] *Id.*

[72] *See* Formal Opin. 341, discussed in Chapter 5, *supra*.

[73] *Id.* As we saw, the majority in Opinion 287 *required* confidentiality only for information communicated by the client. Opinion 341 expressly extended that protection to all information "gained in the professional relationship."

§ 6.13 THE FUTURE CRIME EXCEPTION

The other exception to confidentiality in the Model Code that arguably permits (but, by its terms, would not require) disclosure of client perjury is DR 4-101(C)(3). This is the future crime exception to confidentiality, giving the lawyer discretion to divulge a client's intention to commit a crime and the information necessary to prevent the crime. There are two difficulties with applying this exception to client perjury.

First, as former North Carolina Chief Justice James Exum has written, the future crime exception "does not encompass a client's intent to commit perjury."[74]

> Proposed perjurious testimony by a criminal defendant . . . is intrinsically and inextricably related to the very case in which the lawyer is employed to act both as counselor and as advocate. Disclosure, therefore, must prejudice the defendant in the very matter in which the lawyer is employed to defend him.[75]

The lawyer, Judge Exum adds, "is the defendant's only advocate. He cannot become also his accuser. A conviction, under our system, must be at the hands of the jury, not the defendant's lawyer."[76]

A similar issue has arisen where the defendant in a robbery prosecution tells his lawyer the location of the stolen money and his intention to conceal the money until it becomes safe to enjoy it. Despite the fact that concealing the money is a future or continuing crime, DR 4-101(C)(3) does not permit the lawyer to divulge the location of the stolen money.

The reasoning is the same as Judge Exum's regarding perjury at the criminal trial. That is, "[i]nherent in the disclosure of [the location of the money] is the serious risk of exposing the client as the possessor of the stolen property."[77] In essence, therefore, the lawyer would be disclosing the client's confidential communication regarding the crime for which he is being prosecuted and for which he has sought legal representation.[78]

Moreover, if the future crime exception of DR 4-101(A)(3) did include perjury regarding the client's past crime, it would mean that the model of intentional ignorance had been established by a brief sub-subsection of the Model Code, with no commentary whatsoever. That is, with or without a Miranda warning, clients would learn that some lawyers reveal client perjury to the court, and would thereby be discouraged from confiding in their lawyers. There is no indication in its language or history that subsection (C)(3) was intended to have that far-reaching result.[79]

---

[74] Exum, *supra* note 4, at 22.

[75] *Id.* at 23.

[76] *Id.*

[77] NYSBA COMM. ON PROF. ETHICS, Opin. 405 (1975).

[78] *Id.*

[79] *See, e.g.*, ABA Standard 4-3.2(b) (forbidding the lawyer to "intimate to the client in any way" that the client should withhold potentially damaging facts).

In *Nix v. Whiteside*, 475 U.S. 157, 106 S.Ct. 988 (1984), the Supreme Court said that a defendant who informed his counsel that he was going to commit perjury would have no constitutional right

A second objection to allowing divulgence of client perjury under DR 4-101(C)(3) is that the apparent purpose of permitting disclosure under the future crime exception is not disclosure for the sake of disclosure, but to prevent the crime from taking place. Thus, disclosure is restricted to "the information necessary to prevent the crime." Information that does not serve that end remains protected under DR 4-101(C)(3). If the lawyer tells the judge that her client is about to take the stand and commit perjury, however, that does not change the criminal character of the client's act. To lie on the witness stand is perjury regardless of whether the judge knows the truth.[80]

§ 6.14 FORMAL OPINION 87-353 AND THE MODEL CODE

As noted above, ABA Formal Opinion 87-353 expressly disapproves Informal Opinion 1314, and holds that nothing in DR 7-102(A) "*requires* disclosure of any information protected by DR 4-101."[81] Assuming, without analysis, that the intent of DR 4-101(C)(3) is to include client perjury as a future crime,[82] Opinion 353 holds that the lawyer is permitted under the Model Code to inform the court of the client's intended perjury, but that she is not required to do so. The alternative, by clear implication, is that the lawyer is permitted to go forward in a way that will not reveal the client's perjury to the court. As we have seen, the only way to do that is to present the client's testimony in the normal manner.

In sum, our view is that the client's perjury is not a future crime within the meaning of DR 4-101(C)(3). Therefore, the lawyer is forbidden to reveal it to the court. Further, the lawyer should not move for leave to withdraw, because the motion, directly or indirectly, would reveal the client's confidences to the court (and the motion is almost certain to be denied). The effect of DR 7-102(A)(4), therefore, is to require the lawyer to make good faith efforts to dissuade the client from committing the perjury, which will usually succeed. If the lawyer is unsuccessful, however, she must then go forward in the ordinary way.

The ABA Committee on Ethics and Professional Responsibility both differs and agrees with us in its interpretation of the Model Code. In Opinion 353 the Committee reads DR 4-101(C)(3) as giving the lawyer discretion to reveal

---

under the Sixth Amendment to insist on counsel's silence. 475 U.S. at 174, 106 S.Ct. at 998. The Court did not purport to be analyzing DR 4-101(C)(3), which was not cited in *Nix*. The issue being discussed here is not whether the defendant has a Sixth Amendment right to his counsel's silence, but whether DR 4-101(C)(3) should be construed to permit the lawyer to volunteer that his client intends to commit perjury.

[80] This is no less true, of course, with regard to revealing perjury after the fact. In either case, it might be argued that the lawyer is preventing the judge from being victimized by the client's crime, but that is not what the language of the rule addresses. Also, if the rule were concerned with victimization, then the lawyer would be permitted to directly inform the jury as well.

[81] Emphasis in the original.

[82] Opinion 353 also expressly disapproves of intentional ignorance. (At note 9). Ironically, the opinion overlooks the fact that if lawyers were to make a practice of informing the court of client perjury, we would effectively be adopting intentional ignorance, because clients would learn that you cannot trust your lawyer and would withhold potential crucial information.

client perjury as a future crime. One alternative the Committee offers, therefore, would *permit* the lawyer to inform the judge and to proceed as the judge orders (which may well be to follow the course that we support, albeit with a damaging disclosure en route). However, the ABA Committee would also permit the lawyer to follow the course that we support.

§ 6.15   THE TRILEMMA UNDER THE MODEL RULES

The Model Rules appear to make "a major policy change" from the Model Code and from earlier ethical obligations regarding client perjury.[83] Under MR 3.3(a)(4) the lawyer is forbidden to offer evidence that the lawyer knows to be false. Also, under the same provision, if the lawyer offers material evidence that the the lawyer later learns to be false, the lawyer is required to "take reasonable remedial measures."[84]

ABA Opinion 87-353 explains what it means to take remedial measures. When the lawyer learns that the client intends to commit perjury, she should "warn the client of the consequences," including "the lawyer's duty to disclose it to the court." Having done that, the lawyer "can reasonably believe" that the client will not testify falsely, and she may examine the client in the normal manner. If the client nevertheless testifies falsely, however, the lawyer is then obligated to inform the court.[85]

One problem with that solution is that the lawyer is then in the position of revealing the client's perjury after the fact. The Supreme Court has never addressed the constitutionality of this course, and there is reason to believe that a majority of the Court would hold it to be violative of the right to counsel, the privilege against self-incrimination, and/or due process.[86] Justice White posed precisely that question during the oral argument in *Nix v. Whiteside*[87] and expressed incredulity at the suggestion that the lawyer could disclose the perjury after the fact.[88]

Another problem with MR 3.3 is that it collapses inevitably into intentional ignorance.[89] Indeed, MR 1.2(e) provides for a lawyer-client Miranda warning

---

[83] ABA Formal Opinion 87-353 (1987).

[84] Model Rules 3.3(a)(4); *see also* RESTATEMENT § 120(2):

> If a lawyer has offered testimony or other evidence as to a material issue of fact and comes to know of its falsity, the lawyer must take reasonable remedial measures and may disclose confidential client information when necessary to take such a measure.

[85] *See* Model Rules 3.3, Comment on *Remedial Measures* (1992):

> If perjured testimony or false evidence has been offered, the advocates's proper course ordinarily is to remonstrate with the client confidentially. If that fails, the advocate should seek to withdraw if that will remedy the situation. If withdrawal will not remedy the situation or is impossible, the advocate should make disclosure to the court. It is for the court then to determine what should be done . . . .

[86] *See* Monroe Freedman, *Client Confidences and Client Perjury: Some Unanswered Questions*, 136 PA. L. REV. 1939, 1954–55 (1988).

[87] 475 U.S. 157 (1986).

[88] Freedman, *supra* note 86, at 1954–55.

[89] The Comment to MR 3.3 says that three solutions to the dilemma of client perjury have been proposed. Ironically, the Comment does not refer to (or attempt to defend) intentional ignorance, although that is the one adopted by the Model Rules.

regarding "the rules of professional conduct" and "the relevant limitations on the lawyer's conduct," but not until "the lawyer knows that a client expects assistance not permitted by the rules." This suggests that the rule does not contemplate a fair warning, but one that is delayed until the client has already revealed too much.[90] Thus, lawyers would be eliciting incriminating evidence from their clients and then revealing it to the courts — until word got around the jailhouses and the streets that you can't trust your lawyer.

Interestingly, however, in the 1980 Discussion Draft of the Model Rules, which contained virtually the identical rule,[91] the Comment expressly called for giving the warning in the first interview in every case:

> A new client should be given a general explanation of the client-lawyer relationship. A client should understand the lawyer's ethical obligations, such as the prohibitions against assisting a client in committing a fraud or presenting perjured evidence.

The Comment candidly acknowledged that "[t]he warning may lead the client to withhold or falsify relevant facts, thereby making the lawyer's representation . . . less effective. . . . " When Professor Freedman pointed out that this amounts to intentional ignorance,[92] the Kutak Commission simply deleted the comment — which successfully eliminated the candor but not the problem.

If we paid the price of intentional ignorance by requiring lawyers to reveal client perjury, what would we get in return? The drafters of the Model Rules argued that we would significantly increase truthful results in the criminal process. However, "it is doubtful that a disclosure rule will serve this purpose."[93] Professor Nathan Crystal has pointed out that few criminal defendants who go to trial are acquitted. Thus, a disclosure rule "would affect the outcome in an insignificant number of cases."[94] Moreover, a guilty client, knowing that his lawyer will disclose the information to rectify perjury, will not admit guilt to his lawyer if the client intends to testify falsely.

Opinion 87-353 also suggests that the lawyer can comply with MR 3.3 by "refraining from calling the client as a witness." As Norman Lefstein has

---

[90] Freedman once heard Roy Cohn propose a solution to that problem. The lawyer is to say, "I didn't hear you say that." That, apparently, wipes the information from the ethical slate. A less crude — but no less disingenuous — way to handle the problem is this:

> I'm confused. I understood from what you said before that you didn't do it. But you just said something that might mean that you did do it. Before you go on, let me explain something to you. If you tell me that you did it and that you're going to lie about it in court, I would have to tell the judge. On the other hand, if you're actually telling me you're innocent, then, of course, there's no problem with putting you on the stand. Now, what are you telling me? [Winks and nudges are optional.]

Perhaps that is precisely what MR 1.2(e) contemplates, in conjunction with MR 3.3 and the Model Rules' Terminology definition of "know" as "actual knowledge."

[91] It was then MR 1.4(b), and was the same except that the clauses were in reverse order and there were minor variations in phrasing.

[92] Monroe Freedman, *The Kutak Model Rules v. The American Lawyer's Code of Conduct*, 26 VILL. L. REV. 1165, 1174–75 (1980-1981).

[93] Nathan Crystal, *Confidentiality Under the Model Rules of Professional Conduct*, 30 KAN. L. REV. 215, 242 (1982).

[94] *Id.*

objected, however, "the Model Rules nowhere suggest that this is an appropriate solution."[95] Moreover, "the proposal conflicts with generally accepted principles of professional responsibility."[96]

> The Model Rules recognize [in MR 1.2(a)], as do the ABA Standards and numerous court decisions, that in a criminal case the client, not the lawyer, must be permitted to decide whether to testify. This proposition complements the constitutional principle . . . that a defendant has a constitutional right to testify in his or her own behalf.[97]

Even if the client can be found to "waive" the constitutional right to testify by planning perjury, "surely [that] decision . . . should not be permitted to be made unilaterally by defense counsel."[98] That is, the defendant's right to testify cannot be denied by the unreviewed conclusion of counsel that the defendant is going to commit perjury. As Lefstein reminds us, "We permit no other constitutional right of a defendant . . . to be stripped away in this fashion."[99]

Thus, the defendant is entitled, at the least, to an "on-the-record judicial hearing."[100] That procedure, however, only serves to create further difficulties. If such a hearing is held, the attorney-client relationship will be "torn asunder."[101] As Lefstein demonstrates, therefore, the solution proposed by MR 3.3, as interpreted by Opinion 87-353, is a shambles.[102]

Nix v. Whiteside

Nix v. Whiteside[103] involved a drug-related killing in Iowa. Defendant Whiteside claimed self-defense. At trial he testified to his belief that the victim had been coming at him with a gun, although he did not testify that he had

---

[95] Lefstein, *supra* note 28, at 536.

[96] *Id.*

[97] *Id.* at 536–37 (citations omitted).

[98] *Id.* at 537.

[99] *Id.* at 539. As the Eighth Circuit recognized, "an attorney who acts on a belief of possible client perjury takes on the role of the fact finder, a role which perverts the structure of our adversary system. A lawyer who judges a client's truthfulness does so without the many safeguards inherent in our adversary system. He likely makes his decision alone, without the assistance of fellow fact finders. He may consider too much evidence, including that which is untrustworthy. Moreover, a jury's determination on credibility is always tempered by the requirement of proof beyond a reasonable doubt. A lawyer, finding facts on his own, is not necessarily guided by such a high standard." *United States v. Long*, 857 F.2d 436, 445 (8th Cir. 1988).

[100] *Id.*

[101] *Id.* at 541.

[102] Ironically, the same is true of Lefstein's proposal, which is the narrative solution. Without "any kind of on-the-record judicial hearing," Lefstein would have the lawyer waive the defendant's rights to be questioned by counsel, *Ferguson v. Georgia*, 365 U.S. 570 (1961), and to closing argument, *Herring v. New York*, 422 U.S. 853 (1975). Also, although Lefstein insists that a lawyer does not disclose confidences to the court in adopting the narrative solution, that is clearly contrary to fact.

[103] 475 U.S. 157, 106 S.Ct. 988 (1986).

actually seen a gun.[104] After his conviction, Whiteside moved for a new trial, maintaining that his attorney, Robinson, had improperly coerced him from testifying that he had seen something metallic (not specifically a gun) in the victim's hand.[105]

At one point, Whiteside told Robinson that he had not seen a gun in the victim's hand, but that he had been sure that the victim had been holding one.[106] Shortly before trial, however, Whiteside told Robinson that he had seen something metallic in the victim's hand.[107] When challenged by his lawyer about his belated reference to "something metallic," Whiteside responded, "[I]n Howard Cook's case there was a gun. If I don't say I saw a gun, I'm dead."[108]

Robinson inferred that any testimony about something metallic would be perjurious.[109] He therefore threatened that if Whiteside testified about having seen something metallic, Robinson would "advise the Court of what [Whiteside] was doing" (i.e., committing perjury), and that he "probably would be allowed to attempt to impeach that particular testimony."[110] Robinson also said that he would "ask the Court for permission to withdraw,"[111] which would have left Whiteside with no lawyer.[112]

In response to those threats, Whiteside took the stand in his own defense and testified about his reasonable belief that the victim had been about to shoot him. He said nothing, however, about having seen something metallic. After his conviction, Whiteside's less-than-compelling contention was that his attorney had violated his Sixth Amendment right to effective assistance of counsel by coercing him out of testifying to the perjurious embellishment.

The Supreme Court tested that contention against *Strickland v. Washington*,[113] decided two years earlier. That case had established two criteria for a claim of ineffective assistance: first, the attorney's conduct must have fallen "outside the wide range of professional competence;"[114] second, the attorney's incompetence must have prejudiced the defendant by making the trial so unfair as to "undermine confidence" in the guilty verdict.[115]

All of the justices agreed that, regardless of the issue of attorney competence, Whiteside had not been prejudiced simply by having been dissuaded from testifying falsely about "something metallic." He did testify that he had

---

[104] *See* Petition for a Writ of Certiorari app. F at A55–56, *Whiteside v. Scurr*, 750 F.2d 713 (8th Cir. 1984)(No. 83-1015).

[105] *Id.* at A70–72.

[106] *Id.* at A78–79.

[107] *Id.* at A85.

[108] *Id.*

[109] *Id.*

[110] *Id.*

[111] *Id.* at A88.

[112] Following a previous change of lawyers at Whiteside's insistence, the trial judge told Whiteside that his chances of getting another attorney were about zero. *Id.* at A53.

[113] 466 U.S. 668, 104 S.Ct. 2052 (1984).

[114] 466 U.S. at 690.

[115] 466 U.S. at 694.

thought the victim had a gun, and neither the trial judge nor the jury had learned, directly or indirectly, about his contemplated perjury. As the four concurring justices pointed out, therefore, there was no need for discussion about the ethical propriety of Robinson's conduct.[116]

Nevertheless, Chief Justice Burger and four other justices went on to say that defense attorney Robinson had acted ethically in threatening Whiteside with withdrawal and with exposure of his perjury if he were to go forward with it.[117] Before discussing the ethical issue, however, the Chief Justice cautioned that courts must be careful not to "constitutionalize particular standards of professional conduct and thereby intrude into the State's proper authority."[118]

Justice Brennan took this to mean that "the Court *cannot* tell the states or the lawyers in the states how to behave in their courts, unless and until federal rights are violated."[119] On behalf of the four concurring justices, Justice Blackmun added that a federal habeas corpus case is not "an appropriate vehicle for attempting to resolve [the] thorny problem" of client perjury.[120] And noting that the majority's "essay" on client perjury is "pure discourse without force of law," Justice Brennan concluded that the problem of client perjury "has not now been 'decided.' "[121]

§ 6.16 *NIX V. WHITESIDE*, CLIENT PERJURY, AND THE CONSTITUTION

Nix did, however, decide one important issue. When defense counsel threatened to reveal his client's perjury, his conduct "fell within the wide range of professional responses to threatened client perjury acceptable under the Sixth Amendment."[122] The Court particularly noted, however, that:

> *Robinson divulged no client communications* until he was compelled to do so in response to Whiteside's *post-trial challenge* to the quality of his performance. We see this as a case in which the attorney successfully dissuaded the client from committing the crime of perjury.[123]

Professors Geoffrey Hazard and William Hodes also emphasize that Robinson "merely threatened" to reveal Whiteside's perjury, but "did *not* blow the

---

[116] 475 U.S. at 178, 190, 106 S.Ct. at 1000, 1006.

[117] The Chief Justice's conclusions, analysis, and use of authorities have been severely criticized. Lefstein has observed that the majority opinion "contains a shocking misstatement of the law pertaining to client perjury." Norman Lefstein, *Reflections on the Client Perjury Dilemma and Nix v. Whiteside*, CRIM. JUST. 27, 28 (1986). Another critic of the Chief Justice's inaccuracies is Brent Appel, the Iowa Deputy Attorney General who argued and won *Nix v. Whiteside. See* Brent Appel, Nix v. Whiteside: *The Role of Apples, Oranges, and the Great Houdini in Constitutional Adjudication*, 23 CRIM. L. BULL. 5 (1987). *See also* Monroe Freedman, *The Aftermath of* Nix v. Whiteside: *Slamming the Lid on Pandora's Box*, 23 CRIM. L. BULL. 25 (1987).

[118] 475 U.S. at 165, 106 S.Ct. at 994.

[119] 475 U.S. at 177 (emphasis in the original).

[120] *Id.*

[121] *Id.*

[122] 475 U.S. at 166, 106 S.Ct. at 994.

[123] 475 U.S. at 172, 106 S.Ct. at 997 (emphasis added).

whistle."[124] This factual limitation of the *Nix* case leaves the client perjury issue "still murkier" even than the Chief Justice's misstatements of law and fact in the majority opinion.[125]

Nevertheless, in an earlier edition of their work, the same authors said that *Nix* "closed off the *constitutional* avenue of debate."[126] This is clearly wrong, however, on two counts.

First, as we have seen, the Court itself noted that Robinson "divulged no client communications" at trial, and Hazard and Hodes emphasize that Robinson "did *not* blow the whistle." Clearly, therefore, the Sixth Amendment issue is not foreclosed in the significantly different case in which defense counsel *does* blow the whistle at trial.[127]

§ 6.17 THE CLIENT'S PRIVILEGE AGAINST SELF-INCRIMINATION

The second reason that the constitutional debate has not been foreclosed by *Nix* is that the defendant's Fifth Amendment privilege against self-incrimination was neither argued to the Court nor discussed in the opinions.

One Fifth Amendment case that was not raised in *Nix* is *Estelle v. Smith*,[128] which involved a psychiatrist's examination of a defendant's competency to stand trial. The defendant was not advised of his privilege against self-incrimination, nor was his lawyer informed of the examination. The psychiatrist did not testify at trial regarding the crime at issue. At the post-trial sentencing hearing, however, the psychiatrist gave his opinion that the defendant was likely to commit future crimes.

Writing for the Court, Chief Justice Burger noted that, during the psychiatric evaluation, the defendant "assuredly . . . was 'not in the presence of [a person] acting solely in his interest.'"[129] Rather, the psychiatrist's apparent neutrality changed, and he became at the sentencing trial essentially "an agent of the State recounting unwarned statements made in a postarrest

---

[124] 2 HAZARD & HODES, THE LAW OF LAWYERING § 29.19 (3d ed., 2001).

[125] *Id.*

[126] 1 HAZARD & HODES, THE LAW OF LAWYERING p. 90.1 (Supp., 1987) (emphasis in the original). In the current (third) edition, the authors assert that *Nix v. Whiteside* closed off the main *constitutional* avenue of debate." *Id.*, § 29.19 (3d ed., 2001) (emphasis in the original). They then say, "there is every reason to predict that the end of serious debate about client perjury is close at hand." *Id.*

This is doubly puzzling. First, a serious constitutional issue has always been the defendant's privilege against self-incrimination, which Hazard and Hodes deal with only in cursory fashion, ignoring key cases and arguments. *See id.*, § 29.20. Second, Hazard himself has reopened the debate by changing his prior position on client perjury in criminal cases. *See infra*, this Chapter ("Hazard's Change of Position").

[127] *See also* Freedman, *supra* note 86, 136 PA. L. REV. at 1954–55.

[128] 451 U.S. 454, 101 S.Ct. 1866 (1981). An additional ground of the decision in *Estelle v. Smith* was the right to counsel under the Sixth Amendment. In a similar case, *Satterwhite v. Texas*, 486 U.S. 249, 108 S.Ct. 1792 (1988), the Court applied the harmless error doctrine to the Sixth Amendment right, but found that the psychiatrist's testimony had not been harmless.

[129] *Id.* at 467 (*quoting Miranda v. Arizona*, 384 U.S. 436, 469 (1966).

custodial setting."[130] Accordingly, the defendant's Fifth and Sixth Amendment rights had been violated, and the sentence was vacated.

Another case not cited in *Nix* is *United States v. Henry*.[131] In that case, a government informant who had been placed in the cell with Henry established a relationship of trust and confidence with him. As a result, Henry revealed incriminating information to the informer. Again, Chief Justice Burger wrote the opinion for the Court, vacating Henry's conviction because it had been based in part on the admissions elicited through a false relationship of trust and confidence.

Henry was decided under the Sixth Amendment right to counsel, but its relevance to the Fifth Amendment aspect of client perjury is plain. The Chief Justice's statement of the issue, and the emphasis throughout the opinion, is on the "admission at trial of *incriminating statements* made by [the defendant] to his cellmate."[132] As Justice Powell expressed it, through the cellmate "the government engaged in conduct that . . . is the functional equivalent of interrogation."[133]

It is difficult to understand how a defendant's own lawyer can properly do what the psychiatrist in *Estelle* or the cellmate in *Henry* could not do — that is, establish a relationship of trust and confidence and then "become an agent of the State" by disclosing to the court the incriminating information gained through that relationship. In fact, the role of the lawyer is a more serious one in this regard than that of a cellmate. The Supreme Court has never described trust and confidence between cellmates as "imperative," but it has used that word in describing the relationship of trust and confidence between lawyer and client.[134]

United States v. Henry and *Estelle v. Smith* support the Fifth Amendment point in another way. They show that the privilege against incriminating oneself takes on a special significance once the accused has a lawyer. The government interfered with Henry's right to counsel by conducting "the functional equivalent of interrogation" in the absence of his lawyer.[135] A premise of *Henry*, therefore, was that the defendant was entitled to be warned by his lawyer before making incriminating statements to a cellmate who had established a relationship of trust and confidence and who was eliciting damaging information. As the Court said in *Estelle*, a layman "may not be aware of the precise scope, the nuances, and the boundaries of his Fifth Amendment privilege"; the assertion of that right, therefore, "often depends upon legal advice from someone who is trained and skilled in the subject matter."[136] Accordingly, "a defendant should not be forced to resolve such an important issue without 'the guiding hand of counsel.'"[137] Who, then, has the

---

[130] *Id.*

[131] 447 U.S. 264, 100 S.Ct. 2183 (1980).

[132] *Id.* at 265, 2184 (emphasis added).

[133] *Id.* at 277, 2190 (Powell, J., concurring).

[134] *Trammel v. Unted States*, 445 U.S. 40, 51 (1980).

[135] *Henry*, at 277, 2190 (Powell, J., concurring).

[136] 451 U.S. at 471; 101 S.Ct. at 1877.

[137] *Id.*

responsibility of warning the defendant about the risk of making incriminating statements to his lawyer?

In their cursory discussion of the Fifth Amendment privilege, Hazard & Hodes say:

> [E]ven though the government might discover confidential information because of the presence of a lawyer in situations such as *Nix v. Whiteside*, it simply cannot be said that the government "sent the lawyer in to do its work," or that the lawyer has been "recruited as a listening post" as has sometimes been claimed.

First, that misquotes, or ignores, the arguments made here (or anywhere else by these authors). Nevertheless, let's consider what does happen in a case like *Nix*. The state, through its ethical rules, orders the lawyer to learn everything possible about her client's case. It orders the lawyer, further, that if her client admits that he intends to commit perjury, the lawyer must tell the court. However, the lawyer doesn't warn the client of this in advance of eliciting the information, so as to avoid destroying the relationship of trust and confidence and losing crucial information. (To warn the client in advance would result in intentional ignorance, which has been condemned in ethical rules, standards, and opinions.) Thus, the lawyer elicits, without warning, the incriminating information and, when the client testifies, reveals the incriminating information to the judge (and, under the narrative solution, to the jury as well).[138]

Is it not fair to say that the state has recruited the lawyer (on pain of professional discipline) to elicit incriminating information and to pass it on to the state if the defendant testifies? Is the lawyer in this regard any different from the cellmate in *Henry* or the psychiatrist in *Estelle* in eliciting unwarned admissions and becoming an agent of the state in using them against the defendant?

In view of the interrelationship between the Sixth and Fifth Amendments recognized in *Henry* and in *Estelle*, we believe the answer to those questions is clear. The defendant's own lawyer cannot constitutionally elicit unwarned admissions from her client and then use those admissions in a way that the cellmate and the psychiatrist could not. Indeed, the importance of the Sixth Amendment right to counsel in *Henry* is that the lawyer should have been available to warn the defendant *not* to make incriminating statements to another person (including, presumably, the lawyer herself) that might result in incriminating testimony by that person.

Unquestionably, therefore, the Fifth Amendment privilege against self-incrimination remains, at least, an unresolved issue with respect to client perjury.

---

[138] A chilling illustration of a lawyer failing to warn the client, entrapping him into damaging admissions, and then turning on him, is given in Stephen Ellmann, *Truth and Consequences*, 69 FORDHAM L. REV. 895, 895–899 (2000).

§ 6.18 SELF-INCRIMINATION AND THE FUTURE CRIME EXCEPTION

The Fifth Amendment privilege against self-incrimination is independent of the lawyer-client privilege. Consider, for example, the defendant in *Henry*, who had no lawyer-client privilege (or any other evidentiary privilege) with his cellmate. Nevertheless, the incriminating statements that the defendant had made to the cellmate were excluded.[139] What is important for *constitutional* purposes is not whether there is an evidentiary privilege, but whether unwarned admissions have been elicited from the defendant by someone who then uses those admissions against him in court.

However, the evidentiary lawyer-client privilege has been incorporated into the constitutional privilege against self-incrimination in some contexts.[140] This makes sense, but it can lead to the erroneous notion that if the crime/fraud exception to the *evidentiary* lawyer-client privilege applies, then the client loses his *constitutional* privilege. Although this is a non sequitur, it is worth considering whether a client's intention to commit perjury in denying his guilt is within the future crime exception to the lawyer-client privilege. That is, the client's admission to the lawyer of his guilt is clearly protected by the Fifth Amendment, but does the client's intent to commit perjury constitute a "future crime" that falls outside the lawyer-client evidentiary privilege?

The majority in *Nix* equates perjury with bribing a witness or juror.[141] (Bribery would clearly be a future crime, separate and distinct from the murder for which the defendant was on trial.) However, this was part of what the four concurring justices criticized as the majority's inappropriate *dictum* on professional ethics.[142] As Justice Brennan said, that part of the majority opinion was "pure discourse without force of law."[143] Furthermore, as is

---

[139] Again, *Henry* is indeed a Sixth Amendment case, but the point was that he was entitled to have his lawyer available to warn him before he made the self-incriminating statements to his cellmate.

[140] *E.g.*, in *Fisher v. United States*, 425 U.S. 391, 96 S.Ct. 1569 (1976), the Supreme Court held that a lawyer cannot be compelled to violate the attorney-client evidentiary privilege, because otherwise the client would lose his constitutional privilege simply by communicating with his lawyer. As stated by one authority, "the Supreme Court . . . extended Fifth Amendment protection to the attorney-client privilege for the express purpose of encouraging the uninhibited exchange of information between citizens and their attorneys." CHARLES WHITEBREAD, CRIMINAL PROCEDURE 257 (1976). *See also*, David E. Seidelson, *The Attorney-Client Privilege and the Client's Constitutional Rights*, 6 HOFSTRA L. REV. 693 (1978). *See also* HAZARD & HODES, THE LAW OF LAWYERING § 9.13 (discussing *Fisher*):

> [T]he Supreme Court ruled . . . that there was no Fifth Amendment bar against a subpoena to defense counsel that called for possibly incriminating tax records that the defendants had given to their lawyer [because the privilege is the client's, not the lawyer's]. The government conceded, however, that *if* the documents would have been protected by the Fifth Amendment in the hands of the clients, they must continue to be protected (by the attorney-client privilege) in the hands of the lawyer. The Supreme Court accepted this concession as obvious, for otherwise defendants would de facto lose whatever Fifth Amendment protection they originally had, as a "penalty" for communicating with their lawyers.

[141] 475 U.S. at 174, 106 S.Ct. at 998.

[142] 475 U.S. at 178, 106 S.Ct. at 1000.

[143] *Id.*

characteristic of the most unreliable *dictum*, counsel had failed adequately to argue the point,[144] and the majority opinion does not consider any of the significant differences between perjury and bribing a witness or juror.

As we have seen, perjury has been understood as falling outside of the future crime exception. One reason is that it is "intrinsically and inextricably" related to the crime for which the defendant is being tried.[145] In this respect, it is like the future crime of concealing the proceeds of a theft — that is, to reveal the future crime of concealment is to implicate the client in the crime of theft for which he is being tried, so the "possession and the facts underlying [it] are privileged" despite its future nature.[146] This is not true, of course, of the future crime of bribing a juror. To reveal the client's intent to commit bribery does not require the lawyer to reveal any confidences regarding his guilt of the underlying crime for which he is being tried.

Also, bribery of a juror sabotages the adversary system at its foundation, preventing it from functioning. By contrast, the adversary system takes perjury into account and is designed to deal with it. As Dean Wigmore has written, cross-examination is "the greatest legal engine ever invented for the discovery of truth."[147] A panel on lawyers' ethics was once asked what the defense lawyer should do when a client proposes to commit perjury. "Do me a favor," a United States Attorney on the panel replied, "Let him try it."[148] If the question had related to bribing a juror, however, the United States Attorney would certainly have responded very differently.

In the same paragraph in which it concludes that perjury is "essentially the same" as bribing a juror, the *Nix* majority says that a defendant would have no "right" to insist upon his lawyer's silence regarding bribery of a juror or witness. The analogy cuts the other way, however, because the Court has recognized a defendant's right to insist upon silence regarding his perjury, and, significantly, the context involved the defendant's Fifth Amendment privilege.

In *New Jersey v. Portash*,[149] Portash had been granted use immunity[150] for grand jury testimony. When he was subsequently prosecuted, the trial

---

[144] *See* Freedman, *supra* note 86, at 1949-51.

[145] Exum, *supra* note 4, at 22.

[146] RESTATEMENT § 82, Ill. 4. Ongoing possession of stolen goods remains privileged where the lawyer is "defending the client against criminal charges arising out of the offense." *Id.* Cmt. *e*, "*Continuing crimes and frauds.*" The privilege would be lost, of course, if the confidential communications related to "ways in which Client can continue to possess the stolen goods." *Id.* In the perjury context, this is not the kind of thing that happens when the lawyer makes continued good faith efforts to dissuade the client from committing perjury and avoids coaching the client on how to improve upon the perjury. Note, too, that in the stolen goods case, the lawyer's help in exonerating the defendant or in mitigating the sentence does have the effect of assisting the client in repossessing and enjoying the stolen goods, but that fact does not vitiate the privilege.

[147] 5 J. WIGMORE, WIGMORE ON EVIDENCE § 1367 (Chadbourne rev. ed. 1974).

[148] Salvatore Martoche, Remarks at the Seminar on *Ethics in an Adversary System* (Feb 11, 1984).

[149] 440 U.S. 450 (1979).

[150] Use immunity is given so that testimony can be compelled from a witness who has invoked her Fifth Amendment privilege. The testimony cannot be used against the witness, but can be used against others.

court ruled that if Portash testified to an alibi that contradicted his grand jury testimony, the prosecution would be able to use the grand jury testimony to impeach him. The Supreme Court held that Portash had a constitutional right to present his alibi (which was assumed to be perjured)[151] without being impeached with his grand jury testimony.

Obviously, Portash did not acquire a "right" to commit perjury. The Supreme Court did hold, however, that forfeiture of his Fifth Amendment privilege was not one of the consequences of his perjury.

Moreover, although the lawyer is "an officer of the court and a key component" of a system that is "dedicated to a search for truth,[152] there was no suggestion that Portash's lawyer had acted improperly in attempting to present the perjurious alibi. On the contrary, Portash's conviction was reversed in order to allow him to present the alibi on retrial.

Also bearing upon the future crime exception in the context of the Fifth Amendment privilege is *Estelle v. Smith*.[153] *Estelle* is the case in which the psychiatrist interviewed the defendant without any warning to the defendant that his statements could be used against him in court. The government was therefore barred from using the psychiatrist's testimony as the basis for testimony about the likelihood that the defendant would commit future crimes. Surely, then, if the psychiatrist cannot reveal the defendant's unwarned communications bearing upon future crimes without violating the defendant's Fifth Amendment privilege, the defendant's lawyer cannot do so either.

§ 6.19 WAIVER OF THE FIFTH AMENDMENT PRIVILEGE BY COMMITTING PERJURY

The argument is sometimes made that, despite the Fifth Amendment privilege, lawyers can be required (or permitted) to rectify client perjury by revealing incriminating information received from their clients. The reasoning is based on cases like *Harris v. New York*[154] and *Oregon v. Haas*,[155] where the Supreme Court has held that incriminating statements made by a defendant in violation of his Miranda rights,[156] and therefore inadmissible in the prosecution's case in chief, could nevertheless be used to impeach the defendant if he chose to testify contrary to those admissions. The Court held in *Harris* that the defendant has a privilege to testify in his own defense, but that the privilege to testify "cannot be construed to include the right to commit perjury."[157] "Having voluntarily taken the stand, [Harris] was under an obligation to speak truthfully and accurately," and the prosecution did no more than use "the traditional truth-testing devices of the adversary process."[158]

---

[151] *See* 440 U.S. at 452–453.

[152] *Nix v. Whiteside*, 475 U.S. 157, 174 (1986).

[153] 451 U.S. 454 (1981).

[154] 401 U.S. 222, 91 S.Ct. 643 (1971).

[155] 420 U.S. 714, 95 S.Ct. 1215 (1975).

[156] *Miranda v. Arizona*, 384 U.S. 436, 86 S.Ct. 1602 (1966).

[157] 401 U.S. at 225, 91 S.Ct. 645.

[158] *Id.* at 225, 645-646.

The Court added in *Haas* that inadmissibility of the admissions for impeachment would give the defendant "a right to falsify free from the embarrassment of impeachment evidence from the defendant's own mouth."[159]

Those decisions were strenuously argued by the government in *New Jersey v. Portash* (the case where the defendant was allowed to testify without being impeached with his immunized grand jury testimony). The Court responded, however, that Portash's grand jury testimony had been involuntary, because he had been given use immunity before making the admissions. By contrast, in *Harris* and *Haas* the defendants had made "no claim that the statements made to the police were coerced or involuntary" — that is, neither Harris nor Haas had claimed that his Fifth Amendment privilege had been violated at the time the damaging admissions had been made.[160]

A phrase sometimes used to justify using unwarned admissions against an accused is that "truth has consequences." That is, it is suggested that having chosen to tell the truth (*e.g.*, to a psychiatrist, to a cellmate, or to a lawyer) for some presumed benefit, the defendant has to suffer the consequences in the form of cross-examination. For example, in *Jaffe v. Redmond*, the Supreme Court recognized a therapist-patient privilege, and prohibited use of admissions by the patient to the therapist even for purposes of impeachment.[161] Justice Scalia protested that "[i]t seems to me entirely fair to say that if [the patient] wishes the benefits of telling the truth [to her therapist] she must also accept the consequences [of its use in cross-examination]."[162] On that point, however, Scalia was a lone dissenter. Moreover, in the Fifth Amendment context, the adverse consequences of truth-telling must be fully explained prior to the self-incriminating admissions, and the privilege must be voluntarily waived, before the truth can have adverse consequences in a criminal trial.

Assume, then, that a defendant has made incriminating statements to his lawyer before having been adequately warned that the statements would be communicated to the court if the defendant later chose to commit perjury. As the Supreme Court held in *Estelle v. Smith* (the psychiatrist case), the state's use of unwarned statements made to the psychiatrist would violate the Fifth Amendment privilege similar to any other form of compulsion.[163] The reason is that the Fifth Amendment prevents a defendant from being made "the

---

[159] 420 U.S. at 723, 95 S.Ct. at 1221.

[160] 401 U.S. at 224, 91 S.Ct. at 645; 420 U.S. at 722–723, 95 S.Ct. at 1220–1221. The rule in *Miranda v. Arizona* has since been held to be part of the Fifth Amendment. *Dickerson v. United States*, 530 U.S. 428, 120 S.Ct. 2326 (2000). However, the Court is not likely to change the rule allowing admissions in Miranda-warning cases like *Harris* and *Haas* to be used for purposes of impeachment. In justifying its holding in *Dickerson*, the Court expressly relied on the fact that cases subsequent to *Miranda* had "reduced its impact . . . on legitimate law enforcement" by limiting the effect of the Miranda rule to "evidence in the prosecution's case in chief." 530 U.S. at 443–444, 120 S.Ct. at 2336.

[161] 116 S.Ct. 1923 (1996).

[162] *Id.* at 1935.

[163] "Any effort to compel respondent to testify against his will at the sentencing hearing clearly would contravene the Fifth Amendment. Yet the State's attempt to establish [defendant's] future dangerousness by relying on the unwarned statements he made to [the psychiatrist] similarly infringes Fifth Amendment values." 451 U.S. at 463, 101 S.Ct. at 1873.

deluded instrument of his own conviction."[164] That is, an accused who makes an unwarned confession to the police, as in *Harris* and *Haas*, is obviously dealing with "agents of the state." But the defendant who makes an unwarned confession to his psychiatrist, or to his lawyer, is entitled to believe that he is speaking to someone who is acting "solely in his interest" in a relationship of trust and confidence.[165] Also, unlike cross-examination by the prosecution, as in *Harris* and *Haas*, betrayal of confidences by a defendant's own lawyer is not one of "the traditional truth-testing devices of the adversary process."[166]

A related contention is that by voluntarily choosing to testify after having been warned, the defendant impliedly waives his privilege against self-incrimination. However, "[t]there is a presumption against the waiver of constitutional rights."[167] To be valid, such a waiver "must not only be voluntary, but must also constitute a knowing and intelligent relinquishment or abandonment of a known right or privilege."[168] No such waiver was found, for example, when Portash decided voluntarily to testify and to contradict his truthful grand jury testimony, despite the fact that the trial judge had warned him that if he testified, he could be impeached with his earlier testimony.[169] In the case of incriminating information given to a lawyer, therefore, the point at which the warning must be given is *before* the defendant incriminates himself, in the mistaken belief that he is talking to "[a person] acting solely in his interest."[170] Once the defendant has made unwarned admissions to one who is actually subject to state strictures that have not been explained to him, the warning is too late. The defendant has already become "the deluded instrument of his own conviction."[171]

§ 6.20 *NIX V. WHITESIDE* AND THE QUESTION OF "KNOWING"

Within weeks of the *Nix* decision, the ABA, in conjunction with the American Law Institute, produced a videotape of several experts on the ethics of criminal defense lawyers commenting on the case. The ABA/ALI

---

[164] *Id.* at 462, *citing Culombe v. Connecticut*, 367 U.S. 568, 581, 81 S.Ct. 1860, 1867 (1961).

[165] *See* § 6.17, *supra.*

[166] *Id.* at 225, 645–646.

[167] *Brookhart v. Janis*, 384 U.S. 1, 4, 86 S.Ct. 1245, 1247 (1966).

[168] *Estelle v. Smith*, 451 U.S. at 471, 101 S.Ct. at 1877, n.16, *citing Edwards v. Arizona*, 451 U.S. at 482, 101 S.Ct. at 1883–1884, *quoting Johnson v. Zerbst*, 304 U.S. 458, 464, 58 S.Ct. 1019, 1023 (1938). *See also Mitchell v. United States*, 526 U.S. 314, 323–324, 119 S.Ct. 1307, 1312–1313 (1999), where the defendant was warned of the loss of her Fifth Amendment privilege if she chose to plead guilty, but where the warning was not sufficiently precise and clear to have "brought home" to her that she was waiving her right.

[169] It might be argued that in *Portash* the judge's warning came too late only because the terms of the use immunity had already been set out before Portash had incriminated himself before the grand jury. But the same is true if a client is told by his lawyer to "tell me everything so I can represent you effectively," and is belatedly given a lawyer-client Miranda warning only after he has incriminated himself. Again, the alternative is for the lawyer to give the warning at the outset — returning us to the model of intentional ignorance.

[170] *Estelle v. Smith*, 451 U.S. at 467, 101 S.Ct. at 1875.

[171] *Id.* at 462.

commentators make it clear that the trial lawyer's conduct approved by the majority in *Nix* represented a radical departure from traditional, standard practice.

The defense lawyer in *Nix* is described as having gone "bonkers" in his "brutal" reaction to his client's announced intention to commit perjury. Further, the notion that a criminal defense lawyer might be required to divulge his client's perjury is characterized as "startling," "unworkable," and out-of-touch with the dynamics of the lawyer-client relationship.

One method of coping with the problem created by *Nix* is through the disingenuous use of the standard of "knowing." That is, the lawyer has no obligation to reveal client perjury unless she "knows" that the client is going to commit perjury. All one has to do to nullify *Nix* then, is to define "knowing" in such a way that the obligation virtually never arises.[172]

For example, one commentator on the ABA/ALI videotape says that a lawyer has an obligation to reveal client perjury only if the lawyer has "absolutely no doubt whatsoever" that the client will commit a "serious" fraud on the court. (The perjury in *Nix* is defined on the tape as falling short of "serious" fraud.) Also, soon after *Nix*, the Deputy Attorney General who won the case was quoted in the ABA *Journal* as saying that if the lawyer does not "know for sure" that a witness' evidence is false, the lawyer should put forth the evidence.[173] In the same article a former prosecutor said that a client may stick to a story that "you know in your heart of hearts is false." As long as the client "never admits that it is false," however, most lawyers "suspend judgment and do the best they can." He added that any different standard of "knowing" would be "at war with the duty to represent the client zealously."[174] Similarly, ABA Opinion 87-353 makes sure that it will be "the unusual case where the lawyer does know." The Opinion requires that knowing be established only by the client's "clearly stated intention" that he will commit perjury at trial.

These opinions are consistent with the Model Rules, which narrowly define knowing in the Terminology section as "actual knowledge."[175] The Eighth Circuit has similarly insisted upon a direct client admission of perjury to establish "knowing" or "actual knowledge."[176] The court held that an attorney must use "extreme caution" in deciding that a client intends to commit perjury, and that nothing but "a clear expression of intent" will justify the attorney's disclosure to the judge.[177] The Second Circuit has also adopted a "clearly

---

[172] Our own preference, of course, is to recognize that lawyers know the truth — indeed, that it is our ethical duty to know everything possible about the case — and to confront the ethical issues created by that knowledge.

[173] David O. Stewart, *Drawing the Line at Lying*, ABA J. 84, 88 (May 1, 1986).

[174] *Id.*

[175] The Restatement also defines knowing narrowly in judging the falsity of evidence. The Restatement uses the phrases "actual knowledge" and "firm factual basis." It permits a lawyer to ignore anything that is not "plainly apparent," allows the lawyer to maintain ignorance of information that would have been discovered through reasonable inquiry, and limits "firm factual basis" to facts actually "known to the lawyer or the client's own statements" which indicate that the testimony or other evidence is false. Sec. 120, cmt. *c*.

[176] *United States v. Long*, 857 F.2d 436 (8th Cir. 1988).

[177] *Id.* at 445, 447.

established" or "actual knowledge" standard.[178] In doing so, the court approved of a definition providing that "[i]nformation is clearly established when the client *acknowledges to the attorney* that he has perpetrated a fraud upon a tribunal."[179] The court observed that under any standard less than actual knowledge, courts would be "inundated" with lawyers' reports of perjury.[180]

At another point in its opinion, the Second Circuit went further, indicating that an admission alone will not be sufficient to justify disclosure by a lawyer. After explaining that knowledge by the lawyer means "actual knowledge," the court went on to say that the lawyer should disclose "only that information which [1] the attorney reasonably knows to be a fact and which, [2] when combined with other facts in his knowledge, would [3] clearly establish the existence of a fraud on the tribunal."[181] Thus, even the client's admission does not suffice unless it is corroborated by "other facts" that "clearly establish" the perjury.

This development was forecast in *Nix* itself. The majority opinion characterizes the case as one in which the defendant's "intent to commit perjury [was] communicated to counsel."[182] The concurring justices add that "[e]xcept in the rarest of cases" attorneys who "adopt 'the role of the judge or jury to determine the facts' . . . pose a danger of depriving their clients of the zealous and loyal advocacy required by the Sixth Amendment."[183] Also, Justice Stevens accurately observes that:

> A lawyer's certainty that a change in his client's recollection is a harbinger of intended perjury — as well as judicial review of such apparent certainty — should be tempered by the realization that, after reflection, the most honest witness may recall (or sincerely believe he recalls) details that he previously overlooked.[184]

Finally, when the defense lawyer makes the decision that the client's inconsistent stories do not mean that he intends to commit perjury, presumably the same standard of review will be used as for ineffective assistance — that is, the court must "indulge a strong presumption that counsel's conduct falls within the wide range of reasonable professional assistance."[185] Thus, it is highly unlikely that a lawyer who chooses to honor her client's confidences will run afoul of a proscription (as under MR 3.3) against offering evidence that she "knows" to be false.

Unfortunately, however, the "unusual" cases in which lawyers have acted on their knowledge that their clients are lying have produced a "race and class based double standard," raising serious questions of denial of equal protection

---

[178] *Doe v. Federal Grievance Committee*, 847 F.2d 57 (2d Cir. 1988).

[179] *Id.* at 62 (emphasis added).

[180] *Id.* at 63.

[181] *Id.* at 63.

[182] 475 U.S. at 163, 106 S.Ct. at 993.

[183] *Nix v. Whiteside*, 475 U.S. 157, 189 (1986), quoting in part from *United States ex rel. Wilcox v. Johnson*, 555 F.2d 115, 122 (3d Cir. 1977).

[184] 475 U.S. at 191.

[185] *Nix v. Whiteside*, 475 U.S. 157, 164 (1986), quoting *Strickland v. Washington*, 466 U.S. 668, 689, 104 S.Ct. 2052, 2066 (1984).

of the laws.[186] That is, the cases in which lawyers have revealed client perjury to the court have virtually invariably involved criminal defendants who are poor and members of minority groups. For example, in a case in which counsel has been privately retained, one will not find a case like *People v. DePallo*.[187]

§ 6.21 *NIX V. WHITESIDE* AND MR 3.3 MEET ROY COHN

Perhaps the ultimate method of responding to the *Nix dictum* and of nullifying the requirement to report client perjury under MR 3.3, was provided by Professor Hazard. Appearing on the ABA/ALI videotape, Hazard advises how lawyers can "avoid" or "evade" the *Nix* and Model Rules result. The lawyer, he suggests, can ask the client *what the prosecution is likely to say* about his involvement in the crime. (You will recognize this as a variation on the Roy Cohn solution, discussed above.) In that way, the lawyer can learn the truth without making the client commit himself to a particular version of the facts, and the lawyer then will not have to be concerned about "knowingly" presenting perjury.

This kind of sophistry — which is required by unrealistic rules that appear to require the betrayal of client confidences — is perhaps the best reason to maintain expressly the traditional model of lawyer-client trust and confidence. Under the traditional model, the analytical approach is an open one, requiring moral justification, rather than inviting disingenuous evasions to achieve the same result.

§ 6.22 HAZARD'S CHANGE OF POSITION

As noted earlier, the client perjury trilemma remains unresolved after more than a third of a century of intense discussion. Also, we have acknowledge that we are less than completely satisfied with our own position. It is not surprising, therefore, that even strongly held views on the issue have changed significantly over the years.

One important change in position is that of Professor Geoffrey C. Hazard, Jr., who was the Reporter for the Model Rules and a strong supporter of the requirement of MR 3.3 that lawyers — including criminal defense lawyers — be required to disclose client confidences in order to rectify fraud on the court.[188] Hazard has recently noted, however, that the duties of maintaining a client's confidences and of being candid with the court are "inherently incompatible."[189] Accordingly, he adds, "[s]tatements cast in terms of 'complete loyalty' and 'complete candor' must be regarded as hortatory, hypocrisy, or simply nonsense."[190]

---

[186] Silver, *Truth, Justice, and the American Way: The Case Against Client Perjury Rules*, 47 VAND. L. REV. 339, 358 (1994).

[187] 2001 WL 735739 (N.Y. Ct. App. 2001), discussed *supra* beginning at n.34.

[188] Geoffrey C. Hazard, Jr., *The Client Fraud Problem as a Justinian Quartet: An Extended Analysis*, 25 HOFSTRA L. REV. 1041 (1997). Hazard's article is more thoughtful and complex than this short comment can do justice to.

[189] *Id.* at 1049.

[190] *Id.*

In his wide professional associations, Hazard has found that:[191]

> [M]any judge show strong sympathy for an advocate whose client wants to commit perjury in a criminal case . . . . [T]he inference is that these judges believe that the game of trying to compel counsel to be a gatekeeper in this context is not worth the candle of the additional light of truth that could be achieved.

For his own part, Hazard concludes: "I have come to the view that requiring a criminal defense lawyer to 'blow the whistle' on client perjury is futile or counterproductive."[192]

§ 6.23 FRANKEL'S CHANGE OF POSITION

Another significant development is an article by Marvin Frankel.[193] After about a dozen years as a Federal District Court Judge, Frankel wrote *Partisan Justice*, which is discussed in Chapters 2 and 5 above. Frankel was the most articulate spokesman for less confidentiality and more candor in litigation, and was influential in proposing and drafting MR 3.3(a)(4), which forbids the lawyer to offer known false evidence, and that requires disclosure if the lawyer comes to know that evidence offered was false. After another dozen or so years back in practice, however, Frankel reassessed his position with the same kind of candor that he has championed.

Rules like MR 3.3(a)(4) and DR 7-102(A)(4)[194] are "easily stated," Frankel notes, but are "only the beginning of daunting perplexities" that "continue to baffle us."[195] Despite the rules, there is "no evidence suggest[ing] that there has been a notable increase in truth-telling in the courthouse."[196] This is so for two reasons. First, the problems are "agonizingly difficult." Second, "the status quo, however unsatisfactory in principle, suits us pretty well."[197]

Frankel concludes, therefore:[198]

> . . . That we are not omniscient remains a sound perception and a legitimate comfort in these situations.
>
> Our lack of omniscience has come to seem to me a key fact that we could and should develop more creatively . . . . What we can know is that there is important evidence that contradicts [a witness'] story. We can know, too, that the witness has told a quite different story at another time. We can even know that if our "lives, fortunes, and

---

[191] *Id.* at 1052. At the same time, Hazard argues that the requirement of confidentiality does not have the same force in civil cases as it does in criminal trials. He suggests, therefore, that the balance between candor to the court and confidentiality be struck differently in civil cases. *Id.* at 1052, 1060. *Accord,* MONROE FREEDMAN, LAWYERS' ETHICS IN AN ADVERSARY SYSTEM 40, 53, 56 (1975).

[192] *Id.* at 1060.

[193] Marvin Frankel, *Partisan Justice: A Brief Revisit,* 15 ABA LITIGATION 43 (1989).

[194] Forbidding a lawyer to knowingly use perjured testimony or false evidence.

[195] *Id.* at 43–44.

[196] *Id.* at 44.

[197] *Id.*

[198] *Id.*

sacred honor" depended on it, we would not act on the premise that the witness is telling the truth. But with relatively rare exceptions, we cannot know the "truth" with such a degree of certainty.

The quoted passage appears to be a variation on the sophistry that the lawyer never knows the truth. The key sentence in Frankel's revised position, however, is the one that we omitted from the quotation. It reads: "The more I see of life and the practice of law, the more justifiable I find the stance that *we really ought not to be called upon to 'know'* when someone's story is false."[199]

That is very different from saying that the lawyer does not or cannot know the truth. On the contrary, Frankel impliedly recognizes that lawyers frequently do know the truth, even if not with certainty.[200] On the basis of a wealth of experience in life and in the practice of law, however, he maintains that, in some contexts, lawyers "ought not to be called upon to 'know.'" Specifically, with respect to the false testimony of witnesses, we ought not to be required by rules of ethics to act on our knowledge in a way that threatens the essential relationship of trust and confidence between lawyer and client.

---

[199] *Id.* (emphasis added).

[200] Thus, Frankel is able to maintain his insistence upon more truth in the system on other issues. For example, "at least in civil cases our rules of discovery should be widened to require that lawyers deliver on demand to their adversaries evidence favorable to the other side." *Id.*; *see also* Marvin Frankel, *The Search for Truth Continued: More Disclosure, Less Privilege,"* 54 Colo. L. Rev. 51 (1982); Albert Alschuler, *The Search for Truth Continued, the Privilege Retained: A Response to Judge Frankel*, 54 Colo. L. Rev. 67 (1982).

Chapter 7

COUNSELING CLIENTS AND PREPARING WITNESSES

§ 7.01 INTRODUCTION

Your client in a criminal case has just been convicted and is free on bail pending sentencing in two weeks. He asks you to do one last bit of research for him. "As soon as possible," he says, "give me a list of all of the countries in South America that do not have extradition treaties with the United States." Would you give him the list?

Several years ago, Freedman put that question to two professors at a prestigious law school. Both are experienced trial lawyers, and one has since become a federal judge. One of them said that he would not answer the client's question. The other said that he would. "I am a law book," he explained. That is, if the client had the lawyer's skills in research and analysis, he could go to a law library and answer the question himself. One function of a lawyer is to give people information about the law — information that should be freely, and equally, available to everyone.[1]

Later, Freedman asked each of the professors privately whether he thought the other's response was unprofessional. Each answered No. That is, each considered it to be a matter of discretion with the lawyer whether to give the client the legal advice he sought.

Underlying the discussion in this chapter is the question of how far a lawyer can and should go in giving a client legal advice about potentially unlawful conduct. Does the "I am a law book" philosophy demean the legal profession, or is it an expression of how lawyers fulfill one of their highest functions in a society committed to equal protection of law?

Blue Law Case #1

Assume that one of your firm's principal clients is a major department store that is located near the state line. In your state, there is a Blue Law that forbids the client to remain open on Sundays. In the adjoining state, however, there are no Blue Laws, and just across the state line there are several discount appliance stores that do a heavy business on Sundays. As a result, your client is suffering severe business losses. The client's chief executive officer asks you, therefore, what the penalty would be for staying open on Sunday. Obviously, she wants to do a cost-benefit analysis on law-breaking — to decide, that is, whether crime would in fact pay in this instance.

---

[1] Professor Lon Fuller has maintained that an essential element of the law's inner morality is that the content of the law be readily available to those who are governed by it. LON L. FULLER, THE MORALITY OF LAW 49–51 (1964).

Blue Law Case #2

Assume that you do research the issue and find that the prescribed penalty is $25 for each violation, and that the highest court in the state has interpreted "each violation" to mean each day that business is done, rather than each sale that is made. You inform the client and, predictably, your client opens for business on the next Sunday.

Blue Law Case #3

Assume now that the facts are the same, except that the courts in your state have not yet interpreted the phrase "each violation"? You say to the CEO, "There are two possible penalties. One is that you would have to pay $25 each time the cash register rings." The CEO interjects, "Then we can't possibly go ahead." "On the other hand," you continue, "I think we have a forty-sixty chance of persuading the state supreme court that 'each violation' refers only to each Sunday that the store is open. If you want to give it a try, we'll be glad to litigate it for you." On the basis of your counseling, the CEO decides to take the chance.

§ 7.02 APPLYING THE MODEL RULES[2]

MR 1.2(d) broadly forbids a lawyer to "counsel a client to engage, or assist a client, in conduct that the lawyer knows is criminal or fraudulent." In addition, MR 1.16(a)(1) says that a lawyer shall not represent a client if doing so "will result in violation of the rules of professional conduct or other law." Apart from these mandatory rules, a lawyer may always decline to accept representation of a client at the outset,[3] withdraw with the consent of the client, or withdraw without the client's consent if withdrawal will not have a material adverse effect on the interests of the client.[4] (In a matter before a court or other tribunal, the lawyer might be required by rule of court to obtain permission from the court to withdraw,[5] but that is not relevant here.)

In Case #1, therefore, the lawyer is permitted to research the issue for the client, even though, depending on the results of the research, the client might decide to break the law. Perhaps the lawyer's research will satisfy the client that, in this case at least, crime will not pay because the cost of doing business is too high. Or, even if the price is right, the lawyer might be successful in dissuading the client from violating the law. In short, a lawyer can ethically advise Justice Holmes' "bad man," who wants to know what the law is because he wants to avoid the consequences of breaking the law.[6]

In Case #2, however, the lawyer does do the research and knows that her legal advice (that the penalty is insignificant) is almost certain to result in

---

[2] The results under the Model Code are similar on these issues.

[3] *See* Ch. 3, *supra*.

[4] MR 1.16(b).

[5] *See* MR 1.16(c).

[6] *See* O.W. Holmes, *The Path of the Law*, in Collected Legal Papers 170–171 (1920). The man is bad in the sense that he has no concern with moral right or wrong; however, he has no intention to break the law and risk getting caught.

her client's decision to violate the law. Is the lawyer forbidden, then, to give the client the results of her research?

MR 1.2(d) forbids two kinds of conduct. First, the lawyer shall not "*counsel* a client *to* engage" in criminal conduct. Simply to explain the consequences of a violation of law doesn't do that. Second, the lawyer is forbidden to "*assist* a client . . . *in* conduct the lawyer knows is criminal." Again, that is not what is happening in Case #2. As stated in Comment [6] to MR 1.2: "A lawyer is required to give an honest opinion about the actual consequences that appear likely to result from a client's conduct. The fact that a client uses advice in a course of action that is criminal or fraudulent does not, of itself, make a lawyer a party to the course of action." The comment notes a "critical distinction" between presenting an analysis of legal aspects of questionable conduct and recommending the means by which a crime or fraud might be committed with impunity."[7]

In Case #3, however, the lawyer goes beyond giving the client "an honest opinion of the actual consequences that appear likely to result" from breaking the law. The lawyer is pretty clearly counseling the client to violate the law and see whether the penalty can be kept low enough to make the illegal conduct profitable. Nevertheless, the lawyer's advice is permitted under MR 1.2(d). As we have seen, that rule forbids the lawyer to *counsel* a client *to* engage in unlawful conduct. The rule adds, however, that a lawyer may discuss the legal consequences of any proposed course of conduct with a client "and may counsel or assist a client to make a good faith effort to determine the validity, scope, meaning or application of the law."[8] That is exactly what the lawyer is doing in Case #3.

§ 7.03   THE LAWYER'S INITIATIVE, AND THE SERIOUSNESS OF THE CRIME

Leaving it to the discretion of each lawyer whether to advise a client regarding illegal conduct is satisfactory in the Blue Law case and, perhaps, in the extradition case. On the other hand, we could take the extradition case one step further: It has not occurred to the client that there might be countries that do not have extradition treaties with the United States, so the lawyer raises the issue and offers to do the research. Should the lawyer have discretion to do so? Note that none of the rules we have discussed makes anything turn upon whether the lawyer or the client initiates the discussion.

Also, in neither the Blue Law nor the extradition case is there a victim in the ordinary sense, nor is a crime of violence contemplated. What if the client is planning a bank robbery and wants the lawyer's advice about whether the penalty is higher if she carries an automatic weapon while committing the

---

[7] *See also* N.Y. State Opin. 455 (1976), interpreting New York's DR 7-102(a)(7):

[W]here the lawyer does no more than advise his client concerning the legal character and consequences of the act, there can be no professional impropriety . . . . It is the encouragement of illegal conduct that is proscribed, not the mere giving of advice as to what conduct may be deemed illegal or a discussion of its consequences."

[8] Presumably, the lawyer will also advise the client to voluntarily pay the State $25 each Sunday it remains open for business.

crime? Oddly, none of the rules we have been discussing makes anything turn on the seriousness of the offense.[9] Presumably most lawyers would not take an "I am a law book" approach, and would choose not to advise the client — at least if the answer to the client's question is that carrying an automatic weapon will not increase the penalty. It would appear, however, that such a case should not be a matter of discretion, but that lawyers should be forbidden to give legal advice when to do so would significantly increase the likelihood of criminal conduct that is likely to result in death or serious injury to the person. Similarly, we might be concerned with what the underlying crime is in the extradition case, and with the likelihood that the client will repeat it.

§ 7.04   CREATING FALSE EVIDENCE

Shortly after a serious heart attack, an elderly client of Lawyer *A* decides to make a sizeable gift to his son. *A* advises the client to develop evidence (*e.g.*, write letters to his son and to others) that would help to establish that the gift has not been made in contemplation of death but with a lifetime motive. This evidence could later be used to persuade a court that the client's estate should not have to pay taxes on the gift.   — Has *A* acted unethically?

This fact pattern ("item") was used as part of a pre-test in a study of ethical conduct among lawyers. The purpose of the pre-test was to determine which of the items were effective in identifying lawyers who were unethical. The tax item was eliminated by the pre-test and was not used in the final survey, because the lawyer's conduct was generally approved by lawyers who were regarded as ethical.[10]

The relevant rules of the Model Rules are the following. Under MR 3.4(b), a lawyer is forbidden to "falsify evidence [or] counsel or assist a witness to testify falsely." Under MR 1.2(d), the lawyer is forbidden to assist the client in conduct the lawyer "knows" is criminal or fraudulent. Under 8.4(c), the lawyer is forbidden to engage in "conduct involving dishonesty, fraud, deceit or misrepresentation." Under Rule 3.3(a)(4), the lawyer is forbidden to offer evidence that the lawyer "knows" to be false.

In advising the client to develop evidence of a non-testamentary motive, then, has the lawyer assisted the client in criminal or fraudulent conduct,

---

[9] However, MR 1.16(b)(1) *permits* the lawyer to withdraw if the client "persists" in conduct that the lawyer "reasonably believes is criminal or fraudulent," but the lawyer may do so only if the conduct "involves the lawyer's services." Also, MR 1.16(b)(3) *permits* the lawyer to withdraw if the client "insists on pursuing an objective that the lawyer considers repugnant or imprudent." If the lawyer chose to withdraw, she would also be *permitted* under MR 1.6(b)(1) to reveal information only where necessary to prevent the client from committing a criminal act likely to result in imminent death or substantial bodily harm.

[10] J.E. CARLIN, LAWYERS' ETHICS: A STUDY OF THE NEW YORK CITY BAR 46 (1966). What was deemed to be ethical for purposes of the survey was conduct, like that in the tax case, that was approved by partners in large firms that represented corporations and wealthy individuals. For a critical review of the book, *see* Monroe H. Freedman, *Book Review*, 16 AM. U.L. REV. 177 (1966).

Under the Canons of Professional Ethics, which were then in effect, a lawyer was forbidden to engage in "any manner of fraud or chicane" (Canon 15) or to "deal other than candidly with the facts . . . in the presentation of causes" (Canon 22).

specifically, in creating false evidence, or has the lawyer engaged in conduct involving dishonesty, fraud, deceit, or misrepresentation? And if the lawyer later introduces the letters as evidence of the client's intent to make an *inter vivos* gift, is the lawyer offering evidence that the lawyer knows is false? Surely, the lawyer has *reason to believe* that the client has come to her because he is concerned about dying and wants to "put his affairs in order."[11] But what a reasonable lawyer would believe isn't the test under the ethical rules. Rather, the standard is whether the lawyer has "actual knowledge" of the client's true intent.[12] Should that be the standard?

Part of the problem is that we are concerned here with the client's motive or intent, and motives are frequently mixed or unclear, even to the motivated individual. Nevertheless, there are many situations in which the law makes a person's intent crucial, even when the person may have no "intent" at all in the sense contemplated by the law.

To illustrate the problem of intent as a test of legal consequences, one writer has suggested the following situation.[13] A young man and a young woman decide to get married. Each has $1,000. They decide to begin a business with these funds, and the young woman gives her money to the young man for that purpose. Is their intention to form a joint venture or a partnership? Do they intend that the young man be an agent or a trustee? Is the transaction a gift or is it a loan? Most likely, without counseling regarding legal concepts and legal consequences, the couple's state of mind does not conform to any of the modes of intention that the law might look for. Thus, if they should be advised that their taxes will be lower if the transaction is viewed as a gift, they might "intend" it to be a gift. Undoubtedly, it is their intent to pay no more taxes than the law requires. On the other hand, if making the transaction a loan protects the young woman more effectively from the possibility of serious tort liability, then they might prefer that legal structure.

The illustration is not presented with a cynical intent. As in countless other instances, the rules of law require determinations of "fact" when the facts are truly ambiguous. This is particularly so, of course, with respect to mental states.

The Model Code explicitly recognizes this problem in EC 7-6: whether the proposed action of a lawyer is within the bounds of the law may be a "perplexing question" when the client is contemplating a course of conduct "having legal consequences that vary according to the client's intent, motive, or desires at the time of the action." Under DR 7-102(A)(6), a lawyer may not participate in creating or preserving evidence when the lawyer "knows or it is obvious" that it is false. Nevertheless, EC 7-6 explains that unless the

---

[11] Would the case be different if he had said this in so many words? Lawyers we have spoken to think not.

[12] There is no expressed standard of "knowing" under MR 3.4(b) or 8.4(c). Presumably, though, words like "falsify" and "fraud" (and even the word "misrepresentation" in conjunction with the other words in the same phrase) imply a knowing act of deception. As in MR 1.2(d) and 3.3(a)(4), therefore, these provisions should be interpreted under the Model Rules' standard of "actual knowledge." *See* the discussion of "knowing" in Chapter 6, *supra*.

[13] WURZEL, DAS JURISTISCHE DENKEN 82 (1904), translated in LON FULLER & ROBERT BRAUCHER, BASIC CONTRACT LAW 67 (1964).

lawyer is "certain" as to his client's state of mind, he should "resolve all reasonable doubts in favor of his client" and "assist his client in the development and preservation of evidence of existing motive, intent, or desire."

§ 7.05 RECONSTRUCTING PAST EVENTS THROUGH WITNESSES

A trial is an effort to reconstruct the past under extremely difficult circumstances — two or more parties have different versions of what happened and each has a strong incentive to persuade the trier of fact that his version is the true one. The lawyer's job is to marshal and present her client's case in the most effective way.

An essential step in competently litigating a case is what is called "preparing," "coaching," or "woodshedding" one's witnesses. An article selected by the Section of Litigation of the American Bar Association as part of "A Primer for Trial Lawyers" makes the point without equivocation. "It is axiomatic. Everyone who testifies has to be woodshedded."[14] "The first rule . . . is to woodshed in every instance, rehearsing both direct and cross examination."[15] Professor Anthony Amsterdam has recommended that in a criminal case in which the defendant testifies, it is "frequently desirable to begin the examination of the defendant with a short, *well-rehearsed set piece*, involving crisp, easy-to-remember answers that categorically and emphatically deny guilt and make clear the theory of the defense."[16]

That is, the lawyer must try to elicit all relevant facts and to help the client — who, typically, is not skilled at articulation — to express the relevant facts of his case as persuasively as possible. For example, the poorly educated day laborer who has suffered an injury, and who can only say, "It hurts bad," must be helped to articulate what the pain is like, when it is present, and how it interferes with work, sleep, family life, and recreation.[17] In addition, the statement "I hurt myself on the job" will not be enough. The relevant details must then be sufficiently rehearsed to assure that no material evidence will be overlooked in testimony at trial, where leading questions will not be permitted.[18]

Discussing "litigation practice uniformly followed in the United States," the *Restatement of the Law Governing Lawyers* summarizes practices in witness

---

[14] David H. Berg, *Preparing Witnesses*, in THE LITIGATION MANUAL: A PRIMER FOR TRIAL LAWYERS 466, 469 (2d ed., 1989).

[15] *Id.* at 470.

[16] Anthony Amsterdam, Trial Manual 5 for the Defense of Criminal Cases § 393 (1989); *see also*, §§ 402, 405 (offering guidance for witness preparation of defendants, experts, and character witnesses).

[17] *See* D.C. Bar, Formal Opin. 79 (1979). In an opinion under both the Model Rules and the Model Code, the Committee addressed the ethical limitations on the lawyer's suggesting "the actual language" in which a witness' testimony is to be presented. The opinion concludes that as long as the "substance of the testimony is not, so far as the lawyer knows or ought to know, false or misleading," the lawyer can properly "assist in shaping" the client's testimony.

[18] *See* John M. Conley, William M. O'Barr & E. Allen Lind, *The Power of Language: Presentation Style in the Courtroom*, 1978 DUKE L. JOUR. 1375 (1978).

preparation that are ethically permitted and almost certainly required.[19] These include (among others listed): explaining the law that applies to the facts of the case; telling the witness about other testimony that will be presented and asking the witness to reconsider the witness' own proposed testimony in the light of what others will be saying; suggesting the choice of words that will best make the witness' meaning clear; helping the witness to prepare for probable hostile lines of cross-examination; and rehearsing the witness' testimony.[20]

The process of interviewing and preparing witnesses has been spelled out in three articles in a book compiled under the sponsorship of the Association of American Law Schools.[21] The purpose of the book is to gather together the best legal thought on evidence and trial preparation.[22] Thus, the three articles that we will discuss here — by Lloyd Paul Stryker, Harry S. Bodin, and Edward W. Cleary[23] — can fairly be said to represent a professional consensus of the proper way to interview and prepare witnesses for trial.

In discussing the technique of interviewing the client, Bodin notes that it is generally advisable to let the client tell his own story while the lawyer just listens. If the attorney insists upon getting only answers to specific questions, important points may be screened out, because a lawyer cannot anticipate all the facts in every case.[24] Having gotten the client's story in narrative fashion, the lawyer must then seek additional facts that may have been omitted. That is done by asking questions and by explaining to the client how important the additional information may be to the case. "If the client can be made to understand your thoughts, he may tell you facts which otherwise would have been inadvertently overlooked or consciously and erroneously discarded by him as immaterial."[25]

At the same time the client's story will be affected by a "subconscious suppression, psychologically induced by the wish to put one's best foot forward or by nature's trick of inducing forgetfulness of what one does not like to remember."[26] That is, people will, in perfectly good faith, relate past events in a way that they believe (correctly or incorrectly) to be consistent with their own interests. Necessarily, therefore, in pressing the client for additional information, and in explaining the relevance and importance of that information, the lawyer will be affecting the ultimate testimony. Although it is improper to prompt or suggest an answer to one's witness during the actual testimony, the interview "affords full play to suggestion . . . and evokes in

---

[19] RESTATEMENT § 116, cmt. b; § 52(1) ("a lawyer . . . must exercise the competence and diligence normally exercised by lawyers in similar circumstances.")

[20] Id., § 116, cmt. b. The comment concludes with the sentence: "However, a lawyer may not assist the witness to testify falsely as to a material fact."

[21] SELECTED WRITINGS ON THE LAW OF EVIDENCE AND TRIAL (W. Fryer, ed., 1957).

[22] Id. at v.

[23] LLOYD P. STRYKER, THE ART OF ADVOCACY (1954); HARRY S. BODIN, MARSHALLING THE EVIDENCE (1954); Cleary, Evidence as a Problem in Communicating, 5 VAND. L. REV. 275 (1952).

[24] BODIN, supra note 23, at 13.

[25] Id.

[26] Id. at 14.

advance of trial a complete verbalization, the importance of which cannot be overlooked."[27]

The process of preparing or coaching the witnesses goes far beyond eliciting facts. In the course of polishing the client's testimony, Stryker recommends as many as fifty full rehearsals of direct and cross-examination. During these rehearsals, the testimony is developed in a variety of ways. The witness is vigorously cross-examined, and then the attorney points out where the witness has been "tripped" and how the testimony can be restructured to avoid that result. The attorney may also take the role of witness and be cross-examined by an associate. The attorney's "failures" in simulated testimony are then discussed, and the attorney then may conduct a mock cross-examination of the associate. In that way, "new ideas are developed while all the time the client is looking on and listening. He probably is saying, 'Let me try again.' And you will then go through the whole process once more." By that time, as one might expect, the client "does far better."[28] In fact, after many weeks of preparation, "perhaps on the very eve of trial," the client may come up with a new fact that "may perhaps make a difference between victory and defeat."[29]

Nowhere in these three selections relating to preparation of witness is there any analysis of the ethical implications of the model practices that are set forth. Stryker does say that in repeatedly going over the "hard spots" and the "awkward places" and in showing the client how to "surmount his difficulties," the witness is "still staying well within the truth, the whole truth, and nothing but the truth."[30] Saying that, however, does not make it so. If people do respond to suggestion, and if the lawyer helps the client to "fill in the gaps" and to avoid being "tripped," and does so by developing "new ideas" in the course of repeated rehearsals, it is reasonably clear that the testimony that ultimately is presented in court will have been significantly affected by the lawyer's prompting and by what the client has learned to be in his self-interest. Whether the end product is "well within the truth, the whole truth and nothing but the truth" is subject, therefore, to considerable doubt.

It seems unlikely that a lawyer with Stryker's experience and sophistication was unaware of the impact of suggestion on witnesses, which is recognized in the article by Cleary. Cleary, however, concerns himself only with the problem of how rules of evidence — but not the rules of legal ethics — might be reformed to take into account the psychological realities that he discusses. Bodin also recognizes the "psychologically induced" inclination to remember or forget in a way consistent with one's own interests. However, he ignores the implications of that fact when he discusses how important it is for the lawyer to make the client aware of the significance of information that may have been left out of the client's original narrative.

In addition, the Bodin article (unlike Cleary's) reflects a significant degree of ignorance within the legal profession of the psychological literature regarding memory. For example, Bodin says that, "Experienced trial lawyers have

---

[27] Cleary, *supra* note 23, at 30.

[28] STRYKER, *supra* note 23, at 4.

[29] *Id.* at 3.

[30] *Id.*

learned that even an honest and rational client, who will not *invent* 'facts,' may nevertheless *suppress* facts."[31] Experiments by psychologists, indicate, however, that those experienced trial lawyers are wrong: good faith invention is no less common than good faith suppression. Bodin also states that, "Of first importance in any action are the *facts* — the *exact* facts and *all* the facts."[32] He then explains how the lawyer must seek to elicit "all the important facts" by probing the client's memory with "detailed questioning."[33] The difficulty is that this effort to obtain "*all* the facts" is virtually certain to result in obtaining something very different from "the *exact* facts."[34]

§ 7.06   THE PSYCHOLOGY OF MEMORY

A common misconception about memory is that it is a process of reproducing or retrieving stored information, in the manner of a videotape or a computer. In fact, memory is much more a process of reconstruction. Moreover, the process is a highly creative one, affecting what is "remembered" as much as what is "forgotten."[35] "According to the cliche, memory fades. In fact, however, it grows."[36] Although the initial perception may fade, "every time we recall an event we must reconstruct the memory, and so each time it is changed — colored by succeeding events, increased understanding, a new context, suggestions by others, other people's recollections."[37]

Even before the process of remembering begins, however, the content of what is perceived is often determined by the temperament, biases, expectations, and past knowledge of the witness.[38] A great amount of what is said

---

[31] BODIN, *supra* note 23, at 13 (emphasis in the original).

[32] *Id.* (emphasis in the original).

[33] *Id.* at 13–14.

[34] Since Freedman explored these issues in 1966 and 1975, there has been significantly more sophistication and candor about the ethics of witness preparation. *See,* MONROE FREEDMAN, LAWYER'S ETHICS IN AN ADVERSARY SYSTEM (Ch. 6, *Counseling the Client: Refreshing Recollection or Prompting Perjury?*) (1975). *See, e.g.,* MARVIN E. FRANKEL, PARTISAN JUSTICE 15–16 (arguing that witness preparation frequently leads to subornation of perjury and at the very least "mock[s] the solemn promise of the whole truth and nothing but"); KENNETH MANN, DEFENDING WHITE COLLAR CRIME 137 (1986):

> The attorney has to bring . . . a client to understand how to organize his thoughts and what to emphasize. But it is also true that . . . attorneys . . . improperly influence a client by letting him know, even if only by hinting, what to leave out and what to include and how to shape facts so that an appearance of propriety is created where in fact wrongdoing occurred.

See also John S. Applegate, *Witness Preparation*, 68 TEX. L. REV. 277 (1989); W. William Hodes, *The Professional Duty to Horsehed Witnesses — Zealously, Within the Bounds of the Law*, 30 TEX. TECH. L. REV. 1343 (1999); Richard C. Wydick, *The Ethics of Witness Coaching*, 17 CARDOZO L. REV. 1 (1995); Bennett L. Gershman, *The Prosecutor's Duty to Truth*, 14 GEO. J. Legal ETHICS 309, 343 (2001) (noting the danger of excessive coaching of witnesses by prosecutors); Monroe Freedman, *Ethics, Truth, and Justice in Criminal Litigation*, 68 FORDHAM L. REV. 1371 (2000) (discussing a case in which a detective created highly incriminating testimony from a witness' recollection of what she initially believed to be an innocuous incident).

[35] *See generally* DANIEL L. SCHACTER, THE SEVEN SINS OF MEMORY: HOW THE MIND FORGETS AND REMEMBERS (2001)

[36] ELIZABETH LOFTUS, MEMORY 169 (1980).

[37] *Id.*

[38] FREDERICK C. BARTLETT, REMEMBERING: A STUDY IN EXPERIMENTAL AND SOCIAL PSYCHOLOGY 33 (1967); LOFTUS, *supra*, note 36, at 40; SCHACTER, *supra*, note 35, at 138-60.

to be perceived, therefore, is in fact inferred, a process that has been called "inferential construction,"[39] and "refabrication."[40] Experiencing a situation that is partially unclear or ambiguous, a witness typically "fills up the gaps of his perception by the aid of what he has experienced before in similar situations, or, though this comes to much the same thing in the end, by describing what he takes to be 'fit,' or suitable, to such a situation." Thus, "recall brings greater symmetry or completeness than that which was actually observed."[41] Moreover, the process of unconscious reconstruction continues with the passage of time, probably increasing considerably as the event is left farther behind.[42]

We are not talking about dishonesty. A witness may reconstruct events "without being in the least aware that he is either supplementing or falsifying the data of perception. Yet, in almost all cases, he is certainly doing the first, and in many cases he is demonstrably doing the second."[43] The "vast majority" of testimonial errors are those of the "average, normal honest" person, errors "unknown to the witness and wholly unintentional." Such testimony has been described as "an imaginative reconstruction or construction"[44] that is "*subjectively* accurate but *objectively* false."[45]

For example, in writing a book about a tragic ascent of Mt. Everest in 1996, the author asked three others who had been on the climb to recount a particular incident. "None of us could agree on such crucial facts as the time, what had been said, or even who had been present."[46] Similarly, the book, *Wittgenstein's Poker*, is about a ten-minute incident involving a fireplace poker at a meeting of the Cambridge Moral Science Club. The participants were the world's leading philosophers (including Ludwig Wittgenstein, Karl Popper, and Bertrand Russell) concerned, among other things, with knowledge, understanding, and truth. Ironically, the participants disagreed sharply on crucial elements of the story — the sequence of events, the atmosphere, and how the antagonists behaved. Each of those present had "clear memories" of what had happened, and they were "equally clearly in conflict."[47]

---

[39] BARTLETT, *supra* note 38, at 46.

[40] LOFTUS, *supra* note 36, at 40.

[41] Elon H. Moore, *Elements of Error in Testimony*, 28 ORE. L. REV. 293, 295 (1949); *see also* SCHACTER, *supra*, note 35, at 147 ("People seem almost driven to reconstruct the past to fit what they know in the present. In light of the known outcome, people can more easily retrieve incidents and examples that confirm it.")

[42] BARTLETT, *supra* note 38, at 58, 63ff., 80, 93.

[43] *Id.* at 14.

[44] *Id.* at 213.

[45] Dillard S. Gardner, *The Perception and Memory of Witnesses*, 18 CORN. L.Q. 391 (1933) (emphasis in the original); *cf.* SCHACTER, *supra*, note 35, at 88-137 (discussing misattribution and suggestibility). "When misattribution combines with . . . suggestibility . . . people can develop detailed and strongly held recollections of complex events that never occurred . . . . [S]uch recollections have been linked with deeply troubling events in the therapist's office, the courtroom, and the preschool." *Id.* at 111.

[46] JON KRAKAUER, INTO THIN AIR, Preface (as quoted by Mel Dubnick, Letter to the Editor of the N.Y. TIMES, March 1, 1998).

[47] DAVID EDMONDS & JOHN EIDINOW, WITTGENSTEIN'S POKER (2001): "The poker is red-hot or it is cool. Wittgenstein gesticulates with it angrily or uses it as a baton, as an example, [or] as a tool. He raises it, uses it for emphasis, shakes it or fidgets with it. He leaves after words with Russell or he leaves after Popper has [made a witty rejoinder about a poker]. He leaves quietly or abruptly, slamming the door. Russell speaks in a high-pitched voice or he roars." *Id.* at 20.

An interesting illustration of the tendency to eliminate ambiguities by imaginative reconstruction was provided in the Senate Watergate hearings. John Dean, who had been President Nixon's White House Counsel, was testifying about a meeting he had had with Herbert Kalmbach, who had been Nixon's private attorney. Dean had no incentive to lie about that particular incident; indeed, it was extremely important to him to state the facts with as much exactness as possible.

Dean testified that he had met with Kalmbach in the coffee shop of the Mayflower Hotel in Washington, D.C., and that they had then gone upstairs to Kalmbach's room in the same hotel. Dean was pressed several times on this point, in a way that implied that his questioners had reason to believe that he was not telling the truth as to whether the meeting had taken place at all. Each time, Dean confidently reaffirmed his clear recollection about the incident. Finally, it was revealed that the Mayflower Hotel's register showed that Kalmbach had not been staying at the hotel at the time in question. Dean nevertheless remained certain of the occurrence, putting forth the unlikely theory that Kalmbach had used a false name in registering.

The difficulty was cleared up when someone realized that there was a Mayflower Doughnut Coffee Shop in the Statler Hilton Hotel in Washington — and Kalmbach had been registered at the Statler, under his own name, on the day in question. Thus, Dean's basic story was corroborated. Without realizing it, however, Dean had inaccurately resolved the ambiguity created by the coincidence of the two names by confidently "remembering" the wrong (but more logical) hotel, and by inventing the use of an alias by Kalmbach.[48] He had done so, moreover, in a way that was "subjectively accurate" even though "objectively false."

John Dean is not unusual in this regard. Indeed, "accurate recall is the exception and not the rule."[49] This is true even when the material to be memorized is relative short and simple, and when the witness knows that he will be asked to describe it later.[50] Thus, in portions of "ostensibly factual reporting," we can be sure that "a large proportion of the details will be incorrect, even though presented with the utmost certitude and in good faith."[51] Victims of assault are "notoriously unreliable" witnesses regarding the description of their assailants, but then "so are onlookers who watched in safety."[52] Although stress and fear do inhibit perception and recall,[53] an event need not stir up emotional reactions in order to be "grossly misrepresented" in recollection.[54]

---

[48] This aspect of Dean's testimony was noted in MONROE H. FREEDMAN, LAWYERS' ETHICS IN AN ADVERSARY SYSTEM 66 (1975). Along with other demonstrable errors in Dean's testimony, it is also used in Edmond Blair Bolles, REMEMBERING AND FORGETTING ch. 17 (1988). Bolles notes that Dean became known as "the man with the tape-recorder memory," until the Nixon tapes showed that, in fact, "Dean had a terrible memory." *Id.* at 246.

[49] BARTLETT, *supra* note 38, at 213.

[50] *Id.*

[51] GEORGE A. TALLAND, DISORDERS OF MEMORY AND LEARNING 18–19 (1969).

[52] *Id.* at 19.

[53] LOFTUS, *supra* note 36, at 78.

[54] TALLAND, *supra* note 51, at 18–19.

In the case of John Dean and the Mayflower Hotel/Coffee Shop, it was an unconscious sense of logical consistency that transformed what Dean remembered. The same effect can result from interest or prejudice. A classic example of prejudice is the study in which subjects were shown an illustration of a scene on a subway car, including an African-American man wearing a jacket and tie and a white man dressed in work clothes and holding a razor in his hand. In an experiment in which people serially described the picture to each other (as in the game "telephone"), the razor "tended to migrate" from the white man's hand to that of the African-American man.[55]

A more frightening example of memory distortion has come to be called "false memory syndrome."[56] In the early 1990s, there appeared to be an epidemic of educated middle-class women emerging from psychotherapy with recovered memories of previously forgotten childhood sexual abuse, typically perpetrated by their fathers. As the psychotherapeutic techniques which prompted the "memory" of these "repressed" traumas came under attack — techniques such as hypnosis and guided imagery exercises in which patients imagine possible abuse scenarios — an increasing number of women recanted their accusations.[57]

University of Washington psychologist Elizabeth Loftus, a prominent researcher who had conducted groundbreaking research into how suggested details of an event make their way into the recollections of eyewitnesses, was one of the first psychologists to demonstrate how an entire traumatic autobiographical incident might be implanted in a person's memory. In the "lost in the mall" study, a teenager named Chris was asked by his older brother Jim to try to remember the time Chris was lost in a shopping mall when he was five. Chris initially recalled nothing, but after a few days produced a detailed recollection of the incident. According to Jim and other family members, Chris was never lost in a shopping mall.[58]

At around the same time that adult women were claiming to have "recovered" memories of childhood abuse, there was a sudden outbreak of accusations of bizarre and ritualized child sexual abuse in daycare centers.[59] In the 1980s and early 1990s, highly publicized cases included McMartin in Los Angeles, California; Little Rascals in Edenton, North Carolina; and Fells Acre in Malden, Massachusetts. The alleged victims — preschool children who are

---

55 LOFTUS, *supra* note 36, at 39–40, referring to an experiment reported in Gordon W. Allport & Leo J. Postman, *The Basic Psychology of Rumor*, in READINGS IN SOCIAL PSYCHOLOGY (Eleanor E. Maccoby et al. eds., 1958).

56 *See* SCHACTER, *supra*, note 35, at 123–137; *see also* ELIZABETH LOFTUS & KATHERINE KETCHAM, THE MYTH OF REPRESSED MEMORY: FALSE MEMORIES AND ALLEGATIONS OF SEXUAL ABUSE (1994).

57 *See* SCHACTER, *supra*, note 35, at 123–124.

58 *See id*. at 124–125; Elizabeth Loftus & Jacqueline E. Pickrell, *The Formation of False Memories*, 25 PSYCHIATRIC ANNALS 720–725 (1995). In a subsequent study with twenty-four participants, Loftus demonstrated that after several probing interview, approximately one-fourth of the participants falsely remembered being lost as a child in a shopping mall or similar place. *See also* Ira E. Hyman, et al., *False Memories of Childhood Experiences*, APPLIED COGNITIVE PSYCHOLOGY 9, 181–197 (1995); Ira Hyman & James Billings, *Individual Differences and the Creation of False Childhood Memories*, MEMORY 6, 1-20 (1998); Loftus & Ketcham, *supra*, note 56.

59 *See generally* MARK PENDERGRAST, VICTIMS OF MEMORY: SEX ABUSE ACCUSATIONS AND SHATTERED LIVES (1996).

especially vulnerable to suggestibility — had all been subjected to repeated and highly suggestive questioning by police and/or child-care professionals. Most of these cases have since been discredited.[60]

Another factor that affects both perception and memory is what witnesses understand — correctly or incorrectly — to be in their own interest.[61] Again, we are not referring to deliberate dishonesty, but to what is colloquially called "wishful thinking." For example, a group of people were shown sets of varying numbers of dots, and required to estimate the numbers. The higher the estimate they gave, the higher was the reward they received — but only if the estimate was correct, and an erroneously high estimate resulted in a penalty. Up to the twentieth trial, the people in that group produced more overestimates than did those in another group who were rewarded for correct responses irrespective of the number estimated. However, as it became apparent that overestimates were not effective in winning rewards, overestimation disappeared entirely.[62]

Similarly, we tend to exaggerate our answers in a way that enhances our prestige and self-esteem. We are more likely to "(mis)remember" that we did vote and that we did give to charity.[63] "People tend to rewrite history more in line with what they think they ought to have done than with what they actually did."[64] For example, Brandeis Professor Robert B. Reich, a former U.S. Secretary of Labor, wrote a memoir of his experiences in Washington.[65] "[W]herever C-Span tapes and transcripts of Reich's encounters exist, they demonstrate elaborate and repeated fabrication for dramatic effect."[66] Nevertheless, "[t]his is the way I experienced it," Reich said. "I was absolutely true to my memory."[67] Since Reich was aware of the tapes and transcripts, it is highly likely that he was telling the truth, subjectively, even though what he wrote was demonstrably false.

Another important aspect of constructive remembering is the witness' "readiness to respond and his self-confidence when in fact he ought to be cautious and hedge his statements."[68] In an experiment relating to the ability to remember faces (what lawyers call "eye-witness identification") the person who unconsciously invented more detail than any other in the test group was "completely confident throughout."[69] In another case, referred to by the experimenter as a brilliant example of constructive remembering of a narrative, "it was precisely concerning his inventions that the subject was most pleased and most certain."[70] Moreover, when a witness' "recall" involves a

---

[60] *See* PENDERGRAST, *supra*, note 59, at 361–387; SCHACTER, *supra*, note 35, at 130–137.

[61] *See generally* SCHACTER, *supra*, note 35, at 138–160 (discussing the role of bias in memory).

[62] M.D. VERNON, THE PSYCHOLOGY OF PERCEPTION 206–207 (1962).

[63] LOFTUS, *supra* note 36, at 142.

[64] *Id.*

[65] ROBERT B. REICH, LOCKED IN THE CABINET (1997).

[66] Quoted in Max Frankel, *Ids and Ads*, N.Y. TIMES, § 6, p. 22, July 13, 1997.

[67] *Id.*

[68] TALLAND, *supra* note 51, at 19.

[69] BARTLETT, *supra* note 38, at 78.

[70] *Id.*

mental "visual image," the witness may have an increased sense of confidence that is "entirely out of proportion to any objective accuracy that is thereby secured."[71]

In order to interview and prepare a witness for trial, it is necessary to ask the witness questions. Lawyers should be aware, therefore, that even "straightforward questions of fact" may significantly affect what a witness remembers,[72] and leading or loaded questions can be particularly powerful in inducing good faith errors in memory. Illustrative is a study that showed that witnesses' estimates of the speed of an automobile involved in an accident varied in accordance with the verb used by the interviewer in asking the question. For example, when the question was phrased in terms of one car "contacting" the other, the speed averaged 31.8 miles per hour. The speed of the car increased in the witnesses' memory, however, as the verb was modified: "hit" (34.0 mph), "bumped" (38.1 mph), "collided" (39.3 mph), and "smashed" (40.8 mph).[73] In a case in which the posted speed limit is 40 miles per hour, therefore, the verb used by the questioner can make the difference between due care and negligence per se.

To sum up, remembering is not analogous to playing back a videotape or retrieving information from a computer. Rather, it is a process of active, creative reconstruction, which begins at the moment of perception. Moreover, this reconstructive process is significantly affected by the form of the questions asked and by what we understand to be in our own interest — even though, on a conscious level, we are responding as honestly as we can.

§ 7.07 THE PSYCHOLOGY OF MEMORY AND THE ETHICS OF COACHING

These conclusions might suggest that the conscientious lawyer should avoid giving a client or other witness an understanding of what is relevant and important and should instead rely only upon narrative statements unassisted by questions that seek to elicit critical information. Anyone who has conducted interviews of witnesses will immediately recognize, however, that such a procedure would be highly impractical. An untrained and perhaps inarticulate person cannot be expected to relate all that is relevant without a substantial amount of direction. That is why one of the most important functions of the lawyer is to provide an awareness of what is legally relevant. Moreover, the

---

[71] *Id.* at 60. An example would be the witness who says, "I could never forget that face; it is etched forever on my memory." Loftus has also documented an inverse relationship between confidence and accuracy in eye-witness identification. *See* ELIZABETH LOFTUS & JAMES M. DOYLE, EYEWITNESS TESTIMONY: CIVIL AND CRIMINAL (1987). This human foible is amusing, but it can have tragic consequences. Sixty-five of the seventy-seven wrongful convictions overturned by DNA evidence nationwide in the 1990s resulted from witness errors. Katherine E. Finkelstein, *When Justice Hinges on What Is Seen, and Believed,* N.Y. TIMES, B1, Dec. 4, 2000, referring to statistics compiled by the Innocence Project at the Benjamin N. Cardozo School of Law at Yeshiva University.

[72] BARTLETT, *supra* note 38, at 58; TALLAND, *supra* note 51, at 19.

[73] Loftus, *Psychology Today* 17, 119 (Dec., 1974). In addition, twice as many witnesses reported seeing nonexistent broken glass on the ground when the questioner used the word "smashed" instead of "hit."

same psychological authorities support the necessity of prompting in order to maximize recall. What prompting can do is to trigger recognition, which is a less complex process than remembering. [74] In general, much more of what is observed can be recognized than can be recalled.[75] That is, narrative is "the most accurate" but "the least complete" of all forms of recall.[76] If we rely upon unprompted narrative, therefore, many important facts will be omitted, facts that can be accurately reported if memory is prompted by recognition, as through leading questions.

The lawyer's dilemma, therefore, is that if she fails to probe the client's memory, important facts may be lost; but if she tells the client that a particular fact is important and why it is important, she may induce the client to "remember" the fact even if it did not occur. Furthermore, since the client's memory is inevitably going to be affected by reconstruction consistent with self-interest, a client who has a misunderstanding of her own legal interest could be psychologically inclined to remember in a way that is not only inconsistent with her case, but also inaccurate.

The complexity of the difficulty is heightened, both on a practical and an ethical level, if we reconsider at this point the attorney's professional responsibility to know all the facts the client knows, and if we pose the question of when the lawyer "knows" sufficiently to be on ethical notice.[77] In the area of counseling, these two aspects of knowing are interrelated, but they are also different in important respects. When we speak of the obligation to know everything that the client knows, we refer to the importance of being as fully informed as possible, for tactical purposes, in order most effectively to counsel and to represent the client in an adversarial situation. On the other hand, when we speak of knowing in the sense of being on moral notice, we refer to a state of awareness that is sufficient to compel the conscientious person to recognize that a moral choice has been presented — that is, that there is a situation in which a conscious refusal to make a choice is itself a moral decision.

§ 7.08   THE ANATOMY OF A MURDER "LECTURE"

An effective illustration of the dilemma is the so-called "lecture" in the book, *Anatomy of a Murder*.[78] In the book, a former prosecutor defends an army lieutenant accused of killing his wife's alleged rapist. In the initial interview, the client tells the lawyer an incriminating story — that the accused learned of his wife's assault a full hour before he armed himself, sought out her assailant in a bar, shot him five times in front of a crowd, and then drove home. In response, the lawyer says, in effect: "If the facts are as you have

---

[74] *See, e.g.,* BARTLETT, *supra* note 38, at 195.

[75] *Id.*

[76] Gardner, *supra* note 45, at 404.

[77] *See* Chapters Five and Six, *supra.*

[78] *See* ROBERT TRAVER, ANATOMY OF A MURDER (1958) (25th Anniversary ed., 1983). The name Traver was a pseudonym for John Voelker, then a justice of the Michigan Supreme Court. The book was a best-seller and was later made into an award-winning movie by Otto Preminger, starring Jimmy Stewart and Ben Gazzara. *See* ANATOMY OF A MURDER (Columbia Pictures Corp., 1959).

stated them, you have no legal defense, and you will probably be convicted and given a lengthy prison sentence. On the other hand, if you acted in a blind rage, there is a possibility of getting you off. Think it over, and we'll talk about it tomorrow."[79]

Some lawyers have sought to avoid the implications of this case by arguing that the lawyer's principal fault was in not giving the client the lecture earlier, thereby avoiding the lawyer's knowing too much too soon. These lawyers say that the lawyer in *Anatomy of a Murder* should have prompted the perjurious defense *before* obtaining the client's incriminating story, so that he would have been able to maintain that he did not know the "truth" when he channeled the client's story in the desired direction. Most of those same lawyers would recognize, however, the tactical importance of getting a client's narrative version of the facts before any suggestive prompting by the lawyer begins. Otherwise, as we have seen in the psychological literature, the lawyer may well close off information that would be essential to developing a sound tactical position.

It is difficult to see how the lawyer can have it both ways. If he gives the client the lecture before he has sufficient facts from the client to conclude that the lecture is necessary, then he may foreclose valuable information. But if he waits until it is reasonably clear that the lecture is necessary (because the client's story forecloses any legitimate defense), then he will be participating in the creation of a perjurious defense, with reason to know of its falsity. Nevertheless, under the Model Rules, the lawyer can have it both ways, up to a rather extreme point.

As we have seen, under MR 3.4(b), a lawyer is forbidden to "falsify evidence [or] counsel or assist a witness to testify falsely." Similarly, under MR 1.2(d), a lawyer shall not counsel a client to engage in, or to assist the client in, conduct that the lawyer knows is criminal or fraudulent. Also, under MR 8.4, a lawyer is forbidden to engage in conduct involving dishonesty, fraud, deceit or misrepresentation. And under MR 3.3(a)(4), a lawyer shall not offer evidence that the lawyer knows to be false.

These rules, however, are not as stringent as they appear. All of them, either explicitly or by clear implication, must be interpreted consistently with the

---

[79] The lawyer, Paul Biegler, contemplates his situation before launching into the "Lecture":

> I paused and lit a cigar. I took my time. I had reached a point where a few wrong answers to a few right questions would leave me with a client — if I took his case — whose cause was legally defenseless. Either I stopped now and begged off and let some other lawyer worry about it or I asked him the few fatal questions and let him hang himself. Or else, like any smart lawyer, I went into the Lecture.

Id. at 32

Biegler defines the Lecture as "an ancient device that lawyers use to coach their clients so that the client won't quite know he has been coached and his lawyer can still preserve the face-saving illusion that he hasn't done any coaching. *Id.* at 35. According to Biegler, coaching clients is wrong: "[C]oaching clients, like robbing them, is not only frowned upon, it is downright unethical and bad, very bad." *Id.* However, Biegler continues, by giving the lecture, a lawyer can justifiably claim that "I didn't tell him what to say . . . . I merely explained the law to him, see." *Id.*

The essence of the Lecture is contained in what Biegler calls the "opening salvo." He tells his client: "As things presently stand I must advise you that in my opinion you have not yet disclosed to me a *legal* defense to this charge of murder." *Id.*

Terminology section of the Model Rules. Accordingly, whether the lawyer "knows" that evidence is false requires "actual knowledge"; also, "fraud" "denotes conduct having a purpose to deceive and not merely negligent misrepresentation." The Restatement takes its definition of "knowing" from the Model Rules.[80] Using the phrases "actual knowledge" and "firm factual basis," the Restatement permits a lawyer to ignore anything that is not "plainly apparent," allows the lawyer to maintain ignorance of information that would have been discovered through reasonable inquiry, and limits "firm factual basis" to facts actually "known to the lawyer or the client's own statements" which indicate that the testimony or other evidence is false.[81]

Both the Model Rules and the Restatement say also that "knowledge may be inferred from circumstances." However, that inference precludes only "conscious ignorance,"[82] and allows the lawyer to ignore anything that is not "plainly apparent."[83] Under that definition, therefore, it will be an extreme case where a lawyer could be said to have "actual knowledge" that a client's testimony is false.

Returning, then, to the Lecture in *Anatomy of a Murder*, does Biegler have "actual knowledge" of what happened that night? Is it "plainly apparent" that his client's initial statement was true, and not the product of a client who, in Randolph Paul's phrase, is trying to be too smart for his own good?[84] In fact, the client in *Anatomy of a Murder* believes, erroneously, that his initial story establishes a defense to murder, because he thinks that a husband will be acquitted if he killed to avenge the rape of his wife. It is not plainly apparent, therefore, that the client's initial story is true — indeed, a lawyer, in good faith, might seriously question it.[85] Freedman was wrong, therefore, to say in the earlier edition of this book that the scenario in ANATOMY OF A MURDER is "unambiguous" and that the lawyer "knows beyond any reasonable doubt that the client has told him the truth about the murder."[86]

The scenario in *Anatomy of a Murder* is difficult to assess ethically, but not because the client's initial story is unquestionably true. Rather, the difficulty is created by the author's portrayal of the lawyer as believing the client's initial story, but nevertheless inducing the client to change the story to one that will establish a false defense.[87] The author's depiction of the lawyer's

---

[80] RESTATEMENT § 120, Reporter's Note, *Cmt. c.*

[81] *Id.*, Cmt. c. *See also* § 94, Cmt g.

[82] *Id.*, Reporter's Note, *Cmt. c.*

[83] *Id.*, Cmt. c. *See also* § 94, Cmt g.

[84] *See* Ch. 6, *supra*, note 12.

[85] Especially in a first interview, clients are not always forthcoming. It can be difficult for clients to reconstruct events, including their own state of mind, after a traumatic event. Sometimes clients have their own non-legal reasons for recounting an incident in a certain way, having nothing to do with the truth of what occurred. For example, the accused in ANATOMY OF A MURDER might have thought that it was more "manly" to assert that he had avenged his wife's assault in a deliberate and premeditated fashion.

[86] MONROE H. FREEDMAN, UNDERSTANDING LAWYERS' ETHICS 158 (1990). *Compare* MONROE H. FREEDMAN, LAWYERS' ETHICS IN AN ADVERSARY SYSTEM 69–73 (1975) (same position), *with* Monroe H. Freedman, *Professional Responsibility of the Criminal Defense Lawyer: The Three Hardest Questions*, 64 MICH. L. REV. 1469, 1478 (1966) (approving the Lecture).

[87] *See* note 79, *supra*.

cynical mental state does make for dramatic effect. However, Smith has persuaded Freedman that it should not be the basis for analyzing cases in real life, where both the client's and the lawyer's state of mind are unclear.[88] This conclusion is strongly supported by the behavioral psychology studies discussed earlier in this chapter.

§ 7.09 THE BROKEN ENGAGEMENT

Consider again the case of the young couple who were going to get married and decide to begin a business. Assume that the engagement has been broken off and the young woman consults an attorney about getting her $1,000 back. At the time of the transaction, of course, she had no legally relevant "intent" with regard to the money, and the farthest thing from her mind was a law suit against her fiance to recover it.

As we have seen, in the normal process of remembering/reconstructing, the client's good faith recollection is likely to be affected by what she assumes to be in her best interest. If her lawyer explains to her the legal difference between a gift and a loan, therefore, she will undoubtedly recall that her intent was to make a loan of the $1,000. In a situation like that, which is inherently ambiguous, it would be inappropriate for the lawyer to insist that the client give an uncounseled conclusion of mixed fact and law. Rather, the lawyer should first explain to the client what the relevant law is and what the significance would be of each of her possible responses.

This conclusion is supported by the Restatement, which explicitly approves preparing witnesses by "discussing the applicability of law to the events in issue."[89] Also, EC 7-6 of the Model Code sets forth the commonly accepted view of the lawyer's proper role in "assist[ing] the client in the development and preservation of evidence relevant to the state of mind of the client at a particular time." EC 7-6 recognizes that issues of intent, motives, or desires are perplexing,[90] and instructs the lawyer to "resolve all doubts in favor of his client" unless the lawyer is "certain" about the client's state of mind.

§ 7.10 THE WORKER'S COMPENSATION CASE

A more difficult variation under the ethical rules is a case that turns not on intent but on facts that the client might consciously or unconsciously be withholding from the lawyer. Assume, for example, that Jurisdictions X and Y are adjacent to each other and that many lawyers practice in both jurisdictions. In Jurisdiction X there are a large number of workers' compensation cases in which workers strain themselves while lifting, and recover compensation. In Jurisdiction Y there is an equivalent number of such cases, but in

---

[88] Moreover, in the criminal defense context, a lawyer could not give meaningful counsel to a client about whether to plead guilty or to go to trial if the lawyer did not explain the legal and tactical strengths and weaknesses of a proposed defense.

[89] RESTATEMENT § 116, Cmt. b.

[90] Analogous to intent is the case that calls for expressions of judgment, such as whether something happened quickly or slowly, or frequently or infrequently. See MONROE H. FREEDMAN, LAWYERS' ETHICS IN AN ADVERSARY SYSTEM 71–72 (1975).

all of them the workers who strain themselves while lifting also slip or trip on something in the process. That coincidence is fortunate, because in X it is sufficient for compensation simply that the strain be work-related, while in Y the applicable law requires that the injury be suffered in the course of an "accident" such as a slip or trip. Obviously, the same lawyers whose clients are not testifying about slipping or tripping in X are prompting their clients to recall a slip or a trip when the injury occurs in Y.

In those cases, the issue is not intent but objective fact — did the claimant slip or trip? Nevertheless, even if the client's initial narrative of the incident should omit any reference to slipping or tripping, we believe that the lawyer should explain to the client in Jurisdiction Y that one of the legal requirements for recovery is an accident, such as a slip or trip.

In an article generally critical of the views in this book, John Noonan (then a law professor and now a judge in the United States Court of Appeals for the Ninth Circuit) wrote that a lawyer "should not be paternalistic toward his client, and cannot assume that his client will perjure himself." Noonan added that a lawyer "has an obligation to furnish his client with all the legal information relevant to his case; in fulfilling his duty to inform his client, a lawyer would normally not violate ethical standards."[91]

Judge Noonan's observation is no less true under the Model Code and the Model Rules than it was under the Canons. As we have seen in the experiments by behavioral psychologists, a crucial factual detail might very well be omitted in any witness' narrative for a number of reasons. Along with other difficulties in perception and recall, the witness' understanding of his own self-interest (regardless of whether that understanding is correct or incorrect) is likely to affect the remembering/reconstruction of the incident without any conscious dishonesty. Thus, the client who incorrectly assumes that tripping or slipping would preclude recovery (perhaps because an accident might suggest carelessness) might unconsciously screen out that fact.

The psychological literature makes it clear, therefore, that a lawyer must adopt a skeptical attitude about any witness' story, and that it is the extraordinary case in which the lawyer can accept any narrative statement as "the truth, the whole truth, and nothing but the truth." Despite the risk that a dishonest client might consciously invent a helpful fact, such as a trip or slip, to meet the needs of the litigation, we agree with Noonan that the lawyer should not assume that the client will perjure himself. We believe, therefore, that the attorney should probe the client's memory by explaining the legal relevance and importance of factual aspects of the case that the client may have overlooked or unconsciously suppressed.

§ 7.11   CONCLUSION

In interviewing clients and other witnesses, the lawyer should take into account the psychology of memory. The lawyer should first elicit the facts in narrative form. In doing so, the lawyer has reason to assume a skeptical

---

[91] John T. Noonan, *The Purposes of Advocacy and the Limits of Confidentiality*, 64 MICH. L. REV. 1485, 1488 (1966).

attitude about the accuracy and, particularly, the completeness of the information. In the rare case, even the properly skeptical lawyer will know that the client's story is true. In that event, the lawyer may not provide the client with a tactically better story to testify to at trial, by suggestion or otherwise. In most cases, however, the lawyer can properly give the client relevant legal advice and ask leading questions that might help to draw out useful information that the client, consciously or unconsciously, might be withholding. This procedure presents risks of prompting the client to falsify evidence, but it is necessary to draw out truthful information that the client might have overlooked or might consciously or unconsciously be withholding.

Chapter 8

CROSS-EXAMINING TO DISCREDIT THE TRUTHFUL WITNESS

§ 8.01 INTRODUCTION

Is it ever proper for a lawyer to cross-examine an adverse witness who has testified accurately and truthfully in order to make the witness appear to be mistaken or lying?[1]

Our answer is yes — but the same answer is also given by almost every other commentator on lawyers' ethics. The question is nevertheless worth discussing for two reasons. First, although it is the least controversial of the "three hardest questions,"[2] we consider it to be the most difficult and painful. Second, the discussion can provide a brief introduction to the way that moral philosophy can affect ethical judgments.[3]

§ 8.02 CROSS-EXAMINING THE RAPE VICTIM

The issue was raised effectively in a symposium on legal ethics through the following hypothetical case, which we have revised in form but not substance.[4]

> The accused works at a gas station. He is charged with rape, an offense that carries a lengthy prison sentence. You are his court-appointed defense counsel. The alleged victim is a twenty-two year old graduate student at the divinity school. She is engaged to a young minister. The alleged rape occurred in the early morning hours at a service station where the accused was employed. That is all you know about the case when you have your first interview with your client.

---

[1] Although this chapter can be read by itself, you will have a fuller understanding of it after reading Chapters 2, 4, 5, and 6.

[2] The reference is to Monroe Freedman, *Professional Responsibility of the Criminal Defense Lawyer: The Three Hardest Questions*, 64 MICH. L. REV. 1469 (1966). The other two questions relate to knowingly presenting perjury, and to giving the client legal advice when there is reason to believe that the client might use it as the basis for creating perjury. These issues are discussed in earlier chapters. At the time the Michigan Law Review article was published, even to raise such issues publicly caused reactions of outrage. These included an effort by former Chief Justice Warren Burger (then a federal appellate judge) and two other federal judges to have Freedman disbarred. The story is related in MONROE H. FREEDMAN, LAWYERS' ETHICS IN AN ADVERSARY SYSTEM, PREFACE (1975).

[3] We use the words morals and ethics (and their variants) in a way that is not sanctioned by dictionary definitions of the two words (which we do not find helpful). By morals or morality we mean broad, over-arching principles of right and wrong. By ethics we mean applied morality — rules that apply moral principles to conduct in particular contexts.

[4] Symposium, *Standards of Conduct for Prosecution and Defense Personnel*, 5 AM. CRIM. L.Q. 8 (1966). The case was proposed by former Chief Justice Warren Burger, who was a participant in the symposium.

At first the accused will not talk at all. You assure him that you cannot help him unless you know the truth, and that he can trust you to treat what he says as confidential. He then says that he had sex with the young woman, but that she "told me she really wanted it." He says that he had seen her two or three times before when he was working the day shift at the station, and that she had always started a conversation and, that night, had "come onto me." In fact, he says that after they had talked for a while, she invited him into the car. One thing led to another and, finally, to sex. They were interrupted by the lights of an approaching vehicle which pulled into the station. The accused relates that he got out of the young woman's car to wait on the customer, and the young woman hurriedly drove off.

The accused tells you he was tried for rape in California four years ago and acquitted. He has no previous convictions.

At the grand jury proceedings the complainant testifies that she was returning to her apartment in town from a conference on virtue ethics, where her fiancé presented a paper, when she noticed that her fuel gauge registered empty. She stopped at the first station along the road that was open. The attendant, who seemed to be in sole charge of the station, forced his way into her car, terrified her with threats, and forcibly had sexual intercourse with her. She says he was compelled to stop when an approaching car turned into the station. The alleged victim's fiancé testified as to her timely complaint. No other testimony is presented. The grand jury returns a true bill.

You learn that the complainant has been romantically involved with two men aside from her fiancé. Smith, one of these young men, admits that he and the complainant went together for some time; however, he refuses to say whether he had ever had sex with her or to discuss anything else of an intimate nature, and he says he doesn't think it's any of your business. The other, Jones, apparently a rejected and jealous suitor, tells you right away that he had sex with the complainant early in their relationship, and that he has seen her flirt with strange men. He once took her to a party, he says, and, having noticed she had been gone for some time, discovered her upstairs with Smith, a friend of his, on a bed with some of her clothes off. He appears eager to testify and says that he doubts that the complainant was raped. You believe Jones, but don't like him much.

In a later interview with the accused, after you have won his confidence, the accused admits to you that his first story was false, and that he forced himself on the woman. However, he refuses to plead guilty to the charge or to any lesser offense. He says he knows that he can get away with his story, because he did once before in California.

Should the defense lawyer use the information supplied by Jones to impeach the young woman — if allowed by the rules of evidence — and, if necessary, call Jones as a witness?[5]

§ 8.03   THE MORALITY OF ABSOLUTE AND IMMUTABLE RULES

One of the panelists who spoke to that question was former Chief Justice (then Judge) Warren Burger. The Chief Justice first discussed the question in terms of "basic and fundamental rules." One of those rules, which he characterized as "clear-cut and unambiguous," is that "a lawyer may never, under any circumstances, knowingly . . . participate in a fraud on the court." That rule, he said, "can never admit of any exception, under any circumstances," and no other consideration "can ever justify a knowing and conscious departure" from it. Moreover, only the "naive and inexperienced" would take a contrary position, which is a "perversion and prostitution of an honorable profession." Indeed, Burger held any other view to be "so utterly absurd and that one wonders why the subject need even be discussed among persons trained in the law."[6]

Despite his powerful rhetoric and assertion of absolute principles, Burger's response to the question of cross-examining the truthful witness was similar to ours. The function of an advocate, he declared, and "particularly the defense advocate in the adversary system," is to use "all legitimate tools available to test the truth of the prosecution's case." Therefore, he concluded, "the testimony of bad repute of the complaining witness, being recent and not remote in point of time, is relevant to her credibility."[7] The Chief Justice was

---

[5] Since the time of the symposium at which this hypothetical was presented, virtually every state in the country has enacted a so-called "rape shield statute." Generally speaking, these statutes prohibit cross-examination and the introduction of extrinsic evidence on a rape complainant's sexual history or her reputation for chastity. *See generally* JOSHUA DRESSLER, UNDERSTANDING CRIMINAL LAW § 33.07 (3d ed. 2001). However, rape shield statutes have not rendered the hypothetical obsolete:

> [S]ome jurisdictions permit exceptions that can swallow the rule; lawyers can introduce evidence of previous sexual conduct that establishes a pattern of conduct or that judges find more probative than prejudicial. So, for example, in a Glen Ridge, New Jersey, case involving a gang rape of a retarded girl with a baseball bat, defense counsel presented testimony about prior behavior that painted the victim as promiscuous. Even when courts exclude evidence about complainants' sexual background from trial proceedings, inventive lawyers can leak such information through press reports, pretrial records, and indirect questioning. In the rape prosecution of William Kennedy Smith defense counsel placed the complainant on trial and ensured widespread coverage of her Victoria's Secret underwear, out-of-wedlock child, bar-hopping history, and reputed "wild streak." Similar tactics gained national prominence in a New York City police brutality case. Defense counsel's opening argument suggested that the injuries to a Haitian immigrant could have occurred through a same-sex consensual encounter rather than a police assault.

DEBORAH RHODE, IN THE INTERESTS OF JUSTICE 101 (2000). For a fascinating account of the Glen Ridge rape case, *see* BERNARD LEFKOWITZ, OUR GUYS: THE GLEN RIDGE RAPE AND THE SECRET LIFE OF THE PERFECT SUBURB (1997). For a defense of the tactics in the police brutality case, *see* Abbe Smith, *Defending Defending*, 28 HOFSTRA L. REV. 925 (2000).

[6] Warren E. Burger, *Standards of Conduct for Prosecution and Defense Personnel: A Judge's Viewpoint*, 5 AM. CRIM. L.Q. 11, 12 (1966).

[7] *Id.* at 14–15.

even more explicit in the question period following the panel discussion: he considered it ethical to cast doubt on the young woman's "credibility" by destroying her reputation, even though the lawyer knows that she is telling the truth.

That, of course, is sanction for a deliberate attempt to perpetrate a fraud upon the finder of fact. The lawyer knows that the client is guilty and that the victim is truthful. In cross-examining her, the lawyer has one purpose only: to make it appear, contrary to fact, that the young woman is lying in testifying that she was raped. This, indeed, is what the lawyer will argue to the jury in summation.[8]

There is only one difference in practical effect between presenting the defendant's perjured alibi — which the Chief Justice considered to be clearly improper — and impeaching the truthful victim. In both cases the lawyer participates in an attempt to free a guilty defendant. In both cases the lawyer participates in misleading the finder of fact. In the case of the perjured witness, however, the attorney asks only non-leading questions, while in the case of impeachment, the lawyer takes an active, aggressive role, using his professional training and skill, in a one-on-one attack upon the client's victim.[9] The lawyer thereby personally and directly adds to the suffering of the victim and of those who care for her. In short, under the euphemism of "testing the truth of the prosecution's case," the lawyer communicates a vicious lie to the jury and to the community.

One prominent legal ethics scholar, Professor David Luban, takes a unique view. Luban agrees that defense lawyers generally must attempt to discredit witnesses, even those known to be telling the truth. Nevertheless, he contends that defense lawyers should refrain from cross-examining rape complainants about their sexual history, even when the lawyer believes that the complainant did in fact consent.[10] Luban says that the moral boundaries of zealous criminal defense should be drawn short of allowing cross-examination that "makes the victim look like a whore,"[11] even if she is not telling the truth:[12]

> [T]he cross-examination is morally wrong, even if the victim really did consent to sex with the defendant. Just as the rights of the accused are not diminished when he is guilty, the right of women to invoke the state's aid against rapists without fear of humiliation does not diminish when a [woman] abuses it by making a false accusation. This implies that balancing the defendant's rights against the rape accuser's rights in order to determine the moral bounds of zealous advocacy

---

[8] "Before the trial starts, the advocate knows what he will say to the jury when it is over . . . [including] the part of it that deals with the credibility of the adversary's witnesses . . . ." Irving Younger, *Cicero on Cross-Examination*, in THE LITIGATION MANUAL: A PRIMER FOR TRIAL LAWYERS 532, 533–34 (John G. Koeltl, ed., 2d ed. 1989).

[9] Trial advocacy manuals consistently recommend that lawyers ask only leading questions in cross-examination so that the lawyer, not the witness, is testifying. The lawyer tells the story, and the properly controlled witness is limited to yes and no responses.

[10] *See* DAVID LUBAN, LAWYERS AND JUSTICE: AN ETHICAL STUDY 150–53 (1988).

[11] *Id.* at 151.

[12] *Id.* at 152.

must be done without considering either the defendant's guilt or the accuser's innocence. What's good for the gander is good for the goose.[13]

Luban acknowledges that the question about the "relative threats posed to the defendant by the state and [those posed] to women by . . . the male sex" is "a very close call," but one that he ultimately resolves in women's favor. The constitutional protections afforded an accused (including the right to confront adverse witnesses) do not seem to enter into the balance, nor, apparently, does the fact that the complainant is committing perjury to send an innocent man to prison.[14]

We agree that the question of cross-examining witnesses known to be telling the truth is most painful in the rape context. Insofar as Luban's position is an endorsement of rape shield statutes, and insofar as those statutes do no more than prohibit cross-examination on *irrelevant* sexual history or lifestyle of rape complainants, we agree with him. However, we do not share his view that it is better that an innocent man go to jail than that a woman be called a "whore."[15] We are also concerned about categorical restrictions on cross-examination.[16]

---

[13] Luban does not usually use either cliches or non-sequiturs, although he does both at once in this last sentence.

[14] For example, Luban's view would have prevented Atticus Finch's cross-examination of Mayella Ewell in Finch's much-admired defense of Tom Robinson, who was falsely charged by Ewell with raping her. *See* HARPER LEE, TO KILL A MOCKINGBIRD (1960). *See also* Steven Lubet, *Reconstructing Atticus Finch*, 97 MICH. L. REV. 1339, 1348–1353 (1999):

> . . . Atticus tortured Mayella. He held her up as a sexual aggressor at a time when such conduct was absolutely dishonorable and disgraceful . . . .

> The "she wanted it" defense was particularly harsh . . . . Atticus Finch . . . designed his defense to exploit a virtual catalog of misconceptions and fallacies about rape, each one calculated to heighten mistrust of the female complainant.

> *Fantasy* . . . . According to the defense, Mayella obsessed over Tom for a "slap year," . . . . lur[ing] him into an assignation . . . .

> *Shame* . . . . Atticus told the jury that Mayella lied "in an effort to get rid of her own guilt . . . . " . . . .

> *Sexuality* . . . . Since women can barely control, and sometimes cannot even understand, their desires, they proceed to victimize the men whom they ensnare. As Atticus explained it, "She knew full well the enormity of her offense, but because her desires were stronger than the code she was breaking, she persisted in breaking it . . . . She was white, and she tempted a Negro . . . . No code mattered to her before she broke it, but it came crashing down on her afterwards . . . . "

> *Confusion.* Women may be so confused about sex that they do not even understand what they themselves have done . . . . [Finch says to Ewell:] "You're becoming suddenly clear on this point. A while ago you couldn't remember too well, could you? . . . Why don't you tell the truth, child?"

[15] *See* Abbe Smith, *Rosie O'Neill Goes to Law School: The Clinical Education of a Sensitive, New Age Public Defender*, 28 HARV. C.R.-C.L. L. REV. 1, 42–45 (1993). The authors are lifelong feminists. We believe that most *women* would agree — especially those wrongly accused of crime — that it is better to be called a name than to be imprisoned for something you didn't do (or even something you did do). *See generally* Abbe Smith, *Defending the Innocent*, 32 CONN. L. REV. 485 (2000).

[16] *See State v. Colbath*, 540 A.2d 1212 (N.H. 1988) (opinion by then New Hampshire Supreme Court Justice, and now United States Supreme Court Justice, David Souter holding that rape-shield law must give way to accused's right to confront witnesses against him and present exculpatory evidence under appropriate circumstances).

Still, the authors have chosen different responses to the ethical question of advocacy in a rape case. When Freedman was doing criminal defense work, he stopped taking rape cases because he did not want to be in the position of cross-examining the victim.[17] Smith has represented many indigent adults and juveniles accused of rape, and continues to do so. Although she does not always find it easy to handle these cases,[18] she believes in representing the poor accused notwithstanding the charge — and in doing so zealously.[19]

The case of attacking the credibility of the truthful witness helps us to understand how moral philosophy affects conclusions about ethical conduct. Burger proceeded from a deontological philosophy of moral absolutes — "basic and fundamental rules" that are "clear-cut and unambiguous" and that "can never admit of any exception, under any circumstances." He therefore answers questions of lawyers' ethics by uncritical application of legalistic norms, regardless of the context in which the lawyer may be acting. Lying is wrong. It follows, therefore, that no lawyer, under any circumstances, should knowingly present perjury. Cross-examination, however, is good. It follows, therefore, that any lawyer, regardless of context and consequences, can properly impeach a witness through cross-examination.

§ 8.04   IMMANUEL KANT, AND THE MURDERER AND HIS VICTIM

The classic exponent of a deontological system of moral philosophy is, of course, Immanuel Kant.[20] In assessing moral worth, Kant rejects any concern with consequences, but relies exclusively upon fulfillment of duty as expressed in a maxim of conduct. Thus, says Kant, "the moral worth of an action does not lie in the effect expected from it, nor in any principle of action which

---

[17] See Ch. Three, *supra*, regarding the lawyer's autonomy in deciding whether to accept a particular client or cause.

See also Ch. Ten, *infra*. If a lawyer's reluctance to cross-examine an adverse witness is strong enough to create a significant risk about his ability to do so with maximum effectiveness, the lawyer is required to decline the case or to withdraw. *See* MR 1.7(b), 1.1, and 1.16(a)(1); DR 5-101(A), 6-101(A)(1), and 7-101(A).

[18] See Cookie Ridolfi, *Statement on Representing Rape Defendants, in* LEGAL ETHICS, 279–80 (Deborah L. Rhode & David Luban, eds., 3d ed. 2001):

> Some defense attorneys believe that effective cross-examination can be done in a way that does not demean the complainant. I disagree. No matter what tone of voice is used or how politely the questions are put, a good cross-examination must still ultimately demonstrate that the complaining witness is a liar. . . .
>
> In the conflict between my commitment to defender work and my increasing distress over what is required of me in a sex case, the fact that my own gender is also an issue at trial weighs heavily.

[19] See Abbe Smith, *Defending Defending*, 28 HOFSTRA L. REV. 925, 961 (2000):

> As a matter of professional ethics, criminal defense lawyers are required to thoughtfully consider all lawyering strategies that ethical rules allow and to employ them if they serve the client's interests. Defense lawyers should reject strategies not for reasons of propriety or personal inclination, but only because those strategies are not advantageous to the client.

[20] The discussion that follows is based primarily upon IMMANUEL KANT, FUNDAMENTAL PRINCIPLES OF THE METAPHYSICS OF MORALS (T.K. Abbott, transl., 1949).

requires to borrow its motive from this expected effect." Kant's only test of the validity of a maxim is whether one is prepared to will the maxim to be a universal law. Referring specifically to lying, Kant suggests that it is improper to reason: "I should not lie, because then no one would thereafter believe me." The error in that, Kant says, is that one would then be telling the truth "from apprehension of injurious consequences," rather than from duty to principle.

Assume for example, that one is in a difficult situation that can be avoided only by telling a lie. One might say that everyone may tell a lie in order to escape a difficulty that otherwise cannot be avoided. However: "I presently become aware that while I can will the lie, I can by no means will that lying should be a universal law." From there Kant reasons that telling the truth is a universal law, and that it cannot be violated under any circumstances. Thus, if a victim is fleeing from a murderer, one must answer the murderer truthfully when asked where the victim is hiding. Lying — violation of principle — cannot be justified by mere expediency.

Burger and the ABA are (sometimes) good Kantians.[21] Thus, we have had ethical rules that place a higher value on telling the truth to the court than on saving innocent human life.[22] In a 1988 case,[23] for example, a murderer had falsely implicated an innocent man who was about to be executed. The murderer was then to go on trial himself as an accomplice in the same murder, and his lawyer knew that the murderer planned to commit perjury in order to exculpate himself. The lawyer asked his bar's ethics committee for guidance. He was told, first, that his obligation of confidentiality precluded his volunteering the information necessary to save the life of the innocent man who had been wrongly convicted. He was also told that his obligation of confidentiality was outweighed by the obligation not to participate in presenting a lie to the court; therefore, he was required to reveal the truth to the court if his client should testify falsely in the case in which he was to represent him. In our view, there is something wrong with a system of morality that places a higher value on truth-telling than on the preservation of an innocent person's life.

Moreover, the legal absolutist does not allow for conflicts of principle. In Burger's words, the rules are "basic and fundamental," "clear-cut and unambiguous," and "can never admit of any exception, under any circumstances." What, though, if one had already promised protection to the victim who is

---

[21] Burger did not reject, as Kant does, all selfishly pragmatic concerns. Kant singles out for condemnation the person who says, "I ought not to lie if I would retain my reputation." Burger, however, frequently stressed, at least as a secondary concern, that a lawyer who places confidentiality over candor will suffer in reputation and thereby in effectiveness as an advocate. *See, e.g.,* Burger, *supra* note 6, at 13 (1966). *Compare* the Model Code of Professional Conduct, Preamble: "[I]n the last analysis it is the desire for the respect and confidence of the members of his profession and of the society which he serves that should provide to a lawyer the incentive for the highest possible degree of ethical conduct."

[22] *See* Chapters 5 and 6, *supra*; Monroe Freedman, *Lawyer-Client Confidences Under the Model Rules: Ethical Rules Without Ethical Reason,* 3 CRIM. JUST. ETHICS 3 (1984); Monroe Freedman, *The Life-Saving Exception to Confidentiality: Restating the Law Without the Was, the Will Be, or the Ought to Be,* 29 LOYOLA (L.A.) L. REV. 19 (1996).

[23] David A. Kaplan, *Death Row Dilemma,* NAT'L L. J., Jan. 25, 1988, at 35.

fleeing the murderer? In that case, one could only be truthful to the murderer by breaking one's promise to the victim. That contextual difficulty is similar, of course, to that of the lawyer who has entered into a relationship of trust with her client, and who can avoid violating that trust only by remaining silent about the client's perjury.[24] One can agree with Burger that lying is wrong, and still not know the answer to the question of whether it is worse to lie to the client or to allow the client to lie to the court.

§ 8.05   SYSTEM UTILITARIANISM

There is an important aspect of Kant's rejection of utilitarianism, however, that is frequently overlooked. That is, in holding that one must obey a maxim without regard to consequences, Kant is speaking at the level of personal morality. When he addresses morality in systemic terms, however, Kant becomes pragmatic. Thus, the fundamental question of whether a maxim is valid in the first instance (as distinguished from whether a maxim should be obeyed) is determined by a utilitarian concern with whether the maxim can be universalized, that is, with whether the maxim can be a part of a viable system.

For example, Kant determines that lying in order to extricate oneself from a difficulty cannot be universalized because "with such a law there would be no promises at all, since it would be in vain to allege my intention in regard to my future actions to those who would not believe this allegation, or if they over-hastily did so, would pay me back in my own coin." Hence, he concludes, "my maxim, as soon as it should be made a universal law, would necessarily destroy itself." In short, in judging the morality of a maxim, considerations of individual disadvantage "to myself or even to others" are irrelevant, but systemic practicability — whether the maxim can "enter as a principle in a possible universal legislation" — is crucial.

It is this kind of "system utilitarianism" that we have been advocating, by analyzing the lawyer's obligations in the context of her role in our constitution-alized adversary system.[25] The lawyer is told, for example, "You are under an ethical obligation not to participate in the presentation of perjury, and therefore you are required to reveal your client's confidences if he insists upon committing perjury." The lawyer might respond, in words similar to Kant's, "Let us consider your maxim. If it were to be adopted as a universal law

---

[24] In the rape case, for example, "You assure [the client] that you cannot help him unless you know the truth, and that he can trust you to treat what he says as confidential."

[25] We accept this system because it is founded upon, and gives expression to, deontological values like autonomy (i.e., self-expression, self-determination, and self-fulfillment), human dignity, and equal treatment. These are values expressed in the Constitution and derived from moral philosophy. In addition, Freedman has urged modification of particular rules for the sake of such deontological values as the sanctity of human life. *See* Chapter 6, *supra*.

Michael K. McChrystal has referred to this (in a different but similar situation) as melding deontological and utilitarian concerns. "The values at stake and the consequences of a particular course of action must both be weighed in determining proper conduct. For this reason, categorical preferences for one value . . . over another are of limited use because they ignore the consequences of proposed conduct in particular circumstances." Michael K. McChrystal, *Lawyers and Loyalty*, 33 WM. & MARY L. REV. 367, 385 (1992).

applicable to all lawyers in all circumstances, would the maxim defeat itself and be harmful to the system?"

As we have seen in earlier chapters, proper functioning of the adversary system requires the attorney to know everything that the client knows that is relevant to the case. In order to enable the lawyer to obtain that information, the system provides for an obligation of trust and confidence, designed in part to protect the client from being prejudiced by disclosures to the attorney. In addition, the attorney is required to impress upon her client the obligation of confidentiality in order to induce the client to confide freely and fully in her.

§ 8.06   UNIVERSALIZING THE RULE

Let us return, then, to the case involving the street robbery at 16th and P Streets.[26] The defendant has been wrongly identified as the criminal by one witness, but has been correctly identified by another witness — a nervous, elderly woman who wears eyeglasses — as having been only a block away five minutes before the crime took place. If the woman is not cross-examined effectively and her testimony shaken, it will serve to corroborate the erroneous evidence of guilt. On the other hand, the lawyer could take the position that since the woman is doing her civic duty by testifying truthfully and accurately, she should not be made to appear to be mistaken or lying.

If the latter position were to be adopted as a rule applicable to all cases in which a lawyer has learned from the client that a witness is testifying accurately and truthfully, however, we would defeat the maxim itself and do serious harm to the system. As soon as clients learned that confiding in their lawyers would result in less effective representation, such confidences would rarely be given. The result would be intentional ignorance, the practice in which the client is put on notice that he is not to tell his lawyer anything that might cause the lawyer to be less vigorous in her advocacy. As we have seen, this practice has been condemned as egregiously unprofessional.[27]

More to the present point, a rule protecting the truthful and accurate witness from cross-examination would itself be defeated, because the lawyer, in ignorance of the truth, would conduct the most effective possible cross-examination in virtually every case. It is true that the lawyer would not be doing so knowingly. From the point of view of the witness doing her civic duty, however, the result would be identical. In systemic terms, moreover, the price of the lawyer's maintaining a state of intentional ignorance would be extremely high.[28]

The rape case is, of course, a much harder one, because the injury done to the complaining witness there is far more severe than the more limited humiliation of the public-spirited and truthful witness in the case of the street robbery. In addition, in the rape case, the lawyer is ultimately relying upon the illogical inference that the complainant would voluntarily have sex with

---

[26] *See A Case in Point* in Chapter 6, § 6.04, *supra.*

[27] *See* Chapter 6, *supra.*

[28] *Id.*

a stranger because she has had sexual relations with two men whom she knows in wholly different social circumstances. There is also the implied argument that because she has been sexually active, the fact that she might have been raped is of less importance.[29] Nevertheless, for the reasons given earlier, we come to the same conclusion in the case of cross-examining the rape victim.[30]

Although the justifications differ, there is general agreement that a lawyer can properly cross-examine a truthful and accurate witness to make her appear to be mistaken or lying. Indeed, the prevailing view is that the lawyer is ethically *required* to do so unless tactics dictate otherwise. In the ABA's *Primer for Trial Lawyers*, for example, the lead article on cross-examination says flatly: "The goal of cross-examination . . . is to damage the credibility of the adverse witness, even if the witness is telling the absolute truth."[31] No qualifications of any kind are suggested, including whether the case is criminal or civil.[32] Although reflecting an understandable ambivalence (and apparently a desire to avoid stating the result explicitly) the ABA's Model Code and Model Rules reach the same result.

§ 8.07 THE MODEL CODE

The Model Code requires the lawyer to attack the credibility of the truthful witness, but it does so with some awkwardness and indirection.

EC 7-10 says that the lawyer's duty of zeal "does not militate against his obligation to treat with consideration all persons involved in the legal process

---

[29] Assume, though, that the trial judge bars Jones' testimony that the complainant has flirted with strangers, that she has had sex with Jones, and his testimony regarding the episode with Smith in the bedroom at the party. The prosecutor then argues in summation:

> You have met the young woman and you have heard her testimony about what happened that night. You have heard about her background and about her aspirations as a divinity student. You have also heard the testimony of her fiancé, the minister. And this defendant is now asking you to believe that a woman like this would willingly have sex with him in her car.

If the prosecution can use the "a woman like this" argument, should the defendant be denied it? Also, the same jurors who would be prejudiced against the complainant to learn that she *has* been sexually active would be prejudiced against the defendant if they are allowed to believe, falsely, that she had never before had sex.

[30] *See* especially Chapters 2, 4, 5, and 6.

[31] David Berg, *Cross-Examination, in* ABA THE LITIGATION MANUAL: A PRIMER FOR TRIAL LAWYERS 518, 519 (John G. Koeltl, ed., 2d ed. 1989). *But see* Harry Subin, *The Criminal Lawyer's "Different Mission": Reflections on the 'Right' to Present a False Case*, 1 GEO. J. LEGAL ETHICS 125 (1987); John B. Mitchell, *Reasonable Doubts Are Where You Find Them: A Response to Professor Subin's Position on the Criminal Lawyer's "Different Mission"*, 1 GEO. J. LEGAL ETHICS 339 (1987); Harry Subin, *Is This Lie Necessary? Further Reflections on the Right to Present a False Defense*, 1 GEO. J. LEGAL ETHICS 689 (1988).

[32] After noting general agreement that criminal defense lawyers may attack the credibility of a truthful witness, Wolfram says that "[i]t seems extremely doubtful that it should be extended to civil cases." However, he cites no authority that establishes that limitation. CHARLES WOLFRAM, MODERN LEGAL ETHICS 650–651 (1986). If we were to adopt a special rule for civil cases, should it provide an exception for the witness whose testimony is truthful but misleading? Should there be an exception for the witness whose truthful testimony is serving an unjust cause? Should it be unethical for the lawyer to show on cross-examination that the truthful witness has received an unlawful fee for testifying?

and to avoid the infliction of needless harm." If "needless harm" includes harm to the truthful witness whose credibility is attacked, EC 7-10 would establish that cross-examining the truthful witness is not part of the obligation of zealous representation. However, if the codifiers intended to create such an important exception to the pervasive ethic of zeal,[33] it would be inappropriate to do so in an Ethical Consideration. Rather, we should look to the limitations expressly embodied in the relevant Disciplinary Rules, and particularly to those relating specifically to the obligations of trial lawyers.

DR 7-101(A)(1) is the principal source in the Model Code for the obligation of zealous representation. The second sentence of DR 7-101(A)(1) permits, but does not require,[34] the lawyer to avoid "offensive tactics" and to "treat[] with courtesy and consideration all persons involved in the legal process." The mandatory corollary to this permissive rule is in DR 7-102(A)(1), which says that a lawyer "shall not" take action on behalf of a client when the lawyer knows that the action "would serve merely to harass or maliciously injure another." Were it not for the word "merely," this rule could be read to preclude attacking the credibility of the truthful witness. As we will see, however, attacking credibility, even of the truthful witness, is generally considered to have a legitimate purpose apart from any effect of harassment or malicious injury. Also, DR 7-101 and 7-102 are rules of general application, without specific focus on issues of trial advocacy.

DR 7-106, entitled "Trial Conduct," specifically applies the general obligations of DR 7-101 and 7-102. DR 7-106(C)(2) provides that in appearing before a tribunal, a lawyer "shall not" ask any question that the lawyer has "no reasonable basis to believe is relevant *and* that is intended to degrade a witness or other person."[35] The clause after the "and" is clear: a lawyer is forbidden to ask a question that is intended to degrade a witness. Whenever a lawyer asks questions designed to attack a witness' credibility, however, the lawyer intends to degrade the witness.[36] (Similarly, with reference to DR 7-101(A)(1), attacking any witness' credibility could be viewed as offensive and discourteous — as the witness certainly would view it.)

The crucial question becomes, therefore, whether the lawyer has a "reasonable basis to believe" that the witness' credibility is "relevant," and under the rules of evidence, a witness' credibility is always relevant.[37] In the rape case,

---

[33] *See* Chapter 4, *supra.*

[34] "A lawyer *does not violate* this Disciplinary Rule [requiring zealous representation]. . . . " (emphasis added.)

[35] Emphasis added.

[36] *See supra* note 14.

[37] *See* Justice White's frequently quoted commentary about the professional responsibility of the criminal defense lawyer:

> If [the lawyer] can confuse a witness, *even a truthful one* . . . that will be his normal course. Our interest in not convicting the innocent permits counsel . . . to put the State's case in the worst possible light, regardless of what he thinks or knows to be the truth. . . . [M]ore often than not, defense counsel will cross-examine a prosecution witness, and impeach him if he can, even if he thinks the witness is telling the truth, just as he will attempt to destroy a witness who he thinks is lying. In this respect, as part of our modified adversary system and as part of *the duty imposed on the most honorable defense counsel,* we countenance or require conduct which in many instances has little, if any, relation to the search for truth.

then, the question becomes whether the witness' sexual history is relevant to her credibility. As Burger explained: "[T]he testimony of bad repute of the [truthful] complaining witness, being recent and not remote in point of time, is *relevant to her credibility*."[38] The Model Code, therefore, does not forbid the lawyer to attack the credibility of the truthful witness.

This analysis explains the meaning of DR 7-102(A)(2). Because a witness' credibility is always "relevant" (despite the lawyer's knowledge that the witness' testimony is true), an attack on the witness' credibility cannot be "merely" to harass or to maliciously injure. Similarly, adducing relevant evidence through cross-examination cannot be what is meant in DR 7-101(A)(1) by offensive tactics or discourteous treatment (particularly in a sentence that contains the qualifying clause, "which do not prejudice the rights of his client").[39]

On the contrary, such cross-examination is a "reasonably available means" that is "permitted by law and the Disciplinary Rules" for "seek[ing] the lawful objectives of his client." Accordingly, pursuant to DR 7-101(A)(1), the lawyer "shall not intentionally" fail to pursue that means.[40] That is, discrediting the hostile but truthful witness is not just permitted under the Model Code, it is required.[41]

§ 8.08   THE MODEL RULES

MR 4.4 is intended to deal with the issue of discrediting the truthful witness.[42] The Rule says that a lawyer "shall not use means that have no substantial purpose other than to embarrass . . . or burden a third person." Again, the lawyer's substantial purpose would be impeaching the witness' credibility and, in the criminal case, fulfilling the defendant's constitutional right of confrontation.

United States v. Wade, 388 U.S. 218, 87 S.Ct. 1926 (1967) (White, J., concurring in part and dissenting in part) (emphasis added), citing, *inter alia*, Freedman, *Professional Responsibility of the Criminal Defense Lawyer*, *supra* note 2.

[38] Burger, *supra* note 6, at 14–15 (1966) (emphasis added). This conclusion is, of course, contrary to rape shield laws.

[39] In the criminal case, the rights of the client include the constitutional right to confront witnesses against him.

[40] *See also* the quotation from Justice White's opinion in *United States v. Wade* in note 37, *supra*.

[41] That is subject to an important caveat. Our point is that the lawyer could not justify failing to attack the truthful witness on ethical grounds. However, she might well do so on tactical grounds. That is, if the attempt to discredit the witness is likely to backfire and harm the client's case in the eyes of the jury, then the means of discrediting the witness would not be "reasonably available" to achieve the client's end. *See* Leonard M. Ring, *Cross-Examining the Sympathetic Witness*, in THE LITIGATION MANUAL: A PRIMER FOR TRIAL LAWYERS 608, 620 (John.G. Koeltle, ed., 2d ed. 1989); *see also* Smith, *Defending Defending*, *supra* note 19, at 954–57 (discussing the ethics and tactics of discrediting police abuse victim Abner Louima by suggesting he had engaged in homosexual sex).

Note, however, that if the client insists on the cross-examination, the client's decision should control, particularly in the criminal case where the defendant has a constitutional right to confront witnesses against him. *See supra*, Ch. 3 (esp. section 3.07 on "Objectives vs. Means").

[42] 1 GOEFFREY C. HAZARD & W. WILLIAM HODES, THE LAW OF LAWYERING §§ 40.2, 40.3 (3d ed., 2001).

Hazard and Hodes note that "it is often the *duty* of an advocate to 'burden' or 'embarrass' an adverse witness, if doing so will make the witness less likely to be believed."[43] They add that "[e]ven though cross-examining a *truthful* witness tends to move a trier of fact away from the truth rather than toward it, the advocate may *still* point to a 'substantial purpose' *other* than harassing the witness . . . "[44] However, the authors do not resort to niceties (or euphemisms) about "testing the witness' credibility" in justifying a "substantial purpose." Nor do they advert to the criminal defendant's constitutional right of confrontation. Their justification is that there is "obviously a 'substantial' and legitimate purpose" in attacking a witness' credibility — "namely winning the case at hand."[45]

§ 8.09 CONCLUSION

One of the anomalies about lawyers' ethics is that sometimes the most difficult moral issues receive less attention and are among the least controversial. This is certainly true of the question of cross-examining the witness who is known to be testifying accurately and truthfully in order to make the witness appear to be mistaken or lying. Even those who sought Freedman's disbarment for suggesting that a lawyer can, in some circumstances, knowingly present a criminal defendant's perjury, had no difficulty in concluding that a lawyer can ethically make a liar out of a truthful witness.

On analysis, we too reach that conclusion. The difficulty of the issue, however, is illustrated by Freedman's decision not to accept rape cases in order to avoid cross-examining a truthful rape victim.[46]

---

[43] *Id.*, § 40.3 (emphasis added). No distinction is suggested between criminal and civil cases.

[44] *Id.* (First emphasis in the original).

[45] *Id.* In view of very thoughtful discussion in the remainder of § 40.3, there is clearly a sardonic edge in the authors' use of the last phrase.

[46] *See* text at note 17, *supra*.

Chapter 9

THE IMPARTIAL JUDGE

§ 9.01 INTRODUCTION

An impartial judge is an essential component of an adversary system, providing a necessary counterpoise to partisan advocates. We may tolerate judges who lack wisdom or even good judgment, but if a trial judge is not impartial, there is a "structural defect" in the trial, and reversal is required without consideration of the harmless error doctrine.[1] Indeed, because the right to an impartial tribunal is essential to fundamental fairness, it is one of those "extraordinary" rights that cannot be waived.[2]

Moreover, judges not only must be neutral and detached, they must avoid even reasonable suspicions about possible interest or bias. As long ago as 1270, Henry of Bracton wrote:[3]

> [L]et the suspect judge be removed and one who is not suspect substituted for him . . . . [I]t is a very fearful thing to litigate under a suspect justice and very often results in the saddest outcomes.
>
> But there is only one reason to recuse — suspicion, which arises from many causes . . . .

As that passage indicates, a principal method for ensuring that judges will be neutral and detached is to disqualify judges from cases in which their ability to be impartial might reasonably be questioned.[4]

In the development of modern rules of judicial disqualification, Chief Justice William Rehnquist's role in the case of *Laird v. Tatum* is a dramatic and significant event.[5] The case helped to persuade Congress to broaden substantially the federal judicial disqualification statute. Also, it illustrates the maxim that "no man may be a judge in his own case."[6] As we will see, Rehnquist's partisan interest in the case affected not only his decision on the merits of *Laird v. Tatum*, but also his decision about whether he should have recused himself. In addition, Rehnquist's role in *Laird* provides an introduction to the three major sources of rules relating to judicial disqualification:

---

[1] *Arizona v. Fulminante*, 111 S.Ct. 1246, 1265 (1991).

[2] *United States v. Fay*, 300 F.3d 345, 350–351 (2d Cir., 1962).

[3] John T. Noonan & Kenneth I. Winston, The Responsible Judge 278–279 (1993), *quoting* Bracton, The Laws and Customs of England (1270). The authors call this work "the greatest treatise on English law before Blackstone's Commentaries."

[4] The words *disqualify* and *recuse* are commonly used as synonyms. Technically, *disqualify* is broader than *recuse*; it can be applied to witnesses as well as to judges, and can be used reflexively or nonreflexively. *Recuse* is almost invariably reflexive, i.e., judges are said to "recuse themselves." *See* Bryan A. Garner, A Dictionary of Modern Legal Usage 743 (2d ed. 1995).

[5] 408 U.S. 1 (1972).

[6] I Coke, Institutes *141a, quoted in Note, *Caesar's Wife Revisited — Judicial Disqualification After the 1974 Amendments*, 34 Wash. & Lee L. Rev. 1201, 1202–1203 (1977).

the ABA's Code of Judicial Conduct, the Federal Disqualification Statute, and the Due Process Clause of the United States Constitution.

§ 9.02   CHIEF JUSTICE REHNQUIST, AND *LAIRD V. TATUM*[7]

In 1970, civil rights, civil liberties, and anti-Vietnam War activists filed a case that became, on appeal, *Laird v. Tatum*.[8] The complaint charged that the United States Army was conducting unlawful surveillance of large numbers of individuals and organizations who were engaged in constitutionally protected activities. The Federal District Court dismissed the complaint on the ground that it was not justiciable,[9] and the case was appealed to the United States Court of Appeals for the District of Columbia Circuit.

In 1971, while the appeal was pending, William Rehnquist was the Assistant Attorney General for the Office of Legal Counsel,[10] and testified about *Laird v. Tatum* before the Senate Subcommittee on Constitutional Rights, chaired by Senator Sam J. Ervin, Jr.[11] In Rehnquist's testimony, he asserted that in fact the Army's surveillance activities had stopped. In addition, he contended that such surveillance was constitutional, and he expressly endorsed the District Court's dismissal of *Laird v. Tatum* on the ground that the case was not justiciable.

Later in 1971, the appeal in *Laird v. Tatum* was heard by a panel of the Court of Appeals, which disagreed with the position expressed by Rehnquist.[12] That court reversed the trial court's decision and remanded the case for an evidentiary hearing to determine the nature and extent of military surveillance of lawful political activities, the relationship of such activities to the statutory and constitutional role of the military, whether such activities were inhibiting First Amendment rights of association, speech, assembly, and petition, and, if so, what relief would be appropriate.

The Supreme Court heard *Laird v. Tatum* the following year. Holding that the case was not justiciable, the Supreme Court reversed the Court of Appeals.

---

[7] In addition to specific citations in footnotes, this section relies substantially on the following sources: Jeffrey Stemple, Rehnquist, Recusal, and Reform, 53 BROOK. L. REV. 589 (1987); FRANK ASKIN, DEFENDING RIGHTS (1997) (Askin was General Counsel for the ACLU and lead counsel in the case); JOHN MACKENZIE, THE APPEARANCE OF JUSTICE (1974); *Federal Data Banks, Computers and the Bill of Rights*, Hearings before the Subcommittee on Constitutional Rights of the Committee on the Judiciary of the U.S. Senate, 92d Cong., 1st Sess., Part 1. Confirmation Hearings, William. H. Rehnquist, Nov. 3,4,8-10, 1971; July 29-31, Aug. 1 1986. Interview with Robert E. Jordan, III, former General Counsel of the Army (Dec. 18, 2001).

[8] 408 U.S. 1 (1972). The plaintiff who gave his name to the case was Arlo Tatum, director of the Central Committee for Conscientious Objectors. The defendant was Melvin Laird, Secretary of Defense.

[9] That is, that the case was not suitable for judicial decision.

[10] The position ranks number five in the Department of Justice.

[11] This was a subcommittee of the Senate Committee on the Judiciary. Senator Ervin was the former Chief Judge of the North Carolina Supreme Court and was highly regarded as a constitutional authority. He later chaired the Senate Watergate Committee.

[12] The panel was a conservative one, consisting of Judges Wilkey, Tamm, and MacKinnon. Judge Tamm, for example, had been the third-ranking member of J. Edgar Hoover's FBI. The court's decision was 2-1, with Judge MacKinnon dissenting on the justiciability issue.

The vote was 5-4, with then Justice Rehnquist casting the deciding vote. Without Rehnquist's vote, the Court of Appeal's decision would have stood, and the case would have been litigated in the trial court. Among other things, this would have given the plaintiffs the opportunity to conduct discovery regarding relevant facts and witnesses. As will become clear shortly, Rehnquist would then have become a likely witness and a possible defendant in the case.

According to Senator Ervin, Rehnquist's testimony before the Senate Subcommittee on the merits of *Laird v. Tatum* was sufficient in itself to disqualify him from participating in hearing the case on appeal. However, Ervin (who had joined the case as amicus curiae in support of the plaintiffs) urged that no motion be made to disqualify Rehnquist. His reason was that he fully expected Rehnquist to recuse himself. [13]

What the parties did not know, and what was discovered only after a belated motion to disqualify Rehnquist had been made and denied, was that Rehnquist had testified falsely before the Senate Subcommittee in 1971 when he asserted that Army surveillance had ended. In 1969, when Rehnquist was Assistant Attorney General, his office had been given the responsibility to develop, with representatives of the Army, an Interdepartmental Action Plan for Civil Disturbances. Ironically, the Army had taken a position in accord with the *Laird v. Tatum* plaintiffs, urging that military surveillance of domestic organizations was inappropriate, and that any such law enforcement activities should be transferred from the Army to the Justice Department and the Federal Bureau of Investigation.

The Army's representative in negotiating and drafting the Action Plan was Robert E. Jordan, III, General Counsel of the Army and Special Assistant for Civil Functions to the Secretary of the Army. Rehnquist was his counterpart as "the point man" for the Department of Justice. [14] Generally, it was Rehnquist and Jordan who together drafted the Action Plan. [15] In the course of that process, Rehnquist had successfully overridden the Army's proposal to discontinue military surveillance activities. Accordingly, with continuation of the Army's role included, the Action Plan was forwarded by Rehnquist for President Richard Nixon's approval.

It is reasonable to infer that Rehnquist knew that his testimony was false, therefore, when he told the Senate Committee that such surveillance had ended, because he had been instrumental in assuring its continuance, over the Army's strong objections, only two years before. Further, Rehnquist's central role in developing the Action Plan would have made him a likely witness and a possible party in any trial of *Laird v. Tatum* — a likelihood that he averted with his decisive vote in the case as a Supreme Court Justice. [16]

---

[13] Some of those in attendance were shocked when Rehnquist appeared on the bench at the oral argument of *Laird v. Tatum*. MacKenzie, *supra* note 7, at 211. However, Ervin dissuaded Frank Askin, who was lead counsel, from moving to disqualify Rehnquist, saying, "[H]e's a very honorable man . . . . He will not participate in the decision." ASKIN, *supra* note 7, at 59.

[14] Related by Robert E. Jordan, III, Esquire, to Professor Freedman, Dec. 18, 2001.

[15] *Id.*

[16] The original complaint in the case sought only equitable relief and not money damages, so Rehnquist (no longer responsible for the surveillance activities) would not have been an appropriate defendant. However, in its brief in the Supreme Court the plaintiffs noted their

Rehnquist's role in *Laird v. Tatum* came up again in his 1986 confirmation hearings on his nomination to be Chief Justice. Asked whether he had had personal knowledge of any disputed evidentiary facts in *Laird v. Tatum*, Rehnquist answered no. Since a central issue in the case had been whether military surveillance of domestic organizations was continuing or had stopped, this testimony was not truthful. Regardless of whether he had known that it had stopped or that it was continuing, Rehnquist had had knowledge of a disputed fact.[17]

Return now to 1972 and the belated motion to disqualify Justice Rehnquist after the 5-4 ruling in *Laird v. Tatum*. In denying the motion, Rehnquist wrote a Memorandum opinion justifying his refusal to recuse himself.[18] This opinion serves to highlight important issues in judicial disqualification.

Since the plaintiffs were ignorant of Rehnquist's role in the Action Plan for Civil Disturbances, that role was not mentioned expressly in their motion. They did, however, refer to his "intimate knowledge" of evidence relevant to the case, based on the fact that he had testified about the facts of the case before the Senate Subcommittee only months before deciding the case. In response, Rehnquist quoted a comment from his testimony before the Subcommittee in which he had disclaimed "personal knowledge of every field," and he protested that the plaintiffs' motion was making "a great deal out of very little."[19] Despite the obvious relevance of his role in the Action Plan, Rehnquist made no reference to it in his opinion.

The disqualification motion was based also on the fact that Rehnquist, in his testimony before the Subcommittee, had expressed an opinion on the merits of the controlling legal issue in *Laird v. Tatum*. That issue, of course, was whether the case was justiciable, and the Supreme Court, reversing the Court of Appeals, had held that it was not. In his opinion denying the motion to disqualify him, Rehnquist took the trouble to quote in full an irrelevant factual comment that he had made about *Laird* in his appearance before the Subcommittee.[20] Immediately thereafter — this time without providing the

---

intention to amend their complaint on remand to include allegations of defamation of individuals through widespread dissemination of the surveillance reports about them. This would have made Rehnquist a likely defendant with regard to money damages for the past harmful activities for which he had been in part responsible.

[17] Put otherwise, Rehnquist's answer, to be truthful, would have had to have been either (1) Yes, I did have knowledge of a disputed fact; as I testified in 1971, I knew that the surveillance had stopped, or (2) Yes, I did have knowledge of a disputed fact; as I knew from my work on the Action Plan for Civil Disturbances, the surveillance was still going on. Instead, he testified that he had had no knowledge of any disputed fact.

On the other hand, if he had not had knowledge one way or the other, then he appears to have testified falsely in 1971 when he assured the Senate Subcommittee that it had stopped. "Fraud includes the pretense of knowledge when knowledge there is none." *Ultramares Corp. v. Touche, Niven & Co.*, 255 N.Y. 170, 174 N.E. 441 (1931) (Cardozo, J.). Rehnquist has never cited a memorandum, conversation, or other source other than his own knowledge for his flat assertion to the Senate Subcommittee that the surveillance had stopped.

[18] *Laird v. Tatum*, 409 U.S. 824, 93 S.Ct. 7 (1972).

[19] *Id*. at 826, 93 S.Ct. at 9.

[20] *Id*. at 827, 93 S.Ct. at 10. The reference was to the intended destruction of a print-out from an Army computer relating to the surveillance.

pertinent quotation — he referred to "a discussion of the applicable law" with Senator Ervin. [21]

By obscuring the exact nature of his discussion of law with Ervin, Rehnquist was able to write about his testimony as if he had merely expressed his view about an abstract issue of constitutional law that had turned out to relate to the *Laird* case. Thus, Rehnquist's opinion emphasized an important, but irrelevant, truism — the inevitability that judges, in their previous careers, would necessarily have expressed views on a variety of legal issues that might later come before them as judges. Indeed, "[p]roof that a justice's mind at the time he joined the Court was a complete tabula rasa in the area of constitutional adjudication would be evidence of lack of qualification, not lack of bias." [22] Therefore, the fact that a justice had indicated a "general approach to public affairs, [or even] as to particular issues of law," could not rationally be a disqualifying factor, Rehnquist wrote, "so long as the cases be different." [23]

Particularly in the last phrase, Rehnquist implicitly acknowledged that he should have disqualified himself if his "discussion of the applicable law" with Senator Ervin had indeed been about the case of *Laird v. Tatum* itself. In addition, of course, he clearly implied that his discussion with Ervin had not been about *Laird*. In fact, though, *Laird v. Tatum*, and the controlling issue in that case, was precisely what Rehnquist had commented on in his testimony. Ervin had asserted that "a serious constitutional question arises where any government agency undertakes to place people under surveillance for exercising their first amendment rights." [24] Here is Rehnquist's response, which he omitted from his opinion:

> My point of disagreement with you is . . . whether in the case of *Laird v. Tatum*, that has been pending in the Court of Appeals here in the District of Columbia, that an action will lie by private citizens to enjoin the gathering of information by the executive branch where there has been no threat of compulsory process and no pending action against any of those individuals on the part of the Government. [25]

Thus, Rehnquist had identified "*Laird v. Tatum*, that has been pending in the Court of Appeals here," and had expressly disagreed with Ervin on its justiciability (*i.e.*, "whether . . . an action will lie"), which was the same ground on which he shortly thereafter decided the case as a Supreme Court justice. Accordingly, he acted contrary to his own stated position on the circumstances in which a justice should recuse himself.

In addition, Rehnquist misapplied the version of the Federal Disqualification Statute (28 U.S.C. § 455) that controlled at the time. As Rehnquist recognized, the statute was, in effect, in two parts. The second, or discretionary, part required disqualification where the judge is "so related to or

---

[21] *Id.*

[22] *Id.* at 835, 93 S.Ct. at 13–14.

[23] *Id.*

[24] *Federal Data Banks, Computers and the Bill of Rights*, Hearings before the Subcommittee on Constitutional Rights of the Committee on the Judiciary of the United States Senate, 92nd Cong., 1st Sess. (1971), Part I, at 861.

[25] 409 U.S. at 864–865.

connected with any party or his attorney as to render it improper, in his opinion, for him to sit" in the case. Rehnquist noted that he had had a "total lack of connection" with conducting the defense of *Laird v. Tatum* while at the Justice Department and that he therefore did not fall within that part of the statute.[26] In addition, that part of the statute was discretionary because the justice was to disqualify himself only if, "in his opinion," it would be improper for him to sit, and Rehnquist clearly did not consider that to be the case.

The mandatory part of the statute, however, required disqualification in any case in which the judge "has a substancial interest, has been of counsel, [or] is or has been a material witness." Rehnquist responded simply that he had never been of counsel in the case nor had he been a material witness. Thus, he concluded, "these provisions are not applicable."[27] What he failed to address, however, was the fact that he had had a "substantial interest" in the outcome of the appeal that he had decided. As noted above, if the case had been remanded for discovery and trial, Rehnquist's role in continuing the military surveillance would have come out and he would have become a likely witness and a possible party in the case. By withholding that information, however, Rehnquist managed to ignore entirely the "substantial interest" provision of the disqualification statute.

In addition, Rehnquist relied on holdings that in close questions of disqualification, the judge should resolve the issue in favor of a "duty to sit." He argued that this duty is particularly strong in the case of a Supreme Court justice, because of "the possibility of an affirmance of the judgment below by an equally divided court."[28] However, a divided court affirming the appellate decision below would surely be better than a reversal in which a possibly interested or biased justice has cast the decisive vote.[29] As Professor Frank Askin has noted, Rehnquist's contention means that a judge should disqualify himself only when his vote doesn't matter.[30]

§ 9.03 THE ABA CODE OF JUDICIAL CONDUCT[31]

Rehnquist also acknowledged another important source of judicial disqualification standards, the ABA Code of Judicial Conduct, which had been adopted earlier in 1972.[32] However, he professed not to view the relevant provisions

---

[26] 409 U.S. at 830, 93 S.Ct. at 11.

[27] 409 U.S. at 828, 93 S.Ct. at 10.

[28] *Id.* at 837–838, 15.

[29] *See* Note, Disqualification of Judges and Justices in the Federal Courts, 86 HARV. L. REV. 736, 749–750 (1973) (commenting on Justice Rehnquist's Memorandum in *Laird v. Tatum*).

[30] ASKIN, *supra* note 7, at 60.

[31] Nearly all states and the District of Columbia have adopted codes patterned on the ABA Codes of Judicial Conduct of 1972 and 1990. STEPHEN GILLERS & ROY D. SIMON, REGULATION OF LAWYERS — STATUTES AND STANDARDS 601–602 (2002).

[32] The ABA House of Delegates had approved the Code of Judicial Conduct in August of 1972, prior to Rehnquist's Memorandum opinion. Earlier that year, the Judicial Conference of the United States had taken steps towards adopting the Code for all federal judges. The Judicial Conference adopted the Code (with amendments that are not relevant here) in 1973. Reports of the Proceedings of the Judicial Conference of the United States (1973). The Judicial Conference

of the Code as "materially different" from the disqualification statute.[33] This is a strange observation because the Code marked a radical departure from the statute.[34]

The disqualification provision, Canon 3(C)(1), begins with an extremely broad objective standard, requiring the judge to recuse himself whenever his impartiality "might reasonably be questioned."[35] At the very least, therefore, this provision should have put Rehnquist on notice of the importance of his testimony before the Ervin subcommittee and of his role in the Interdepartmental Action Plan, which made him a potential witness and defendant in a remanded case. Either of these matters might cause a reasonable person to question Rehnquist's ability to judge *Laird v. Tatum* impartially, and would therefore have required him to recuse himself.

§ 9.04 THE DUE PROCESS CLAUSE AND JUDICIAL DISQUALIFICATION

Rehnquist's Memorandum opinion also omits any reference to three relevant Supreme Court decisions requiring disqualification of judges under the Due Process Clause of the Constitution. These cases began in 1927 with *Tumey v. Ohio*.[36] There the Supreme Court held unanimously, in an opinion by Chief Justice Taft, that due process is violated if there is "a *possible temptation* to the average . . . judge . . . which *might* lead him not to hold the balance nice, clear, and true . . . . "[37] *Tumey* was a misdemeanor prosecution in which the judge received $12 as his share of the $100 penalty assessed against the defendant. In vacating the conviction for violating due process, the Court held that unless the judge's interest is so "remote, trifling, or insignificant," as to be de minimis, the judge must be disqualified.[38] In *Tumey*, the judge's receipt of $12 was held to be sufficient to require disqualification.

The Court in *Tumey* held also that in determining what constitutes due process in disqualification cases, it would consider the statutory and common

---

revised the Code in 1992 (150 F.R.D. 307), and revised it again in 1998. *Code of Conduct for United States Judges,* 175 F.R.D. 363 (1998).

In adopting the Code, the Judicial Conference determined that, in cases in which a judge has an interest in the litigation, "where the Code is more restrictive [than the Federal Disqualification Statute], the Code prevails." Reports of the Proceedings of the Judicial Conference of the United States (1973).

[33] 409 U.S. at 825, 93 S.Ct. at 9.

[34] Rehnquist subsequently acknowledged this. *See* text and footnotes at n. 52–54. The 1972 Code was also a sharp departure from the ABA's earlier Canons of Judicial Ethics. *Cf.* Canons 13 and 29.

[35] In the 1994 version of the ABA Code of Judicial Conduct, this is Canon 3E(1).

[36] 273 U.S. 510, 47 S.Ct. 437.

[37] 273 U.S. at 532, 47 S.Ct. at 444 (emphasis added).

[38] *Id.* at 531–532 and 444. In *Ward v. Village of Monroeville*, 409 U.S. 57, 93 S.Ct. 80 (1972), decided one month after Rehnquist's Memorandum in *Laird*, the Court vacated a traffic conviction on due process grounds. There, the mayor who acted as judge received no share in the petitioner's fines of $100, but such fines were a substantial part of the village's revenues. Under state law, petitioner could have had a trial de novo before a judge, but the Supreme Court held that due process entitled him to a "neutral and detached judge in the first instance." 409 U.S. at 62, 93 S.Ct. at 84. Justices White and Rehnquist dissented.

law of England prior to adoption of the Constitution. That would include the fundamental principle, already established in the early seventeenth century, that "no man may be a judge in his own case."[39]

In *In re Murchison*[40] the Supreme Court reversed a conviction on due process grounds where a state judge had held a defendant guilty of contempt for conduct before a prior grand jury proceeding where the same judge had presided. As noted by the dissent in *Murchison*, the judge had had no pecuniary interest in the case, nor was there any showing or contention that the judge had become embroiled in the case, or that he had been in any way biased.[41] Nevertheless, the Court held that "to perform its high function in the best way, 'justice must satisfy the appearance of justice.' "[42] Accordingly, even if the judge has no interest or bias in fact, "no man is permitted to try cases where he has an interest in the outcome."[43]

The third Supreme Court decision ignored by Justice Rehnquist is *Commonwealth Coatings Corp. v. Continental Casualty Co.*[44] That case held that standards of due process relating to disqualification of judges apply equally to arbitrators under the United States Arbitration Act. Three justices dissented on the ground that arbitrators should be treated differently from judges but, significantly, the Court ruled unanimously that a judge, as distinguished from an arbitrator, would have to be disqualified on the facts of the case.[45] That is, every member of the Supreme Court concurred that a judge "not only must be unbiased but also must avoid even the appearance of bias."[46]

The ground for disqualification in *Commonwealth Coatings* was that one of the three arbitrators had had sporadic business dealings with one of the parties and had not revealed that fact to the other party; however, there had been no business between the arbitrator and the party for about a year, and the payments the arbitrator had received had been a very small part of his income. Also, there was no claim of any bias in fact on the part of the arbitrator, and the Court noted that "we have no reason, apart from the undisclosed business relationship, to suspect him of any improper motive."[47] Moreover, the arbitration panel's decision had been unanimous. Nevertheless, the Supreme Court reversed the arbitration decision because the arbitrator had withheld information which *"might* create an impression of *possible* bias.' "[48]

---

[39] I Coke, Institutes *141a, quoted in Note, "Caesar's Wife Revisited — Judicial Disqualification After the 1974 Amendments," 34 WASH. & LEE L. REV. 1201, 1202–1203 (1977).

[40] 349 U.S. 133, 75 S.Ct. 623 (1955).

[41] 349 U.S. at 141, 75 S.Ct. at 623 (Reed, J., dissenting).

[42] 349 U.S. at 136, 75 S.Ct. at 625, quoting *Offutt v. United States*, 348 U.S. 11, 14.

[43] *Id.*

[44] 393 U.S. 145, 89 S.Ct. 337 (1968).

[45] As Justice Fortas wrote in dissent: "Arbitration is . . . obviously designed to protect the integrity of the process with a minimum of insistence upon set formulae and rules. *The Court applies to this process rules applicable to judges* . . . . " 393 U.S. at 154–155, 89 S.Ct. at 342 (emphasis added).

[46] 393 U.S. at 150, 89 S.Ct. at 340.

[47] 393 U.S. at 147, 89 S.Ct. at 338.

[48] 393 U.S. at 149, 89 S.Ct. at 339 (emphasis added). The Court did not clarify whether the impression of possible bias might result from gratitude for past business, or hope of future business, or both.

These cases are clearly relevant to Justice Rehnquist's role in *Laird v. Tatum*. Rehnquist's interest in the outcome in *Laird* was substantially more personal, direct, and significant than was the judge's interest in the outcome in *Murchison* (the grand jury contempt case).[49] Also, as in *Tumey v. Ohio* (where the judge received only $12), Rehnquist's interest in the outcome in *Laird* presented "a possible temptation to the average . . . judge . . . which might lead him not to hold the balance nice, clear, and true . . . ." In addition, as in *Commonwealth Coatings* (the arbitration case), Rehnquist withheld facts (and misleadingly distorted others) that "might create an impression of possible bias." Moreover, unlike the panel in *Commonwealth Coatings*, the court in *Laird* was not unanimous; rather, the justice whose impartiality was subject to question cast the decisive vote in the case. Yet, despite research into previous cases of recusal by members of the Supreme Court, which he reviewed at some length in his Memorandum opinion,[50] Rehnquist made no reference to the cases applying the Due Process Clause to judicial disqualification.

§ 9.05 THE FEDERAL JUDICIAL DISQUALIFICATION STATUTE

In 1974, two years after Justice Rehnquist refused to recuse himself in *Laird v. Tatum*, Congress amended the Federal Judicial Disqualification Statute (28 U.S.C. § 455) to conform with the ABA's 1972 Code of Judicial Conduct.[51] As Chief Justice Rehnquist has acknowledged, the 1974 amendment "substantially revised" the statute, making "massive changes" in the statutory law of judicial disqualification.[52] Specifically, subsection § 455(a) is an "entirely new 'catchall' recusal provision, covering both 'interest or relationship' and 'bias or prejudice' grounds . . . but requiring them *all* to be evaluated on an *objective* basis, so that what matters is not the reality of bias or prejudice but its appearance."[53]

The catchall provision of subsection 455(a) is sparse in phrasing and sweeping in scope. It says: "Any justice, judge or magistrate of the United States shall disqualify himself in any proceeding in which his impartiality might reasonably be questioned." As the Supreme Court has recognized, "[q]uite simply and quite universally, recusal [is] required whenever 'impartiality might reasonably be questioned.' "[54]

---

[49] The Court in *Murchison* also noted that the judge in that case had knowledge of what had happened before the grand jury, and that therefore (like Rehnquist in *Laird)* he might have been a material witness. 349 U.S. at 138–139, 75 S.Ct. at 626–627.

[50] 409 U.S. at 831–834, 93 S.Ct. at 11–13.

[51] One addition Congress made to the ABA Code might be called "The Rehnquist Amendment." Section 455(b)(3) requires recusal when the judge "has served in governmental employment and in such capacity . . . expressed an opinion on the merits of the particular case in controversy."

[52] *Liljeberg v. Health Services Acquisition Corp.*, 486 U.S. 847, 108 S.Ct. 2194, 2207 (1988) (Rehnquist, C.J., dissenting); *Liteky v. United States*, 510 U.S. 540, 546, 114 S.Ct. 1147, 1153 (1994) (Rehnquist, C.J., joining in majority opinion). These opinions contradict Rehnquist's assertion in his Memorandum opinion in *Laird v. Tatum*, 409 U.S. at 825, 93 S.Ct. at 9, that the 1972 ABA Code was not "materially different" from the pre-1974 version of § 455.

[53] *Liteky v. United States*, 510 U.S. at 548, 114 S.Ct. at 1153–1154 (emphasis in the original).

[54] 510 U.S. at 548, 114 S.Ct. at 1154.

Then, in subsection 455(b), the statute requires disqualification "also" in specified situations, the most important of which are: actual bias or prejudice;[55] personal knowledge of disputed evidentiary facts concerning the proceeding;[56] a financial interest, however small, in the outcome of the proceedings;[57] or any other interest that could be substantially affected by the outcome.[58]

The most important interpretation of § 455 is the Supreme Court's decision in *Liljeberg v. Health Services Acquisition Corp.*,[59] where the Court gave effect to the plain meaning of § 455(a). *Liljeberg* was a declaratory judgment suit that centered on which party owned a certificate of need from the State of Louisiana to build a new hospital. Loyola University was not a party to the litigation but, because of a contract between Loyola and Liljeberg, the University did have a substantial financial interest in Liljeberg's obtaining the certificate.

After a trial, Federal District Judge Robert Collins awarded the certificate to Liljeberg. Ten months later, the losing party, Health Services Acquisition Corp., learned that Judge Collins had been a member of Loyola's board of trustees at the time of the trial. Accordingly, Health Services moved to vacate the judgment and to retry the case before an impartial judge.[60]

As a board member, Judge Collins had been present at meetings when Loyola's contract with Liljeberg had been discussed. However, another federal district judge, who conducted a hearing on the motion to vacate the judgment, found as a fact that Judge Collins had forgotten about Loyola's interest in the matter during the trial, and the Supreme Court accepted this finding in its discussion of § 455(a).[61] This did not answer the question, however, of whether a reasonable person "might" nevertheless "question" whether Judge Collins had really forgotten what he had known, and therefore question his impartiality.[62] The problem, the Court noted, is that members of the public too often have "suspicions and doubts" about the integrity of judges.[63] Congress enacted § 455(a) to eliminate such suspicions and doubts and to avoid the appearance of impropriety "whenever possible."[64]

---

[55] 28 U.S.C. 455(b)(1).

[56] *Id.*

[57] 28 U.S.C. 455(b)(4) and (d)(4). Ownership in a mutual or common investment fund that holds securities in not a "financial interest" in the securities unless the judge participates in the management of the fund. Sec. 455(d)(4)(i).

[58] 28 U.S.C. 455(b)(4) (1974).

[59] 486 U.S. 847, 108 S.Ct. 2194 (1988).

[60] The motion was made under Fed. Rules Civ. Proc. 60(b)(6) (allowing a court to relieve a party from a final judgment for "any . . . reason justifying relief"), because § 455 does not prescribe any particular remedy for a judge's failure to recuse himself when required to do so.

[61] 486 U.S. at 864, 108 S.Ct. at 2205.

[62] The Court posited a reasonable person "knowing all the circumstances" (which included Judge Collins' insistence that he had had no recollection of Loyola's interest in the case). *See also Paulo State of the Federal Republic v. American Tobacco Co.,* Inc. 122 S.Ct. 1290, 1292 (2002).

[63] 486 U.S. at 864, 108 S.Ct. at 2205. As shown *supra* at note 3, suspicions of judicial bias or interest were recognized as grounds for disqualification as early as 1270.

[64] *Id.* at 864–865 and 2205.

The Supreme Court discussed appearances not only from the perspective of the "reasonable

In addition, the District Court found as a fact that eight days after he had entered judgment in the case, Judge Collins had received actual knowledge of Loyola's financial interest in who won the certificate of need. The Supreme Court held that this constituted a separate violation of § 455(b)(4), which requires disqualification if a judge *"knows* that he . . . as a fiduciary . . . has a financial interest in the subject matter in controversy or . . . any other interest that could be substantially affected by the outcome."[65] If Judge Collins had revealed his interest upon receiving knowledge of Loyola's interest, Health Services could have filed a motion for a new trial within the ten-day period allowed for such motions.[66]

The holding in *Liljeberg* makes it clear that there can be a violation of each subsection of § 455 in the same case; that is, although subsections (a) and (b) overlap considerably, they are complementary. In *Liljeberg* there was a violation of subsection (a) because, despite the finding that the judge had forgotten about Loyola's interest, a reasonable person might nevertheless question whether the judge had forgotten about it. In addition, there was a violation of subsection (b)(4) because the judge ultimately had received knowledge of the ground for disqualification — which is a distinct requirement of subsection (b)(4) — and had done nothing about it. This dual result is consistent, of course, with the introductory language of subsection (b): "He shall *also* disqualify himself in the following circumstances . . . . "[67]

Chief Justice Rehnquist dissented, contending that actual knowledge, which is expressly required under subsection 455(b)(4), should be read into subsection 455(a), where it is not mentioned.[68] Even in dissenting, however, Rehnquist recognized that the 1974 amendment of the statute was intended to avoid the appearance of impropriety,[69] that it replaced the subjective standard for disqualification with an objective one,[70] and that it eliminated "the so-called 'duty to sit.' "[71] Also, § 455 "placed the obligation to identify the existence of those grounds upon the judge himself, rather than requiring recusal only in response to a party affidavit."[72] The same observations are true, of course, of the disqualification provision of the ABA's 1972 Code of

---

person," but also from the perspective of "the public" and "the skeptic." 486 U.S. at 860 and 865, n.12, 108 S.Ct. at 2203 and 2205, n.12. The phrase "the public" (implying the whole public or perhaps a majority of the public) would require disqualification in far fewer cases. The phrase "the skeptic" (who might be considered reasonable, but who is, at most, only a subset of the "reasonable person") would require disqualification in more cases.

[65] 486 U.S. at 867, 108 S.Ct. at 2206 (emphasis added).

[66] 486 U.S. at 851, 108 S.Ct. at 2198.

[67] Emphasis added.

[68] Congress specified actual knowledge as a requirement for disqualification under subsections (b)(1), (b)(4) and (b)(5), but not under subsections (a), (b)(2) and (b)(3).

Rehnquist did not address the majority's point that Judge Collins did have actual knowledge (which he did not reveal to the parties) within the ten-day period during which Health Services was allowed to file a motion for a rehearing.

[69] 486 U.S. at 872, 108 S.Ct. at 2209.

[70] *Id.*

[71] 486 U.S. at 871, 108 S.Ct. at 2208.

[72] *Liteky v. United States*, 510 U.S. 548, 114 S.Ct. at 1153 (Scalia, J., in majority opinion joined by Rehnquist, C.J.).

Judicial Conduct, Canon 3C, and of the ABA's 1990 Code, Canon 3E, which are substantially the same as § 455.[73]

§ 9.06   WHAT A REASONABLE PERSON "MIGHT," "COULD," AND "WOULD" DO

There can be no disagreement about what § 455 says: "Any . . . judge . . . shall disqualify himself in any proceeding in which his impartiality *might* reasonably be questioned."[74] In addition to the plain meaning of the statute, the legislative history shows that disqualification is required when there is "any reasonable factual basis for doubting the judge's impartiality."[75]

Also, as a matter of constitutional due process, a judge is required to recuse himself if there is "a *possible temptation* to the average . . . judge . . . which *might* lead him not to hold the balance nice, clear, and true . . . ."[76] or if the circumstances "*might* create an *impression* of *possible* bias."[77] It would be anomalous, of course, if the statute were to be less demanding of judicial impartiality than the Due Process Clause.

Nevertheless, there is a tendency for some judges and commentators — and particularly for advocates opposing disqualification — to slip away from the statutory language, turning "might" into "could" or "would."[78] The differences

---

[73] The 1990 Code has a new Canon 3B(1), which reads: "A judge shall hear and decide matters assigned to the judge *except those in which disqualification is required*" (emphasis added). In light of the "except" clause, this obligation to hear and decide assigned matters is subordinate to the obligation of disqualification under Canon 3E.

It has been suggested, however, that the new 3B(1) affirms a duty to sit. Lisa L. Milord, The Development of the ABA Judicial Code 17 (1992) ("The views expressed are those of the author" and "have not been approved" by the ABA. *Id*. at ii). Whatever the author means by a duty to sit, the text of the disqualification provision (now Canon 3E) remains unchanged, and that text was purposefully drafted to eliminate the idea of a duty to sit in the sense of a makeweight in close cases. The old notion of a duty to sit has not been revived, therefore, as a consideration in deciding an issue of disqualification. On the contrary, the language of Canon 3E still "clearly mandates that it would be preferable for a judge to err on the side of caution and disqualify himself in a questionable case." *Potashnick v. Port City Construction Co.*, 609 F.2d 1101, 1112 (5th Cir., 1980) (construing § 455).

[74] Emphasis added.

[75] *Potashnick v. Port city Const. Co.*, 609 F.2d 1101, 1111 (5th Cir., 1980), *quoting* 1974 U.S. Code Cong. & Admin. News, 6351, 6354–55.

[76] *Tumey v. Ohio*, 273 U.S. 510, 532, 47 S.Ct. 437, 444 (1927) (emphasis added).

[77] *Commonwealth Coatings Corp. v. Continental Casualty Co.*, 393 U.S. 145, 149, 89 S.Ct. 337, 339 (1968) (emphasis added).

[78] A striking instance of an inadvertent shift from "might" to "would" is in *Potashnick v. Port City Const. Co.*, 609 F.2d 1101 (5th Cir., 1980), *cert. den.*, 449 U.S. 820. In disqualifying the trial judge, the Fifth Circuit wrote: "Use of the word '*might*' in the statute was intended to indicate that disqualification should follow if the reasonable man, were he to know all the circumstances, *would* harbor doubts about the judge's impartiality." 609 F.2d at 1111 (emphasis added). At the same time, the court recognized that disqualification is required if there is "any reasonable factual basis for doubting the judge's impartiality." *Id.*

Even in the Supreme Court, similar slips have occurred. For example, in *Liljeberg* Justice Stevens adopted the language of the Court of Appeals, saying, "a reasonable person *would expect* that Judge Collins would remember that Loyola had some dealings with Liljeberg . . . ." 486 U.S. at 851–852, 108 S.Ct. at 2198. Under the Court's holding in that case, however, it was sufficient that a reasonable person might have had suspicions or doubts about the matter.

are important. The word "might" is used to express "tentative possibility;" "could" is used to express "possibility;" while "would" connotes what "will" happen or is "going to" happen.[79] Accordingly, the word "would" requires significantly more than a tentative possibility of doubt regarding a judge's impartiality, and use of the word "would" therefore produces a subtle but substantial change in the meaning of the statute.

For example, when Justice Stephen Breyer was nominated for the United States Supreme Court, Professor Freedman argued against his confirmation. The reason was that Breyer, when sitting in the First Circuit, had written an opinion that could well have had a devastating impact on Breyer's own financial well-being as a member of Lloyd's of London.[80] Freedman maintained that Breyer had acted unethically in failing to recuse himself. Then White House Counsel Lloyd Cutler contended that reasonable people differed about whether Breyer's impartiality in the case was questionable, and that Breyer therefore was not required to recuse himself.

That argument would have force if the statute required disqualification only when a reasonable person *would* question the judge's impartiality. In that event, if reasonable people disagreed about whether the judge's impartiality is questionable, one could not say that a reasonable person *would* question it — only that she might or might not — and recusal would not be required. Under the statute as enacted, however, if reasonable people do disagree, then clearly a reasonable person *might* question the judge's impartiality, and recusal is required. That is, under § 455(a) a judge can properly stay in a case only if no reasonable person might question the judge's impartiality.[81]

In a letter to the Senate Judiciary Committee, Professor Stephen Gillers introduced a similar alteration of the statutory language. The point had been made that Breyer had also violated subsection 455(b)(4), which requires recusal when a judge "knows that he . . . has a financial interest in the subject matter in controversy . . . that *could* be *substantially* affected by the outcome of the proceeding." Gillers wrote that "Professor Freedman cannot say with any degree of confidence that the decision [written by Breyer] . . . *would* have a *direct and* substantial effect on his [financial interests]."[82] That was, of course, true. What Freedman had said with confidence, however, was that Breyer's decision "could" have had a "substantial" effect on his financial interests (a matter that was beyond reasonable dispute), and that is all that the statute does or should require.

Since Breyer has been on the Supreme Court, he has disqualified himself in a number of cases that have not been as serious as the one he decided in

---

[79] RANDOM HOUSE WEBSTER'S COLLEGE DICTIONARY (2d ed., 1997).

Using WEBSTER'S NEW WORLD COLLEGE DICTIONARY (3rd ed., 1997), Professor Leslie W. Abramson defines "might" as "expressing especially a shade of doubt or a lesser degree of possibility." Leslie W. Abramson, *Appearance of Impropriety: Deciding When a Judge's Impartiality 'Might Reasonably Be Questioned,"* 14 GEO. J. LEGAL ETHICS 55, 58 (2000).

[80] Letter from Monroe H. Freedman to Sen. Joseph R. Biden, Chair, Committee on the Judiciary, 140 CONG. REC., Sen. 10075 (1994). The case against Justice Breyer is also set forth in Freedman, *Breyer Won — Ethics Lost*, LEGAL TIMES, Aug. 23, 1994.

[81] *See* Abramson, *supra* note 79, at 59.

[82] 140 CONG. REC., Sen. 10075 (1994) (emphasis added).

the First Circuit.[83] In addition, "at a hefty price," he has reinsured his liability in Lloyd's.[84]

§ 9.07 THE PRACTICAL ADVANTAGES OF AN APPEARANCES RULE

The use of a disqualification rule based on the appearance of impropriety has important practical advantages. First, some lawyers are reluctant to make disqualification motions for fear of antagonizing judges, particularly those before whom they expect to appear again.[85] The professional obligation to seek disqualification in appropriate cases is made easier when the lawyer need not accuse the judge of bias in fact. Rather, the lawyer can acknowledge that the particular judge is "pure in heart and incorruptible," but that he is nevertheless subject to disqualification on an objective, appearances standard.[86]

Also, some judges are reluctant to recuse themselves out of concern that to do so would be an embarrassing admission of a disabling bias. The appearances standard, by disqualifying even the judge who is "pure in heart and incorruptible," avoids this concern as well. In addition, as illustrated by Chief Justice Rehnquist's opinion denying disqualification in *Laird v. Tatum*, it can be difficult to act impartially as a judge in one's own case. An objective standard, and the elimination of the duty to sit, make it less likely that a judge will be able to successfully avoid recusal when it is warranted.

A related problem arises when a judge's decision not to recuse himself is reviewed by fellow judges in an appellate court or by a colleague on the same bench. A desirable collegiality among judges can be adversely affected by a decision by one judge that another is biased, or (as a federal district judge was called upon to decide in *Liljeberg*) that a fellow judge had not really forgotten information that he claimed to have forgotten. Also, the Supreme Court recognized a further concern in *Liljeberg*:[87]

> A finding by another judge — faced with the difficult task of passing upon the integrity of a fellow member of the bench — that his or her colleague merely possessed *constructive* knowledge, and not *actual* knowledge [and therefore is not subject to disqualification], is unlikely to significantly quell the concern of the skeptic.

That is, despite the fact that a fellow judge has accepted the word of a judicial colleague that the latter has forgotten relevant facts, a reasonable member

---

[83] *See* Letter to the Editor from Freedman, *Justice Breyer Takes Ethics Seriously*, N.Y. TIMES, Nov. 9, 1994, *See, e.g., General Electric Capital Corp. v. National Union fire Insur. Co.*, 513 U.S. 916, 115 S.Ct. 293 (1994) (denying cert.). *See also* Tony Mauro, *Wave of Recusals Marks Breyer's Debut*, LEGAL TIMES, Oct. 10, 1994, at 8.

[84] Neil A. Lewis, *Justice Breyer Buys Policy to Sever Ties to Lloyd's*, N.Y. TIMES, Nov. 11, 1994.

[85] For example, a lawyer believed in one case that a Supreme Court justice "[w]ithout question . . . should have recused himself." Nevertheless, "like most lawyers in similar situations," he decided not to make a motion for recusal "for strategic reasons." He explained that "[y]ou risk offending not only the justice but the whole body." Tony Mauro, *Thomas Ruling Spurs Recusal Spat*, LEGAL TIMES, Aug. 19 & 26, 1996.

[86] *Liljeberg*, 486 U.S. at 860, 108 S.Ct. at 2203.

[87] 486 U.S. at 865, n.12, 108 S.Ct. at 2205, n.12.

of the public might nevertheless question whether the judge truly had forgotten what he admittedly had once known.

For these reasons, the broad language of § 455(a) has sound practical justification apart from assuring that justice will not only be done but that it will appear to have been done.

§ 9.08   THE POTENTIAL EFFECTS OF *REPUBLICAN PARTY OF MINNESOTA V. WHITE*

Republican Party of Minnesota v. White [88] is an intriguing case in several respects. The issue before the Supreme Court was whether a candidate for an elective state judgeship could be prohibited from "announc[ing] his views on disputed legal or political issues." This prohibition came from what is called the "announce" clause of Canon 7(B) of the ABA Model Code of Judicial Conduct (1972). [89]

The Court, dividing 5-4, struck down the announce clause. It held that such speech is at the core of First Amendment freedoms because it relates to the qualifications of candidates for public office. Accordingly, the announce clause had to withstand strict scrutiny, which means that the state had to meet the burden of proving that the restriction (1) served a compelling state interest and (2) was narrowly tailored to avoid unnecessarily limiting protected expression. The majority opinion was written by Justice Scalia, joined by Rehnquist, O'Connor, Kennedy, and Thomas. The dissenters were Stevens, Souter, Ginsburg, and Breyer.

Most commentators have strongly condemned the decision. [90] We believe, however, that the decision is consistent both with the First Amendment and with a desirable degree of realism about the substantial, demonstrable influence of judges' political ideologies on their decisions. [91] Nevertheless, we acknowledge that judicial decisions are not consistently determined, or

---

[88] 536 U.S. 765, 122 S.Ct. 2528 (2002).

[89] "(1) A candidate, including an incumbent judge, for a judicial office . . . (b) should not . . . announce his views on disputed legal or political issues . . . ." ABA Model Code of Judicial Conduct, Canon 7B(1)(b) (1972).

Canon 5A(3)(d)(ii) of the 1990 Code changed this language to read: "(3) A candidate for a judicial office . . . (d) shall not . . . (ii) make statements that commit or appear to commit the candidate with respect to cases, controversies or issues that are likely to come before the court . . . ."

[90] *See, e.g.,* Geoffrey C. Hazard, Jr., *"Announcement" by Federal Judicial Nominees,* _____ HOFSTRA L. REV. _____ (2004).

[91] *See, e.g.,* David A. Schkade and Cass R. Sunstein, *Judging by Where You Sit,* N.Y. TIMES, June 11, 2003:

> The effect of ideology on panel decisions is clear. Consider, for example, a case in which a woman has complained of sex discrimination. In front of an appellate panel of three Democratic appointees, she wins 75 percent of the time . . . . With two Democratic and one Republican appointee, she wins 49 percent of the time; with one Democratic and two Republican appointees, she wins 38 percent of the time. And with a panel of three Republican appointees, she wins just 31 percent of the time.

The authors report similar results, influenced by political ideology, in other areas of the law. *See also,* Deborah Sontag, *The Power of the Fourth [Circuit],* N.Y. TIMES MAGAZINE, March 9, 2003, at 38.

predictable, by reference to a judge's political ideology. In *White* itself, for example, it was five Republican justices who upheld the First Amendment, and the two Democratic plus two Republicans justices who favored restrictions on speech.[92]

Beyond the immediate First Amendment issue in *White*, the opinions in that case could have profound effects on other important issues relating to judicial impartiality. We turn to those now.

[1] The Definition of Impartiality

The compelling interests asserted by the state in *White* were preserving the impartiality of the judiciary and preserving the appearance of impartiality. Scalia devotes a significant part of his opinion to defining impartiality.[93] He rejects definitions that equate impartiality with either open-mindedness or a lack of a preconceived view of the law, and concludes that the word means "the lack of bias for or against either *party* to the proceeding."[94] What is not clear is why Scalia takes such pains with establishing this definition, because he finds that impartiality fails to justify the announce clause under any of the three definitions he discusses.

Also, Scalia refers with approval to *Aetna Life Ins. Co. v. Lavoie*,[95] characterizing it as a case in which due process was violated because it was in the judge's financial interest to find against Aetna, thereby establishing bias against a party. This is accurate, but misleading. In *Lavoie*, a judge in the Alabama Supreme Court, Judge Embry, was himself litigating against two insurance companies (neither of them Aetna). In one case he was attempting to recover punitive damages for a tortious bad-faith refusal to pay a claim. The law in Alabama had not clearly established such a tort. In *Lavoie*, the Alabama Supreme Court did recognize the tort, thereby establishing a favorable precedent for Embry in his own case.

Although Aetna had contended that the judge was biased against insurance companies as *parties*, the U.S. Supreme Court expressly rejected that argument.[96] Instead, the Court held that due process was denied because Embry had participated in establishing a precedent favorable to himself on the *issue* of tortious bad faith, and was therefore acting as "a judge in his own case."[97]

---

[92] To further complicate the issue, *see Florida Bar v. Went For It*, discussed *infra*, § 12.06. The case involved a restriction on lawyer advertising, which is protected as commercial speech. A four-to-one Republican majority (O'Connor joined by Rehnquist, Scalia, Thomas, and Breyer) upheld the speech restriction, while three Republican and one of the Democratic appointees voted to uphold the First Amendment (Kennedy joined by Stevens, Souter, and Ginsburg). The only justice who was consistent in the two cases is Kennedy, a Republican appointee, who supported the First Amendment right in both cases.

[93] 536 U.S. at 775–779, 122 S.Ct. at 2535–2537.

[94] *Id.* at 775, 2537 (emphasis in the original).

[95] 475 U.S. 813, 106 S.Ct. 1580 (1986).

[96] "[I]t is likely that many claimants have developed hostile feelings from the frustration in awaiting settlement of insurance claims . . . . [Aetna's] allegations of bias and prejudice on this general basis, however, are insufficient to establish any constitutional violation." 475 U.S. at 821.

[97] *Id.* at 824.

Thus, the judge was biased against the *party*, Aetna, only in the sense that he had a personal financial interest in the *issue* in the case.[98]

Scalia's definition of impartiality is therefore dictum and based on questionable analysis. In addition, it does not hold a majority of the Court. Justice O'Connor, who is part of the majority of five in *White*, expressly disagrees with Scalia on the definition of impartiality. In the second paragraph of her concurring opinion, O'Connor ignores Scalia's analysis, and defines impartiality as being "free from any personal stake in the outcome of the cases . . . ."[99]

The potential significance in how impartiality is defined is its critical importance in § 455(a) of the Federal Disqualification Statute.[100] Conceivably, Scalia was attempting to narrow the definition of impartiality, and thereby to reduce the occasions for judicial disqualification under § 455(a) as well as in cases under the Due Process Clause of the Fourteenth Amendment. In either event, as indicated above and as discussed further in the next subsection, he does not appear to have been successful.

[2] The Potential Relevance of *White* to Disqualification Under § 455(a)

As we have seen, § 455(a) requires a judge to recuse herself if her impartiality might reasonably be questioned. If impartiality referred only to a lack of bias against a *party*, therefore, the scope of § 455(a) would be considerably narrowed. In *Laird v. Tatum*,[101] for example, the grounds for disqualifying Rehnquist related to (1) his having taken a position on the merits of the *issue* in that very case in his testimony before Congress on behalf of the government, and (2) his *personal interest* (or, to use O'Connor's word, his "stake") in avoiding becoming a witness and a defendant in the case. Neither of these reasons made him biased against the plaintiffs *as parties*. Scalia's definition, emphasizing bias against a party, is therefore artificially narrow.[102]

Also, in an interesting exchange with Stevens in *White*, Scalia acknowledges that a judge's announced position on an issue can, in some circumstances, manifest a bias against a party or a class of parties. Stevens wrote:

> Even when "impartiality" is defined in its narrowest sense to embrace only "the lack of bias for or against either *party* to the proceeding," the announce clause serves that interest. Expressions that stress a candidate's unbroken record of affirming convictions for rape, for example, imply a bias in favor of a particular litigant (the prosecutor) and against a class of litigants (defendants in rape cases). Contrary to the Court's reasoning in its first attempt to define impartiality, an

---

[98] *See also* Scalia's concession that an announced position on an issue can manifest bias against a party, discussed *infra*, § 9.08[2].

[99] 536 U.S. at 788, 122 S.Ct. at 2542.

[100] *See* § 9.05, *supra*.

[101] *See* § 9.02, *supra*.

[102] As Justice Ginsburg points out in *White*: "Our Due Process Clause cases do not focus solely on bias against a particular party, but rather inquire more broadly into whether the surrounding circumstances and incentives compromise the judge's ability faithfully to discharge her assigned duties." 536 U.S. at 815, 122 S.Ct. at 2556, n.3.

interpretation of the announce clause that prohibits such statements serves the State's interest in maintaining both the appearance of this form of impartiality and its actuality . . . .

In response, Scalia said:

Some of the speech prohibited by the announce clause may well exhibit a bias against parties — including Justice Stevens' example of an election speech stressing the candidate's unbroken record of affirming convictions for rape . . . .[103]

Thus, it appears that the Supreme Court is unanimous in recognizing that some speech relating to issues may well require a judge's disqualification under § 455(a). The implications of this are discussed further in § 9.09 of this chapter.

[3] Elected Judges and Denial of Due Process

The most important potential significance of *White* is the strong suggestion in the opinions of Justices O'Connor and Ginsburg (writing for a total of five justices) that no judge subject to reelection can decide a controversial case without violating due process. As discussed earlier in this chapter,[104] due process is denied if there is a *"possible* temptation to the average . . . judge . . . which *might* lead him not to hold the balance nice, clear, and true . . . ."[105] There is substantial reason to believe that elective judges are influenced in controversial cases by the threat of being voted out of office. Particularly in a case involving issues like the death penalty or abortion rights, therefore, there is a strong argument that a decision by such a judge violates the Due Process Clause of the Fourteenth Amendment.[106]

Indeed, Justice O'Connor's concerns ultimately go beyond the controversial case, to challenge the entire system of electing judges. She concurs separately to express her objections to "judicial elections generally."[107] Referring to the state's claim of a compelling interest in "an actual and perceived . . . impartial judiciary," she notes that "the very practice of electing judges undermines this interest."[108] Defining impartiality as being free of any stake in the outcome of a case, she explains that when judges are subject to regular elections, "they are likely to feel that they have at least some personal stake in the outcome of every publicized case."[109] That is, elected judges "cannot help being aware that if the public is not satisfied with the outcome of a particular case, it could hurt their reelection prospects."[110] Moreover, even when judges succeed in overcoming their concern with voters' displeasure, "the public's confidence in

---

[103] 536 U.S. at 800, 122 S.Ct. at 2548.

[104] *Supra*, § 9.04.

[105] 273 U.S. 510, 532, 47 S.Ct. 437, 444 (1927) (emphasis added).

[106] In addition, as pointed out by Justice O'Connor, fundraising for judicial elections creates problems even in cases that are not of great public interest. See *infra*, this section.

[107] *Id.* at 788, 2542.

[108] *Id.*

[109] *Id.* at 788–789, 2543.

[110] *Id.* at 789, 2543.

the judiciary could be undermined simply by the possibility that judges would be unable to do so."[111]

O'Connor refers to a law review article that quotes former California Supreme Court Justice Otto Kaus' statement that ignoring the political consequences of controversial cases is like "ignoring a crocodile in your bathtub."[112] She also relies on an article that cites statistics indicating that judges who face elections are far more likely to override jury sentences of life without parole and impose the death penalty.[113]

In addition, O'Connor discusses the pernicious effects of campaign fundraising in judicial elections, noting, for example, that the thirteen candidates in a partisan election for five seats on the Alabama Supreme Court in 2000 spent an average of $1,092,076 on their campaigns.[114] Not surprisingly, lawyers and litigants who appear before the judges are among the major contributors to judges' campaigns,[115] and "relying on campaign donations may leave judges feeling indebted to certain parties or interest groups."[116]

When lawyers and litigants appear to be buying influence with campaign contributions, the appearance of partiality goes beyond the highly publicized case, tainting any case in which money may have passed.[117] Thus, O'Connor's ultimate due process challenge is to the entire system of judicial election of judges, in cases of both major and minor public interest.

Justice Ginsburg analyzes some of the Court's most important cases requiring disqualification of state judges on due process grounds.[118] Her analysis provides three conclusions. First, a litigant is deprived of due process where the judge who hears his case has a "direct, personal, substantial and pecuniary" interest in ruling against him.[119] Second, the judge's interest is sufficiently "direct" if the judge knows that "his success and tenure in office depend on certain outcomes."[120] Third, due process does not require a showing that the judge is biased in fact as a result of his self-interest. Rather, the cases have "always endeavored to prevent even the probability of unfairness."[121]

---

[111] *Id.*

[112] Eule, *Crocodiles in the Bathtup: State Courts, Voter Initiatives and the Threat of Electoral Reprisal*, 65 U. COLO. L. REV. 733, 739 (1994).

[113] Bright and Keenan, *Judges and the Politics of Death: Deciding Between the Bill of Rights and the Next Election in Capital Cases*, 75 B.U.L. REV. 759, 793–794 (1995). *See also* Ronald J. Tabak, *Why an Independent Appointing Authority is Necessary to Choose Counsel for Indigent People in Capital Punishment Cases*, 31 HOFSTRA L. REV. 1105, 1106–1108 (2003).

[114] *Citing* Roy Schotland, *Financing Judicial Elections, 2000: Change and Challenge*, 2001 L. REV. MICH. STATE U. DETROIT COLLEGE OF LAW 849, 866.

[115] *Citing* Barnhizer, *"On the Make": Campaign Funding and the Corrupting of the American Judiciary*, 50 CATH. U.L. REV. 361 (2001); Thomas, NATIONAL L.J., March 16, 1998, p. A8, col. 1; Greenberg Quinlan Rosner Research, Inc., and American Viewpoint, National Public Opin. Survey Frequency Questionnaire 4 (2001) (http://www.justiceatstake.org/files/JASNationalSurveyResults.pdf) (indicating that 76 percent of registered voters believe that campaign contributions influence judicial decisions).

[116] 536 U.S. at 790, 122 S.Ct. at 2542.

[117] *See* n. 115, *supra.*

[118] *Id.* at 813–820, 2555–2558.

[119] *Quoting Aetna Life Ins. Co. v. Lavoie*, 475 U.S. at 824.

[120] *Citing Ward v. Monroeville*, 409 U.S. 57, 60.

[121] *Quoting In re Murchison*, 349 U.S. 133, 136.

Ginsburg's immediate focus in *White* is on the judge who has made or implied a commitment to voters to decide cases a certain way, and who fears voter retaliation if she fails to deliver. Ginsburg's remarks, however, apply equally to any judge whose reelection may depend upon not offending voters in the next election. Such a judge may be thought to have a direct, personal, substantial, and pecuniary interest in ruling against certain litigants, Ginsburg notes, "for she may be voted off the bench and thereby lose her salary and emoluments" if her decision displeases the voters.[122] Quoting The Federalist No. 79, she adds, "In the general course of human nature, a power over a man's subsistence amounts to a power over his will."[123]

The Chair of the ABA Commission on the 21st Century Judiciary agrees. "The commission found," he has written, "that the greatest threats to the impartiality and independence of judges, whether real or perceived, are posed by the prospect of ouster from office based on the content of judicial decisions."[124]

Because states can no longer prevent judicial candidates from announcing views on legal and political issues, some states will very likely abandon judicial elections. To the extent that they do not, a litigant in a case involving a controversial issue will have a strong argument that due process requires disqualification of any judge who is subject to reelection.[125]

§ 9.09   SOME IMPLIED EXCEPTIONS TO DISQUALIFICATION

When a statute is drafted broadly, as § 455(a) is, a literal interpretation will inevitably yield some consequences that are so impractical or absurd as to be obviously inconsistent with the intent of the legislature. When that happens, "implied" or judge-made exceptions must be made pursuant to a rule of reason.[126] The challenge to the courts in such cases is to find a rational and principled way to avoid the impractical or absurd result.

[1]   The Judicial Source Exception

One important exception to § 455(a) was made in *Liteky v. United States*.[127] The case arose from a 1991 prosecution of three Catholic priests who were charged with vandalism, including spilling human blood on walls and objects

---

[122] 536 U.S. at 816, 122 S.Ct. at 2556.

[123] *Id.* at 817, 2557.

[124] Letter to the ABA JOUR. from Edward W. Madeira, p. 10, Dec., 2003.

[125] The Rule of Necessity (see § 9.08[4], *infra*) is intended to apply in sporadic or incidental cases. It should not be sufficient to overcome due process concerns, therefore, when what is at issue is the constitutional validity of the judicial system in every case of public importance.

[126] For example, § 1 of the Sherman Antitrust Act says that "[e]very contract . . . in restraint of trade . . . is . . . illegal." As Justice Brandeis pointed out, however, an essential purpose of every contract is to restrain trade. Read literally, therefore, the statute would outlaw every private contract. Accordingly, the Supreme Court has held that the statute should not be read literally but must be read in accord with the rule of reason. *See National Society of Professional Engineers v. United States*, 98 S.Ct. 1355, 1363 (1978).

[127] 510 U.S. 540, 114 S.Ct. 1147 (1994).

at the Fort Benning Military Reservation, as part of a political protest. [128] In 1983, eight years before this trial, one of the defendants and others had been prosecuted before the same judge for similar offenses.

In the 1991 case, the defendants moved to disqualify the judge on the ground that in the earlier trial, the judge had displayed "impatience, disregard for the defense and animosity" toward the defendants and their beliefs. [129] The specifications related to how the judge had conducted the trial, particularly with regard to evidentiary rulings restricting the defendants' efforts to justify their conduct by introducing facts and arguments relating to government policies of which they disapproved. The defendants asserted that the most serious ground for disqualification was that the judge had interrupted the closing argument of a defendant, instructing him to stop introducing new facts and to limit himself to discussion of evidence already presented. [130]

The judge denied the disqualification motion, and the Court of Appeals affirmed, on the ground that "matters arising out of the course of judicial proceedings are not a proper basis for recusal." [131] That is, the court held that only bias or prejudice deriving from an extrajudicial source — a source outside a judicial proceeding — can be the basis for disqualification under § 455(a).

The practical reasons justifying an extrajudicial source doctrine are that a judge's job is to develop reactions, sometimes strong ones, for and against litigants as the case unfolds; that a judge's improper rulings and conduct at trial can be remedied on appeal; that permitting disqualification for trial rulings can interfere with a judge's responsibility to conduct the trial; and that efficiency is promoted by having the same judge preside over successive cases involving the same parties or issues. Accordingly, a majority of the Supreme Court held that: [132]

> opinions formed by the judge on the basis of facts introduced or events occurring in the course of the current proceedings, or of prior proceedings, do not constitute a basis for a bias or partiality motion unless they display a deep-seated favoritism or antagonism that would make fair judgment impossible.

Four justices concurred in affirming denial of disqualification under § 455(a). They pointed out, however, that the Court's standard — whether "fair judgment is impossible" — is not in the statute. Indeed, they protested, that test "bears little resemblance to the objective standard Congress adopted in § 455(a): whether a judge's impartiality 'might reasonably be

---

[128] One of the defendants, Charles Joseph Liteky, had earned a Congressional Medal of Honor as a Chaplain in Vietnam and, in another act of protest, had thrown away his medal at the Vietnam War Memorial.

[129] 510 U.S. at 542, 114 S.Ct. at 1151.

[130] 510 U.S. at 542–543, 114 S.Ct. at 1151.

[131] 973 F.2d 910 (1992).

[132] 510 U.S. at 555, 114 S.Ct. at 1157.

questioned.' "[133] The relevant consideration under the statute, they noted, is the appearance of impropriety, not where the impropriety originated.[134]

Ironically, the majority opinion was written by Justice Antonin Scalia — the fervent champion of applying statutes in accordance with their textual meaning, regardless of the judge's views of what would be better policy.[135] Nevertheless, for the reasons given above, the Court's extra-statutory exception does make the statute a wiser one than Congress enacted.[136]

[2] Disqualification Based on a Judge's Prior Commitment to Issues or Causes

A serious practical problem relating to judicial disqualification is a judge's commitment to issues or causes before becoming a judge. For example, under a literal reading of § 455(a), one might well conclude that Justice Thurgood Marshall should have recused himself from all cases involving civil rights, that Justice Ruth Bader Ginsburg should not sit in cases involving women's rights, and that Ninth Circuit Judge John T. Noonan, Jr., who wrote books and articles opposing abortion before becoming a judge,[137] would have to recuse himself from cases involving abortion rights. Surely a reasonable person might question the ability of former partisans, with strong ideological commitments, to be neutral and detached in such cases.

As Chief Justice Rehnquist observed in his Memorandum in *Laird v. Tatum*, however, anyone qualified to be a judge will inevitably have expressed views on issues of law and public policy prior to becoming a judge. The fact that a justice has expressed opinions in his previous career could not be a disqualifying factor, however, because "[p]roof that a justice's mind at the time he joined the Court was a complete tabula rasa in the area of constitutional law would be evidence of lack of qualification, not lack of bias."[138] Moreover, the views expressed by judicial candidates on issues of law and public policy can be critical considerations in the candidates' selection for the bench.[139] It makes little sense, therefore, to disqualify a judge for the very kind of

---

[133] 510 U.S. at 563, 114 S.Ct. at 1161 (Kennedy, J., concurring). Ironically, Justice Kennedy himself misstated the statutory standard in his opinion in *Liteky*, saying that the statute guarantees that "no reasonable person *will* have [the] suspicion" that the judge is partial. *See supra* at 27–32.

[134] 510 U.S. at 558, 114 S.Ct. at 1158–1159.

[135] *See, e.g.*, ANTONIN SCALIA ET AL., A MATTER OF INTERPRETATION 20–23 (1997) ("Congress can enact foolish statutes as well as wise ones, and it is not for the courts to decide which is which and rewrite the former.")

[136] Applying the extrajudicial source doctrine to successive cases before the same judge is not justifiable, however, either as a textual reading of the statute that Congress enacted or as a matter of wise policy. Whatever the gain in judicial efficiency, there is a greater, and easily avoidable, loss in the appearance of justice.

[137] *E.g.*, JOHN T. NOONAN, JR., THE MORALITY OF ABORTION (1970); A PRIVATE CHOICE (1979); John T. Noonan, *Liberal Laxists*, HUM. LIFE REV. 32, 38 (1981).

[138] *Laird v. Tatum*, 409 U.S. at 835, 93 S.Ct. at 14. This does not mean, of course, that a judge can properly sit in a case when he has previously, in an extrajudicial context, expressed an opinion on the merits of that very case. *See* text at notes 23–25, *supra*.

[139] *Republican Party of Minnesota v. White*, 536 U.S. 765 (2002).

experience and viewpoint that qualified him in the first place.[140] Also, if a judge could not decide an issue on which he had previously expressed an opinion in a book or a law review article, an authority like Professor Laurence Tribe could not be a Supreme Court justice, because there are few issues of constitutional importance on which he has not expressed opinions in highly regarded scholarly works.

Indeed, Marshall and Ginsburg were made justices partly because of their longtime experience advancing civil rights, and Noonan was made a judge partly because of his impressive scholarship on important issues of public concern, including abortion. As one would expect, therefore, the drafters of the ABA's Model Code (on which § 455 is patterned) did not intend to require recusal of a judge on the ground of "a fixed belief about the law."[141] This means, then, that a line has to be drawn that has not been expressed in the text of § 455(a) and that has not been adequately articulated by any case or commentary.[142]

Our proposal is that a judge's recusal not be required where the judge has developed a point of view based on the judge's life experience. This means that Justice Marshall properly sat in civil rights cases, that Justice Ginsburg can properly decide cases involving women's rights, and that Judge Noonan can properly sit in abortion cases. These are issues on which these judges' prior involvement presumably commended them to the President and the Senate in nominating and confirming them as judges. In addition, as a practical matter, these issues, and other life-experience issues like them, represent major categories of cases coming before the federal courts.

On the other hand, we propose that recusal be required in cases in which the issue is the constitutional or statutory validity — and, therefore, the continued existence — of a judge's own work product, *e.g.*, a statute or regulation that the judge was instrumental in drafting and/or getting enacted. In a case like that, the judge can be expected to have an especially strong proprietary interest in the viability of the particular subject matter of the dispute. In addition, unlike the generality of life-experience issues, this category of cases is small enough to be manageable.

A useful illustration is the case of Griffin Bell. During the late 1950s, when the South was in the throes of court-ordered desegregation, responsible leadership and wise counsel were desperately needed. Griffin Bell responded

---

[140] For example, Harvard Law Professor Charles Ogletree has noted that the representation of women and minorities "serves to ensure that the judicial system reflects the broad perspectives of society":

> Describing the immense contribution that Justice Thurgood Marshall made in this regard, Justice Sandra Day O'Connor explained, "At oral arguments and conference meetings, in opinions and dissents, Justice Marshall imparted not only his legal acumen but also his life experiences, pushing and prodding us to respond not only to the persuasiveness of legal argument but also to the power of moral truth."

Charles T. Ogletree, *Why Has the G.O.P. Kept African-Americans Off Federal Courts?* N.Y. TIMES, Op. Ed., Aug. 18, 2000.

[141] E. WAYNE THODE, REPORTER'S NOTES TO CODE OF JUDICIAL CONDUCT 61 (1973).

[142] As we have seen in § 9.08[1], *supra*, Justice Scalia's attempt to exclude issues altogether from the definition of impartiality neither works, nor does it have the support of a majority of the Court.

by taking leave from his law firm to serve as volunteer chief of staff to Governor Vandiver of Georgia. As reported by The Atlanta Constitution, however, Bell's job was not to further orderly compliance with the Supreme Court's desegregation decree, but to lead in the effort in "reinforcing Georgia's anti-integration armor."[143]

Part of the strategy that Bell helped to devise was a plan that imposed discriminatory standards on African-American students who tried to transfer to white schools. For example, African-American students were required to pass a special "personality interview" and had to achieve higher scores than white students on a standardized test. Bell's racist school plan was successful for years. Ultimately, however, it was challenged in the federal courts. When the case reached the Fifth Circuit, the court split 2-1. The majority opinion, upholding Bell's school plan, was written by Judge Griffin Bell.[144]

Presumably, in the minds of those who promoted Bell's judgeship, his segregationist background was a qualifying factor. In any event, like Marshall's and Ginsburg's backgrounds in civil rights and Noonan's in anti-abortion scholarship, Bell's background represented knowledge and a commitment on an important issue of public policy founded on the judge's life experience. Accordingly, just as Marshall and Ginsburg could properly sit in cases involving civil rights, and Noonan could properly sit in cases involving abortion, Bell could properly have decided cases involving segregation. Indeed, he could properly have brought his expertise to bear in a case involving the interpretation of his own segregationist school plan.

What Bell should not have done, however, was pass on the constitutional validity of the very plan that he had played a leading role in devising. Maintaining the legality and continued existence of his own particular work product involved a high degree of personal identification with the subject matter of the dispute, going beyond bringing experience, knowledge, and ideology to an important issue of public policy.

Another useful illustration is Justice Stephen Breyer's major role, before he joined the Court, in drafting and in persuading Congress to establish the United States Sentencing Commission to draft sentencing guidelines.[145] The validity of that legislation was later attacked on constitutional grounds.[146] If Breyer had been on the Court when that attack was made, it would have been improper for him to have participated in determining the viability of the work product in which he had invested so much time, judgment, and commitment. On the other hand, Breyer has properly contributed his expertise to interpreting the meaning of the statute; this includes determining the validity of a guideline, promulgated by the Commission, that was challenged as inconsistent with the language of the statute.[147]

---

[143] Gene Britton, *Vandiver Names Anti-Integration Team of Lawyers*, ATLANTA CONSTITUTION, p. 1, July 13, 1959.

[144] *Calhoun v. Latimer*, 321 F.2d 302 (5th Cir., 1976). Other unsavory aspects of Bell's career are related in Monroe Freedman, *When It Comes to Ethics, This Bell Rings Hollow*, NEWSDAY, April 13, 1989.

[145] 28 U.S.C. § 991.

[146] *Mistretta v. United States*, 488 U.S. 361, 109 S.Ct. 647 (1989). The legislation was upheld, with only Justice Scalia (correctly, in our view) dissenting.

[147] *United States v. LaBonte*, 520 U.S. 751, 762, 117 S.Ct. 1673, 1679 (1997) (Breyer, J., dissenting).

In sum, here is the implied exception that we would suggest to § 455(a) regarding prior commitments to issues or causes. When a judge has experience regarding an important issue in a case, recusal is not required, even though the judge may have expressed strong views on the issues. On the other hand, when the issue in the case is the validity and viability of the judge's own particular work product, recusal is required. We are not aware of any authority drawing the line this way,[148] but as a practical matter, a line has to be drawn, and this one seems to be both rational and principled.

[3] Disqualification Based on an Implied Bias for or Against a Class of Litigants

The opinions of Justices Scalia and Stevens in *Republican Party of Minnesota v. White*[149] suggest that all members of the Supreme Court agree that a judge's extra-judicial statement on an *issue* may well exhibit a bias for or against a *party*.[150] The illustration is of a candidate for a judgeship who stresses his unbroken record of affirming convictions for rape, thereby indicating a bias against defendants in rape cases and in favor of prosecutors. Certainly under the broad language of § 455(a), a reasonable person might question that judge's impartiality in rape cases.

Again, however, the disqualification of a judge in such a case could have practical consequences that could not have been intended by the legislature. The difficulty is that a similar inference of bias could be drawn if a judge publicly stated that habeas corpus cases are unduly crowding the federal docket (bias against habeas petitioners), or that products liability litigation reflects a lack of self-responsibility on the part of injured people and discourages marketing of desirable products (bias in favor of manufacturers). Indeed, any judge who has expressed a position on an issue or a commitment to a cause could be said to have implied a bias for or against particular parties in such cases. Where, then, would be the stopping point if a position on an issue could be understood to manifest a bias against a party?

The answer might lie in cases where a stated position on a legal issue is combined with other circumstances that go beyond the expression of a point of view. For example, we have previously said that Judge John T. Noonan, Jr., should not be required to disqualify himself in cases involving abortion rights, where the motion for disqualification is based on his having written books and articles against abortion.[151] However, Noonan has gone beyond stating a strongly-held position on the issue of abortion. He has referred to abortionists as "those who maim and kill."[152] This powerfully negative, personalized characterization justifies an inference of a bias against

---

[148] Note, however, Justice O'Connor's approving reflection about Justice Thurgood Marshall, that "[a]t oral arguments and conference meetings, in opinions and dissents, Justice Marshall imparted not only his legal acumen but also *his life experiences.*" Note 140, *supra* (emphasis added).

[149] 536 U.S. 765, 122 S.Ct. 2528 (2002).

[150] *See* § 9.08[2],*supra.*

[151] *See* § 9.09[2], *supra.*

[152] Noonan, *Liberal Laxists*, Hum. rts. Rev. 32, 38 (1981).

abortionists that is stronger than the inference of bias in the rape-defendant hypothetical in Stevens' and Scalia's opinions in *White*. Also, the guilt of a rape defendant is always at issue, but the fact that one party is an abortionist is a given in any litigation involving abortion rights. Accordingly, we believe that Noonan should be disqualified from sitting in cases involving abortion rights.[153] This is so not because of his previous opposition to abortion, but because his opposition has been accompanied by particularly harsh language about abortionists as persons.

Another illustration of circumstances going beyond the statement of a viewpoint is a speech by Scalia about the phrase "under God" in the Pledge of Allegiance. Scalia made it clear in that speech that he sees no merit in the argument that the First Amendment forbids the inclusion of that phrase when the pledge is recited in public schools. When the issue came before the Supreme Court in *Elk Grove Unified School District v. Newdow*,[154] Scalia recused himself from the case, but without giving any explanation.

A possible reason for Scalia's recusal is that he announced his position on the issue in *Elk Grove* before the case was argued before the Court. Consistent with Scalia's agreement with Stevens regarding the rape-defendant illustration, one might conclude that Scalia recused himself from *Elk Grove* because, in expressing a view on the *issue*, he indicated a bias against the *party* who is now pressing the issue before the Court.

In his opinion in *White*, however, Scalia is emphatic that the fact that a judge has expressed a view on a legal issue does not in itself establish that the judge lacks impartiality in a case involving that issue. "A judge's lack of predisposition regarding the relevant legal issues in a case has never been thought a necessary component of equal justice, and with good reason," Scalia holds, adding that "it is virtually impossible to find a judge who does not have preconceptions about the law."[155] Moreover, "even if it were possible to select judges who did not have preconceived views on legal issues, it would hardly be desirable to do so."[156]

Clearly, therefore, Scalia does not mean that bias against a party is established whenever a judge has stated a position on an issue contrary to that party's contention. It appears that something more is necessary to justify an inference of bias.

Precisely what that may be is not clear, but there are additional facts regarding Scalia's speech about the issue in *Elk Grove* that appear to be material to his recusal. First, the speech was to a chapter of the Knights of Columbus, and that organization has filed an *amicus curiae* brief in *Elk*

---

[153] Professor Freedman is a friend of Noonan's, admires him deeply, and has no doubt about Noonan's ability to judge such a case impartially. However, subjective judgments about the character of a particular judge is not material under § 455(a). The issue is whether a reasonable person might question the judge's impartiality, and, as held in *Tumey v. Ohio*, 273 U.S. 510, 532, 47 S.Ct. 437, 444 (1927), the concern is with the "average" judge's ability to be, and to appear to be, impartial.

[154] No. 02-1624.

[155] 536 U.S. at 777, 122 S.Ct. at 2536.

[156] *Id.* at 778, 2536.

Grove.[157] Second, Scalia made express reference to the Ninth Circuit's decision in *Elk Grove* — the very case that was soon to be heard by the Supreme Court.[158] Either one of those additional facts should be enough to have required recusal. The first implies a bias in favor of the Knights of Columbus, which is appearing before the Court; the second expresses a prejudgment of the very case before the Court. Together, these facts evidently persuaded Scalia that he should not sit in the case.

The problem this leaves is that the circumstances that might accompany a statement of position on an issue, and thereby manifest bias for or against a party, are subject to infinite variations. The best one can say, therefore, is that a judge's statement of a position on an issue will not in itself justify an inference of bias for or against a party. However, accompanying circumstances might justify an inference of bias. Such circumstances include, among others, the language used by the judge in stating the position, whether the judge has referred to the specific case, and whether the statement has been addressed to a party in the case.

[4]   The Rule of Necessity

Another exception to judicial disqualification is the Rule of Necessity. That is, where disqualification would deny a litigant the right to a trial or appeal, the judge is required to hear the case.[159] There is, of course, no reference in the text of § 455 to an exception on grounds of necessity. Nevertheless, in 1980 the Supreme Court held unanimously, in *United States v. Will*, that § 455 "was not intended by Congress to alter the time-honored Rule of Necessity."[160]

The case involved a challenge under the Compensation Clause of the Constitution[161] to a statute that adversely affected the compensation of all federal judges, thereby effectively disqualifying all of them from passing on the constitutionality of the statute. The Supreme Court in *Will* relied in significant part on the legislative history of § 455, which indicated that Congress assumed that a disqualified judge would be replaced by another judge who is not subject to disqualification; thus, Congress expected in passing the legislation that the litigants would be able to have their cases heard.[162]

Later, in *United States v. Hatter*,[163] a similar issue arose, but not all judges' salaries were affected. There had been decisions in the case in the Court of Federal Claims[164] and in the Court of Appeals for the Federal Circuit,[165] but

---

[157] Tony Mauro, *Scalia's decision to remove himself from a case sparks debate on judges' speech*, LEGAL TIMES, p. 13, Oct. 20, 2003.

[158] *Id.*

[159] In the case of a trial judge who would be deciding the case without a jury, the judge might consider appointing a master to determine the facts.

[160] *United States v. Will*, 449 U.S. 200, 217, 101 S.Ct. 471, 482 (1980). The Court traced the Rule of Necessity back to 1430. *Id.* at 239 and 480.

[161] Art. III, § 1.

[162] 449 U.S. at 481, 101 S.Ct. at 481.

[163] 519 U.S. 801, 117 S.Ct. 39 (1996).

[164] 31 Fed.Cl. 436.

[165] 64 F.3d 647.

the Supreme Court, for lack of a quorum of six, was not able to hear the case. As a result, the decision of the Federal Circuit was affirmed.[166] This was done pursuant to 28 U.S.C. § 2109, which provides that when the Supreme Court does not have a quorum, it shall enter an order affirming the court of appeals decision.

Presumably, the Supreme Court did not invoke the Rule of Necessity in *Hatter* because of § 2109. In addition, the Supreme Court did not rely on necessity in *Hatter* because there had already been appellate review in the Federal Circuit, so that further review in the Supreme Court was therefore not "necessary" to give the litigants appellate review. In *Will*, by contrast, the court of appeals had also been disqualified, leaving the Supreme Court as the only available appellate forum. As the Court said in *Will*, there was in that case, "no other appellate tribunal to which under the law [the appellant] could go."[167]

[5] Friendships Between Judges and Lawyers Appearing Before Them

Might not a reasonable person question a judge's impartiality when the judge and one of the lawyers appearing before the judge are friends? Certainly, if a judge has enough regard for a lawyer to maintain a friendship with the lawyer, then that lawyer's interests and continuing good will might be of importance to the judge. In Professor Charles Fried's definition, a friend is one who "enters into a personal relationship with you" and who "acts in your interests, not his own; or rather he adopts your interests as his own."[168] Even in the more prosaic dictionary definition, a friend is "a person attached to another by feelings of affection or personal regard."[169]

When a judge and a lawyer appearing before the judge have an attachment of affection or personal regard, surely a reasonable person might question the judge's impartiality. Nevertheless, unless there is some indication of a close relationship between the judge and the lawyer, disqualification would be impractical in a system in which friendships between judges and lawyers are common. The reason for such friendships is that judges begin their careers as lawyers, long-term friendships are often formed at that time, and those friendships are naturally continued after those who were once lawyers become judges;[170] in addition, new friendships are often formed between judges and

---

[166] Five years later, the case came back to the Supreme Court, and the justices then on the Supreme Court were able to hear and decide the case. 532 U.S. 557, 121 S.Ct. 1782 (2001).

[167] 449 U.S. at 215, 101 S.Ct. at 480, quoting *Evans v. Gore*, 253 U.S. 245, 247–248, 40 S.Ct. 550, 550–551 (1920).

[168] Charles Fried, *The Lawyer as Friend: the Moral Foundations of the Lawyer-Client Relation*, 85 Yale L.J. 1060, 1071 (1976).

[169] Random House Webster's College Dictionary (2nd ed., 1997).

[170] In continental European countries, those planning careers as judges (magistrates) go to special schools for that purpose. Unlike in the United States, therefore, they do not go to the same schools as those planning to be lawyers, and thereafter magistrates and lawyers do not ordinarily associate with each other outside the courtroom.

lawyers because of their common, often desirable, involvement in professional activities.[171]

An excellent illustration of the difficulties in this area (and of some other issues related to disqualification) is *United States v. Murphy*.[172] This was a highly publicized prosecution of a corrupt judge in Cook County, Illinois, who had been exposed as a result of an elaborate federal investigation called Operation Graylord. The principal lawyer for the prosecution was Dan K. Webb, then the United States Attorney. Charles Kocoras was the judge in the case.

Webb and Judge Kocoras were the best of friends, going back to when they were Assistant United States Attorneys together early in their careers. Before Murphy's trial, Webb and the judge had planned a vacation together, with their families, at Calloway Gardens Resort in Pine Mountain, Georgia, where they had arranged for adjoining cottages. In order to leave for the joint vacation on time, the judge advanced the date of sentencing in Murphy's case. Moreover, the Webb and Kocoras families had vacationed together at Calloway Gardens two years before. Judge Kocoras did not reveal this planned trip, so there was no opportunity for a waiver of disqualification on that ground under § 455(e).

The Seventh Circuit applied a test for disqualification that is different from and more difficult to meet than that in § 455(a) — whether "an objective observer fully informed of the facts . . . *would* entertain a *significant* doubt that justice would be done in the case."[173] Even under that standard, however, the court concluded that the particular relationship between Webb and Kocoras went significantly beyond ordinary friendship, and that "an objective observer reasonably would doubt" the judge's ability to be fair in the case.[174] "A social relationship like this," the court said, "implies extensive personal contacts between judge and prosecutor, perhaps a special willingness of the judge to accept and rely on the prosecutor's representations."[175]

Accordingly, when the case had been assigned to Kocoras, he had been under an obligation to recuse himself, or, pursuant to § 455(e), to put the disqualifying facts on the record and invite the parties to consider waiving disqualification. Even so, the Seventh Circuit did not vacate the conviction and order a

---

[171] The practical problem can be even more acute in smaller communities where "trial judges often know most, if not all, of the attorneys who practice before them. They may have attended the same schools, churches, or belong to the same civic clubs. Most are members of the same bar association." *Matthews v. Rodgers*, 279 Ark. 328, 333, 651 S.W.2d 453, 456 (1983).

Even so, in cases of close friendships, it should not be difficult to invite a neighboring judge to sit or to change the venue to a nearby city or town. The problem is mitigated in South Carolina, where judges ride circuit, and no judge sits in his or her own community.

[172] 768 F.2d 1518 (7th Cir., 1985).

[173] 768 F.2d at 1538 (emphasis added).

[174] 768 F.2d at 1538.

[175] *Id.* The court added:

The U.S. Attorney lays his own prestige, and that of his office, on the line in a special way when he elects to try a case himself. By acting as trial counsel he indicates the importance of the case and of a conviction, along with his belief in the strength of the government's case. It is a particular blow for the U.S. Attorney personally to try a highly visible case such as this and lose. A judge could be concerned about handing his friend a galling defeat on the eve of a joint vacation.

new trial before another judge. The reason is that lead defense counsel in the case, Matthias Lydon, was well aware of the special relationship between Webb and Kocoras, having shared a similar relationship with both of them since the time when he, along with Webb and Kocoras, had been an Assistant United States Attorney. Although Lydon did not know about the impending vacation trip to Calloway, he and his family had made the trip to the same resort with Webb and Kocoras two years before. Also, Murphy himself knew of the long-standing relationship among Lydon, Webb, and Kocoras.[176]

The defense's awareness of this special relationship did not excuse Kocoras' failure to raise the issue himself. As the Seventh Circuit noted, § 455(e) "requires waiver on the record, not waiver by implication."[177] Similarly, the Supreme Court has unanimously held that the statute "placed the obligation to identify the existence of [grounds for disqualification] upon the judge himself, rather than requiring recusal only in response to a party affidavit."[178] The judge's duty of recusal, in short, is "self-enforcing."[179]

The issue in *Murphy*, however, was not whether the judge had had an obligation to recuse himself, but whether this justified vacating the conviction and retrying the case. Courts are understandably unwilling to allow a litigant to withhold or to consciously avoid pursuing knowledge of disqualifying facts, waiting to see how the case comes out, and then, only if the result is not satisfactory to the litigant, to make a belated motion to vacate the judgment.[180] Thus, the court would not give Murphy "two trials when a timely assertion of the right [to disqualify Kocoras] would have held the number to one."[181]

Murphy is frequently cited as a case in which the issue that was decided was whether the judge should have recused himself because of the joint vacation that followed immediately after the trial. The basis for the court's refusal to vacate the judgment suggests, however, that the projected vacation was not essential to the conclusion that Kocoras should have recused himself. In deciding that the defense had had sufficient information to raise the issue of disqualification even without knowledge of the impending vacation, the court apparently held that there had been grounds for Kocoras' recusal because the friendship between him and Webb was a close one. This was demonstrated in part by the joint vacation two years *before* the trial, and regardless of the projected vacation immediately after it.

An interesting variation on this theme is *Beazley v. Johnson*,[182] in which Napoleon Beazley was convicted and sentenced to death for murder. The

---

[176] 768 F.2d at 1540.

[177] 768 F.2d at 1539.

[178] *Liteky v. United States*, 510 U.S. 540, 548, 114 S.Ct. 1147, 1153 (1994).

[179] *United States v. Conforte*, 624 F.2d 869, 880 (9th Cir., 1980) (Kennedy, J.).

[180] This is sometimes called the "lying in wait doctrine." *See Hall v. Small Business Administration*, 695 F.2d 175, 179 (5th Cir. 1983). Courts are understandably disinclined to encourage this kind of "bad faith manipulation . . . for litigious advantage." *Delesdernier v. Porterie*, 666 F.2d 116, 121 (5th Cir. 1982).

[181] 768 F.2d at 1540. For a powerful criticism of the result in *Murphy*, see Steven Lubet, *Judicial Impropriety and Reversible Error*, CRIM. JUST. 26 (Spring, 1988).

[182] 533 U.S. 969 (mem.) (2001). This account is taken from Debra Lyn Bassett, *Judicial Disqualification in the Federal Appellate Courts*, 87 IOWA L. REV. 1213, 1214–1216 (2002).

victim's son was J. Michael Luttig, who was a judge in the Fourth Circuit. Judge Luttig was not, of course, a party in the case. However, he relocated his office from Virginia to Texas during the murder trial, consulted regularly with the prosecutors, and testified at sentencing. Shortly before the scheduled execution, Beazley moved for a stay of execution in the Supreme Court.

Judge Luttig (the victim's son) had particularly close professional relations with three members of the Supreme Court. These relations apparently resulted in friendships and, in two cases, an apparent sense of personal obligation. First, Luttig had clerked for Justice Scalia, who immediately recused himself.[183] Second, Beazley's lawyer requested that Justice Thomas recuse himself, alleging that Luttig had helped to prepare Thomas for his Senate confirmation hearings and that Thomas believed that Luttig was responsible for his confirmation. In response, Thomas did recuse himself. Third, Luttig had also helped to prepare Justice Souter for his confirmation hearings, and Souter also recused himself.

Our conclusion is that the distinction that must be drawn regarding judge-lawyer friendships is between an ordinary acquaintance/friendship, which does not require disqualification, and a close friendship, which does require disqualification. Unavoidably, this is not a bright-line distinction. Relevant considerations would include the frequency and nature of social contacts, their duration, the number of people present on such occasions, the opportunity for ex parte communications during such contacts, the frequency and nature of exchanges of gifts, a basis for an inference of personal obligation on the part of the judge, and honorary status such as godparent to children. In a case close to that line, the plain meaning of the statute should resolve the issue, tipping the balance in favor of recusal.

§ 9.10 JUSTICE SCALIA'S DENIAL OF RECUSAL IN THE CHENEY CASE

A particularly dramatic and controversial case of judicial disqualification is Justice Antonin Scalia's denial of a motion that he recuse himself in *Cheney v. U.S. District Court for the District of Columbia*.[184] The case relates to a National Energy Policy Development Group, created by President Bush to establish a national energy policy, and chaired by Vice President Richard B. Cheney.

The Sierra Club and others allege that unidentified industry representatives participated as *de facto* members of the energy group, and the plaintiffs seek to compel disclosure of the identities of the industry members.[185] Cheney, however, has denied that anyone other than government employees participated in the group as members or as *de facto* members. As stated by the

---

[183] We do not take this to mean that a former clerk can never appear before a judge. In this case, the former clerk had a strong emotional stake in the case. Reasons of practicality would also argue against recusal in all cases in which former law clerks are lawyers for parties.

[184] Memorandum Opin. of Scalia, J., 541 U.S. _____ (March 18, 2004).

[185] A federal district court ordered that the names be produced in discovery, *Judicial Watch, Inc. v. Nat. Energy Policy Development Group*, 219 F.Supp.2d 20 (2002). The U.S. Court for the District of Columbia affirmed. *In re Cheney*, 334 F.3d 1096 (2003).

Justice Department, representing Cheney, the first issue before the Supreme Court relates to the allegation that the energy group had not truthfully reported who its members were.[186]

The basis for the recusal motion under the Federal Disqualification Statute, § 455(a), was that while the case was pending before the Supreme Court, Scalia and Cheney, who are old and close friends, went on a duck-hunting trip together. In a 21-page Memorandum Opinion, Scalia denied the motion.[187] The opinion is both disappointing and disingenuous.

The applicable federal law is clear. The Federal Disqualification Statute expressly applies to justices of the Supreme Court. As we have seen, it requires disqualification whenever a justice's impartiality "might" reasonably be "questioned," and the Supreme Court has interpreted that language broadly to avoid "suspicions and doubts" about the integrity of judges.[188]

The close and long-standing friendship between Scalia and Cheney might cause a reasonable person to question Scalia's impartiality in a case of such importance to Cheney, especially in a presidential election year in which energy and environmental issues are being debated.

In addition, a situation that is universally recognized as relevant to a judge's impartiality is the acceptance of something of value from a litigant. For example, in 2002, Justice Scalia recused himself in *Kahvedzic v. Republic of Croatia*.[189] Just before that case had come before the Supreme Court, Justice Scalia had been reimbursed by Croatia for a trip to meet Croatian judges in Zagreb.[190]

Another situation that is universally recognized as relating to a judge's impartiality is ex parte communications. For example, like every other code of judicial conduct, the Code of Conduct for United States Judges[191] says that a judge shall "neither initiate nor consider ex parte communications on the merits, or procedures affecting the merits, of a pending or impending proceeding." Although the Code applies to all federal judges except Supreme Court justices, Scalia makes it clear in his opinion that he is well aware of the relevance of that issue to his own disqualification under § 455(a).[192]

A justice's close friendship with a litigant, his acceptance of something of value from a litigant, and the potential for ex parte communications with a litigant, are all implicated in Scalia's duck-hunting trip with Cheney.

---

[186] Mem. Opin. of Scalia, J., Slip Opin. at 8. Cheney's lawyers are challenging the applicability of the Federal Advisory Committee Act, and are contending that the federal district court does not have power to compel disclosure of the members' names through discovery. *Id.*

[187] *Id.*

[188] *Liljeberg v. Health Services Acquisition Corp*, 486 U.S. 847, 864, 108 S.Ct. 2194, 2205 (1988).

[189] No. 02–5917. *See* Tony Mauro, *Decoding High Court Recusals*, LEGAL TIMES, March 1, 2004.

[190] Mauro, *supra* note 189. Also, Scalia routinely recuses himself in cases involving Tulane University, in whose summer programs he teaches. When he first recused himself in a Tulane case in 1991, he had called the law school dean to find out whether the Tulane entity in the case also sponsored the law school program. *Id.*

[191] 175 F.R.D. 364 (1998), Canon 3A(4).

[192] Scalia asserts that "we said not a word about the present case" (opin. at 3), and "the Vice President and I . . . never discussed the case" (opin. at 13). The significance of those denials are discussed *infra* .

First, the facts. Scalia is caustic about errors that have been made in the recusal motion and in news reports and editorials relating to the trip — errors that could have been avoided if Scalia had been forthright at the outset.[193] There is nothing new in Scalia's recitation of the facts, however, that is material to the motion for his disqualification. Indeed, one error Scalia points to is that it was not his daughter who accompanied him and the Vice President on Air Force Two, but his son and his son-in-law — which means that the value of the flight to the Scalia family was 150% greater than had been stated in the recusal motion.

The friendship between Scalia and Cheney goes back over a quarter of a century. Scalia has been going on duck-hunting trips to Louisiana for about five years. Several months prior to the most recent trip, Scalia suggested to his host that Cheney be invited, "subject, of course, to any superseding demands on the Vice President's time." (While recognizing that later events might interfere with the Vice President's trip, Scalia omits any reference to the possibility of superseding demands on his own responsibilities as a justice.) Scalia acknowledges that he and Cheney were together for the flight, during a car ride, during a boat trip, and during all meals. He also acknowledges they might have walked alone together going to or from a boat, or going to and from dinner. There were thirteen guests in all, plus staff and security personnel.

All of those facts can be taken at face value. Scalia adds, however, that he and Cheney did not talk to each other about the pending case. That may or may not be true, but Scalia's saying it is irrelevant to a recusal motion under § 455(a). That is, a denial of impropriety by the judge whose impartiality might reasonably be questioned, is not sufficient to remove the question.

For example, the issue in *Liljeberg* centered on which party owned a certificate of need from the State of Louisiana to build a new hospital. Loyola University was not a party to the litigation but, because of a contract between Loyola and Liljeberg, the University did have a substantial financial interest in Liljeberg's obtaining the certificate. After a trial, Federal District Judge Robert Collins awarded the certificate to Liljeberg. Ten months later, the losing party, Health Services, learned that Collins had been a member of Loyola's board of trustees at the time of the trial. Accordingly, Health Services moved to vacate the judgment and to retry the case before an impartial judge, which the Supreme Court did.

As a board member, Collins had been present at meetings when Loyola's contract with Liljeberg had been discussed. However, Collins testified at a hearing on the motion that he had forgotten Loyola's interest in the matter and had made no connection between Loyola and the *Liljeberg* case (to which Loyola had not been a party). Also, a different district judge, who presided over the motion to vacate, found as a fact that Collins' testimony was truthful, and the Supreme Court accepted that finding in its discussion of § 455(a).[194]

That did not answer the question, however, of whether a reasonable person might nevertheless question whether Collins had really forgotten what he had

---

[193] *See* § 455(e) (Provided it is preceded by a "full disclosure on the record" by the judge, disqualification under § 455(a) can be waived by the parties.).

[194] 486 U.S. at 864, 108 S.Ct. at 2205.

known, and therefore question the judge's impartiality. Significantly, the Court posited a reasonable person "knowing all the circumstances" — and Judge Collins had asserted under oath that he had had no recollection of Loyola's interest in the case. For purposes of disqualification, however, Collins' own testimony was not material as a "circumstance."[195] As the Second Circuit held in an analogous situation, "[w]e are confident that [there was in fact no impropriety]. However we cannot impart this same confidence to the public by court order."[196]

In sum, even though Scalia has asserted that he and Cheney did not discuss the case, a reasonable person might nevertheless question whether ex parte communications might have occurred during their trip together while the case was pending.

Scalia expressly recognizes that friendship between a judge and a litigant is a ground for recusal when a friend is sued personally.[197] He contends, however, that because Cheney is being sued in his capacity as chair of the energy advisory group, Cheney has no personal interest in the outcome of the case. Acknowledging that disqualification would be appropriate if Cheney's "reputation and integrity" were at stake, Scalia says that this is not the case here. "This is a run-of-the-mill legal dispute about an administration decision," Scalia insists.[198]

But, despite Scalia's italics, this is *not* a routine administrative matter. The Justice Department, representing Cheney, stated the issue that was accepted for review. The case, according to Cheney's lawyers, relates to the allegation that the "advisory group was not constituted as . . . the advisory group reported."[199] That is, the issue is whether Cheney, as chair of the advisory group, has been lying about how the group was constituted. That goes to Cheney's "reputation and integrity" in the most significant way, and is of particular importance to him in an election year.

But Scalia turns that fact into a disingenuous play on words. Admitting that the decision in the case can have "political consequences," and that an adverse decision can do "political damage" to his good friend,[200] Scalia says that "political consequences" are not, and should not be, his concern as a judge.[201] Thus, Scalia characterizes the undeniable impact on Cheney's "integrity and reputation" as mere "political damage," which he then transforms into an abstract proposition about the propriety of isolating judges from politics. What remains true, however, is that Scalia's good friend has a great deal more at stake — personally — in this case than does a government official named as a pro forma party in the typical administrative law case.

Scalia also contends that a four–four tie in the Supreme Court is such a bad thing that the disqualification statute doesn't mean the same thing for

---

[195] *See also Paulo State of the Federal Republic v. American Tobacco Co., Inc.*, 122 S.Ct. 1290, 1292 (2002).

[196] *Cinema 5 Ltd. v. Cinerama, Inc.*, 528 F.2d 1384 (2nd Cir., 1976).

[197] Opin. at 17.

[198] *Id.* at 7 (emphasis in original).

[199] *Id.* at 8, n.1.

[200] *Id.* at 9.

[201] *Id.*

Supreme Court justices as for all other judges. But the statute makes no distinction at all between judges and justices, and Scalia himself has written, "Congress can enact foolish statutes as well as wise ones, and it is not for the courts to decide which is which and rewrite the latter."[202] Moreover, Scalia's rewrite of the statute would mean that a four–four tie, affirming a decision by a federal appellate court, is somehow worse than having the Supreme Court's decision determined by a justice whose vote is crucial to protecting his friend's reputation and integrity.[203]

A substantial part of Scalia's opinion is a catalogue of instances in which justices have socialized with presidents and other government officials. His list begins with Chief Justice John Marshall, who attended dinner parties given by President John Quincy Adams. His latest illustration is a skiing trip that Justice Byron White took with Bobby Kennedy in 1963, when Kennedy was about to make an argument before the Court as Attorney General. These illustrations demonstrate, Scalia says, that there is no impropriety in social contacts between justices and government officials who are involved in litigation in their official capacities.

The fallacy in characterizing this as an ordinary official-capacity case is discussed *supra*. But Scalia goes on to refute a non-argument. "Of course it can be claimed," he says, "that 'times have changed,' and that what was once considered proper — even as recently as Byron White's day — is no longer so."[204] The point, however, is not that *times* have changed since 1963. The fact is that the *law* relating to disqualification has undergone what Scalia himself has called "massive changes."[205]

Until 1974, the disqualification statute used a subjective standard for disqualification. That is, if the judge herself believed that she could be impartial, she was not only permitted to sit, but had a duty to do so. Both the subjective standard and the notion of a "duty to sit" were abrogated by the 1974 amendment to § 455. As noted at the beginning of this comment, the standard today is whether a reasonable person might question the judge's impartiality. If so, the judge is required, *sua sponte*, to recuse herself, regardless of her own opinion of her impartiality.

When the motion was made to recuse Scalia, "8 of the 10 newspapers with the largest circulation in the United States . . . and 20 of the 30 largest have called on Justice Scalia to step aside."[206] Moreover, "not a single newspaper has argued against recusal."[207] Unless we are to believe that all these editorialists are unreasonable people, the conclusion is inescapable that a reasonable person *might question* Scalia's impartiality in the case.

Finally, Scalia misstates the law. Stating "[t]he question, simply put," he asks rhetorically whether one "would reasonably *believe* that I cannot decide

---

[202] ANTONIN SCALIA, ET AL., A MATTER OF INTERPRETATION 20–23 (1997).

[203] A corollary to that notion is that a justice should recuse herself only when her vote doesn't matter.

[204] Opin. at 17.

[205] *Liteky v. United States*, 510 U.S. 540, 546, 114 S.Ct. 1147, 1153 (1994).

[206] Opin. at 13, quoting the Motion to Recuse 3–4. Scalia does not contradict these figures.

[207] *Id* .

[the case] impartially because I went hunting with [a] friend and accepted an invitation to fly there with him on a Government plane."[208] Of course, the question is not what a reasonable person *believes* about the justice's impartiality, but whether a reasonable person *might question* his impartiality. And the point is not that Scalia in fact *cannot* decide the case impartially, but, again, that a reasonable person *might question whether* he can do so.

Scalia then links his misstatement of the law to what he claims to be the inconsequential value of the flight on Air Force Two for himself and two family members. The issue then becomes whether he can be "bought so cheap."[209] He even makes the disingenuous point that "[o]ur flight cost the Government nothing," because the Vice President was going on the duck-hunting trip anyway, and the space was "available."[210]

"I dare say," Scalia adds, "that, at a hypothetical charity auction, much more would be bid for dinner for two at the White House than for a one-way flight to Louisiana [for three] on the Vice President's jet [with the Vice President]."[211] (And how much, one might wonder, would be bid for a commercial flight for one to Croatia?) But, of course, this vacuous speculation about auctions hardly establishes that Scalia received nothing of value from Cheney while Cheney's case was pending. Nor does it respond in any way to the undeniable opportunities for ex parte discussion of the pending case, which a reasonable person might suspect took place during flights, rides, walks, dinners, and casual conversations.

In short, Scalia's opinion denying the recusal motion engages in fallacious arguments and misstates and misapplies the Federal Disqualification Statute. A justice of the Supreme Court of the United States owes the litigants, and the public, a greater respect for the law of the United States.

§ 9.11   CONCLUSION

As long ago as 1270, Bracton recognized that "suspicion" about whether a judge is impartial is "a very fearful thing" for litigants, requiring recusal of the judge.[212] That ancient truism is the premise of our three major sources of law relating to judicial recusal: the Due Process Clause of the Constitution, the Federal Judicial Disqualification Statute, and the Code of Judicial Conduct. In the unanimous view of the Supreme Court, due process requires a judge's disqualification when the circumstances "*might* create an impression of *possible* bias."[213] And under both the Disqualification Statute, § 455(a), and the Code of Judicial Conduct, Canon 3E(1), judges are required to recuse themselves when their impartiality "*might* reasonably be *questioned*." Echoing Bracton, the Supreme Court has explained that this means that judges are

---

[208] *Id.* at 20 (second emphasis in the original).

[209] *Id.*

[210] *Id.* at 10.

[211] *Id.* at 11.

[212] Note 3, *supra*.

[213] *Commonwealth Coatings Corp. v. Continental Casualty Co.*, 393 U.S. 145, 149, 89 S.Ct. 337, 340 (1968) (emphasis added).

to avoid "suspicions and doubts" about the integrity of the judiciary "whenever possible."[214]

In this way, the fearful prospect of a judge who might be impaired by bias or interest is minimized, and the integrity of the administration of justice is strengthened, in appearance as well as in fact.

---

[214] *Liljeberg v. Health Services Acquisition Corp.*, 486 U.S. 847, 864–865, 108 S.Ct. 2194, 2205 (1998).

Chapter 10

CONFLICTS OF INTEREST: THE ETHIC OF PREVENTION AND OF APPEARANCES

§ 10.01 INTRODUCTION

Conflicts of interest are among the most frequent and difficult problems that a lawyer confronts. Sanctions for conflicts of interest include disciplinary action, disqualification from representing a client, and malpractice liability, which can result in compensatory damages, forfeiture of fees, and even punitive damages.

Despite the array and severity of these sanctions, conflicts of interest are not inherently immoral. They are, rather, an inescapable aspect of the human condition. That is because, whenever there is a reasonable possibility that you will be unable to satisfy fully the legitimate needs or desires of two or more people (including yourself), you have a conflict of interest. If you get married or enter a committed relationship, there is a reasonable possibility that you and your partner will disagree about some significant aspect of your life together; you therefore have a conflict of interest. If you and your partner have a child, you have a further conflict of interest. If you have another child, you have more conflicts of interest. If you have a family and an employer, you have additional conflicts of interest, that is, additional legitimate demands on your time, attention, and loyalty that you might not be able to meet.

§ 10.02 LAWYER-CLIENT CONFLICTS OF INTEREST DEFINED

As indicated in the preceding paragraph, the term conflict of interest refers to a situation where there is a reasonable *possibility* that you will not be able to fulfill all of the legitimate demands on your time, attention, and loyalty. Crediting the first edition of this book, Professors Hazard and Hodes refer to this focus "on the *potential* for harm rather than the harm itself" as the "modern approach" to conflicts of interest.[1] That is, a conflict of interest exists "whenever the attorney-client relationship or the quality of the representation is 'at risk,' *even if no substantive impropriety — such as a breach of confidentiality or less than zealous representation — in fact eventuates.*"[2] They add,

---

[1] 1 Geoffrey C. Hazard, Jr., & W. William Hodes, The Law of Lawyering § 10.4 (3d ed., 2001). Hazard and Hodes note that "the first explicit use of this approach" was in Monroe H. Freedman, Understanding Lawyers' Ethics 174–179 (1st ed. 1990)). *Id.*, n. 1. *See also* Kevin McMunigal, *Rethinking Attorney Conflict of Interest Doctrine*, 5 Geo. J. Legal Ethics 823 (1992).

[2] *Id.*

however, that this modern approach is entirely consistent with earlier authority.[3]

The Restatement adopts the same analysis.[4] For example, § 121 provides that there is a conflict of interest whenever there is a "substantial risk" that the lawyer's "representation" of the client will be "materially and adversely affected by the lawyer's own interests or by the lawyer's duties to another current client, a former client, or a third person."

To be "substantial," the risk of an adverse effect on the representation must be "more than a mere possibility."[5] However, it need not be "immediate, actual, and apparent."[6] On the contrary, as explained in the comment to Restatement § 121, a risk can be substantial, within the meaning of the rule, even if it is "potential or contingent," and despite the fact that it is neither "certain or even probable" that it will occur.[7] The ultimate test is that there be a "significant and plausible" risk of adverse effect on the representation of the client.[8]

§ 10.03 KINDS OF CONFLICTS OF INTEREST

Conflicts of interest can exist between the client's interests and those of the lawyer herself, between the interests of a former client and those of a new client, between two or more current clients, and between a client and a non-client third party.

[1] Conflicts Relating to the Lawyer's Own Interests

Some conflicts of interest are inherent in the lawyer-client relationship, and are tolerated out of necessity.[9] A potential client considers retaining you. Because the fee that you consider necessary and appropriate is likely to be more than the client would prefer to pay, you immediately have a conflict of

---

[3] *Id.* at n. 2:

> . . . [A]lthough a separation between risk of harm and actual harm had not previously been made explicit in the literature and in the decided cases, virtually every authority had implicitly followed such an approach for years. Consequently, the cases — even the earlier cases — may all be analyzed according to this new scheme.

[4] RESTATEMENT OF THE LAW GOVERNING LAWYERS §§ 121–135 (2000).

[5] *Id.*, Cmt. *c(iii)*.

[6] *Id.*

[7] *Id.*

[8] *Id.* The potential adverse effect of the conflict of interest is expressed in § 121 with respect to the effect on the lawyer's "representation of the client." In the Model Rules, the phrases used are "adversely affect the relationship" (MR 1.7(a)(1)) and "materially limit" or "materially affect" the "representation." (*See* MR 1.7(b)). In the Model Code, the reference is to the impairment of the lawyer's "independent professional judgment" on behalf of a client. *See* Canon 7. All of these phrases are used to mean the same thing. The question consistently relates to the risk that the lawyer will, "to an unacceptable degree, be diverted from the main task of loyally serving the client." HAZARD & HODES, *supra* note 1.

[9] That is, the *risk* that the lawyer will take unfair advantage of the client is tolerated out of necessity. Nevertheless, if the lawyer is charged with succumbing to the risk, for example, by charging an excessive fee, the burden of proof is on the lawyer, as a fiduciary, to justify the fairness of the fee. *See* MR 1.5; DR 2-106.

interest. Also, if you charge your client by the hour for conducting litigation, it will be less in your interest than your client's to settle the case at an early stage, because your hourly fee will end with the case. If you charge a contingent fee, however, it may be more in your interest than your client's to settle the case for a lesser amount at an early stage, because the potential increase in the ultimate recovery may not justify the additional time that you otherwise will have to invest in the case. Even if you charge no fee at all, because you are dedicated to the cause that the client's case represents, there may come a time when the client wants to settle the case on terms that do not, in your view, adequately serve the cause that motivated you to take the case.[10]

However, other conflicts between the lawyer's interests and the client's are restricted by ethical rules. For example, a lawyer is generally forbidden to enter into a business transaction with a client unless certain safeguards are observed.[11] Such business transactions include obtaining a security interest in, say, the client's residence or other property to ensure payment of the lawyer's fee. The lawyer must fully explain the transaction to the client, advise the client of the desirability of seeking the advice of independent legal counsel, give the client a reasonable opportunity to seek independent advice, and be prepared to demonstrate that the terms are fair to the client. The underlying principle is that, consistent with the lawyer's fiduciary duties to the client, the lawyer should not take advantage of the lawyer's special skills, the client's trust in the lawyer, or the client's dependence upon the lawyer.

For similar reasons, a lawyer should not arrange for a substantial gift from a client to the lawyer,[12] and a lawyer should not begin a sexual relationship with a client during the lawyer-client relationship.[13] Other lawyer-client conflicts are discussed below in this chapter and in Appendix B.

[2] Conflicts Between a Former Client and a New Client

A common conflict of interest is that between a lawyer's on-going obligations to a former client and the lawyer's obligations to a new client who has interests adverse to the former client. The principal basis for this conflict is the lawyer's obligation of confidentiality, which extends indefinitely, beyond the end of the lawyer-client relationship.[14] Thus, a lawyer is forbidden to take on a new

---

[10] For example, the named plaintiffs in an employment discrimination case might want to accept a settlement in which only their own salary and working conditions would be improved, even though the proposed settlement also provides that demands for systemic reform would be dropped.

[11] *See* MR 1.8, DR 5-104. The drafting of MR 1.8 is superior to DR 5-104. The New York Code has much the same language as MR 1.8 in the New York version of DR 5-104.

[12] MR 1.8(c); New York Code EC 5-5, 5-6.

[13] MR 1.8(j); New York Code DR 5-111. The first rule forbidding initiation of a sexual relationship with a client was in the American Lawyer's Code of Conduct 8.8 (Public Discussion Draft, 1980) (Monroe Freedman, Reporter). The Kutak Commission ignored this proposal, but the ABA amended its Model Rules to adopt this provision in 2002, more than two decades later.

[14] In addition, a lawyer is forbidden to attack her own former work product, such as a contract or a will that the lawyer drafted.

client, or to continue to represent a client, if there is a reasonable possibility that the lawyer learned confidences in the former representation that might be used to the former client's disadvantage in the new representation.[15] The assessment of this risk is referred to as the "substantial relationship" test.

The conflict of interest relates here to the possibility that the lawyer will fail to fulfill her ethical obligations either to the former client or to the new client. If the lawyer were to use a former client's confidences in the new matter, the lawyer would, of course, be violating her duty of confidentiality to the former client. On the other hand, if she failed to use those confidences to benefit the new client, she would be violating her duties of zeal, competence, and communication to the new client.

Assume, for example, that a lawyer formerly represented a national franchiser of ice cream dealerships. That prior case involved an action for breach of contract against the franchiser by one of the franchise dealers. The litigation ended in a settlement a year ago, and the lawyer has had no contact with the franchiser since then. The lawyer is now approached by a different ice cream franchise dealer who wants to sue the franchiser for breach of contract. That is, the lawyer is being asked to sue her former client, the franchiser. However, the franchiser objects to the lawyer's accepting the new client.

The lawyer should not take the case. There is a reasonable possibility that the lawyer learned confidences or secrets from the franchiser in the course of the earlier representation. These include the franchiser's policies and practices in carrying out (or not carrying out) its contracts with its franchise dealers. If the lawyer accepted the new client, therefore, her obligations to the new client of zeal, competence, and communication would require her to make use of her confidential knowledge about the former client's business practices. If she did that, however, she would be violating her obligation of confidentiality to the former client. In short, there is a significant risk that the lawyer would be disloyal to one client or the other.[16]

The franchiser's business policies and practices relate to issues and facts that are likely to be common to the former breach-of-contract case and to the present one. Another kind of knowledge about a former client that is important is called "playbook" information. This refers to the lawyer's knowledge of the former client's policies and practices relating to how it handles disputes with franchisees, *e.g.*, the former client's ability to finance litigation, its willingness to settle, and on what terms. As noted by Professor Richard Zitrin (an ethics expert who also has had extensive experience in both civil and criminal

---

[15] Apart from situations in which there are possible violations of confidentiality, however, a lawyer is not generally forbidden to take action adverse to former client.

[16] We are assuming here that the prior representation of the franchiser was only a year before. However, if sufficient time elapses between the two representations, the information might become unimportant. *Cf. State ex rel. Ogden Newspapers, Inc. v. Wilkes*, 198 W.Va. 587, 482 S.E.2d 204 (1996) (lawyers disqualified when two years had elapsed); *State ex rel. Ogden Newspapers, Inc. v. Wilkes*, 211 W.Va. 423, 566 S.E.2d 560 (2002) (same lawyers not disqualified in similar matter when nine years had elapsed).

litigation), playbook information can be even more valuable to the litigator than issue-related information.[17]

In short, therefore, the new client's litigation against the lawyer's former client is substantially related to the prior representation of the former client, and the lawyer is forbidden to take on the new matter.

[3]   Conflicts Between Current Clients

The most obvious conflict between current clients is where the lawyer is representing two or more clients whose interests are adverse to each other. For example, a lawyer could not represent two or more clients who are competing for the same asset. Also, a lawyer could not represent a client who is suing a defendant who happens to owe money to another client of the lawyer, at least not where success in the law suit might jeopardize the ability of the lawyer's other client to collect its debt from the defendant.

Another form of current-client conflict can arise when a lawyer is representing multiple clients, that is, two or more clients who are on the same side of a litigation. Assume, for example, that the driver and the passenger in a car are injured when their car is rear-ended by another car. It might appear that a lawyer could represent both of them in suing the driver of the other car. However, the passenger might also have a claim against the plaintiff driver under, say, an uninsured motorist provision in the driver's policy. Also, two or more criminal defendants accused of jointly committing the same crime have conflicts of interest, despite the strong advantages that they might have in maintaining a united front. One such conflict relates to the possibility that one defendant will be able to escape punishment by a plea bargain that includes agreeing to provide evidence against the other.[18]

[4]   Conflicts Relating to Non-Client Third Parties

A lawyer has a conflict between the client's interests and a non-client third party when, for example, someone other than the client is paying the lawyer's fee.[19] A common situation of this kind is when the lawyer has been retained by an insurer to represent its insured (discussed below). Another is when the employee of an organization is represented by a lawyer who is being paid by the organization.[20]

---

[17] Professor Zitrin was the first scholar to point out the practical importance to litigators of this kind of information, at the Hofstra Ethics Conference in 1996. Zitrin analogized the information to a "tell" in poker B how a player unconsciously reveals whether, for example, he is bluffing or has gotten a strong hand. Professor Charles Wolfram was the first to use the "playbook" analogy, also at the Hofstra Conference. *See* Charles Wolfram, *The Vaporous and the Real in Former Client Conflicts*, 1 JOUR. INST. FOR STUDY OF LEGAL ETHICS 133, 138 (1996).

For an excellent opinion on disqualification for conflict of interest, including discussion of playbook information, *see Mitchell v. Metropolitan Life Insurance Company*, 2002 WL 441194 (U.S.D.C.,S.D.N.Y., March 20, 2002) (Pauley, J.). *See also* ABA Formal Opin. 99-415.

[18] *See also* § 11.17, *infra*.

[19] *See* MR 1.8(f); DR 5-107.

[20] *See, e.g.*, §§ 11.16 and 11.17, *infra*.

§ 10.04   LOYALTY AND THE LAWYER'S FIDUCIARY DUTY

We have identified confidentiality, zeal, competence, and communication as the ethical concerns that are typically threatened by conflicts of interest. In addition, although loyalty is not the subject of a distinct rule in either the Model Rules or the Model Code, loyalty is often cited as a particular ethical concern in discussions of conflicts of interest.[21]

For example, the comment to MR 1.7 (titled "Conflict of Interest: General Rule") begins: "Loyalty is an essential element in the lawyer's relationship to a client." Also, EC 5-1 says that "[n]either the lawyer's personal interests, the interests of other clients, nor the desires of third persons should be permitted to dilute the lawyer's loyalty to the client." Similarly, in a leading case in which a lawyer was disqualified on grounds of conflicts of interest, the court referred to the "absolute loyalty" and the "undivided fidelity" that a lawyer owes to the client.[22] Also, Professor Hazard has said that "above all" a lawyer is required to demonstrate loyalty to the client,[23] and Professor Wolfram has emphasized that the lawyer-client relationship is "founded on the lawyer's virtual total loyalty to the client and the client's interests."[24]

Loyalty can be equated with zeal, and, like zeal, it pervades the lawyer-client relationship. Loyalty can also serve as a convenient shorthand, incorporating zeal, confidentiality, competence, and communication. In addition, loyalty manifests a concern with maintaining the lawyer-client relationship of trust and confidence, and it is an expression of the lawyer's fiduciary obligation to the client. Justice Cardozo explained the obligation of a fiduciary this way:[25]

> Many forms of conduct permissible in a workaday world for those acting at arm's length, are forbidden to those bound by fiduciary ties. A trustee is held to something stricter than the morals of the market place. Not honesty alone, but the punctilio of an honor the most sensitive, is then the standard of behavior. As to this there has developed a tradition that is unbending and inveterate. *Uncompromising rigidity has been the attitude of courts of equity when petitioned to undermine the rule of undivided loyalty* by the "disintegrating erosion" of particular exceptions. . . .

---

[21] For an excellent article discussing loyalty, *see* Michael K. McChrystal, *Lawyers and Loyalty,* 33 WM. & MARY L. REV. 367 (1992).

[22] *T.C. Theatre Corp. v. Warner Bros.*, 113 F.Supp. 265, 268 (1953) (citing Canon 6 of the 1908 Canons of Professional Ethics).

[23] Geoffrey C. Hazard, Jr., *Triangular Lawyer Relationships: An Exploratory Analysis*, 1 GEO. J. LEGAL ETHICS 15, 21 (1987), quoted in Michael K. McChrystal, *Lawyers and Loyalty*, 33 WM. & MARY L. REV. 367 (1992).

[24] CHARLES W. WOLFRAM, MODERN LEGAL ETHICS 146 (1986), quoted in Michael K. McChrystal, *Lawyers and Loyalty*, 33 WM. & MARY L. REV. 367 (1992).

[25] *Meinhard v. Salmon*, 249 N.Y. 458, 164 N.E. 545, 546 (1928). The case involved neither a lawyer nor a guardian, but a businessman described as a "joint adventurer."

One importance in the lawyer's role as a fiduciary is that the breach of a fiduciary duty — as in a conflict of interest — can result in punitive damages.

§ 10.05   THE PREVENTIVE RATIONALE

Note, again, that the conflict of interest arises in the ice cream franchise case regardless of whether the lawyer would in fact misuse, or fail to use, information gained from the former client on behalf of the new one. If she did in fact misuse the former client's confidences, she would have violated her obligation of confidentiality, and if she did in fact fail to use her knowledge on behalf of the new client, she would have violated her obligations of competence and zeal. The conflict of interest arises, however, before that point is reached. That is because proscriptions of conflicts of interest are designed for prophylactic reasons and for reasons of appearances.

The prophylactic rationale is to prevent a situation that might result in the violation of a substantive ethical obligation (such as a breach of confidentiality, or a failure of zeal or competence). The appearances rationale avoids a situation in which a fair-minded person would have grounds to suspect that an ethical obligation has been violated — that is, to avoid an "appearance of impropriety" even when no ethical violation has occurred in fact.

We have already adverted to the preventive rationale in the case of the ice cream franchise dealer. There is a likelihood that the lawyer has learned confidences and secrets from the franchiser when she represented it in the earlier litigation. If she were now to accept the franchise dealer as her client, therefore, she might at some point violate her professional responsibilities either to the former client or to the new one. The proscription on conflicts of interest prevents that point from being reached.[26]

One of the most common instances of conflict of interest occurs when a lawyer is chosen and paid by an insurance company to represent its insured pursuant to an insurance policy. It is not necessarily improper for one party to pay the lawyer's fee for another. Whenever this occurs, however, the relationships must be carefully scrutinized to avoid conflicts of interest. On its face, the insurance situation does not present a conflict, because it is usually in the interest of both the insurer and the insured to minimize the liability. Some lawyers who have this kind of practice assume, therefore, that they represent both the insurer and the insured and that there is no problem.

In fact, however, a number of serious conflicts are present. Assume, for example that the policy amount is $500,000. The plaintiff is willing to settle for that amount, but nothing less, and the defendant-insured wants to dispose of the case on that basis. However, the insurance company might reason that it has nothing to lose by litigating the case. That is, the jury might award substantially less than the face amount of the policy, in which case the company would come out ahead; and if the jury were to award substantially in excess of the policy amount, the company would lose nothing, because the insured would be responsible for the additional amount.[27]

---

[26] Professor McMunigal suggests an analogy to reckless driving, which is a punishable offense even if no harm actually occurs. Keven McMunigal, *Rethinking Conflicts of Interest Doctrine*, 5 GEO. J. LEGAL ETHICS 823, 835 (1992).

[27] This kind of reasoning by the insurance company is increasingly risky under developing statutory and case law.

On the other hand, if the insured is a lawyer or a doctor charged with malpractice, she might be unwilling to accept a settlement for an amount substantially less than the full insurance coverage. In her view, only by litigating the case can she defend her reputation and vindicate herself professionally. The insurer, however, might be eager to settle for the lesser amount rather than risk a higher judgment.

Moreover, it is possible that a lawyer, in the course of representing an insured, will discover facts that could be the basis for an argument that the insured is not entitled to the insurance coverage at all. For example, in filling out the insurance application, the insured might have made statements that are arguably false and material, justifying a contention by the insurance company that the policy is voidable. If the lawyer informed the insurance company of the facts learned from the client, she would violate her obligation of confidentiality to the insured. On the other hand, if the insurance company were viewed as her client, the lawyer would be required to keep the company fully informed of all material developments in the case, including the possibility of voiding the policy.

Even if the lawyer and the insurance company understood that only the insured is the lawyer's client, there is nevertheless a conflict of interest because the lawyer has a financial incentive to maintain the good will of the insurance company. The company, not the insured, is the ongoing source of the lawyer's business, and the lawyer's loyalty to the client (the insured) could be significantly impaired by the desire for repeat business from the insurer. Professors Hazard and Hodes have recognized the lawyer's temptation to "curry favor" of the insurance company and referred to this as a "hidden conflict of interest" which raises the realistic risk that the lawyer "will *not* properly represent the insured" but will favor the insurer when the interests of the two become adverse.[28]

Consider another illustration of the preventive rationale. Lawyers, like other fiduciaries, are forbidden to commingle funds, that is, to put their clients' money into their own bank accounts. A client's funds must be kept in an account that is identifiable as a client trust account.[29] Obviously, there is nothing inherently immoral in commingling funds. It raises, however, three possibilities. First, the lawyer might unintentionally overdraw her own money

---

[28] HAZARD & HODES, THE LAW OF LAWYERING 250.2 (Supp., 1992) (emphasis in the original). This insurance illustration is not included in the third edition of Hazard & Hodes, but there is a similar one in a banking context. *See* 1 HAZARD & HODES, THE LAW OF LAWYERING § 10.10, Ill. 10-1 (3d ed., 2001).

See also Greene v. Grievance Committee, 54 N.Y.2d 118, 429 N.E.2d 390, 444 N.Y.S.2d 883 (1981), where the lawyer asked real estate brokers to recommend his services to buyers of real estate. The Court of Appeals held that the lawyer had a conflict of interest in representing buyers recommended by the brokers, because the brokers were a desired source of future business for the lawyer. The problem, of course, is that the lawyer might, consciously or unconsciously, curry favor with the source of potential business (the broker) by being less than zealous on behalf of the lawyer's client (the buyer).

See also ABA Formal Opin. 95-390 (1995) (a desire to remain "in the good graces" of a valued client can cause a "material limitation on the lawyer's ability properly to represent a[nother] client].").

See also note 36, *infra*.

[29] MR 1.15(a); DR 9-102(A).

and invade the client's portion of the account. Second, the lawyer might succumb to the temptation of having the client's money readily available in an account under her own name, and "borrow" — that is embezzle — some of it simply by writing a personal check. Indeed, without even withdrawing the client's money, the lawyer might use the commingled funds as a basis for establishing her own credit for a loan. Third, an account under the lawyer's name might be attached by the lawyer's creditors, to the client's detriment.

In most cases, none of these possibilities will come to pass. Nevertheless, we know from experience and common sense that these kinds of problems do occur. This experience and common sense justify a preventive rule to reduce the risk.

§ 10.06　THE APPEARANCES RATIONALE

A familiar and fundamental principle of due process is that "any tribunal permitted by law to try cases and controversies must not only be unbiased but also must avoid even the appearance of bias."[30] That is, "to perform its high function in the best way, justice must satisfy the appearance of justice."[31] Accordingly, if a judge's impartiality "might reasonably be questioned," the judge should recuse herself, even though she is not in fact biased.[32]

Unlike judges, lawyers are required to be partial, indeed, zealously so. Like judges, however, lawyers are an integral part of the administration of justice, and it is essential that fair-minded people have no reasonable grounds to suspect that the administration of justice is being impaired by the improper conduct of lawyers. The appearance of impropriety is, therefore, an appropriate concern of lawyers' ethics.

When we talk about the appearance of impropriety, however, we are referring to concerns of substance.[33] Unless the appearance of impropriety is related to a specific, identifiable ethical imperative, the concept is unduly vague, either for purposes of giving adequate notice to lawyers of what conduct is proscribed, or for purposes of rational enforcement. Note, therefore, that in each of our prior illustrations appearances are of the highest importance. A judge's impartiality goes to the essence of her function, as does a lawyer's zeal or competence or her trustworthiness with respect to confidences. Maintaining these professional qualities, in appearance as well as in fact, is essential to the administration of justice.

In our ice cream franchise case, for example, we would have reasonable grounds to believe that the lawyer might use confidences or secrets of the former client, the franchiser, on behalf of the new client, the franchise dealer. In the course of zealously representing the present client, it is likely that — intentionally or unintentionally — the lawyer will be using information gained in her earlier representation of her current adversary. Similarly,

---

[30] *Commonwealth Coatings Corp. v. Continental Casualty Co.*, 393 U.S. 145, 150 (1968).

[31] *Aetna Life Insurance Co. v. Lavoie*, 475 U.S. 813, 825, 106 S.Ct. 1580, 1587 (1986), *quoting In Re* Murchison, 349 U.S. 133, 136, 75 S.Ct. 623, 625 (1955).

[32] *See generally* Ch. 9, *supra*.

[33] We distinguish, therefore, a concern with superficial appearances, familiarly referred to in the public relations term "image."

anyone who has ever overdrawn a checking account or received a bad check will have reason to suspect that commingled accounts will cause some lawyers, intentionally or unintentionally, to misappropriate client's funds. In these cases, therefore, the appearance of impropriety refers to a justifiable suspicion of particular wrongdoing.

§ 10.07 SUBSTANTIAL RELATIONSHIP AND SIGNIFICANT ROLE

It is worth repeating: Conflicts of interest can exist even though no substantive impropriety has in fact occurred. That is so whether we are talking about the preventive or the appearances rationale. Under either of these rationales, the concept of conflict of interest turns upon reasonable possibility based upon experience and common sense.

Returning again to the ice cream franchiser case, let us assume that there is no direct evidence that the lawyer learned any confidences or secrets from her former client, the franchiser, that would be relevant to the new litigation. However, the two cases are substantially related — each involves a dispute over the franchiser's performance of the same franchise contract. Also, we are assuming that the lawyer's role in the previous case was a significant one and not merely peripheral. This means that it is reasonably possible that the lawyer learned information in the first matter that might be useful against the former client in the new matter.

The franchiser might well agree that the lawyer has no confidences or secrets of any consequence, and the former client might therefore have no objection to the lawyer's taking the new client.[34] If the former client does object, however, what should the lawyer do? Again, we have been assuming a case in which the two matters are substantially related to each other, and in which the lawyer's role in the earlier case was significant. Both of these elements are necessary to justify the inference of a reasonable possibility that the lawyer obtained client confidences in the earlier representation.

One way for the lawyer to avoid a finding of a conflict of interest, therefore, would be to show that the two matters are not substantially related. This could not be done on the facts of our ice cream franchise case, since both cases involve litigation relating to performance under the franchise contract. If, however, the earlier matter had instead involved only an application on behalf of the franchiser to obtain a zoning variance, the two matters would not be substantially related, and the lawyer would be permitted to represent the second client in a contract action against the former client.

Even if the two matters are substantially related, as in our original ice cream franchise hypothetical, the lawyer might avoid a finding of a conflict of interest if her role in the earlier franchise litigation had been peripheral. For example, the lawyer might be able to establish that she had served only as a summer clerk in the firm that had represented the franchiser, that she had had no access to the franchiser's file, and that she had been responsible only for researching the issue of whether a clause in the franchise agreement

---

[34] The issue of client consent is dealt with below.

rendered it illusory. On those facts, it would be extremely unlikely that she had obtained any client confidences in the earlier litigation, and she would be permitted to accept the new client.

Let us again assume, however, that the two matters are substantially related and that the lawyer's role in the earlier matter was significant. There would then be a conflict of interest unless the lawyer could prove a negative — that, despite the substantial relationship between the two matters and the lawyer's central role in the earlier one, she nevertheless obtained no client confidences or secrets. She can reiterate that she has no client confidences, of course, but there is no way for her to prove it. Moreover, experience and common sense suggest that in a significant number of such cases, the self-interested denials of at least some lawyers will not be entirely reliable.

The ordinary evidentiary solution in a situation like this is to put the burden of proof on the party who is in the position to prove the affirmative. Here, all the former client needs to do is state what confidences the lawyer has that the client does not want revealed. The problem with that, though, is obvious. In order to protect its confidences, the client would be required to disclose them.

The case is appropriate, therefore, for the following presumption: Where the two matters are substantially related and the lawyer's role in the earlier case was significant, it is presumed that the lawyer obtained relevant confidences or secrets from the client in the earlier matter. The lawyer would be precluded from taking the second client to prevent placing a burden on the former client to expose its confidences in order to preserve them.

The presumption that relevant information was obtained in the prior representation is based in part on the ethical obligation the lawyer had to obtain all relevant information during the representation of the former client. This presumption is joined with another to create the conflict of interest. The second presumption is that the lawyer will honor her ethical obligations to the new client of zealous representation and communication, which includes using the information obtained in the prior representation for the benefit of the new client. In addition, it has been recognized that a lawyer, "perhaps, unintentionally" or "even unconsciously," might use the previously obtained information.[35]

§ 10.08 POSITIONAL CONFLICTS OF INTEREST

Assume that a lawyer represents Mr. Lessor, who owns an apartment building. The lawyer has drafted a form lease for Lessor and represents him whenever litigation arises between Lessor and his lessees.

The lawyer receives a call from Mr. Tenant, who is not a lessee in the client's building but who wants to sue his own landlord because of alleged negligence in the maintenance of the building in which Tenant lives. Tenant's lease contains a clause, similar to one that the lawyer had drafted for Lessor's form lease, exculpating the landlord from liability for negligence. In order to prevail in the litigation, therefore, the lawyer would have to argue that the clause

---

[35] *T.C. Theatre Corp.*, 113 F.Supp. at 269.

in Tenant's lease — similar to the one drafted by the lawyer for Lessor — is voidable on grounds of unconscionability or public policy.

The conflict is not as obvious and direct as it would be if the lawyer were called upon to sue a current client. Here the conflict is created by the contradictory positions that the lawyer would be taking on an issue relating to the representation of two separate clients in different contexts. It is referred to, therefore, as a positional conflict of interest (or, sometimes, an "issue conflict of interest").

If the lawyer chooses to represent Tenant, she has a conflict of interest with respect to both clients. As to Tenant, there is a significant possibility that the lawyer's zeal and competence will be impaired by her desire to maintain Lessor as a client.[36] Also, the clause that she would be attacking as unconscionable and contrary to public policy is similar to one that she drafted, so her pride in her drafting skills might adversely affect the force of her advocacy.[37]

With respect to Lessor, the lawyer has a conflict of interest because her zealous advocacy of Tenant's cause is inconsistent with her obligation of zeal in maintaining Lessor's rights. We could also say that Lessor might well feel a justifiable sense of betrayal. This refers back to the idea of loyalty and a concern with impairment of the lawyer-client relationship of trust and confidence.

§ 10.09   IMPUTED DISQUALIFICATION

Assume that the lawyer in each of our hypotheticals has a law partner. If the lawyer cannot represent the ice cream franchise dealer or the insured or the tenant, can her partner do so?

Once again, we look to experience and common sense. Partners share profits and losses. They also share file cabinets, computer systems, and conversations. Moreover, it is virtually impossible to police conversations between partners. If we are concerned, therefore, that a conflict of interest might impair the lawyer's own zeal or competence, or that it might induce her to misuse confidences, then we must recognize that the risks are substantially the same when her partner undertakes the same representation.

---

[36] This is the "currying favor" concern discussed *supra* at n. 28. Another illustration of currying favor in the context of a positional conflict of interest is provided by HAZARD AND HODES, *supra*, note 1. They posit the case of a lawyer, L, who is counsel to a regional bankers' association and represents a number of banks. L is asked to defend a debtor who is being sued by another bank — a bank which is neither a client nor a member of the association. On behalf of the debtor, a sound argument can be made to narrow the scope of the state's holder-in-due-course rule. In analyzing that case, the authors recognize the realistic concern that the lawyer's personal interest in future business from banks might affect his zeal on behalf of the debtor:

> Due to his *personal interest in maintaining* the trust (and therefore *the business*) of his present banker clients, L, if he took the debtor's case, might underplay the contemplated defense, or might be too ready to urge a quiet settlement upon his new client. While such temptations can be overcome, *any lawyer who claims he would be wholly uninfluenced by them is deluding himself and his clients.*

Id., § 10.10, Ill. 10-1 (emphasis added).

[37] A more pointed illustration is a lawyer who represented a criminal defendant at trial, now responsible for deciding whether to argue on appeal that the defendant had been denied effective assistance of counsel.

Accordingly, when a lawyer is disqualified because of a conflict of interest, her partner is similarly disqualified. You will find this referred to as imputed disqualification.[38]

§ 10.10 "POTENTIAL," "ACTUAL," AND "APPEARANCE OF" CONFLICTS

As we have seen, a conflict of interest can exist even though no actual impropriety (i.e., breach of confidentiality, zeal, competence, or communication) has occurred and even though no actual impropriety will in fact take place. This is because conflicts of interest are forbidden in order to guard against potential improprieties and against the appearance of impropriety.

It should be clear, therefore, that a conflict of interest is nothing more than a "potential" impropriety or an "appearance" of impropriety. Nevertheless, you will find references to a "potential conflict of interest," to an "actual conflict of interest," and to an "appearance of a conflict of interest."

When commentators refer to an "actual" conflict of interest, they ordinarily mean that one or more of the substantive improprieties that the conflict of interest rule was designed to prevent have taken place. Thus, two distinct ideas — the initial conflict of interest and the resultant breach of zeal or confidentiality — are misleadingly collapsed into the single phrase, "actual conflict of interest." It would be more accurate to say, therefore, that the lawyer had been involved in a conflict of interest which then resulted in a breach of confidentiality.[39]

The imprecise expression "actual conflict of interest" has led to use of the redundant phrase, "potential conflict of interest." The phrase is redundant because, as we have seen, every conflict of interest is "potential" in the sense that the proscription seeks to prevent a substantive ethical violation from occurring. For those who use the expression "actual" conflict of interest, however, there is a need to distinguish the conflict of interest that is not "actual" (that is, the conflict that has not yet resulted in a substantive ethical violation). Thus, we have the "potential conflict of interest."

The idea of "an appearance of a conflict of interest" is probably most often the result of sloppy thinking, but might be a variation on the "potential conflict of interest." Whatever its source, the phrase is at best redundant because, as we have seen, one thing that "conflict of interest" connotes is "an appearance

---

[38] The same idea is sometimes expressed with the phrase "vicarious disqualification," which is now used infrequently.

"Vicarious disqualification" should not be confused with the term "vicarious client." If a lawyer sues a company that is *not* the lawyer's client, but the company is a member of a trade association that *is* the lawyer's client, the company may be referred to as a vicarious client. Whether the lawyer should be disqualified in such a case depends upon a case-by-case assessment of the same concerns that we have been considering. *See, e.g., Gluek v. Jonathan Logan, Inc.*, 653 F.2d 746, 749 (2d Cir. 1981).

[39] Consider again Professor McMunigal's analogy of conflict of interest to reckless driving. *See* note 26, *supra*. Like conflict of interest, reckless driving is punishable because it presents an unacceptable risk of harm, regardless of whether harm actually occurs. It is unnecessary, and would make no sense, therefore, to refer to "potential reckless driving" and to "actual reckless driving" to distinguish reckless driving from, say, vehicular homicide.

of impropriety." Thus, "an appearance of a conflict of interest" translates into "an appearance of an appearance of an impropriety." Because this would mean a substantive impropriety twice removed, the relationship between the asserted conflict of interest and the impropriety could be extremely tenuous.

Since sloppy thinking and redundancy are all too common in the law,[40] there is little that can be done about it, but you should understand that these usages are often careless and can be confusing or misleading. Also, as we will see, the corruption of "appearance of impropriety" into "appearance of a conflict of interest" has contributed to the depreciation of the idea of the "appearance of impropriety." This is unfortunate, because the concept of an appearance of impropriety is not only valuable but is one of constitutional significance.[41]

§ 10.11   CONSENT TO CONFLICTS OF INTEREST

This book argues for a client-centered system of lawyers' ethics that is designed in significant part to give expression to each client's autonomy.[42] In the context of conflicts of interest, client autonomy means that the affected clients should have the power to waive conflicts of interest, as long as the clients act voluntarily and with full knowledge of all of the risks of the conflict.[43]

In the ice cream franchise hypothetical, for example, even if the lawyer has confidences from the previous representation, the franchiser might nevertheless have no objection to the lawyer's representing the franchise dealer in the new litigation. There would, therefore, be no reason to deny the dealer his choice of counsel. That is, as long as the former client is willing to waive its objections to the use of its confidences, there is no breach of confidentiality to guard against, nor is there any appearance of impropriety.

Similarly, in our insurance hypothetical, the insured, having been fully advised about and understanding the risks of being represented by a lawyer selected and paid by the insurance company, might be perfectly willing to accept that lawyer. If so, there is no ethical concern that would justify interfering with the parties' decision. It would not be sufficient, however, to rely upon the insured's apparent agreement in the insurance policy to accept any lawyer chosen by the insurance company. In most cases, the insured is probably unaware that there is such a clause in the policy. Moreover, it is doubtful that in any case the insured has in fact agreed to accept the lawyer with full knowledge of the risks of doing so. Even if such a clause in a policy were found to be binding between the insurer and the insured as a matter of contract

---

[40] A teacher of Contracts would suggest, for example, "binding contract" or "valid contract" for "contract," and "firm offer" when what is meant is "offer" (and not an offer that by its terms is to be kept open for a stated time).

[41] *See* text at notes 30–22, *supra.*

[42] *See* Chapter 3.

[43] There will be circumstances, however, in which the lawyer will be unable to seek an informed consent from one client or potential client because to do so would require the lawyer to reveal a confidence or a secret of another client. In such a case, of course, an informed consent could not be obtained.

law, the clause would not justify the lawyer in ignoring her own ethical responsibilities with respect to conflicts of interest.

Again, however, if the insured makes a fully informed and voluntary decision to waive any conflict, the insured's decision should be respected. Such a waiver by the insured should satisfy any ethical concerns that others — the bar, the court, or the public — might have, either of substance or of appearances.[44] Indeed, we cannot think of any conflict of interest that should not be waivable, as long as the judgment can fairly be made that all persons potentially affected by the conflict had a complete understanding of the risks and made a voluntary decision to accept the risks that come with the particular lawyer.[45] The appropriate question in cases of conflict of interest, therefore, is whether the lawyer is able to obtain a voluntary and informed consent from the client or former client before undertaking or continuing the representation.

United States v. Schwarz[46] illustrates the situation where the defendant could not have acted voluntarily and/or with a complete understanding of the risks in consenting to his lawyer's conflict of interest. Accordingly, the Second Circuit found the conflict of interest "unwaivable." *Schwarz* grew out of a notorious episode of police brutality, in which Officer Volpe forced a broomstick up the rectum of a prisoner, Abner Louima, in a bathroom of a station house.

A critical factual issue in Officer Schwarz's trial was whether Schwarz had been in the bathroom at the time of the attack. There was substantial evidence (including the victim's testimony) that there had indeed been a second officer in the bathroom, but there was conflicting testimony as to whether it had been Officer Schwarz or Officer Weise. Thus, there was an extremely high likelihood that the jury would find that there *was* a second officer in the bathroom. It followed that Schwarz's strongest defense was that the other officer had been Weise. Indeed, Volpe (after pleading guilty) offered to testify that the officer who had been with him was not Schwarz. Nevertheless, Schwarz's lawyer did not introduce evidence, or argue to the jury, that the second officer had been someone other than Schwarz; rather, he took the untenable position that Volpe had acted alone.

What created the conflict of interest was that Schwarz's lawyer was Stephen Worth, whose firm had recently gotten a two-year, $10,000,000 retainer agreement with the Policeman's Benevolent Association to represent its members. The retainer agreement had been signed by the PBA president, Matarazzo, the fee was payable in monthly installments (with part held back for quarterly payments to assure satisfaction), and the agreement was subject to cancellation on thirty days notice.

---

[44] This assumes, of course, that the person who provides the waiver is not herself subject to a conflict of interest.

[45] Although a lawyer is permitted to accept a client who has effectively waived a conflict of interest, there are many cases in which the lawyer would not be acting prudently to do so. After the case is over, the client might well take the position that the lawyer had been less than zealous and that the client had not fully understood the conflict of interest when giving the waiver. Even if the lawyer is confident that such charges would not be justified, the possibility is not one that a lawyer should invite without careful consideration.

[46] 283 F.3d 76 (2002).

The conflict of interest arose from the fact that the victim, Louima, had filed a civil lawsuit against the PBA and Matarazzo, alleging a police conspiracy to injure Louima and cover it up. This meant that the PBA and Matarazzo had a critical interest in maintaining that Volpe was a rogue cop who had acted on his own and that no other officer had been complicit in any way. Thus, Worth, in order to maintain the favor of the PBA and Matarazzo, had a personal interest in taking the untenable tactical position (as he did at trial) that Volpe had acted alone. Since the jury, predictably, rejected that contention, Schwarz was left without any significant refutation of the prosecution's evidence that he had been the second officer.

The Second Circuit was therefore "convinced that no effective conflict-free defense attorney would have acted as Worth did, and thus, only Worth's conflict could explain his actions."[47] Accordingly, the court characterized Worth's conflict of interest as "unwaivable."[48] The court explained "unwaivable" to mean that a conflict cannot be waived "if, in the circumstances of the case, no rational defendant would knowingly and intelligently desire that attorney's representation."[49] That is, the court inferred that Schwarz did not fully understand the risks of the conflict and that, therefore, his waiver had been ineffective.[50] Accordingly, the court vacated Schwarz's conviction.

§ 10.12 CONFLICT OF INTEREST AS A GROUND FOR COURT-ORDERED DISQUALIFICATION

Lawyers' ethical rules have been drafted specifically for purposes of disciplinary actions against lawyers.[51] They are being used increasingly, however, as the basis for disqualification motions against opposing counsel. Indeed, no litigating lawyer can afford to ignore the potential tactical advantages — and disadvantages — of disqualification.

The most common ground for court-ordered disqualification is conflict of interest.[52] Courts have been most responsive to claims that the moving party

---

[47] *Id.* At 95.

[48] *Id.*

[49] *Id.*

[50] An alternative inference is that Schwarz had not acted voluntarily, because he was dependent on having a lawyer paid for by the union and/or because he was intimidated by union members and representatives to go along with the rogue-cop theory.

[51] The Model Code does not "undertake to define standards for civil liability of lawyers." Model Code, Preliminary Statement. The Model Code, in the Scope note, are more emphatic and explicit:

> Violation of a Rule should not give rise to a cause of action nor should it create any presumption that a legal duty has been breached. The rules . . . are not designed to be a basis for civil liability. Furthermore, the purpose of the rules can be subverted when they are invoked by opposing parties as procedural weapons. . . . [N]othing in the Rules should be deemed to augment any substantive legal duty of lawyers or the extra-disciplinary consequences of violating such duty.

Nevertheless, the ethical rules are widely used as evidence of malpractice as well as in disqualification cases.

[52] Other ethical rules may also be relevant to disqualification. *See, e.g., W.T. Grant Company v. Haines*, 531 F.2d 671 (2d Cir. 1976) (giving legal advice to an unrepresented adverse party, in violation of DR 7-104(A)(2)).

might suffer prejudice because opposing counsel obtained relevant confidences while representing the moving party in a prior matter. A major advantage of disqualification, therefore, is that it eliminates counsel who is likely to have an unfair advantage gained through violation of ethical rules. In addition, disqualification delays the litigation and deprives the adversary of counsel knowledgeable about the case. The adversary's case is thereby derailed and its expenses increased.

Thus, disqualification motions can make unethical conduct extremely costly. This is a salutary development, especially in view of the limited resources of disciplinary offices and the reluctance of too many bar counsel to bring charges against attorneys with large firms. Disqualification motions have made major law firms conscious of the ethical rules in a way that ineffective disciplinary action has failed to do. Some courts, however, have not been enthusiastic about disqualification motions, in part because the court's calendar is likely to be delayed by disqualification of counsel.

When presented with disqualification motions, courts frequently mention that such motions are often made to obtain a tactical advantage. One would hope, however, that such motions are *always* made to obtain a tactical advantage; certainly, a motion to disqualify opposing counsel should not be made if it is to the moving party's disadvantage.[53] As with any motion, the issue for the court should not be whether the moving party has a tactical motive for making the motion, but whether the motion is meritorious.[54]

Another reason that weighs against disqualification is that it deprives a party of counsel of his choice. That is unquestionably an important concern. If the motion is meritorious because of a potential for prejudice, however, one party's right to select counsel must give way to the other party's right to a fair trial.

Recognizing that avoiding prejudice is the most important concern in litigation, some courts make disqualification turn upon whether the attorney's conduct "tends to taint the trial," as where the attorney is "at least potentially in a position to use privileged information concerning the other side [obtained] through prior litigation."[55] However, if a lawyer's conduct has been so

---

[53] We do not mean to disparage rules requiring lawyers to report unethical conduct. *See* DR 1-103(A) and MR 8.3(c). On the contrary, such rules are extremely important. Some lawyers oppose these as "squeal rules," which expresses a norm that might be appropriate to the street or the alley, but that cannot be an acceptable norm for a profession concerned with the administration of justice and that prides itself on self-policing.

However, the obligation to report unethical conduct is subordinate to rules protecting clients' confidences and secrets.

[54] Even substantial delay in filing a meritorious disqualification motion is not grounds for denying it, unless the delay has in fact prejudiced the other party. *Emle Industries, Inc. v. Patentex, Inc.*, 478 F.2d 562, 574 (2d Cir. 1973) (three year delay insufficient to justify denying motion to disqualify counsel). An unexplained delay by a party who had full knowledge of the ground for disqualification could be taken to constitute consent, but consent should be revocable if there has been no detrimental reliance on it. A better ground for denying disqualification because of delay in objecting would be the likelihood that any confidences would already have been communicated, which would mean that disqualification could no longer eliminate trial taint.

[55] *See, e.g., Board of Education v. Nyquist*, 590 F.2d 1241, 1246 (2d Cir., 1979). The Nyquist court also suggested that disqualification might be granted when the court is concerned that the attorney's zeal on behalf of her own client might be impaired. *Id.* This ground would be appropriate, however, only upon a finding that the attorney's client is incapable of giving an informed and voluntary waiver.

egregious as to "diminish . . . the integrity of the judicial process," a court might well be moved to disqualify the lawyer, whether as a means of punishment or out of a felt need to dissociate the court from the offensive conduct. [56]

Even if a conflict of interest does not tend to taint a trial and therefore does not occasion court-ordered disqualification, the lawyer's conduct might warrant disciplinary action. Also, not all conflicts of interest arise in litigation. There may be conflicts between the client's interests and the lawyer's own, for example, when the lawyer is handling a business matter for the client.

§ 10.13   THE IMPORTANCE OF CONTEXT IN CONFLICT OF INTEREST

How conflicts of interest are dealt with depends in significant part on the context in which the issue is presented. As noted earlier, the ethical codes were written primarily for disciplinary purposes, that is, to protect members of the public and the administration of justice from lawyers who are incompetent, untrustworthy, or otherwise unfit to practice. In the context of a disciplinary matter, therefore, there is no rule of "no harm, no foul." That is, if a lawyer violates a disciplinary rule, appropriate disciplinary action should follow regardless of whether a client or the administration of justice has actually suffered as a result of the particular act of misconduct. Thus, a lawyer might well be disciplined for violating the conflict of interest rules regardless of whether the conflict has resulted in a breach of confidentiality or other substantive rule of ethics. Again, it would be analogous to punishing someone for reckless driving even though no accident has occurred.

On the other hand, in the typical lawyer malpractice case, a lawyer cannot be held liable for damages unless the lawyer's failure to give reasonably skilled and competent service has caused provable harm to the client. However, the fact that the lawyer is a fiduciary can justify a reduced burden of proof regarding causation of damages. [57] In addition, in a case of conflict of interest, the lawyer may be subject to fee forfeiture [58] as well as punitive damages [59] without a showing of actual harm.

In the context of disqualification of counsel from representing a client in a trial or appeal because of a conflict of interest, the principal concern should be whether the conflict presents an unacceptable risk of unfairness in the

---

[56] See Beiny v. Wynyard, 522 N.Y.S.2d 511, 515, 132 A.D.2d 190 (App. Div., First Dept. 1987). In Beiny, the law firm was disqualified for unlawfully and deceitfully obtaining a mass of documents which it knew included privileged materials. Although the court made reference to prejudice to the other party (which had already occurred), the disqualification was clearly a response to the serious affront to the administration of justice.

[57] See, e.g., Meinhard v. Salmon, 249 N.Y. 458, 465, 164 N.E. 545, 547 (1928); Lewis v. Dobyns, 1997 WL 133525 (Ohio App., 1997), app. not allowed, 79 Ohio St.3d 1450, 680 N.E.2d 1022 (Ohio, 1997).

[58] See, e.g., Silbiger v. Prudence Bonds Corp., 180 F.2d 917, 920–921 (1950) (L. Hand, J.); Woods v. City Nat. Bank & Trust Co. of Chicago, 312 U.S. 262, 269, 61 S.Ct. 493, 497 (1941); Condren v. Grace, 783 F.Supp. 178, 185–187 (1992).

[59] See, e.g. Brown v. Coates, 253 F.2d 36, 40 (1958) (Burger, J.); Chase Manhattan Bank v. Perla, 411 N.Y.S.2d 66, 69 65 A.D.2d 207, 211 (1978).

proceeding. This would occur, for example, if the lawyer on one side might be in a position to take advantage of confidential information learned from the adverse party in a former representation of that party.

Another contextual difference that has proved to be important is the impact of conflicts of interest on the Sixth Amendment right to effective assistance of counsel in criminal cases. In view of the importance of conflicts of interest in civil litigation, one would expect courts to be particularly attentive, in cases involving life and liberty, to assure that defendants are represented by counsel who are not burdened by conflicting obligations. The *Schwarz* (Abner Louima) case, in which the Second Circuit vacated the conviction, is a good illustration of a court's recognition of how a defendant can be denied the effective assistance of counsel because of his lawyer's conflict of interest.[60] Also, as we have seen, prosecutors have been successful in disqualifying defense lawyers on grounds of conflicts of interest, even over the objections of defendants.

Unfortunately, however, some courts, including the Supreme Court, have shown less regard for unfairness to criminal defendants than courts generally show for unfairness to civil litigants in cases involving conflicts of interest. Illustrative is *Mickens v. Taylor*.[61] Walter Mickens was charged with the capital murder of Timothy Hall. At the time of his death, Hall had been the defendant on an assault and concealed weapons charge, and was being represented by a court-appointed attorney, Bryan Saunders. Upon learning of Hall's death, the Virginia trial judge relieved Saunders of his appointment and, on the next court day, appointed Saunders to represent Mickens. Saunders said nothing about his representation of Hall, but the Supreme Court accepted a finding that the judge either had known or should have known that she had appointed the victim's lawyer to represent his accused murderer.

Frequently, a criminal defendant will insist upon his complete innocence in early interviews with his lawyer. This is especially true in the case of clients who have not chosen their lawyers, but who are represented by strangers sent by the court. Apart from an understandable distrust of the lawyers on the part of many such clients, there is a common assumption that appointed counsel will only give effective representation if they believe the client to be innocent.[62] It is not only appropriate but necessary, therefore, that defense counsel explain to the client the law of defenses to the charge and mitigation of the punishment.[63]

When Mickens told Saunders that he had not known Hall and that he had not been at the scene of the murder, however, Saunders did not explain the implausibility of this testimony in the light of other evidence. In addition, Saunders did not tell Mickens how other facts — facts that were damaging to the reputation of Saunders' former client, Hall — could have avoided the death penalty. The "outrageously and wantonly vile" conduct that justified the death penalty in Mickens' case was the jury's finding that the murderer

---

[60] *See* "Consent to Conflicts of Interest," *supra.*

[61] 122 S.Ct. 1237 (2002).

[62] *See, e.g.,* PHILIP B. HEYMANN, ASSAULT WITH A DEADLY WEAPON (with Allen & Kelly) (1977).

[63] *See, supra,* § 7.08, "The Anatomy of a Murder 'Lecture.'"

had forcibly sodomized Hall before killing him.[64] In fact, though, evidence was available that Hall had been a prostitute and that he had been killed in an area known for prostitution.[65] Thus, the argument could have been made that Hall had consented to the sodomy. Without proper counseling from Saunders, however, Mickens maintained his original denial of any involvement, foreclosing use of the mitigating evidence.[66]

Nevertheless, in an opinion by Justice Scalia, a 5-4 majority upheld the conviction. Scalia acknowledged that there was a conflict of interest, but only in what he deprecated as "a mere theoretical division of loyalties."[67] Also, Scalia recognized that in *Holloway v. Arkansas*[68] the Supreme Court presumed that representation of multiple defendants undermined the adversary process and reversed the conviction. The *Holloway* Court noted that a trial conducted by a lawyer representing conflicting interests is inherently suspect, and that assessing prejudice on review is difficult when the record has been made by a lawyer who has been burdened by a conflict.[69] Accordingly, the defendant in *Holloway* had not been required to show prejudice as a condition of reversal.

However, Scalia distinguished *Holloway* on the ground that counsel in that case had protested the conflict, and the judge had nevertheless failed to conduct an inquiry. In *Mickens*, although the judge had known about the conflict, Saunders had not objected to it. On this thin distinction, Scalia held, therefore, that no inquiry into the conflict had been necessary despite the judge's awareness of the conflict and despite the fact that she had created it. Accordingly, Mickens had been required to show an "actual conflict." Scalia explained that "for Sixth Amendment purposes, [an actual conflict] is a conflict of interest that adversely affects counsel's performance."[70] Since the Fourth Circuit had held (incredibly) that Saunder's performance had not been adversely affected,[71] Mickens' conviction and sentence were upheld.[72]

This inappropriate use of the phrase "actual conflict" is unfortunate, and the way in which courts have used it to minimize the serious problem of conflicts of interest in criminal cases is deplorable. As we have seen, if a

---

[64] 122 S.Ct. at 1249 (Stevens, J., dissenting).

[65] *Id.* at 1248–1249.

[66] *See id.* at 1247 (Kennedy, J., concurring). Also, at the sentencing hearing, Hall's mother testified that "all [she] lived for was that boy." Saunders failed to rebut that "victim impact testimony" by bringing out (as he had known) that Hall's arrest on the assault and battery charges had been on a warrant sworn out by Hall's mother. *Id.* at 1249, n.4 (Stevens, J., dissenting).

[67] *Id.* at 1243. A large number of specialists in lawyers' ethics, including Professor Freedman, joined an amicus brief prepared by Lawrence Fox, urging reversal on grounds of Saunders' conflict of interest.

[68] 435 U.S. 475, 98 S.Ct. 1173 (1978).

[69] *Id.* at 489–490.

[70] 122 S.Ct. at 1244, n.5.

[71] 240 F.3d 348, 360 (2001) (en banc).

[72] Adverse effect on counsel's performance is also referred to as "prejudice." In addition to such adverse effect, or prejudice, Mickens would also have been required to show that, but for counsel's errors, there was a reasonable probability that the result of the proceeding would have been different. *Id.* at 1241, *relying on Strickland v. Washington*, 466 U.S. 668, 694, 104 S.Ct. 2052 (1984).

conflict of interest adversely affects counsel's performance (*e.g.*, in a lack of zeal, a failure to communicate, or a breach of confidentiality), the lawyer has gone beyond conflict of interest to a substantive violation of her ethical obligations. In civil cases, the conflict of interest alone — the significant and plausible risk of a substantive violation — is enough to require the lawyer's disqualification. This is so regardless of whether the lawyer objects on the record to her own conflict of interest and without any showing that a substantive violation has occurred. The standard should be at least as stringent in criminal cases under the Sixth Amendment.

Moreover, we agree with Justice Breyer that the representation of an accused murderer by his victim's lawyer constitutes a conflict of interest that is "egregious on its face," that "the conflict is exacerbated by the fact that it occurred in a capital murder case," and that "the Commonwealth itself *created* the conflict in the first place."[73] Accordingly, the conviction should have been reversed because of a "structural defect affecting the framework within which the trial [and sentencing] proceeds, rather than simply an error in the trial process itself."[74]

§ 10.14 CONFLICTS OF INTEREST UNDER THE MODEL CODE

Canon 5 of the Model Code deals with various aspects of conflicts of interest. The Canon reads: "A Lawyer Should Exercise Independent Professional Judgment on Behalf of a Client."[75] DR 5-101(A) requires the lawyer to obtain the client's consent before accepting employment when the lawyer's own interests create a conflict with the client's interests. DR 5-105 requires the lawyer to obtain consent in cases of multiple representation. Canon 9 requires that "A Lawyer Should Avoid Even the Appearance of Impropriety." In addition, EC 4-5 and 4-6 refer to protecting confidences in the context of representing more than one client, either simultaneously or one after the other.

We noted earlier that rules relating to conflicts of interest guard against the appearance of impropriety and the risk of impropriety. Canon 9 refers expressly to the appearances rationale, while Canon 5 and EC 4-5 and 4-6 place principal emphasis on the prophylactic purpose of conflict of interest rules.

---

[73] *Id.* at 1264 (Breyer, J., dissenting) (emphasis in the original).

[74] *Id.*, quoting *Arizona v. Fulminante*, 499 U.S. 310, 111 S.Ct. 1246 (1991).

[75] Throughout Canon 5 the drafters have avoided reference to the term conflict of interest, but the language and substance of Canon 5 indicate that "independent professional judgment" is intended to include the same concerns that are associated with conflicts of interest. In the Index to the Model Code, the phrase "Conflicting interests" is cross-referenced to "Adverse effect on professional judgment of lawyer." Also, EC 5-1 appears to equate the exercise of professional judgment with "loyalty" and with avoiding "compromising influences and loyalties." In addition, EC 5-2 refers to adverse effect upon "the advice to be given or services to be rendered" a client. Further, DR 5-105 uses the phrase "differing interests," which is defined at the end of the Model Code as including "every interest that will adversely affect either the judgment or the loyalty of a lawyer to a client, whether it be a conflicting, inconsistent, diverse or other interest."

One troublesome aspect of the conflicts of interest provisions of the Model Code is that they suggest differing standards for determining whether there is a conflict of interest. The two key sections are DR 5-101 and DR 5-105. DR 5-101 relates to conflicts created by "the lawyer's own financial, business, property, or personal interests." DR 5-105 relates generally to potential impairment of the lawyer's professional judgment by concurrent representations.

The test under DR 5-101(A) is whether the lawyer's judgment "will be or *reasonably may be*" adversely affected. Both DR 5-105(A) and (B), however, refer to whether the lawyer's judgment "will be or is *likely* to be adversely affected" by the multiple representation or whether it "would be *likely* to involve him in representing differing interests."[76] There is no indication, however, of a conscious decision to vary the standard depending upon the context.

Thus, it is unclear whether the test is a reasonable possibility[77] or a probability[78] of an adverse effect.[79] Since each of the disciplinary rules under Canon 5 allows client consent to override the conflict, we prefer "reasonable possibility," because it requires the lawyer to inform the client and obtain consent in more rather than in fewer circumstances.

Consent alone is sufficient to overcome a conflict of interest under Model Code DR 5-101(A). New York has modified this provision, however, to add to consent a requirement that a disinterested lawyer "would believe that the representation of the client will not be adversely affected" by the conflicting interest. Also, New York has added a similar "disinterested lawyer" limitation on consent under DR 5-105, making the two sections consistent.[80]

A serious drafting problem in the Model Code is the failure to deal explicitly with the important conflict of interest between a former client and a current one. This led to the need for some fancy construction,[81] which has been avoided in New York by the addition of DR 5-108, dealing specifically with the issue of the former client. Oddly, though, consent is sufficient under DR 5-108 without the additional "disinterested lawyer" proviso. DR 5-108 also includes provisions relating to imputed disqualification.

---

[76] The phrase "differing interests" is defined (at the end of the Model Code) as including every interest that "will" adversely affect the lawyer's judgment or loyalty. However, the context makes the "likely" standard controlling.

[77] Pursuant to dictionary definitions, we understand "may" to suggest possibility as distinguished from probability.

[78] Pursuant to dictionary definitions, we understand "likely" to suggest probability as distinguished from possibility.

[79] The Ethical Considerations suggest other standards. EC 5-2 says that a lawyer should not assume a position that would "tend" to make his judgment less protective of the client, but also refers to a "reasonable probability." EC 5-15 refers to "potentially differing interests," and adds that the lawyer "should resolve all doubts against" the propriety of the representation.

[80] The Model Code versions of DR 5-101(A) and DR 5-105(C) are inconsistent with each other. Also, the provision in Model Code DR 5-105(C) is drafted particularly poorly; because of the New York amendment, however, there is no need to review those issues here. The difficulty is discussed in the first edition of this book at pages 187–188.

[81] *See* the first edition of this book at page 188.

§ 10.15 CONFLICTS OF INTEREST UNDER THE MODEL RULES

Some of the drafting problems of the Model Code have been resolved under the Model Rules, but new ones have been created. The relevant provisions are Rules 1.7 through 1.13 and 2.2. We are concerned here only with the core concepts of conflicts of interest under the Model Rules and with some of the more interesting problems of policy and drafting.

MR 1.7 gives the general rules that are applicable to a conflict of interest between clients, between a client and the lawyer's own interest, or between the client and the lawyer's responsibility to a third person. MR 1.7 is in two subsections, but, for reasons that we explain, subsection (a) is, at best, unnecessary. Let us begin, therefore, with MR 1.7(b), which is the basic conflict of interest provision.

§ 10.16 CONSENT, PLUS "REASONABLE BELIEF," UNDER THE MODEL RULES

The original MR 1.7(b) (still in effect in most states) defines a conflict of interest as one in which the lawyer's representation of a client "may be materially limited" by the lawyer's responsibilities to another client or to a third person or by the lawyer's own interests. When that possibility[82] exists, the lawyer cannot represent the client unless (1) the lawyer "reasonably believes the representation will not be adversely affected," and (2) the client consents after consultation.[83]

The difficulty is with the requirement that the lawyer "reasonably believe[]" that the representation "will not" be adversely affected. The problem is that, by hypothesis, the lawyer's representation "may be" materially limited as a result of a conflict; otherwise we would not be into 1.7(b) at all. Taking that as a given, the lawyer cannot "reasonably believe[]" that the representation "will not" be adversely affected.[84] In other words, given that the representation *may be materially limited*, how could the lawyer ever reasonably believe that the representation *will not be adversely affected*?[85]

---

[82] As under the Model Code, we understand the phrase "may be" in its dictionary sense of indicating a possibility rather than a probability.

[83] Consultation is defined in the Terminology section of the Model Rules as "communication of information reasonably sufficient to permit the client to appreciate the significance of the matter in question."

[84] The lawyer could reasonably believe that the representation *probably* will not be adversely affected, but "probably" is not in the rule.

[85] Discussing "reasonable belief" in the context of MR 1.7, Hazard and Hodes note that "a lawyer who plunges ahead, oblivious to obvious threats to the continued vitality of the client-lawyer relationship, would ordinarily have violated Rule 1.7(a), even if all of the parties were in fact able to muddle through." 1 GEOFFREY C. HAZARD & W. WILLIAM HODES, THE LAW OF LAWYERING § 11.5 (3d. ed., 2001). Again, this would appear to be every case under MR 1.7(b), because every time the lawyer sought consent under MR 1.7(b)(2), she would be acknowledging that there is a threat to the continued vitality of the lawyer-client relationship, the existence of which would render the consent irrelevant.

The analysis of MR 1.7 by Hazard and Hodes is considerably different from that presented here. They do not address the problem now under discussion.

If, then, MR 1.7(b)(1) requires that the lawyer reasonably believe that there is no risk when, by hypothesis, there is a foreseeable risk, the rule would appear to say that the lawyer can never represent a client when there is a conflict of interest, regardless of the client consent provision in MR 1.7(b)(2). One obvious problem with that reading, however, is that there is a simpler way of saying that a client's consent is never effective when there is a conflict of interest.[86]

We are compelled, therefore, to interpret MR 1.7 to avoid a plain-meaning result that could not have been intended by the drafters. The best solution would appear to be to refer to MR 1.2(c), which allows the lawyer to "limit the objectives of the representation" if the client consents after consultation. Thus, if the client consents to the representation under MR 1.7(b)(2), the client will, in effect, have consented to a limitation of the representation as permitted under MR 1.2(c).[87] Once consent has been given, the lawyer can reasonably believe, therefore, as required by MR 1.7(b)(1), that the representation (which has been *defined* by the *consent*) will no longer be materially *limited* by the *conflict*.

Recasting MR 1.7(b) in accord with the foregoing analysis, it means that there is a conflict of interest whenever "the representation of [a] client may be materially limited by the lawyer's responsibilities to another client or to a third person, or by the lawyer's own interests." The conflict of interest is waivable, however, if two conditions are met. First, the client must consent, knowingly and voluntarily, to limit the representation to the extent required by the conflict. Second, the lawyer must reasonably believe that the client has fully understood the implications of the conflict and that the representation, as limited, will not be adversely affected by the conflict in any way that has not been consented to by the client.

§ 10.17   THE REDUNDANCY OF MR 1.7(a)

The original MR 1.7(b) (still in effect in most states) forbids a lawyer to represent a client where the representation of that client will be "directly adverse" to the representation of another client.[88] In such a case, however, the representation of one client inevitably "may be materially limited" by the lawyer's responsibilities to the other client, which is what MR 1.7(b) is about. It follows that the case of direct adversity is covered by the more general provision of MR 1.7(b). For that reason, MR 1.7(a) adds nothing of substance to MR 1.7(b).

It is difficult to understand, therefore, why direct adversity — which is necessarily included in MR 1.7(b) — is treated separately under 1.7(a). Also

---

[86] In fact, the Comment to MR 1.7 says: "A client may consent to representation notwithstanding a conflict." Unfortunately, however, the remainder of that paragraph refers to circumstances in which the lawyer "cannot properly . . . provide representation on the basis of the client's consent."

[87] In partial support of this construction, the Comment to MR 1.7 says, "Consideration should be given to whether the client wishes to accommodate the other interest involved."

[88] This includes "act[ing] as an advocate against a person the lawyer represents in some other matter, even if it is wholly unrelated." MR 1.7, Cmt.

difficult to understand is why two different standards of "reasonable belief" have been adopted in the two subsections of MR 1.7. Under subsection (b) the lawyer must reasonably believe that "the *representation* will not be adversely affected." Under subsection (a), however, the lawyer must reasonably believe that "the representation will not adversely affect *the relationship with the other client*."[89]

Which of these reasonable-belief requirements is harder to fulfill? (Bear in mind that neither of them is relevant unless the client consents after consultation, because subsection (2) is identical under 1.7(a) and 1.7(b).) As shown above, on a plain-meaning reading of subsection (b) it will be impossible for the lawyer to fulfill (b)(1); only by fancy interpretation can the consent/reasonable-belief provisions of 1.7(b)(1) ever work as the drafters apparently intended.

Without the need for any construction, however, subsection (a)(1) is easily complied with. If the client fully understands the conflict of interest inherent in a directly adverse representation and voluntarily consents to it, then the client has made the crucial decision that the client's *relationship* with the lawyer will not be adversely affected. As observed by Professors Hazard and Hodes, "clients know their own feelings better than the lawyer does."[90] If the client consents to representation that is directly adverse, therefore, the lawyer can reasonably believe, under MR 1.7(a)(1), that the lawyer-client relationship will not be adversely affected by the simultaneous representation.[91]

This leaves the question of whether the case of directly adverse representation must pass muster under 1.7(b) as well as under 1.7(a). That is, even if the lawyer reasonably believes that the *relationship* will not be adversely affected by directly adverse representation of two clients, the *representation* of the clients might nevertheless be adversely affected. Therefore, should not 1.7(b) also be complied with? If so, it would appear that subsection (b) is going to be more important than subsection (a). As we have seen, the client's consent should put to rest any concerns about the *relationship*, but the client's consent might not be sufficient to eliminate all concerns about the *quality of the representation*. Thus, assuming client consent, the real hurdle is 1.7(b) and not 1.7(a). In that event, subsection (a) is, again, redundant.

The alternative is to conclude that in cases of direct adversity, subsection (a) applies exclusive of (b). It is not apparent, however, why the only concern in cases of direct adversity is the lawyer-client *relationship*, which is the focus of subsection (a), as distinct from the adequacy of the *representation*, which is the focus of (b). If anything, cases of direct adversity would seem to raise the most acute questions regarding the adequacy of the representation. Yet

---

[89] For purposes of this discussion, we are assuming that there is some significant difference between these two concepts (as implied by the text of MR 1.7). In practical fact, however, we have difficulty with the idea that the lawyer-client relationship can be impaired without thereby impairing the representation, or that the representation can be impaired without thereby impairing the lawyer-client relationship.

[90] HAZARD & HODES, *supra* note 85. However, Hazard and Hodes adopt a different analysis of MR 1.7 than is presented here.

[91] Of course, the client may be less likely to consent in the case of directly adverse representation, but that does not justify putting direct adversity under a separate subsection.

the lawyer is not required under subsection (a) to make any judgment about the quality of the representation, but only about the relationship.[92]

We therefore have two choices. First, cases in which the representation of one client is directly adverse to that of another is covered exclusively by 1.7(a). In that event, the lawyer's reasonable belief standard is easier to fulfil in direct adversity cases than in cases of indirect adversity. Second, cases of direct adversity are covered by both 1.7(a) and 1.7(b). In that event, 1.7(a) is redundant.

Our own preference is to view 1.7(b) as the controlling provision because the standard of subsection (b) — whether the representation "may be materially limited" — better expresses the concerns of conflicts of interest than does the limited standard of subsection (a) — whether the representation "will be directly adverse" to another client."[93] In addition, the consent provision of 1.7(b) (reasonable belief about whether the representation will be adversely affected) is broader and more important that the consent provision of 1.7(a) (reasonably belief about whether the relationship with the client will be adversely affected). The reason is that the latter proviso is fulfilled by the client's decision to consent, while the former requires a more complex calculation and is not necessarily satisfied by the client's consent.

§ 10.18   THE FORMER CLIENT UNDER THE MODEL RULES

The Model Rules deal explicitly with the problem of the former client whose interests are adverse to those of a present client. This is done not in MR 1.7, however, but in a separate rule, MR 1.9.[94]

MR 1.9 is superior to MR 1.7 in important respects. For example, consent of the former client is sufficient under MR 1.9(a) to permit the lawyer to accept the representation despite the conflict of interest. There is no additional (and

---

[92] As noted earlier, we have difficulty in making a distinction between the two concepts. The distinction is not ours, however, but the drafters'.

[93] Note the subordinate standard of MR 1.7(a)(1), which relates to whether the lawyer "reasonably" believes that the representation will not "adversely affect the relationship with the other client." This would make the conflict turn upon the first client's subjective, but reasonable, feelings about whether the lawyer-client relationship of trust and confidence will be impaired by new retainer. *See* note 75, *supra*. In the context of MR 1.7(a), however, this subordinate standard is generally meaningless, because in a case of direct adversity, the client is almost certain to feel a reasonable sense of betrayal. At the same time, the client's reasonable sense of betrayal is necessarily included under MR 1.7(b), because the impairment of trust and confidence is a material limitation that adversely affects the representation.

[94] It would have been preferable to have included the former client in MR 1.7(b) by saying: "A lawyer shall not represent a client if the representation of that client may be materially limited by the lawyer's responsibilities to another client, *to a former client*, or to a third person, or by the lawyer's own interests. . . . " As observed in the Comment to MR 1.9: "The principles in Rule 1.7 determine whether the interests of the present and former client are adverse."

Other provisions in 1.9 could then have been distributed appropriately; for example, the imputed disqualification material of 1.9(b) could have been dealt with under MR 1.10.

puzzling) requirement that the lawyer have a reasonable belief that the former client's interests will not be adversely affected.[95]

Also, the phrase used in MR 1.9 to describe a conflict of interest is whether the new client's "interests are materially adverse" to the interests of the former client.[96] This is an improvement over the use in MR 1.7 of four different phrases — whether the representation will be "directly adverse," whether the representation will "adversely affect the relationship" with the other client, whether "the representation . . . may be materially limited," and whether "the representation will . . . be adversely affected." Also, the comment to MR 1.7 compounds the difficulty by identifying "[t]he critical question" as the likelihood that a conflict will materially interfere with the lawyer's "independent professional judgment." Thereby, the comment collapses all four standards of MR 1.7 into the inferior rubric of Canon 5 of the Model Code, which appears to have been purposely (and wisely) discarded in the text of the Model Rules.[97]

A shortcoming of MR 1.9 is that it could leave a lawyer with a misunderstanding of her obligations with respect to conflicts of interest involving a former client. Throughout MR 1.9, the lawyer is permitted to accept the new client on condition that the former client consent after consultation. That is appropriate. There is no suggestion in MR 1.9 or its Comment, however, that the lawyer might have to obtain an informed consent *from the new client.*

For example, the former client might have been a source of retainers in the past, and the lawyer might well be, or reasonably appear to be, desirous of maintaining the good will of the former client in hopes of future retainers.[98] This problem is covered by the reference in MR 1.7 to "the lawyer's own interests." However, a lawyer who is looking up her obligations in a former-client context might assume that the consent provisions of MR 1.9 are the only ones that she has to be concerned with. An explicit cross reference in the Comment would therefore be useful.

§ 10.19 WHAT INFORMATION IS "GENERALLY KNOWN"?

MR 1.9(c) and New York DR 5-108(a) generally forbid a lawyer to use information of a former client to the former client's disadvantage. One exception that could be significant, but that should not be, is when the information has become "generally known."[99]

---

[95] This reinforces the inference that the reasonable-belief provision of MR 1.7 is not intended to override the client's consent.

Pursuant to the criticism of MR 1.7 in the first edition of this book, the ABA in 2002 changed MR 1.7 to eliminate the reference in 1.7 (a) to the"relationship." However, the discussion in the text is still relevant because thus far, no state has adopted the change.

[96] The phrase appears to be compounded of two standards from MR 1.7: "directly adverse" and "materially limited."

[97] There is no evidence that the multiple standards in MR 1.7 represent finely nuanced drafting. On the contrary, as we have seen, they produce unnecessary confusion. Moreover, the use of yet another (and preferable) phrase in MR 1.9 is further indication of a lack of care in drafting MR 1.7.

[98] *See* notes 28 and 36, *supra.*

[99] MR 1.9(c)(1); N.Y. DR 5-108(a)(2).

With few exceptions, the phrase "generally known" has appropriately been limited quite strictly. EC 4-4 notes that a lawyer must guard a client's secrets regardless of the fact that "others share the knowledge." Also, as explained by Professor Roy Simon, the phrase "generally known" in the New York Code means "much more than publicly available or generally accessible."[100] Rather, it must have "already received widespread publicity" or be a matter of "considerable public notoriety."[101] This is consistent with the definition of "known" in the Model Rules as denoting "actual knowledge."[102]

Thus, it should not be enough that the former client's information is accessible to any member of the public who knows or can discover where to look for it.[103] Rather, by a plain-meaning reading, the exception created by MR 1.9(c)(1) and by New York's DR 5-108(a)(2) should not apply unless members of the public "generally" have "actual knowledge" of the information.

§ 10.20 THE ETHICAL ILLUSION OF SCREENING

One of the most controversial issues in lawyers' ethics currently is screening.[104] The issue of screening arises, for example, when a lawyer who has been representing, say, the defendant in a case, becomes a partner in the firm representing the plaintiff in the same case. Understandably, the defendant will be concerned that its confidences and secrets will be made available to its adversary. Until a short time ago, such "side-switching" always resulted in mandatory disqualification not only of the migrating lawyer but also of that lawyer's new firm (unless, of course, the migrating lawyer's former client

---

[100] Roy Simon, The New York Code of Professional Responsibility Annotated 624 (2003).

[101] Id. at 624–625.

[102] In Florida, however, "generally known" has been given "anything but its plain meaning." Lawrence J. Fox, *Former Clients in Florida Beware: Your Former Lawyer May Become Your Worst Enemy*, The Professional Lawyer 2 (Summer, 2002). The Florida Supreme Court has defined the phrase to include only information that could not be uncovered in public records or through discovery procedures — that is, anything that is not protected by the attorney-client or work-product privileges. Thus, a client's former lawyer will be able to "frame discovery requests, follow investigative leads, and evaluate the responses thereto employing confidential information that otherwise is not available to any other lawyer." *Id.*

[103] This conclusion goes back at least to the leading case of *T.C. Theatre Corp. v. Warner Bros. Pictures, Inc.*, 113 F.Supp 265 (1953) (Weinfeld, J.), where the lawyer unsuccessfully argued that he could use the former client's information because "the government had fully exposed and *made publicly available* all the [former client's] files and records" in the prior litigation. *Id.* at 268 (emphasis added).

In *Jamaica Public Service Co. Ltd. v. AIU Insurance Company*, 92 N.Y.2d 631, 707 N.E.2d 414, 684 N.Y.S.2d 459 (1998), the N.Y. Court of Appeals held, first, that the law firm's prior representation of the client was not substantially related to the current matter. In that context, the court then went on to hold that a narrow category of information — the identities of the prior client's subsidiaries — was generally known, because it was "readily available in such public materials as trade periodicals and filings with State and Federal regulators." *Id.* at 417, 462, 637–638. Presumably, it is also material to the decision that the information had already been made available to the trade and to the public by the client itself.

[104] Another term for screening is "Chinese Wall," a term that was coined by *supporters* of the practice because it suggests impregnability. Unfortunately, the phrase has on occasion been misperceived as a slur, and it therefore will not be used here. Occasionally, you will also see the phrase "cone of silence" to express the same idea.

consented). That is, neither the migrating lawyer nor any of her new partners would be permitted to oppose the former client in the same matter.[105]

Screening would allow the plaintiff's firm — even over the defendant's objections — to continue in the case. It consists of assurances by the plaintiff's firm to the defendant that the migrating lawyer will not have access to files of the case, will not communicate with lawyers who are handling the case, and will not share directly in fees from the case. Those who support screening do so despite tradition and the obvious jeopardy to client confidences, because they want to increase lawyers' job mobility. The practice therefore mocks the claim that the law is a profession and not a business.

Screening was not a significant issue until the mid-1970s, and then only with regard to lawyers moving from government service to private law firms. Until that time, when a lawyer left the government to join a private firm, two things followed. First, the lawyer was disqualified from opposing the government in any matter in which the lawyer had been personally and substantially involved on behalf of the government. Second, the lawyer's new firm was similarly disqualified through imputed disqualification. As the result of an intensive effort by large law firms in Washington, D.C., and New York, for whom the government/private-practice revolving door was a way of professional life, imputed disqualification was effectively eliminated by allowing screening of the former government lawyer from involvement in the case.[106]

In the ensuing years, there has been a significant increase in movement of lawyers between law firms. Again, the large law firms find it in their interest to use screening to avoid disqualification because of conflicts of interest caused by migrating lawyers. The Model Code does not allow screening in any cases. The New York Code[107] and the Model Rules[108] do allow screening, but only in cases involving former government lawyers, and not when lawyers move between private firms.[109]

---

[105] *See, e.g.,* MR 1.9(a) and MR 1.10(a); N.Y. Code, DR 5-108(a)(1) and 5-105(d).

[106] Ironically, the principal argument that was made at that time was that screening was necessary — but only in the government-to-private-firm situation — to encourage "the best" lawyers to serve in the government (for brief periods, of course). This argument has been conveniently forgotten now that the debate has shifted to lawyers who migrate between private firms. For a general discussion of the history of this debate, *see* MONROE H. FREEDMAN, UNDERSTANDING LAWYERS' ETHICS 205–211 (1st ed., 1990).

[107] DR 9-101(b). *See also Kassis v. Teacher's Insurance and Annuity Ass'n,* 93 N.Y.2d 611, 717 N.W.2d 674 (1999) (Where lawyer had played "an appreciable role" as counsel for plaintiff, defendants' conclusory averments that lawyer had not acquired confidences during the prior representation "failed to rebut that presumption as a matter of law," and erection of a screen was, therefore, "inconsequential.") *Id.,* 93 N.Y.2d at 618–619, 717 N.E.2d at 678–679.

[108] MR 1.11(a).

[109] The Restatement has a very limited screening provision for avoiding imputed disqualification when a lawyer moves from one private firm to another. The provision is odd because it is so limited that it is unlikely ever to be used — not, at least, according to its terms. As stated in The Professional Lawyer, "the Restatement recognizes screening only in situations where it is not really needed." Robert A Creamer, *Screening Plays in Peoria,* 10 THE PROF. LAWYER 1 (1999).

Section 124 permits screening of the lawyer who moves from one firm to another, but only where any confidential information communicated to the personally prohibited lawyer is "unlikely to be significant in the subsequent matter." § 124(2)(a). This is illustrated by a case in which "a junior lawyer in a law firm [provided] minimal assistance on a peripheral element of a transaction, thereby gaining little confidential information that would be relevant in the later matter." *Id.,*

In order to understand the problems raised by screening, consider a typical case. Attorney is with firm A&B and is heavily involved in representing Plaintiff. In the middle of the litigation, Attorney switches to firm Y&Z, which is representing Defendant in the same case. As noted earlier, the traditional rule of ethics has been that both Attorney and firm Y&Z are disqualified from representing Defendant in that case. As we have seen, the rule relies on presumptions that are based upon common sense and the practicalities of proof.

The first presumption is that Attorney learned confidences from Plaintiff while serving as its lawyer. This presumption is justified in part by Attorney's ethical obligation to learn everything that might be relevant to Plaintiff's case. Moreover, the presumption that Attorney learned confidences from Plaintiff avoids making Plaintiff reveal its confidences in order to protect them.

The second presumption is that Attorney, having switched sides, might use Plaintiff's confidences on behalf of Defendant. This presumption is based in part on the fact that Attorney, if he were permitted to represent Defendant, would be ethically required to be loyal to Defendant, to act zealously on its behalf, and to communicate to Defendant all information material to the representation. Thus, the traditional rule of disqualification recognizes that Plaintiff could reasonably believe that its confidences were being betrayed, and the rule respects this legitimate client concern.

The imputed disqualification of firm Y&Z is also based upon common sense and practicalities of proof. Even if Attorney is not personally representing Defendant at his new firm, there is a reasonable possibility that Attorney, having switched allegiances, might disclose Plaintiff's confidences to his new partners. As observed in the *Harvard Law Review*, Attorney's new colleagues have a "significant incentive" to elicit the confidences, and Attorney has a similar incentive to prove his allegiance to his new firm by cooperating.[110] Thus, there is a "distinctive danger" that Attorney will reveal Plaintiff's confidences to Defendant's lawyers.[111] Moreover, such violations would be virtually impossible to police. It is extremely unlikely that Plaintiff would ever be able to discover and prove a brief conversation in someone's office, or during a private dinner, or in a phone call to Attorney's home.[112]

In short, the traditional presumption underlying disqualification in such cases is based upon a high level of temptation, a low level of visibility, and

---

Cmt. *d(i)*. Also, the "lawyer or law firm seeking to remove imputation has the burden of persuasion that there is no substantial risk that confidential information of the former client will be used with material adverse effect on the former client." *Id.*

[110] *See Developments in the Law — Conflicts of Interest in the Legal Profession*, 94 HARV. L. REV. 1244, 1361 (1981).

[111] *Id.*

[112] "The experience of any attorney who has represented clients teaches that extremely confidential matters which are privileged may be communicated in a conversation of less than a few minutes, irrespective of whether . . . billable time is generated." *Carbo Ceramics, Inc. v. Norton-Alcoa Proppants*, 155 F.R.D. 158 (1994).

a near-impossible burden if Plaintiff were required to prove a specific breach of its confidences.[113]

Of course, Plaintiff might consent to Attorney's representation of Defendant, or might consent to Y&Z's continued representation of Defendant with the understanding that Attorney would not be involved in that representation. Plaintiff might be willing to consent, for example, in order to avoid delaying the case. And if Plaintiff does consent, there is no need for disqualification. But what if Plaintiff, understandably, refuses to consent? As noted earlier, the answer under both the Model Rules and the Model Code is that the firm is disqualified.

Allowing Y&Z to erect a screen would defeat that result. That is, the lawyers at Y&Z would write to Plaintiff saying that Attorney will not work on the case or talk about it with the lawyers who represent Defendant. Nothing else would change. The temptations to violate Plaintiff's confidences would be just as high, violations would still be virtually impossible to police, and Plaintiff would still be under an impractical burden to uncover and to prove a violation.

Supporters of screening contend that objections to screening reflect skepticism, even cynicism, about lawyers' ethics. That may be. There is, sad to say, some skepticism in that regard among members of the public. Indeed, a major purpose of the conflict of interest rules is to allay that skepticism, and an unpoliceable assurance of screening by a law firm is not likely to achieve that goal. As noted in a recent federal case:[114]

> In an age of sagging public confidence in our legal system, maintaining confidence in that system and in the legal profession is of the utmost importance. In this regard, courts should be reluctant to sacrifice the interests of clients and former clients for the perceived business interests of lawyers.

Another contention by supporters of screening is that violations of screening have not been reported in those few jurisdictions that permit it, or in cases of former government lawyers. But, again, a major part of the problem is that violations of screening are so unlikely to be revealed. We cannot really expect lawyers to admit that they were subject to screening but nevertheless violated client confidences.[115]

---

[113] In the words of Professor Charles W. Wolfram:

In the end, there is little but the self-serving assurance of the screening-lawyer foxes that they will carefully guard the screened-lawyer chickens. Whether the screen is breached will be virtually impossible to ascertain from outside the firm. On the inside, lawyers whose interests would all be served by creating leaks in the screen and not revealing the leaks would not regularly be chosen as guardians by anyone truly interested in assuring that leaks do not occur.

C.W. WOLFRAM, MODERN LEGAL ETHICS, § 7.6.4, at 402 (1986).

[114] *Roberts & Schaefer Co. v. San-Con, Inc.*, 898 F.Supp. 356, 363 (U.S.D.C., W.V. 1995).

[115] The ABA's Ethics — 2000 Commission recommended adoption of screening, on the reasoning that it had "heard no evidence to suggest that [the] objections [to screening] have a factual basis." 87 A.B.A.J. 61 (May, 2001). In response, Professor Andrew L. Kaufman wrote, incredulously: "Did the Commission really expect firms to confess to negligence or worse, with loss of business and lawsuits to follow? Really?" Andrew L. Kaufman, *Ethics 2000 — Some Heretical Thoughts*, THE PROFESSIONAL LAWYER 1, 2 (Symposium Issue, 2001).

The Commission's proposal for screening was defeated in the ABA House of Delegates in August, 2001.

Nevertheless, such cases have on occasion come to light. In one case, a client, Maritrans, learned that the law firm that had been representing it in labor negotiations, Pepper, Hamilton & Scheetz, had begun to represent four of its competitors.[116] Pepper, Hamilton & Scheetz is an old and reputable Philadelphia firm. The law firm had obtained highly sensitive client information from Maritrans that would be extremely valuable to its competitors.[117] When Maritrans objected to the law firm's representation of its competitors, the law firm proposed that the lawyers in the firm who represented Maritrans would be screened off from those who were representing the competitors; the law firm also proposed that it would limit its representation of Maritrans' competitors to the four companies that the firm already represented.[118] Maritrans agreed to this proposal primarily because it did not want the law firm to represent any additional competitors, and especially not Bouchard.[119]

The law firm then broke its word in two ways. First, it violated the screen by passing information from the lawyers who represented Maritrans to the lawyers representing the competitors.[120] Second, the law firm "parked" Bouchard and a sixth competitor with another labor lawyer. The other lawyer was then working at a different law firm, but was negotiating to join Pepper, Hamilton & Scheetz, and soon after, he did so, bringing Bouchard and the other competitor with him.[121] In the meantime, Pepper, Hamilton "for all intents and purposes, was representing Bouchard" as well as the five other competitors.[122]

The law firm's scheme in the *Maritrans* case came to light because of two unusual circumstances. First, three months after Pepper, Hamilton & Scheetz promised Maritrans that it would not represent Bouchard, the law firm terminated its representation of Maritrans. Second, the lawyer with whom Bouchard had been parked joined Pepper, Hamilton, and he brought Bouchard with him as a client. These facts alerted Maritrans and led to a law suit against Pepper, Hamilton & Scheetz, in which discovery uncovered the law firm's deceitful conduct.[123]

Another case, with an issue analogous to screening, provides additional compelling evidence that assurances of confidentiality — again, at a large, prestigious law firm — are less than reliable.[124]

Procter & Gamble sued Bankers Trust Company, alleging in an amended complaint that Bankers Trust is a racketeer-controlled organization. The court issued a protective order, sealing the amended complaint, in order to protect Bankers Trust's reputation while the matter was being adjudicated. Bankers Trust was represented by Sullivan & Cromwell. The law firm is more than

---

[116] *Maritrans GP Inc. v. Pepper, Hamilton & Scheetz*, 529 Pa. 241, 602 A.2d 1277 (1992).

[117] *Id.*, 529 Pa. at 247–248, 250, 602 A.2d at 1280, 1281.

[118] *Id.*, 529 Pa. at 249, 602 A.2d at 1281.

[119] *Id.*

[120] *Id.*, 529 Pa. at 251, 602 A.2d at 1282.

[121] *Id.*, 529 Pa. at 249, 602 A.2d at 1281.

[122] *Id.*

[123] *Id.*

[124] The account here is based on John Morris, *How Could Anyone Lose This Case?*, AMERICAN LAWYER, Nov. 1995.

a century old and widely respected. Sullivan & Cromwell has strict rules and established procedures about safeguarding confidential documents. Nevertheless, when a *Business Week* reporter, Linda Himelstein, telephoned a Sullivan & Cromwell partner and asked for a copy of the sealed complaint, he sent it to her by messenger the same day.

The partner is Steven Holley. He had not worked on the Bankers Trust case, and he did not know that the amended complaint was under seal. In response to Himelstein's request, Holley simply asked an associate for a copy, and the associate gave it to him, without asking why Holley wanted it and without telling him about the court's order sealing it. The amended complaint was not kept in a secure place, nor was the copy stamped on its face that it was under seal. Nor did Holley follow Sullivan & Cromwell policy by checking first with the partner in charge of the case before giving the complaint to Himelstein.

It gets even worse. Himelstein testified that she had learned the following day that the complaint had been sealed and that she immediately called Holley to tell him. Under oath, Holley several times denied the call (which explained why he had failed for a week thereafter to tell his partners what he had done). In fact, he testified, at the time Himelstein said she had called him, he had not been at his office, but at home. Then, on cross-examination, Holley was impeached with telephone records showing a telephone call from Himelstein to his home that day.[125]

The way Sullivan & Cromwell dealt with a highly sensitive document has to give pause to anyone who considers screening to be an ethical and practical way to avoid conflicts of interest. But the analogy isn't perfect. In fact, the case of Sullivan & Cromwell and Bankers Trust is even more compelling than the usual screening case in showing the fallibility of law firms in protecting sensitive documents. First, Sullivan & Cromwell had requested that the complaint be sealed in order to protect its own client. Second, Sullivan & Cromwell hadn't simply given assurances to an adversary, it had been ordered by a court to maintain confidentiality; thus, the law firm was subject to contempt of court and to sanctions for releasing the document. Third, giving the sealed complaint to a reporter was guaranteed to alert the world that there had been a leak somewhere.

Moreover, the disputed testimony about the telephone call to Holley's home underscores the difficulties of proving a breach of confidentiality. In the Sullivan & Cromwell case, Himelstein had no incentive to go along with Holley's false denial of their telephone conversation. In the typical screening case, by contrast, both parties to any conversation about a former client's confidences will have an incentive to cover it up.

Another illustration of the unreliability of screens is the case of the New Hampshire Supreme Court.[126] Judges who are disqualified from participation

---

[125] Holley next came up with the unlikely surmise that his answering machine had picked up the call and that the message had then somehow been erased.

[126] David E. Rovella, *Ethics Scandal Swamps N.H. Supreme Court*, NAT'L L. JOUR., p. 1, April 17, 2000; Sandra J. Holien, *I have to sit this case out, but hey, guys, can we talk?*, NAT'L L. JOUR., p. A7, May 1, 2000; Carey Goldberg, *New Hampshire's House Impeaches Chief Justice*, N.Y. TIMES, July 13, 2000; Carey Goldberg, *Humbling Days for Top New Hampshire Court*, N.Y. TIMES, p. A24, Sept. 24, 2000; *Chief Justice Admonished*, N.Y. TIMES, p. A10, April 21, 2001 (reporting that

in a case are not supposed to participate in deciding the matter in any way. In effect, they are screened from the case. Ordinarily, we can expect, or hope, that judges will not tolerate violations of screens by their colleagues, if only because there are usually not the same financial incentives as there are in private practice. Nevertheless, a clerk of court revealed that the chief judge had been allowing colleagues to participate in cases in which they had been disqualified, and even, in one case, to control an important decision.[127] During an impeachment investigation, the chief judge then lied repeatedly when questioned about the screening violations.[128]

The final irony is that proponents of screening have relied on the experience of the major accounting firms. As Professors Rhode and Hazard have put it, "The approach developed in accounting firms of 'insulation walls' to segregate employees with conflicts of interest has . . . gained support in the legal profession as well."[129] That is, it has been suggested that law firms emulate the screening mechanisms used by accounting firms.

Accounting firms, like Arthur Anderson, have divisions that are set up to provide the public with objective audits of their client companies, like Enron. At the same time, the accounting firms have divisions that sell lucrative consulting services to those same companies. It is important to keep those functions separate, of course, so that the accuracy of the audits won't be influenced by the desire to sell the consulting services. Thus the use of insulation walls, or screening, by the accounting firms. The scandal relating to Arthur Anderson's audits of Enron is only one of too many illustrations of how those accounting-firm screens have failed to function.

Similar scandals have implicated major Wall Street brokerage firms, like Merrill Lynch, which have bypassed screens to commit massive frauds on investors. The brokerage firms purport to provide objective research, analysis, and recommendations about stocks to investors. They also sell investment banking services to companies whose stocks are being researched. These two functions have been screened from each other.

As has recently been revealed, however, the brokerage firms have been violating the screens, using unjustifiably favorable ratings of the stock of their investment banking customers as a marketing tool to sell banking services. As reported in the *New York Times*, Merrill emails revealed "negotiations between the firm's bankers and their corporate clients over what a stock's

---

Chief Justice David Brock had been impeached by the N. H. House, but then acquitted in the State Senate on the ground that he had suffered enough in the impeachment; he was then admonished by the Judicial Discipline Committee for "serious violations," including lying during the impeachment investigation.).

[127] Again, the circumstances that led to exposure of the practice were unusual. The chief judge had told the clerk to appoint a particular judge to preside over the disqualified judge's divorce litigation. Then, at the behest of the disqualified judge, the chief judge had countermanded that order. It was then that the clerk felt compelled to reveal what had happened. Carey Goldberg, *Clerk Challenges System, and Finds That It Works*, N.Y. TIMES, Oct. 15, 2000.

[128] Carey Goldberg, *Humbling Days for Top New Hampshire Court*, N.Y. TIMES, p. A24, Sept. 24, 2000, at A24.

[129] DEBORAH L. RHODE & GEOFFREY C. HAZARD, PROFESSIONAL RESPONSIBILITY AND REGULATION 125 (2002).

rating by the supposedly independent analysts should be."[130] In short, the supposed screen separating Merrill's researchers from its bankers was "more like Swiss cheese."[131]

It appears, therefore, that the skeptics have some significant justification for their concerns about the efficacy of screening.

At the time of this writing, screening in cases of lawyers moving from one firm to another is permitted by ethics rules or court decision in only a small minority of jurisdictions. In August, 2001, the ABA House of Delegates rejected a proposal of the Ethics 2000 Commission to amend the Model Rules to allow screening. However, the issue is not likely to die there.

---

[130] Editorial, *Disinformation on Wall Street*, N.Y. TIMES, April 11, 2002, at A32.
[131] *Id.*

Chapter 11

PROSECUTORS' ETHICS[1]

§ 11.01 INTRODUCTION

Special ethical rules are appropriate for prosecutors because the role of the prosecutor is significantly different from that of other lawyers. In the words of Justice Felix Frankfurter, the prosecutor "wields the most terrible instruments of government."[2] This "formidable"[3] power of the prosecutor includes discretion to initiate and direct investigations, to decide whether to prosecute, to designate the crimes to be charged, to affect the punishment, and to accept or reject a plea of guilty to a lesser offense. In the words of a former United States Attorney, "The power to investigate and prosecute is the power to destroy."[4]

In the course of exercising this extraordinary discretion over the lives of other citizens, the prosecutor frequently makes decisions that no other lawyer has the power to make. Moreover, even when attorneys for private clients do participate in similar kinds of decisions, they are required to abide by their clients wishes.[5] To say that a prosecutor is subject to special ethical rules

---

[1] The treatment of prosecutors' ethics in this chapter is necessarily selective. For a broader coverage, *see* BENNETT L. GERSHMAN, PROSECUTORIAL MISCONDUCT (1985). For an examination of the ethics of prosecution generally, *see* Abbe Smith, *Can a Good Person Be a Good Prosecutor?*, 14 GEO. J. LEGAL ETHICS 335 (2001). For a sample of influential or especially thoughtful articles on prosecutors' ethics, *see* Albert Alschuler, "Courtroom Misconduct by Prosecutors and Trial Judges," 50 TEX L. REV. 629 (1972); Albert W. Alschuler, *The Prosecutor's Role in Plea Bargaining*, 36 U. CHI. L. REV. 50 (1968-69); Stanley Z. Fisher, *In Search of the Virtuous Prosecutor*, 15 AM. J. CRIM. LAW 197 (1988); Bennett L. Gershman, *The New Prosecutors*, 5 U. PITT. L. REV. 393 (1992) (discussing the growing power and diminishing accountability of prosecutors); Bruce Green, *Why Should Prosecutors Seek Justice?*, 26 FORDHAM URB. L.J. 607 (1999); James Vorenberg, *Decent Restraint of Prosecutorial Power*, 94 HARV. L. REV. 1521 (1981); Ellen Yaroshefsky, *Cooperating with Federal Prosecutors: Experiences of Truth Telling and Embellishment*, 68 FORD. L. REV. 917 (1999).

There are references in this chapter to the AMERICAN LAWYER'S CODE OF CONDUCT, which was sponsored by the Roscoe Pound/American Trial Lawyers Foundation (1980), and to the DISTRICT OF COLUMBIA RULES OF PROFESSIONAL CONDUCT (1990). Freedman was the Reporter for the AMERICAN LAWYER'S CODE. He was also a member of the Jordan Commission, which thoroughly rewrote the MODEL RULES FOR THE DISTRICT OF COLUMBIA in the mid-1970s, and a member of its Subcommittee on Prosecutors' Ethics, which recommended the additional provisions that were adopted as part of MR 3.8 in the District of Columbia.

[2] *See* Letter to The New York Times, Mar. 4, 1941, *quoted*, *Martin v. Merola*, 532 F.2d 191, 196 (2d Cir. 1976) (Lumbard, J. concurring); *see also* *McNabb v. United States*, 318 U.S. 332, 343 (1943) (Justice Frankfurter referring to the "awful instruments of the criminal law").

[3] ABA STANDARDS RELATING TO THE ADMINISTRATION OF JUSTICE: THE PROSECUTION FUNCTION, INTRODUCTION (3d ed. 1993).

[4] Joseph E. diGenova, *Investigated to Death*, N.Y. TIMES, Dec. 5, 1995.

[5] For example, "[a] lawyer shall abide by a client's decision whether to accept an offer of settlement of a matter." MR 1.2(a). Specifically, in a criminal case, a defense attorney must "abide by the client's decision . . . as to a plea . . . ." *Id. See also*, DR 7-101(A)(1); EC 7-7 and 7-8.

relating to the exercise of prosecutorial discretion, therefore, is simply to recognize that the prosecutor is the lawyer who has that discretion to exercise.[6]

Also, as we have seen, the defense lawyer's professional responsibilities are determined in large part by her client's constitutional and related rights, which protect the dignity of the individual in a free society. These rights include the effective assistance of counsel, the presumption of innocence, the privilege against self-incrimination, and confidentiality between lawyer and client. The prosecutor, who does not represent a private client,[7] is not affected by these considerations in the same way. On the contrary, prosecutors are ethically obligated to assure that the rights of their adversaries are protected.[8]

For example, the defense attorney is entitled, and may be professionally bound, to withhold material evidence; defense counsel may advise a guilty defendant to remain silent and put the government to its proof. The Constitution guarantees the defendant nothing less.[9] The prosecutor, however, is not similarly entitled to withhold material evidence. Indeed, she is forbidden to do so.[10]

Similarly, a defense lawyer can ethically cross-examine a prosecution witness to make the witness appear to be inaccurate or untruthful, even though the lawyer knows that the witness is testifying accurately and truthfully.[11] Even some of the strongest proponents of the view that counsel should never mislead the court agree with that conclusion.[12] They reach that result on the reasoning that the defense is entitled to "put the government to its proof,"[13] and to "test the truth of the prosecution's case,"[14] whereas we base the same conclusion on the necessities of the lawyer-client relationship of trust and confidence. None of those rationales, however, would justify a prosecutor in making a defense witness appear to be testifying inaccurately

---

[6] *See* RESTATEMENT THIRD OF THE LAW GOVERNING LAWYERS § 97, Cmt. *h* (2000): "Unlike lawyers in private practice, a government lawyer with power to file and conduct criminal or civil proceedings against citizens is subject to special limitations in doing so."

[7] *See* H. Richard Uviller, *The Neutral Prosecutor: The Obligation of Dispassion in a Passionate Pursuit*, 68 FORD. L. REV. 11695 (2000): "The prosecutor doesn't have a client; he has a constituency . . . . Free of client control, [prosecutors] have the luxury and burden of developing the standards for the exercise of public authority."

[8] *See* ABA, PROSECUTION FUNCTION, *supra* note 3, at 3–3.1, Comment: "Prosecutors, as representatives of the people in upholding the law, should take the lead in assuring that investigations of criminal activities are conducted in accordance with the safeguards of the Bill of Rights . . . . "; RESTATEMENT § 97, Cmt. *h* ("Lawyers empowered by law to bring and press criminal charges have an authority that must be exercised with care to protect the rights of both the innocent and the guilty."

[9] U.S. CONST., Amend. V.

[10] *Brady v. Maryland*, 373 U.S. 83, 83 S.Ct. 1194 (1963); *United States v. Agurs*, 427 U.S. 97 (1976); *United States v. Bagley*, 105 S.Ct. 3375 (1985); Model Code DR 7-103(B); Model Rules 3.8(d).

[11] *See* Chapter 8, *supra*.

[12] *See, e.g.*, Warren E. Burger, *Standards of Conduct for Prosecution and Defense Personnel: A Judge's Viewpoint*, 5 AMER. CRIM. L.Q. 11, 14–15 (1966).

[13] David G. Bress, "Professional Ethics in Criminal Trials: A View of Defense Counsel's Responsibility," 64 MICH. L. REV. 1493, 1494 (1966).

[14] Burger, *supra* note 12.

or untruthfully when the prosecutor knows that the witness is testifying accurately and truthfully. The defendant, who is presumed innocent, does not have a burden of proof to be tested, nor does the prosecutor have a lawyer-client relationship or client confidences to maintain when conducting a trial.

In addition, the prosecutor represents the majesty of our government. Conduct that is tolerable on the part of a private person may be intolerable when done under color of law, on behalf of the United States or a state. As the Supreme Court has held:

> The United States Attorney is the representative not of an ordinary party to a controversy, but of a sovereignty whose obligation to govern impartially is as compelling as its obligation to govern at all; and whose interest, therefore, in a criminal prosecution is not that it shall win a case, but that justice shall be done. As such, he is in a peculiar and very definite sense the servant of the law, the twofold aim of which is that guilt shall not escape nor innocence suffer.[15]

Because the prosecutor speaks and acts on behalf of the sovereign, she must do so with due regard to the majesty of her office.

In recognition of the distinctive role of the prosecutor, the American Bar Association and the Association of American Law Schools, in their Joint Conference Report on Professional Responsibility, concluded that "[t]he public prosecutor cannot take as a guide for the conduct of his office the standards of an attorney appearing on the behalf of an individual client. The freedom elsewhere wisely granted to partisan advocacy must be severely curtailed if the prosecutor's duties are to be properly discharged."[16] This is not to say that the prosecutor's ethical standards are "higher," but only that they are different as a result of the prosecutor's distinctive role in the administration of justice.

The ABA has recognized the differing roles of prosecutor and defense lawyer by adopting a separate set of standards for each in the Standards for Criminal Justice. As noted in The Prosecution Function Standards, the prosecutor's role has been described as "quasi-judicial":

> Although the prosecutor operates within the adversary system, it is fundamental that the prosecutor's obligation is to protect the innocent as to convict the guilty, to guard the rights of the accused as well as to enforce the rights of the public. Thus, the prosecutor has sometimes been described as a "minister of justice" or as occupying a quasi-judicial position.[17]

The Model Code also recognizes that the responsibility of the prosecutor "differs from that of the usual advocate; his duty is to seek justice, not merely to convict."[18] The Model Rules similarly state that the prosecutor "has the responsibility of a minister of justice and not simply that of an advocate."[19]

---

[15] *Berger v. United States*, 295 U.S. 78, 88 (1935).

[16] ABA-AALS, JOINT CONFERENCE REPORT ON PROFESSIONAL RESPONSIBILITY (1958).

[17] ABA, PROSECUTION FUNCTION, *supra* note 3, at 3-1.1; *see also id.* at 3-1.2 (prosecutors must "seek justice [and] not merely convict").

[18] EC 7-13.

[19] MR 3.8, Comment.

This responsibility carries with it "specific obligations to see that the defendant is accorded procedural justice."[20]

As we will see, however, the ABA's Model Code, Model Rules, the Prosecution Function Standards, and the American Law Institute's Restatement Third of the Law Governing Lawyers, all fail to establish rules of ethical conduct that are adequate to the special role that they so clearly recognize.[21]

§ 11.02 ENEMIES LISTS AND SELECTIVE PROSECUTION

The first major issue of prosecutorial discretion is the decision to investigate. Justice Robert Jackson (who had been Attorney General of the United States) called that "the most dangerous power of the prosecutor," because it enables the prosecutor to "pick people he thinks he should get rather than pick cases that need to be prosecuted."[22] Irving Younger, reflecting on his own experience as a prosecutor, similarly observed that "[a] prosecutor's power to damage or destroy anyone he chooses to indict is virtually limitless."[23] Bennett Gershman, another former prosecutor who is one of the most thoughtful commentators on prosecutors' ethics, noted that "[t]he prosecutor's decision to institute criminal charges is the broadest and least regulated power in American criminal law."[24]

When a prosecutor focuses on a person, Jackson said, it is "not a question of discovering the commission of a crime and then looking for the man who has committed it, it is a question of picking the man and then searching the law books or putting investigators to work, to pin some offense on him." At that point, law enforcement "becomes personal, and the real crime becomes that of being unpopular with the predominant or governing group, being attached to the wrong political views, or being personally obnoxious to or in the way of the prosecutor himself."[25]

Jackson went on to observe that, with the law books filled with a great assortment of crimes, a prosecutor has a good chance of pinning at least a technical violation on almost anyone. The Justice's concern, therefore, was with the prosecutor's improper motive in targeting someone; the prosecutor's subsequent success in obtaining a conviction does not justify the improper targeting.

This kind of "selective prosecution" is illustrated by *Yick Wo v. Hopkins*.[26] In *Yick Wo*, a San Francisco ordinance made it unlawful for any person to

---

[20] *Id.*

[21] The rules that apply specifically to prosecutors are DR 7-103, EC 7-13, and 7-14 of the Model Code, MR 3.8 of the Model Rules, and § 97 of the RESTATEMENT.

[22] Justice Robert Jackson, Address, Second Annual Conference of U.S. Attorneys, April, 1940.

[23] Irving Younger, *Memoir of a Prosecutor*, 62 COMMENTARY, Oct. 1976, at 66.

[24] Bennett L. Gershman, *A Moral Standard for the Prosecutor's Exercise of the Charging Discretion*, 20 FORD. URB. L. J. 513, 513 (1993); *see also* Vorenberg, *supra* note 1, at 1523 (noting prosecutors' "essentially unreviewable discretion").

[25] Robert Jackson, Address, Second Annual Conference of U.S. Attorneys, April, 1940. The other side of the same problem is, of course, the abuse of prosecutorial discretion to *favor* someone for personal, political, or other improper motives.

[26] 118 U.S. 356, 6 S.Ct. 1064 (1886).

maintain a laundry in a wooden building without getting a license from the Board of Supervisors. Yick Wo was convicted of violating the ordinance and imprisoned for not paying the fine. The record in the case showed that virtually all applications for licenses that had been filed by Chinese had been denied, and that virtually all licenses requested by non-Chinese had been granted. Thus, the prosecutions of Yick Wo and others were founded in discriminatory treatment based upon racist motives.

The Supreme Court held that "[t]hough the law itself be fair on its face and impartial in appearance, yet, if it is applied and administered by public authority with an evil eye and an unequal hand, so as practically to make unjust and illegal discriminations between persons in similar circumstances, material to their rights, the denial of equal justice is still within the prohibition of the Constitution." Even though Yick Wo had in fact committed the offense, the prosecution was wrongful because it had been motivated by a discriminatory purpose.

Another illustration of Jackson's point is President Richard Nixon's Enemies List, compiled by John Dean, for the purpose of getting or, in Dean's word, "screwing" those who had displeased Nixon in some way.[27] Another example is a similar list circulated among the United States Attorneys' offices when Robert Kennedy was Attorney General. The Kennedy Enemies List included Jimmy Hoffa and Roy Cohn, both of whom had earned Kennedy's enmity in years past. In addition, there was a Get-Hoffa Squad (it was actually called that) in the Department of Justice,[28] and Irving Younger, then a young Assistant United States Attorney, was directed to spare no expense to find grounds for prosecuting Roy Cohn.[29]

§ 11.03 THE ENEMIES LIST UNDER THE ETHICAL RULES

Justice Jackson's concern with selective prosecutions, therefore, was not fanciful. How, then, do the Model Code and the Model Rules deal with that critical issue? The answer is: Not at all. Neither of the ABA's ethical codes even addresses the problem of a prosecutor targeting people for investigation

---

[27] Shortly before the exposure of Nixon's Enemies List, Professor Alexander M. Bickel defended such practices. He wrote that it was "unexceptional" for a prosecutor to target members of dissident political groups in an effort to "get" them, as long as the prosecutor ultimately succeeded in developing a "plausible" case, even though the case proved to be "quite flimsy." Alexander M. Bickel, *Judging the Chicago Trial*, COMMENTARY 31, 36, 37, 39 (Jan. 1971). As Jackson pointed out, this would justify selective prosecution of virtually anyone, for the worst of motives, because a determined prosecutor can make a plausible case for some offense against almost anyone.

[28] During Robert Kennedy's tenure as Attorney General, there were more prosecutions against Hoffa than there were civil rights prosecutions in the state of Mississippi, and more prosecutions against officers of Hoffa's Teamsters Union than there were civil rights prosecutions in the entire country. In view of the fact that Kennedy was said to have had a "commitment" to civil rights, his devotion to putting Hoffa in jail bordered on obsession. The first product of that extraordinary diversion of government resources was a two-month trial of Hoffa on a misdemeanor charge. *See* VICTOR NAVASKY, KENNEDY JUSTICE, Chapter 9 (1971).

[29] Younger, *Memoir of a Prosecutor*, *supra* note 23, at 66. Younger's account has been challenged by Robert M. Morgenthau and others. *Id.*, vol. 63, no. 1, p. 4 (Jan. 1977). Roy Cohn was in fact prosecuted three times, each time unsuccessfully.

and prosecution on the basis of an Enemies' List. This is particularly ironic with regard to the Model Rules, because the Rules were often said to be a response to the criticisms directed against lawyers (like Richard Nixon and John Dean) who had been implicated in the Watergate scandal. By contrast, the American Lawyer's Code of Conduct (1980), Rule 9.1, provides:

> A lawyer serving as public prosecutor shall not seek evidence to support a prosecution against a particular individual unless that individual is identified as a suspect in the course of a good faith investigation into suspected criminal conduct.

There has, however, been some progress in this area. The American Lawyer's Code of Conduct also provides, in Rule 9.2, that "[i]n exercising discretion to investigate or to prosecute, a lawyer serving as public prosecutor shall not show favoritism for, or invidiously discriminate against, one person among others similarly situated." This led to Rule 3.8(a) in the District of Columbia Rules of Professional Conduct: "The prosecutor in a criminal case shall not: (a) in exercising discretion to investigate or to prosecute, improperly favor or invidiously discriminate against any person." Also, the third edition of the ABA's Prosecution Function Standards (1993) includes Std. 3-3.1(b):

> It is unprofessional conduct for a prosecutor to invidiously discriminate against or in favor of any person on the basis of race, religion, sex, sexual preference, or ethnicity in exercising discretion to investigate or to prosecute. A prosecutor should not use other improper considerations in exercising such discretion.

There is a growing recognition, therefore, that targeting someone for selective prosecution constitutes unethical prosecutorial conduct.

Unfortunately, the Restatement appears to go in the opposite direction. The Restatement not only ignores the problem of selective prosecution, it seems to condone political partisanship as a basis for prosecutor decision-making. Explaining a government lawyer's "powers of decision," the Restatement says that a government lawyer "is empowered to take partisan political considerations into account to the extent consistent with the objectives and responsibilities of the governmental client."[30]

§ 11.04 THE POWER TO INDICT

The next important issue of prosecutorial discretion relates to whether to charge someone with a crime and, if so, which crime.[31]

---

[30] § 97, Cmt. *g*. The breadth of this statement seems to be contradicted by other language in the comment: "Courts have stressed that a lawyer representing a governmental client must seek to advance the public interest in the representation and not merely the partisan or personal interests of the government entity or officer involved." *Id*., Cmt. *f*. However, that limitation is in turn contradicted in the next sentence in the comment: "In many instances, the factor is stressed for hortatory rather than definitional purposes." *Id*.

[31] If the charge is made by a grand jury, the action, technically, is not the prosecutor's. As a matter of practical fact, however, the grand jury is the instrument of the prosecutor, and it is the rare grand jury that fails to follow the prosecutor's lead (thus, the expression, "runaway grand jury"). As it is sometimes said, a prosecutor could get a grand jury to indict Abel for the murder of Cain.

To be formally charged with a crime is, in itself, a punishing experience. The defendant's reputation is immediately damaged, frequently irreparably, regardless of an ultimate acquittal.[32] Anguish and anxiety become a daily presence for the defendant and for the defendant's family and friends. The emotional strains of the criminal process have been known to destroy marriages and to cause alienation or emotional disturbance among the accused's children. Also, the financial burden can be enormous. A criminal charge may well result in loss of employment because of absenteeism due to pretrial detention, attendance at hearings and the trial, or simply because the accused has been named as a criminal defendant.[33] The trial itself, building up to the terrible anxiety during jury deliberations, is a harrowing experience.[34]

The prosecutor sets these events into motion simply by exercising the awesome discretionary power to have a fellow citizen charged with a crime. Expressing the idea that the government seeks justice, not convictions, it is said that the government wins its point even when a not-guilty verdict is returned. That is also true in a less idealistic, more cynical, sense: the prosecution wins even when the defendant is found innocent because, typically, the defendant will carry for life the severe wounds of his encounter with justice. In the words of one former federal prosecutor, "[t]he power to indict is the power to destroy."[35]

---

[32] A notorious example of the damage that can be done by a mere accusation — with or without the formal imprimatur of an indictment — is the FBI's targeting of security guard Richard Jewell as the prime suspect in the 1996 Olympics bombing in Atlanta, Georgia. Jewell, who was never formally charged, but who became a social pariah by public condemnation, endured months of intense law enforcement and media scrutiny before it was determined that he was innocent. *See* Kevin Sack, *A Man's Life Turned Inside Out By Government and the Media*, N.Y. TIMES, Oct. 28, 1996, at A1 (discussing the Richard Jewell case, which "provides a fresh object lesson about the immense power of the Federal government to disrupt the lives of those it only suspects of misdeeds, even with the thinnest of evidence . . . . ").

In another notorious case, in 2000, American nuclear scientist Wen Ho Lee was falsely accused of being a spy for China. Dr. Lee faced a multiple-count felony indictment, and prosecutors announced that his traitorous acts "could truly change the world's strategic balance" and had put millions at risk of nuclear annihilation. He ultimately pleaded to a single misdemeanor and was freed from jail. *See* Joseph E. Persico, *Life Under Suspicion*, N.Y. TIMES BOOK REVIEW, Feb. 17, 2002, at 9; Robert Scheer, *No Defense: How the* New York Times *Convicted Wen Ho Lee*, THE NATION, Oct. 23, 2000, at 11 (examining the Wen Ho Lee case, and arguing that the New York Times and other media were as blameworthy as the government in pursuing Lee).

[33] Consider also the conditions under which an accused can be held for up to two full days, before being found guilty of any offense, while waiting for arraignment:

> There are no mattresses, no bedding, no clean clothing and no showers. The toilets, where there are toilets at all, are open bowls along the walls and often encrusted and overflowing. . . . [continued]
>
> . . . Some [prisoners] were threatened by other prisoners. Others were chained to people who were vomiting and stinking of the streets. With few phone privileges, many felt as if they were lost in a hellish labyrinth far from the lives they had been plucked from.

William Glaberson, *Where Fear and Filth Meet: The Nightmare of New York's Holding Pens*, N.Y. TIMES, Mar. 23, 1990, at A1.

[34] See Justice Lewis Powell's opinion for the majority of the Supreme Court in *Gerstein v. Pugh*, 420 U.S. 103, 114, 95 S.Ct. 854, 863 (1975).

[35] Carl H. Lowenson, *The Decision to Indict*, 24 LITIGATION 13 (1997).

Recognizing that truth, conscientious prosecutors do not put the destructive engine of the criminal process into motion unless they are satisfied beyond a reasonable doubt that the accused is guilty. In a thoughtful and candid exploration of the exercise of prosecutorial discretion, Professor John Kaplan observed that the "first and most basic standard" is that, "regardless of the strength of the case," a prosecutor who does not "actually believe" that the accused is guilty does not feel justified in prosecuting. In Kaplan's experience as a prosecutor, the attitude "was more than a mere question of prosecutorial policy." The "great majority, if not all" of the Assistant United States Attorneys took the position that it was "morally wrong" to initiate a prosecution unless one was "personally convinced" of guilt.[36]

A different point of view has been expressed by Professor Richard Uviller, who suggests the following case.[37]

An elderly white man is suddenly grabbed from behind in a dimly-lit vestibule by a black youth who shows a knife and takes the victim's wallet. The entire incident takes thirty seconds. Some days later, the victim sees someone in the neighborhood whom he believes to have been the assailant and has him arrested. Although the prosecutor presses him hard, the victim swears he has picked the right man. There is nothing unusual about the defendant's appearance, the victim never saw him except during those few moments of terror in a dim light, and the victim admits that he does not know many black people. However, he remains certain because, he says, his attacker's face was "indelibly engraved on [his] memory." The defendant has an alibi: his mother will testify that at the time of the crime he was at home watching television with her.

As Uviller acknowledges, reasonable doubt will be "clear" to the prosecutor. Uviller also recognizes, however, that juries "regularly convict in such cases."[38] Nevertheless, he suggests that the prosecutor can properly, and perhaps even should, go forward in such a case.[39] Athough Uviller concedes that the prosecutor should not proceed when there is a "substantial likelihood" of innocence, or when there is "good reason to believe" that a prosecution witness is lying about a material fact, he goes so far as to say that when the issue "stands in equipoise" in the prosecutor's mind, there is "no flaw" in the conduct of the prosecutor who puts the accused to the burden of a criminal prosecution.

---

[36] John Kaplan, The Prosecutorial Discretion — A Comment," 60 Nw. L. Rev. 174, 178–79 (1965). Kaplan noted some deviation from that standard in some special cases. *See also* Lowenson, *supra* note 35, at 14:

> . . . [A]ny prosecutor who indicts based solely on probable cause — perhaps in the hope that the defendant will plead guilty or that more evidence will turn up by trial — exhibits a woeful disregard for the rights of the accused, the purposes of the criminal justice system, the limited resources of the prosecutor's office, and probably the prosecutor's own career. Probable cause may be enough to obtain an arrest warrant on a complaint or to justify a search warrant, but is not sufficient to justify an indictment.

[37] H. Richard Uviller, *The Virtuous Prosecutor in Search of an Ethical Standard: Guidance from the ABA*, 71 Mich. L. Rev. 1145, 1157–59 ((1973).

[38] *Id.* On the fallibility of eye witness identification, *see* Ch. 7, *supra*; Daniel L. Schacter, The Seven Sins of Memory (2001); Elizabeth F. Loftus & James M. Doyle, Eyewitness Testimony (1997) (examining problems associated with eyewitness identification and demonstrating that the certainty of an identification has no relationship to its accuracy).

[39] *Id.*

Uviller's principal justification for this view is that the prosecutor should not preempt the function of the judge and jury in doubtful cases. If we follow his scenario to its likely conclusion, however, that rationale does not hold up. This is what will happen in almost every case of the kind he describes.

The charge in the case of the mugging at knifepoint will be armed robbery, which may carry a penalty ranging from thirty years to life in prison. The defendant will insist that he is innocent; however, his lawyer will explain to the young man that if he goes to trial on a charge involving the use of a weapon, and he is convicted, he may not get out of prison until he is a very old man. The defendant will protest, of course, that conviction is impossible, because he is innocent and because his mother will confirm that he was at home. The defense lawyer will know, as well as Uviller and the prosecutors do, however, that "juries regularly convict in such cases," and the lawyer will have to tell that to the defendant.

The defendant will also learn that his lawyer will try to negotiate a plea of guilty to assault with intent to rob. The maximum penalty for that offense may be fifteen years, but if the defendant saves the government the expense of a trial, the judge may be lenient and give him only three to nine years in prison. If the defendant is extremely lucky, he will be permitted to plead guilty to simple assault, for which the maximum penalty is only one year of his freedom, and he might actually be out of jail in a matter of months. Regardless of the sentence, the young man will be burdened for life with a criminal record. Although the defendant is innocent, that presents no problem with the bargained plea. The law, in its even-handed majesty, permits the innocent as well as the guilty to plead guilty in order to avoid the coercive threat of extended imprisonment.[40]

Thus, although Uviller rationalizes his conclusion on the ground that the prosecutor should not preempt the function of the judge and jury, the fact is that in the majority of cases that is precisely what will happen, through plea bargaining, in the kind of case that he suggests.

---

[40] *North Carolina v. Alford*, 400 U.S. 25, 91 S.Ct. 160 (1970). The prosecutorial practice of offering a lenient plea in a case where the government's case is weak and where there is a strong claim of innocence raises serious ethical questions. *See* Smith, *Can You Be a Good Person and a Good Prosecutor, supra* note 1, at 391 (recounting a case in which a prosecutor offered to recommend probation when confronted with compelling evidence that someone other than the accused was the perpetrator of felony child abuse).

Also raising serious ethical questions is the practice of coercing a plea by binding one accused to another with the threat of a harsher sentence if either accused exercises the right to trial. For example, New York criminal defense lawyer David Stern represented a woman who was charged with drug offenses carrying a minimum sentence of fifteen years to life. The woman's husband was charged with the same crime. The evidence against the husband was overwhelming, but the woman had a good chance of an acquittal and may well have been innocent. However, the prosecutor's position was that if the woman went to trial, he would not allow her husband to plead guilty to a lesser charge and thereby obtain a reduced sentence. Complicating things further, the couple had a two-year-old daughter. In the end, the woman decided to plead guilty rather than make a choice that could deprive her child of her father forever. Still, her plea deprived her child of both parents for some years. *See* Abbe Smith, *Defending the Innocent*, 32 CONN. L. REV. 485, 494 n. 58 (2000); Bruce Green, *"Package" Plea Bargaining and the Prosecutor's Duty of Good Faith*, 25 CRIM. L. BULL. 507 (1989) (urging prosecutors to exercise restraint when offering "packaged" pleas).

Uviller's response to that analysis presents an even more serious ethical problem. A guilty plea will probably not result in the case we are discussing, he says, because guilty pleas are "far more likely to come in cases where the state's case . . . is strong."[41] The case at issue is strong, however, in the sense that there is a likelihood of conviction; as Uviller acknowledges, juries regularly convict in such cases. What he seems to mean, therefore, is that the case is not "strong" in the sense that the prosecutor recognizes the significant possibility that the defendant is innocent.

Thus, his point is that the prosecutor should reject a guilty plea in such a case — thereby compelling the defendant to proceed to trial, to a probable conviction, and to an extended prison term. In short, the defendant who the prosecutor thinks may well be innocent is deprived of the benefits of the plea bargain that would be made available to the defendant who is clearly guilty.

In major part because of the unacceptable consequences of Uviller's position, we agree with those prosecutors who will not go forward unless they are satisfied beyond a reasonable doubt that the accused is guilty. Beyond that, we believe that a prosecutor should be professionally disciplined for proceeding with a prosecution if a fair-minded person could not reasonably conclude, on the facts known to the prosecutor, that the accused is guilty beyond a reasonable doubt.

A variation on this position was adopted by Justice Byron R. White, with the concurrence of retired Chief Justice Warren E. Burger and present Chief Justice William Rehnquist. "Unless prosecutors are incompetent in their judgments," Justice White wrote, "the standards by which they decide whether to charge a capital felony will be the same as those by which the jury will decide the questions of guilt and sentence."[42] That is, a prosecutor's failure to use a beyond-a-reasonable-doubt standard in exercising charging discretion constitutes unethical conduct on the prosecutor's part.[43]

§ 11.05   THE POWER TO INDICT UNDER THE ETHICAL RULES

There is a problem, however, with imposing a beyond-a-reasonable-doubt standard as an ethical requirement with threat of disciplinary action. Prosecutors have pointed out that every time there is an acquittal, it could (and perhaps would) be contended that the prosecutor acted unethically in proceeding with the case. In addition, judges might be reluctant to grant judgments of acquittal because of the implication that the prosecutor acted unethically in proceeding to trial. Although the conscientious prosecutor should use a standard of beyond a reasonable doubt, a disciplinary rule to that effect might well be undesirable.

---

[41] H. Richard Uviller, *Prosecutorial Discretion: Another View of Ethics*, 172(76) N.Y.L. J. 4 (1974).

[42] *Gregg v. Georgia*, 428 U.S. 153, 225 (1976) (White, J., concurring).

[43] *See* MR 1.1 ("Competence"); DR 6-101 ("Failing to Act Competently"). Although the justices were referring to a capital case, the standard for the conscientious prosecutor should be no different in any criminal case.

Reflecting these concerns, the National District Attorneys Association in its National Prosecution Standards, adopted the significantly lower standard that a prosecutor "shall file only those charges which he reasonably believes can be substantiated by admissible evidence at trial."[44] That is, the prosecutor cannot ethically go forward unless he believes he can make a prima facie case against the accused. (A prima facie case is one that is sufficient to make out the offense charged and survive a motion for judgment of acquittal at the close of the government's case.)

The standard set by the ABA's Model Code, Model Rules, and Prosecution Function Standards, and the ALI's Restatement all fall short even of the prima facie evidence standard adopted by the National District Attorneys Association. The Model Code does say that "in our system of criminal justice the accused is to be given the benefit of all reasonable doubts."[45] Contrary to that promise, however, the Model Code and the Model Rules both say only that the prosecutor shall not institute criminal charges when he knows that the charges are "not supported by probable cause."[46]

Probable cause, of course, may be satisfied by less than a substantial likelihood of guilt, and may be based upon evidence that would be inadmissible in court. The ABA standard appears to mean that the prosecutor can ethically go forward under the Model Code and the Model Rules regardless of whether he personally believes that the accused is guilty, and even though he knows that there is insufficient evidence against the accused to survive a motion for judgment of acquittal at the close of the government's case.

The ABA's Prosecution Function Standards are not much better. Standard 3.9(a) uses the NDAA's prima facie evidence test only as an aspirational guide (by using the phrase "should not"), but adopts the lesser probable cause standard as its disciplinary rule (by using the phrase "unprofessional conduct"). Likewise, the Restatement does not go beyond the probable cause standard.[47]

Thus, the American Bar Association and the American Law Institute have consistently permitted the prosecutor to institute charges on a lesser discretionary standard than the National District Attorneys Association considers appropriate as a minimal ethical standard.[48] The best that can be said for

---

[44] NDAA, NATIONAL PROSECUTION STANDARDS, Std. 43.3 (2d ed., 1991).

The Introduction to the NDAA's STANDARDS declares that "[t]hese standards are quite literally the voice of prosecution present and future. (At 7).

[45] EC 7-13.

[46] DR 7-103(A); MR 3.8(a). The Model Code includes the phrase "or it is obvious" after the word "knows."

[47] At first glance, the language in § 97(3) looks promising. In filing criminal proceedings, a prosecutor must base his decision on "probable cause and *the lawyer's belief, formed after due investigation, that there are good factual and legal grounds to support the step taken.*" (Emphasis added). In the corresponding Comment, however, the drafters make plain that there is no "substantive difference" between § 97(3) and the "traditional standard . . . [of] probable cause." *Id.*, Comment *h*.

[48] The CALIFORNIA UNIFORM CRIME CHARGING STANDARDS (1974) provides: "The prosecutor should charge only if the prosecutor has considered the probability of conviction by an objective fact-finder hearing the admissible evidence." *Quoted in* John Jay Douglass, *Charging Crime in England and America*, The Prosecutor 27, 30 (Summer, 1992).

the codifications of the ABA and ALI, therefore, is that they do not preclude a conscientious prosecutor from declining to go forward unless she is personally satisfied beyond a reasonable doubt that the accused is guilty.

§ 11.06 CONFLICTS OF INTEREST AND SPECIAL PROSECUTORS

Freedman once wrote that Jimmy Hoffa was a marked man from the day he stuck his finger under Bobby Kennedy's nose and told him that he was nothing but a rich man's kid who never had to earn a nickel in his life. Freedman added that when Kennedy became Attorney General, satisfying that grudge became the public policy of the United States of America. [49]

Professor Richard Uviller replied: "[I]f Robert Kennedy as Attorney General was convinced that the Teamsters Union and Hoffa in particular was destructive to trade unionism and a powerful, dangerous, and gangster-ridden force in the economy of the nation, would not his pursuit of Hoffa seem more ethical than if . . . Kennedy resolved to imprison Hoffa in revenge for a trivial personal insult . . . ?" [50] There is obvious merit in Uviller's response. Motive is, of course, a primary consideration in making judgments regarding the ethical quality of conduct, and it is possible (although, in our view, highly unlikely) that Robert Kennedy was indifferent to Hoffa's insult.

Nevertheless, a resolution of the ethical problem raised by the Kennedy-Hoffa problem lies elsewhere. We are concerned here with the attorney as public official, wielding enormous governmental powers, and responsible for assuring not only that justice be done but that it appear to be done. It does not matter, therefore, whether Freedman is right in believing that Kennedy was bent upon satisfying a personal grudge, or whether Uviller is right in suggesting a worthier motive. Rather, both the possibility and the appearance that Kennedy's professional judgment might have been affected by a personal interest created a conflict of interest that required Kennedy to abstain from any direct or indirect role in Justice Department actions against Hoffa. [51]

Prosecutors are, of course, subject to the same ethical rules as other lawyers, [52] including rules dealing with conflicts of interest. Specifically, the

---

The CODE FOR CROWN PROSECUTORS in England provides: "The Crown prosecutor service does not support the proposition that a bare prima facie case is enough but rather will apply the test of whether there is a realistic prospect of a conviction." *Id.*

The DISTRICT OF COLUMBIA RULES OF PROFESSIONAL CONDUCT (1990) takes an intermediate position. Under Rule 3.8(b), the prosecutor shall not "file in court or maintain a charge that the prosecutor knows is not supported by probable cause." Under 3.8(c), however, the prosecutor shall not "prosecute to trial a charge that the prosecutor knows is not supported by evidence sufficient to establish a prima facie showing of guilt."

[49] *See* note 28, *supra. See also* Bruce Fein, *Time to Rein in the Prosecution*, ABA JOUR. 96 (July, 1994) (agreeing that the "Get Hoffa Squad" in Kennedy's Justice Department was the result of Kennedy's "personal vendetta" against Hoffa).

[50] Uviller, *The Virtuous Prosecutor in Quest of an Ethical Standard, supra* note 37, at 1152.

[51] *See* Chapter 10, *supra.*

[52] ABA, PROSECUTION FUNCTION STANDARDS, 3-1.2(e). "Like other lawyers, the prosecutor is subject to disciplinary sanctions for conduct prohibited by applicable codes of professional conduct in his or her jurisdiction." *Id.*, Cmt.

ABA's Prosecution Function Std. 3-1.3(f) says that a prosecutor "should not permit his or her professional judgment or obligations to be affected by his or her own political, financial, business, property, or personal interests." Moreover, the NDAA's National Prosecution Standards explicitly recognize that when the prosecutor has a conflict of interest, "it is his responsibility to seek a special prosecutor."[53] Under NDAA Std. 7.4d, "[i]n those jurisdictions where the prosecutor does not have authority to appoint a special prosecutor, he may petition the court to assign a special prosecutor . . . . "[54]

§ 11.07   POLICE MISCONDUCT AND THE PROSECUTOR'S DUTY

The prosecutor must maintain a close working relationship with the police.[55] The prosecutor's job may be extremely onerous if he does not have the willing cooperation of the police, both in investigating cases and in presenting evidence in court. As a consequence, the prosecutor may be under considerable pressure to ignore or to cover up police misconduct, such as perjury, unlawful arrests, unlawful searches and seizures, unlawful interrogation, and brutality.

Irving Younger, a former prosecutor, observed, for example, that "[e]very lawyer who practices in the criminal courts knows that police perjury is commonplace."[56] Another former prosecutor, Professor Richard Uviller, has confirmed that "every lawyer" who is aware of perjurious testimony by police officers includes prosecutors.[57] Even when police perjury is clear, however, the offending officer is "as likely to be indicted by his co-worker, the prosecutor, as he is to be struck down by thunderbolts from an avenging heaven."[58] Moreover, the clear implication of what every prosecutor knows about police

---

[53] NDAA Std. 7.4 ("The Special Prosecutor"), Cmt., at 25.

[54] NDAA Std. 7.4d.

[55] *See* ABA, PROSECUTION FUNCTION STANDARDS, COMMENT TO STD. 3-2.8.

[56] Irving Younger, *The Perjury Routine*, 3 CRIM. L. BULL. 551 (1967). For legal scholarship on the routine nature of police perjury, *see, e.g.*, Morgan Cloud, *The Dirty Little Secret*, 43 EMORY L.J. 1311 (1994); Stanley Z. Fisher, *"Just the Facts, Ma'am": Lying and the Omission of Exculpatory Evidence in Police Reports*, 28 NEW ENG. L. REV. 1 (1993); Myron W. Orfield, Jr., *Deterrence, Perjury, and the Heater Factor: An Exclusionary Rule in the Chicago Criminal Courts*, 63 U. COLO. L. REV. 75, 83 (1992). For reports by blue ribbon commissions from three major cities documenting widespread police misconduct, including perjury, *see* COMMISSION REPORT OF THE CITY OF NEW YORK COMMISSION TO INVESTIGATE ALLEGATIONS OF POLICE CORRUPTION AND THE ANTI-CORRUPTION PROCEDURES OF THE POLICE DEPARTMENT (1994) (Mollen Commission Report); REPORT OF THE BOSTON POLICE DEPARTMENT MANAGEMENT REVIEW COMMISSION (1992) (St. Clair Commission Report); REPORT OF THE INDEPENDENT COMMISSION ON THE LOS ANGELES POLICE DEPARTMENT (1991) (Christopher Commission Report). As the Mollen Commission Report states:

> Police perjury and falsification of official records is a serious problem facing the . . . criminal justice system — largely because it is often a 'tangled web' that officers weave to cover for other underlying acts of corruption or wrongdoing. . . . [T]he practice of police falsification in connection with . . . arrests [for drugs and guns] is so common in certain precincts that it has spawned its own word: 'testilying.' "

Supra, at section 4, p. 36.

[57] Uviller, *The Virtuous Prosecutor in Search of an Ethical Standard*, *supra* note 37, at 1158.

[58] Younger, *The Perjury Routine*, *supra* note 56, at 551.

perjury is that prosecutors are knowingly presenting police perjury to obtain convictions.[59]

In addition, prosecutors have sometimes gone so far as to cover up police crimes. For example, some years ago in our nation's capital, two black men were stopped, interrogated, and searched for no apparent reason other than that they were walking with a white woman. They disputed the propriety of the arrest and, as a result, were charged with disorderly conduct.[60] The police officers attempted to justify the initial arrest by swearing under oath that the men corresponded to a description of two burglars that had been broadcast over the squad-car radio that evening. The police log book revealed, however, that no such burglary had taken place, and no such description had been broadcast.

The prosecutor made strenuous efforts to prevent defense counsel from examining the log book, which indicates that the prosecutor was aware of the perjury and was attempting to prevent its exposure. A police trial board subsequently found the officers guilty of unlawful arrest and perjury. (It subjected them only to small fines, however, rather than to dismissal from the force.) Despite demands of civic organizations, the United States Attorney for the District of Columbia failed to prosecute the officers. No disciplinary action was ever taken against the prosecutor for attempting to cover up the police officers' perjury at the trial of the two men.

In a more recent civil action, a jury found that five police officers had shot at two men, beaten them, causing concussions, broken ribs, and other injuries, and had then charged the men with attempted murder, all without justification.[61] The jurors subsequently told *The New York Times* that they had been "shaken" by the testimony. One commented that "[t]he officers didn't show remorse [and] quite frankly, they scared us."[62] Despite the extreme facts and the impact of the case on the civil jury, the District Attorney professed to have been unable to satisfy a grand jury that there was probable cause to indict the officers.[63]

Two recent cases (one arguably more clear-cut than the other) demonstrate the continuing problem of race-based police brutality. In the 1996 Abner Louima case, a white New York City police officer, allegedly aided by others, sexually assaulted a Haitian immigrant with a broom handle in a precinct bathroom as revenge for the mistaken belief that Louima had punched him in a brawl outside a nightclub.[64] In the 1999 Amadou Diallo case, four white New York City police officers killed an unarmed West African immigrant, shooting him dozens of times outside his apartment.[65] The criminal trial in

---

[59] *See* Model Code DR 7-102(A)(4); Model Rules R. 3.3(a)(4).

[60] *District of Columbia v. Mills*, Crim. No. D.C. 3135–64 (D.C. Ct. Gen. Sess., Jan. 22, 1965).

[61] Craig Wolf, *Jury Awards Two Men $76 Million in Police Brutality Case*, N.Y. TIMES, Mar. 8, 1990, at B1.

[62] *Id.*

[63] *Id.* at B6. *See* n. 31, *supra*.

[64] *See* Abbe Smith, *Defending Defending: The Case for Unmitigated Zeal on Behalf of People Who Do Terrible Things*, 28 HOFSTRA L. REV. 925 (1999).

[65] *See* Kevin Flynn, *Police Killing Draws National Notice*, N.Y. TIMES, Feb. 8, 1999 at B5.

the Louima case resulted in a mid-trial guilty plea and a thirty year sentence for the chief perpetrator. The civil case resulted in a nine million dollar settlement. The prosecution of the officers in the Diallo case — in which the accused testified that they had believed Diallo had pulled a gun, fired their own guns in self-defense, and felt genuine remorse about Diallo's death — resulted in an acquittal.

Conscientious prosecutors are sensitive to race and poverty issues, and the longstanding police practice of abusing those with little power. Conscientious prosecutors ought not be complicit when police try to cover up their misdeeds. They should be skeptical of implausible police accounts relating to the use of force, and mindful of the police strategy of charging victims of brutality with disorderly conduct, resisting arrest, or assaulting a police officer. They should also prosecute the officers who commit these crimes and who reveal them by making patently false charges against their victims.[66]

§ 11.08 POLICE MISCONDUCT AND RELEASE-DISMISSAL AGREEMENTS

In order to protect police officers or private security guards from civil actions for tortious conduct, some prosecutors will condition a *nolle prosequi* or other alternative disposition on the defendant's release of civil claims. In one case, the prosecutor admitted in court that the prosecution had been reinstituted, after having been dropped, solely because the defendant had made a complaint against the arresting police officer:

> [T]hree months later he comes in and makes a formal complaint. So we said, "if you are going to play ball like that why shouldn't we proceed with our case?" . . . *I had no reason to file until he changed back* on his understanding of what we had all agreed on. *That is done in many criminal cases.*[67]

On appeal, the United States Court of Appeals for the District of Columbia Circuit reversed the conviction, holding that the prosecutor had committed a "gross abuse of discretion."[68] Other courts have similarly reversed convictions or have refused to enforce release-dismissal agreements on grounds of public policy.[69]

---

[66] In the alternative, as discussed *supra*, § 11.06, the prosecutor should recognize that he has a conflict of interest because of his working relationship with the police, and have a special prosecutor appointed.

[67] *District of Columbia v. Dixon*, Nos. 4071, 4072 (D.C. Ct. App., June 13, 1967) (emphasis added).

[68] *Dixon v. District of Columbia*, 394 F.2d 966 (D.C. Cir., 1968). The prosecutor's conduct was criminal as well as unethical:

> Whoever . . . threatens to accuse any person of a crime . . . with intent . . . to compel the person accused or threatened to do or to refrain from doing any act, and whoever with such intent publishes any such accusation against another person shall be imprisoned for not more than five years or be fined not more than one thousand dollars, or both. 22 D.C. Code 2305 (1961).

[69] *See, e.g., MacDonald v. Musick*, 425 F.2d 373 (9th Cir.), *cert. denied*, 400 U.S. 852 (1970); *Boyd v. Adams*, 513 F.2d 83 (7th Cir., 1975).

As explained by Justice Sandra Day O'Connor, the central problem with such agreements is that "public criminal justice interests are explicitly traded against the private financial interest of the individuals involved in the arrest and prosecution."[70] Justice O'Connor noted further that the risk and expense of a criminal trial "can easily intimidate even an innocent person whose civil and constitutional rights have been violated."[71] Accordingly, she added, the coercive power of criminal process "may be twisted to serve the end of suppressing complaints against official abuse, to the detriment not only of the victim of such abuse, but also of society as a whole."[72]

Nevertheless, the Supreme Court held in that case, *Town of Newton v. Rumery*, that an agreement by an accused to release a civil rights action under 42 U.S.C. § 1983 in exchange for dismissal of criminal charges is not *per se* invalid.[73] The Court noted, however, that when a prosecutor either brings unwarranted charges or dismisses meritorious charges to protect the interests of other officials, that conduct "properly [has] been recognized as unethical."[74]

§ 11.09   RELEASE-DISMISSAL AGREEMENTS AND THE PROSECUTOR'S DUTY UNDER THE RULES OF ETHICS

In referring to the ethics of release-dismissal agreements in *Rumery*, the Supreme Court cited DR 7-105 of the Model Code. This rule forbids every lawyer from presenting or threatening to present criminal charges solely to obtain an advantage in a civil matter. The release-dismissal agreement appears to be the most extreme form of doing that.[75] Unfortunately, there is no parallel to DR 7-105 in either the Model Rules, the ABA Prosecution Function Standards,[76] or the Restatement. However, the National District

---

[70] *Town of Newton v. Rumery*, 480 U.S. 386, 401, 107 S.Ct. 1187, 1196 (1987) (O'Connor, J., concurring).

[71] *Id.* at 400.

[72] *Id.* at 400.

[73] *Town of Newton v. Rumery*, 107 S.Ct. 187 (1987). The Court held that the agreement was enforceable under the facts in that case. Rumery's decision was found to have been voluntary because (1) he was a sophisticated businessman; (2) he was represented by an experienced defense lawyer; (3) the lawyer drafted the release agreement; (4) the lawyer spent about an hour explaining the release to Rumery, and (5) Rumery then considered it for three days before deciding to sign it.

In addition, the case was a "particularly sensitive" one, because the witness against Rumery was the victim of an alleged aggravated sexual assault. Thus, the prosecutor was motivated by an "independent, legitimate reason" — a desire to avoid the trauma to the victim of a sexual assault of having to testify in either a criminal or a civil case. *Id.* at 395, 390.

Further, four members of the Court favored a "strong presumption" against the enforceability of such releases, and a fifth concluded that the burden should be on the proponent of the release to prove that it is neither involuntary nor the product of an abuse of the criminal process. *Id.* at 418 (Stevens, J. dissenting) and 399 (O'Connor, J. concurring).

[74] *Id.* at 395, n.4, citing DR 7-105.

[75] There would be no violation of this rule on the facts in *Rumery*, because the prosecutor had an "independent, legitimate reason" for making the agreement. 408 U.S. at 399. *See* note 73, *supra*. Therefore, he did not act "solely" to obtain an advantage in the civil action against the police.

[76] In the District of Columbia, the Jordan Committee and the Bar's Board of Governors

Attorneys Association says flatly that the prosecutor "should not file charges for the purpose of obtaining from a defendant a release of potential civil claims against victims, witnesses, law enforcement agencies and their personnel, or the prosecutor and his personnel."[77]

As Justices Stevens and O'Connor recognize in their opinions in *Rumery*, the release-dismissal agreement implicates the prosecutor in a serious conflict of interest. Justice Stevens points out that the conflict is "obvious . . . between the prosecutor's duty to enforce the law and his objective of protecting members of the police department who are accused of unlawful conduct."[78]

As discussed earlier, conflicts of interest are forbidden not only by DR 5-101(A) and MR 1.7(b), but also by the ABA's Prosecution Function Standards, the Restatement, and the NDAA's National Prosecution Standards. Further, under both the Prosecution Function Standards and the National Prosecution Standards, the proper course for the prosecutor in cases of conflict of interest is to seek the appointment of a special prosecutor and withdraw from the case. These rules apply in any case in which there is a non-frivolous issue of police misconduct to be resolved, including those that might result in a release-dismissal agreement.

§ 11.10 TRIAL PUBLICITY BY PROSECUTORS[79]

As discussed above,[80] the First Amendment right to freedom of speech is never more important to an individual than when he or she is the accused in a criminal prosecution. In contrast to the defense lawyer, however, the prosecutor is not the spokesperson for a private citizen. Rather, the prosecutor acts under color of law as an agent of the government. In that official capacity, the prosecutor is privileged to publish to the world — including the defendant's family, friends, neighbors, and business associates — the most heinous and defamatory charges, in an indictment.

Despite this devastating impact on the life and the reputation of the accused, it is essential that indictments be open to public scrutiny; secret indictments are familiar weapons of tyrannous governments. In addition, in a particular case, a prosecutor may find a compelling law enforcement purpose justifying public announcements, such as to notify the public that the accused is at large and dangerous. Also, the prosecutor should be permitted to respond

---

recommended a *per se* rule forbidding a prosecutor to "condition a dismissal of charges, nolle prosequi, or similar action on the accused's relinquishment of the right to seek civil redress." However, the Court of Appeals deleted this provision. (In the Jordan Committee discussions, there was no objection to applying the *per se* rule to the release of rights against public officials. Strangely, the only objection was that the prosecutor should be free to protect private security guards through such agreements.) Nevertheless, the D.C. Rules do include a Rule 8.4(g), which adopts DR 7-105.

[77] NDAA, National Prosecution Standards, Std. 43.5.

[78] 480 U.S. at 412.

[79] For a fuller discussion of this issue, *see* Monroe H. Freedman & Janet Starwood, *Prior Restraints on Freedom of Expression by Defendants and Defense Attorneys: Ratio Decidendi v. Obiter Dictum*, 29 Stan. L. Rev. 607 (1977).

[80] *See* § 4.08.

publicly if the defense accuses the prosecutor of unlawful or unethical conduct in the case.

Beyond those limited situations, however, there is no legitimate reason for a prosecutor, as an agent of the government, to engage in pretrial publicity that heightens the public condemnation of the accused. Of course, the defendant can also, as a practical matter of fact, be deprived of a fair trial. Nevertheless, as we have seen, it is virtually impossible for a prosecutor to deprive a defendant of a *constitutionally* fair trial through pretrial publicity.[81] It makes little sense, therefore, to forbid a prosecutor to engage in pretrial publicity that impairs the defendant's constitutional right to a fair trial (although, as discussed below, conscientious prosecutors will not do so).

The serious problem that remains, however, and that can be addressed effectively in ethical rules, is that pretrial publicity by prosecutors condemning the accused can be a severe form of punishment without due process of law. Illustrative is the following statement that was made by a United States Attorney at a press conference that was called to announce an indictment:[82]

> Ladies and Gentlemen, I am very happy to be here and to be . . . part of something which I perceive to be probably the largest corruption, criminal investigation, probably in the history of the nation. It crosses city lines, it crosses state lines, it crosses federal lines. Also it has its tentacles in Puerto Rico and probably in Hawaii. . . . I suspect that the bottom line is that corruption or greed has no bias.

Thus, the clear thrust of the prosecutor's statement was that the defendants (who were identified by name) were not only guilty, but guilty of "the largest corruption . . . in the history of the nation."[83] The court found the prosecutor's statement to have been "egregious."[84]

Despite that finding, of course, the prosecutor's statement, along with other "massive publicity"[85] adverse to the defendants, did not constitute grounds for overturning the convictions in the case. The point here, however, is the manner in which the prosecutor inflicted severe punishment on the defendants — the modern equivalent of the pillory — before the defendants had even had their day in court. For example, after he was acquitted of criminal charges involving dishonesty, former U.S. Secretary of Labor Ray Donovan bitterly commented, "Now tell me where I can go to get my good name back."[86]

---

[81] *Id.*

[82] *United States v. Simon*, 664 F.Supp. 780, 794, n. 17 (1987). The same case illustrates a related area of prosecutorial abuse:

> [T]he history of this case points up what the court can only describe as a shameful abuse of grand jury secrecy. . . . Following Mr. Simon's indictment . . . there was massive publicity concerning the targets of the ongoing grand jury investigation, the allegations being presented before the grand jury, and in some instances the identities and testimony of witnesses before the grand jury. . . .

See also, Application of Dow Jones & Co., Inc., 842 F.2d 603, 605 (1988).

[83] The case was not Teapot Dome, Watergate, or Enron, but Wedtech — a name that is not likely to make the list of historic scandals.

[84] *Simon*, 664 F.Supp. at 794, n. 17.

[85] *Id.* at 792.

[86] *See, How Do I Repair Reputation? Donovan After his Trial*, CHI. TRIB., May 27, 1987, at C4.

Another case never did get to trial. Patricia Emory had been named as one of her county's five outstanding school principals. However, she was arrested and branded by prosecutors as "part of the largest marijuana operation in the history of [the county]," and a "member of the board of directors of a massive criminal enterprise." Ultimately, Ms. Emory was not indicted. However, the prosecutor effectively punished her without the need for a trial, and discouraged school officials from rehiring her, by announcing that "we didn't have sufficient evidence to convict and therefore we didn't request an indictment, *at least at this time.*"[87]

Recognizing the pernicious effect of pretrial publicity by prosecutors, as well as the fact that such publicity too frequently serves no legitimate prosecutorial purpose, the American Lawyer's Code of Conduct (1980) provides:

> 9.11. A lawyer in public service shall not engage in publicity regarding a criminal investigation or proceeding, or an administrative investigation or proceeding involving charges of wrongdoing, until after the announcement of a disposition of the case. However, the lawyer may publicize information that is (a) necessary to protect the public from an accused who is at large and reasonably believed to be dangerous; (b) necessary to help in apprehending a suspect; or (c) necessary to rebut publicized allegations of improper conduct on the part of the lawyer or the lawyer's staff.

A similar position was taken in 1989 by the Committee on Professional Responsibility of the Association of the Bar of the City of New York.[88] The Committee disapproved of press conferences by prosecutors where "the principal effect is to heighten public condemnation of the accused before a conviction has been fairly won in the courtroom."[89] The Committee added that it "can be unethical for a prosecutor to impose the penalty of public condemnation before trial."[90]

Conscientious prosecutors do not feel a need for pretrial publicity. For example, the Department of Justice has adopted guidelines forbidding release of information where no law enforcement function would be served.[91] The guidelines note further that particularly in the period approaching and during trial, statements to the press "ought strenuously to be avoided."[92] Also, when Second Circuit Chief Judge Jon O. Newman was United States Attorney for

---

[87] David A. Harris, *Loose Talk Prejudges Defendant*, NAT'L L.J., April 5, 1993, at 17. Consider also the case of the American nuclear scientist Wen Ho Lee. Dr. Lee was falsely accused in 2000 of being a spy for China, based partly on racial profiling. He faced a multiple-count felony indictment, and prosecutors announced that his traitorous acts "could truly change the world's strategic balance" and had put millions at risk of nuclear annihilation. He ultimately pleaded to a single misdemeanor and was freed from jail. *See* Joseph E. Persico, *Life Under Suspicion*, N.Y. TIMES BOOK REVIEW, Feb. 17, 2002, at 9 (reviewing DAN STOBER & IAN HOFFMAN, A CONVENIENT SPY (2002), and WEN HO LEE WITH HELEN ZIA, MY COUNTRY VERSUS ME (2002).

[88] Freedman was a member of the committee at the time.

[89] Letter from Meredith M. Brown, Chair, Comm. on Prof. Resp., Ass'n of the Bar of the City of N.Y., 44 Record 803 (Dec. 1989).

[90] *Id.*

[91] 28 C.F.R. § 50.2(b)(3)(iv) (1984), quoted in *Simon*, 664 F.Supp. at 795, n. 19.

[92] *Id.* § 50.2(b)(5).

the Connecticut District in 1964, he issued a memorandum forbidding prosecutors in his office to disclose to the press prospective evidence, statements of witnesses, reports of investigative agencies, and opinions regarding the guilt of the accused. Close questions were to be resolved against disclosure. "To put it simply," Judge Newman said, "if in doubt, keep silent."[93] Clearly, therefore, the relatively few prosecutors who glorify themselves by heightening the public condemnation of defendants are acting against, not pursuant to, acceptable standards of prosecutorial conduct.

§ 11.11   PRETRIAL PUBLICITY UNDER THE ETHICAL RULES

Until as recently as 1994, the ABA's ethical rules had it backwards. Under the double standard of both MR 3.6 and DR 7-107, the prosecutor was given broad scope to engage in pretrial publicity, while the defense lawyer was forbidden to speak even in response to a televised press conference by the prosecutor dramatically publicizing the charges in the indictment.[94] In recent years, however, the ABA in its rules, and the ALI in its Restatement, have gone a long way towards adopting the position urged in the American Lawyer's Code of Conduct and in the first edition of this book.[95]

The first significant change in the earlier rules was in the District of Columbia. Under the D.C. version of MR 3.6, lawyers generally are forbidden to communicate with the public only if doing so will create a "serious and imminent threat to the impartiality of the judge or jury."[96] At the same time, the Comment expressly recognizes that "litigants have a right to present their side of a dispute to the public, and the public has an interest in receiving information about matters that are in litigation." With specific reference to the attorney as the defendant's spokesperson to the public, the Comment continues: "Often a lawyer involved in the litigation is in the best position to assist in furthering these legitimate objectives."

Moreover, the D.C. pretrial publicity standard for prosecutors, Rule 3.8(f), speaks directly to the concerns expressed above. It expressly forbids the prosecutor from making extrajudicial comments that "heighten condemnation of the accused," except for statements that are "*necessary* to inform the public of the nature and extent of the prosecutor's action *and* which serve a legitimate law enforcement purpose."[97] Also, in contrast to the Model Code

---

[93] *Simon*, 664 F.Supp. at 796, n. 19, *citing* DONALD GILLMORE, FREE PRESS AND FAIR TRIAL 39–40 (1966).

[94] *See* MONROE H. FREEDMAN, UNDERSTANDING LAWYERS' ETHICS 232–235 (1st ed., 1990).

[95] *See also* Monroe H. Freedman & Janet Starwood, *Prior Restraints on Freedom of Expression by Defendants and Defense Attorneys*, 29 STAN. L. REV. 607 (1977).

[96] The D.C. Court of Appeals deleted a comment by the Bar that read: "[T]his Rule applies only to extrajudicial statements made after jury selection has begun." However, the relevant text was not changed, *i.e.*, the limitation applies only to "a case *being tried* to a judge or jury". Thus, it is not clear that the Court intended to change the Bar's desired meaning — that prior to the point at which jury selection has begun, and the case is "being tried," there are no restrictions on lawyers' speech about impending litigation.

[97] Emphasis added.

and Model Rules provisions allowing the prosecutor to publicize anything that she chooses to put into a public record, including the charges in the indictment, the comment to District of Columbia Rule 3.8(f) says that the prosecutor may "respond" to press inquiries "to clarify" such things as "technicalities of the indictment. . . ."[98]

In sum, the thrust of District of Columbia Rule 3.8(f) is that "a prosecutor should use special care to avoid publicity, such as through televised press conferences, which would unnecessarily heighten condemnation of the accused."[99]

As amended in 1994, the ABA's Model Rule 3.8(g) provides that a prosecutor shall "refrain from making extrajudicial comments that have a substantial likelihood of heightening public condemnation of the accused." The only exception in 3.8(g) is for statements that are "necessary to inform the public of the nature and extent of the prosecutor's action and that serve a legitimate law enforcement purpose."

A serious problem remains, however, because the prosecutor is still permitted, under MR 3.6(b)(2) to publicize "information contained in a public record," e.g., an indictment. In addition, under MR 3.6(b)(7)(i), the prosecutor is still permitted to publicize "the identity, residence, occupation and family status of the accused."

The improvement in this regard is that in the 1994 amendment, MR 3.6(c) permits a criminal defense lawyer (as well as a lawyer in a civil case) to "protect a client from the prejudicial effect of recent publicity not initiated by the lawyer or the lawyer's client." This corrects the former imbalance, under which the prosecutor could publicly condemn the accused, but the defense lawyer was forbidden to publicly respond.

In addition, as was pointed out in Chapter Four above, defense lawyers can also take advantage of the public-record exception, by filing motions in limine and other pretrial pleadings in which they (just as prosecutors have been doing for decades in indictments) can provide the basis for permissible pretrial publicity.

Even more encouraging is the position taken in Restatement § 109. Under § 109(2), the prosecutor must "refrain from making extrajudicial comments that have a substantial likelihood of heightening public condemnation of the accused." The only exception is for statements "*necessary* to inform the public of the nature and extent of the prosecutor's action *and* that serve a legitimate law-enforcement purpose." In addition, along with other lawyers, the prosecutor is forbidden under § 192(1) to make a public statement that will have a substantial likelihood of "materially prejudicing a juror or influencing or intimidating a prospective witness."

At the same time, the speech rights of defendants and their lawyers are recognized in § 192(1), which also provides that a lawyer "may in any event" make a public statement "to mitigate the impact on the lawyer's client of

---

[98] The Comment also properly permits the prosecutor to respond, "insofar as necessary, to any extrajudicial allegations by the defense of unprofessional or unlawful conduct on the part of the prosecutor's office."

[99] Comment to D.C. Rule 3.8(f).

substantial, undue, and prejudicial publicity recently initiated by one other than the lawyer or the lawyer's client."

§ 11.12   PROSECUTORS' RELIANCE ON QUESTIONABLE SCIENTIFIC EVIDENCE

Serious questions are being raised about the accuracy and reliability of certain kinds of forensic "science," such as the identification of illegal drugs,[100] hair and fibers,[101] blood and body fluids,[102] and DNA.[103] The techniques employed by most police laboratories do not begin to meet the standards and practices in high caliber medical or science laboratories. By and large, these laboratories are run not by educated, independent professionals, but by "law enforcement officers in lab coats."[104] It is impossible to estimate how many innocent people have been wrongly imprisoned or sentenced to death on the basis of shoddy and dishonest science.[105] The stories continue to unfold.

In May, 2001, Jeffrey Pierce was released from an Oklahoma prison after DNA tests proved that he had served fifteen years for a rape he did not commit. The prosecution's case had rested largely on testimony by Joyce Gilchrist, a supervisor in the Oklahoma City police laboratory, who linked Pierce to the crime through hair evidence.[106] Prosecutors continued to use Gilchrist notwithstanding criticism by judges and reputable forensic scientists.[107] Gilchrist assisted prosecutors in over 3000 cases for a period of thirteen years, and helped obtain convictions in twenty-three capital trials.[108]

In 1992, Glen Dale Woodall was released from a West Virginia prison after serving five years for a kidnap and rape he did not commit. He had been convicted of the crime largely because of expert testimony by Fred S. Zain,

---

[100] *See, e.g.*, Juan Forero, *Review of Police Lab Faults Chemists, Hindering Accreditation*, N.Y TIMES, Nov. 30, 1999, at B6 (reporting that six police chemists in New York employed inadequate procedures for identifying drugs). These same problems occur in police laboratories across the country.

[101] *See, e.g.*, Jim Yardley, *Inquiry Focuses on Scientist Employed by Prosecutors*, N.Y. TIMES, May 2, 2001, at A14 (reporting about discredited Oklahoma City police laboratory scientist Joyce Gilchrist, who often testifies about hair and carpet fibers).

[102] *See id*; *see also* Francis X. Clines, *Work by Expert Witness is Now on Trial*, N.Y. TIMES, Sept. 5, 2001, at A12 (reporting about the criminal prosecution of Fred S. Zain, a "serology specialist" who is alleged to have faked scores of test findings and engaged in other fraudulent conduct in hundreds of cases in a dozen states).

[103] *See, e.g.*, Gina Kolata, *Simpson Trial Shows Need for Proper Use of Forensic Science, Experts Say*, N.Y. TIMES, Oct. 11, 1995, at A20 (noting that DNA tests are being performed under poor conditions in many police laboratories).

[104] *Id.*

[105] David Johnston, *F.B.I. Chemist Says Experts Are Pressured to Skew Tests*, N.Y. TIMES, p. B4, Sept. 15, 1995 (The chemist accused officials at the agency's crime laboratory of "pressuring forensic experts to commit perjury or to skew tests to help secure convictions in hundreds of criminal cases."

[106] *See* Yardley, *supra* note 101.

[107] *See id.* (quoting Barry Scheck: " 'She has always been identified as a problem . . . . She had been criticized by her peers. It's a real failure of oversight by the district attorney's office.").

[108] As of 2001, eleven of those inmates had been executed. Twelve remain on death row. *See id.*

a crime laboratory expert who helped convict hundreds of defendants across a dozen states. Zain's testimony that Woodall's blood and body fluid matched the perpetrator was directly contradicted by a DNA test.[109]

In a 1992 rape trial in Chicago, police lab analyst Pamela Fish did not disclose exculpatory serological results, contributing to a wrongful conviction. The defendant was exonerated seven years later by DNA tests. New questions have been raised about Fish's conduct in other cases.[110]

Police and prosecutors persist in using the questionable testimony of demonstrably unreliable witnesses and in justifying the unsound techniques that lead to wrongful convictions.[111] They also persist in relying on "experts" who are often lazy, incompetent, or corrupt.[112] Using this kind of evidence at trial — or in order to obtain a plea — is contrary to the prosecutor's responsibility to do justice. As the Comment to Model Rule 3.8 states: "A prosecutor has the responsibility of a minister of justice and not simply that of an advocate. This responsibility carries with it specific obligations to see that the defendant is accorded procedural justice and that *guilt is decided upon the basis of sufficient evidence.*"[113] Clearly, unreliable or inaccurate evidence is not "sufficient" evidence, particularly when a human being's life or freedom is at issue. As the Ethics 2000 Commission Report said:

> As a minister of justice and not simply an advocate, the prosecutor has the obligation to see that both guilt and punishment are decided on the basis of sufficient evidence, including consideration of exculpatory and mitigating evidence known to the prosecution. This obligation goes beyond the duty imposed upon prosecutors by constitutional law. Evidence tending to negate the guilt of the accused includes evidence that materially tends to impeach a government witness."[114]

Conscientious prosecutors should not be relying on experts whom they know — or have reason to know — lack expertise. Conscientious prosecutors do not simply "put on the case," deferring to the factfinder, when there are "inadequacies or injustices" in the administration of justice.[115] Prosecutors who persist in using experts whose credentials or practices have been called

---

[109] *See* Clines, *supra* note 102.

[110] *See* Barry Scheck & Peter Neufeld, *Junk Science, Junk Evidence*, N.Y. TIMES, May 11, 2001, at A35.

[111] *See* Scheck & Neufeld, *supra* note 110.

[112] *See* Roberto Suro, *Ripples of a Pathologists Misconduct In Graves and Courts of West Texas*, N.Y. TIMES, p. 22, Nov. 22, 1992 at 22: Dr. Ralph R. Erdmann "left a trail of faked autopsies, botched blood samples and missing organs." The doctor testified as an expert in as many as twenty capital cases and dozens of others over a ten-year period. According to a special prosecutor, prosecutors continued using him as an expert despite "clear indications that a number of people in law enforcement considered him weird and questioned his competence because he regularly messed up evidence."

[113] Model Rules 3.8, Cmt. [emphasis added]; *see also* ABA The Prosecution Function, Std. 3-1.2(c) ("The duty of the prosecutor is to seek justice, not merely to convict").

[114] Ethics 2000 Commission Report, Rule 3.8, Comment [3].

[115] ABA PROSECUTION FUNCTION, Std. 3-1.2(d). As the Standards state: "It is an important function of the prosecutor to seek to reform and improve the administration of criminal justice. When inadequacies or injustices in the substantive or procedural law come to the prosecutor's attention, he or she should stimulate efforts for remedial action." *Id.*

into question have, at the very least, a duty to share this information with defense counsel.[116] Instead, too many prosecutors have simply turned a blind eye to highly dubious competence and honesty on the part of their experts — which is, of course, seriously unethical.[117] Moreover, prosecutors have also knowingly used, defended, and even strived to cover up such incompetence and dishonesty.

In New York, two state troopers were found to have falsified fingerprints and other evidence in dozens of cases.[118] One explained how he had used a photocopy machine to fabricate fingerprints. He said also that the county district attorney had been present when he had altered the date on a piece of fingerprint evidence.[119] Defense lawyers in the county observed that the prosecutors should have been alerted by the fact that so many fingerprints were being found in so many tough cases. The county district attorney did not deny the suspicious nature of the troopers' success, but responded, "in our relationship with the police, we have to trust the police."

In addition, prosecutors have sometimes resisted the use of reliable scientific evidence in order to maintain wrongful convictions. In one recent case, for example, Bruce Godschalk was exonerated by DNA evidence after having served fifteen years in prison for two rapes he had not committed.[120] While he was in prison, Godschalk's sister, his father, and his mother had died. In her will, Godschalk's mother had left him $10,000 for DNA testing. Despite the fact that Godschalk had been convicted in part on particularly questionable eye-witness identification,[121] the prosecutor tried to prevent Godshcalk from having the DNA test performed. Even after two DNA laboratories, one chosen by the defense and one by the prosecution, had concluded that Godschalk could not have been the rapist, the district attorney continued to fight his release.

§ 11.13 PROSECUTION USE OF SNITCHES

Neither the ABA nor the ALI offer guidance to prosecutors using cooperating witnesses or "snitches." Yet, this is an increasingly troublesome area for prosecutors, who regularly obtain information and testimony from people who can incriminate others in exchange for promises of leniency. Indeed, in some

---

[116] *See id.*

[117] For example, a forensic dentist in Mississippi who has testified in numerous capital cases was censured in April, 1994, by the American Academy of Forensic Sciences for misrepresenting evidence and for failing to meet professional standards. Four months later, however, he was scheduled by prosecutors to testify as an expert witness in three capital murder cases. Paul C. Giannelli, *When the Evidence Is a Matter of Life and Death*, N.Y. TIMES, Op. Ed., Aug. 21, 1994.

[118] This account is taken from the N.Y. TIMES, April 16, 1993. The matter came out when one of the troopers, applying for a job with the CIA, boasted of his prowess in fabricating evidence. *Id.*

[119] The district attorney denied it. *Id.*

[120] *See* Sara Rimes, *DNA Testing in Rape Cases Frees Prisoner After 15 Years*, N.Y. TIMES, Feb. 15, 2002, at A12.

[121] "Six months after the two rapes, after studying Mr. Godschalk's picture in a mug shot array for more than on hour, one victim identified him as her rapist. The second victim could not make an identification." *Id.* Godschalk also gave a confession that he later repudiated, but which was used against him in trial. *Id.*

cases, because of lack of adequate evidence, it would be difficult, if not impossible, to prosecute without such "cooperation."

The problem is that the substantial incentives for cooperation — the prospect of a lesser charge or sentence (or no charge at all), early release from prison, witness relocation and/or protection — do not always result in truthful information or testimony.[122] Too often, such testimony has been the principal evidence in a wrongful conviction of an innocent accused. For example, of sixty-four cases of exoneration through DNA technology, snitch testimony was a factor in twenty-four percent of the wrongful convictions.[123]

The criticism of the use of snitches spans the ideological spectrum. A federal court denounced the practice as a form of bribery.[124] There are some criminal defense lawyers who eschew the representation of snitches altogether as contrary to the role of defense advocacy.[125] Several commentators have noted that further study of the cooperation process is needed.[126]

Even prosecutors have expressed serious misgivings about relying on snitches.[127] For example, a 1988 U.S. Department of Justice publication discusses "the general nature" of informants, describing many of them as "outright conscienceless sociopaths to whom 'truth' is a wholly meaningless concept."[128] "[R]emarkably manipulative and skillfully devious," their willingness to do anything to avoid prison can include "lying, committing perjury, manufacturing evidence, soliciting others to corroborate their lies with more lies, and doublecrossing anyone with whom they come into contact."[129] That assessment was written by Stephen Trott, then Associate Attorney General of the United States and now a federal judge.

There will always be cooperators. It can be very much in an accused's interest to cooperate, in view of stringent state and federal sentencing guidelines and harsh sentences generally.[130] However, that is precisely why

---

[122] See generally Symposium, *The Cooperating Witness Conundrum: Is Justice Obtainable?*, 23 CARDOZO L. REV. 746 (2002); Graham Hughes, *Agreements for Cooperation in Criminal Cases*, 45 VAND. L. REV. 1, 7–12 (1992).

[123] See JIM DWYER, ET AL., ACTUAL INNOCENCE 156, app. 2 (2000).

[124] See *United States v. Singleton*, 144 F.3d 1343 (10th Cir. 1998) (panel of 10th Circuit finding that government violated federal bribery statute by offering leniency to a cooperating witness and thereby violated Rule 3.4(b) of the Rules of Professional Conduct by "offer[ing] an inducement to a witness that is prohibited by law"); *but see United States v. Singleton*, 165 F.3d 1297 (10th Cir. 1999) (finding that Congress did not mean to include in the federal bribery statute the longstanding practice of prosecutors offering leniency to codefendants for truthful testimony).

[125] See Daniel C. Richman, *Cooperating Clients*, 56 OHIO ST. L. J. 69, 69 (1995) (describing Los Angeles criminal defense lawyer Barry Tarlow " 'general policy not to represent clients in negotiations with the government concerning cooperation [because he found them] personally[,] morally and ethically offensive.' "); *see also id.* at 76, 126–38. *See also* Monroe H. Freedman, *The Lawyer Who Hates Snitches*, LEGAL TIMES, May 3, 1993 (defending Tarlow's against charges of unethical conduct).

[126] See David A. Sklansky, *Starr, Singleton, and the Prosecutor's Role*, 26 FORDHAM URB. L.J. 509 (1999).

[127] See Ellen Yaroshefsky, *Cooperation with Federal Prosecutors: Experiences of Truth Telling and Embellishment*, 68 FORDHAM L. REV. 917, 931–34 (1999).

[128] PROSECUTION OF PUBLIC CORRUPTION CASES, Ch. 10, 117–118 (1988).

[129] *Id.* at 118.

[130] See Ian Weinstein, *Regulating the Market for Snitches*, 47 BUFF. L. REV. 563, 563–564 (1999) (noting these are "boom times for the sellers and buyers of cooperation").

conscientious prosecutors should exercise caution. Information or testimony by cooperators should be corroborated by other credible witnesses or physical evidence, and testimony by "career informants" should be avoided.[131] As one such informant, Leslie White, acknowledged, "Every time I come in here [prison], I inform and get back out."[132] How could the prosecutors not have known?[133]

§ 11.14   PROSECUTOR'S DUTY TO ENSURE FAIR TRIAL FOR ACCUSED

Prosecutors have special responsibilities toward the court and the accused at trial. This reflects the prosecutor's duty to "seek justice" rather than convictions.[134] These obligations are also consistent with the protections afforded the accused by the presumption of innocence and burden of proof. The prosecutor's duties at trial include avoiding offering false, misleading, or inadmissible evidence,[135] avoiding any conduct that might prejudice the factfinder,[136] not commenting on the accused's silence,[137] not expressing a personal opinion about the credibility of any testimony or the guilt of an accused,[138] and disclosing all exculpatory evidence.[139]

---

[131] *See* Cheryl W. Thompson, *DEA Shielded Tainted Informant*, WASH. POST, July 19, 2001, at A1 (reporting that a confidential informant who worked for the Drug Enforcement Administration for sixteen years earning nearly two million dollars had concealed his own criminal record and testified falsely in dozens of criminal prosecutions across the country); *see also* Alan Berlow, *The Wrong Man*, ATLANTIC MONTHLY, Nov. 1999, at 66, 77 (quoting Walter F. Rowe, a professor of forensic science at George Washington University: " 'The dirty little secret in this country, and it's not such a secret, is that if you perjure yourself for the prosecution, no one's going to prosecute you."); *id.* (referring to an inmate at the Los Angeles County Jail who "acknowledged that he had fabricated a dozen 'confessions' by fellow inmates, which he reported to authorities in exchange for more lenient treatment").

[132] *A Snitch's Story*, TIME, Dec. 2, 1988.

[133] As a result of this career informant's confession, and the resultant adverse publicity, the district attorney's office reviewed every conviction of a major crime obtained with jailhouse testimony in the preceding ten years. The investigation turned up 120 questionable cases. *Id.* *See also* Martin Berg, *D.A. Memo Airs Private Suspicions of Snitch Misuse*, L.A. DAILY JOUR., Aug. 17, 1989, at 1. Nevertheless, the state prosecutors' office opposed reopening any of the convictions obtained through White's testimony.

[134] *See supra* notes 8-22; *see also* Bruce Green, *Why Should Prosecutors Seek Justice?*, 26 FORDHAM URB. L.J. 607, 612–14, 625–37 (discussing the ethical duty of prosecutors to seek justice above all else).

[135] *See* Model Rule 3.3(a)(1), 3.4(e); Model Code DR 7-102(A)(4), (5), DR 7-106(C)(1); Prosecution Standards 5.6, 5.8; *see also* Saltzberg, note 141, *infra*.

[136] *See* ABA PROSECUTION FUNCTION, Std. 5.9(c), (d) (recommending that prosecutors avoid making arguments that appeal to prejudice or otherwise distracts the jury from its proper function). Unfortunately, this sort of prosecutorial misconduct is not rare. *See, e.g.,* Ken Armstrong & Steve Mills, *Death Row justice derailed*, CHICAGO TRIBUNE, Nov. 14, 1999, at 1, (reporting that in order to win a death sentence, prosecutors in Illinois have routinely failed to disclose exculpatory evidence, engaged in racial discrimination during jury selection, exaggerated the criminal backgrounds of defendants, lied to jurors about the possibility of parole, and browbeat jurors by telling them if they failed to send the defendant to the death chamber they will have violated their oaths and "lied to God").

[137] *See Griffin v. California*, 380 U.S. 960 (1965).

[138] *See* MR 3.4(e); DR 7-106(C)(4); ABA PROSECUTION FUNCTION, Std. 5.8(b).

[139] *See* following notes and text.

Disclosure of material exculpatory evidence by prosecutors on request of the defense is constitutionally mandated.[140] With respect to the prosecutor's ethical duties, however, both the ABA and ALI go further, requiring prosecutors to disclose exculpatory evidence without a defense request and without a materiality limitation. MR 3.8(d) requires the prosecutor to make "timely disclosure to the defense of all evidence or information known to the prosecutor that tends to negate the guilt of the accused or mitigates the offense." Restatement § 97, Cmt. *h* is similar, as is DR 7-103(B), which adds the phrase, "or reduce the punishment."

Nevertheless, there are longstanding problems with prosecutors who fail to disclose exculpatory evidence notwithstanding constitutional and ethical requirements to do so.[141] In a characteristically trenchant analysis, Professor Stephen A. Saltzburg illustrates the continuing problem of prosecutors failing to disclose critical exculpatory evidence (even prosecutors who purport to have an "open file policy") and how this leads to false and misleading testimony.[142]

A less noted prosecutorial obligation at trial relates to the accused's right to counsel. Conscientious prosecutors should be concerned not only with helping to assure that the accused is represented by counsel,[143] but with safeguarding the accused's right to *competent* counsel.[144] Although some examples are more notorious than others,[145] every jurisdiction has its drunk,

---

[140] *See Brady v. Maryland*, 373 U.S. 83 (1963) (holding that failure to disclose material exculpatory evidence upon request violates due process); *Kyles v. Whitley*, 514 U.S. 419 (1995); *United States v. Bagley*, 473 U.S. 667 (1985) (same); *United States v. Agurs*, 427 U.S. 97 (1976) (same); *see also Giglio v. United States*, 405 U.S. 140 (1972) (nondisclosure of promise of leniency to key prosecution witness violates due process).

[141] *See* Stephen A. Saltzberg, *Perjury and False Testimony: Should the Difference Matter So Much?*, 68 FORDHAM L. REV. 1537 (2000).

[142] *Id. See also* Stanley Z. Fisher, *The Prosecutor's Ethical Duty to Seek Exculpatory Evidence in Police Hands: Lessons From England*, 68 FORDHAM L. REV. 1379 (2000) (urging an ethical rule that would require prosecutors to make reasonable efforts to obtain access to exculpatory evidence known to the police).

[143] MR 3.8(b) ("The prosecutor in a criminal case shall make reasonable efforts to assure that the accused has been advised of the right to, and the procedure for obtaining, counsel and has been given [a] reasonable opportunity to obtain counsel. . . . ").

[144] *See generally* Vanessa Merton, *What Do You Do When You Meet A "Walking Violation of the Sixth Amendment," If You're Trying to Put That Lawyer's Client in Jail?*, 69 FORDHAM L. REV. 997 (2000). We are not talking about *constitutionally* ineffective assistance of counsel, which has become a nearly impossible standard for an accused to meet no matter how poorly he or she was represented. *See Strickland v. Washington*, 466 U.S. 668 (1984); *see also Brown v. Harris*, 1999 U.S. Dist. Lexis 6409 (N.D. Ca. 1999) (suggesting that it is constitutionally acceptable for defense counsel to sleep from time to time during an attempt murder trial); *but See Burdine v. Johnson*, 66 F.Supp. 2d 854 (S.D. Tex. 1999) (finding that counsel who slept during "substantial portions" of a capital murder trial was ineffective). *Burdine v. Johnson*, 262 F.3d 336 (2001) (affirmed). Prosecutors who are concerned about justice are necessarily concerned about the problem of incompetent counsel.

[145] *See* Sara Rimer & Raymond Bonner, *Texas Lawyer's Death Row Record a Concern*, N.Y. TIMES, June 11, 2000, at A1 (reporting about Texas defense lawyer Ronald G. Mock, who may be responsible for more people on death row than any prosecutor in the country, and who bragged about flunking criminal law as a law student).

See also Steve Mills, Ken Armstrong, & Douglas Holt, *Flawed Trials Lead to Death Chamber*, CHICAGO TRIBUNE, June 11, 2000, at 1 (reporting that forty-three of the attorneys who defended

hung-over, and sleeping lawyers, or lawyers so incompetent that even the most dyspeptic, world-weary court staff cringe when they enter the courtroom.[146] The more serious the case, the more painful the reality. Ineffective assistance of counsel is a significant factor even in wrongful capital convictions.[147]

Despite the prevalence of incompetent defense counsel, prosecutors virtually never halt a trial in the face of plainly incompetent defense counsel, or raise a concern in advance of trial.[148] The right to competent counsel is central to every other right of the criminally accused,[149] and the denial of this right destroys the foundation of adversarial justice.[150] Because the problem of incompetent counsel is most often visited upon the indigent accused (the overwhelming majority of criminal cases), the legitimacy of our legal system is called into serious question.[151] Prosecutors have an ethical obligation, therefore, to take affirmative corrective action — rather than take advantage — when they encounter a plainly ineffective defense lawyer.[152] At the very least,

---

the 131 people executed under Governor George W. Bush had been sanctioned for misconduct by the State Bar of Texas and others were "convicted felons . . . [and] attorneys who were inexperienced or . . . inept").

[146] See Merton, *supra* note 144, at 1007–1014 (vividly recounting a student prosecutor's encounter with an incompetent, ineffectual defense lawyer). Merton offers a memorable portrait of a truly bad lawyer, in the best tradition of Charles Dickens — or perhaps Tom Wolfe:

> All along, he had been leaning against a wall, scribbling with a pencil on a stack of files. He had no brief case or satchel or backpack to hold a handy CPL or Penal Law. He was, to put it politely, unkempt: flushed, uncombed, unshaven, shirt-tails hanging out of his trousers, and extremely distracted looking. My first thought was he must be unusually dedicated to come to court when he was so obviously sick with the flu.
>
> As it developed, that didn't seem to be the problem. . . .
>
> "OK, here it is — Sanchez, yeah, another car thief. Probably young, though, you know? Maybe not such a bad kid — maybe he does it to support his dear mother. (Head thrown back in, a gleeful guffaw over his own wit.) What are you looking for? These guys don't care if they get a conviction as long as there's no jail. How 'bout a fine? He can always steal another car to pay it." (Another raucous guffaw that descended into a giggle. Then he started working on something in his ear.)

Id. at 1007–08.

[147] See Stephen Bright, *Counsel for the Poor: The Death Penalty Not for the Worst Crime, but for the Worst Lawyer*, 103 YALE L. J. 1835 (1994) (discussing the pervasiveness of shoddy representation of indigent defendants in capital cases); Fox Butterfield, *Death Sentences Being overturned in 2 of 3 Appeals*, N.Y. TIMES, June 12, 2000, at A1 (reporting that two out of three death penalty convictions in the United States were overturned on appeal because of ineffective assistance of counsel, prosecutorial misconduct, and police overreaching).

[148] See Fisher, *supra* note 1, at 222 (noting that "[p]rosecutors are uniquely positioned to observe incompetent and lazy representation of defendants").

[149] See supra at Ch. 2.

[150] See *Handford v. United States*, 249 F.2d 295 (5th Cir. 1957) (noting that a prosecutor "owes a heavy obligation to the accused . . . of fairness," an obligation "so important that Anglo-American law rests on the foundation: better the guilty escape than the innocent suffer.").

[151] See David L. Bazelon, *The Defective Assistance of Counsel*, 4 U. CIN. L. REV. 1, 4 (1973) ("[W]e pretend to do justice by providing an indigent defendant with a lawyer, no matter how inexperienced, incompetent or indifferent.").

[152] See Monroe Freedman, *The Professional Responsibility of the Prosecuting Attorney*, 55 GEO. L. J. 1030, 1039–40 (1967) (discussing the problem of prosecutors actively covering up ineffective assistance of defense counsel); Bruce Green, *Her Brother's Keeper: The Prosecutor's Responsibility When Defense Counsel Has a Potential Conflict of Interest*, 16 AM. J. CRIM. L. 323, 341–42 (1989) ("[W]hen it becomes apparent that defense counsel may be denying the accused adequate legal assistance, the prosecutor, as a representative of the State, should take reasonably available steps to remedy the problem.").

a conscientious prosecutor should approach the bench and make a record of the incompetence she observes, rather than ignoring it.[153]

This position is grounded in the ethical codes. As the Comment to MR 3.8 states: "A prosecutor has the responsibility of a minister of justice and not simply that of an advocate. This responsibility carries with it specific obligations to see that the defendant is accorded procedural justice." Also, the ethical codes uniformly forbid a lawyer to "engage in conduct that is prejudicial to the administration of justice.[154] Because the problem of incompetent counsel is prejudicial to the administration of justice in the most fundamental sense, and because it remains far too prevalent, a prosecutor should not remain silent when the alternative is to participate in a judicial proceeding that denies justice.

Some prosecutors might protest that this it is not their job to help eliminate incompetent defense lawyers from the criminal courts. Prosecutors have not hesitated, however, to seek disqualification on ethical grounds of highly *effective* criminal defense lawyers from participation in criminal trials.[155] In the case of incompetent defense lawyers, at least, no one could question their motives.

§ 11.15　THE FAILURE OF PROFESSIONAL DISCIPLINE OF PROSECUTORS

Historically, the bar has failed to take disciplinary action against prosecutors who violate the few clear rules of ethical conduct that exist. Some prosecutors have been disbarred for extreme misconduct, but typically significant discipline is imposed only for the commission of a felony, like embezzlement of state funds. As noted by Professor Bennett L. Gershman, discipline of prosecutors is "so rare as to make its use virtually a nullity."[156]

---

[153] Of course, judges are also implicated when trials proceed with incompetent defense lawyers.

[154] See MR 8.4; DR 1-102(A)(5); Restatement § 5(3).

This obligation to report incompetence to the court is also implicit in provisions requiring a lawyer to report to appropriate authorities conduct by another lawyer that raises a substantial question as to that lawyer's fitness to practice law. See MR 8.3(a); DR 1-103(A); Restatement § 5(3).

We are not urging prosecutors to casually or routinely report defense lawyers to courts and disciplinary boards. Such an action is serious, could easily be misused, and should not be undertaken lightly. See Restatement § 5, Cmt. I (noting that some lawyers have objected to the duty to report wrongdoing because it invites unprincipled lawyers to unfairly threaten opposing counsel). The chief concern of a conscientious prosecutor should be for the fair administration of justice, which necessarily includes ensuring that an accused is competently represented.

See United States ex rel. Williams v. Twomey, 510 F.2d 634 (7th Cir. 1975) ("While a criminal trial is not a game in which the participants are expected to enter the ring with a near match in skills, neither is it a sacrifice of unarmed prisoners to gladiators"); see also Green, Her Brother's Keeper, supra note 152, at 325 ("[T]he duty to promote the fairness of criminal proceedings includes, as a corollary, a duty to avoid the public perception that criminal proceedings are unfair.")

[155] See infra (Sections on "Government Motions to Disqualify Defense Counsel" and "A Qualification by Professor Freedman").

[156] See GERSHMAN, PROSECUTORIAL MISCONDUCT § 1.8(d), at 1-52, § 13.6, at 13-16 to 13-18 (1985).

One computerized review has shown that there have been only 100 reported cases of professional discipline of prosecutors, nationwide, federal and state, in the past century — an average of only one disciplinary case a year.[157] This paucity of cases is not limited to those in which prosecutors have unethically suppressed evidence, knowingly used false evidence, or otherwise violated the rights of criminal defendants. On the contrary, they relate, for the most part, to cases of bribery, extortion, conversion, and embezzlement of government funds. Moreover, the few cases in which prosecutors were disciplined for such egregious conduct as presenting false evidence and misleading or deceiving a tribunal, have usually resulted in the minimal discipline of censure or reprimand, or no disciplined at all.[158]

An illustration of the reluctance of disciplinary committees to impose discipline on prosecutors is *In re Bonet*.[159] There, a prosecutor in Washington told a defense witness that if he did not testify for the defense, the prosecutor would dismiss criminal charges that were pending against him.[160] When the witness' lawyer asked the prosecutor to put the agreement in writing, the prosecutor replied, "no, because that wouldn't look good."[161] Later, during a disciplinary hearing, the prosecutor falsely denied that there had been an agreement.[162] Having found these facts, the Disciplinary Board held that no sanction was appropriate and dismissed all charges against the prosecutor.[163] On appeal, the Washington Supreme Court held that the offer of an inducement to the witness not to testify was unethical, and remanded the case with directions to impose some discipline.[164] Three years later, Westlaw reveals no disciplinary action having been taken.

Another example involves a lawyer with the Organized Crime Strike Force of the U.S. Department of Justice.[165] The prosecution's chief witness was to be Dennis DiRicco, an unindicted coconspirator in a prosecution involving money laundering and narcotics. The prosecutor had a transcript of previous testimony by DiRicco, under oath, that *constituted a complete and detailed denial of any wrongdoing . . . by any of the defendants in this case.*[166]

Nevertheless, the prosecutor did not reveal this testimony to the grand jury when he obtained an indictment; on the contrary, he "extracted a story from [DiRicco] that was diametrically opposed to his prior trial testimony in every

---

[157] Fred C. Zacharias, *The Professional Discipline of Prosecutors*, 79 N.C. L. Rev. 721, 744–745 and note 86 (2001). *See also* Monroe H. Freedman, *The Professional Discipline of Prosecutors: A Reply to Professor Zacharias*, 30 Hofstra L. Rev. 121 (2001).

[158] *See id.* at 746–47. The harshest punishment was for misleading the court. *See also* Greg Rushford, *"No Action Has Been Taken"* Legal Times, p. 1, Jan. 28, 1991 ("U.S. Prosecutors Rapped by Judges Rarely Face Any Discipline").

[159] *In re Bonet*, 29 P.3d 1242 (2001).

[160] *Id.* at 1244.

[161] *Id.*

[162] *Id.* at 1245. Two detectives testified that they had heard the prosecutor make the deal. *Id.* at 1244.

[163] *Id.* at 1249.

[164] *Id.*, citing MR 3.4(b), 8.4(b), and 8.4(d).

[165] *United States v. Isgro*, 751 F.Supp. 846 (U.S.D.C., C.D. Calif., 1990).

[166] *Id.* at 847 (emphasis in original).

important detail."[167] Also, he did not turn over the transcript as *Brady* material when such material was requested by the defense, and he "repeatedly denied the existence of material which would tend to exonerate the defendants."[168]

In the course of their own investigation, however, defense counsel learned about DiRicco's former testimony. The prosecutor's response was to "flatly den[y] that there was any inconsistency between the two sets of testimony," despite the fact that they were "completely contrary to each other."[169] Federal District Judge James M. Ideman found that the prosecutor's reaction was "to stonewall and simply deny the obvious."[170] Summing up the situation, Ideman observed that "having been caught with a smoking pistol, the Government, having previously denied that it had a pistol, now denied that the pistol smoked."[171] Accordingly, the judge dismissed the indictment.[172]

The Ninth Circuit reversed the dismissal of the indictment, but joined Ideman in "condemning" the government's "intolerable" behavior.[173] The Court of Appeals also referred the case to the Attorney General for possible departmental discipline.[174] Three years and three months after Ideman's opinion exposing the prosecutor's misconduct, however, no disciplinary action had been taken against the prosecutor.[175]

There are, however, some hopeful developments. Recent federal legislation, the Ethical Standards for Federal Prosecutors Act (the "McDade Amendment"), subjects federal prosecutors to the same state laws and rules as other attorneys in each state.[176] Even though state prosecutors have been infrequently disciplined under those laws and rules, this legislation is an indication of a developing concern at the highest levels of government. Also, there is a growing body of legal scholarship addressing the regulation and discipline of prosecuting attorneys.[177] In time, these developments can lead to more careful

---

[167] *Id.* at 848.

[168] *Id.*

[169] *Id.*

[170] *Id.* at 851. Ideman's career before being appointed to the bench had been as a district attorney.

[171] *Id.* at 852.

[172] Ideman noted that "this is not the first instance of misconduct by the prosecuting attorneys in this case." Another federal judge had found that the Strike Force lawyers had been "guilty of outrageous . . . misconduct by coercive tactics used towards a defendant and by misrepresentations to [the court]." *Id.*

[173] 974 F.2d 1091, 1099 (1992).

[174] *Id.*

[175] *United States v. Isgro*, Hearing, Dec. 6, 1993.

[176] 28 U.S.C.A. § 530B (Supp. IV 1998). As a result of this statute, the prosecutor would have been subject to disciplinary action for misleading the grand jury. *See* MR 3.8, Cmt. [1], which says that grand jury proceedings are included under MR 3.3(d). The latter rule says that "[i]n an ex parte proceeding, a lawyer shall inform the tribunal of all material facts known to the lawyer which will enable the tribunal to make an informed decision, whether or not the facts are adverse."

The Supreme Court has held that it is not a violation *of the accused's constitutional rights* if a prosecutor withholds evidence from a grand jury, but that decision does not bind a state court in applying its ethical rules for disciplinary purposes.

[177] *See, e.g.,* Leslie Griffin, *The Prudent Prosecutor*, 14 Geo. J. Legal Ethics 259, 275 (2001);

oversight of prosecutors and to higher standards of practice generally by prosecuting attorneys.

§ 11.16   GOVERNMENT MOTIONS TO DISQUALIFY DEFENSE COUNSEL

In recent years, prosecutors have begun to use the tactic of disqualifying defense lawyers from representing certain clients, usually on the ground of conflict of interest. The tactic was first used prominently in 1991, when prosecutors successfully moved to disqualify New York defense attorney Bruce Cutler from representing John Gotti. Gotti had prevailed in three earlier prosecutions, but after Cutler was disqualified, Gotti was convicted and sentenced to life in prison. After this, disqualification became one of the Government's preferred weapons in organized crime cases.[178]

In order to remove so called "mob lawyers," prosecutors use the legal reasoning of the 1991 case, which was approved by the United States Court of Appeals for the Second Circuit two years later.[179] In that case, *United States v. Locascio*,[180] the Second Circuit ruled that an accused "does not have the absolute right to counsel of her own choosing."[181] The court affirmed Cutler's disqualification on the grounds that Cutler had represented not merely John Gotti, but the Gambino Crime Family as a whole, amounting to his being "house counsel," and that Cutler was in a position to be an unsworn witness for Gotti because of his first-hand knowledge of the events presented at trial.[182] The court acknowledged that disqualification is a "drastic remedy,"

Rory K. Little, *Who Should Regulate the Ethics of Federal Prosecutors?*, 6 FORDHAM L. REV. 355 (1996); Richard A. Rosen, *Disciplinary Sanctions Against Prosecutors for* Brady *Violations: A Paper Tiger*, 65 N.C. L. REV. 693 (1987); Fred C. Zacharias, *Who can* Best *Regulate the Ethics of Federal Prosecutors, or, Who should Regulate the Regulators?: Response to Little*, 65 FORDHAM L. REV. 429 (1996); Fred C. Zacharias & Bruce A. Green, *The Uniqueness of Federal Prosecutors*, 88 GEO. L. J. 207 (2000); Richard A. Rosen, *Disciplinary Sanctions Against Prosecutors for* Brady *Violations: A Paper Tiger*, 65 N.C. L. REV. 693 (1987).

[178] William Glaberson, *Effort to Oust Gotti Lawyer Reopens Debate on Tactics*, N.Y. TIMES, May 4, 1998, at B6. In 1998, federal prosecutors moved for the removal of Cutler from the racketeering trial of Gotti's son, John A. Gotti. The grounds for the motion were that Cutler was so involved with the Gambino crime family that he should be considered "house counsel" — the same claim that had been made in 1991. *See id.* Cutler rejected this assertion: " 'I am not now, I never was and I never would be "house counsel" to any organized crime group.' " William Glaberson, *Gotti Lawyer Says Prosecutors' Fear of His Past Victories Is Behind Effort to Disqualify Him*, N.Y. TIMES, April 25, 1998, at B4. He countered that prosecutors wanted him off the case because of the three times he defeated prosecutors before the senior Gotti was convicted (represented by a different defense lawyer after Cutler was removed): " 'I am not blowing my own horn. . . . I have a unique ability to try a case. People like me.' " *Id*

[179] *See United States v. Locascio*, 6 F.3d 924 (2d Cir. 1993), *cert denied*, 511 U.S. 1070 (1994). In 1988, the Supreme Court held that a trial court had the discretion to disqualify a defense attorney who has a "serious potential for conflict." *Wheat v. United States*, 486 U.S. 153, 164 (1988). Prior to *Wheat*, the Supreme Court and lower federal courts generally professed faith that most defense lawyers would comport with the general ethical standards of the legal profession regarding conflict of interest. *See Holloway v. Arkansas*, 435 U.S. 475 (1978); *Cuyler v. Sullivan*, 446 U.S. 335 (1980).

[180] 6 F.3d 924 (2d Cir. 1993).

[181] *Id.* at 931.

[182] *See id.* at 932–33.

but found that Cutler had entangled himself in the activities of the Gambino Crime Family "to an extraordinary degree."[183]

This tactic has been employed beyond organized crime, in a range of situations from multiple client representation,[184] to cases where a lawyer previously represented a witness or co-defendant[185] — even where the clients have been willing to waive any challenge to such representation. The growing use of this tactic is disturbing for a number of reasons. A motion to disqualify counsel can threaten the attorney-client relationship by eroding attorney-client confidentiality and trust. Neither the court nor the prosecution should be privy to the details of a client's relationship to his lawyer. The autonomy of the individual client is also threatened.[186] What could be more important than the client's choice of an attorney?[187] It should also be noted that prosecutors tend to use disqualification motions against zealous, skilled lawyers — not lawyers who pose no threat to the government's case.[188]

§ 11.17 A QUALIFICATION BY PROFESSOR FREEDMAN

The preceding section has been written by Professor Smith, and Freedman is sympathetic to the concerns expressed. Disqualification of defense counsel can be used as a divide-and-conquer tactic when two or more defendants justifiably want to present a common defense, and it can interfere with the defendant's choice of counsel. In addition, disqualification in some cases has the appearance of selective disbarment or suspension without due process. Moreover, the lawyer's efforts to oppose disqualification (for example, by proving that he is not "house counsel," or by otherwise distancing himself from the client) can violate confidentiality and can otherwise impair the lawyer-client relationship. Nevertheless, there are instances when it is appropriate to disqualify defense counsel from representing a particular defendant.

---

[183] *Id.* at 934. The court noted that the case was unusual:

> [Cutler] is recorded on government tapes when discussions of allegedly illegal activity took place; he is allegedly involved in the tax fraud count against Gotti; his role as house counsel could be used to prove the criminal enterprise; and his representation of government witnesses caused a conflict with his representation of Gotti.

Id.

[184] *See generally* Bruce Green, *"Through a Glass, Darkly": How the Court Sees Motions to Disqualify Criminal Defense Lawyers*, 89 COLUM. L. REV. 1201 (1989) [hereinafter Green, *"Through a Glass, Darkly"*]; David Rudovsky, *Legitimate Means or "Chilling Wedges?": The Right to Counsel Under Attack*, 136 U. PA. L. REV. 1965, 1967 (1988).

[185] *See* Green, *"Through a Glass, Darkly," supra* note 184, at 1232–33.

[186] *See id.* at 1232–38.

[187] *See Wheat v. United States*, 486 U.S. 153, 172 (Stevens, J., dissenting) (referring to the Court's "paternalistic view of the citizen's right to select his or her own lawyer" as reflected in the "inadequate weight [it gives] to the informed and voluntary character the of the clients' waiver of their right to conflict-free representation"); *but see United States v. Locascio*, 6 F.3d 924, (2d Cir. 1993) ("Although we are cognizant of the right of the accused to secure representation, we are also conscious of the institutional interest in protecting the integrity of the judicial process. If an attorney will not perform his ethical duty, it is up to the courts to perform it for him.").

[188] *See* William Glaberson, *Effort to Oust Gotti Lawyer Reopens Debate on Tactics*, N.Y. TIMES, May 4, 1998, at B6.

One clear case is where the lawyer has previously represented someone who is to be a witness for the prosecution, and where the witness is unwilling to waive the conflict of interest. The risk is that the lawyer will use information gained in the prior representation in cross-examining the former client. A related problem is where the lawyer does not conduct a vigorous cross-examination of the witness out of concern that the witness will implicate the lawyer in prior wrongdoing involving the witness and the lawyer.

A more difficult situation is illustrated by the following case. Freedman once represented five defendants charged with the same offense. The government's case was very strong. Although a united front was desirable for four of the clients, who were principals in the offense, it was not in the best interest of the fifth, who was considerably less culpable, if culpable at all. That is, although a united front strengthened the position of all of the defendants, making a favorable plea bargain more likely, the fifth defendant unquestionably could have done better on his own. However, the fifth was unsophisticated and had no idea that he was jeopardizing his own case through the multiple representation. In short, the fifth defendant was not capable of exercising his autonomy (his informed judgment) on the issue. Acting contrary to the interests of the four principals, therefore, Freedman told the fifth defendant that he would have to get separate representation.[189] Only immediately afterwards did he inform the other four of what he had done.[190]

There is ground for concern that in a case like that, some lawyers would put the interests of the group above those of the individual client, even when the individual is less culpable, has a stronger position alone, and is not aware of the unnecessary risk he is taking. This is part of the concern with a lawyer who is believed to be "house counsel" — that is, a lawyer whose overriding loyalty is to the organization rather than to the individual client whose representation is being financed by the organization.[191]

Another problem in such cases is what the Second Circuit referred to as the lawyer serving as "unsworn witness" for the defense. In the Gotti case

---

[189] This did not necessarily mean that the fifth defendant would abandon a common defense, but it gave him the option to do so if, with the benefit of unconflicted counseling, he decided that to be in his best interest.

[190] Freedman's conflict of interest had begun, of course, when he agreed to represent all five defendants. He had, in fact, gotten a waiver of a variety of conflicts of interest, based on informed consent by all of the clients, but he had failed to anticipate this particular (though foreseeable) problem, and he had not included it in the waiver discussions. Accordingly, he found himself forced to be disloyal either to the four principals or to the one less culpable defendant — which is precisely what the conflict of interest rules are designed to avoid.

Smith feels strongly that a single lawyer should never represent multiple defendants in a criminal case, even if each of the defendants gives a fully informed and voluntary waiver. Although it would not be unethical under the rules, she considers it essential that each client have his or her own lawyer to discuss individual concerns and issues, including pretrial motions, trial strategy, and (perhaps most important) sentencing. Cf. MR 1.7, Cmt. [7]: "in a criminal case . . . ordinarily a lawyer should decline to represent more than one co-defendant."

Freedman continues to believe that there are cases in which a united front is the strongest defense for each and all joint defendants (as it ultimately proved to be in the case mentioned), and that this can most effectively be achieved with a single lawyer (which is why prosecutors try to force each defendant to have a separate lawyer). This issue is the subject of the philosophical/mathematical conundrum called "the prisoner's dilemma."

[191] See *United States v. Locascio*, 6 F.3d at 932–933, 935.

(*Locascio*) the evidence included tape recordings of conversations that the government maintained were incriminating, and at which Cutler (the lawyer) had been present. In disputes over what had been said on the tapes (*i.e.*, where the tapes were unclear) or over what was actually meant by particular words or phrases, Cutler's arguments to the jury about what had been said and about what had been meant would have amounted to "unsworn testimony," not subject to cross-examination.[192] This could give the defense an unfair advantage.

Also, the court may have been concerned that Cutler's presence as counsel could imply an endorsement by the court of the propriety of the taped discussions in which he had taken part.[193] In addition, although the court did not mention it, the prosecution might have wanted to counter these advantages by attacking Cutler's culpability and credibility, which would have raised serious evidentiary questions.[194]

On balance, therefore, Freedman has serious reservations about the views in the preceding section, while sharing the concern regarding potential prosecutorial abuse in disqualifying defense counsel.

§ 11.18   CHOOSING TO BE A PROSECUTOR

Law students who are interested in doing public interest work and who know of Freedman's background in civil liberties and indigent criminal defense, sometimes express surprise when he urges them to consider becoming prosecutors. In fact, however, Freedman believes you can do more good as a conscientious prosecutor than as a zealous criminal defense lawyer. A defense lawyer, for example, may be able to expose unlawful law enforcement and prosecutorial abuses; a prosecutor of "honor, temperament, and professionalism," however, can prevent it from ever happening.[195]

However, Freedman cautions that because the prosecutor "wields the most terrible instruments of government," a prosecutor can also do more harm. Perhaps the most difficult aspect of the prosecutor's job is to help to protect society from antisocial people without helping to create an antisocial state.[196]

Smith is skeptical about the ability of even conscientious prosecutors to do good under the current criminal justice regime.[197] She believes that the culture of prosecution fosters rigidity, cynicism, and a tendency to engage in wilful or careless abuse of official power. She disagrees with Freedman that you can do more good as a conscientious prosecutor than as a zealous defense

---

[192] *Id.* at 933–934.

[193] *See id.* at 935 (discussing the disqualification of George Santangelo as counsel for Locascio).

[194] Insofar as the issue is disadvantage to Gotti (*e.g.*, by a government attack at trial on Cutler) Gotti certainly should have been permitted to waive the conflict. But the other concerns raise issues of unfairness to the government that go, as the court said, to the integrity of the proceeding. *Id.* at 932.

[195] The quoted phrase is Irving Younger's. Younger, *Memoir of a Prosecutor*, *supra* note 23, at 70.

[196] We use antisocial in the sense of "opposed or hostile to social order or the principles on which society is constituted." THE RANDOM HOUSE DICTIONARY (Revised ed., 1982).

[197] *See* Smith, *Can You Be a Good Person and a Good Prosecutor*, *supra* note 1.

lawyer. She therefore urges students interested in advancing criminal and social justice to represent the indigent accused (and convicted), growing numbers of whom fill our nation's already overcrowded prisons.

§ 11.19   CONCLUSION

Summing up his account of the effort by the Department of Justice to "get" Roy Cohn, Irving Younger wrote, with extraordinary candor: "I read over this narrative and I am not proud. When [the United States Attorney] said, 'The Department wants Cohn,' I replied, with enthusiasm, 'I'll get him.' " Younger then summarized the improprieties in the course of that effort, and concluded: "It was the power of power. If I possibly could, I was going to be the one to do the job the Department wanted done. Not once did I stop to think what it was a Department of."[198]

---

[198] Younger, *Memoir of a Prosecutor, supra* note 23, at 70. *See, e.g.*, Raymond Bonner, *Death Row Inmate is Freed After DNA Test Clears Him*, NY TIMES, Aug. 24, 2001, at A10 (quoting a prosecutor's response to the exoneration by DNA of a man who had been on death row for eighteen years: "It really doesn't change my opinion that much that [he is] guilty!").

Chapter 12

SOLICITATION OF CLIENTS: THE PROFESSIONAL RESPONSIBILITY TO CHASE AMBULANCES

§ 12.01 INTRODUCTION

A five-year-old boy named Ernest Gene Gunn was seriously injured when he was hit by a car driven by John J. Washek. Shortly after the accident, the boy's mother was visited at home by an adjuster from Washek's insurance company. The adjuster told Ms. Gunn that there was no need for her to hire a lawyer, because the company would make a settlement as soon as Ernest was out of his doctor's care. If Ms. Gunn was not satisfied at that time, he explained, she could get a lawyer and file suit.

Ernest's injuries were sufficiently severe to require a doctor's care for twenty-three months. During that time, the adjuster was regularly in touch with Ms. Gunn. At the end of Ernest's medical treatment, however, despite several efforts on her part to reach him, the adjuster was unavailable. Finally, she retained a lawyer, who promptly filed suit for her. Ernest Gunn never had his day in court, however, because the insurance company successfully pleaded a two-year statute of limitations.[1]

Before examining how the ethical rules affect unsophisticated people like Ernest Gunn and his mother, we should review briefly some issues that we have considered in previous chapters.

§ 12.02 USING THE STATUTE OF LIMITATIONS UNJUSTLY

A lawyer is not required to represent a client whose claim or defense is morally offensive to the lawyer.[2] In fact, if the lawyer's feelings are sufficiently strong, she should decline the case on conflict of interest grounds.[3] If the lawyer does choose to represent the client, however, the lawyer is ethically bound under DR 7-101(A)(1) of the Model Code "to seek the lawful objectives of his client through reasonably available means permitted by law and the Disciplinary Rules."[4] MR 1.2(a) of the Model Rules is less clear on this point,

---

[1] *Gunn v. Washek*, 405 Pa. 521, 176 A.2d 635 (1961). The same court has recognized that the statute can be tolled by "fraud in the broad sense, i.e. inclusive of an unintentional deception." *Nesbitt v. Erie Coach Co.*, 416 Pa. 89, 96, 204 A.2d 473 (1964). However, that rule is applied only in "*clear* cases of fraud, deception or concealment." *See, e.g.*, *Walters v. Ditzler*, 424 Pa. 445, 227 A.2d 833, 835 (1967) (emphasis in original), citing *Gunn* with approval and refusing to toll the statute.

[2] *See* Chapters 3 and 4, *supra*.

[3] DR 5-101(A); MR 1.7(b). *See* Chapter 10, *supra*.

[4] *See* Chapters 3 and 4, *supra*.

because the lawyer is required to "abide by" the client's decision with regard to "objectives" of the representation, but need only "consult" with the client with regard to the "means" of pursuing the client's ends.[5] The question arises under the Model Rules, therefore, whether pleading the statute of limitations is an objective or a means?

The Comment to MR 1.2 acknowledges that the distinction between objectives and means is not a clear one, and suggests that "means" include only "technical and legal tactical issues."[6] This could mean that the statute of limitations is a means, because the statute is often used a paradigm of a "technical" defense.[7] Giving the terms "technical" and "tactical" a narrow reading, however, Professor Geoffrey C. Hazard, Jr., the Reporter for the Model Rules, has interpreted MR 1.2 to be identical to DR 7-101(A)(1).[8] With specific reference to the statute of limitations, "[a] lawyer counseling a creditor cannot withhold the . . . defense if the client wants it asserted," Hazard says, "no matter how piteous the claimant, no matter how great her need."[9]

Although the client's decision is controlling on such an issue, it would be entirely appropriate for the lawyer to urge the client not to defend against a just claim or to forgo using a technical defense.[10] Indeed, we consider it to be unprofessional for a lawyer to preempt a client's judgment on such an issue by asserting the defense without consulting with the client.[11]

What we have said so far assumes that the plaintiff has allowed the statute of limitations to run without the duplicitous inducement of the defendant. In a case like Ms. Gunn's, for example, the insurance company's lawyer would be forbidden to "counsel [the] client to engage, or assist [the] client, in" the adjuster's fraudulent conduct.[12] In addition, a lawyer is forbidden to "[c]ircumvent a Disciplinary Rule through the actions of another."[13] Thus, the

---

[5] Id.

[6] See Ch. 3, supra.

[7] See, e.g., DAVID LUBAN, LAWYERS AND JUSTICE, 9–10 (1988). In a sense, the ethical issue is preempted by the law of malpractice. The most common basis for malpractice actions against defense attorneys is the failure to plead a defense. RONALD E. MALLEN & JEFFREY M. SMITH, LEGAL MALPRACTICE, § 24.20 (3d ed. 1989).

[8] "[T]he client has authority to instruct the lawyer what course of action to pursue, so long as the course of action is within the limits of the law." Geoffrey Hazard, My Station As a Lawyer, 6 GA. ST. L. REV. 1, 4–5 (1989), citing MR 1.2.

[9] Id. at 5. Explaining that position, Hazard wrote:

I think the statute of limitations defense is not simply a tactical device but a meritorious defense, just as I regard estoppel to invoke the defense as a meritorious contention by a plaintiff. I don't see why the client doesn't have the last word on such matters.

Letter to Monroe H. Freedman, March 5, 1990.

[10] EC 7-8, 7-9; MR 2.1. See also Chapters 3 and 4, supra.

[11] Id.

[12] MR 1.2(d). The language of DR 7-102(A)(7) is similar. With regard to whether the adjuster's promises constitute fraud, see Edgington v. Fitzmaurice, 29 Chan. 459 (1882) (Bowen, L.J.) [continued]:

"[Fraud requires] a misstatement of an existing fact: but the state of a man's mind is as much a fact as the state of his digestion." Fraud exists, therefore, "[w]hen a promise is made with no intention of performance, and for the very purpose of accomplishing a fraud."

[13] DR 1-102(A)(2); MR 8.4(a).

lawyer would be forbidden, through the adjuster, to engage in "conduct involving dishonesty, fraud, deceit, or misrepresentation,"[14] or to advise Ms. Gunn *not* to get a lawyer.[15] Furthermore, even if the lawyer did not know until after the fact that the adjuster had deceitfully induced Ms. Gunn to allow the statutory limit to pass, the lawyer would be forbidden to ratify the adjuster's conduct by taking advantage of the statute of limitations.[16]

The focus of the present chapter, however, is not on the responsibilities of the lawyer for the defendant insurance company, but on the way in which the rules of lawyers' ethics can impede or enhance the opportunity for people like Ms. Gunn to achieve equal protection and due process of law.

§ 12.03   HOW THE LEGAL PROFESSION FAILED ERNEST GUNN

The legal profession failed in its responsibilities when a plaintiff's lawyer was not at Ms. Gunn's doorstep at least as soon as the insurance adjuster. As Justice Musmanno noted in dissent in a case similar to *Gunn*:[17]

> [The plaintiff] knew nothing about the statute of limitations. He had an eighth grade education. He had five small children [one of whom lost all power of speech and locomotion in the accident at issue]; he lived in a renovated garage. Neither his sociological status nor his limited studies would acquaint him with a statute of limitations.

Referring to just such a person, former Attorney General Ramsey Clark has remarked, "A citizen who is unaware of his rights is hard to distinguish from a subject who has none."

Nor is Ms. Gunn's problem a unique one. Half a century ago, Illinois Supreme Court Judge Bristow observed that "insurance companies, railroads, airlines and other industries in whose operation some people are certain to be maimed or killed have highly organized mechanisms of defense."[18] Unfair tactics of claim agents for these corporations range from "excessive zeal to . . . shocking fraud."[19] Obviously, "[e]ven the most scrupulous claim agent cannot fairly represent both claimant and defendant."[20] Thus, only through "timely arrival of the solicitor" can a claimant hope to receive "an amount that a court and jury deem adequate and just."[21]

The response of the organized bar to the plight of the aggrieved individuals has been to denounce as "ambulance-chasers" the lawyers who seek to give

---

[14] DR 1-102(A)(4); MR 8.4(c).

[15] DR 7-104(A)(2): "[A] lawyer shall not . . . [g]ive advice to a person who is not represented by a lawyer, other than the advice to secure counsel, if the interests of such person are or have a reasonable possibility of being in conflict with the interests of his client."

In a puzzling piece of drafting, the Model Rules omits this restriction in MR 4.3 but then includes it in the Comment.

[16] MR 5.3(c)(1). This result is less likely under DR 1-102(A)(2).

[17] *Walters v. Ditzler*, 424 Pa. 445, 227 A.2d 833, 837 (1967).

[18] *In re Cohn*, 10 Ill.2d 186, 139 N.E.2d 301, 305–06 (1957) (Bristow, J., concurring).

[19] *Id.*

[20] *Id.*

[21] *Id.* at 306.

them their day in court before it is too late. Illustrative of the bar's attitude is a $125,000 study of lawyers' ethics undertaken by the Philadelphia Bar Association not long after *Gunn v. Washek* was decided. The resulting report recognized the need "to counter the activity of [insurance] carriers' adjusters."[22] It suggested, however, that the problem could be dealt with "by the exercise of restraint on the part of carriers."[23] There was no reference in the report to any professional responsibility on the part of those lawyers who are house counsel to insurance carriers or who regularly represent them in litigation. On the contrary, the substance of the report was dedicated to the need to stamp out "ambulance chasing."

Ironically, the report did acknowledge the "social value" of automobile wrecking companies listening to police calls in order to be the first to arrive at accident scenes to carry off the damaged vehicles.[24] The report found no social value, however, in a similar effort by lawyers to protect the rights of the injured people (which would include the preservation of relevant evidence that might be hauled off and destroyed by the wrecking companies).

§ 12.04 SOCIOECONOMIC ASPECTS OF THE RULES AGAINST SOLICITATION

The bar's rules against solicitation are an integral part of the inglorious history of the ABA's ethical codes.[25] In both design and enforcement, the 1908 Canons of Professional Ethics discriminated in favor of a White Anglo-Saxon Protestant legal establishment (and their clients)[26] and against recently arrived Jewish and Catholic lawyers from Eastern Europe, Italy, and Ireland (and their clients).[27] The principal means of restricting the practice of these new lawyers was through anticompetitive rules of "ethics" forbidding advertising and solicitation. Indeed, anticompetitive issues so dominated the work of the ABA's Committee on Professional Ethics under the 1908 Canons of Professional Ethics that "there has been a tendency . . . to assume that this is the exclusive field of interest of the Committee and that it is not concerned with the more serious questions of standards and obligations."[28]

---

[22] Jaffe, Report to the Committee of Censors of the Philadelphia Bar Association of the Investigation into Unethical Solicitation by Philadelphia Lawyers 41 (March 1, 1971). The Report also mentioned the possibility of remedial legislation, but no effort appears to have been made by the Bar Association toward that end.

[23] *Id.*

[24] *Id.* at 40.

[25] *See* Chapter 1, *supra.*

[26] "Native-born Americans dominated the profession at the end of the nineteenth century. Only 3 percent of lawyers practicing in Massachusetts in 1870 or admitted to its bar between 1870 and 1890 were born abroad." Richard L. Abel, American Lawyers 85 (1989). Contributing to this homogeneity were "[e]xplicit, sometimes de jure, ethnoreligious, racial, and sexual discrimination (by law schools, bar examiners, bar associations, and employers)." *Id.* at 6.

Discrimination on grounds of race and gender were particularly severe, and has continued. [continued] For example, in 1960, African Americans were 10.6 percent of the population but only 0.8 percent of the bar. *Id.* at 100. Women were less than 5 percent of the profession until the 1970s. *Id.* at 90.

[27] Jerold Auerbach, Unequal Justice, ch. 2 and 4 (1976).

[28] Model Code of Professional Responsibility, Preface (1969).

Although that observation was made in the Preface to the Model Code in 1969, it did not signal a lessening of the established bar's concern with advertising and solicitation. The "axiomatic norm" of Canon 2 did recognize that "A Lawyer Should Assist the Legal Profession in Fulfilling its Duty to Make Legal Counsel Available."[29] Nevertheless, the first five disciplinary rules under Canon 2 were devoted not to assuring adequate information about the availability and cost of legal services but, rather, to denying the communication of relevant information to people who would most need it.[30]

Thus, DR 2-104 read: "A lawyer who has given unsolicited advice to a layman that he should obtain counsel or take legal action shall not accept employment resulting from that advice. . . ." DR 2-103 said: "A lawyer shall not recommend employment as a private practitioner of himself, his partner, or associate to a non-lawyer who has not sought his advice."

Those rules appear on first reading to be broad and absolute. For a particular class of lawyers and clients, however, they are practically meaningless because of certain exceptions. For example, DR 2-104 also provided that "[a] lawyer [who has volunteered advice] may accept employment by a close friend, relative, [or a] former client." That means, of course, that those who are accustomed to retaining lawyers, say, to do their tax or estates work, and those who have lawyers as friends and relatives, can be solicited despite the rule. As to that socioeconomic class of people, there is no impropriety in solicitation.

Thus, "opulent lawyers and large law firms" have been known to spend "large sums of money for memberships in country clubs [and] entertainment in fashionable surroundings . . . [for] . . . the primary purpose of . . . attract[ing] . . . law business."[31] This is "attested by the fact that such lawyers regularly claim and the Internal Revenue Department regularly allows deductions for these expenditures as 'business' and not 'personal' expenses."[32] This has been considered "not only a dignified method of solicitation that is generally recognized, but it has the unique advantage of having the United States government pay a substantial portion of its cost."[33]

---

[29] Also, EC 2-1 said:

> The need of members of the public for legal services is met only if they recognize their legal problems, appreciate the importance of seeking assistance, and are able to obtain the services of acceptable legal counsel. . . .

EC 2-2 added that "[t]he legal profession should assist laymen to recognize legal problems because such problems may not be self-revealing and often are not timely noticed."

[30] DR 2-101 forbad a lawyer to use any means of commercial publicity; DR 2-102 imposed narrow limitations on the use of professional cards, letterheads, and telephone directory listings; DR 201-3 forbad a lawyer to recommend that a non-lawyer retain the lawyer's services if the non-lawyer had not initiated the contact by seeking legal advice; DR 2-104 said that a lawyer who has given unsolicited legal advice to a member of the public shall not accept employment resulting from that advice; and DR 2-105 forbad a lawyer to indicate a specialization in a particular area of the law. However, as discussed below, each of those rules included arbitrary exceptions for the benefit of lawyers seeking to represent corporations and wealthy clients.

[31] In re Cohn, 10 Ill.2d 186, 139 N.E.2d 301, 306 (1957) (Bristow, J., concurring).

[32] Id.

[33] Id. Another means of selective enforcement of the rules against advertising and solicitation are "law lists," which are privately operated advertising books (like MARTINDALE-HUBBELL) that are certified by the ABA Standing Committee on Law Lists. Law lists contain self-laudatory

That is the way that solicitation has been carried on with impunity by lawyers seeking to represent those of wealth and privilege. The problem of impropriety has arisen principally for lawyers seeking to represent the socioeconomic group typified by Ernest Gunn's mother, or tenants as distinguished from landlords, or consumers as distinguished from manufacturers. For this group — comprised of people who are likely to be less sophisticated and therefore more in need of information about their rights — the established bar has erected "ethical" barriers that block the access to the legal system that is promised by Canon 2.

MR 7.3 continues this socioeconomic double standard. In MR 7.3a, a lawyer is forbidden to solicit employment in person, by telephone, or by real-time electronic contact from a person with whom the lawyer has no family, close personal, or prior professional relationship.

An oddity about MR 7.3 is that the codifiers felt a need for a blanket rule barring in-person, telephone, or real-time solicitation in any case;[34] if the concern is with the possibility of abusive practices, the rule could simply have forbidden the abusive practices. This is in fact done in MR 7.3(b), where the lawyer is forbidden to solicit a relative or former client if (1) the person has made known to the lawyer a desire not to be solicited, or (2) the solicitation involves coercion, duress, or harassment. If the reason for the blanket proscription is that it would be difficult to prove these kinds of abuses in fact occurred, that difficulty could be avoided by putting the burden on the lawyer to prove that she did not commit any abuses, rather than putting it on disciplinary counsel to prove that she did.

In what may be a significant advance in this area of lawyers' ethics, the Restatement has no section generally forbidding a lawyer to solicit or advertise for clients.[35] The only section relating to this issue is § 9, which relates to the limited situation of a lawyer who is leaving a law firm and who wants to solicit the firm's clients to go with her. In the comment to that section, and in the reporter's note, there are cursory references to the fact that there are limitations on solicitation under lawyer codes.[36]

---

announcements (euphemistically called "cards") and are directed to potential clients and forwarders of clients. However, not every attorney is permitted to compete by listing her professional autobiography, prestigious associations, and important clients in MARTINDALE-HUBBELL. One must await an invitation from the publisher to apply for an "a" rating, which can be achieved only upon submission of favorable references from 16 judges and lawyers who have already received an "a" rating themselves. For a pointed illustration of the advertising purpose behind the law list, see MONROE H. FREEDMAN, LAWYERS' ETHICS IN AN ADVERSARY SYSTEM 117 (1975).

[34] MR 7.3, Cmt. [4].

[35] In this regard, the RESTATEMENT is similar to the AMERICAN LAWYER'S CODE OF CONDUCT (1980). Unlike the RESTATEMENT, however, the ALCC does have limitations on abusive methods of solicitation, such as misleading a potential client or continuing solicitation after being told that the person does not want to be solicited. See ALCC, Rules 7.1–7.5.

[36] See RESTATEMENT § 9, Cmt. i, Reporter's Note i.

§ 12.05 ADVERTISING FOR CLIENTS — "THIS NEW REVOLUTION IN LAW PRACTICE"

The first attack on the Model Code restrictions on advertising and solicitation was in 1970.[37] The Stern Community Law Firm in Washington, D.C., a public-interest law firm of which Freedman was Director, advertised in newspapers, magazines, and on the radio seeking clients for two cases that the firm wanted to litigate. The first of these cases related to child adoption. At that time the District of Columbia kept a larger proportion of its homeless children in public institutions than did any other American city. These institutions were notoriously overcrowded and understaffed, and the children were being neglected and abused. Nevertheless, many people who wanted to adopt the children were being barred from doing so solely because they were single, because both parents were working, or because they were white (virtually all of the homeless children were African American). The firm therefore advertised for clients who wanted to adopt children but who were unable to do so because of these rules.[38]

Similarly, when the Food and Drug Administration refused to take action regarding toys that presented a risk of maiming and killing children, the firm published a list of the toys and their manufacturers and offered to represent anyone who had bought one of the toys and was having difficulty getting a refund.[39]

Complaints by judges and lawyers about the Stern Firm's advertisements resulted in a proceeding against Freedman and the firm before the Bar's Committee on Legal Ethics and Grievances. In its brief to the Grievance Committee, the firm argued that advertising and solicitation by lawyers is protected under the First Amendment as freedom of speech by the attorney and as an essential aspect of the client's right to petition for redress of grievances.[40] The firm also argued that it is important to the profession as

---

[37] *See also* MONROE FREEDMAN, *Solicitation of Clients: For the Poor, Not the Privileged*, 1 JURIS DOCTOR 10 (1971); Monroe Freedman, *Access to the Legal System: The Professional Obligation to Chase Ambulances*, in LAWYERS' ETHICS IN AN ADVERSARY SYSTEM, ch. 10 (1975); Monroe Freedman, *Advertising and Solicitation by Lawyers: A Proposed Redraft of Canon 2 of the Code of Professional Responsibility*, 4 HOFSTRA L. REV. 183 (1976).

Freedman also testified as an expert witness in two cases challenging the ABA's restrictions on advertising, *Consumers Union v. ABA*, No. 75-0105-R (E.D.Va. 1975), and *United States v. ABA*, No. 76-C-3475 (N.D.Ill.1976). In the latter case, Hazard served as an expert witness on behalf of the ABA. Hazard has since changed his position on the issue. *See* Goeffrey Hazard, Russell G. Pearce & Jeffrey W. Stempel, *Why Lawyers Should Be Allowed to Advertise: A Market Analysis of Legal Services*, 58 N.Y.U. L. REV. 1084 (1983).

[38] As a result of the Stern Firm's publicity and litigation, overcrowded and abusive institutions were closed, and adoption standards were liberalized.

[39] In response to a suit brought by a firm attorney, Harriet Rabb (subsequently Assistant Dean at Columbia Law School and later a Deputy at the Department of Health and Human Services), the FDA did list the toys, but then failed to issue regulations regarding returns and refunds.

[40] Although now conventional, this argument was considered novel, if not frivolous, at the time. Even five years later, in the course of a bar-sponsored debate on lawyer advertising, Antonin Scalia (then Assistant Attorney General in Charge of the Office of Legal Counsel) said in exasperation, "I do wish Dean Freedman would forget about the First Amendment and stick to the merits."

Of course, Justice Scalia might yet have the last word on the subject. *See Shapero v. Kentucky Bar Ass'n*, 486 U.S. 466, 108 S.Ct. 1916 (1988), where Scalia and the Chief Justice joined in a

well as to the public that lawyers be seen reaching out to serve members of the community and not just corporations and other wealthy clients. Although the Committee began with an openly hostile attitude, it ultimately issued the first Bar Association opinion in the country approving advertisements for clients by public interest lawyers serving without fees.[41]

Despite this limitation,[42] Fred Graham wrote in the *New York Times* that "for a profession that has forbidden lawyers to wear tie clasps bearing their state bar emblem or to send Christmas cards to prospective clients, on the ground that such activities were unethical 'advertising,' the activities approved in the new ruling are unprecedented."[43] In introducing federal legislation to override the Bar's decision, a member of Congress complained that "[c]lient soliciting, this new revolution in law practice . . . can be expected to usher in a new era of encouraged litigation from so-called poor people, class action by groups, and idealists in the areas of consumerism and ecology, etc."[44]

§ 12.06   LAWYER ADVERTISING IN THE SUPREME COURT

It did that and more. Six years later, in *Bates v. State Bar of Arizona*,[45] the Supreme Court agreed that advertising by lawyers is protected under the First Amendment.

In response to the contention that advertising has an adverse effect on professionalism, the Court found any connection between advertising and the erosion of "true professionalism" to be "severely strained."[46] Because "professionalism" is frequently a euphemism for public image, the Court pointed out that the failure of lawyers to advertise may be viewed by the public as a professional failure to reach out and serve the community.[47] Elaborating on

---

dissent by Justice O'Connor. Referring to the line of cases protecting lawyer advertising as protected speech, the dissenters denounced it as "built on defective premises and flawed reasoning." 108 S.Ct. at 1925. However, O'Connor has since acknowledged that it is "now well established that lawyer advertising is commercial speech and, as such, is accorded a measure of First Amendment protection." *Florida Bar v. Went for It*, 115 S.Ct. 2371, 2374 (1995).

[41] The opinion was issued in March, 1971, but is published in 41 D.C. BAR J. 102 (1974).

[42] Another limitation in the Committee's opinion, was that advertisements had to be in the name of the firm alone and could not carry the name of a particular lawyer. (Freedman's name was included in the first Stern Firm ads at the request of other lawyers in the firm, who did not want to be unnecessarily at risk of professional discipline.) Ironically, MR 7.2(d) of the Model Rules now *requires* that advertising "include the name of at least one lawyer responsible for its content."

[43] Fred Graham, *D.C. Bar Supports Some Law Ads*, N.Y. TIMES, March 10, 1971, at A25. The WASHINGTON POST commented that the decision is expected to have "far-reaching effects for [public interest] lawyers who have sought to offer legal assistance to individuals and in 'class actions' on behalf of groups, such as the poor, minorities, consumers and environmental organizations." Id. at A1.

[44] *The Nonprofit Practice of Law — A Threat to the American Judicial System*," Extension of Remarks of Rep. John R. Rarick, CONG. REC., E1769, March 11, 1971.

[45] 433 U.S. 350, 97 S.Ct. 2691 (1977).

[46] *Bates*, 433, U.S. at 368, 97 S.Ct. at 2701.

[47] *Bates*, 433 U.S. at 370 n.21, 97 S.Ct. at 2702 n.21, *citing* MONROE H. FREEDMAN, LAWYERS' ETHICS IN AN ADVERSARY SYSTEM 115–16 (1975).

that point, the Court noted that "cynicism with regard to the profession may be created by the fact that it long has publicly eschewed advertising, while condoning the actions of the attorney who structures his social or civic associations so as to provide contacts with potential clients."[48]

Nor did the Court find persuasive the contention that advertising is "inherently misleading." "[W]e view as dubious," the Court said, "any justification that is based on the benefits of public ignorance."[49] In any event, "the bar retains the power to correct omissions that have the effect of presenting an inaccurate picture."[50] "If the naivete of the public will cause advertising by attorneys to be misleading," the Court added, "then it is the bar's role to assure that the populace is sufficiently informed as to enable it to place advertising in its proper perspective."[51]

Further, the Court said, "we cannot accept the notion that it is always better for a person to suffer a wrong silently than to redress it by legal action."[52] Underlying cases like *Button* and the union cases that followed it was "the Court's concern that the aggrieved receive information regarding their legal rights and the means of effectuating them," and "[t]his concern applies with at least as much force to aggrieved individuals as it does to groups."[53]

Replying to the contention that advertising will have an adverse effect on the quality of legal work, the Court made the common-sense observation that "[r]estraints on advertising are an ineffective way of deterring shoddy work. An attorney who is inclined to cut quality will do so regardless of the rule on advertising."[54]

Because advertising by lawyers for fee-paying clients is "commercial speech,"[55] however, the Court held that those attacking the bar's restrictions could not rely on the First Amendment "overbreadth" doctrine.[56] That is, the

---

See also 433 U.S. at 370 n.22, 97 S.Ct. at 2702 n.22, citing Petition of the Board of Governors of the District of Columbia Bar for Amendments to Rule X of the Rules Governing the Bar of the District of Columbia (1976), reprinted in the App. to Brief for the United States as *Amicus Curiae.* The Petition of the Board of Governors was also published as Monroe Freedman, *Advertising and Solicitation by Lawyers: A Proposed Redraft of Canon 2 of the Code of Professional Responsibility,* 4 HOFSTRA L. REV. 183 (1976).

[48] *Bates,* 43 U.S. at 371, 97 S.Ct. at 2702.

[49] *Bates,* 433 U.S. at 375, 97 S.Ct. at 2704.

[50] *Id.*

[51] *Bates,* 433 U.S. at 375, 97 S.Ct. at 2705. There is some irony to this point. One of the arguments against permitting individual lawyers to advertise was that it is preferable to inform members of the public about their legal rights through educational programs carried out by the bar. *See* EC 2-2. The problem was that the organized bar never carried out that function, perhaps because there was no profit motive in doing so.

[52] *Id.*

[53] *Bates,* 433 U.S. at 377 n.32, 97 S.Ct. at 2705 n.32. The *Button* line of cases is discussed in this chapter, *infra.*

[54] *Bates,* 433 U.S. at 378, 97 S.Ct. at 2706.

[55] Commercial speech is speech that "proposes a commercial transaction." It receives a lower level of First Amendment protection than does other speech. *See Virginia Pharmacy Board v. Virginia Consumer Council,* 425 U.S. 748, 761, 96 S.Ct. 1817, 1825 (1976); *Bigelow v. Virginia,* 421 U.S. 809, 95 S.Ct. 2222 (1975).

[56] *See Broadrick v. Oklahoma,* 413 U.S. 601, 610, 93 S.Ct. 2908, 2914 (1973).

disciplinary rule at issue could not be attacked on its face on the ground that speakers not before the court might be chilled in the exercise of First Amendment rights by the statute's breadth.[57]

Since the bar did not have to cope with an overbreadth attack on its disciplinary rules, it could have prevailed simply by carrying the burden of proving that the advertisement at issue was misleading. The bar attempted to do this on the ground that the ad used the title "legal clinic," that it referred to "very reasonable" prices, and that it omitted the fact that a lawyer is not needed in order to obtain a name change (one of the legal services offered in the ad). The Court found, however, that the bar had failed to carry its burden of showing "unambiguously" that the advertising at issue had been misleading in any of those respects[58] and reversed the disciplinary sanctions against the lawyers.

The response of the established bar was to attempt to avoid the clear implications of *Bates* and of subsequent decisions on lawyer advertising through a series of redrafts of the ethical rules. One of these efforts was the "laundry list" — a listing of specific kinds of information that could be published, with the expressed or implied proscription against publishing any other information.[59] The pettiness of the bar's resistance to *Bates* is illustrated in the disciplinary proceeding *In the Matter of R.M.J*,[60] where one ground for disciplining the lawyer was that he had used the words "real estate" in his printed advertisements, instead of the laundry-listed word "property."

Other charges in *R.M.J.* were that the lawyer had advertised the unlisted words "contracts" and "securities" in describing his practice; that his advertisement had stated (truthfully) that he was licensed to practice in Missouri and Illinois and before the United States Supreme Court; and that he had sent cards announcing the opening of his practice to "persons other than lawyers, clients, former clients, personal friends, and relatives."[61] In an opinion by Justice Lewis Powell, the Supreme Court unanimously brushed aside these charges.[62]

---

[57] *Bates*, 433 U.S. 381–82, 97 S.Ct. at 2707–08. "Ordinarily, the principal advantage of the overbreadth doctrine for a litigant is that it enables him to benefit from the statute's [unconstitutional] application *to someone else*," even if the statute is constitutional as applied to him. *Board of Trustees of the State University of New York v. Fox*, 492 U.S. 469, 483, 109 S.Ct. 3028, 3036 (1989).

[58] *Bates*, 433 U.S at 382, 97 S.Ct. at 2708.

[59] *See, e.g.*, DR 2-101(B), listing 25 categories of information that may be communicated if "presented in a dignified manner." *But cf.* MR 7.2, Cmt. [3]: "Questions of . . . taste in advertising are matters of speculation and subjective judgment."

[60] 455 U.S. 191, 102 S.Ct. 929 (1982).

[61] The lawyer had also omitted a required disclaimer, stating that he had not been formally certified to practice in the areas of law mentioned in the advertisement. The lawyer did not challenge the constitutionality of the disclaimer provision, and it was not at issue before the Supreme Court. 455 U.S. at 204, 102 S.Ct. at 938.

[62] The Court found it to be "[s]omewhat more troubling" that R.M.J. had listed his membership in the bar of the United States Supreme Court in large boldface type. Since such membership is a formality for a member of any state bar, "[t]he emphasis of this relatively uninformative fact is at least bad taste." 1455 U.S. at 205, 02 S.Ct. at 938; *see also Shapero v. Kentucky Bar Ass'n*, 486 U.S. 466, 479–80, 108 S.Ct. 1916, 1925 (1988) (plurality opinion). Nevertheless, the burden is on the bar to prove that an advertisement is false or misleading, and the bar therefore lost on this issue because "[t]here is nothing in the record to indicate that the inclusion of this information was misleading." *Id.*

Using a test that comes from *Central Hudson Gas & Electric Corp. v. Public Service Comm'n of New York*, the opinion in *R.M.J.* explained the burden on the state in a case involving a limitation on commercial speech.[63] As the *Central Hudson* test has evolved,[64] it provides a two-part test of "intermediate scrutiny" of restrictions on commercial speech. The first part of the *Central Hudson* test posits that the government may freely regulate commercial speech that concerns unlawful activity or that is misleading. The second part of the test has three "prongs." First, the state must assert a "substantial interest" in support of its regulation. Second, the government must show that the restriction on commercial speech "directly and materially advances that interest." Third, the regulation must be "narrowly drawn."[65] Inherent in these is the requirement of *Bates* that the state must carry the burden of proving "unambiguously" that the evils that justify the regulation are in fact present in the particular advertising that the state seeks to suppress.[66]

The next Supreme Court decision on lawyer advertising after *R.M.J.* was *Zauderer v. Office of Disciplinary Counsel*.[67] Again the bar sought to discipline a lawyer on petty grounds, this time that he had solicited clients in an advertisement that explained the rights of women who had been injured, some of them severely, through the use of the Dalkon Shield intrauterine device. The bar was also concerned that the advertisement had contained an illustration of the Dalkon Shield, under which was the question, "Did you use this IUD?"[68] Two women who had retained the lawyer to represent them testified that they would not have known of their legal rights had it not been for the lawyer's ad. The Supreme Court reversed the state's disciplinary action against the lawyer with respect to these charges.

The Court upheld the state's power to discipline the attorney on two other grounds, however, with respect to advertising statements that were in fact misleading. The Dalkon Shield ad said that the client would not be responsible for any fees unless she recovered a judgment in the case. This was misleading to those members of the public who would not realize that the client would be responsible for costs (which could be substantial). Also, in an ad for clients charged with drunk driving, the same lawyer had said that legal fees would be returned in full if the client were "convicted of drunk driving." What the ad failed to say was that most drunk driving defendants plead guilty to a lesser offense than drunk driving, in which event the fee would not be refundable.

---

[63] *Central Hudson Gas & Electric Corp. v. Public Service Comm'n of New York*, 447 U.S. 557, 100 S.Ct. 2343 (1980).

[64] *See Florida Bar v. Went For It*, 115 S.Ct. 2371, 2375–2376 (1995).

[65] This does not require the state to use, in regulating commercial speech, "the least restrictive means" to achieve its end. Nor, on the other hand, is review limited to the less rigorous "rational basis" test. What is required in a commercial speech case is that there be "a fit that is not necessarily perfect, but reasonable; that represents not necessarily the single best disposition but one whose scope is 'in proportion to the interest served,' that employs not necessarily the least restrictive means but . . . a means narrowly tailored to achieve the desired objective." *Id*. at 2380.

[66] *Bates*, 97 S.Ct. at 2708–09.

[67] 471 U.S. 626, 105 S.Ct. 2265 (1985).

[68] The Office of Disciplinary Counsel stipulated that the information in the ad was not false, fraudulent, or deceptive, and that the illustration was an accurate representation of the Dalkon Shield. *Id*. at 634, 2273.

Accordingly, the Court upheld a rule requiring the inclusion of clarifying information in such advertisements.

Not long after, in *Shapero v. Kentucky Bar Association*,[69] the Supreme Court again struck down bar restrictions on truthful advertising. Shapero had sought permission to send a letter to members of the public whose homes were the subject of foreclosure suits. The letter was found to be neither false nor misleading.[70] Nevertheless, the Kentucky Supreme Court held that it would be unethical to advise people who were about to lose their homes that Federal law might allow them additional time to pay, and then to represent those people to enforce their rights.

The state court based its decision on the 1984 version of MR 7.3, which forbad a letter directed to a recipient "known to need [the] legal services" offered by the lawyer.[71] That is, what made the letter unethical under MR 7.3 was that it was directed to people who were known to need the information because their homes were in fact in jeopardy, rather than being directed to an amorphous group of people who might or might not find such services useful.[72]

The Supreme Court's response had a sardonic edge. "Generally, unless the advertiser is inept, the latter group would include members of the former," the Court said, adding, "the First Amendment does not permit a ban on certain speech merely because it is more efficient; the State may not constitutionally ban a particular letter on the theory that to mail it only to those whom it would most interest is somehow inherently objectionable."[73] In short, the bar cannot categorically forbid targeted mailings that are neither false nor misleading.

In 1995, in *Florida Bar v. Went For it, Inc.*,[74] the Supreme Court limited the scope of *Shapero*. *Went For It* involved a challenge to provisions in Florida's Rules of Professional Conduct that prohibited direct mail advertising of legal services to victims or victims' relatives within thirty days of an accident or disaster. A lawyer and his referral service (Went For It, Inc.) challenged the new rules on First Amendment grounds.

Justice Sandra Day O'Connor wrote a five-to-four majority opinion upholding Florida's thirty-day limitation on solicitation. She was joined by Chief Justice Rehnquist and Justices Scalia, Thomas, and Breyer. Applying the *Central Hudson* test, O'Connor first found that the state has a substantial interest, both in regulating the practice of professions and in protecting the privacy of citizens from intrusion.[75]

With respect to the second prong of *Central Hudson*, O'Connor held that the thirty-day limitation directly and materially advances the state's interest. She based this holding on a 106-page summary of a two-year study of lawyer

---

[69] 486 U.S. 466, 108 S.Ct. 1916 (1988).

[70] *Id.* at 468, 1919.

[71] 486 U.S. at 479, 108 S.Ct. at 1920.

[72] *Id.* at 373. The ABA filed a brief *amicus curiae* in support of the Kentucky position. *Id.* at 476.

[73] 486 U.S. at 473–74, 108 S.Ct. at 1921–22.

[74] 515 US. 618, 115 S.Ct. 2731 (1995).

[75] *Id.* at 2376–2377.

advertising and solicitation submitted by the Florida Bar, which concluded that a majority of the public views direct mail solicitation immediately after an accident as "an intrusion on privacy that reflects poorly on the profession."[76] O'Connor acknowledged that the Bar, which had the burden of proof, failed to provide crucial backup information regarding sample size, selection procedures, and copies of the actual surveys.[77] Without that support information, a summary of the results of a survey is worthless. Nevertheless, O'Connor found the data to be "sufficient" to show that the restriction "targets a concrete, nonspeculative harm."[78]

Turning to the third prong of *Central Hudson*, O'Connor held the Bar's rule to be "reasonably well-tailored to its stated objective of eliminating targeted mailings whose type and timing are a source of distress to Floridians, distress that has caused many of them to lose respect for the legal profession."[79] She also noted that there are other ways for lawyers to reach potential clients, including advertising on prime-time television and radio, newspapers and other media, and by renting billboards; she referred also to the allowable use of "untargeted letters to the general population."

This last point (the fact that untargeted mailings are permitted) undercuts the reasoning in *Went For It*, because, as the Court noted in *Shapero*, unless the advertiser is inept, the untargeted general public will include all of the same targeted accident victims.[80] The result would therefore be the identical asserted invasion of privacy and impairment of the image of the bar. The only practical difference appears to be that a general mailing (like prime-time television, billboards, etc.) are likely to be prohibitively expensive for most lawyers.

Justice Anthony Kennedy dissented, joined by Justices Stevens, Souter, and Ginsburg.[81] Kennedy pointed out (and the majority did not disagree) that "when an accident results in death or injury, it is often urgent at once to

---

[76] *Id.* at 2377. The opinion also relies upon an "anecdotal record" submitted by the bar, that is "noteworthy for its breadth and detail." *Id.* Much of this came from newspaper articles and editorials critical of lawyers, a subject that is discussed *infra* § 12.10.

[77] *Id.* at 2378.

[78] *Id.*

[79] *Id.* at 2380.

[80] 486 U.S. at 473–74, 108 S.Ct. at 1921–22. The Court added that "the First Amendment does not permit a ban on certain speech merely because it is more efficient; the State may not constitutionally ban a particular letter on the theory that to mail it only to those whom it would most interest is somehow inherently objectionable." *Id.*

[81] For a comment by Ginsburg on *Went For It*, *see* Ruth Bader Ginsburg, *Supreme Court Pronouncements on the Conduct of Lawyers*, 1 J. INST. STUD. LEGAL ETHICS 1, 11 (1996) (noting that the dissent was "strong," and wondering whether the case was "an entering wedge to an eventual volte-face on lawyer advertising, or . . . an isolated exception to the general run of First Amendment/commercial speech precedent"). Ginsburg also noted the subtitle of this chapter in the first edition of this book: "The Professional Responsibility to Chase Ambulances." *Id.*

See also John Phillips, *Six Years After* Florida Bar v. Went For It, Inc.: *The Continual Erosion of First Amendment Rights*, 14 GEO. J. LEGAL ETHICS 197, 203–09 (2000) (listing states that have enacted similar bans).

One year after Went for It, Kentucky made it a criminal offense to solicit plaintiffs within thirty days of an accident. Ky. Rev. Stat. § 21A.300.

investigate the occurrence, identify witnesses, and preserve evidence."[82] Accordingly, the banned communications may be "vital to the recipients' right to petition the courts for redress of grievance" under the First Amendment.[83] Also, quoting *Zauderer*,[84] he noted that "the mere possibility that some members of the population might find advertising . . . offensive cannot justify suppressing it. The same must hold true for advertising that some members of the bar find beneath their dignity."[85]

Kennedy also pointed to the bar's failure to carry its burden of demonstrating the reality of the asserted harm. Noting the lack of backup information for the survey summary, Kennedy observed that the anecdotal evidence (which the majority had found "noteworthy for its breadth and detail") was "noteworthy for its incompetence."[86]

Perhaps Kennedy's strongest point is the practical one, that the problem asserted by the state is "largely self-policing."[87] That is, if members of the public really find the banned solicitation to be offensive, such solicitation will stop because it will fail to attract clients. On the contrary, however, the fact that some 280,000 direct mail solicitations are sent to accident victims and their survivors in Florida each year is an indication of a positive public response to the practice.[88]

Unfortunately, what may have been the most effective argument before this Supreme Court was not made in *Went For It*. Kennedy mentioned in his opinion that while plaintiffs' personal injury lawyers were barred from contacting victims or their survivors, there is no similar ban against potential defendants, their lawyers, and their adjusters. This, he said, "makes little sense."[89] Actually, this discriminatory treatment between the two adverse sides is more serious than that, and the constitutional authority for striking it down is significant.

Just as there is anecdotal evidence that some people resent the intrusion of a plaintiffs' lawyer on their privacy, there is evidence that people similarly resent intrusion by insurance adjusters. One source for this is the Wall Street Journal (not a friend to plaintiffs' lawyers). For example, an adjuster for Liberty Mutual Group knocked on the door of the family of a New Jersey woman, just thirteen hours after she had been killed in a wreck, to discourage them from getting a lawyer and to propose settlement with a waiver of their rights.[90] The insurer defended the practice as a benefit to those solicited.[91] In another case, this one from Florida, a woman briefly considered dealing

---

[82] 115 S.Ct. at 2381.

[83] *Id*. at 2382.

[84] 431 U.S. 626, 648.

[85] 115 S.Ct. at 2383.

[86] *Id*. at 2384. Kennedy also argued that the ban is overinclusive, and that there is a "wild disproportion between the harm supposed and the speech ban enforced." *Id*.

[87] *Id*. at 2385.

[88] *Id*. at 2386.

[89] *Id*. at 2382.

[90] Leslie Scism, *Insurers Stir Anger by Contacting Victims*, WALL ST. J., Feb. 2, 1997.

[91] *Id*.

directly with an adjuster but "became suspicious" after the claims representative repeatedly stressed that a lawyer wasn't necessary.[92] And, of course, additional anecdotal evidence can be found in published cases, like the case of Ernest Gene Gunn, recounted above.

Discouraging victims and their survivors from retaining lawyers is a familiar practice of insurance companies. Here, for example, are questions and answers from a document distributed to victims and their survivors by Allstate Insurance Company:[93]

1) AM I REQUIRED TO HIRE AN ATTORNEY TO HANDLE MY CLAIM?

No. In fact, each year Allstate settles claims directly with many accident victims with no attorneys involved in the claim settlement process.

2) WILL AN ATTORNEY MAKE THE CLAIM SETTLEMENT PROCESS FASTER FOR ME?

A recent study . . . found that people who settle insurance claims without and attorney generally settle their claims more quickly than those who have hired attorneys.

3) HOW MUCH ARE ATTORNEYS' FEES AND WHO PAYS FOR THEM?

Attorneys often take up to one-third of the total settlement you receive from an insurance company, plus expenses incurred. If you settle directly with Allstate, however, the total amount of the settlement is yours.

Clearly, this is a controversy of public importance — whether an accident victim should retain a lawyer to assert her First Amendment right of petition, and whether a particular settlement is in the interest of a particular victim. Just as clearly, one side of that controversy is being permitted to speak, while the other is being gagged. This is "viewpoint discrimination," which was declared unconstitutional in *R.A.V. v. City of St. Paul* just three years before *Went For It*.[94] The opinion in *R.A.V.* was written for the Court by Justice Scalia, who was in the 5-4 majority in *Went For It*.[95] For those of us, like Freedman, who believe that Scalia tries to be principled (despite occasional

---

[92] *Id.*

[93] *See Commonwealth of Pennsylvania v. Allstate Insurance Company*, 729 A.2d 135, 138 (Pa. 1999); *Allstate Insurance Company v. West Virginia State Bar*, 233 F.3d 813 (4th Cir. 2000).

[94] 505 U.S. 377, 391, 112 S.Ct. 2538, 2547 (1992).

[95] The case involved a hate-crime ordinance that made it a crime to put a symbol on public or private property that the actor "knows or has reasonable grounds to know arouses anger, alarm or resentment in others on the basis of race, color, creed, religion or gender." Scalia held the ordinance to be unconstitutional because one side of a controversy was gagged while the other wasn't. "One could hold up a sign saying, for example, that all 'anti-Catholic bigots' are misbegotten; but not that all 'papists' are." *Id.* at 391–392, 2547–2548.

It's the same in Went for It. One can intrude on a person's grief to say, "You don't need a lawyer, and this is a good settlement," but not to say, "You do need a lawyer to find witnesses and evidence before it's too late, and that settlement they're offering you is inadequate."

lapses, as in *Liteky v. United States* [96]), there is reason to hope that he would come out differently if confronted with his opinion in *R.A.V.* [97]

In this analysis of *Went For It*, the regulation would be constitutional as long as both sides were barred from speaking during the thirty-day period. This still would give an advantage to the insurer in most cases, because it is the victim who has the burden of proof and who urgently needs to find witnesses and to gather physical evidence before it has been lost or destroyed. Nevertheless, such a balanced rule would be a significant improvement and would avoid the constitutional concerns of *R.A.V.* [98]

§ 12.07 "ACTUALLY," "INHERENTLY," AND "POTENTIALLY" MISLEADING

Another important Supreme Court decision on lawyer advertising is *Peel v. Attorney Registration and Disciplinary Commission of Illinois.* [99] In *Peel*, the lawyer truthfully stated on his letterhead that he had been certified by the National Board of Trial Advocacy (NBTA). Illinois censured him under a disciplinary rule that categorically forbad a lawyer to hold himself out as certified or as a specialist.

The Supreme Court struck down the disciplinary rule as applied to Peel. In doing so, the Court discussed three kinds of misleading advertising — "actually," "inherently," and "potentially." We are not sure precisely what each of these terms means. What is clear, however, is that the state may categorically ban advertising that is either "actually" or "inherently" misleading. Together, these terms include situations in which the state shows that a "potential client or person was actually misled or deceived," [100] and situations in which the statement is true but deceptive. An illustration of the latter category is where the state presents evidence that "the certification [has] been issued by an organization that [has] made no inquiry into [the lawyer's] fitness, or by one that [issues] certificates indiscriminately. . . . " [101]

Peel's letterhead, however, was "neither actually nor inherently misleading" because "there is no dispute about the bona fides and the relevance of NBTA certification." [102] Thus, the state's blanket proscription was unconstitutional as applied to Peel. The Court added that the state's concern about "the possibility of deception in hypothetical cases is not sufficient to rebut the

---

[96] Discussed *supra*, Ch. 9, § 9.08[1].

[97] This could happen in an appeal of a criminal conviction for post-accident solicitation, as under the Kentucky statute, *supra*, note 81.

[98] Under this analysis, the federal anti-solicitation statute would be constitutional. It bars unsolicited communications concerning potential personal injury litigation by "an attorney . . . *or any potential party to the litigation*," made to the victim or a relative within forty-five days of the accident. 49 U.S.C. § 1136(g)(2) (1997) (emphasis added).

[99] 496 U.S. 91, 110 S.Ct. 2281 (1990).

[100] *Id.* at 101. It was not sufficient that the Illinois Supreme Court found "as a matter of law" that Peel's letterhead was "necessarily misleading." *Id.* at 101.

[101] *Id.* at 102. This distinction was anticipated in the AMERICAN LAWYER'S CODE OF CONDUCT (1980) at p. 703, Ill. 7(a) and 7(b).

[102] *Id.* at 110–11.

constitutional presumption favoring disclosure over concealment."[103] Nevertheless, a holding that a total ban is unconstitutional "does not necessarily preclude less restrictive regulation of commercial speech."[104]

We understand the reference to "the possibility of deception" to mean that the statement was "potentially" misleading, in the sense, for example, that a member of the public might infer that the NBTA is affiliated with the state or federal government. Therefore, as emphasized in Justice Marshall's concurrence, the state could use "less restrictive measures" than a total ban to prevent deception.[105] One way to do that would be to require a statement that the certifying organization is private.

§ 12.08   IN-PERSON SOLICITATION

The struggle to allow lawyer advertising that is not false or misleading appears to have largely been won. As indicated in *Went For It*, the last ditch still being defended by much of the established bar is in-person solicitation.

Going well beyond the rule in *Went For It*, MR 7.3(a) categorically forbids in-person solicitation "when a significant motive for the lawyer's doing so is the lawyer's pecuniary gain."[106] As noted earlier, MR 7.3(a) nevertheless permits the lawyer to solicit for pecuniary gain when the lawyer has a "family, close personal *or prior professional* relationship" with the prospective client. The justification for this, as expressed in the comment, is that a lawyer is less likely to engage in abusive practices against one with whom the lawyer has a prior professional relationship. However, this proposition is not self-evident. For example, how does a previous representation of the client give assurance that the lawyer will not engage in "private importuning" of the prospective client, who "may already feel overwhelmed by the circumstances"?[107]

The real problem of the potential client who may feel overwhelmed by circumstances is illustrated by the following case. A woman arrives at a busy, crowded metropolitan courthouse holding a small boy by the hand. She speaks almost no English. She is intimidated by the imposing surroundings, and she is frightened and confused by the bustle and the noise. All she knows is that she is required to be some place in that building because her son has gotten into trouble or her landlord is attempting to evict her family. People brush by her, concerned with their own problems. Then a man appears, smiles at her, and asks her in her own language whether he can help her. Through him, the woman meets and retains the man's employer, a lawyer who gives her competent representation at a fair fee.

In our view, that lawyer should have been given an award as Attorney of the Year. Instead, Solomon Cohn, whose practice consisted of cases like that

---

[103] *Id.* at 111.

[104] *Id.* at 110 n.17.

[105] *Id.* at 116. (Marshall, J., concurring).

[106] New York's DR 2-103 is somewhat different, but does categorically forbid in-person solicitation, and it exempts solicitation of a former client or current client.

[107] *See* MR 7.3, Cmt. [1].

one, was prosecuted as a criminal[108] and convicted of the misdemeanor of soliciting business on behalf of an attorney.[109] Professional disciplinary proceedings then followed. Giving favorable weight to Cohn's "expressions of self-reproach and the humiliation he has already suffered," the court in the disciplinary case decided to treat him with "leniency."[110] This meant humiliating him further by publicly censuring him on the front page of the *New York Law Journal*.[111]

In a similar case in Illinois,[112] members of the bar testified without contradiction on behalf of the lawyer's "integrity and the fidelity and effectiveness with which he [had] handled the business of his clients."[113] One of the judges in the case added that [f]or a quarter of a century [the lawyer] . . . enjoyed an unblemished record."[114] Nevertheless, the Bar Association sought a five-year suspension. As stated by Justice Schaefer (who agreed with the Bar and dissented from the leniency of censure) the fact that the lawyer represented his clients effectively and treated them fairly was "not particularly relevant." What justified a five-year suspension, Schaefer explained, was that the lawyer had "overreached the other members of the bar" by competing for clients through solicitation.[115]

§ 12.09 SOLICITATION AT THE BEDSIDE

The classic horror for those who decry ambulance-chasing is solicitation of a tort victim at the bedside. Consider, then, the following case.

Laura Eagle is a sole practitioner in a large city. One evening an acquaintance who is a social worker mentioned to Eagle the terrible conditions he had seen that day on a visit to a private nursing home in the city — filth, poor food, and neglect, even to the point of one patient who had maggots growing in her flesh. Because the patients are poor, elderly, bedridden, and rarely visited by anyone, they have no way to help themselves or to get help. Eagle asked the social worker to return to the nursing home, explain to some of the patients about the possibility of litigation on their behalf, and sign up one or more of them on a contingent fee. She made it clear that the social worker was not to mislead or pressure the patients in any way, and he followed her instructions.

As a result, Eagle became attorney for the patients. Before taking any action on their behalf, she discussed possible courses of action with them, explaining the advantages and disadvantages of each course. The patients unanimously

---

[108] *See* N.Y. Judiciary Law §§ 479, 482, and 485. These provisions are still law in New York. *But see Attorney Advertising and Solicitation Should Not Be a Crime (The Case for Repeal of Judiciary Law Sections 479 and 482)*, Report of the Committee on Professional Responsibility of the Ass'n of the Bar of the City of New York, THE RECORD 634 (1989).

[109] *In re* Solomon Cohn, N.Y.L.J. p. 1:6-7, 3:3 (Feb. 19, 1974).

[110] *Id.*

[111] *Id.*

[112] *In re* Saul E. Cohn, 10 Ill.2d 186, 139 N.E.2d 301 (1957).

[113] 139 N.E.2d at 305 (Justice Bristow, concurring).

[114] *Id.* at 306.

[115] 139 N.E.2d at 304.

decided on a class action against the nursing home. Eagle obtained a substantial recovery for the patients and a court order protecting their rights to adequate care. She also received a substantial fee on the normal one-third contingency basis.

At Eagle's disciplinary hearing for violating MR 7.3 and 8.4(a) (violating a disciplinary rule through another), she admitted that a significant motive for her taking the case was to earn the fee. She pointed out that she could not have afforded to handle such a difficult and time-consuming case on a *pro bono* basis.

Eagle was suspended from practice for one year, while the lawyer who represented the nursing home spent the same year serving as President of the State Bar Association.

Eagle's case is a variation on a hypothetical that Freedman used as a panelist at an ABA convention.[116] The purpose was to point out the importance that solicitation can have in helping the profession to "Fulfill[] Its Duty to Make legal Counsel Available." Possible responses might have been either that the Eagle hypothetical is unrealistic (although there have in fact been cases like it) or that the application of the anti-solicitation rule in such circumstances is inappropriate. No one, however, made either of those responses. On the contrary, Freedman's co-panelist, Professor Michael Davis, found the case to be "relatively easy to decide."[117] While recognizing that Eagle "achieved the sort of good the legal profession aims at," Professor Davis insisted that "she *is* guilty of unprofessional conduct."[118]

The moral of the story, and of the bar's anti-solicitation rules, appears to be that it is better to have maggots feeding on your flesh than to have a lawyer sitting at your bedside.[119]

A real-life variation on the Eagle hypothetical was subsequently provided in an opinion by the Alabama State Bar Disciplinary Commission.[120] The facts, as accepted by the Commission were these. A lawyer represents twenty-five members of a class of people who had had experimental surgery performed on them without their consent by a surgeon who was acting on behalf of a company. There are about 150 other members of the class who do not know

---

[116] ABA Conference on Professionalism, Denver, Colorado, June 25, 1987.

[117] *See* Michael Davis, *Professionalism Means Putting Your Profession First*, 2 GEO. J. LEGAL ETHICS 341, 349 (1988). Davis did find it troubling that "Eagle is, in many ways, a good lawyer. She gave legal help to some who, though needing it desperately, might not have gotten it but for her." *Id.* In part for that reason, Davis would limit the sanction to a thirty-day suspension from practice. (An article based on Freedman's talk at the conference was also submitted to the same journal, but it was rejected by the editors.)

[118] *Id.* (Emphasis in the original).

[119] That is the view, at least, of the legal establishment. Hospitals, however, have started programs to provide on-site legal services. In September of 2001, the Boston Medical Center hosted a conference for medical and legal professionals around the country interested in starting additional legal assistance programs in hospitals. A hospital official at the Medical Center commented that "[p]eople are just thrilled to find a lawyer right on the premises." Margaret Graham Tebo, *Just What the Doctor Ordered*, A.B.A. JOUR., p. 28, Oct., 2001.

[120] Opin. 89-57 (June 2, 1989), ABA/ALI LAWYERS' MANUAL ON PROFESSIONAL CONDUCT 267 (1984).

that they have rights and that their rights will be terminated shortly by a statute of limitations.

Because these potential clients are mostly elderly and uneducated, they are unlikely to understand or to be able to respond to a written communication about the case. The lawyer therefore proposed to speak with them directly to inform them of what he has discovered and to advise them that they may choose to do nothing, to seek the advice of other attorneys, or to become members of the class the lawyer represents. The lawyer does not want "to do anything unethical but cannot simply sit by and allow this injustice . . . to go unchallenged and unknown by most of the victims."[121]

Like Professor Davis, the Commission found the case to be a clear one: the lawyer "may not contact these individuals in person or by telephone to 'solicit' his employment."[122]

§ 12.10 SOLICITATION AT THE DISASTER SITE

After a major disaster in the United States, two groups rush to the site. One group is comprised of members of the news media, the other of lawyers. Each group is there to further First Amendment rights[123] and each has a financial interest in doing so. Not infrequently the reporters ask intrusive and offensive questions like, "How did you feel when you learned that your child was one of those that burned to death on the school bus?" In a letter to the editor, the parent of a student killed in the explosion of TWA Flight 800 complained of the abusive conduct by reporters: "We can endure no more."[124]

Then, after they have tired of the story, the reporters and editorialists devote their attention to harsh criticism of the way in which lawyers invade the privacy of the victims and their grieving families by offering them legal services.

---

[121] *Id.*

[122] *Id. But see Gulf Oil Company v. Bernard*, 452 U.S. 89, 101 S.Ct. 2193 (1981).

[123] With regard to the client's First Amendment right to petition for redress of grievances through litigation, *see* Chapter 2, *supra*, and this chapter, *infra*.

[124] *See* Donald Nibert, *Media Add to Grief of Victim's Families*, USA TODAY, Letter to the Editor, p. 14A, Sept. 14, 1996:

> . . . Peter Jennings' ABC news team, *Newsweek, Time* and a New York newspaper added greatly to the already unbearable sorrow we had to endure . . . .

> And an ABC news staffer also asked my son, "Can't you identify your own sister?" when he was trying to identify her on a VCR tape dancing with 12 young women all dressed the same. How can anyone be so cruel to a grieving sibling?

> *Newsweek* published a picture of the recovery team loading a naked victim into a boat . . . . [W]hat if that had been one our own children? How much additional anguish would have been created?

> A reporter for a New York newspaper trespassed on cemetery property while my wife and I were selecting a burial plot and published the picture taken.

> TV crews stalked our school, stuck microphones into the faces of students and asked, "How did you feel?"

> We can endure no more. We have given all we have.

See also the cover story of BRILL'S CONTENT, Oct., 1999: *Kids? Grieving Families? Is Anyone Ever Off-Limits?* (The magazine was a rare publication that criticized the media. It has not survived.)

Consider, for example, a story in *The New York Times* relating to an accident in which twenty-one children drowned and sixty others were injured when a school bus plunged into a water-filled gravel pit in Alton, Texas. Fully four months after the accident, the *Times* ran a front-page story with a three column headline: "Where 21 Youths Died, Lawyers Wage a War."[125] The story tells of a "parade of lawyers" that began almost immediately after the accident, and of "fierce competition" among the lawyers to represent the families.[126] On page one, the *Times* identifies "one benefit, if that is what it is: a poor and undereducated community, made up largely of Hispanic field laborers, has acquired a new kind of sophistication."[127] This questionable benefit, according to the *Times*, is that people who wanted to grieve without the intrusion of lawyers are now saying, "When this happens to you, you hire a lawyer and you get money."[128]

The important part of the story is on an inside page, at the very end, and is written in a way that makes it appear to be unrelated to the main story that preceded it. There we learn that the 3,000 people who live in Alton have returned to "the anonymous, poverty-stricken lives they led before the bus crashed into the water." Because the students who died were among the poorest in the high school, the response among the other students was "much less than if it was the star quarterback."[129]

With the filing of that story, the last of the reporters also left Alton. Although the *Times'* prominent and lengthy critique of the "parade of lawyers" did not mention the fact, only the lawyers remained, to serve the members of this "poor, undereducated community, made up largely of Hispanic field laborers." Subsequently, in a brief item buried on an inside page, the *Times* reported that the lawyers for sixteen of the families whose children had been killed had obtained a settlement of $67.5 million for their clients.[130]

In short, the legal system succeeded in providing equal protection and due process of law to poverty-stricken people whom all others were content to abandon. That is the story that deserved, but never received, a front-page headline.

Similarly, in a disaster in Bhopal, India, in 1984, 3,100 people were killed and 30,000 were severely disabled when poisonous gas was released from a Union Carbide pesticide plant. Predictably, Union Carbide mounted a legal defense at a cost of more than $7,000,000 — per year.[131] Its court documents

---

[125] Lisa Belkin, *Where 21 Youths Died, Lawyers Wage War*, N.Y. TIMES, Jan. 18, 1990, at A1. The defendant was Coca-Cola Enterprises, the nation's largest bottler of Coke soft drinks, with annual sales of $3.9 billion. *Settlement is Reached in Texas Bus Deaths*, N.Y. TIMES, Apr.19, 1990, at A16. This means that the defendant had deep pockets, but also that it was a formidable adversary with enormous resources for litigation.

[126] *Id.* at B6. We are not defending alleged abuses that sometimes accompany solicitation. For example, MR 7.3(b)(1) forbids solicitation of a client who has indicated to the lawyer that she does not want to be solicited, and MR 7.3(b)(2) forbids solicitation that involves coercion, duress, or harassment. These abuses can and should be punished.

[127] *Id.* at A1.

[128] *Id.* at B6.

[129] *Id.* at B6.

[130] *Settlement is Reached in Texas Bus Deaths*, N.Y. TIMES, Apr. 19, 1990, at A16.

[131] Andrew Blum, *Four Years Later, No End in Sight; Bhopal Disaster Litigation Lingers*, NAT. L. J., Dec. 19, 1988, at 23.

have been described as mountainous. [132] Nevertheless, the American lawyers who went to India to offer to take on this multinational conglomerate on behalf of its victims were frequently referred to as "vultures." Imagine: we have developed a system of justice in which some of the best lawyers in the world travel thousands of miles to offer their services to impoverished people, and instead of celebrating that fact, there are those who decry it. [133]

§ 12.11   SOLICITATION OF CLIENTS AND THE FIRST AMENDMENT

Unfortunately, those who condemn in-person solicitation in cases like those we have been discussing include the ABA and the state bars, which have uniformly adopted the anti-solicitation provisions. [134] It is necessary to consider, therefore, the extent to which solicitation is protected under the First Amendment. In fact, lawyers who solicit clients in person, in fee-paying cases, have a significant degree of constitutional protection, and lawyers like Laura Eagle cannot be disciplined under rules like MR 7.3.

In *NAACP v. Button* [135] the Supreme Court considered solicitation by the NAACP to recruit plaintiffs for school desegregation cases. The NAACP called a series of meetings, inviting not only its members and not only poor people, but all members of the community. At these meetings, the organization's staff attorneys took the platform to urge those present to authorize the lawyers to sue in their behalf. The lawyers had a clear pecuniary interest, because they were paid for the litigation they conducted. [136] Also, the NAACP maintained the ensuing litigation by defraying all expenses, regardless of the financial means of any particular client. Further, as pointed out by the dissenting Justices, common-law prohibitions of champerty, barratry, and maintenance are of long standing. [137]

Nevertheless, the Supreme Court held that "the State's attempt to equate the activities of the NAACP and its lawyers with common-law barratry, maintenance and champerty, and to outlaw them accordingly, cannot obscure

---

[132] *Id.*

[133] Even the WALL STREET JOURNAL complained editorially that the Bhopal lawyers were really interested in making money. In any other context, the WSJ would have recognized this as an example of the profit motive working at its best.

An editorial took note of the fact that India had sought jurisdiction in an American court on the ground that the plaintiffs could not get justice in an Indian court. John P. MacKenzie, *India Salutes American Justice*, NEW YORK TIMES, Dec. 23, 1985, at A16. Even in an editorial on the superiority of American justice, however, there was gratuitous criticism of the American lawyers who were serving the people of Bhopal. The editorial concludes, "Perhaps this tribute to American procedures can compensate for the damage done to our reputation by the American lawyers who raced to India to sign up plaintiffs."

[134] As noted earlier, however, the ALI has chosen virtually to ignore the issue, and the RESTATEMENT has no general proscription of solicitation.

[135] 371 U.S. 415, 83 S.Ct. 328 (1963).

[136] 371 U.S. at 457 (Harlan, J., dissenting).

[137] *Id.* at 456. "Put simply, maintenance is helping another to prosecute a suit; champerty is maintaining a suit in return for a financial interest in the outcome; and barratry is a continuing practice of maintenance or champerty." *In re* Primus, 436 U.S. 412, 424–25 n.15, 98 S.Ct. 1893 1900–01, n.15.

the serious encroachment . . . upon protected freedoms of expression."[138] The Court added that "it is no answer to the constitutional claims asserted by petitioner to say . . . that the purpose of these regulations was merely to insure high professional standards and not to curtail free expression. For a State may not, under the guise of prohibiting professional misconduct, ignore constitutional rights."[139]

A year later, in *Brotherhood of Railroad Trainmen*,[140] the Supreme Court considered a union's legal services plan that resulted in channeling all or substantially all of the union members' personal injury claims, on a private fee basis, to lawyers selected by the union and touted in its literature and at meetings. Asserting that this constituted unlawful solicitation, the Virginia State Bar obtained an injunction against the legal services plan. The Court again upheld the solicitation on constitutional grounds, despite the objections of the two dissenting Justices that by giving constitutional protection to the solicitation of personal injury claims, the Court "relegates the practice of law to the level of a commercial enterprise," "degrades the profession," and "contravenes both the accepted ethics of the profession and the statutory and judicial rules of acceptable conduct."[141]

In the *United Mine Workers* case three years thereafter,[142] the Court dealt with the argument that *Button* should be limited to litigation involving major political issues, like school desegregation, and not be extended to personal injury cases. The Court recognized that the litigation at issue was "not bound up with political matters of acute social moment," as in *Button*.[143] It held, nevertheless, that "the First Amendment does not protect speech . . . only to the extent that it can be characterized as political. 'Great secular causes, with small ones, are guarded.' "[144]

The next case in this line was *United Transportation Union v. State Bar of Michigan*.[145] At that time, commercial speech was still wholly without constitutional protection,[146] and *United Transportation Union* presented a case of commercial speech by lawyers in a classic (if not extreme) form of in-person solicitation. As Justice John Marshall Harlan said, the state decree was designed "to fend against 'ambulance chasing,' an activity that I can hardly suppose the Court thinks is protected by the First Amendment."[147]

The facts were that the United Transportation Union maintained a cadre of paid accident "investigators" (commonly referred to in the literature of solicitation as runners, cappers, or touters). Their job was to keep track of

---

[138] 371 U.S. at 438–39.

[139] *Id.*

[140] *Brotherhood of Railroad Trainmen v. Virginia*, 377 U.S. 1, 84 S.Ct. 1113 (1964).

[141] 377 U.S. at 9 (Clark, J., dissenting).

[142] *United Mine Workers v. Illinois State Bar Ass'n*, 389 U.S. 217, 88 S.Ct. 353 (1967).

[143] 389 U.S. at 223.

[144] *Id.*

[145] 401 U.S. 576, 91 S.Ct. 1076 (1971).

[146] *Valentine v. Chrestensen*, 316 U.S. 52 (1942), was not overruled until 1975, four years after United Transportation Union. *See Bigelow v. Virginia*, 421 U.S. 809 (1975), and *Virginia Pharmacy Board v. Virginia Consumer Council*, 425 U.S. 748 (1976).

[147] 401 U.S. at 597, 91 S.Ct. at 1088 (Harlan, J., dissenting).

accidents, to visit the injured members, to make contingent fee contracts with them, and to urge the injured members to retain private attorneys who had been selected by the union. Even if the runners were unsuccessful in signing up victims, they were paid by the union for their time and expenses in transporting potential clients to the designated lawyers' offices, where the lawyers themselves could induce the victims to retain them.

In holding this conduct to be constitutionally protected, the Court reiterated that "collective activity to obtain meaningful access to the courts is a fundamental right within the protection of the First Amendment."[148] What is important to bear in mind, however, is that: (1) the attorneys were not in-house counsel for the union, but were private practitioners; (2) the attorneys earned substantial fees; (3) the cases were ordinary personal injury cases; (4) the attorneys were retained as a result of the activities of runners paid by the union to find out where accidents had occurred, to visit the victims as promptly as possible after the accident, to "tout" the particular lawyers, and, if necessary, to take the victim to the lawyers' office so that the lawyer, in person, could solicit the victim to sign a retainer agreement.

The Court did not decide whether the runners could have been paid directly by the lawyers. The dissenting Justices would have disapproved payment, while the majority did not reach that issue, on the ground that it was not in the record before them. It is difficult to see, however, why anything should turn on who pays the runner. An unsophisticated person like Ms. Gunn, or helpless and friendless patients in a nursing home, need information about their rights regardless of who is paying the investigator or the social worker. Nevertheless, MR 7.2(c) forbids a lawyer to "give anything of value to a person for recommending the lawyer's services,"[149] other than payment for advertising that is permitted under MR 7.2(a). This has the irrational effect of permitting a lawyer to pay an actor to recommend her services in television commercials, while forbidding Solomon Cohn to employ his Spanish-speaking runner to recommend his services to the woman in the courthouse lobby, who would not otherwise have understood her rights.

In *Button* and the union cases the Court happened to be dealing with legal services provided by associations, and there are therefore references in those cases to the First Amendment right of association. However, the cases also recognized "the right of individuals" to be represented in lawsuits[150] and to obtain "meaningful access to the courts."[151] Again, the aggrieved person who has no association or union to turn to (perhaps because she has no job) is even more in need of information about her rights than one who has the advantages of association. Recognizing this, the Supreme Court has held that the "[u]nderlying . . . concern" of *Button* and the union cases was that "the aggrieved receive information regarding their legal rights and the means of

---

[148] 401 U.S. 585, 91 S.Ct. at 1082.

[149] An alternative, in order to guard against overreaching or other improper conduct by a runner, would be a rule holding the lawyer professionally responsible for any misconduct on the part of the runner.

[150] *See, e.g., Brotherhood of Railroad Trainmen v. Virginia,* 377 U.S.1, 7 (1964).

[151] *United Transportation Union,* 401 U.S. at 585, 91 S.Ct. at 1082.

effectuating them."[152] This concern, the Court added, "applies with at least as much force to aggrieved individuals as it does to groups."[153]

§ 12.12 *PRIMUS* AND *OHRALIK* — TWO DIFFERENT LEVELS OF CONSTITUTIONAL PROTECTION

We have not yet considered two very important solicitation cases, *Primus*[154] and *Ohralik*,[155] which were decided by the Supreme Court in 1978, one year after *Bates*. On the facts of *Primus* (solicitation for a social cause) the Court reversed discipline of the lawyer, while on the facts of *Ohralik* (solicitation of a personal injury case) the Court affirmed discipline. *Ohralik* is frequently cited as holding that when solicitation is done for the lawyer's pecuniary gain, it is without any constitutional protection. However, that is a misinterpretation.

Primus involved an effort by the American Civil Liberties Union to litigate a case on behalf of pregnant mothers on public assistance who were being sterilized or threatened with sterilization as a condition of continued receipt of medical assistance under Medicaid. Edna Smith Primus was a cooperating (*i.e.*, unpaid) attorney with the ACLU. She met with a group of women who had been sterilized by Dr. Clovis H. Pierce, explained their rights to them, and suggested the possibility of a lawsuit.[156] Primus then followed up this in-person contact by writing to one of the women, Mary Etta Williams, asking her to become a plaintiff in an ACLU lawsuit against Pierce.[157] As a result, Primus was subjected to professional discipline for soliciting a client.

In upholding the disciplinary action, the South Carolina Supreme Court noted that the ACLU "would benefit financially [through court-awarded fees] in the event of successful prosecution of the suit for money damages."[158] In addition, Primus herself had a pecuniary interest in the sterilization case, because she acted in part in her capacity as a retained lawyer for the South Carolina Council on Human Relations (a private, nonprofit organization).[159] Nevertheless, the Supreme Court described the case as one that was not

---

[152] *Bates v. State Bar of Arizona*, 433 U.S. 350, 376 n.32. 97 S.Ct. at 2705 n. 32.

[153] *Id.*

[154] *In re* Primus, 436 U.S. 412, 98 S.Ct. 1893 (1978).

[155] *Ohralik v. Ohio State Bar Ass'n*, 436 U.S. 447, 98 S.Ct. 1912, (1978).

[156] *Primus*, 436 U.S. at 415, 98 S.Ct. at 1896.

[157] Shortly after receiving the letter, Williams visited Pierce for a medical consultation, which proved to be a legal consultation. At the doctor's office, she was confronted by his lawyer, who induced her to sign a release of liability in the doctor's favor and to call Primus on the doctor's telephone to turn down her offer of free legal assistance.

There is no indication that the disciplinary committee showed any concern with the conduct of Dr. Pierce's lawyer. *But see* DR 7-104(A)(2). Note that the stated concerns of the anti-solicitation rules are that a lawyer might use undue influence, overreach, misrepresent, invade privacy, and have a conflict of interest, all of which appear to characterize the conduct of Pierce's lawyer.

[158] *Primus*, 436 U.S. at 420, 98 S.Ct. at 1899.

[159] *Primus*, 436 U.S. at 415 n.3, 98 S.Ct. at 1896 n.3. Also, Primus had a professional relationship with Herbert Buhl, who was a paid staff member of the ACLU.

in-person solicitation "for pecuniary gain," because Primus herself would not receive a share of any recovery.[160]

The Supreme Court reversed the disciplinary action against Primus. The Court noted that the ACLU "engages in litigation as a vehicle for effective political expression and association, as well as a means for communicating useful information to the public."[161] Accordingly, the Court held that Primus had been exercising "core First Amendment rights" in soliciting Williams, and that the state's action in punishing Primus had to withstand "exacting scrutiny."[162] The state therefore had to carry the burden of demonstrating that it had a "subordinating interest which is compelling," and that the regulation used in furtherance of that interest is "closely drawn" to avoid unnecessary abridgment of First Amendment rights.[163]

In response, South Carolina contended that it had a compelling interest in preventing such evils as undue influence, overreaching, misrepresentation, invasion of privacy, and conflict of interest. The Court replied, however, that "the Disciplinary Rules in question permit punishment for mere solicitation unaccompanied by proof of any of the substantive evils that [the state] maintains were present in this case."[164] Moreover, even assuming that the Disciplinary Rules were not overbroad, the state had not carried its burden of proving the presence of the asserted evils. "The record does not support [the state's] contention that undue influence, overreaching, misrepresentation, or invasion of privacy _actually occurred_ in this case."[165]

Primus, therefore, illustrates the highest level of constitutional protection for "core" First Amendment speech — advertisement or solicitation where the lawyer is using litigation as a form of political expression. _Bates_ illustrates the intermediate level of constitutional protection afforded to speech, in writing, that proposes a commercial transaction. In such a case, the _Central Hudson_ test applies, including the requirement inherent in that test that the state carry the burden of proving "unambiguously" that the evils that justify the regulation are in fact present in the particular advertising that the state seeks to suppress.[166]

Ohralik v. Ohio State Bar Association,[167] illustrates the third level of constitutional protection in the area of advertising and solicitation by lawyers. This lowest level of protection is accorded to commercial speech when it

---

[160] _Primus_, 436 U.S. at 422, 98 S.Ct. at 1899–1900. The Court expressly reserved decision on whether the result would be the same if the ACLU permitted cooperating lawyers like Primus to share in court-awarded fees. 436 U.S. at 430–31 n.24, 98 S.Ct. at 1904 n.24.

[161] _Primus_, 436 U.S at 431, 98 S.Ct. at 1904. There is merit to Justice Rehnquist's point that it can be difficult to distinguish litigation on behalf of Ms. Williams from any other personal injury litigation. 436 U.S. at 442, 98 S.Ct. at 1910. A lawyer who specializes in representing the victims of drunk drivers, for example, might well have a strong political view about the evils of drunk driving and about the importance of using litigation to discourage drunk driving and to educate the public about how dangerous it is.

[162] _Primus_, 436 U.S. at 432, 98 S.Ct. at 1905.

[163] _Id_.

[164] _Primus_, 436 U.S. at 433, 98 S.Ct. at 1905.

[165] _Primus_, 436 U.S. at 434–35, 98 S.Ct. at 1906 (emphasis added).

[166] _Bates_, 97 S.Ct. at 2708–09.

[167] 436 U.St. 447, 98 S.Ct. 1912 (1978).

involves in-person solicitation, as distinguished from the core political speech in *Primus* (full First Amendment protection) and the written advertisements in *Bates, Shapero,* and *Went for It, Inc.*(intermediate, commercial-speech protection). At this third level of protection, the state need not prove that the evils that justify the regulation are present; rather the state enjoys a presumption that the evils are present, and the burden is shifted to the lawyer to prove that her solicitation was in fact free of those evils. Nevertheless, the important — and often overlooked — point is that even in-person solicitation enjoys some degree of First Amendment protection as commercial speech.

Ohralik arose under the Model Code.[168] Having learned that a young woman named Carol McClintock had been injured in an automobile accident, an attorney named Albert Ohralik called her home and was told that she was in the hospital. When he suggested that he visit McClintock there, her parents requested that he first stop by to speak with them. In Ohralik's conversation with McClintock's parents, they told him that she had been driving the family car when she was hit by an uninsured motorist. They also told him that McClintock's passenger (Wanda Lou Holbert) had also been hospitalized. McClintock's parents expressed concern that they might be sued by Holbert, but Ohralik advised them that such an action would be precluded by Ohio's guest statute. He then suggested that they retain a lawyer for their daughter, and they replied that their daughter should make that decision.

Ohralik then went to the hospital, where he found McClintock lying in traction in her room. He asked her to sign a retainer agreement, but she said that she would have to discuss it with her parents.

Ohralik next picked up a tape recorder, which he used to secretly record subsequent conversations with McClintock, her parents, and Holbert, both before and after the young women had retained him.[169]

When Ohralik returned to McClintock's parents, they told him that their daughter had telephoned to say that he could represent her. (Although the opinion is unclear as to whether the parents considered themselves, along with their daughter, to be Ohralick's clients, they were at least acting as her agents in their relations with him.) Two days later Ohralik had McClintock sign a retainer agreement providing for a one-third contingent fee. While at the McClintock home, Ohralik reexamined their insurance policy and discovered that it provided benefits of up to $12,500 each for McClintock and Holbert under an uninsured-motorist clause. McClintock's mother again indicated to Ohralik that they did not want Holbert to make a claim against them or their policy, telling him that "Wanda swore up and down she would not do it."

Intending to solicit Holbert as a client to sue against the McClintocks' insurance policy, but telling them only that he had to ask Holbert some

---

[168] The statement of facts that follows is from the Court's opinion, 436 U.S. at 449–53, 98 S.Ct. at 1915–17.

[169] Several ethics opinions had held surreptitious recording of a conversation to be a violation of DR 1-102(A)(4) ("A lawyer shall not engage in conduct involving dishonesty, fraud, deceit, or misrepresentation.") *See, e.g.,* ABA Opin. 337 (1974). Whether there is a disciplinary violation can turn on whether making a recording without the knowledge and permission of both parties is a violation of law in the jurisdiction. Also, Ohralik violated his "fiduciary obligation fairly and fully to disclose to clients his activities affecting their interests." *Ohralik,* 98 S.Ct. at 1926, citing EC 4-1 and 4-5 (Marshall, J., concurring); *see also* EC 9-2.

questions about the accident,[170] Ohralik obtained her name and address from the McClintocks. In his visit to Holbert, Ohralik told her that he had a "little tip" for her — the McClintocks' insurance policy had an uninsured motorist clause that might provide her with up to $12,500.[171]

During the same visit, Ohralik got Holbert to retain him on a one-third contingent fee.[172] In doing so, he told her that if there was no recovery, she would not have to pay him anything.[173] Holbert was eighteen years old and had not graduated from high school. The next day, Holbert's mother called Ohralik on her daughter's behalf and repudiated the agreement to retain him. Ohralik refused to withdraw as Holbert's lawyer,[174] and advised his client through her mother that she could not get out of her agreement with him.[175]

McClintock also discharged Ohralik, and another attorney represented her in concluding a settlement with the insurance company for the full $12,500. However, the insurance company refused to release the check to her because Ohralik was asserting a claim for $4,166 against the settlement.[176]

All of these facts were reported to the Board of Commissioners on Grievances and Discipline of the Supreme Court of Ohio. We have catalogued over a dozen disciplinary violations, many of them clear and some involving dishonesty, fraud, deceit, or misrepresentation, as well as betrayal of his own client. Yet, consistent with the bar's long-standing preoccupation, the only charges against Ohralick were that he had engaged in solicitation of clients

---

[170] *See* DR 1-102(A)(4).

[171] Ohralik thereby violated DR 4-101(B)(1), (2), and (3) by revealing a confidence or secret of his client, by using it to his client's disadvantage, and by using it to his own advantage and to the advantage of a third person. He also gave legal advice to a person who was not represented by a lawyer and whose interests were or had a reasonable possibility of being in conflict with the interests of his client. DR 7-104(A)(2).

[172] This was a violation of DR 5-105(A) because his judgment or loyalty on behalf of each of the young women was, or was likely to be, adversely affected by his representation of the other. *See also* Definition (1) at the end of the Model Code.

[173] This was a misrepresentation, in violation of DR 1-102(A)(4). *See* DR 5-103(B), which provides (improperly, in our view), that the client must be "ultimately liable" for any litigation costs paid by the lawyer. *See also Zauderer v. Office of Disciplinary Counsel of the Supreme Court of Ohio*, 471 U.S. 626 (1985).

[174] A violation of DR 2-110(B)(4).

[175] At this point, Ohralik had a personal conflict of interest with his client (in effect, he was representing his own interests), but continued to give her legal advice. *See* DR 5-101(A) and DR 7-104(A)(2). In fact, his advice was inaccurate, which was at least a violation of Canon 6 ("A Lawyer Should Represent a Client Competently") and probably of DR 1-102(A)(4).

Ohralik's subsequent action against Wanda Lou Holbert for a fee was dismissed with prejudice. Moreover, his suit against Holbert was contrary to representations that Ohralik had made at his disciplinary hearing, that he was abandoning his claim against her on ethical grounds. This raises further questions under DR 1-102(A)(4).

[176] This action (and similar conduct regarding Holbert's check) would not be improper, except for the fact that Ohralik had forfeited his fee by his conflict of interest. *See, Silbiger v. Prudence Bonds Corp.*, 180 F.2d 917, 920–921 (2d Cir.), *cert. denied*, 340 U.S. 831 (1950); *Financial General Bankshares, Inc. v. Metzger*, 523 F.Supp. 744 (D.C. 1981), *rev'd on other grounds*, 680 F.2d 768 (D.C. Cir. 1982). Arguably, therefore, he violated DR 7-101(A)(3) by holding up the check and thereby damaging his client. There was in fact no professional relationship at that point, but Ohralik was insisting that there was. Also, even upon withdrawal, Ohralik was required under DR 2-110(A)(2) to take reasonable steps to avoid prejudice to his client. Further, Ohralik violated DR 2-106(A) by charging a clearly excessive fee.

in violation of DR 2-103(A) and DR 2-104(A). As a result, he was indefinitely suspended from the practice of law — a sanction that is more than justified by the charges that were *not* brought against him.

The Supreme Court affirmed the disciplinary action against Ohralik and used the case to refine the constitutional law applicable to in-person solicitation of clients in fee cases. Because the case involved commercial speech, Ohralik was unable to rely upon overbreadth analysis.[177] That is, he could not argue that the statute on its face could be applied to cases of protected speech; rather, he had to argue that, as applied to him, the disciplinary rules were unconstitutional.[178] Attempting to use the rule established in the advertising cases,[179] therefore, Ohralik argued that the state had failed to carry its burden of proving that the evils said to be associated with solicitation were present in his case.

Ohralik conceded, and the Court agreed, that the state had a compelling interest in preventing "those aspects" of solicitation that involve fraud, undue influence, intimidation, overreaching, and other forms of "vexatious" conduct.[180] That concession would end the case, the Court said, "but for his insistence that none of those evils was found to be present in his acts of solicitation."[181] "We agree," the Court added, "that the appropriate focus is on [Ohralik's] conduct," which requires the Court to "undertake an independent review of the record to determine whether that conduct was constitutionally protected."[182]

Ohralik lost, however, at the next point in his argument, in which he contended that the state had failed to prove "actual harm" to Carol McClintock or Wanda Lou Holbert.[183] In response, the Court declined to apply the rule that imposes the burden on the state to demonstrate that the evils sought to be prevented by the disciplinary rules were in fact present in the case at issue. "Unlike the advertising in *Bates*," the Court explained, "in-person solicitation is not visible or otherwise open to public scrutiny."[184] In such cases, therefore, it may be "difficult or impossible to obtain reliable proof of what actually took place."[185] Accordingly, if the state had to carry the burden of proving actual injury to those solicited, "in-person solicitation would be virtually immune to effective oversight and regulation." For this reason, "the

---

[177] 98 S.Ct. at 1922, n. 20.

[178] *Ohralik v. Ohio State Bar Ass'n*, 436 U.S. 466, 462 (1978).

[179] *See Bates v. State Bar of Arizona*, 433, U.S. 350, 381, 97 S.Ct. 2691, 2708 (1978) ("The record does not unambiguously reveal some of the relevant facts in determining whether the nondisclosure is misleading. . . . We conclude that it has not been demonstrated that the advertisement at issue could be suppressed.").

[180] *Ohralik*, 436 U.S. at 462, 98 S.Ct. at 1921.

[181] *Id.* at 460–63.

[182] *Id.* at 463.

[183] *Id.* at 466. This was, at best, a questionable proposition on the undisputed facts of the case, but one has to sympathize with Ohralik's lawyer, who did not have a lot to work with.

[184] *Id.* at 466.

[185] *Id.* The same is true, of course, of every initial interview between a lawyer and client, when the lawyer, in private and in person, advises the client about whether she has rights that are worth pursuing and sets the fee. The Court did not explain why lawyers who solicit are more likely to take unfair advantage of clients than are lawyers who do not solicit.

absence of explicit proof or findings of harm or injury is immaterial,[186] because the state is entitled to a presumption of such harm.[187] Nevertheless, in-person solicitation does enjoy First Amendment protection, although at a lower level of judicial scrutiny. This lower level of scrutiny involves shifting the burden to the lawyer to prove the absence of harmful conduct, rather than requiring the state to prove that harm was present.[188]

Thus, although "the appropriate focus is on [Ohralik's] conduct," and the Court "must undertake an independent review of the record,"[189] Ohralik lost. The reason is that he failed to carry the burden of proof which had been shifted to him by the presumption of harm that is afforded the state in a case of in-person solicitation. This failure of proof was shown "[o]n the basis of the *undisputed* facts of record," which justified the conclusion that "the Disciplinary Rules *constitutionally could be applied to appellant* [Ohralik]."[190] As the Court has subsequently explained, what justified disciplining Ohralik was "not so much that he solicited business for himself, but rather the circumstances in which he performed that solicitation and the means by which he accomplished it."[191]

§ 12.13 MS. GUNN, THE WOMAN IN THE COURTHOUSE, THE NURSING HOME PATIENTS, AND THE DISASTER VICTIMS

Recall the cases of Ms. Gunn, of the confused woman in the courthouse, of the abused patients in the nursing home, and of the impoverished people of Bhopal, India, and Alton, Texas. What the foregoing section shows is that those people need not remain abandoned, without knowledge of their rights and without a "champion against a hostile world." Lawyers who seek to represent them do not have the full First Amendment protection accorded to core speech, or the intermediate protection accorded to commercial speech that is in writing. However, in-person solicitation does enjoy a third level of "entitlement . . . to the protection of the First Amendment."[192] Under this lowest level of constitutional protection, the lawyer who can show that her solicitation did not in fact involve evils like misrepresentation, overreaching, or harassment cannot properly be disciplined.

This means that lawyers like Laura Eagle and Solomon Cohn — lawyers who give competent legal services at a fair fee to those who need their help — cannot be treated like common criminals or even like lawyers who are guilty of unprofessional conduct. On the contrary, such lawyers should be lauded in the pages of bar journals for "Assist[ing] the Legal Profession in Fulfilling Its Duty to Make Legal Counsel Available."[193]

---

[186] *Id.* at 468.

[187] *Id.* at 464–66.

[188] Ohralik, 436 U.S. at 457, 98 S.Ct. at 1919.

[189] *Id.* at 462.

[190] *Id.* at 467 (emphasis added).

[191] *Shapero v. Kentucky Bar Ass'n*, 486 U.S. 466, 474–75, 108 S.Ct. 1916, 1922 (1988), *quoting Ohralik*, 436 U.S. at 470, 98 S.Ct. at 1926 (Marshall, J., concurring).

[192] *Ohralik,* 436 U.S. at 470, 98 S.Ct. at 1918.

[193] Model Code of Professional Responsibility Canon 2 (1970).

APPENDIX A

REPRESENTING THE UNPOPULAR CLIENT:
THE CASE OF DR. BERNARD BERGMAN

During the summer of 1976, Professor Freedman represented Dr. Bernard Bergman at his sentencing hearing. Bergman was implicated in widely publicized nursing home scandals in New York, and was vilified in the news media where he was called "the meanest man in New York." The most sustained attacks on Bergman were in The New York Times *and the* Village Voice. *When Bergman was sentenced to four months in prison by Federal District Court Judge Marvin Frankel, the sentence was denounced in the news media, including in a* New York Times *editorial, as outrageously inadequate.[1] As a result, Freedman and Frankel were also vilified in the press.*

At that time, Freedman was Dean of the Hofstra University Law School. For two months, he posted prominently on the Dean's Bulletin Board one of the worst of the attacks (a column from the Village Voice *by Jack New-field). This produced considerable student concern over Freedman's role in the case, which led to the following talk to the student body. The talk is included here because of its bearing on some of the most important issues in this book — the lawyer's moral accountability in choosing clients, lawyers' freedom of speech on behalf of clients, and the adversary system.*

The New York Times *covered the talk, reporting that Freedman addressed the students "angrily."[2] You can judge the fairness of that characterization (and of the coverage in general) when you read the talk itself.*

I have never been more proud to be associated with this Law School than I am now. I am here because questions have been asked of me by Hofstra Law School students about my representation of Dr. Bergman, and I think that the fact of your concern with what a lawyer does and whom he represents does you credit and is a tribute to the kind of people we have at Hofstra. I have been asked, in fact, whether I don't resent such questions. On the contrary. You are entitled to ask, and I am here to account to you.

I am not going to tell you that everybody is entitled to a lawyer. Everybody is, but that really is not relevant to my acceptance of a retainer in this case. Nor am I going to tell you that a lawyer is bound to represent everybody who walks in the door. That is not true and never has been true. Lawyers select and reject clients for a wide variety of reasons, including whether the case is in the area of law in which the lawyer has chosen to practice, or whether the client is one who can afford the lawyer's fee, or

---

[1] The *New York Times* editorial, some of the *Times* news articles, and Judge Marvin Frankel's sentencing opinion in the *Bergman* case are excerpted in Wayne R. LaFave, MODERN CRIMINAL LAW 28–42 (West, 2d ed., 1988).

[2] *See id.*, 37–38.

for any number of other reasons or lack of reasons. That freedom of choice on the part of the lawyer is sanctioned by the Code of Professional Responsibility and by the history of practice.

Some lawyers view themselves as hired guns. They will represent anybody in their area of practice if that person can afford the fee and if the lawyer is not overcommitted at that time. Others represent only people they love, and there is a good deal of argument as to which of those is the proper stand. In fact, our profession is pluralistic, and I believe that is a good thing. There are no inflexible standards for taking or rejecting clients, and there need not be. There may be an extraordinary case in which you are the only lawyer in town and someone accused of a crime will have to go to trial without a lawyer unless you take the case. In that situation you may well be under a professional obligation to take the case despite whatever reservations you might otherwise have. But I have never seen that happen outside the movies, and it is not likely that anybody here will. And that, too, is irrelevant to this particular case.

My own position for some time has been that I do not take a case unless in some significant respect it involves a cause that I think worth devoting my time to. Why, then, did I choose to represent Bernard Bergman?

Let me begin with my reasons for disapproving of the death penalty. I think the least appropriate way for us, as a society, to manifest our abhorrence of the taking of human life is by executing people—that is, by taking human life. I think that we should observe, as a society, the most civilized standards we can. Similarly, I have an abhorrence of the mistreatment of old and sick people, and I think that the least appropriate way that we as a society should manifest that sense of abhorrence is by taking an old, sick man—and that is what Bernard Bergman is—and mistreating him: locking him up in a cage like an animal, brutalizing him, subjecting him to the inhumane conditions of our prison system.

In addition, this case posed an extremely important and unique opportunity for law reform in an area in which very little has been done. This case appeared very likely to focus on the propriety of using general deterrence alone as a rationale for a prison sentence. For example, shortly before the Bergman sentencing, Eugene Hollander was sentenced in Judge Jack Weinstein's court in another nursing home prosecution. Judge Weinstein said that he was satisfied that Hollander had suffered enough and that there was no necessity to send him to prison for specific deterrence or to incapacitate him from doing the same thing again. What this case comes down to, Judge Weinstein said, is the message that we communicate to the rest of the community—to other people who might be inclined to do the same thing. That is, the judge decided to punish one man for the good of the rest of society—to make an example of him even though, in the judge's view, he had already been punished enough. In short, the judge chose to use a man as a means, rather than an end in himself.

There are many of us who feel that is impractical, immoral, and unconstitutional. Indeed, a new committee was recently formed by the New York

Civil Liberties Union to work on just that problem: sentencing generally, with a particular focus on the propriety of general deterrence as a rationale for criminal sentencing. I spent a good bit of time with the members of that committee, and it is my judgment that the only reason that NYCLU did not enter the Bergman case as friend of the court was because the issue arose early in the summer, the Board had not established policy on the issue and was not to meet again until September or October, and the committee could not on its own authorize an NYCLU lawyer to enter the case. Members of the committee agreed with me, however, that the Bergman case was a unique opportunity to raise that issue, particularly because the case was being heard by Judge Marvin Frankel, who is one of the world's greatest authorities on sentencing, who has written one of the leading books on sentencing, and who might well be expected to write an important, landmark decision on the issue. I once said, in response to a reporter's question, that I would not have represented Dr. Bergman without a fee, because it happened that he could afford to pay a fee. If asked by ACLU, however, I would have entered the case on a pro bono basis, as I have done many times as an ACLU volunteer lawyer, because of my belief in the importance of the issue.

Another reason for my taking the case is that I practice law for a living. I do not do much practice for a fee. I take perhaps one or two cases a year at the most, and since I have been at Hofstra Law School, it has been less than that because of conflicts in time with my responsibilities as Dean. My major involvement in time in this case, however, was during the summer, and that made it a particularly appropriate case to me in terms of giving everything I could to the case with minimal interference with my primary responsibilities here.

I should add, however, that I believed most of what I had heard about Dr. Bergman at that time, and I had a number of discussions with my wife and with my closest friend about whether I should get into the case in view of what I believed. It was therefore relevant to my decision that Dr. Bergman had already pleaded guilty when I came into the case, and that the issue was not whether he would go without a declaration of his guilt and without any penalty at all. Rather, the only issue was whether he would have to go to prison in addition to a number of very severe penalties that he had already suffered or was committed to suffer.

Those penalties included, first, complete restitution of every dollar that was unlawfully or improperly his. Second, the anguish and the expense of litigation, which nobody who has seen the criminal process close up would minimize. Third, the destruction of his reputation, which was enormous. Dr. Bergman had been widely and highly honored—and, as I will discuss with you later, deservedly so . . . deservedly so—and all of that went down the drain. In addition, as a direct result of this case, he suffered severe impairment of his health. He was a healthy man two years ago. As a result of the pressures of this case, he has developed what has been diagnosed by a doctor whom I recommended—my personal physician—as a precarious cardiovascular condition which he had never had before. And so the issue was, in addition to all of that, including complete restitution, should a 64-year-old man, broken in spirit and broken in health, serve time in a prison.

Those were the initial reasons for my entering this case, and in all candor, I needed no other. But I came to find, as I got further and further into the case, that Dr. Bergman has been the victim of some of the most irresponsible and malicious character assassination that I have ever seen. Note that I feel no compulsion to say that by way of justification for my role in the case. As I have just explained to you, it was wholly without that justification that I entered the case in the first place, and I am prepared to take a stand on that. My determination that Dr. Bergman has been grossly defamed came after that fact.

The *Village Voice* article that I have had posted for a couple of months now on the Dean's bulletin board is an adequate illustration, although not by any means the worst example, of the unfair treatment that Dr. Bergman has received in the news media. But that article is a useful one for me to speak to, because it refers to things in which I have been personally and directly involved.

I was interviewed, on tape, by another reporter, and it is obvious to me that Jack Newfield, who wrote the piece, was relying on the tape. Mr. Newfield, the investigative reporter, never—never once—made an effort to contact me about that story, never once attempted to verify a word in it with me. And in some respects it wasn't necessary for him to do so, because he had a one-hour taped interview which another reporter had conducted.

In that interview I said, in response to a question, "Since I left full-time practice with a big firm two decades ago, I have never been a hired gun. What I have been doing, 95 percent of the time, for twenty years now, has been civil rights, civil liberties, and indigent criminal defense work, for most of which I have received no fee whatsoever. Therefore, for the five percent, at most, of my professional time for which I charge anything, my time comes high." And what did Mr. Newfield find of value to quote out of all of that? Only the last four words: "So Dean Freedman, for a generous fee, ('my time comes high') entered the case." It is little wonder, therefore, that readers of Mr. Newfield's article have written to accuse me of being interested in nothing but how much money I can make in a case.

Newfield also raised the question of how I can appear before a judge who is my employee, whose job depends upon remaining in my good graces, and who is therefore beholden to me. First, I would like to consider with you how this guilty secret was smoked out by the diligent investigative reporter. The first day I appeared in court, my appearance was moved by one of my co-counsel, because I am not a member of the bar of the Southern District. As he stood up and began to say briefly why I was qualified to be admitted *pro hoc vice*, he said, "Mr. Freedman is . . . ." Judge Frankel interrupted to say, "I know the Dean," and shortly thereafter the Judge said, speaking directly to me, "I teach at your law school." That was said with several dozen people present, including over a dozen reporters. That's how the guilty secret was smoked out. The prosecutor, who of course was also there, was aware of those facts, but has never then or at any other time objected to any unfairness in my being involved in the case.

Nor, in fact, was there any unfairness. Indeed, as Newfield knew, the transcript is not accurate where it has the judge saying, "I *teach* at your law school." Last winter, before I was ever invited to be in the Bergman case, Judge Frankel made the decision that it was simply too much trouble to travel out to Long Island each week to teach one seminar. (His home is in Westchester.) He therefore made arrangements last spring to return to Columbia Law School, where some years ago he had taught full time and where, except for the two semesters here, he had always taught part time. His last day at Hofstra, therefore, was in April of this year. My first appearance in the case was in June. Most significantly, the judge's decision in Dr. Bergman's case was June 17th, which was almost two months after teaching his last class at Hofstra Law School.

That discussion assumes, indeed, that there would have been something improper if Judge Frankel had still been teaching here. But, as everyone knows who has done part-time teaching, you don't do it for the money. Judge Frankel was never beholden to me in any significant sense of the word. Apart from the fact that Columbia is not as good a school as Hofstra, Judge Frankel always had the option to return to Columbia at precisely the same salary. Would anybody, knowing Judge Frankel, think for a minute that he would cave in simply because I walked into his courtroom?

Let me tell you about an experience that he and I had shortly after he was hired to teach at Hofstra, but before he had received his first paycheck. Judge Frankel gave the Cardozo Lecture before the Association of the Bar of the City of New York. In the course of that lecture, which was subsequently published in the Pennsylvania Law Review, Judge Frankel mentioned me by name, referred to one of my positions on legal ethics, and said, obviously trying to butter me up, "That is a crass and pernicious idea unworthy of a public profession." If anyone wants to check that, it's at 123 Pennsylvania Law Review on page 1056. Thereupon, obviously trying to ingratiate myself with a judge before whom I might some day practice, I wrote in response that Judge Frankel was "radically wrong" and that his proposals "neither resolve confusion nor dispense truth." That's at pages 1060 and 1066 in the same issue of the Pennsylvania Law Review, published early in 1975.

All of that was known to Jack Newfield when he falsely wrote,[3] in July 1976, that Judge Frankel "teaches" at my law school and "works" on my faculty, and that I had therefore acted unethically in appearing before him.

---

[3] In 1970, Newfield supported Bella Abzug for Congress. Two years later, he opposed her, and made the following admission: "I was there when Bella said . . . in 1970 she was against jets for Israel . . . . I lied, and denied she ever said it, so that she might defeat Barry Farber." VILLAGE VOICE, Sept. 28, 1972, p.4. Newfield has since claimed that his admission that he lied proves that he has become honest, but he neglected to mention that the admission was occasioned by his switch of allegiance from Abzug to her new opponent.

Not long ago *Time Magazine* planned to do a follow-up on Jack Newfield's story. They talked with me for over an hour. They even sent a photographer to take a picture. They were all ready to go, but at the last minute they killed the story, obviously having reached the decision, on the basis of their investigation of the facts as distinguished from Newfield's falsehoods, that there isn't much of a story in the fact that two guys who teach legal ethics didn't do anything unethical after all.

This, as you have seen, is the picture at the top of Newfield's story. It's a very flattering picture of Dr. Bergman, actually, with his head thrown back, laughing. And then Newfield explains that. He says, "on June 17, when he received his four-month sentence, *Bergman left the courthouse laughing* . . . . As soon as Bergman left Frankel's sight the old con artist couldn't contain himself. *Watching Bergman exit laughing* I thought . . . ." *etcetera*. That is a lie—and the picture is a fraud. This picture, which purports to show Dr. Bergman exiting laughing, unable to contain himself as he walked out of the courtroom, is an outright, deliberate fraud on Newfield's readers.

I was with Dr. Bergman for every minute of time, from the sentencing, when I was sitting next to him, until he was almost back at his apartment, well over an hour later. He was a very sad man. He did not laugh, I can tell you, and as he left the courtroom there were no pictures taken. He was led by the marshal directly to a back stairway, where there were no reporters or photographers. He then went into the U.S. Attorney's office, where he sat for a considerable amount of time. Then he went down the stairs and out the back, where there were some photographers and where some pictures were taken. In one picture he appeared to be smiling—not laughing; in fact he was grimacing, upset that the photographers were there at all. The picture Newfield published, however, was not taken at that time, but had been taken some months previously, in happier times. When Dr. Bergman left the courtroom, I was talking to him; I know what he was thinking; I know what he was feeling.

Incidentally, you may be interested to know, his first words to me (this 64-year-old man who had just been sentenced to prison)—his first words to me as we left the courtroom were, "I saw how much the sentence affected you." And it had. I was bitterly disappointed. I thought it was a gross injustice. And Bernard Bergman's first comment to me was not, "Look what has been done to me," but, "I saw how much the sentence affected you."

There is another theme that runs through this case, also expressed in Newfield's article, that is: this is rich man's justice. It is illustrated by the lead-off quote, right under the byline. "If you steal a loaf of bread, you get a year in jail, but if you steal a railroad, you get into the social register. (George Bernard Shaw)." That is what passes on the *Village Voice*, apparently, for investigative reporting. If you want to find out what sentence you get when you steal a loaf of bread, you pick up a book of familiar quotations and read what George Bernard Shaw said was the condition in England half a century ago—then you know what happens on the streets of Manhattan in 1976.

That also is false. That is not what happens. If you steal a loaf of bread in Manhattan and you have no convictions, as is Dr. Bergman's situation, the District Attorney will probably dismiss the charges against you, or, in a rare case, if the District Attorney for some reason does not dismiss the case, then he will probably take a plea of petty larceny and there will be an unconditional discharge. If you want to do your own investigative reporting, talk to any experienced prosecutor in Manhattan and I guarantee that that is what you will be told. Indeed, even in the case of a first offense for a street mugging, there is a substantial likelihood that the criminal will spend no time in jail. That's not rich man's justice . . . it's the way the system works, for better or worse.

Or take the poor person's equivalent of Medicaid fraud—welfare fraud. Will a poor person who cheats the government suffer a more severe penalty than Dr. Bergman's four-month jail term? I asked a Legal Aid attorney who, over the past four-and-a-half years, has handled and observed about 400 welfare fraud cases. She told me that in 399 of them, there was not even a prosecution. In the sole case that was prosecuted, there was a conviction, but no jail time.

What was Dr. Bergman's crime? In the state court he pleaded guilty to one count. The count was—not as it has frequently been characterized, bribery—but a lesser offense (as lawyers, we know that there are significant differences) of giving something of value to a public official in order to influence his official conduct. That is the only charge to which there was a plea in the state court. The Special Prosecutor accepted that charge.

Now think of this. Of all the criticisms that have been thrown around, with all the vilification that you can read in the media about everybody who has been associated with this case, including the lawyers and even the judge, no one to my knowledge has ever hinted that the Special Prosecutor is less than honest and competent. There is no reason to believe otherwise. Why then, other than—as was admitted to Dr. Bergman's lawyers, that this was a bad case—why then would the Special Prosecutor accept a plea to a knocked-down charge of one count of giving something of value to a public official? And how, incidentally, can you criticize the judge for sentencing on the plea that was given and taken? What does plea bargaining mean if you plead guilty to one reduced charge and then may be sentenced for everything that the prosecutor has bargained away plus anything else the news media may have dreamed up?

That state count itself is of some interest. The public official was Assemblyman Blumenthal. What happened was this. Dr. Bergman was having trouble getting a license for a nursing facility which was modern and well-equipped. He went to Blumenthal, who was his representative, and he exercised his right—I'm not being facetious—he exercised his constitutional right to petition for redress of grievances by going to his elected representative to say, "Can you find out what the problem is? Is there anything you can do for me to cut through this bureaucratic snarl?" Blumenthal said yes, he thought he could and that he'd try. And Blumenthal said to Bergman, "In addition to your nursing home in my district, there is also a federally-funded job-training program for minority group members. If your home opens up, will you permit the minority group members to receive job training at the nursing home?" And Dr. Bergman—lowest of the low, in the depths of his venality—said, "Yes, I will let the federally-funded job-training program use the facilities of the nursing home to train minority group members." That was it. That is what Dr. Bergman gave as a "bribe."

There is another aspect to this. Blumenthal knew—although Dr. Bergman did not—that the job-training program was being represented by Blumenthal's law firm, and therefore Blumenthal received some $800 as a fee to his law firm from the job-training program. And that, indeed, was something of value that Blumenthal received, but which Bergman did not give and knew nothing about. That was the only count to which Dr. Bergman pleaded, and to which the Special Prosecutor willingly accepted a plea, in the state court. The same charge—the counterpart charge—against Blumenthal was thrown out on the legal ground that although he had gotten something of value, his acts were not related to his official conduct as an assemblyman.[4]

The more serious charges to which Dr. Bergman pleaded in the federal court were two: one was conspiracy to defraud the government on Medicaid payments, and the other was filing a false tax return. However, as Judge Frankel expressly found, the fraud to which Dr. Bergman pleaded, and which was accepted by the prosecutors, "is by no means the worst of its kind; it is by no means as flagrant or as extensive as has been portrayed in the press; it is evidently less grave than other nursing-home wrongs for which others have been convicted . . . ."

With respect to the false tax return charge, as far as we know, prior to the Bergman case, the government had never charged anyone on that kind of violation. The charge was this. Dr. Bergman filed an HP2E tax form. On the form he was asked to name all of his partners during the preceding year. During the year there had been a group of people who were trying to buy one of his nursing homes. Ironically, Dr. Bergman was trying to get out of the nursing home business. The agreement, however, was conditional on the buyers' getting approval as operators of a nursing home from the Health Department of the State of New York. During the course of the year they had been unable to obtain the approval, and Dr. Bergman's lawyer wrote to their lawyer and said, "We have a contract to sell to you, but it is conditional upon your getting approval. The condition has not been fulfilled and therefore the sale is off."

Were those people partners of Dr. Bergman during that period of time? Dr. Bergman was advised not, and did not list them. That was the false return. But this is the more important thing. That return affected not one penny of anybody's tax—not Dr. Bergman's, not the buyers', nobody's. That

---

[4] The same judge later sentenced Bergman to one year in prison —which is a bit like saying that Fred Astaire did the tango with Ginger Rogers, but Ginger Rogers didn't dance with Fred Astaire.

return—let's assume it was false—had no effect whatsoever on the collection of revenues by the government. That's the charge. We are talking about a man who had been accused of everything from killing old people in their own excrement to being involved with the Mafia, and what was the Special Prosecutor able to come up with? —He filed a false HP2E form, leaving off some names which affected nobody's taxes.

And then the more serious charge—the only one that approaches being called a serious charge—was that Dr. Bergman conspired to defraud the government out of large sums of money. Those sums of money are in dispute; the dispute is being worked out, and there is going to be full restitution as determined by one of the leading accounting firms in the country. That was done at Dr. Bergman's suggestion. He suggested that the government select one of the top eight accounting firms in the country, and that he pay whatever amount that firm decided he owed.

One of the things about the conspiracy to defraud is very interesting. Dr. Bergman's lawyers felt that the plea was in his interest for a number of reasons. Among others, he was being blackmailed by the prosecutor—I use the word advisedly—blackmailed by the prosecutor, who threatened to prosecute his children and his wife if he did not plead guilty. His attorneys urged him to accept the plea, but he wouldn't do it for quite some time—for one reason. The prosecutor was insisting that he say that he *knowingly* defrauded the government, and he would not say that. They kept telling him that it was just a matter of words, that it didn't matter. Dr. Bergman answered that he hadn't known, that he would say that he had had reason to know, that if he had been more vigilant, he would have caught his accountant. But he did not know, and he would not say in court that he did know.

Finally, after considerable wrangling (and I've seen the correspondence—his own lawyers were getting impatient) they decided that Dr. Bergman could say that he should have known, instead of that he did in fact know, and he took the plea on that basis. But that was a matter of considerable importance to him. He had pointed out all along that the frauds were committed by his accountant, that at no other Bergman homes were there such frauds except at the one at which that accountant was employed, and that at other people's nursing homes where the same accountant was employed, the same frauds occurred.

After all that was over, Dr. Bergman, on his own, went to the leading lie detector laboratory in New York, the one that is used by the prosecutors, and he took a lie detector test. He was asked on the lie detector test, "Prior to January 1975 did you know that you were getting money from Medicaid to which you were not entitled?" Answer: "No." Conclusion: The answer was truthful. He did not know prior to 1975, when the public charges were made, that Medicaid frauds were taking place. And that has never been reported! That was revealed in open court, with over a dozen reporters present, and you haven't seen it in the newspapers, you haven't seen it on television, and you haven't heard it on the radio. Can you imagine, if Dr. Bergman had taken a lie detector test and it had shown that he was guilty? Can you imagine the headlines? Can you imagine the television features?

There are, I think, two reasons that dramatic event has never been reported. First, it is inconsistent with the media mythology that Dr. Bergman is guilty. Another reason is that it is inconsistent with the portrayal that was being made of Marvin Frankel, who has always been regarded as one of our fairest, most intelligent, most conscientious judges. Because if the lie detector test had been reported, then Judge Frankel's reaction to the lie detector test would have had to be reported. Judge Frankel, who was beholden to me; Judge Frankel, who stands up when I walk into his courtroom [Laughter], Judge Frankel's response was, "I will give that zero weight. I don't know enough about lie detector tests. I don't know whether they're reliable. I won't credit it."

Newfield also says, "So the whole process was dehumanized by Frankel. It all became a clever legal exercise with his peer, Monroe Freedman. Reality—infected bed sores, rotten food, old people's pain—was inadmissible. Without any evidence or any adversary proceeding, Frankel said, 'It now appears to be undisputed that Dr. Bergman has been vilified in the media (and by people who wanted to be featured in the media) for many kinds of evildoing of which he has in fact been innocent.'"

Now listen to that quote again. One of the most respected judges in the country, having sat on this case, said: "It now appears to be undisputed that Dr. Bergman has been vilified in the media (and by people who wanted to be featured in the media) for many kinds of evildoing *of which he has in fact been innocent.*"

Now I ask you, fellow lawyers and law students, what is Newfield's complaint with that? His complaint is that Judge Frankel came to that conclusion "without any evidence or any adversary proceeding." That means the man was presumed guilty. In Newfield's scheme of criminal justice, if there is no evidence and no adversary proceeding, then Bernard Bergman is guilty of every crime attributed to him in the news media. Happily, our system is just the other way around. *If* there is no evidence, *if* there is no adversary proceeding, *if* the prosecutor (whose honesty, integrity, and competence nobody has questioned) never even *charged* Dr. Bergman with those crimes, how does Newfield dare to presume that infected bed sores, rotten food, or old people's pain have anything to do with this case?

Incidentally, you will have heard and read a lot of hearsay, hearsay many times removed, that seems to implicate Dr. Bergman in wrong-doing. I have over 300 letters of praise for Dr. Bergman's homes—not from reporters who visited a home once or twice, but from people who have lived there, from the children of people who have lived there, and from social workers who have worked there. If anyone asks me later, I will be pleased to read to you from those letters. What they show is a well-run home where people enjoyed their life and liked the people who cared for them.[5]

---

[5] One such letter, from a doctor at a New York hospital, praised Dr. Bergman's nursing homes for accepting patients from the hospital who had difficult care problems and for

Newfield also wrote an article headed. "Is Bergman Laundering the Mob's Money?" It started out, "The ultimate sinister layer of Bernard Bergman's venality is about to be peeled away . . . his involvement in organized crime." What happened to that charge? We have a man charged in the press with involvement in organized crime, but no charge by the special prosecutor's office and no charge by the federal government. And this is a man who was subjected for over a year-and-half to the most thorough investigation by no less than 14 agencies of state and federal government, and with a special grand jury sitting for over a year and a half with the powers of subpoena.

Let me tell you briefly what the link to organized crime was. Dr. Bergman hired as a security guard at one of his nursing homes a man who has the misfortune to be named Rocco Scarfone. Every investigative reporter looking at that name knew that Rocco Scarfone had to be involved with organized crime. I haven't told you the whole story. In addition, it was discovered that Rocco Scarfone had more than once visited Miami, Florida, where he had cashed paychecks from Dr. Bergman.

Rocco Scarfone, it turns out, was simply a former police officer in the New York City Police Department. The *Village Voice*, however, has never printed a correction of that gross slander against Dr. Bergman and Mr. Scarfone.

I don't have time to deal with all the errors in this one piece by Newfield, but let me point up one thing which I expect every law student would have caught, but which I do not expect members of the public generally to have seen through. "Curiously, in another decision, the same Judge Frankel took exactly the opposite judicial view on sentencing." That is a serious charge. "On September 3, 1970, Judge Frankel sentenced Martin Sweig to 30 months in prison for one count of perjury. He was acquitted on 14 other counts. At the time Judge Frankel wrote in his opinion, 'I am more or less required to take into account the responsible things stated by the government's representative even beyond what is proved in evidence at a trial when I come to sentence. There was substantive evidence at the trial [which Judge Frankel himself heard—subject to cross-examination and confrontation] which indicated gross irregularities, misuse of facilities, abuse of government trust, and whatever.' "

Despite Newfield's charge of inconsistency, that was clearly a different case. In Dr. Bergman's case there was a guilty plea instead of a trial. There was, therefore, no other evidence before Judge Frankel whatsoever. The Sweig case went to trial. Judge Frankel is on record for the proposition (with which I happen to disagree) that it is appropriate to sentence more heavily where there is a conviction as the result of trial, and he is certainly right in saying that he can take into account evidence that he himself saw presented in an adversary proceeding.

---

accepting patients without regard to race. He added: "As for the care of . . . patients [we sent to] these nursing homes, it was excellent, so good that I took my mother to the Park Crescent Nursing Home when she was gravely ill." Letter from Walter Liebling, M.D., April 7, 1976.

Copies of this and similar letters are available from Professor Freedman on request.

The two cases therefore are not alike. But I doubt that anybody other than a law student or a lawyer, reading it, would appreciate the fact that Newfield was not able to find any inconsistency in Judge Frankel's sentencing record.

I think that one of the cruelest things that has been done to Dr. Bergman is the deprecation of his philanthropic activities. What is often said—and Newfield does it—is that Dr. Bergman gave some money, which he stole anyway, to some charities, and thereby bought his way into positions of prominence and honor. That is not accurate. Bernard Bergman, over the decades, has given enormously of himself. Before there was a Soviet Jewry movement, Dr. Bergman was in Russia, at his own expense, getting people out. During the Nazi period, Dr. Bergman helped people to escape, through direct personal involvement. At the end of the war, when displaced persons were coming to this country out of the camps, arriving at the docks in New York, penniless and friendless, it was Bernard Bergman, not Jack Newfield or any of Dr. Bergman's other detractors, who was at the dock to meet them, to take them into his own home, to feed and clothe them, and to find them jobs—I have letter after letter attesting to that—when he had no hope whatsoever of anything in return from those people.

One of the books on the recommended reading list for entering law students is *The Ox Bow Incident*. It's about a man who allows himself to be talked into becoming a member of a vigilante group, and participating in the lynching of three men on what appeared at the time to be adequate evidence. He finds out afterward that if time had been taken for due process, the complete evidence would have shown that the men were innocent, and he lives to be ashamed of his act. If any of you were taken in by Newfield, and by other news media lies about Bernard Bergman, you now know what it's like to be duped into becoming part of a vigilante lynch mob.

The Ox Bow Incident, essentially, is about due process of law. It's about the presumption, not of guilt, but of innocence. That, ultimately is what the Bergman case is about, and that, in the final analysis, is why I am proud to be representing Bernard Bergman. [Applause]⁶

---

[6] After this address was transcribed, a magazine asked to publish it and, with Freedman's acquiescence, invited Newfield to answer it. Newfield declined the invitation.

APPENDIX B

MUST YOU BE THE DEVIL'S ADVOCATE?[1]

By Monroe Freedman

Item. A lawyer at New York's Sullivan & Cromwell recently turned down a court appointment to represent Mahmoud Abou-Halima, who is charged with involvement in the car-bombing of the World Trade Center. A Sullivan & Cromwell partner explained to the Wall Street Journal that the firm did not want to dedicate its resources to the case, because the bombing was "such a heinous crime" and because the defendant is "so personally objectionable." The partner added that Abou-Halima is "anti-Semitic in the most dangerous way." And the firm was also concerned about adverse reactions from some if its current clients.

Item. Michael Tigar, a professor at Texas Law School,[2] recently argued in a federal appeals court that John Demjanjuk should be allowed to return to the United States when he leaves Israel. The Israeli Supreme Court has reversed Demjanjuk's conviction for participating in the mass murder of Jews in the gas chambers of Treblinka. The court was won over by compelling evidence that Demjanjuk has an alibi. Because he had been engaged in the mass murder of Jews at other Nazi camps, Demjanjuk couldn't possibly have been a guard at Treblinka.

Was Sullivan & Cromwell right to refuse to defend Abou-Halima? Was Tigar right to represent Demjanjuk? And what do the rules of ethics say about it?

Before answering those questions, we should recall the ethical obligations that a lawyer assumes by agreeing to represent a client. Under the traditional view, a lawyer is bound to represent a client zealously, using all reasonable means to achieve the client's lawful objectives. Some academics would like to do away with the ethic of zeal and substitute a more "communitarian" approach, while some practitioners favor a more paternalistic role for the lawyer. In short, these critics would replace democratic equality under law with the elitist discretion of lawyers. But the traditional view, which recognizes the client as a free person in a free society, is still the dominant ideal among American lawyers, as it has been for well over a century.

That does not mean that lawyers should disregard moral concerns in representing clients. On the contrary, if a lawyer believes that what the client proposes is immoral or even simply imprudent, the client is entitled to the lawyer's judgment and counsel. But "[i]n the final analysis . . . the lawyer should always remember that the decision whether to forgo legally available objectives or methods because of non-legal factors is ultimately

---

[1] LEGAL TIMES, Aug. 23, 1993, page 19.

[2] Professor Tigar now teaches at American University Law School.

for the client and not for himself." American Bar Association Model Code of Professional Responsibility, EC 7-8.

Thus, a lawyer's decision to represent a client may commit that lawyer to zealously furthering the interests of one whom the lawyer or others in the community believe to be morally repugnant. For that reason, the question of whether to represent a particular client can present the lawyer with an important moral decision—a decision for which the lawyer can properly be held morally accountable, in the sense of being under a burden of public justification.

That would not be so if each lawyer were ethically bound to represent every client seeking the lawyer's services. If there were no choice, there would be no responsibility. Under both rule and practice, however, lawyers have always been free to choose whether to represent particular clients. Ethical Consideration 2-27 of the ABA Model Code does urge lawyers not to decline representation because a client or a cause is unpopular, but EC 2-26 says flatly that a lawyer has "no obligation" to take on every person who wants to become a client. And the Model Rules of Professional Conduct say similarly that a lawyer ordinarily is "not obligated to accept a client whose character or cause the lawyer regards as repugnant."

Thus, Sullivan & Cromwell violated no ethical rule in declining to defend Mahmoud Abou-Halima. Indeed, on the facts as reported, the firm would have acted unethically if it had taken the case. Under Disciplinary Rule 5-101 of the ABA Model Code, which is controlling in New York, a lawyer has a conflict of interest [requiring rejection of a matter], if the exercise of her professional judgment on behalf of her client "reasonably may be affected" by her own personal or business interests.

And this is precisely the position of the lawyers at Sullivan & Cromwell who find the potential client so personally objectionable that they don't think the partnership should put its resources into the case, who find the crime so heinous that they don't want to be associated with its defense, and who are worried about how other clients and potential clients will view the representation. Certainly those powerful concerns may reasonably be expected to affect the zeal with which those lawyers would represent that client.

What then about Michael Tigar's representation of John Demjanjuk?

I said earlier that a lawyer's decision to represent a client is a decision for which the lawyer is morally accountable. But I must confess that this has not always been my position. At one time I argued that it is wrong to criticize a lawyer for choosing to represent a particular client or clause. If lawyers were to be vilified for accepting unpopular clients or causes, I said, then those individuals who are most in need of representation might find it impossible to obtain counsel.

But I was mistaken. Lawyers have always been vilified for taking unpopular cases, even by other lawyers and judges, and lawyers have nonetheless been found to represent the most heinous of clients. In the face of the harshest invective, lawyers have represented "The Meanest Man in New York" (whom I represented) and even Nazis, to advocate their right to march in Skokie, Ill.

What ultimately changed my mind on the issue of moral accountability was a debate I participated in about 25 years ago. It was sparked by the picketing of D.C.'s Wilmer, Cutler, & Pickering by a group of law students led by Ralph Nader. The demonstrators were protesting the firm's representation of General Motors in an air-pollution case. I took the position that the protesters were wrong to criticize a firm for its choice of clients.

My opponent argued that it was entirely proper for the demonstrators to challenge lawyers at the firm to ask themselves: "Is this really the kind of client to which I want to dedicate my training, my knowledge, and my skills as a lawyer? Did I go to law school to help a client that harms other human beings by polluting the atmosphere with poisonous gasses?

Although I didn't realize it for some time, my opponent won the debate in the most decisive way—by converting me to his position. The issue is not whether General Motors should be represented. Of course they should, and there will always be someone who will do it. The real issue for each of us is: Should *I* be the one to represent this client, and if so, why?

And so I now ask my victorious opponent in that long-ago debate: Mike Tigar, is John Demjanjuk the kind of client to whom you want to dedicate your training, your knowledge, and your extraordinary skills as a lawyer? Did you go to law school to help a client who has committed mass murder of other human beings with poisonous gases? Of course, someone should, and will, represent him. But why you, old friend?

SETTING THE RECORD STRAIGHT ON THE DEFENSE OF JOHN DEMJANJUK[3]

By Michael E. Tigar

All of Monroe Freedman's statements about me in this newspaper are wrong, except two: We are—or were—old friends. And I do represent John Demjanjuk.

Until today, I thought that a reasonable legal newspaper would not publish personal attacks on lawyers without making some effort to check the facts. Professor Freedman's commentary accuses me of violating legal ethics and of being faithless to my own principles by arguing that John Demjanjuk be allowed to return to this country and that the federal court decisions involving him be vacated. The commentary is false and defamatory as to both me and Mr. Demjanjuk. A single telephone call from *Legal Times* would have established that the facts and imputations are false.

Professor Freedman is wrong about the Israeli Supreme Court decision and about the American judicial decisions that caused Demjanjuk to linger in a death cell for years, for a crime he did not commit.

---

[3] LEGAL TIMES, Sept. 6, 1993, page 22.

John Demjanjuk was extradited to Israel to stand trial as "Ivan the Terrible" of Treblinka, one of the worst mass murderers of the Holocaust. It turned out that crucial exculpatory evidence—that someone named Ivan Marchenko, not Demjanjuk, was Ivan the Terrible—was withheld from the defense. The evidence was not an "alibi"; it had to do with tragically mistaken identification and the U.S. government's failure to live up to its obligations of candor to its adversary and to the courts.

Freedman is wrong about what the Israeli Supreme Court did once it found doubt that Demjanjuk was Ivan. That court did not, as Freedman asserts, hold that Demjanjuk was guilty of other crimes. The Israeli court did consider whether Demjanjuk should be convicted as having served at other Nazi death camps, but found that Demjanjuk never had a fair opportunity to rebut evidence of service at other camps.

In 1981, a U.S. district judge found that Demjanjuk should be denaturalized. The judge found that Demjanjuk was Ivan the Terrible, a decision that is now universally conceded to have been wrong. There is powerful evidence that government lawyers suppressed evidence that would have shown that decision to have been wrong when made.

The U.S. judge also considered the question of whether Demjanjuk served at other camps. The judge found that, since Demjanjuk was Ivan and denied being Ivan, he probably should not be believed when he denied other culpable conduct at other camps. Thus, the judge's decision, now argued by the government as barring judicial review of Demjanjuk's right to enter the United States, was taken in the shadow of these now-discredited allegations.

Those are the facts. I represent Mr. Demjanjuk *pro bono*, along with the federal public defender, in an American judicial proceeding. The proceeding will, we hope, vacate earlier judgments against Demjanjuk and leave the government free — if it wishes — to bring and try fairly its allegations that John Demjanjuk served at death camps. If, as Professor Freedman says, there is evidence of such service, which Mr. Demjanjuk has denied, my client is entitled to a fair trial where the evidence can be tested.

I am mindful of the limitations on my rights, as counsel, to use public media to air my views. Here is some of what the record shows:

John Demjanjuk has lived for more than 16 years under a cloud of government allegations that he was Ivan the Terrible. Since at least 1978, the government has had solid evidence that these charges were false. In 1980, a government lawyer on the case wrote a memo saying that the case should not be pursued. The government failed to turn over the exculpatory material. Its lawyers violated their obligations to their adversary and to the judicial system. As a result, Demjanjuk was sentenced to death for a crime he did not commit. Whether the government's lawyers fraudulently committed misconduct was argued to the U.S. Court of Appeals for the Sixth Circuit on Sept. 3. The briefs and record are there for anyone to read. My argument on that score is being made in court, not in the media.

As I write, the Israeli Supreme Court is considering its next step. Under international law, its duty to release Mr. Demjanjuk is clear.

We must remember the Holocaust, and we should pursue and punish its perpetrators. We dishonor that memory and besmirch the pursuit if we fail to accord those accused of Holocaust crimes the same measure of legality and due process that we would give to anyone accused of wrongdoing. Precisely because a charge of culpable participation in the Holocaust is so damning, the method of judging whether such a charge is true should be above reproach.

So much for the factual difficulties in which Professor Freedman finds himself. Let us turn to his analysis of the ethical issues.

Professor Freedman begins by lauding a major law firm for refusing a court appointment to represent an unpopular indigent defendant. The firm doesn't like the client, doesn't like that fact that he is accused of a "heinous crime," and is afraid that its other clients will object. OK, says Freedman, those are good reasons for the law firm to refuse.

Let us all hurry to the library, and rewrite *To Kill a Mockingbird*. Atticus Finch is not a hero after all. He should have thought more of maintaining his law practice and refused to represent someone charged with a heinous— and possibly racially motivated—crime. Clarence Darrow should have stayed with the railroad, instead of taking on those Commie unionists as clients. The lawyers who lost their licenses for daring to represent the colonial newspaper editor John Peter Zenger for the heinous crime of seditious libel were chumps. And John Hancock, that notorious tax evader, had no right to have John Adams as his counsel.

Maybe Sullivan & Cromwell has the right to refuse a court appointment, and maybe it should have that right. I have represented plenty of unpopular folks in my 25 years at the bar and have always stood up to the task of telling my paying clients that they just have to understand a lawyer's responsibility in such matters, or they should take their business elsewhere.

From praise of Sullivan & Cromwell, Professor Freedman then makes a giant leap. He invents a new rule of legal ethics. Based on the supposed right to refuse a court appointment, we are told that every lawyer must bear "a burden of public justification" for representing someone accused of odious crimes. There is no rule of professional responsibility that so provides, and several rules cut directly against his assertions.

If Atticus Finch decides to represent an indigent defendant, Freedman will require him not only to incur the obloquy of his friends and clients, but to undertake a public defense of his ethical right to accept the case.

To put lawyers under such a burden of public justification undermines the right to representation of unpopular defendants. It invites the kind of demagoguery that we are now seeing in the attacks on lawyers for defendants in capital cases. It even invites the kinds of unwarranted attacks on zealous advocacy that have often been directed—and quite unjustly—at Professor Freedman.

I undertook the *pro bono* representation of John Demjanjuk in the Sixth Circuit after a thorough review of the facts and law. I can no more be under a duty to make a public accounting of why I took the case than I can be under a duty to open the files of all my cases to public view.

Professor Freedman does not end matters by inventing a pernicious rule. He also claims to remember what he calls a "debate" of 25 years ago. We did, in fact, meet on stage at the George Washington University law school some 23 years ago. I did not make the statement he attributes to me.

I did say then, and still believe, that lawyers have a responsibility to their own conscience for the kinds of clients that choose to represent and the positions they choose to advance. The lawyers who have upheld that principle, from Sir Thomas More to Lord Brougham to Clarence Darrow, are rightly celebrated.

Having misquoted me, Freedman (who is still at this point in his diatribe calling me his "friend") wonders why I would choose to use my talent for John Demjanjuk, instead of letting some other lawyer do it. I am not sure what alternative scenario he sees being played out here. Maybe he thinks I should represent some of Sullivan & Cromwell's clients instead.

I have answered that question for myself, and it is insulting for Professor Freedman to suggest that I am faithless to my principles. When the most powerful country on earth gangs up on an individual citizen, falsely accuses him of being the most heinous mass murderer of the Holocaust, and systematically withholds evidence that would prove him guiltless of that charge, there is something dramatically wrong. When that man is held in the most degrading conditions in a death cell based on those false accusations, the wrong is intensified. When the government that did wrong denies all accountability, the judicial branch should provide a remedy. I have spent a good many years of my professional life litigating such issues. I am proud to be doing so again.

THE MORALITY OF LAWYERING[4]

By Monroe Freedman

My views are "worse than absurd." They are "dangerous" and pernicious." "Joe McCarthy," I am told, "would be proud of you." I am, it appears, the devil personified, and all because I asked a simple question: Why you?

The question was directed to Professor Michael Tigar in my column titled "Must *You* Be the Devil's Advocate?". Tigar represents John Demjanjuk, who is accused of having covered up his past as a Nazi death-camp guard in order to gain entry into the United States.

My question to Tigar relates to one of the most fundamental issues of lawyer's ethics and the nature of the lawyer's role. That issue is frequently posed by asking whether one can be a good person and a good lawyer at

---

[4] LEGAL TIMES, Sept. 20, 1993.

the same time. Or whether the lawyer forfeits her conscience when she represents a client. Or whether the lawyer is nothing more than a hired gun. Essentially, these questions ask whether the lawyer, in her role as a lawyer, is a moral being. There are three answers to that question:

The amoral lawyer. The answer has been dubbed "the standard conception." It holds that the lawyer has no moral responsibility whatsoever for representing a particular client or for the lawful means used or the ends achieved for the client. Critics have accurately pointed out that under the standard conception, the lawyer's role is at best an amoral one and is sometimes flat-out immoral.

Moral control of the client. A second answer insists that the lawyer's role is indeed a moral one. It begins by agreeing with the standard conception that the lawyer's choice of client is not subject to moral scrutiny. But it holds that the lawyer can impose his moral views on the client by controlling both the goals pursued and the means used during the representation.

According to this view, the lawyer can properly stop the client from using lawful means to achieve lawful goals. For example, the lawyer, having taken the case and having induced the client to rely upon her, can later threaten to withdraw from the representation—even where this would cause material harm to the client—if the client does not submit to what the lawyer deems to be the moral or prudent course. I recently criticized this view in my column titled "ALI to Clients: Drop Dead!".[5]

Choice of client as a moral decision. The third answer also insists that the lawyer's role is a moral one. It begins by agreeing with the standard conception that the client is entitled to make the important decisions about the client's goals and the lawful means used to pursue those goals. But this answer recognizes that the lawyer has the broadest power—ethically and in practice—to decide which clients to represent. And it insists that the lawyer's decision to accept or to reject a particular client is a moral decision. Moreover, that decision is one for which the lawyer can properly be held morally accountable.

Although critics have erroneously, and repeatedly, identified me with the standard conception, I have consistently advocated the third answer for 17 years. It is refreshing, therefore, to be criticized at last for what I believe, rather than for what I don't believe.

Some of the responses to my column suggest that a lawyer can't "know" that a potential client or cause is morally repugnant until there has been a trial by jury that has determined guilt or innocence. But this confuses a legal adjudication of guilt with the lawyer's personal decision about what is true or false and what is right or wrong based upon the available evidence.

And we make that kind of personal decision all the time. For example, if you have express your opinion that either Clarence Thomas or Anita Hill

---

[5] LEGAL TIMES, May 31, 1993, page 26.

was telling the truth, you have necessarily condemned the other as a perjurer even though that person has not had the benefit of trial by jury.

As to Demjanjuk, there is more than enough basis to convince me, for purposes of a personal decision, that he is guilty of participating in genocide. The Israeli Supreme Court, with honesty and courage, did indeed reverse his conviction on charges that he was "Ivan the Terrible" of Treblinka. But the court's further conclusion cannot be ignored, as Demjanjuk's supporters would have us do. The court also found an accumulation of "clear and unequivocal evidence" that, while Demjanjuk was not Ivan of Treblinka, he was the Ivan who voluntarily participated in genocide at Sobibor and other Nazi death camps.

Specifically, the court concluded that Demjanjuk "volunteered to serve in the S.S." as a member of the *Wachmanner* unit—a unit "devised to establish and operate the Extermination Camps in Sobibor, Lodz and Treblinka" in order to achieve the genocidal Final Solution. In addition, the court found that the possibility that Demjanjuk's *Wachmann* identity card was a forgery, as Demjanjuk argued, was "reduced to zero" by the clear and unequivocal evidence. Indeed, in the final paragraph of its opinion, the court designates him using the title and name on his Nazi SS identity card— "*Wachmann* Ivan Demjanjuk."

In short, while reversing Demjanjuk's conviction of one loathsome crime, the Israeli Supreme Court condemned him for committing a similar one. Because that was not the specific charge that Demjanjuk had been extradited and tried on, however, the court properly reversed his conviction.

But assurance that Demjanjuk is guilty of a heinous crime does not mean that no lawyer could conscientiously represent him. People who do things that are morally repugnant can have causes that are morally justifiable. That is one significance of the decision of the Israeli Supreme Court. And so it was not merely a rhetorical question when I asked Michael Tigar: Why are you representing John Demjanjuk in his effort to re-enter the United States? Why does that cause deserve your extraordinary talents?

One letter in response to my column said that the question was "impertinent." No lawyer, the writer said, should be under a burden of pubic moral accountability. That, indeed, is the standard conception. As I have indicated, one reason I reject that view is that I believe that the lawyer's role is neither an immoral nor an amoral one.

Moreover, we are a profession that exists for the purpose of serving the public, and we hold a government-granted monopoly to do so. As the U.S. Supreme Court has repeatedly held, lawyers are an essential part—a constitutionally required part—of the administration of justice. It is therefore contrary to democratic principles for lawyers to contend that we owe the public no explanation of what we do and why we do it. Further, I believe that a major reason for lawyer-bashing (which is not a new phenomenon) is that our profession has failed to explain and to justify the true nature and importance of the lawyer's role in American society.

Seventeen years ago, I also was asked "impertinent" questions about my representation of Dr. Bernard Bergman, a nursing-home owner who was falsely characterized in the press as "The Meanest Man in New York." My response was a two-hour public explanation, which began: "I have been asked whether I don't resent such questions. On the contrary, you are entitled to ask, and I am here to account to you."[6]

It is no surprise that Tigar, in response to my question, has come through with a powerful, persuasive explanation—a moral explanation—of his decision to represent John Demjanjuk.

First, he notes that the memory of the Holocaust should not be dishonored by denying even its perpetrators the fullest measure of legality. One lesson of the Holocaust is that the vast powers of government must constantly be subjected to the most exacting scrutiny in order to guard against their abuse.

Further, Tigar refers to "powerful evidence" that lawyers in the Department of Justice suppressed evidence that would have shown that Demjanjuk should not have been extradited on charges of being Ivan the Terrible. (Note that these government lawyers have not been found guilty after trial by jury, but Tigar nevertheless—and properly—finds enough evidence of their guilt to justify his personal moral decision.) This kind of corruption of justice is an intolerable threat to American ideals, regardless of one's opinion of the accused.

And Tigar concludes: "When the government that did wrong denies all accountability, the judicial branch should provide a remedy. I have spent a good many years of my professional life litigating such issues. I am proud to be doing so again."

Thus, Tigar's moral response to my question illuminates a crucial issue of enormous public importance about what lawyers do and why they do it. And it illustrates why I am proud to call Mike Tigar my friend.

A Comment on the Tigar-Freedman Debates

As mentioned in the proceeding exchange, Professors Tigar and Freedman had another debate in 1971. The occasion was the picketing of a law firm, Wilmer, Culter & Pickering, by a group of law students led by Ralph Nader. The pickets were objecting to the firm's defense of General Motors in an air pollution case, and were challenging the lawyers to justify that representation. Freedman argued against the picketing, contending that it was wrong to criticize lawyers for zealously representing even the most heinous clients.

Tigar sided with the picketers. Arguing that it was proper to publicly challenge the lawyers in the firm for their choice of clients, he said:[7]

---

[6] *See* App. A, *supra*.

[7] These quotations are from a transcript which was made at the time from an audiotape of the debate. (On file with Professor Freedman).

I am not criticizing Wilmer, Culter & Pickering for [going all out on behalf of their clients]. I am criticizing them for the choice of their clients that they choose to go all out on behalf of. And that, you see, is an important difference.

Tigar explained to the law students in the audience that "you have to make a decision, just as [every other lawyer] has to make a decision." He continued:

The decision is: Which side are you on? The decision is whether or not you will commit your skills, your talents, your resources to the vindication of the interests of the vast majority of Americans or the vindication of the interests of . . . the minority of Americans who own instruments of pollution and repression.

"What I am proposing," he said, "is a moral decision."

Tigar went on to defend the picketers in their demand for a public justification from the lawyers in the firm:

[T]hey say, many of the people in that firm, that they believe in certain things, and I think that it is all right to ask them whether in fact their conduct in fact belies the assertion that they believe in certain things.

In sum, Tigar argued: first, that every lawyer has to decide, in representing a client or cause, whether to commit "your skills, your talents, your resources" to that client or cause; second, that the lawyer's decision is a moral one; and, third, that it is appropriate to publicly ask a lawyer to justify the choice that he has made.

Illustrating the lawyer's discretion to decline a client, Tigar has said:

I am not interested in defending anyone having anything to do with the Enron business. I am so horrified by their conduct that I don't think I would be an effective lawyer for any of those folks.[8]

---

[8] WASHINGTON LAWYER, p. 41 (Sept., 2002).

APPENDIX C

TAKING ADVANTAGE OF AN ADVERSARY'S MISTAKE

The following is excerpted from an on-line discussion on Lexis/Counsel Connect in the 1990s. It is in the original discussion format because it effectively expresses differing views on lawyers' professional obligations, and because it illustrates how lawyers can refine and change their thinking in the course of arguing out conflicting positions. The full original discussion (edited here) includes some additional hypotheticals and some interesting digressions into related issues, and is available on request.

Neal Goldfarb — Ingersoll and Bloch — Wash

I've been meaning to pass on a story I heard at a mandatory "professionalism" CLE program sponsored by the Virginia bar.

Husband and Wife are in the process of getting a divorce. Husband is represented by an experienced divorce practitioner, Wife by someone who doesn't know what he's doing (and who happens to be a friend of the husband's lawyer). The parties are negotiating various points, and Wife's lawyer decides for some reason that he wants a decree entered sooner rather than later. He drafts a proposed decree and sends it to Husband's lawyer with a letter asking for his signature and saying the decree doesn't address alimony, but that they can deal with that issue after the decree is entered.

What Wife's lawyer doesn't know (but Husband's lawyer does) is that in Virginia alimony must be included in the decree or else it is irrevocably lost. Husband's lawyer realizes that Wife's lawyer is committing malpractice. He goes to Husband, explains the situation, and asks permission to tell Wife's lawyer that if the decree is entered as drafted, the wife cannot later get alimony. Husband says, "No way—sign the decree." (Apparently it was not an amicable divorce.)

After much agonizing, the lawyer signs the decree and sends it back to Wife's lawyer, who files it with the court. A short time later, Wife's lawyer says, "OK, now let's talk about alimony." To which Husband's lawyer says, "Sorry, too late."

Wife moves for relief from the decree. The motion is denied on the ground that her lawyer made a unilateral mistake of law.

Wife sues her lawyer, who it turns out was in the process of switching firms or something like that and had no coverage.

David L. Haron — Frank, Stefani & Haron — Troy

Neal: What's the question? Was it a "nice" thing to do? Was it ethically permissible? Was it "professional"?

Stephen Gillers — NYU Law School — New York

If I were the husband's lawyer, I would not agree to do it. If my client insisted, I'd withdraw and not say why. Am I exposing myself to something

393

or other? Maybe. I don't know. I hope not. I doubt a court would come down on me. Let hubby go get another sonofabitch to do it for him. I don't have to. It's repugnant within the meaning of the Rule.[1]

Scot C. Stirling — Sacks Tierney, P.A. — Phoenix

You can't always quit when you want to, so withdrawing because your client wants you to be a sonofabitch isn't always an option.

If a date has been set for trial, under our rules you can't withdraw without getting the court's permission and it's not all that easy to get. If the client doesn't consent to your withdrawal, you have to explain your reasons for quitting to the court and get permission, and your hands are still tied by the ERs about what you can say to explain your reasons for wanting to quit. Unless what the client wants you to do is unethical, you'd have a hard time getting out under our rules.

But, how often does it happen that a lawyer corrects another lawyer's misapprehension about the law, rather than take advantage of the other lawyer's ignorance? I think it happens all the time. Is there anything in the rules that would have prevented the husband's lawyer from saying to the wife's lawyer, when the suggestion was first made, "No, we can't come back and deal with the alimony later, because it has to be in the decree or it's waived. So we need to resolve that issue before we stipulate to the entry of a decree."

Frankly, I think that's what I would have done, in response to the wife's lawyer's suggestion, and I wouldn't have consulted the client first. I think that is the lawyer's judgment call, just like most other decisions about how to handle the case and comply with all the rules.

I think lawyers make judgments like that all the time, without consulting their clients. In the facts described here, the court refused to grant the wife relief from the decree, but I'm not sure that it couldn't have turned out differently. There is a good argument to be made, I think, that the husband's lawyer impliedly agreed to come back and do the alimony part later when he accepted the suggestion by the wife's lawyer to enter the decree first.

Making an agreement with no intention of honoring it is fraud. Maybe it's "other misconduct" under Rule 60—the husband's lawyer was agreeing to do something that the rules do not permit, which is not good, or he was agreeing to do something with no intention of doing it, which is also not good. And in both cases, some additional litigation is likely.

Couldn't the husband's lawyer have reasonably made the judgment, without consulting the client, that it makes no sense to start down that road by trying to take advantage of the other lawyer's ignorance, and instead just tell him straight up— "we can't do what you have proposed—the rules require that the decree include the provision for alimony, if there is going to be any." I say that he could have and probably should have done just that.

---

[1] *See* MR 1.16(b)(3); *but compare* DR 2-110(C)(1)(e). *See also* Ch. 3, *supra.* —Eds.

Lawyers are supposed to be problem solvers as well as advocates. I often talk to opposing lawyers about different ways of addressing a problem, and while trying to solve a problem, will sometimes brainstorm with the opposing lawyer, as openly and as candidly as possible. Most of the lawyers that I think are any good deal with me in the same way. You still have to be careful, before concluding a deal, to make sure that you've thought through all of its consequences, but that doesn't mean that you can't point out errors in your opponent's thinking about a proposed solution to a problem, rather than rush to take advantage of it.

Monroe Freedman — Hofstra University — Hempstead

It's easy to be generous with one's client's rights and money, and to pride oneself on being "professional."

It just might be, though, that the client's adversary, or the adversary's lawyer, doesn't happen to be the client's favorite charity.

Scot C Stirling — Sacks Tierney, P.A. — Phoenix

Doesn't it beg the question to suggest that doing anything but taking advantage of another lawyer's ignorance whenever you can is being "generous" or "charitable" with your client's money?

Monroe Freedman — Hofstra University — Hempstead

Yes, it does beg the question. It's also just rhetoric. Here's my reasoning.

A lawyer is a fiduciary who is required to do for the client everything that is lawful, ethical, and tactically desirable to further the client's lawful interests as the client perceives them.[2] The lawyer can and should counsel a client to do what the lawyer considers to be the right thing to do. "In the final analysis, however, the lawyer should always remember that the decision whether to forgo legally available objectives or methods because of non-legal factors is ultimately for the client and not for himself."EC 7–8.

Consider one of the cases discussed in "Civility Runs Amok," Legal Times, Aug. 14, 1995. On well-established legal grounds, the court refused to open the default. Then some of the judges castigated the lawyer for having been "unprofessional."

No, they weren't criticizing the lawyer who negligently failed to file the answer. They criticized the lawyer who entered the default and who—on lawful instructions of his client—didn't tell his "brother lawyer" about it.

There are two ironies here. One is that the court expected the plaintiff's lawyer to give the defendant greater rights than the court itself was willing to give. The second is that the court had no problem with a lawyer's enforcing a default against an apparently unrepresented defendant. It was only when a "brother lawyer" entered the picture that the conduct of the plaintiff's counsel became "shocking" and "unprofessional."

I'm interested in where the professionalism movement draws the line in not taking advantage of adversaries' mistakes.

---

[2] See Ch. 3, *supra*. —Eds.

What if the other lawyer misses a statute of limitations?

What if the other lawyer doesn't plead a statute of limitations, thereby waiving it?

What if the other lawyer, in response to a discovery request, sends a smoking-gun document that could have been protected by asserting a privilege?

What if the plaintiff's lawyer closes his case without introducing available evidence on an essential element?

As you know, the list is endless. Where, in that long list, is the professionalism movement's stopping point?

Neal Goldfarb — Ingersoll and Bloch — Washington

1. I don't agree with Scot that Husband's lawyer should have corrected the other lawyer's mistake without even telling the husband. Arguably the wife's proposal was a settlement offer that Husband's lawyer was required to pass on to his client. The suggestion that Husband's lawyer was being deceptive by failing to disclose the mistake raises some interesting questions. I tend to doubt that the argument would succeed if Husband's lawyer did nothing more than sign the decree and if he didn't affirmatively lead the other lawyer to believe that they could deal with alimony later.

And I certainly don't think it would have been clear to Husband's lawyer that he would be committing fraud. At most, he might reasonably believe that he was operating in a grey area, and that there was some risk he would be found to have committed fraud. Of course, that's a legal issue as well as an ethical issue, and let's remember that the husband prevailed on the legal issue. I don't know whether the wife argued fraud, but in any event Husband's lawyer's legal analysis was ultimately vindicated.

2. Although it is true that what Husband's lawyer did was likely to (and did) spawn further litigation, I assume the lawyer disclosed that risk to Husband (remember, the lawyer asked Husband's permission to correct Wife's lawyer's mistake) and Husband made an informed decision to proceed. And as I've mentioned, he won the litigation.

3. I think Steve is right in his (implicit) suggestion that if you don't want to do what the client wants in this situation, your remedy is to withdraw rather than disobey the client's instructions.

Monroe Freedman — Hofstra University — Hempstead

First, I'm not sure how one can agree with Scot's approach, because he hasn't yet given us his stopping point.

Second, the court could easily have exercised its discretion to open up the default. In fact, I believe that the court subsequently changed its rules to expressly change the result. That's the way such problems ought to be dealt with, rather than expecting lawyers to take the initiative by disregarding the law to the disadvantage of their clients. (Note that the fact of the default was a client secret,[3] so the judges who criticized the lawyer were demanding

---

[3] *See* MR 1.6(a); DR 4-101. —Eds.

that, in the name of professionalism, he violate the disciplinary rules that they themselves had promulgated.)

Third, I draw the line between taking advantage of an adversary's mistake (when he drafts the agreement), and myself purposefully drafting the agreement in a way contrary to what I agreed to in order to trick the other lawyer.

On the first point, I would only take advantage of the mistake after (a) deciding that it would be tactically desirable to do so, and (b) failing in an effort to persuade my client that we shouldn't do it regardless of the tactical advantage.

With respect to the question you're thinking regarding (b), the answer is, yes, I have succeeded in persuading a client not to take advantage of an adversary's mistake; in one case it was a multimillion-dollar mistake that an adversary had made in drafting a contract.

Scot C. Stirling — Sacks Tierney, P.A. — Phoenix

I don't mean to suggest that this is such an easy case for me, or that it is so obvious that the husband's lawyer should have done what I suggested, or that it is necessarily improper to do what the husband's lawyer did in this case. I think we may be reading the facts at the top of the discussion a little differently, which is a point I will come back to in a minute.

I am also wondering exactly where or how the line is drawn between asserting your own client's rights zealously and acting "professionally." I am really griped by the case that Monroe mentions, where a court refused to set aside a decree, but chastised the lawyer who refused to stipulate to it for being "unprofessional." In fact, the change in our rule about entering defaults (requiring the two weeks written notice before it became effective) was the result of that kind of situation—the judges of our Supreme Court adopted the rule authorizing defaults to be taken, and then bitched at all the lawyers who took defaults and refused to set them aside when another lawyer showed up two days later and asked for relief.

By the way, when that was the rule, I would never stipulate to set aside a default after it was entered without getting my client's consent—but if somebody called me up on the day that I was going to enter a default and asked for more time, I would almost invariably grant more time to answer, without consulting my client, unless I knew there was some reason why pushing the case fast was important to my client. I always considered the latter request the type of call that was mine to make. So we all recognize that the lines have to be drawn somewhere, but I admit I'm not too clear about where the line is in some of these situations.

Anyway, to get back to the situation described at the top of this discussion, the important point for me is that—the way I read these facts—the wife's lawyer was making a proposal that had two parts to it: (a) a decree to be entered now, and (b) the alimony to be decided later. I don't think the husband's lawyer can sign the decree and return it in these circumstances without at least implicitly representing to the wife's lawyer that he is accepting the proposal made by the wife's lawyer. That was the deal that was proposed, and if the husband's lawyer signals his assent to it by signing and returning the decree, *without any intention of honoring the second part of "the deal,"* I think he is being dishonest.[4] Not adversarial, not zealous, not hard-nosed, but dishonest. I don't think he has any obligation to his client to do that, and I don't think it's proper. If he wants to sign the decree and return it with a message that he is not agreeing to the rest of the wife's proposal about the alimony to be decided later, of course he can do that.

Now, if the wife's lawyer had simply proposed a decree that was very favorable to the husband (because it didn't include any provision for alimony), I don't think the husband's lawyer would have any obligation to point out the omission to the wife's lawyer before signing it.

Neal Goldfarb — Ingersoll and Bloch — Washington

Perhaps Husband's lawyer's silence in these circumstances constitutes an implied representation but you could undoubtedly find lots of authority supporting the contrary position. The two lawyers were adversaries, and Husband's lawyer was not under a generalized duty to disclose. This *might* fit within the principle of a partial disclosure that is misleading because it is incomplete. Or maybe not. Also, any reliance by Wife's lawyer was not reasonable.

Stephen Gillers — NYU Law School — New York

Soul Not For Sale

I also blame the judge for not allowing the default to be opened.

If I could not withdraw, and I determined that the decision belonged to the client, which I suppose though I'm not entirely sure it does, then I guess I'd have no choice and I'd just condemn a system that forced me to aid a despicable act. Then I'd change my retainer agreement to say I could withdraw if the client wanted me to engage in a legal and ethical but despicable act.

I don't have to behave this way and I won't if I can avoid it. If I can't avoid it, so what can I do?

Where do we draw the line? Hell, I don't know. I was never good at art, anyway. I can draw a line around an act without knowing where I'd stop the line and where I'd continue. If I had to know that before acting, I would be paralyzed.

Here the lawyer is proposing to do something stupid, and I think I have a moral duty to point it out. If a lawyer forgets to assert the statute of limitations in an answer, well, I see a difference. I feel no need to call up and recommend a list of affirmative defenses. I don't even know why he did it. In the problem, it's pretty clear that the lawyer is laboring under a serious misconception and I know it and am being asked to agree to an act that will clinch it.

---

[4] *See* MR 8.4(c); DR 1-102(A)(4). —Eds.

I'm sure there are gray areas where I'm not sure what I'd do. I'm sure someone could say I contradict myself. But as Emerson said, contradictions are hobgoblins of little minds. Or something like that.

Maybe that means someone won't hire me to be his or her lawyer because I won't behave the awful way the client might wish, assuming I can avoid the behavior. You know what I say to that? Good.

Monroe Freedman — Hofstra University — Hempstead

First, I still have pending the question of where the professionalism stopping point is with regard to not taking advantage of an adversary's mistake. (Incidentally, it's a *foolish* consistency that Emerson said is the hobgoblin of small minds.) I don't think I have gotten an answer, except that no line can be drawn (and we're not talking art, we're talking ethics). "Professionalism" seems to be just an ad-hoc, feel-good, holier-than-thou kind of thing that judges and lawyers can shmooze about at Inns of Court, condemning those who take zealous representation seriously.

Second, let's assume that it is "dishonest," "fraudulent," and/or "unprofessional" for a lawyer to let another lawyer's mistaken assumption pass about the effect of the clients' contract that he has drafted. If so, consider this.

As a lawyer, you regularly contract with clients. You know that all, most, or at least some clients assume that you will do for them everything that is lawful and ethical to achieve their lawful rights. But you know that you have no intention of doing that in all cases. Nevertheless, you take on the client, without disabusing her of her erroneous understanding of your intentions.

Are you guilty of some form of dishonesty, fraud, and/or unprofessionalism?

Note that there's an important difference between this case and the one of taking advantage of an adversary lawyer's mistake. The other lawyer knows that he's in an arm's length situation, representing his client against yours. He knows that you'll take advantage of at least *some* of his mistakes. He might even know that there are ethical rules that require you to do so, and malpractice actions to back them up.

Your client, on the other hand, is entrusting you to be her fiduciary, to be her champion against a hostile world, and she's a lot less sophisticated than your lawyer adversary.

Are you, then, going to do as Steve suggests. Are you going to tell every client up front that you might, in the course of representing her, do less than what is lawful and ethical to achieve her lawful goals? Are you going to tell her in advance that *you* will decide what is "repugnant or immoral," and—even if she disagrees about what's "repugnant" —that you will be prepared to cause "material harm" to her interests rather than use such means?

Stephen Gillers — NYU Law School — New York

The Code and Rules do now have a rule permitting lawyers to withdraw when the client's "objective" is "repugnant or imprudent." Court approval may be needed. I've never like imprudent, myself, but I'm comfortable with repugnant. (A line?) I don't read "objective" to mean only the object but to include the means.

So far no one seems to disagree with a concrete situation identified in an earlier discussion where a lawyer, though legal and ethically permitted to do so, and even if (assume) it would advantage the client, declines to go back on his unenforceable oral agreement with an opposing lawyer and file papers while the other lawyer is on a trip to the (inaccessible) Amazon. To do so would be repugnant. I won't do it and don't feel any need to have alerted my client to that situation specifically or generically before declining. I'd frankly be surprised if clients believed that when they hire a lawyer they get complete subservience of the lawyers' own standards of decency to the client's objectives. If they do, too bad. It'll be a warm day in hell before a court ordered me to pay damages for refusing the instruction.

Frankly, I also agree with Scot that many lawyers would immediately correct the inexperienced lawyer's misunderstanding in the divorce situation, and it'd be an equally warm day in hell before any court would surcharge them for doing that. Surely, that prediction of what the courts would do in fact must tell us something. I quote Judge Posner: "Refusal to violate professional ethics—or even to approach as near to the line as humanly possible—is not professional misconduct. A scrupulous lawyer, a lawyer who takes Law Day rhetoric seriously, sincerely believes that he has a dual duty, to his client and to the law, and acts on his belief, may lose some clients to his less scrupulous competitors but he should not be deemed to be courting a tort judgment." 39 F.3d 812, 817.

Last, I note that the fact pattern at the start of the discussion posited that the erroneous lawyer was a friend and without malpractice insurance. Not that those facts are critical to my behavior, but I sure hope that in accepting a representation I haven't ceded my authority to decline to hurt a friend this way.

As before, if I have misread the autonomy I have after accepting a matter, and must do the deed, so be it. There are few rules I'd break at the cost of my license, but probably not none. But I don't read the rules that way and I'm confident that nothing would happen to me if I remained true to my values on the facts offered.

Scot C. Stirling — Sacks Tierney, P.A. — Phoenix

If another lawyer sent to me a stipulation to dismiss his plaintiff client's case, already signed by him, with a letter saying that his client was willing to walk away from the case right now, and only wanted a cash payment of $10,000 before the end of the month—could I sign the stipulation and file it, and then tell him after the case was dismissed that my client has no intention of paying his client any money?

He obviously thought that this letter was an offer to settle for $10,000, and the already-signed stipulation was supposed to be the carrot dangling right in front of my nose to make the offer seem more attractive, but unfortunately for him, the letter was badly drafted. All it says is that his client is willing to walk away, and that he also wants some money. If only the letter had said that he was willing to walk away in exchange for the payment of money. Well, too bad. My client certainly understands that his client wants some money, but has no intention of paying it.

However, my client is willing to walk away from the case. So I sign the stipulation and *then* we refuse to pay, after the case has been dismissed.

How is that different from the situation where the wife's lawyer tenders a stipulation with a suggestion that the alimony be decided later, when the latter suggestion is clearly supposed to be part of the deal? If the deal is legally "impossible," then how can you accept it? Or pretend to accept it?

This *isn't* simply a question of the wife's lawyer not understanding the legal consequences of the decree that he drafted. It's also a question of pretending to accept a deal that you have no intention of honoring—whether because you don't want to or can't doesn't matter. Contributory negligence and stupidity are not defenses to fraud, and I still think that's what this is.

What is more, even if I thought I had the better of the argument that the wife's lawyer (or the wife) could not reasonably rely upon my implicit but false representation that I was accepting their proposal, so that I had a good defense to the fraud claim—I don't think I have any obligation to my client to lie to them in the first place.

And by the way, if the facts as described at the top of the discussion were clearly established, I think the judge erred in refusing to set aside the decree for fraud or other misconduct under Rule 60.

Monroe Freedman — Hofstra University — Hempstead

Earlier I acknowledged that I was begging the question. Can we agree that resolving the issue by saying that one's soul is not for sale, etc., is also begging the question?

The issue, after all, isn't whether to be moral or immoral. If it were that simple, we wouldn't be discussing it with such intensity. The issue is, Who deserves your primary allegiance? Either way, there's an arguable "betrayal" of someone and of some moral imperative that most of us would give some degree of weight to.

Also, perhaps it's time to unload (or reload) one of the sets of facts.

Let's say that the lawyer on the other side in a matrimonial case is with a big firm that has heavy insurance. He's not a friend, indeed, he's been rather overbearing and a bit rude during your relationship in the case.

Does that add a bit of pull to a different answer?

Scot C. Stirling — Sacks Tierney, P.A. — Phoenix

No, it doesn't, at least not for me it doesn't change anything, because none of the facts that you rearranged made any difference to me in the first place. I didn't remember that the wife's lawyer was a friend of the husband's lawyer until you changed the facts to make him not a friend, and a jerk to boot. So what?

And with all respect, I don't think the issue is to whom your primary allegiance is owed, because that is also an obvious and loaded question. The issue is what your allegiance to your client requires you to do, when you think that what your client wants is either (a) unwise, (b) distasteful to you, (c) maybe dishonest, but probably not actionable, (d) dishonest and maybe actionable, but you'll probably get away with it, or (e) fraudulent, and if you were the judge, not only would you set the decree aside, but you might also sanction the crap out of somebody for doing something like this.

Apparently, we aren't seeing eye to eye on the point that I think is most critical. Monroe and Neal seem to think this conduct by the husband's lawyer is acceptable, and therefore expected and required of the husband's lawyer if it will benefit the husband, even if the lawyer finds it personally distasteful. I don't know if we just aren't seeing the facts the same way, or what the real difference is in our views of this situation. The way I read these facts, I think what the husband's lawyer has done is just as fraudulent as the conduct of the lawyer in the hypothetical situation I described, where a lawyer accepts the stipulation to dismiss when he has no intention of paying the settlement that was obviously expected by the lawyer who offered the stipulation. I think this case falls somewhere in the range of my (d) and (e) options listed above.

I don't think we get anywhere by pretending that the issue is where your duty lies—with your own client or with the opposing lawyer—we all know the answer to that question. The issue is what your duty to your client requires you to do. I don't think it requires you to cheat the opposing counsel or his client, and I think this is cheating. Unless we focus on that aspect of the problem, I don't think this discussion is going anywhere. The fact that we are expected and required to take advantage of another lawyer's mistake in many other situations doesn't mean that all of those situations are identical, or that it is always permissible to take advantage of such a mistake.

Monroe Freedman — Hofstra University — Hempstead

Here are two retainer clauses that ought to be considered if we are really serious about "civility" and "professionalism" as they relate to taking, or not taking, advantage of an adversary's mistake:

Clause One:

In the course of representing you, I may be negotiating with your adversary's lawyer. Those negotiations may require me to give my word to the other lawyer. I will only do that when you have authorized me to do so, or when doing so will not materially prejudice your interests. Once I have given my word, I will not break it, even if you tell me to do so.

Clause Two:

In the course of representing you, I may realize that the lawyer representing your adversary has made a mistake that might help you to achieve your goal. If that should happen, I might decide to correct or not take advantage of the lawyer's mistake. I will do that even if (a) it would materially affect your interests if I corrected the mistake, (b) it would be lawful and ethical for me to take advantage of the mistake, and (c) you told me that I should take advantage of the mistake.

I don't have any difficulty with Steve's position on this discussion, because, as I understand it, he would add Clause Two to his retainer. Whether anyone else would do so is one of the questions I have asked but haven't gotten an answer to.

Also unanswered is whether a lawyer who *intends* to follow Clause Two but doesn't tell the client up front, is being any less "fraudulent" with the client than is the lawyer who takes advantage of an adversary's mistake.

Also unanswered are my stopping-point questions.

The question that is pending to me is how I can justify keeping my word to the lawyer honeymooning in the Amazon that I will give him an extension until he returns. The answer is in Clause One. I think that what is stated there is generally recognized by clients, something that is assumed in the lawyer-client relationship that doesn't need stating. But I would have no hesitation about putting it into a retainer.

This is very different from Clause Two, because I believe that what is stated in Two is very different from what all/most/many clients assume they are getting when they retain a lawyer. As Steve says, he might well lose clients because of such a clause, and he responds, "Good."

That leads me to ask again: How many of those who agree with Steve *really* agree with Steve, and will be putting Clause Two into their retainers?

Neal Goldfarb — Ingersoll and Bloch — Washington

Let me expand a bit on why I don't think it's so clear that the husband's lawyer was being dishonest.

Scot says this is a case of accepting a proposed deal with no intention of performing. But what was the supposed deal? Not, I would assume, to come to a binding agreement on alimony—you can't have an agreement to agree—but rather to negotiate some more about alimony. What kind of deal is that? Suppose the husband's lawyer thought at the time, "Sure I'm willing to negotiate about alimony. But the first thing I'm going to say is that the negotiations are useless because the decree has been entered."

More broadly, is it *dishonest* to tell an opponent that you are willing to negotiate when you know that your client will never agree to any deal that is offered? Is that *fraudulent*?

In short, even if you accept Scot's argument that the husband's lawyer was agreeing to some kind of deal, the deal he was agreeing to was meaningless. The client had no obligation to agree to anything. And of course the wife wasn't interested in the negotiations because she enjoyed negotiating, she wanted them as a means for obtaining alimony. In an ordinary divorce case, if negotiations fail the remedy isn't to get an order compelling further negotiations but to litigate (right?)—and in that event the husband presumably has the right to argue that the wife shouldn't get alimony at all.

So what, exactly, was the husband's lawyer agreeing to do?

Maybe the line here between honesty and dishonesty just isn't that clear.

Stephen Gillers — NYU Law School — New York

This has been a remarkably valuable discussion and has revealed several distinct views. In the end, I suppose, one must choose and I have without ever thinking hard about the choice. I suppose the choice is made in life before and apart from professional life.

In 30 years of practice, it would never have occurred to me to think, when the opposing lawyer in the opening story, proposed divorcing now and agreeing later: "Ah, I've got him. I'll sign the decree then say 'too late.'" Or even: "What a shame. I think it stinks to take advantage of this but it's my client's call."

So maybe people who want a lawyer like that shouldn't hire me. Not maybe. They shouldn't. Yet, I have to admit that I would not explain all this at the outset of the representation. I hope I don't have to. If I do, I will though I don't know how I'd word all the various permutations.

As for Monroe's two retainer clauses, I must confess that it would never have occurred to me, until now, to include the first, much less the second. Maybe I should do that now—if I still had clients whose work justified it— but I don't think I would even then.

I'm sure what I'd say in the story posed is: "We can't do that under the new rules," or whatever.[5] Would it matter that the lawyer was not my friend or his client a miserable person? No. It might matter if I felt that the other lawyer were treating me that way. I recognize the difficulty in determining that, but my presumption would be otherwise—especially if it were someone with whom I'd dealt in the past and whom I found to be candid and fair. I don't want to start the rush to the cellar.

I wonder what those of you who disagree with me would do if the other lawyer was not only a friend but someone who in a prior litigation saved you from a blunder of equivalent magnitude and same degree of oversight. Would you now say, "Lucky for me, but what a dumb move. He screwed his client, but I'm going to screw him."? I look forward to an answer.

At the end of the day, no one can cite me authority that faults me for doing what I said above I'd do or which reveals that I'd be found in violation of a disciplinary rule[6] or liable in malpractice. Until that happens, I'm going to assume that the professional norms are in sync with my own.

Frankly, I think a client who sued me because I didn't take advantage of the blunder stated in the opening story would be laughed out of court.

---

[5] *Question*: Do you prefer Professor Gillers' present position, or the one he expressed in his first response to the hypothetical?

[6] *Question*: Can you cite such authority?

"Judge, I could have avoided paying my wife any alimony, although I owe her big, but for my lawyer's warning to her lawyer. Now he owes me big." To me, that lawsuit would a joke.

As for line drawing: As an academic I'm committed to it, of course, and try to do it. I never expect to draw the perfect categories, though, and know that there'll always be rough edges. As an actor on the stage of real life, I can't wait until the lines are even nearly drawn before choosing. If the question Neal posed arose today, I'd have to act on an imperfect set of lines.

Last, I must also say that as a civil litigant I'd rather I and my adversary hire someone who thought like I did than the other way. I don't want to screw anyone in the manner described and don't want to be the screwee in that manner.

If the reply to this is that since I can't be sure that the other side will be as noble as I'm prepared to let my lawyer be, it is a formidable reply and commands an honest answer. Here it is:

That view only encourages the worst behavior. I'd be prepared to take my chances, relying on my lawyer's assessment of the other side's standards. I don't want to start the race downward by assuming the worst of others. If my lawyer tells me we have a real s.o.b. on the other side, I may have no choice. As someone who actively litigated in private practice in Manhattan for 9 years, I could pretty accurately evaluate the decency of my opponents. I'd rather think well of people if I can. Does that expose me to some risk? I guess so. Will the world be a better place if others thought this way? I think so, but I can't know.

Socrates said he'd rather be the victim of injustice than do injustice. I feel pretty much that way. I realize there are limits and dangers and uncertainties, but it's a good guide.

Monroe Freedman — Hofstra University — Hempstead

I still don't know where you stand, Steve. Where's the stopping point?

Would you tell the other lawyer that a statute of limitations was going to run out the day after tomorrow on a suit he's been threatening against your client?

Would you tell the other lawyer that he neglected to raise the statute of frauds as a defense and it would be waived if he didn't amend his answer?

Would you pass up a motion for a directed verdict if your adversary omitted to introduce evidence on an essential element for which you knew evidence was available?

Would you tell your adversary that the time for opening a default was about to run out, if no rule of court required you to do so and your client told you not to do so?

Would you teach your students that the ethical rules in New York allow them to answer yes to those questions?

Would you tell your client that you had a conflict of interest because the lawyer on the other side had, in another case, saved you from embarrassment and you feel you owe him?

Does the fact that after all this time I can't get an answer constitute an answer?

Stephen Gillers — NYU Law School — New York

For me this is partly contextual so it is not always easy to answer generic questions Monroe asks absolutely. But I think I can make some headway.

I begin by accepting and supporting the adversary system and leave it to the other side to make its own tactical judgments. Ninety-nine times out of 100 my view of their "mistakes" will probably be my error about their actual strategies because of my ignorance of the "different" picture they see.

1. The statute question. No. I'd wait it out. If the lawyer called me—as the original hypo posited—and said I have until next month to sue and I knew he was wrong, I wouldn't say anything. If he said "right?", I'd say "don't ask me to do your research for you." In the original hypo, I am being asked to cooperate by filing the divorce. That matters to me. In this hypo, I'm passive and will defer to the ordinary expectations of adversary justice.

2. Statute of frauds. Essentially the same answer for the same reason plus I'd assume he had his reasons which I can try to figure out or will eventually learn. Nor would I expect him to tell me the same (ditto for the prior example).

3. Directed verdict. I'd make the motion for the same reasons. I assume in the ordinary case, the court will let the adversary supply the missing evidence. If I know where it is and he doesn't, then tough. I don't have to do his investigation for him. I would expect the same from him and would not expect him to feel betrayed if he later learned that I knew what he didn't.

4. Opening the default. Same answer for the same reasons. This seems very different from the original hypo to me. Let me make it harder. The adversary calls and asks me to agree to an extra seven days to open the default. I know that an oral agreement is not binding—maybe a new case came down two days ago. Would I say sure intending to trap him after the time runs and he fruitlessly files to open the default thereafter but within the 7 day extension I "granted" him? No way. What would others do on my revised facts?

5. My students. I would teach them just what I said here. In fact, I do. I would also teach them (and do) that they can answer the question in the original hypo differently than I, but that I don't know any law that would get them into trouble if they acted as I would. I would also tell them that I think the standards in their communities are important to know about and that reputations are won or lost for lots of reasons. I'm not sure I've done this lately.

6. Would I tell my client about a conflict? No. I don't feel I have a conflict. I would act the way I described whether the lawyer had "saved me" or not.

But I wonder how others would act on this variation because if they would act differently than I would on the hypo, then it seems to me they have a conflict. I notice that my question based on the hypo has not yet been answered. I'd like to know what the answers are to it and to my variation in paragraph four above. Here's the original question:

"I wonder what those of you who disagree with me would do if the other lawyer was not only a friend but someone who in a prior litigation saved you from a blunder of equivalent magnitude and same degree of oversight. Would you now say, "Lucky for me, but what a dumb move. He screwed his client, but I'm going to screw him.""? I look forward to an answer."

I see a clear distinction between the questions Monroe posed and the original hypo. Maybe I'm seeing an illusion but it's an illusion that worked. I happen to believe clients were better off in that community of lawyers, too.

In my practice circles in large and nasty Manhattan, people would have been astonished if the lawyer in the hypo did not correct the misimpression but rather sought to exploit it. I mean it would never even have occurred to me. And they would not have been astonished if lawyers acted as I've described in responding to Monroe's questions. But maybe I'm living in a dream world.

I'm beginning to think—dare I say it? —that maybe there is something called professionalism after all, and that it's an amalgam of dignity and decency, self-respect and self-restraint. Anyway, that's the way I want to practice and did practice and nothing untoward ever happened. I was successful beyond what I ever expected when I opened my own practice at age 29.

Anyway, I've answered the questions. How about others? What do others think? And who will answer the several questions I have outstanding.

Scot C. Stirling — Sacks Tierney, P.A. — Phoenix

Sorry, I've been away from this discussion for a while. I had to get my response to a motion filed today, so I could take advantage of one of my opponent's mistakes before he had a chance to catch it. His motion was trying to take advantage of a glitch in our pleadings. When we are finished taking advantage of each other's mistakes, the district court judge will make some mistakes of his own, and then one of us will appeal.

But seriously, folks . . . .

I don't agree with Neal that the agreement about reserving the issue of alimony for later was "meaningless" anyway, so that nothing was agreed and therefore no harm was done by pretending to go along with the proposal made by the wife's lawyer. Obviously it is true that there was no agreement on the amount of alimony, or whether there would be any alimony, or how it would be paid. That doesn't mean the agreement offered by the wife's lawyer was meaningless. You can agree to resolve an issue on the merits, and you can also make a meaningful agreement about the procedure for resolving an issue on the merits.

For example, I don't think anybody would say that an agreement to arbitrate the issue of alimony would be meaningless, even though there is no agreement on the amount of alimony, or whether or how alimony will be paid. In this case, what was proposed by the wife's lawyer was an agreement on procedure—the decree would be entered now, and the issue of alimony would be reserved and decided later, by agreement if the parties could agree, or by arbitration if they later agreed to arbitrate, or by litigation if they didn't agree on some other way to resolve the issue.

I think it is clear that the decree was tendered to the husband's lawyer with that understanding. If the husband's lawyer didn't *want* to accept that offer, or knew that he *couldn't* accept that offer because the rules don't allow it, then I don't think he can sign off on the decree and file it, or sign and return it to the wife's lawyer without saying so. If he does either of those things, he is (I think) accepting or pretending to accept the offer that was made to him, without any intention of performing, and that's as good as lying about his and his client's intentions.

Now, for the revisions to my retainer agreements. I don't have anything like either Monroe's proposed retainer provision number 1 or number 2. I do meet with clients and go over in some detail how they would like to see their particular problem resolved, and what kind of "attitude" they think the other side is bringing to the issues.

When I sense that a client is looking for a real sonofabitch to handle the case, I tell the client that I'm not the guy he or she is looking for, and they should keep looking. I try to solve problems. I think my clients are pretty clear about how I intend to go about representing them, although I don't spend nearly enough time with any of them to assure that they are completely educated on the ERs and how I interpret each one of them.

If you hired Salvador Dali to paint your portrait, I don't think you would be surprised if the finished product doesn't look like it was done by Leonardo da Vinci, even though I don't think either one would tell you in advance exactly what the finished picture would look like. So it is with lawyers—I tell clients what I can about their problems and how I recommend they should proceed to solve them, but I don't try to predict each stroke of the brush on canvas and I don't consult the client at every step, either.

I would not use the language in Monroe's retainer agreement provision number 2, because I don't think that describes what I am saying. I think there is a middle ground between the point described in provision number 1 ("I honor my agreements with opposing counsel, even if you don't like it") and number 2 ("If the other lawyer just screws up, I'm going to let him off the hook, even if you don't like it")—and that is that I am not going to use dishonest methods (and I will be the judge of what I think is dishonest) to trick the opposing lawyer into making a mistake, and I won't try to take advantage of his (or his client's) ignorance or gullibility by making an agreement that neither you nor I have any intention of performing.

If the opposing lawyer misses the statute of limitations, that's too bad for him and his client. If he allows his client's default to be taken, and my client doesn't want to stipulate to set it aside, that's also too bad for him and for his client. If he agrees to settle his client's case for half of the amount my client would have agreed to pay, a deal is a deal.

Monroe Freedman — Hofstra University — Hempstead

I infer some substantial agreement that we would all take advantage of many (perhaps the overwhelming majority) of tactical blunders that are made by other lawyers. What I don't see, though, is the expression of a principled basis for drawing a different line from my own. Scot's is: "I am not going to use dishonest methods (and I will be the judge of what I think is dishonest)." I can understand that that's a satisfying response on a personal level, but I doubt that Scot would claim it to be one that can be generalized in a principled way.

Stephen Gillers — NYU Law School — New York

What would you do on the original hypo if the person (or the partner of the person) you were talking to, who was about to make the serious error, had saved you from a similar error a while back? Or just last month. Would you still not tell him his error? Would you have thought back then "Fool" and think now "I'm not going to do what you did?"

Scot C. Stirling — Sacks Tierney, P.A. — Phoenix

As for generalizing my position with respect to this particular situation in a principled way, I think it's simple. What is more, my principled position is consistent with the law that applies to everybody else in the world, and not just lawyers. You can't agree to something when you have no intention of doing it. That's fraud in Arizona, and in most other states as well, I think. In this case, when the husband's lawyer waited for the call from the wife's lawyer inquiring about how to take up the alimony issue, I think it was too late to say "too late."

I wouldn't have any problem with a lawyer representing the husband who says he doesn't want to pay any alimony—let him take that argument into court and see what happens. I also don't have a problem with making a settlement offer to the wife including no alimony; she can say yes or no. The distinction that I am making is based on the methods used to achieve that result—not on the fairness of the result itself—and that is a principled distinction that the law makes all the time.

Does that mean that I am assuming that I know more about ethical issues than my client? Not necessarily, especially if you are including ethical issues outside the rules of professional responsibility. (If that were the relevant inquiry, there is no question *at all* in my mind that what the husband and the husband's lawyer did in this case is unethical. See the Golden Rule.) But one of the things that I have and that my client probably doesn't have is objectivity—so even if my ethical sense is no better than my client's, I am more likely to identify the ethical issues and to analyze them more clearly than my client can in his or her own case. That more objective view and analysis is one of the things that I am supposed to provide to my client, so he doesn't drive himself off a cliff while trying to run down his wife.

I also know more about the law of fraud, and I know that I have the right, even as against my client, not to go down that road.

Monroe Freedman — Hofstra University — Hempstead

In answer to Steve's question: In any case in which I found myself on the other side from that lawyer, I would tell my client that I have a conflict of interest. The client could waive the conflict, that is, authorize me, if the occasion arose, to tell the other lawyer about his error. Or the client could decide to go with another lawyer.

Neal Goldfarb — Ingersoll and Bloch — Washington

I think Scot pushes his point too far in contending that the husband's lawyer didn't just act dishonestly, but committed legal fraud. Dishonesty alone isn't enough to constitute fraud, and there are grounds on which a claim for fraud could easily be rejected even if you assume the lawyer was dishonest. E.g., it wasn't reasonable for the wife's lawyer to rely on opposing counsel's statement of the law. Although the dishonesty question is a close one, in my opinion, the fraud question isn't.

Stephen Gillers — NYU Law School — New York

Monroe: I think you avoided the dilemma posed. Or you did only by making it a no-brainer by adding a fact. It could well happen that you would not have had an opportunity to raise that issue (or your special relationship with the other lawyer) with your client at the outset. As I said, what if the other lawyer helped you out a month ago, long after you took the case. What if he helped out your partner or his partner helped you out a month ago. What if your partner brought in the client and then you took over the case. Then the dilemma arises. There are many ways in which the dilemma can arise without a pre-existing agreement with the client about how you would differently treat the adversary lawyer because of a past favor.

Scot C. Stirling — Sacks Tierney, P.A. — Phoenix

I think I have admitted a couple of times that I also have some doubts about the strength of a legal claim for fraud, because there is some question about the right to rely. I admit that there is a distinction between dishonesty and legal fraud, and I also think this is more clearly dishonest than fraudulent (in the sense that it would be actionable as fraud). I think that fraud for purposes of Rule 60 is not necessarily the same thing as common law fraud, and I have also noted that Rule 60 provides for relief for "fraud," as well as for "misrepresentation" and other "misconduct."

However, I have continued to speak of fraud, because there are a couple of ways of looking at these facts, and a fraud claim is weaker or stronger depending upon which view you take.

If you interpret the husband's lawyer's actions as an implied representation to the wife's lawyer (which is what you are doing when you refer to the "opposing lawyer's statement of the law"), you are interpreting the facts in a way that makes it much more likely that the fraud claim will be shot down because the wife's lawyer doesn't have the right to rely on the husband's lawyer for an explanation of the law.

If you interpret the husband's lawyer's actions as indicating agreement to do something that the husband and his lawyer have no intention of doing, I think the odds of succeeding on a claim of fraud go up. In those fraud cases that are based upon making an agreement with no intention of performing it, I don't think most courts are going to analyze the right to rely issue in the same way, or allow the husband's lawyer to get off by saying the misrepresentation, if there was one, concerned a legal issue, and not a fact—such as the husband's intentions or present state of mind. I am inclined to this latter interpretation of these facts.

I'm not sure how much the distinction between dishonesty and actionable fraud matters. As I think I said somewhere earlier in this discussion, I don't think I have an obligation to be dishonest, even if my dishonesty wouldn't be actionable as fraud. Do I have an obligation to my client to make a false representation about a fact, knowing that it is false, and intending that the other party will believe me and rely upon the truth of my representation—because I know that the other guy can't prove that he had a right to rely on my representation? I don't think so. In those circumstances, what I am doing is not legal fraud, because one of the elements (the right to rely) is missing. I still don't think it's proper, or that I have any obligation to my client to make that false representation.

Monroe Freedman — Hofstra University — Hempstead

Scot, you were right.

I think that, in the most fundamental sense, we have all been agreeing in principle all along. The apparent disagreement has been in the area that Neal has properly described as gray.

On one side of the gray area, I believe that we all agree that we wouldn't volunteer to the opposing lawyer that a statute of limitations will bar his client's cause of action in two days. We *will* take advantage of another lawyer's mistake.

On the other side of the gray area, we agree that we wouldn't make a promise to the opposing lawyer intending to break it. That would be fraud.

All of the thunder and lightning has been directed at the relatively narrow gray area—the cases where Neal and I don't see the conduct as fraud, and Scot and Steve do. But we have all recognized, I think, that these are cases where reasonable lawyers can differ in our conclusions as to whether there have in fact been implied promises, what the scope of the promises are, and whether the other lawyer has been reasonable in relying on the implied promise (assuming there was one). It's on those factual/legal issues that the differences turn.

I disagreed with Scot's insistence that he will make the factual/legal determination in the gray area. But he was right. The lawyer *has* to make that decision. I would add only that the lawyer's judgment can't be arbitrary; it must be reasonable. The appropriate phrasing is in Model Rule 1.16(b)(1)— "conduct that *the lawyer reasonably believes* is criminal or fraudulent."

That leaves room for honest disagreement about how each of us might act in a particular case in that relatively small gray area.

In the alimony matter, I didn't understand that I had promised anything. That is, I didn't understand the facts, as Steve does, as one where "the lawyer asked you *to agree* to . . . alimony later." As I saw it, he says, "Will you sign the decree now? We can talk about the alimony later." I say nothing about alimony; I say only, "I'll have to ask my client about expediting the divorce by signing the decree now." Then I send him the signed decree.

Steve and Scot see that as an implied promise on my part, "I will negotiate the alimony issue with you in good faith after the decree is signed." That's not an unreasonable reading. It just isn't my reading, and I think that my reading is reasonable too. Also, I don't think an opposing lawyer can reasonably rely on my silence as meaning that I will educate him about alimony law. Again, if we disagree, I don't think either of us is being unreasonable.

In short, I see the alimony case as closer to remaining silent about the statute of limitations than it is to the case in which I promise to extend the time on the default.

But, again, I don't think anyone who sees the alimony case as being closer to the default case is unreasonable.

Finally, on Steve's reply to my conflict of interest response. The outset of the lawyer-client relationship isn't the only time that one might (or is required) to inform the client about a conflict of interest. If the other lawyer "helped [me] out a month ago, long after [I] took the case," then the time to tell the client about the conflict was a month ago, when the conflict arose.

But I'm sure that Steve can come up with facts that will force the issue (altho with each hypo, I think we get a little further from something that is likely to occur in real life). In any event, I think I have been clear all along that, if the choice is forced upon me to choose between fidelity to my client and friendship with the other lawyer, I feel my stronger obligation to my client. That's where my soul is, and, to quote someone eminently quotable, My soul is not for sale.

Stephen Gillers — NYU Law School — New York

Anticipating that this discussion will go in some history book about legal ethics in the 20th century, I want to clarify a few points and pose a letter to Monroe.

1. I am glad to see Monroe use the phrase "gray area" because I agree with him and used that phrase in explaining my inability to draw perfect lines.

2. I did not say, and do not believe, that responding as Monroe and Neal would to the opening hypo would be fraud. Monroe attributes Scot's position

to me. I respect Scot's position. It is not mine. I said I would alert the other lawyer because that's where my values are.

3. Similarly, contrary to Monroe's ascription to me, I did not say there was an implied promise on the part of the lawyer who signed the divorce decree to negotiate alimony. I did not rely on legal duties for my analysis.

I understand Monroe to answer my first hypothetical to say that he would not take advantage of the other lawyer's ignorance of the jurisdictional bar in seeking an extension of time to open the default.

Now let me restate my other issue this way:

Dear Professor Freedman:

I was in your legal ethics class several years ago and you said we could come to you if we had a problem. I hope you can help me.

I represent Joe in a divorce case [the letter proceeds to lay out the opening hypo]. The wife's lawyer, Neal, sent me this decree, thinking we could talk about alimony later, but I know, and he doesn't know, that we can't.

Now it happens that just last week I learned that Neal took in a partner, Scot. Amazingly, Scot saved me from just this sort of sorry oversight in connection with the filing of a notice of appeal a few months ago, when he was at another firm. (I didn't realize that you couldn't extend the time to file by stipulation. I called Scot and asked him to do so because I was then solo and in the middle of a trial. Scot told me he would agree but it wouldn't matter because the time limit was jurisdictional. Whew! We won the appeal. If I had missed the deadline, I would have had to declare bankruptcy—well, close.)

Anyway, I know that Neal's firm (just Neal and Scot) have very little malpractice coverage. The alimony here, conservatively, is $100,000 yearly and maybe a lot more. So if I don't warn them, they're really in trouble.

What do I do Professor Freedman? I feel terrible about this. I don't want to hurt them by taking advantage of their ignorance. But you taught me to have strong duties to my client. Do I sign the divorce decree and send it back? Do I ask my client? If my client says sign it, can I disregard the instruction? Do I have to ask my client? Can I just warn Neal? Can I withdraw? I got an A in your class but I don't recall a problem as hard as this one.

I'm sorry to load this on you so suddenly by e-mail but I'm really in trouble and learned a lot from your course.

Thanking you in advance. . . . .

    John Marshall

P.S. I tried calling Professor Gillers, when I couldn't reach you, but he wanted a retainer because I wasn't in his class.

Monroe Freedman — Hofstra University — Hempstead

(1) I don't want to answer JM's letter.

(2) I wouldn't answer JM's letter.

(1) I don't want to answer the letter because I think the discussion has played itself out. Any longer and we're going to become an artifact of the 21st century.

More important, I'm satisfied that the discussion has served to provide me, and perhaps some others, with a principled way to deal with a vexing problem.

With regard to your own formulation ("because that's where my values are"), I have no doubt that it's satisfying to you, but it can't be the basis for a principled response to an issue of lawyers' professional responsibilities—not unless the principle becomes, "Do whatever is consistent with your own values." (If that's what you teach, it's an easy A for every student, unless, of course, you penalize them for having values different from your own.)

(2) I wouldn't answer the letter, because the issue is too important to my client, and I really don't know what he wants to do. In fact, I'm not sure *he* knows yet what he wants to do. I am going to have to sit down with my client and do some lawyer-client counseling.

Our discussion would cover the same ground that this discussion has, but more. More, because I want to know what *JM's* values are respecting fidelity to clients and loyalty to friends, how much risk *he's* willing to take, and how much malpractice coverage *he* has.

Note: *My* client is JM, so my concern is with his interests as he perceives them, not his client's interests, and not the interests of Scot, Neal, the system, myself, or anyone else.

He says in his letter that he feels terrible about this and doesn't want to hurt Scott and Neal. I've had clients say the same thing (about not hurting their own clients, who had put the lawyers in difficult positions). But it became apparent after we had talked about it at length that what they really wanted was to be told that, in the circumstances, they *should* take the action that would hurt their clients and avoid professional discipline.

In one case, on my suggestion, my client (the lawyer) decided that I should speak directly to his client to tell the client that the lawyer's decision to do something that would hurt the client was based on my advice that that's what the lawyer was ethically required to do (as in fact he was required to do). In short, the lawyer wanted me to take some of the heat that he would get from an irate client, and I did.

On the other hand, maybe JM *really* doesn't want to hurt Scot and Neal. Our discussions would reveal the most prudent (i.e., self-protective) way to go about achieving that end. But I would want to make sure that, while he was worrying about Neal's and Scot's exposure, he was acutely aware of his own potential liability. If the facts of this case could happen (as you said of your own facts: "Amazingly . . ."), then JM's client might learn what he had done, and the $100,000 shoe could be pinching JM's foot.

TABLE OF CASES

[References are to pages.]

INDEX

[References are to pages, appendices and footnotes.]

[References are to pages, appendices and footnotes.]

[References are to pages, appendices and footnotes.]

[References are to pages, appendices and footnotes.]

[References are to pages, appendices and footnotes.]

M

[References are to pages, appendices and footnotes.]

N

O

[References are to pages, appendices and footnotes.]

[References are to pages, appendices and footnotes.]

[References are to pages, appendices and footnotes.]